GUIDE TO GAAP

by

Stephen W. Lindsey, CPA
Marilyn Z. Rutledge, CPA
Cheryl Wilson, CPA

Contributing Editor
David R. Frazier, CPA

Third Edition (October 1997)
Practitioners Publishing Company
Fort Worth, Texas
(800) 323-8724
www.ppcinfo.com

ISSN 1087-2167

ISBN 0-7646-0299-3

PRINTED IN THE UNITED STATES OF AMERICA

TABLE OF CONTENTS

PREFACE

Generally accepted accounting principles (GAAP) include the measurement and disclosure principles that apply to all financial statements (except those prepared on an other comprehensive basis of accounting). They govern the recognition of transactions (that is, they specify when a transaction will be recorded and the amounts to be recorded) and dictate the numbers and other information that must be presented in financial statements. SAS No. 69, *The Meaning of "Present Fairly in Conformity with Generally Accepted Accounting Principles" in the Independent Auditor's Report,* outlines the following hierarchy of sources of GAAP for nongovernmental entities:

   a. Pronouncements of an authoritative body designated by the AICPA Council to establish accounting principles pursuant to Rule 203 of the AICPA *Code of Professional Conduct* (This level includes Financial Accounting Standards Board (FASB) Statements of Financial Accounting Standards, FASB Interpretations, Accounting Principles Board (APB) Opinions, and AICPA Accounting Research Bulletins.)

   b. Pronouncements of groups composed of expert accountants, that deliberate accounting issues in public forums for the purpose of establishing accounting principles or describing existing accounting practices that are generally accepted, provided the pronouncements have been exposed for public comment and have been cleared by a body referred to in category (a) (This level includes AICPA Industry Audit Guides and Accounting Guides, AICPA Statements of Position, and FASB Technical Bulletins.)

   c. Pronouncements of groups organized by an authoritative body listed in (a) and composed of expert accountants, that deliberate accounting issues in public forums for the purpose of interpreting or establishing accounting principles or describing existing accounting practices that are generally accepted or pronouncements referred to in category (b) that have been cleared by a body in category (a) but have not been exposed for public comment (This level includes consensus positions of the FASB Emerging Issues Task Force and AcSEC Practice Bulletins.)

   d. Practice or pronouncements that are widely recognized as being generally accepted because they represent prevalent practice in a particular industry or the knowledgeable application to specific circumstances of pronouncements that are generally accepted

(This level includes AICPA Accounting Interpretations, "Qs and As" published by the FASB staff, and practices that are widely recognized and prevalent in the industry.)

e. Other accounting literature (This level includes AICPA Issues Papers and Technical Practice Aids, FASB Statements of Financial Accounting Concepts, Statements of International Accounting Standards, pronouncements of other professional associations or regulatory agencies, and accounting textbooks and articles.)

Accounting principles in category (a) are undisputed as generally accepted accounting principles. If a principle in category (a) does not cover the accounting treatment of a particular transaction or event, the accounting principles specified by category (b), (c), or (d) should be considered. (Accountants should follow the treatment specified by the source in the higher category if a principle in more than one of those categories is relevant.) Generally, accountants should only consider other accounting literature, category (e), in the absence of relevant accounting principles in category (a), (b), (c), or (d).

Guide to GAAP presents the accounting principles in category (a) of the GAAP hierarchy (and related pronouncements in the other categories) in a single, easy-to-use source. Its clear, concise guidance covers all FASB Statements of Financial Accounting Standards (SFASs), FASB Interpretations (FASBIs), FASB Technical Bulletins (FTBs), APB Opinions (APBs), and Accounting Research Bulletins (ARBs). It also covers relevant AICPA Statements of Position (SOPs) and consensus positions of the EITF. With its numerous examples, practice aids, and practical considerations, accountants will find the *Guide* to be a valuable, time-saving tool for applying generally accepted accounting principles.

PEER REVIEW OF THIS *GUIDE*

To ensure that the quality control materials in this *Guide* are reliable aids to users in complying with professional standards and to help users minimize the costs of their peer reviews or quality reviews, Practitioners Publishing Company has voluntarily elected to undergo a peer review of its system for the development and maintenance of these quality control materials.

The unqualified peer review report covering this *Guide* has been accepted by the Private Companies Practice Section (PCPS) and the SEC Practice Section (SECPS) of the AICPA Division for CPA Firms and is reprinted on the following page. (There were no items that required a letter of comments.) If your firm is undergoing a peer review, you should provide a copy of this report to the captain of your review team. Because of the timing of the peer review (the review cannot begin until after the edition is published), the review report refers to the second edition of *Guide to GAAP*. However, as established by the AICPA Division for CPA Firms, the report is valid for three years. Accordingly, the report also covers this edition of your *Guide*. PPC will continue to have each edition of this *Guide* peer reviewed.

The Board of Directors
Practitioners Publishing Company
Fort Worth, Texas

We have reviewed the system of quality control for the development and maintenance of Guide to GAAP *(Second Edition)* (materials) of Practitioners Publishing Company (the company) in effect for the year ended December 31, 1996, and the resultant materials in effect at December 31, 1996, in order to determine whether the materials are reliable aids to assist users in conforming with those professional standards the materials purport to encompass. Our review was conducted in accordance with the standards for reviews of quality control materials promulgated by the Peer Review Committee of the SEC Practice Section of the AICPA Division for CPA Firms. Our review did not cover the development and maintenance of the continuing professional education programs included in the materials.

In performing our review, we have given consideration to the following general characteristics of a system of quality control. A company's system for the development and maintenance of quality control materials encompasses its organizational structure and the policies and procedures established to provide the users of its materials with reasonable assurance that the quality control materials are reliable aids to assist them in conforming with professional standards in conducting their accounting and auditing practices. The extent of a company's quality control policies and procedures for the development and maintenance of quality control materials and the manner in which they are implemented will depend upon a variety of factors, such as the size and organizational structure of the company and the nature of the materials provided to users. Variance in individual performance and professional interpretation affects the degree of compliance with prescribed quality control policies and procedures. Therefore, adherence to all policies and procedures in every case may not be possible.

Our review and tests were limited to the system of quality control for the development and maintenance of the aforementioned quality control materials of Practitioners Publishing Company and to the materials themselves and did not extend to the application of these materials by users of the materials nor to the policies and procedures of individual users.

In our opinion, the system of quality control for the development and maintenance of the quality control materials of Practitioners Publishing Company was suitably designed and was being complied with during the year ended December 31, 1996, to provide users of the materials with reasonable assurance that the materials are reliable aids to assist them in conforming with those professional standards the materials purport to encompass. Also, in our opinion, the quality control materials referred to above are reliable aids at December 31, 1996.

Cherry, Bekaert & Holland, L.L.P.

Greensboro, North Carolina
January 24, 1997

HOW TO USE
GUIDE TO GAAP

Guide to GAAP can be used as a desktop practice tool, library reference source, or training tool for staff members. It provides clear, concise coverage of generally accepted accounting principles in an easy-to-use topical format. The *Guide* is divided into the following major sections:

- GENERAL STANDARDS discusses the generally accepted accounting principles that apply to most entities. The chapters are arranged alphabetically, by topic, with each chapter containing an overview, accounting requirements section, disclosure requirements section, and references to authoritative literature and related topics.

- INDUSTRY STANDARDS covers the more specialized pronouncements that apply to not-for-profit organizations and entities operating in certain industries.

- CROSS-REFERENCE TO AUTHORITATIVE LITERATURE lists all of the Accounting Research Bulletins, APB Opinions, FASB Statements, FASB Technical Bulletins, and FASB Interpretations that have been issued and refers to the chapters in the *Guide* in which they are discussed.

- DISCLOSURE CHECKLISTS summarizes the primary disclosures that should be included in financial statements of nongovernmental entities. Although the main focus of this section is on the disclosures required by generally accepted accounting principles, the checklists presented also cover the disclosures normally made in practice but not specifically required by GAAP.

While every effort has been made to make *Guide to GAAP* as accurate and reliable as possible, it should be emphasized that the *Guide* is not a substitute for a careful study of authoritative technical literature or the professional judgment that must be applied by practitioners. Consequently, references are made throughout the *Guide's* accounting requirements and disclosure requirements sections to original authoritative pronouncements. The references, which appear in parentheses at or near the end of most paragraphs, refer to specific paragraphs in Accounting Research Bulletins (ARBs), APB Opinions (APBs), FASB Statements of Financial Accounting Standards (SFASs), FASB Interpretations (FASBIs), FASB Technical Bulletins (FTBs), consensus positions of the FASB Emerging Issues Task Force (EITFs), and AICPA Statements of Position (SOPs).

Organization of the *Guide*

The beginning of each major section of the *Guide* contains a page marker to make it easy to find. To locate a particular major section, refer to the table of contents printed on the back cover, gently bend the pages in half, and look along the page edges for the corresponding black page marker.

Each paragraph of the *Guide* has been assigned a four or five digit paragraph number (X.XXX or XX.XXX). The first digit (or two digits in a five digit number) relates to the chapter number. The last three digits relate to sections within the chapter. (Numbers 100–199 refer to paragraphs in the overview section, numbers 200–499 refer to paragraphs in the accounting requirements section, and numbers 500–599 refer to paragraphs in the disclosure requirements section.) Chapter tables of contents and the topical index refer to paragraph numbers. Paragraph numbers also are presented on the bottom of each page.

Pages in *Guide to GAAP* are numbered consecutively within each chapter. The page numbers begin with the chapter number followed by a dash and the individual page number, for example, 1-1, 1-2, etc. Page numbers appear on the top of each page.

Suggestions for Improvement

The authors encourage users of the *Guide* to offer any comments or suggestions they may have to improve the usefulness of future editions. Of special interest are your comments about the usefulness of individual chapters and recommendations for additions to *Guide to GAAP.* Please address your comments and suggestions to:

> Practitioners Publishing Company
> Attn: *Guide to GAAP*
> P.O. Box 966
> Fort Worth, TX 76101

ACKNOWLEDGMENTS

We are grateful to the many individuals who contributed to *Guide to GAAP.* In particular, we express our appreciation to Senior Technical Editors at PPC, Ken Koskay, CPA; Melissa Snow, CPA; and David R. Frazier, CPA; Technical Editor at PPC, Mark Wells, CPA, and to Gary Gillette, CPA, Director of Product Systems for PPC, for their technical as well as literary assistance. Special recognition is also due the Product Systems department of Practitioners Publishing Company for the patient and dedicated teamwork that made this book a reality. Finally, we are especially thankful to our families and friends for their patience and encouragement.

Stephen W. Lindsey
Marilyn Z. Rutledge
Cheryl Wilson

ABOUT THE AUTHORS . . .

Stephen W. Lindsey, CPA, is an Executive Editor for Practitioners Publishing Company where he is responsible for the technical content of a number of PPC's guides and continuing education courses. He is a coauthor of PPC's *Guide to Accounting for Income Taxes, Guide to Write-up Services, Guide to Managing an Accounting Practice, Guide to Nonprofit GAAP,* and *Guide to Health Care Consulting.* Before joining PPC, he was in public practice for over eight years with KPMG Peat Marwick and a local firm in Fort Worth, Texas. His experience providing accounting, auditing, and tax services to clients ranging from small businesses to multinational companies ensures that *Guide to GAAP* contains practical, as well as authoritative, guidance.

Marilyn Z. Rutledge, CPA, is Vice President/Publisher of Accounting and Auditing Publications for Practitioners Publishing Company where, among her many duties, she closely monitors the development of literature by the FASB and AICPA. She was formerly a manager with the Auditing Standards Division of the AICPA and has eight years of local firm experience. While at the AICPA, Ms. Rutledge was in charge of drafting SSARS Nos. 1 and 2 and was the staff liaison for the small business audit committee. She is a coauthor of PPC's *Guide to Auditor's Reports, Guide to Forecasts and Projections, Guide to Real Estate, Guide to Homeowners' Associations and Other Common Interest Realty Associations,* and *Guide to HUD Audits.* In addition, she has coauthored several articles in the *Journal of Accountancy* and other professional publications and is coauthor of several continuing education courses.

Cheryl Wilson, CPA, is a Technical Editor for Practitioners Publishing Company. She is currently responsible for the technical content of a number of PPC books and courses, including Guide to Preparing Financial Statements, Guide to Accounting for Income Taxes, and Guide to Real Estate. In addition, she is coauthor of Guide to Health Care Consulting and PPC's Annual Auditing and Accounting Update course. Prior to joining PPC, she was Accounting Director for the Fort Worth Independent School District and was in public practice with Deloitte & Touche. Her solid technical background and over 13 years of "hands on" experience ensure that the guidance in Guide to GAAP is accurate and relevant to CPAs in public practice and industry.

AND THE CONTRIBUTING EDITOR

David R. Frazier, CPA, is a Senior Technical Editor for Practitioners Publishing Company, where he is an author of PPC's *Guide to Start-up Businesses* and a contributing author of PPC's *Guide to Audits of Small Businesses*. He is also coauthor of several continuing education courses and PPC's *Accounting and Auditing Update* newsletter. Before joining PPC, he spent several years in public practice with Ernst & Young, where he was an audit manager. Mr. Frazier's extensive experience includes providing audit and consulting services to a wide range of governmental, nonprofit, and small business clients.

GENERAL STANDARDS

Table of Contents

GENERAL STANDARDS

Table of Contents (Continued)

GENERAL STANDARDS

Table of Contents (Continued)

ACCOUNTING CHANGES

Table of Contents

ACCOUNTING CHANGES

Table of Contents (Continued)

ACCOUNTING CHANGES

OVERVIEW

1.100   There are three broad categories of accounting changes:

a. changes in an accounting principle,

b. changes in an accounting estimate, and

c. changes in the reporting entity.

Corrections of errors are not accounting changes. (Correcting errors is discussed in Chapter 42.)

1.101   An overall presumption in financial statement preparation is that the accounting principles adopted by an entity will be applied consistently from period to period. However, entities sometimes change accounting principles to use a preferable method of accounting. Changes in accounting principles are recorded through either (a) a cumulative effect adjustment that is reported in net income of the period of the change, (b) retroactive restatement of prior year financial statements, or (c) prospective accounting. Disclosures are required in the year of the change.

1.102   Changes in accounting estimates are common in practice and result from new events or occur as a company gains more experience or obtains additional information. Changes in estimates are reported in the period the estimate is revised or in both the current and future periods if the change affects future periods.

1.103   A change in reporting entity is a change that results in financial statements that are, in effect, the statements of a different entity. Changes in reporting entity are generally limited to changes in the companies or subsidiaries that are included in combined or consolidated financial statements. Changes in reporting entity are accounted for by restating the financial statements of prior periods.

ACCOUNTING REQUIREMENTS

1.200   How accounting changes are reported depends on whether the change is a change in accounting principle, accounting estimate, or reporting entity. EXHIBIT 1-1 resents a flowchart that summarizes the accounting for each type of change while EXHIBIT 1-2 summarizes the accounting, reporting, and disclosure requirements for the changes. The remaining paragraphs discuss each type of accounting change in more detail.

CHANGE IN ACCOUNTING PRINCIPLE

Definition of a Change in Accounting Principle

1.201   A change in accounting principle is generally defined as a change from one acceptable principle to another or a change in the method of applying an acceptable accounting principle. (APB 20, par. 7) A change to an unacceptable method, including the use of a tax or cash method of accounting for an item in GAAP financial statements, results in a GAAP departure. A change from an unacceptable method to an acceptable method is a correction of an error and not a change in accounting principle as defined by GAAP.

Practical Consideration. The authors believe that a change from a comprehensive basis of accounting other than GAAP (e.g., tax basis or cash basis) to GAAP also should be accounted for as a correction of an error. Accounting errors are treated as prior period adjustments and are discussed in Chapter 42.

EXHIBIT 1-1

ACCOUNTING CHANGES

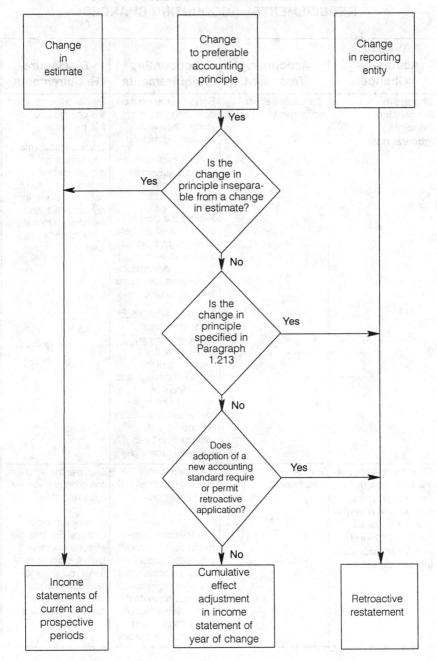

EXHIBIT 1-2

SUMMARY OF ACCOUNTING AND DISCLOSURE
REQUIREMENTS—ACCOUNTING CHANGES

Type of Accounting Change	Accounting Treatment	Accounting Requirements	Disclosure Requirements
Change in Accounting Principle (general rule)	Cumulative effect adjustment.	Report current period operating results using the new accounting method. Present prior period financial statements as previously reported. Record the cumulative effect adjustment in the current period income statement between the captions of extraordinary items and net income. The cumulative effect is the difference between retained earnings at the beginning of the period of change and the amount of retained earnings that would have been reported if that change had been applied retroactively.	Disclose the nature of the change and why it is preferable. Disclose pro forma information on income before extraordinary items, net income with the net tax effect, and per share information for all periods presented.
Change in Accounting Principle (for the exceptions to the general rule discussed in Paragraph 1.213 and some new accounting standards)	Retroactive restatement.	Restate financial statements for all prior years presented. The financial statements for all years presented should reflect an adjustment of beginning retained earnings equal to the cumulative effect of the change on net income of prior years.	Disclose the nature of the change and why it is preferable. In the year of the change, disclose the effect on income before extraordinary items, net income, and earnings per share for all prior periods presented.

EXHIBIT 1-2 (Continued)

Type of Accounting Change	Accounting Treatment	Accounting Requirements	Disclosure Requirements
Change in Accounting Principle (prospective changes; for example, a change to the LIFO method of accounting for inventory)	Current and prospective periods.	Record the change in income statements of current and future periods.	Disclose the nature of the change and why it is preferable. Disclose the effect of the change on current year income. Disclose the reason for the absence of cumulative effect and pro forma information.
Change in Estimate	Current and prospective periods.	Record in income statements of current and future periods. Report current and future financial statements on the new basis. Present prior period financial statements as previously presented.	If the change affects future years, disclose the effect on income before extraordinary items and net income.
Change in Reporting Entity	Retroactive restatement.	Restate the financial statements for all prior years presented. Determine operating results of prior years based on the new reporting entity.	For the period of the change disclose— (1) the nature and the reason for the change. (2) the effect on income before extraordinary items and net income for all periods presented.

1.202 Circumstances That Are Not Changes in Accounting Principle. The following events or circumstances are not considered to be accounting changes:

    a. Adoption of a new accounting principle for new events or transactions, substantially different events or transactions, or material events or transactions that previously were immaterial (APB 20, par. 8)

    b. Changes in classification

    c. A change in accounting principle for income tax purposes only

> **Practical Consideration.** Although changes in classification are not considered to be changes in accounting principles, material changes in classification and material reclassifications made in previously issued financial statements to enhance comparability with current financial statements should be disclosed.

1.203 Change in Components of Inventory Cost. Under generally accepted accounting principles, inventory is stated at cost. Generally, inventory costs include the cost of raw materials, direct labor, purchased finished goods, and allocated indirect costs. A change in inventory cost components (for example, to allocate insurance costs to inventory) is considered a change in accounting principle. (FASBI 1, par. 5)

> **Practical Consideration.** As a result of changes in income tax inventory capitalization rules, many companies are reconsidering the costs capitalized for GAAP reporting. For example, inventory storage costs, such as rent, depreciation, insurance, etc., generally must be capitalized for tax purposes but may not have been capitalized for GAAP reporting. The authors believe that accounting for a change in the components of inventory cost depends on whether the change is due to a change in circumstances (for example, a change in the production process) or because costs that should have been capitalized in prior periods were not. A change due to a change in circumstances should be accounting for as a change in accounting principle, while a change due to incorrect past capitalization policies should be accounted for as a correction of an error. EITF Issue No. 86-46, *Uniform Capitalization Rules for Inventory under the Tax Reform Act of 1986,* states that a change in tax law is not a change in circumstances that would, in itself, justify a change in accounting principle.

1.204   Changes Prescribed by AICPA Statements of Position and Practice Bulletins, FASB Technical Bulletins, or EITF Consensuses. A change in accounting principle that is made to conform with the requirements of an AICPA Statement of Position or Practice Bulletin, a FASB Technical Bulletin, or a consensus of the FASB's Emerging Issues Task Force should be reported as prescribed by the pronouncement. If the pronouncement does not provide guidance on accounting for the change, the change should be reported as discussed in this chapter. (SFAS 111, par. 10 and FASBI 20, par. 5)

1.205   Justifying Changes in Accounting Principles. Changes in accounting principle are permitted only if an entity justifies the use of an alternative acceptable accounting principle on the basis that it is preferable. (APB 20, par. 16) For example, there are acceptable alternative methods of accounting for certain items, and companies may change among those alternative methods. However, a company should not change an accounting principle unless the proposed new principle is in conformity with GAAP and management believes that the new principle is preferable in the circumstances.

1.206   In addition to choosing among acceptable alternative methods of accounting, FASB Statements that either create new accounting principles, express a preference for accounting principles, or reject specific accounting principles are sufficient support for changes in accounting principles, as are all pronouncements in categories (b), (c), and (d) of the revised GAAP hierarchy. (SFAS 111, par. 7) If a conflict between accounting principles occurs, the accounting principle specified in the higher category of the GAAP hierarchy should be followed. (SFAS 111, par. 17) (The GAAP hierarchy is discussed in the preface to this *Guide.*)

Practical Consideration. The authors believe the primary reason for voluntarily changing methods of accounting typically is the belief that (a) a different method more accurately reports the financial results for the company's operations or (b) the change to a new method reflects the methods used by competitors. The latter reason allows investors and other financial statement users to better compare the operating results of competing companies. The authors believe those reasons are justification for a change in accounting principle based on preferability. However, as stated in Paragraph 1.201 the new accounting principle must be in conformity with GAAP.

Accounting Treatment of a Change in Accounting Principle

1.207   The following summarizes the various methods used to account for changes in accounting principles:

     a. Cumulative effect adjustment

(1) Voluntary changes in accounting principle made by an entity should be accounted for through a cumulative effect adjustment. For example, a company may decide that depreciating existing assets using the straight-line method of accounting is preferable to the previously used accelerated method.

b. Retroactive restatement

(1) Many recent FASB pronouncements require or permit retroactive application when new accounting principles prescribed by them are adopted.

(2) GAAP requires a limited number of special changes in accounting principle to be applied retroactively. (See Paragraph 1.213)

c. Prospective change

(1) Prospective changes in accounting principle are less common; the most notable prospective change is a change to the LIFO method of inventory valuation. (APB 20, par. 26) (Paragraphs 1.215–.216 provide other examples of prospective changes.)

(2) The issuance of a new pronouncement may allow prospective accounting.

The accounting and reporting requirements for changes in accounting principles are discussed in the following paragraphs.

1.208 **Determining the Cumulative Effect.** Most voluntary changes in accounting principle, i.e., changes in the selection of principles among acceptable alternatives, should be recognized by including the cumulative effect adjustment of changing to a new accounting principle, based on a retroactive computation, in net income of the period of the change. The cumulative effect of changing to a new accounting principle is the difference between—

a. the amount of retained earnings at the beginning of the period of change and

b. the amount of retained earnings that would have been reported if the change had been applied retroactively.

The cumulative effect of changing to a new accounting principle should be presented net of related income tax effects as a separate line item after extraordinary items, if any. Per share amounts may be presented on the face of the income statement or in the notes. (APB 20, paras. 19–20) Accounting changes that are recognized by restating the financial statements of prior periods are discussed in Paragraphs 1.212–1.214.

1.209 **Pro Forma Information.** In addition to presenting the cumulative effect of an accounting change as described in the preceding paragraph, income before extraordinary items and net income (and, for public companies, per share amounts) computed on a pro forma basis (net of tax) should be shown on the face of the income statement for all periods presented as if the newly adopted accounting principle had been applied to all periods affected. However, because of space limitations, pro forma amounts are sometimes disclosed in the notes or a separate schedule following the financial statements. (In such cases, public companies should repeat the disclosures of actual per share amounts for comparative purposes.) In addition, if an income statement is presented for the current period only, the actual and pro forma amounts for the immediately preceding period should be disclosed. (APB 20, paras. 19 and 21)

1.210 Pro forma amounts should include both the direct effects of the accounting change and any nondiscretionary items that would have been recognized in prior periods. Examples of nondiscretionary items include royalties, profit-sharing expense, and bonuses that would have been recognized had the accounting change taken place in those prior periods. However, nondiscretionary items should not be considered in determining the cumulative effect of the accounting change unless those nondiscretionary adjustments are actually recorded. Income tax effects should be recognized for both direct effect and nondiscretionary adjustments when determining pro forma information. (APB 20, par. 19)

1.211 **Reporting Changes in Accounting Principles—Interim Periods.** Changes in accounting principles that are to be reported by including the cumulative effect of the change should be recognized in the first interim period regardless of when the change was actually made. The dollar effect of the change should be determined as of the end of the previous year. Thus, if a change in accounting principle is made in the second quarter, the cumulative effect of the change would not be reported in net income of the second quarter, but in the first quarter. Both quarters would be presented as if the accounting change was effective at the beginning of the year, that is, net income before extraordinary items would be based on the new accounting principles. (SFAS 3, paras. 9–10) In other words, all interim period statements would be based on the new principle and any interim period beginning with the first day of the year, such as the month of January, quarter ended March 31, or year-to-date through June, would include the cumulative effect of the change as of the end of the previous year.

1.212 Restatement of Prior Period Financial Statements. In certain circumstances, a change in accounting principle is accounted for retroactively. A restatement of the financial statements is made by restating the statements of prior years on a basis consistent with the new accounting principle. Unlike a cumulative effect adjustment, pro forma information is not presented since a restatement is handled retroactively by restating retained earnings for all periods presented. In addition, disclosure is made of the income effect of the change for all periods presented.

1.213   The following specific changes in accounting principle should be recognized by restating prior period financial statements:

     a. A change from the LIFO method of pricing inventory to another method

     b. A change in the method of accounting for long-term construction contracts

     c. A change to or from the full cost method of accounting in extractive industries (APB 20, par. 27)

     d. A change from retirement-replacement-betterment accounting to depreciation accounting for railroad track structures (SFAS 73, par. 2)

     e. Accounting changes that result in financial statements that are, in effect, those of a different reporting entity (See Paragraphs 1.219–.224.)

Retroactive application also is allowed, but not required, for changes made in connection with an initial public distribution of securities by a closely held company. (APB 20, par. 29)

1.214   When changes in accounting principle are recognized by restating prior period financial statements, the current year financial statements should reflect an adjustment of beginning retained earnings for the cumulative effect on net income of prior years. In other words, the dollar amount of an accounting change is the same whether the change is accounted for as a restatement or a cumulative effect adjustment; only where the change is recorded differs (retained earnings vs. income statement).

Changes in Depreciation Methods

1.215 Adopting a New Depreciation Method. A new depreciation method may be adopted in either of the following ways depending on the circumstances: (APB 20, par. 24)

- *Prospective*—It is applied only to new assets, and old assets continue to be depreciated using the old method.

- *Retroactive*—It is applied to both existing assets and future acquisitions.

Under the first option, GAAP does not require any special measurement or presentation. However, a retroactive change requires a cumulative effect adjustment as of the beginning of the year in which the change becomes effective. The adjustment changes the book value of depreciable assets owned at the beginning of the year to what it would have been if the new depreciation method had always been used for those assets, and it is included in current earnings rather than being recorded directly to retained earnings. Depreciation for the year of the change is computed using the new method.

1.216 Planned Change in Depreciation Method. Since declining balance methods do not depreciate to zero, some companies adopt a policy of using a declining balance method until depreciation drops below what straight-line depreciation would have been and then switch to straight-line depreciation. The book value of the asset when the change is made is depreciated on a straight-line basis over the asset's remaining useful life. For example, a company may establish a policy that for a certain type of asset, it will use the double declining balance method for the first two years (assuming two years is the break-even point), then switch to the straight-line method. The policy is acceptable for GAAP and would actually reflect the economic decline in value of many assets. GAAP specifically states that the consistent application of a policy to change to the straight-line method at a specific point in the service life of an asset does not constitute a change in accounting principle. (APB 20, par. 9)

CHANGE IN ACCOUNTING ESTIMATE

1.217 A change in accounting estimate results from additional information or new developments. Examples of accounting estimates that periodically change are allowances for bad debts, useful lives or salvage values of depreciable assets, and inventory obsolescence. (APB 20, par. 10) The effects of changes in estimates should be reported in the period of change and subsequent periods. Restatement of prior periods is not appropriate. (APB 20, par. 31) For example, a change in the estimated useful lives of assets would be accounted for by adjusting depreciation expense in the current and future periods to depreciate the carrying value of assets at the date of the change over their remaining (new) useful lives. Changes in estimates that are inseparable from changes in accounting principle, such as a change from deferring and amortizing a cost to expensing it as incurred because of a reassessment of future benefits, should be accounted for as changes in accounting estimates. (APB 20, par. 11)

Change in Salvage Value and Estimated Useful Life

1.218　Changes in salvage value and estimated useful life are normally changes in estimates caused by, for example, changing market conditions or better information. (APB 20, par. 32) To illustrate, assume that a repair shop buys a press for $12,000 and estimates that it will have a useful life of five years. However, at the end of the fourth year, management believes it can use the press for four more years. Using the original estimate, annual depreciation is $2,400 ($12,000 divided by 5), but using the revised estimate, annual depreciation should have been $1,500 ($12,000 divided by 8). As a result, there is an overstatement of depreciation of $900 ($2,400 − $1,500) for each of the first four years (for a total of $3,600), which should be spread over depreciation of years five through eight. The undepreciated cost at the time of the change in estimate of $2,400 ($12,000 − $9,600) should be allocated to the remaining four years at $600 per year as follows.

Year	Depreciation
1	$ 2,400
2	2,400
3	2,400
4	2,400
5	600
6	600
7	600
8	600
	$ 12,000

Practical Consideration. The "catchup" method, which would reduce depreciation in the preceding example by $3,600 in the year of change, is a departure from GAAP.

CHANGE IN REPORTING ENTITY

Definition of a Change in Reporting Entity

1.219 A change in reporting entity refers to a change that results in financial statements that are, in effect, the statements of a different reporting entity. Typically, such changes are limited to changes in the companies or subsidiaries that are included in combined or consolidated financial statements. (APB 20, par. 12) Changes in the legal form of businesses, for example, sole proprietorship to corporation, are not changes in the reporting entity.

Identifying a Change in Reporting Entity

1.220 Determining when a change in reporting entity occurs is important because it should be accounted for by restating the financial statements of prior periods to show financial information for the new reporting entity for all periods. (APB 20, par. 34) A change in reporting entity takes place when the following occurs: (APB 20, par. 12)

 a. Consolidated or combined statements are presented in place of the statements of individual companies.

 b. Specific subsidiaries comprising the group of companies for which consolidated financial statements are presented change.

 c. Companies included in combined financial statements change.

Practical Consideration. APB Opinion No. 20 does not view a change caused by transactions or events as a change in reporting entity. Consequently, the authors believe acquiring or disposing of a controlling interest, either all at once or in steps, is not a change in reporting entity because it is prompted by a transaction. (However, see Paragraph 1.221.) Similarly, a change in reporting entity does not occur if an investor owning a majority voting interest consolidates its investment in one year but does not in the next because it no longer controls the subsidiary (for example, because the subsidiary is in bankruptcy proceedings) since the change is prompted by an event.

Practical Consideration (Continued).

Guidance about what constitutes a change in reporting entity also is found in SAS No. 1 at AU 420.06-.10, which was issued to provide guidance on whether an audit report should be modified for a consistency exception when certain accounting changes occur. Although it was not intended to modify APB Opinion No. 20's guidance, it made two observations about what constitutes a change in reporting entity—(1) the purchase or disposition of an investee is not a change in reporting entity and (2) changing among the cost, equity, and consolidation methods is such a change. While the first observation clearly rules out acquisitions and dispositions that occur all at once, the second observation has created two views about whether step acquisitions and dispositions are changes in reporting entity. Those that believe they are such a change typically base their view on a literal reading of the second observation. The authors believe, however, that step acquisitions and dispositions do not result in changes in reporting entity because they result from transactions. Furthermore, ARB No. 51 and APB Opinion No. 18 generally do not permit restatements for step transactions. Thus, even if step acquisitions and dispositions were considered changes in reporting entity, the APB Opinion No. 20 restatement requirement could not be met. The authors believe the second observation was included in SAS No. 1 because, prior to SFAS No. 94, majority-owned subsidiaries with nonhomogeneous operations were not required to be consolidated, and investors could elect to account for such subsidiaries through consolidation, the equity method, or cost method.

The authors believe changes in reporting entity generally occur when an entity has a choice between acceptable alternatives and changes its policies about which entities are included in consolidated or combined financial statements. (In other words, it occurs as a result of the entity's change in policy rather than a transaction or event.) Thus, a change in reporting entity generally will be limited to one of the following:

> a. *An investee not required to be consolidated is consolidated in one year but not in another.* While SFAS No. 94 requires only majority-owned subsidiaries to be consolidated, it does not preclude an investor from consolidating an investee that is controlled by a means other than through majority ownership, such as through a management agreement. In such cases, if the investor changes its policy and does not consolidate the investee in a subsequent year, a change in reporting entity has occurred. (The authors believe the key factor is whether the consolidated entities change as a result of a change in policy or the occurrence of an event or transaction. In this example, a change in reporting entity has occurred because the investor changed its consolidation policy to another acceptable policy. However, if the investor did not change its policy and did not consolidate the investee as the result of an event, such as the expiration of the management agreement, a change in reporting entity would not have occurred.)

Practical Consideration (Continued).

    b. *Different entities are included in combined statements.* Although not required to do so, companies sometimes present combined financial statements because they result in a more meaningful presentation (for example, when two or more companies with related operations are controlled by the same individual). The authors believe changing the entities included in combined statements is a change in reporting entity if the change is prompted by a change in policy. A change in reporting entity does not occur, however, if the change is prompted by a transaction or event, such as the individual's gain or loss of control over a company.

1.221   A business combination accounted for under the purchase method does not constitute a change in reporting entity. The financial statements for a purchase-method business combination should not be retroactively restated. (APB 16, par. 11) A business combination accounted for under the pooling of interests method does constitute a change in reporting entity, however. Accordingly, the financial statements must be restated as if the combination took place at the beginning of the earliest year presented. (APB 20, par. 12)

Practical Consideration. Although APB Opinion No. 20 states that a business combination accounted for as a pooling of interests results in a change in reporting entity, as a practical matter, APB Opinion No. 16, rather than APB Opinion No. 20, sets the measurement and disclosure requirements for poolings. Chapter 3 discusses accounting for a business combination under the pooling of interests method in further detail.

1.222   In all cases, the key issue in deciding whether a change qualifies as a change in reporting entity is to determine if the change results in financial statements that are, in effect, those of a different reporting entity. (APB 20, par. 12) The concept of a different reporting entity differs from that in which the reporting entity is the same but whose mix of assets and liabilities has changed. The latter situation does not constitute a change in reporting entity.

DISCLOSURE REQUIREMENTS

SUMMARY OF DISCLOSURE REQUIREMENTS

1.500   The following is a summary of disclosure requirements for accounting changes:

    a. *Changes in accounting estimates.* The effect of the change on net income (and income before extraordinary items, if applicable) and related per share amounts should be disclosed if the change affects future years, such as the estimated useful lives of property and equipment. Disclosure of routine changes, such as uncollectible accounts, is only required if they are material. (APB 20, par. 33)

b. *Changes in reporting entity.* Disclosure and reason for the change should be made in the period of change, and the effect on net income (income before extraordinary items, if applicable), and related per share amounts also should be disclosed for all periods presented. (APB 20, par. 35)

c. *Changes in accounting principles, excluding changes in accounting estimates inseparable from changes in accounting principles.* Disclosure should include the following:

   (1) Nature of the change and why it is preferable (APB 20, par. 17)

   (2) The effect of adopting the new principle on net income and income before extraordinary items, if applicable (and for public companies, on related per share amounts) of the period of change or, if the change in principle is accounted for by restating prior period financial statements, the effect for all prior periods presented. (APB 20, paras. 17 and 28)

   (3) For changes in accounting principles to be accounted for through a cumulative effect adjustment, pro forma net income and income before extraordinary items, if applicable (and for public companies, related per share amounts) as if the new principle had been applied during all periods presented. (If an income statement is presented for the current period only, the actual and pro forma amounts for the immediately preceding period should be disclosed. (APB 20, par. 21)

Practical Consideration. Changes in accounting principles that are inseparable from changes in estimates should be treated as changes in accounting estimates.

DISCLOSURE OF CHANGES IN ACCOUNTING PRINCIPLE—UNUSUAL CIRCUMSTANCES

1.501   Exceptions to the typical circumstances surrounding a change in accounting principle occasionally may be encountered in practice. The following summarizes the presentation and disclosure required in unusual circumstances.

     a. *An accounting change is not material in the current period but will have a material effect in later periods.* Disclose the change when financial statements for the period of change are presented. (APB 20, par. 38)

     b. *Cumulative effect is not determinable, for example, a change from FIFO to LIFO.* Disclose effect of change on current results of operations (and per share amounts, if presented) and describe why cumulative effect and pro forma amounts for prior years have been omitted. (APB 20, par. 26)

     c. *Pro forma amounts are not determinable, for example, because information is unavailable.* Present cumulative effect adjustment and related disclosures; explain why pro forma amounts have been omitted. (APB 20, par. 25)

Practical Consideration. In practice, the primary motivation for switching to LIFO is tax benefits, and the IRS conformity rules are the only reason LIFO is used for financial statement reporting. However, that does not constitute "preferable" accounting and, accordingly, the authors recommend reference to the matching concept in disclosing justification for the change.

Prospective Adoption of a New Depreciation Method

1.502   As explained in Paragraph 1.215 companies sometimes adopt a new depreciation method for assets acquired after the effective date of the change but continue to depreciate assets previously acquired using the old method. In such cases, the following disclosures are required: (APB 20, par. 24)

     a. Nature of the change

     b. The effect on net income and income before extraordinary items, if applicable, (and for public companies, the related per share amounts)

The effect on net income is measured by the after tax difference between depreciation of assets acquired after the date of the change as computed under the new method versus the depreciation of those assets determined under the method used for previously acquired assets. Preferability of the change need not be justified because it is the adoption of a new principle rather than the change of an existing one.

DISCLOSURE OF CHANGES IN ACCOUNTING PRINCIPLE—INTERIM PERIODS

1.503   The disclosures required in interim financial statements for changes in accounting principle that are accounted for by reporting the cumulative effect of the change in net income are as follows: (SFAS 3, par. 11)

a. The nature and justification for the change should be disclosed in the interim statements in which the new principle is adopted.

b. The effect of the change on income from continuing operations and net income (and for public companies, related per share amounts) for the interim period in which the change is made should be disclosed.

c. When the change is made in other than the first interim period, the period of change should also disclose:

(1) the effect of the change on income from continuing operations and net income (and for public companies, related per share amounts) for each pre-change interim period of the fiscal year, and

(2) the restated income from continuing operations and net income (and for public companies, related per share amounts) for each pre-change interim period.

d. In the interim period in which the new principle is adopted, income from continuing operations and net income (and for public companies related per share amounts) computed on a pro forma basis for the interim period in which the change is made and any interim periods of prior fiscal years for which financial information is being presented should be disclosed.

(1) If financial information is not being presented for prior fiscal years, disclosure should be made in the period of change of the actual and pro forma amounts of income from continuing operations and net income (and for public companies related

per share amounts) for the interim period of the immediately preceding fiscal year corresponding to the interim period in which the change is made.

    (2) The pro forma amounts should be computed and presented in conformity with the guidance in Paragraphs 1.209–.210.

e. In year-to-date and last twelve-months-to-date financial statements that include the interim period in which a new principle is adopted, the disclosures specified in items a., b., and d. should be made.

f. In financial statements of subsequent (post-change) interim periods, the effect of the change on income from continuing operations and net income (and for public companies, related per share amounts) for the post-change interim periods should be disclosed.

DISCLOSURE OF FUTURE ACCOUNTING CHANGES

1.504   When the accounting principles currently being followed are acceptable, an entity does not have to implement a FASB Statement prior to its effective date. However, entities that have not yet implemented, due to a future effective date, a recently issued Statement that will require retroactive application and is expected to have a material effect on results of operations or financial position should consider whether disclosure of the following is necessary for adequate disclosure:

a. A brief discussion of the new Statement, the date that implementation is required, and the date that the entity plans to implement the Statement

b. A discussion of the effect that implementation of the Statement is expected to have on the financial statements or, if the effect is not known or is not reasonably estimable, a statement to that effect

---

Practical Consideration. If the estimated effect of implementing a new Statement is material, disclosure may be made by supplementing the financial statements with pro forma information as if the adjustment had occurred as of the balance sheet date. The information may be presented in the notes to the financial statements, in a column alongside the statements, or in separate pro forma statements following the financial statements.

AUTHORITATIVE LITERATURE AND RELATED TOPICS

AUTHORITATIVE LITERATURE

APB Opinion No. 16, *Business Combinations*
APB Opinion No. 20, *Accounting Changes*
SFAS No. 3, *Reporting Accounting Changes in Interim Financial Statements*
SFAS No. 73, *Reporting a Change in Accounting for Railroad Track Structures*
SFAS No. 111, *Rescission of FASB Statement No. 32 and Technical Corrections*
FASB Interpretation No. 1, *Accounting for Changes Related to the Cost of Inventory*
FASB Interpretation No. 20, *Reporting Accounting Changes under AICPA Statements of Position*

RELATED PRONOUNCEMENTS

EITF Issue No. 86-46, *Uniform Capitalization Rules for Inventory Under the Tax Reform Act of 1986*
EITF Issue No. 92-4, *Accounting for a Change in Functional Currency When an Economy Ceases to be Considered Highly Inflationary*
EITF Issue No. 93-13, *Effect of a Retroactive Change in Tax Rates on Deferred Taxes that is Included in Income from Continuing Operations*
Accounting Interpretations of APB Opinion No. 20, *Accounting Changes*

RELATED TOPICS

Chapter 2—Accounting Policies, Nature of Operations, and Use of Estimates Disclosures
Chapter 23—Income Statement
Chapter 29—Interim Financial Reporting
Chapter 42—Prior Period Adjustments

ACCOUNTING POLICIES, NATURE OF OPERATIONS, AND USE OF ESTIMATES DISCLOSURES

Table of Contents

ACCOUNTING POLICIES, NATURE OF OPERATIONS, AND USE OF ESTIMATES DISCLOSURES

OVERVIEW

2.100   Applying generally accepted accounting principles often involves choosing from a number of acceptable accounting principles and methods. For example, the LIFO, FIFO, specific identification, or average cost methods may be used to value inventory. Selecting one alternative over another may result in significantly different financial results. Consequently, all significant accounting policies should be disclosed when a balance sheet, income statement, or statement of cash flows is presented.

2.101   Entities are also required to disclose certain information about the nature of their operations and that management's estimates were used in preparing the financial statements.

DISCLOSURE REQUIREMENTS

SUMMARY OF SIGNIFICANT ACCOUNTING POLICIES

General Requirements

2.500   Accounting policies are the specific accounting principles and methods of applying those principles that an entity uses to prepare its financial statements. APB Opinion No. 22, *Disclosure of Accounting Policies,* requires an entity to disclose its significant accounting policies whenever it issues one or more of the basic financial statements (that is, a balance sheet, income statement, or statement of cash flows). An accounting policy is significant if it materially affects the determination of financial position, cash flows, or results of operations. In particular, APB Opinion No. 22 requires disclosing accounting principles and methods that involve any of the following: (APB 22, par. 12 and SFAS 95, par. 152)

- A selection from existing acceptable alternatives

- Industry peculiarities

- Unusual or innovative application of GAAP

2.501   The format, including the location, of the disclosure is flexible. However, APB Opinion No. 22 states that it is preferable to title the information "Summary of Significant Accounting Policies" and present it in a separate summary preceding the notes or in the first note to the financial statements. (APB 22, par. 15)

> **Practical Consideration.** Accounting policies need not be disclosed in interim financial statements unless an accounting policy has changed. In practice, however, accounting policies usually are disclosed when interim financial statements include notes to the financial statements.

Applying the General Requirements

2.502   Often, a specific authoritative pronouncement will require an accounting policy to be disclosed when acceptable alternative policies exist. Also, authoritative literature frequently provides guidance on accounting policies peculiar to specific industries. However, there is little guidance on disclosing unusual or innovative applications of GAAP. In general, financial statement preparers should assume that readers have a fundamental, but not expert, knowledge of accounting principles. That means, for example, that the accounting treatment of changes in a company's tax status might be considered unusual and should be disclosed.

2.503   Accounting policies disclosures need not duplicate information presented elsewhere in the financial statements. Consequently, in some instances it may be appropriate for the accounting policies note to refer to information that may be found in other parts of the financial statements. For example, a change in accounting policy may be described by referring to an "Accounting Change" note that contains the required disclosures of the current effect of the change and the pro forma effect of retroactively applying the change. (APB 22, par. 14)

> **Practical Consideration.** The authors offer the following suggestions when applying the general requirements:
>
> - If an accounting method approximates a generally accepted accounting principle or method, the authors recommend using the GAAP description. Describing both the GAAP method and the method that approximates it only serves to confuse the reader. If the difference between methods is not material, the fact that a method only approximates GAAP is not significant.

Practical Consideration (Continued).

- Normally, the accounting policies note should only deal with policies, and numbers should be excluded. However, the authors believe exceptions to that policy are justified when an additional note would have to be used only to disclose the number.

- In some cases, more than one accounting method may be used (for example, for inventory or depreciation). Since the accounting policy disclosure is intended to identify policies that significantly affect the financial statements, the accounting policy note generally should describe only the primary method(s) used. Thus, if one method accounts for most of the effect on the financial statements, only that method need be identified. If two methods significantly affect the financial statements, both should be described.

- In addition to the other disclosures required for a change in accounting principle (see Chapter 1), the authors believe that the relevant accounting policy note should be expanded to describe the use of different methods during the periods covered by the financial statements.

Specifically Required Accounting Policy Disclosures

2.504   Authoritative pronouncements often require an entity to disclose a specific accounting policy. For example, accounting policies related to the following are specifically required to be disclosed:

- *Inventory.* ARB No. 43, *Restatement and Revision of Accounting Research Bulletins* (Chapter 4—Inventory Pricing), requires disclosure of the basis for stating inventories and the method of determining cost. (ARB 43, Ch. 4, par. 14)

- *Depreciation.* APB Opinion No. 12, *Omnibus Opinion—1967,* requires a general description of the methods used to compute depreciation for major classes of depreciable assets. (APB 12, par. 5)

- *Amortization of intangibles.* APB Opinion No. 17, *Intangible Assets,* requires disclosure of the method and period used to amortize intangible assets. (APB 17, par. 30)

- *Pension plans.* SFAS No. 87, *Employers' Accounting for Pensions,* requires an employer to describe its pension plan, if applicable, including the employee groups covered, type of benefit formula, funding policy, types of assets held, and significant non-benefit liabilities. (SFAS 87, par. 54)

- *Cash and cash equivalents.* SFAS No. 95, *Statement of Cash Flows,* requires disclosure of the policy used to determine whether a short-term investment is treated as a cash equivalent in the statement of cash flows. (SFAS 95, par. 10)

- *Recognition of interest on impaired loans.* SFAS No. 118, *Accounting by Creditors for Impairment of a Loan—Income Recognition and Disclosures,* require disclosing the method used to recognize interest income related to impaired loans. (SFAS 118, par. 6)

- *Tax leases.* FASB Technical Bulletin 82-1, *Disclosure of the Sale or Purchase of Tax Benefits through Tax Leases,* requires disclosure of the method used to account for the sale or purchase of tax benefits through tax leases. (FTB 82-1, par. 4)

In addition, APB Opinion No. 22 states that the basis of consolidation and method of recognizing profit on long-term construction-type contracts are examples of accounting policies that typically should be disclosed. (APB 22, par. 13)

Practical Consideration. In addition to disclosures required by specific pronouncements, the authors recommend disclosing the accounting methods prescribed by authoritative literature that are relatively complex, such as the following:

- The accounting treatment of unrealized gains and losses of investments in debt or equity securities classified as trading securities, held-to-maturity securities, or available-for-sale securities

- A description of how deferred taxes are calculated

- The "lag" in reporting if the investee's year-end differs from the investor's year-end

---

NATURE OF OPERATIONS DISCLOSURES

2.505   A for-profit entity's financial statements should disclose information about the entity's major products or services and its principal markets, including the location of the markets. (A nonprofit entity should describe the principal services it provides and the revenue sources for those services.) An entity that operates more than one business should also indicate the significance of each business to the entity as a whole and the basis used in determining the significance (for example, based on assets, revenues, or earnings). The disclosure need not quantify the significance of each business to the entity as a whole, however. Rather, the entity may indicate the significance of a business by using terms such as "principally," "major," or "about equal." (SOP 94-6, par. 10)

USE OF ESTIMATES TO PREPARE FINANCIAL STATEMENTS

2.506   Preparing financial statements usually requires the use of estimates. For example, it is necessary to estimate an asset's useful life to compute depreciation. SOP 94-6 requires financial statements to disclose that they were prepared using management's estimates. (SOP 94-6, par. 11)

> **Practical Consideration.** The disclosure may be made by including language such as the following in the accounting policies note:
>
> > Management uses estimates and assumptions in preparing financial statements in accordance with generally accepted accounting principles. Those estimates and assumptions affect the reported amounts of assets and liabilities, the disclosure of contingent assets and liabilities, and the reported revenues and expenses. Actual results could vary from the estimates that were assumed in preparing the financial statements.

AUTHORITATIVE LITERATURE AND RELATED TOPICS

AUTHORITATIVE LITERATURE

APB Opinion No. 22, *Disclosure of Accounting Policies*
SOP 94-6, *Disclosure of Certain Significant Risks and Uncertainties*

RELATED TOPICS

Chapter 1—Accounting Changes
Chapter 49—Segment Reporting

BUSINESS COMBINATIONS

Table of Contents

BUSINESS COMBINATIONS

OVERVIEW

3.100   The combination of two or more businesses into one entity should be accounted for under either the purchase or pooling of interests method. The method used depends on the attributes of the combining companies, how the combination is accomplished, and whether certain planned transactions exist. If certain criteria are met, a combination should be accounted for using the pooling of interests method. Otherwise, the purchase method should be used. The primary difference between the two methods is that the purchase method views the combination as an acquisition of one company by the other, whereas the pooling of interests method treats the combination as a uniting of ownership interests.

3.101   Under the purchase method of accounting, the acquiring company should record an acquisition on the basis of the fair value of the consideration given or the fair value of the acquired net assets, whichever is more clearly evident. The purchase price should be allocated to the assets acquired and the liabilities assumed as follows:

a. Assets and liabilities should be recorded at their fair values as of the acquisition date.

b. If the cost of the acquired company exceeds the sum of the amounts assigned to the assets and liabilities acquired, the excess should be recorded as goodwill.

c. If the values assigned to the assets acquired and liabilities assumed exceed the cost of the acquired company, the amounts assigned to noncurrent assets acquired (other than long-term investments in marketable securities) should be reduced by a proportionate part of the excess. After the noncurrent assets have been reduced to zero, any excess of assigned values over cost of the acquired company should be recorded as negative goodwill.

3.102   Under the pooling of interests method, the historical costs of the separate companies' assets and liabilities are combined and become the recorded amounts of the combined company's assets and liabilities. The combining companies' stockholders' equity accounts also are combined. However, because the combined company's outstanding common stock at par or stated value may not equal the separate companies' combined amounts of common stock, the following considerations apply:

a. If the combined company's outstanding common stock at par or stated value is less than the separate companies' combined amounts of common stock, the difference should be added to paid-in capital.

b. If the combined company's outstanding common stock at par or stated value exceeds the separate companies' combined amounts of common stock, the difference should be deducted first from combined paid-in capital and then from combined retained earnings.

3.103   Regardless of the method of accounting used, a business combination should be fully disclosed in the acquiring company's financial statements.

ACCOUNTING REQUIREMENTS

ACCOUNTING METHODS

3.200   A business combination occurs when a company and one or more businesses are brought together into one accounting entity. (APB 16, par. 5) Business combinations usually take one of the following forms:

- An existing company acquires the stock of another company and liquidates the acquired company.

- An existing company acquires the stock of another company and retains the acquired company as a subsidiary.

- A newly formed company acquires the stock of two or more existing companies and either retains the companies as subsidiaries or liquidates them.

- An existing company acquires the assets of one or more companies and, in some cases, assumes their liabilities.

Business combinations are accounted for under either the purchase method or the pooling of interests method. (APB 16, par. 42)

Determining Whether the Purchase or Pooling of Interests Method Applies

3.201   The pooling of interests method should be used to account for a business combination if certain criteria are met. Otherwise, the purchase method should be used. To use the pooling of interests method, a business combination must meet all of the following criteria:

Attributes of the Combining Companies

a. Each of the combining companies is autonomous and has not been a subsidiary or division of another corporation within two years before the plan of combination is initiated. (A plan of combination is initiated on the date the major terms of the plan are formally made known, either by public announcement or in writing, to the stockholders of one of the combining companies.)

b. At the dates the plan of combination is initiated and consummated, the combining companies are independent of each other. A combining company is independent if it does not hold more than 10 percent of the outstanding voting stock of the other combining company excluding shares acquired to effect the combination after the plan of combination is initiated. (APB 16, paras. 45–46) A business combination initiated before November 1, 1970, and completed after that date need not meet the independence requirement to be considered a pooling-of-interests. (SFAS 10, paras. 1–3)

Manner of Combining Interests

c. The combination is effected by a single transaction or is completed in accordance with a specific plan within one year after the plan is initiated.

d. A corporation offers and issues only common stock with rights identical to those of the majority of its outstanding voting common stock in exchange for substantially all of the voting common stock of another company at the date the plan of combination is consummated. (The requirement essentially means that the corporation must exchange its voting common stock for 90 percent or more of the outstanding common stock of the other company between the date the plan of combination is initiated and the date the plan is consummated.) In a business combination initiated before November 1, 1970, and completed after that date, however, 90% of the interest *not held on October 31, 1970,* must be acquired. (SFAS 10, paras. 1–3)

e. None of the combining companies changes the equity interest of the voting common stock in contemplation of effecting the combination either within two years before the plan of combination is initiated or between the dates the combination is initiated and consummated. Changes made in contemplation of effecting the combination include distributions to stockholders (other than normal dividends) and additional issuances, exchanges, and retirements of securities.

f. A combining company reacquires shares of its voting common stock only for purposes other than business combinations (such as for stock option plans or other recurring distributions), and no company reacquires more than a normal number of its shares between the date the plan of combination is initiated and the date it is consummated.

g. The ratio of the interest of an individual common stockholder to those of other common stockholders in a combining company remains the same as a result of the exchange of stock to effect the combination.

h. The common stockholders in the resulting combined corporation can exercise their voting rights. A voting trust or other mechanism may not be used to deprive or restrict stockholders from exercising their voting rights.

i. The combination is resolved at the date the plan is consummated, and no provisions of the plan relating to the issue of securities or other consideration are pending. (Thus, for example, the combined corporation may not agree to contingently issue additional shares of stock at a later date to the former shareholders of a combining company.) (APB 16, par. 47)

Absence of Planned Transactions

j. The combined corporation does not agree directly or indirectly to retire or reacquire all or part of the common stock issued to effect the combination.

k. The combined corporation does not enter into other financial arrangements for the benefit of the former stockholders of a combining company, such as a guaranty of loans secured by stock issued in the combination, that in effect negates the exchange of equity securities.

l. The combined corporation does not intend to dispose of a significant part of the assets of the combining companies within two years after the combination (excluding disposals in the ordinary course of business of the formerly separate companies or to eliminate duplicate facilities or excess capacity). (APB 16, par. 48)

Practical Consideration. The conceptual difference between the purchase and pooling of interests methods is that the purchase method views the business combination as an acquisition or purchase of one company by another, whereas the pooling of interests method treats the combination as a uniting of ownership interests. Consequently—

- Assets acquired and liabilities assumed are recorded at their fair values under the purchase method, but at their book values under the pooling of interests method. Thus, goodwill may arise in a combination under the purchase method, but not under the pooling of interests method.

- Under the purchase method, the earnings of the acquiring company include its share of the earnings of the acquired company only from the date of the acquisition forward. Under the pooling of interests method, the acquiring company's earnings include its share of the acquired company's earnings as if the combination had taken place at the beginning of the earliest period presented.

- Combination expenses (for example, attorney's fees incurred in effecting the combination) are treated as part of the cost of the consideration given under the purchase method, but as a period expense under the pooling of interests method.

Transfers between Entities under Common Control

3.202   A parent company may transfer the net assets of a wholly owned subsidiary to itself and liquidate the subsidiary, or it may transfer its interest in several partially owned subsidiaries to a new wholly owned subsidiary. Such transfers or exchanges between entities under common control should be accounted for at historical cost in a manner similar to a pooling of interests. That is, the acquirer should record the net assets acquired at their book values. (APB 16, par. 5)

Practical Consideration. Acquiring part of a minority interest is not considered a transfer or exchange by entities under common control. The purchase method should be used if the effect of a transfer or exchange is to acquire all or part of the outstanding shares held by a minority interest.

PURCHASE METHOD

3.203   The purchase method treats a business combination as the acquisition or purchase of one enterprise (the acquired company) by another (the acquiring company). Accordingly, the accounting for the combination should follow the historical cost principle for acquisitions in general. That is, the acquiring company should record the acquisition on the basis of the fair value of the consideration given (for example, assets, debt, or stock) or the fair value of the acquired assets less liabilities assumed, whichever is more clearly evident.

3.204   The acquiring company should allocate the total cost (purchase price) of the acquired company to the assets acquired and liabilities assumed. All identifiable assets acquired should be assigned a portion of the total cost equal to their fair values at the date of the business combination. Similarly, all liabilities assumed should be recorded based on their fair values at the date of the combination. Any excess of the cost of the acquired company over the sum of amounts assigned to identifiable net assets acquired should be recorded as goodwill. (APB 16, paras. 66–68)

Determining the Cost of the Acquired Entity

3.205   The cost of the acquired entity is the fair value of the consideration given. It includes cash paid, the fair values of other assets distributed, and the fair values of liabilities incurred to purchase the acquired company. (The fair value of a debt security incurred equals its present value, and a premium or discount should be recorded if the security has a fixed interest rate that materially differs from effective rates or current yields of comparable securities.) The cost of the acquired entity also includes direct acquisition costs. Thus, for example, the fair value of equity securities issued to effect a combination should be reduced by the cost of registering and issuing the securities. (APB 16, paras. 72 and 76) Costs incurred to close duplicate facilities are not included in the cost of the acquired entity, however. (FTB 85-5, par. 1)

> **Practical Consideration.** The cost of an acquired entity does not include indirect expenses related to the acquisition. Such costs should be included in income when incurred.

3.206   **Contingent Consideration.** A business combination agreement may require a company to issue additional shares of stock or transfer other consideration if certain future events occur. Contingent consideration should be disclosed in the financial statement but not recorded as a liability or as additional stock issued until the contingency is determinable beyond a reasonable doubt. (The fact that the contingent consideration is being held by an escrow agent until the contingency is resolved does not alter that treatment.) (APB 16, paras. 77–78) When contingent consideration is recorded, the following guidelines apply:

- *Consideration contingent on achieving a certain level of earnings should be included in the cost of the acquired company.* (APB 16, par. 80)

- *Consideration contingent on whether the security issued to effect the combination maintains or exceeds a specified market price does not affect the cost of the acquired company.* (APB 16, par. 82) For example, assume a company issued 10,000 shares of its stock to acquire another company. The acquiring company agrees that if the value of its stock, which was $15 per share on the acquisition date, is not at least $15 per share at the end of two years, it will issue additional stock equal to the decline in value. At the acquisition date, the cost of the acquired company would be $150,000 ($15 × 10,000). If, at the end of two years, the value of the company's stock drops to $10 per share, the acquiring company would (a) issue another 5,000 shares at $10 per share (for a total cost of $50,000) and (b) reduce the value of the original stock issued to $10 per share (for a total cost of $100,000). Issuing the contingent consideration does not affect the cost of the acquired company. The cost of the acquired company remains the same ($150,000), and only the number of shares issued changes.

- *Contingent consideration that is intended to provide compensation for services or use of property should be recorded as an expense in the period the contingency is resolved.* (APB 16, par. 86)

3.207   Interest and dividends paid or accrued on debt or equity securities held in escrow pending the outcome of the contingency should not be recorded as interest expense or dividend distributions until the contingency is resolved. At that time, any interest or dividends distributed to the former stockholders should be added to the cost of the acquired company. (APB 16, par. 84)

Allocating Cost to Assets Acquired and Liabilities Assumed

3.208   The cost of a purchased subsidiary should be allocated among assets acquired and liabilities assumed as follows: (APB 16, par. 87)

a. All identifiable assets acquired and liabilities assumed (whether or not they are shown in the financial statements of the acquired company) should be assigned a portion of the cost of the acquired company. Normally, the amount assigned to an asset or liability is equal to the asset's or liability's fair value at the date of acquisition.

b. Any excess of the cost of the acquired company over the amounts assigned to assets and liabilities should be recorded as goodwill. If the sum of the fair values of assets acquired less liabilities assumed exceeds the cost of the acquired company, the values otherwise assigned to noncurrent assets acquired (other than long-term investments in marketable securities) should be reduced by a proportionate part of the excess. A deferred credit may be recorded for any excess of assigned values over cost of the acquired company that remains after all noncurrent assets acquired (other than long-term investments in marketable securities) have been reduced to zero. (The deferred credit is sometimes referred to as "negative goodwill.")

3.209 An acquiring company should not record as a separate asset any goodwill previously recorded by the acquired company. In addition, an acquiring company should not record any deferred income taxes recorded by the acquired company before the business combination. (APB 16, par. 88) Instead, a deferred tax asset or liability should be recorded based on the temporary differences between the assigned values and the tax bases of the assets acquired and liabilities assumed. (SFAS 109, par. 30) (Accounting for income taxes is discussed further in Chapter 24.)

Practical Consideration. If the acquiring company expects to sell a portion of the acquired company within one year after the purchase, EITF Issue No. 87-11, *Allocation of Purchase Price to Assets to Be Sold*, requires that the expected cash flows from the operations to be sold be considered in the purchase price allocation. To illustrate, assume that the fair value of the net assets of a division of an acquired company is $100,000. The division is expected to be sold within a year of its acquisition and is expected to earn $20,000 from operations during the holding period. Furthermore, interest on the additional debt needed to finance the purchase of the division is expected to be $8,000. The purchase price allocated to the division's net assets should be $112,000 ($100,000 + $20,000 − $8,000) and should be reported as a single item in the balance sheet. Differences between expected and actual results during the holding period should be charged or credited to the investment account. If sold within one year, any gain or loss on the sale should result in a reallocation of the purchase price of the remaining assets of the acquired company. The gain or loss should not be included in earnings of the continuing business.

Practical Consideration (Continued).

If the business has not been sold after a year but management still intends to sell it, EITF Issue No. 90-6, *Accounting for Certain Events Not Addressed in Issue No. 87-11 Relating to an Acquired Operating Unit to Be Sold,* requires the company to report the results of operations of the business from that point forward as a single line item in its income statement (and continue to report the investment in the assets offered for sale as a single line item in its balance sheet). If management decides not to sell the business, the following applies:

   a. If the decision not to sell was made during the one-year holding period, (1) the purchase price should be reallocated as if the assets had never been held for sale and (2) the provision for expected cash flows from operations should be reversed. The resulting adjustment should be reported as a cumulative effect adjustment and included in the company's results of operations for the year in which the decision was made.

   b. If the decision not to sell was made after the one-year holding period, the purchase price should not be reallocated. Instead, the carrying amount of the investment in the business as of the date that the decision was made should be allocated to the current fair values of the business's identifiable assets and liabilities on that date. The remainder, if any, should be allocated to goodwill.

3.210   The following are guidelines for valuing various types of assets and liabilities:

   a. *Marketable securities*—current net realizable values

   b. *Receivables*—present values of amounts to be received less allowances for uncollectibles and collection costs

   c. *Inventories:*

   (1) *Finished goods and merchandise*—estimated selling prices less the sum of costs of disposal and a reasonable profit allowance

   (2) *Work in process*—estimated selling prices of finished goods less the sum of costs to complete, costs of disposal, and a reasonable profit allowance

   (3) *Raw materials*—current replacement costs (APB 16, par. 88)

d. *Plant and equipment:*

(1) *To be used*—current replacement costs for similar capacity

(2) *To be sold*—fair value less cost to sell (SFAS 121, par. 20)

e. *Identifiable intangible assets*—appraised values

f. *Other assets*—appraised values

g. *Liabilities*—present values of amounts to be paid determined at appropriate current interest rates. (APB 16, par. 88)

Practical Consideration. APB Opinion No. 16 requires valuing identifiable intangible assets, land, natural resources, nonmarketable securities, and other assets at their appraisal values. Most accountants view that as requiring measurement at whatever value would be set between a willing buyer and seller on a going concern basis. The term appraisal value refers to fair value; presumably, it was used to avoid the complexity of addressing the determination of fair value for the variety of assets that are encountered. The following are common valuation methods:

- *Customer lists*—discounted cash flow, with the period depending on the length of time the entity is benefited

- *Franchises*—current cost

- *Favorable leases*—difference between discounted cash flow at current and market rates

- *Land*—fair market value or discounted cash flows

- *Nonmarketable securities*—discounted cash flows

3.211 **Contingent Assets Acquired and Contingent Liabilities Assumed.** Contingent assets acquired and contingent liabilities assumed should be assigned a portion of the cost of the acquired company when (a) the fair value of the preacquisition contingency can be determined during the allocation period or (b) information available prior to the end of the allocation period indicates that it is probable that an asset existed, a liability had been incurred, or an asset had been impaired, and the amount of the asset or liability can be reasonably estimated. The allocation period is the period required to identify and quantify the assets acquired and the liabilities assumed. It ends when the acquiring company is no longer waiting for information that it has arranged to obtain and that is known to be available or obtainable. The

one year from the date the business combination was consummated. (SFAS 38, paras. 4–5)

3.212 Pension Plan Assets and Liabilities. When a defined benefit plan is acquired as part of a business combination accounted for under the purchase method, a portion of the purchase price should be allocated to a liability for a projected benefit obligation in excess of plan assets. Similarly, cost should be allocated to an asset for an excess of plan assets over the projected benefit obligation. Recognizing a new pension asset or liability at the date of purchase results in the elimination of any (a) unrecognized net gain or loss, (b) unrecognized prior service cost, and (c) unrecognized net obligation or asset that existed when SFAS No. 87, *Employers' Accounting for Pensions,* was adopted. (SFAS 87, par. 74)

3.213 Postretirement Benefit Plan Assets and Liabilities. When a defined postretirement benefit plan (other than a pension plan) is acquired as part of a business combination accounted for under the purchase method, a portion of the purchase price should be allocated to (a) a liability for the accumulated postretirement benefit obligation in excess of the fair value of plan assets or (b) an asset for the excess of the fair value of plan assets over the accumulated postretirement benefit obligation. The acquiring company should measure the accumulated postretirement benefit obligation based on its own assumptions about future events and based on the terms of the plan that it will provide if they differ from the terms of the acquired entity's plan. (SFAS 106, par. 86)

3.214 If plan benefits are improved as a result of the business combination and the improvement is attributable to employee service rendered before the purchase was consummated, the following applies: (SFAS 106, par. 87)

- If the improvement is made as a condition of the business combination, its effect should be included in the accumulated postretirement benefit obligation assumed.

- If the improvement is not made as a condition of the business combination, its effect should be accounted for as prior service cost to the extent it is attributable to prior service cost.

3.215 Assets Associated with Research and Development Activities. In a business combination, a portion of the purchase price should be assigned to acquired identifiable intangible and tangible assets resulting from research and development activities and to those used for research and development activities. Upon completion of the business combination, costs assigned to assets *used for* research and development activities should be charged to expense unless they have an alternative future use. (See Chapter 47.) (FASBI No. 4, paras. 4-5.)

> **Practical Consideration.** Identifiable assets *resulting from* research and development activities of the acquired entity include patents, blueprints, formulas, and specifications and designs for new products. Identifiable assets *used for* research and development activities include materials and supplies, equipment and facilities, and research projects in progress.

Financial Institutions

3.216   When a banking or thrift institution is acquired in a business combination, the assets acquired and liabilities assumed should be recorded at their fair values at the acquisition date. The net-spread method, which values the acquired company as a whole based on the spread between interest rates received on the loan portfolio and interest rates paid on deposit accounts, should not be used. (FASBI 9, par. 4) The fair value of identifiable intangible assets related to loans or deposits should be based on relationships that exist at the acquisition date. Relationships with new depositors or borrowers that occur after the acquisition date should not be considered. (SFAS 72, par. 4)

POOLING OF INTERESTS METHOD

3.217   The pooling of interests method views the business combination as a uniting of two separate interests. Stockholders of the combining companies do not withdraw or invest assets, but exchange stock based on a ratio that determines their interests in the combined enterprise. As discussed in Paragraph 3.201 the pooling of interests method may only be used if certain conditions dealing with the attributes of the combining companies, manner of combining interests, and absence of planned transactions are met. (APB 16, par. 45)

Recording Assets and Liabilities

3.218   Under the pooling of interests method, the historical costs of the separate companies' assets and liabilities are combined and become the recorded amounts of the combined company's assets and liabilities. If the separate companies used different methods of accounting to record assets and liabilities, adjustments may be made so that the same method of accounting is used (but only if the change in accounting method otherwise would have been appropriate for the separate company). Changes to conform accounting methods should be retroactively applied, and prior period financial statements should be restated, if presented. (APB 16, paras. 51–52) (See Paragraph 3.224 regarding the presentation of prior period financial statements.)

3.219 **Disposition of Assets.** The combined company may dispose of assets to eliminate duplicate facilities or excess capacity or in the normal course of its operations. Losses or estimated losses on those disposals should be deducted to determine the combined company's net income. Other significant asset disposals may require special treatment, however, because the company would not have been allowed to use the pooling of interests method if it *planned or was committed to make* significant disposals as a result of the combination. (See Paragraph 3.201, item l.) Profits or losses from such disposals should be classified as extraordinary items, net of any related tax effects if (a) the profit or loss is material to the combined company's net income and (b) the disposition is within two years of the combination. (APB 16, paras. 59–60)

Recording Stockholders' Equity

3.220   The separate companies' stockholders' equity accounts also are combined under the pooling of interests method. Thus, the separate companies' recorded amounts of capital stock are combined to become the combined company's capital stock amount; the separate companies' paid-in capital amounts are combined to become the combined company's paid-in capital amount; and the separate companies' retained earnings or deficits are combined to become the combined company's retained earnings or deficit. The combined company's outstanding common stock at par or stated value may not equal the separate companies' combined amounts of common stock. In such cases, the following guidelines apply: (APB 16, par. 53)

- If the combined company's outstanding common stock at par or stated value is less than the separate companies' combined amounts of common stock, the difference should be added to paid-in capital. For example, assume that Company A had 2,000 shares of $15 par common stock outstanding and Company B had 1,000 shares of $20 par value common stock outstanding. If Company A issues 1,000 shares of its common stock in exchange for all of Company B's common stock, the combined company's common stock and paid-in capital amounts would be determined as follows:

Company A's common stock before the combination (2,000 × $15)	$ 30,000
Company B's common stock before the combination (1,000 × $20)	20,000
	50,000
Combined company's common stock (3,000 × $15)	45,000
Increase to paid-in capital	$ 5,000

- If the combined company's outstanding common stock at par or stated value exceeds the separate companies' combined amounts of common stock, the difference should be deducted first from combined paid-in capital and then from combined retained earnings. For example, in the preceding illustration, if Company A had issued 2,000 shares of its common stock in exchange for all of Company B's common stock, the combined company's common stock, paid-in capital, and retained earnings accounts would be determined as follows:

Company A's common stock before the combination (2,000 × $15)	$ 30,000
Company B's common stock before the combination (1,000 × $20)	20,000
	50,000
Combined company's common stock (4,000 × $15)	60,000
Decrease to other capital accounts	$ (10,000)

The $10,000 decrease to other capital accounts would first be applied to paid-in capital. The decrease remaining after paid-in capital has been reduced to zero would then be applied to retained earnings.

3.221   The following guidance applies when a combining company owns treasury stock or stock in other combining companies: (APB 16, paras. 54–55)

a. If the acquiring company issues treasury stock to effect the combination, it should treat the treasury stock as retired. (Retiring treasury stock is discussed in Chapter 51.) It should then consider the shares the same as it would any previously unissued shares.

b. If an acquired company has an investment in the common stock of the acquiring company, the combined company should account for the investment as treasury stock since the investment in effect has been returned to the issuing company.

c. Investments in the common stock of acquired companies (that is, those not issuing stock to effect the combination) in effect are exchanged in the combination for shares of the acquiring company. Thus, investments in the common stock of acquired companies should be treated as stock that is retired as part of the combination.

Combination Expenses

3.222   All expenses related to the business combination should be deducted from the combined company's net income in the period in which they are incurred. Such costs should not be recorded as asset additions or reductions to stockholders' equity. Examples of expenses related to business combinations include registration fees, costs of furnishing information to stockholders, consultants' fees, and costs and losses resulting from combining operations of the previously separate companies. (APB 16, par. 58)

Reporting Considerations

3.223   Under the pooling of interests method, the combined company should report its operations for the period in which the combination occurs as if the combination occurred at the beginning of the period. Similarly, balance sheets and other financial information as of the beginning of the period should be presented as though the company had been combined. The effects of intercompany transactions on current assets, current liabilities, revenue, and cost of sales for periods presented and on retained earnings at the beginning of the periods presented should be eliminated to the extent possible. The effects of nonrecurring intercompany transactions involving long-term assets and liabilities need not be eliminated, although their nature and effects on earnings per share should be disclosed. Certain disclosures are also required about the results of operations of each of the separate companies from the beginning of the period to the date the combination is consummated. (APB 16, paras. 56–57) (Disclosure requirements are discussed further in Paragraphs 3.500–.504.)

3.224   Prior period financial statements and financial information, if presented, should be restated on a combined basis to aid comparisons to the current period. The restated information should clearly indicate, however, that it is the combined information of previously separate companies. (APB 16, par. 57)

3.225   **Financial Statements of Combining Companies.** A business combination that will qualify for pooling of interests accounting may be initiated but not consummated as of the date of a combining company's financial statements. In such cases, the combining company should record any common stock of the other combining companies acquired before the financial statement date as follows: (APB 16, par. 62)

a. Common stock purchased with cash or other assets or by incurring liabilities should be recorded at cost.

b. Stock acquired in exchange for common stock of the issuing company should be recorded at the proportionate share of underlying net assets as of the date the stock was acquired.

The equity method should be used to account for the investment until the combination is consummated. (Chapter 20 discusses the application of the equity method of accounting.) In addition, the combining company should include certain disclosures about the combination in its financial statements. (See Paragraphs 3.503–.504.)

DISCLOSURE REQUIREMENTS

PURCHASE METHOD

3.500   The acquiring company should disclose the following in its financial statements for the period a business combination accounted for by the purchase method occurs: (APB 16, par. 95)

a. Nature and brief description of the acquired company

b. Method of accounting for the combination (that is, by the purchase method)

c. Period for which the acquired company's results of operations are included in the acquiring company's income statement

d. Cost of the acquired company and, if applicable, the number of shares of stock issued or issuable and the amount assigned to the issued and issuable shares

e. Description of the plan for amortizing acquired goodwill, including the amortization method and period

  f. Contingent payments, options, or commitments specified in the acquisition agreement and their proposed accounting treatment

  g. Consideration that is issued or issuable at the end of a contingency period or that is held in escrow (APB 16, par. 78)

3.501   An acquiring company that is publicly held (SFAS 79, par. 6) also should present the following supplemental, pro forma information:

  a. Results of operations for the current period as though the companies had combined at the beginning of the period (unless the acquisition was at or near the beginning of the period)

  b. If comparative statements are presented, the results of operations for the immediately preceding period as though the companies had combined at the beginning of that period

At a minimum, the supplemental information should disclose revenue, income before extraordinary items, net income, and earnings per share amounts. (APB 16, par. 96)

POOLING OF INTERESTS METHOD

3.502   When the pooling of interests method is used, the combined company should disclose in its financial statements that a combination accounted for by the pooling of interests method occurred during the period. The disclosure, which includes the basis of the current presentation and a reference to the restatement of prior year information if presented, should be made through appropriate financial statement captions or references to the notes to the financial statements. In addition, the combined company should disclose the following in its notes for the period the combination occurs: (APB 16, paras. 63–64)

  a. Name and brief description of the companies combined

  b. Method of accounting for the combination (that is, by the pooling of interests method)

  c. Description and number of shares of stock issued in the business combination

  d. Details of the results of operations of the previously separate companies for the period before the combination is consummated that are included in current combined net income (The details should include revenue, extraordinary items, net income, other changes in stockholders' equity, and amount of and manner of accounting for intercompany transactions.)

e. Nature of adjustments of net assets of the combining companies to adopt the same accounting practices and, if prior period financial statements are presented, the effects of the adjustments on net income reported previously by the separate companies

f. If a combining company changed its fiscal year as a result of the combination, details of any increase or decrease in retained earnings as a result of the change (At a minimum, the details should include revenues, expenses, extraordinary items, net income, and other changes in stockholders' equity for the period that are excluded from the reported results of operations.)

g. Reconciliations of the acquiring company's previously reported revenue and earnings to combined amounts currently presented (The acquiring company is the company that issues the stock to effect the combination. If a new company is formed to effect the combination, the earnings of the separate companies that comprise combined earnings for prior periods may be disclosed instead.)

h. The nature of and effects on earnings per share of nonrecurring intercompany transactions involving long-term assets and liabilities that were not eliminated from current period income (APB 16, par. 56)

3.503   A combining company should disclose information about a business combination that (a) occurs before it issues its separate financial statements but (b) is either incomplete or not initiated as of the financial statement date. The disclosure should include the effects of the combination on revenue and net income (and for public companies, earnings per share) and the effects of anticipated changes in accounting methods as if the combination had been consummated at the financial statement date. The disclosure should be made for all periods presented. (APB 16, par. 65)

3.504   In addition, if a transaction expected to be treated as a pooling has been initiated, and a portion of the stock has been acquired, but the pooling is not consummated at the balance sheet date, combined results of operations of all prior periods presented and the entire current period should be disclosed. The disclosure should be disclosed in the same manner as it would be presented if the combination is later accounted for as a pooling. (APB 16, par. 62)

AUTHORITATIVE LITERATURE AND RELATED TOPICS

AUTHORITATIVE LITERATURE

APB Opinion No. 16, *Business Combinations*

SFAS No. 10, *Extension of "Grandfather" Provisions for Business Combinations*

SFAS No. 38, *Accounting for Preacquisition Contingencies of Purchased Enterprises*

SFAS No. 72, *Accounting for Certain Acquisitions of Banking or Thrift Institutions*

SFAS No. 79, *Elimination of Certain Disclosures for Business Combinations by Nonpublic Companies*

SFAS No. 87, *Employers' Accounting for Pensions*

SFAS No. 106, *Employers' Accounting for Postretirement Benefits Other Than Pensions*

SFAS No. 109, *Accounting for Income Taxes*

SFAS No. 121, *Accounting for Impairment of Long-Lived Assets and for Long-Lived Assets to be Disposed Of*

FASB Technical Bulletin 85-5, *Issues Relating to Accounting for Business Combinations*

FASB Interpretation No. 4, *Applicability of FASB Statement No. 2 to Business Combinations Accounted for by the Purchase Method*

FASB Interpretation No. 9, *Applying APB Opinion Nos. 16 and 17 When a Savings and Loan Association or Similar Institution Is Acquired in a Business Combination Accounted for by the Purchase Method*

RELATED PRONOUNCEMENTS

EITF Issue No. 84-22, *Prior Years' Earnings per Share following a Savings and Loan Association Conversion and Pooling*

EITF Issue No. 84-23, *Leveraged Buyout Holding Company Debt*

EITF Issue No. 84-35, *Business Combinations: Sale of Duplicate Facilities and Accrual of Liabilities*

EITF Issue No. 85-4, *Downstream Mergers and Other Stock Transactions between Companies under Common Control*

EITF Issue No. 85-14, *Securities That Can Be Acquired for Cash in a Pooling of Interests*

EITF Issue No. 85-43, *Sale of Subsidiary for Equity Interest in Buyer*

EITF Issue No. 85-45, *Business Combinations: Settlement of Stock Options and Awards*

EITF Issue No. 86-9, *IRC Section 338 and Push-Down Accounting*

EITF Issue No. 86-10, *Pooling with 10 Percent Cash Payout Determined by Lottery*

EITF Issue No. 86-14, *Purchased Research and Development Projects in a Business Combination*

EITF Issue No. 86-29, *Nonmonetary Transactions: Magnitude of Boot and the Exceptions to Use of Fair Value*

EITF Issue No. 87-11, *Allocation of Purchase Price to Assets to Be Sold*

EITF Issue No. 87-15, *Effect of a Standstill Agreement of Pooling-of-Interests Accounting*

EITF Issue No. 87-16, *Whether the 90 Percent Test for a Pooling of Interests Is Applied Separately to Each Company or on a Combined Basis*

EITF Issue No. 87-27, *Poolings of Companies That Do Not Have a Controlling Class of Common Stock*

EITF Issue No. 88-16, *Basis in Leveraged Buyout Transactions*

EITF Issue No. 88-19, *FSLIC-Assisted Acquisitions of Thrifts*

EITF Issue No. 88-26, *Controlling Preferred Stock in a Pooling of Interests*

EITF Issue No. 88-27, *Effect of Unallocated Shares in an Employee Stock Ownership Plan on Accounting for Business Combinations*

EITF Issue No. 89-19, *Accounting for a Change in Goodwill Amortization for Business Combinations Initiated Prior to the Effective Date of FASB Statement No. 72*

EITF Issue No. 90-6, *Accounting for Certain Events Not Addressed in Issue No. 87-11 Relating to an Acquired Operating Unit to Be Sold*

EITF Issue No. 90-10, *Accounting for a Business Combination Involving a Majority-Owned Investee of a Venture Capital Company*

EITF Issue No. 90-12, *Allocating Basis to Individual Assets and Liabilities for Transactions within the Scope of Issue No. 88-16*

EITF Issue No. 90-13, *Accounting for Simultaneous Common Control Mergers*

EITF Issue No. 92-9, *Accounting for the Present Value of Future Profits Resulting from the Acquisition of a Life Insurance Company*

EITF Issue No. 93-2, *Effect of Acquisition of Employer Shares for/by an Employee Benefit Trust on Accounting for Business Combinations*

EITF Issue No. 93-7, *Uncertainties Related to Income Taxes in a Purchase Business Combination*

EITF Issue No. 95-3, *Recognition of Liabilities in Connection with a Purchase Business Combination*

EITF Issue No. 95-8, *Accounting for Contingent Consideration Paid to the Shareholders of an Acquired Enterprise in a Purchase Business Combination*

EITF Issue No. 95-12, *Pooling-of-Interests with a Common Investment in a Joint Venture*

EITF Issue No. 95-14, *Recognition of Liabilities in Anticipation of a Business Combination*

EITF Issue No. 95-19, *Determination of the Measurement Date for the Market Price of Securities Issued in a Purchase Business Combination*

EITF Issue No. 95-21, *Accounting for Assets to Be Disposed of Acquired in a Purchase Business Combination*

EITF Issue No. 96-5, *Recognition of Liabilities for Contractual Termination Benefits or Changing Benefit Plan Assumptions in Anticipation of a Business Combination*

EITF Issue No. 96-7, *Accounting for Deferred Taxes on In-Process Research and Development Activities Acquired in a Purchase Business Combination*

EITF Issue No. 96-8, *Accounting for a Business Combination When the Issuing Company Has Targeted Stock*

EITF Issue No. 97-8, *Accounting for Contingent Consideration Issued in a Purchase Business Combination*

EITF Issue No. 97-9, *Effect on Pooling-of-Interests Accounting of Certain Contingently Exercisable Options or Other Equity Instruments*

FASB Technical Bulletin 85-6, *Accounting for a Purchase of Treasury Shares at a Price Significantly in Excess of the Current Market Price of the Shares and the Income Statement Classification of Costs Incurred in Defending Against a Takeover Attempt*

Accounting Interpretations of APB Opinion No. 16, *Business Combinations*

RELATED TOPICS

CASH FLOWS STATEMENT

Table of Contents

CASH FLOWS STATEMENT

Table of Contents (Continued)

CASH FLOWS STATEMENT

OVERVIEW

4.100   A statement of cash flows is required to be presented as part of a full set of financial statements prepared in accordance with generally accepted accounting principles. The statement shows a company's cash receipts and payments during a period, classified by principal sources and uses. The cash receipts and payments are categorized as operating, investing, and financing activities. In addition, noncash transactions that affect financial position must be disclosed.

4.101   A statement of cash flows must be included for each period that an income statement is presented along with a balance sheet. If a balance sheet or income statement is presented separately, a statement of cash flows is not required.

ACCOUNTING REQUIREMENTS

WHEN SHOULD THE STATEMENT BE PRESENTED?

4.200   A statement of cash flows shows the changes in an entity's cash and cash equivalents during a period. (SFAS 95, par. 7) It should be presented as a basic financial statement when each of the following conditions is met:

a. The entity is a profit-oriented business enterprise or nonprofit organization. Individuals are not required to present the statement. (SFAS 95, par. 3 and SFAS 117, par. 30)

b. The financial statements are prepared in accordance with generally accepted accounting principles. A statement of cash flows is not required if the financial statements are prepared on a basis of accounting other than GAAP.

c. Both a balance sheet and an income statement are presented. (A statement of cash flows should be provided for each period for which an income statement is presented.) (SFAS 95, par. 3)

Practical Consideration. Authoritative literature does not prohibit presenting a statement of cash flows when the preceding requirements are not met. Thus, for example, a company could present a statement of cash flows and not present a balance sheet or income statement.

4.201   The following entities are exempt from the requirement to present a statement of cash flows, however:

a. Defined benefit pension plans and employee benefit plans presenting financial information similar to that of defined benefit pension plans (SFAS 102, par. 5)

b. If the following conditions are met, investment companies subject to the requirements of the Investment Company Act of 1940 (and those with essentially the same characteristics as those subject to the Act) and common trust funds, variable annuity accounts, or similar funds maintained by a trustee, administrator, or guardian (SFAS 102, paras. 6–7)

   (1) Substantially all investments during the period were highly liquid.

   (2) Substantially all investments are carried at market value.

   (3) The entity had little or no debt, based on average debt outstanding during the period, in relation to average total assets.

   (4) The entity presents a statement of changes in net assets.

All other entities meeting the requirements in Paragraph 4.200 are required to present a statement of cash flows regardless of their legal form (for example, partnership, proprietorship, limited liability company, S corporation, or C corporation) or whether they normally classify their assets and liabilities as current and noncurrent. In addition, the requirement to present a statement of cash flows applies to both interim and annual financial statements.

DEFINITION OF CASH AND CASH EQUIVALENTS

4.202   As discussed in Paragraph 4.200 the statement of cash flows presents information about changes in cash and cash equivalents. Cash includes currency on hand and demand deposits with banks or other financial institutions. It also includes other accounts that have the general characteristics of demand deposits in that the customer may deposit or withdraw funds at any time without prior notice or penalty. Examples of cash include certificates of deposit (unless penalties or terms associated with them effectively restrict withdrawal of funds), money market accounts, and repurchase agreements that have the preceding characteristics. (SFAS 95, paras. 7 and 9)

> **Practical Consideration.** Some companies do not include cash overdrafts in the definition of cash. Instead, they consider overdrafts to be current liabilities similar to accounts payable. Thus, they present cash overdrafts as an operating activity in the statement of cash flows. The authors believe, however, that a cash overdraft generally should be included in the definition of cash. Although there is a financing element to a cash overdraft, the time required for the overdraft to be eliminated usually is insignificant.
>
> In addition, because cash restricted for special purposes should be separated from cash available for general operations and, normally, excluded from current assets, the authors believe restricted cash should not be included in the definition of cash or cash equivalents.

4.203   Cash equivalents are short-term, highly liquid investments that (a) are readily convertible to known amounts of cash and (b) are so near to their maturity that they present an insignificant risk of changes in value because of changes in interest rates. Examples include Treasury bills, commercial paper, money market accounts that are not classified as cash, and other short-term investments whose *original* maturity is three months or less. (SFAS 95, par. 8) (Equity securities never meet the definition of cash equivalents.) Paragraphs 4.225–.226 provide further guidance on distinguishing between investments and cash equivalents.

> **Practical Consideration.** Only investments that meet the preceding criteria and mature three months or less from the date they were purchased qualify as cash equivalents. For example, a three-month Treasury bill and a three-year Treasury note purchased three months from maturity both qualify as cash equivalents. A Treasury note purchased three years ago does not become a cash equivalent when its remaining maturity is three months, however.

4.204   Throughout this chapter, the authors use the term cash to include cash equivalents.

BASIC ELEMENTS OF THE STATEMENT OF CASH FLOWS

4.205   A statement of cash flows has five basic elements:

- Cash flows from operating activities

- Cash flows from investing activities

- Cash flows from financing activities

- Net change in cash during the period

- Supplemental disclosure of noncash investing and financing activities

Accordingly, all cash receipts and payments should be classified as operating, investing, or financing activities, and noncash transactions involving investing and financing activities, such as acquiring assets by assuming liabilities, should be disclosed separately rather than within the body of the statement. (SFAS 95, par. 6) When a cash receipt or cash payment qualifies for more than one classification, it should be included in the category that represents the predominant source of cash flows for the item. (SFAS 95, par. 24) EXHIBIT 4-1 shows how a typical company's transactions would be classified into operating, investing, and financing activities.

Presenting Gross and Net Cash Flows

4.206 As a general rule, cash flows from investing and financing activities should be reported in gross rather than net amounts. The presumption is that gross cash receipts and disbursements are more relevant than net amounts. (SFAS 95, par. 11) Thus, for example, both proceeds from sales of assets and cash payments for capital expenditures should be shown in the cash flows statement rather than the net change in property and equipment. In addition, both proceeds from short-term debt and payments to settle short-term debt should be shown rather than the net change in short-term debt.

4.207 While the general rule calls for reporting gross cash flows, net cash flows may be reported from the following activities:

a. Cash receipts and payments from purchasing and selling cash equivalents (SFAS 95, par. 11)

b. Cash receipts and payments related to investments that are not cash equivalents, loans receivable, and debt when the original maturity of the asset or liability is three months or less (Amounts due on demand and credit card receivables of financial services operations with original maturities of three months or less are considered to be loans.) (SFAS 95, par. 13)

EXHIBIT 4-1
TYPES OF CASH FLOWS

STATEMENT OF CASH FLOWS

OPERATING	INVESTING	FINANCING	NONCASH INVESTING AND FINANCING TRANSACTIONS
CASH RECEIPTS FROM: • Sale of goods and services • Short and long-term notes receivable from customers arising from sales of goods or services • Interest and dividends • Other cash receipts not arising from investing or financing activities, such as amounts received to settle lawsuits or refunds from suppliers • Sale or maturity of trading securities	**CASH RECEIPTS FROM:** • Sale of property and equipment • Sale of available-for-sale or held to maturity securities • Collections on loans • Insurance proceeds relating to transactions classified as investing	**CASH RECEIPTS FROM:** • Short-term borrowings • Long-term borrowings • Issuance of stock	• Acquiring nonoperating assets, e.g., property and equipment or a subsidiary, by assuming liabilities • Issuing stock in exchange for subscriptions receivable or other noncash consideration • Converting debt to equity or one class of stock to another, e.g., common to preferred • Stock dividends or distributions of property as dividends • Converting notes receivable to investments
CASH PAYMENTS FOR: • Inventory • Short and long-term notes payable to suppliers for materials or goods • Wages • Other operating expenses • General and administrative expenses • Interest (excluding amounts capitalized) • Taxes • Other cash payments not related to investing or financing activities, such as cash contributions and cash refunds to customers • Purchase of trading securities	**CASH PAYMENTS FOR:** • Property and equipment (including capitalized interest) • Available-for-sale or held-to-maturity securities • Loans to others	**CASH PAYMENTS FOR:** • Dividends • Repayment of amounts borrowed, e.g., short-term debt, long-term debt, and capital lease obligations • Treasury stock	

    c. Cash receipts and payments from agency transactions (that is, transactions for which the company is holding or disbursing cash on behalf of its customers) (SFAS 95, par. 12)

    d. For banks, savings institutions, and credit unions, cash receipts and payments related to:

        (1) Deposits placed with other financial institutions

        (2) Customer time deposits

        (3) Loans made to customers (SFAS 104, par. 7)

4.208   Although GAAP permits reporting net cash flows from the preceding activities, netting is not required. Presenting gross cash flows for those activities may be preferable in some instances. For example, it may create an unnecessary recordkeeping burden to segregate cash flows from investments with a maturity of three months or less from those of investments with longer maturities.

Practical Consideration. Should cash flows from revolving lines of credit be presented on a gross or net basis? A difference of opinion exists among CPAs in practice. Some firms have taken the position that there must be a series of 90-day notes for the cash flows to be presented net. If the borrower signs a single note with a term of more than three months for the maximum amount of the line of credit, they believe that GAAP requires gross amounts to be presented. Others, however, present all cash flows related to revolving lines of credit net. The authors believe that either method is acceptable.

CASH FLOWS FROM OPERATING ACTIVITIES

What Is Included?

4.209   Cash flows from operating activities are defined by exception; operating activities include all transactions and events that are not investing or financing activities. Generally, however, operating activities meet the following three criteria:

    a. The amounts represent the cash effects of transactions or events.

    b. The amounts result from a company's normal operations for delivering or producing goods for sale and providing services.

c. The amounts are derived from activities that enter into the determination of net income.

Thus, cash flows from operating activities include cash received from sales of goods or services and cash used in generating the goods or services, such as for inventory, personnel, and administrative and other operating costs. Cash receipts from both short and long-term notes receivables from customers arising from sales of goods or services are also classified as operating activities. Similarly, principal payments on customers' accounts and both short and long-term notes payable to suppliers for materials or goods also should be classified as operating activities. In addition, interest and dividend income and interest expense are considered to be operating activities even though they are not precisely consistent with the preceding criteria. (SFAS 95, paras. 21–23)

4.210   Cash flows from operating activities exclude (a) amounts not derived from cash receipts and cash payments (for example, accruals, deferrals, and allocations such as depreciation), and (b) amounts considered to be derived from investing or financing activities rather than from operations (for example, cash receipts and payments related to property and equipment and dividends paid).

Formats for Presenting Cash Flows from Operations

4.211   Cash flows from operations may be presented in either of two basic formats: the direct method or the indirect method. The following paragraphs describe both methods.

Practical Consideration. The authors believe that GAAP permits an entity to present cash flows using the direct method in one year and the indirect method in the next (or vice versa). If presented for comparative purposes, however, the authors recommend restating prior year cash flows to conform to the current year presentation and disclosing the fact that the prior period was restated.

4.212   **Direct Method.** The direct method begins with cash receipts and deducts cash payments for operating costs and expenses, individually listing the cash effects of each major type of revenue and expense. At a minimum, the following categories of cash receipts and cash payments are required to be presented:

- Cash collected from customers, including lessees and licensees

- Interest and dividends received

- Other operating cash receipts, if any

- Cash paid to employees and other suppliers of goods or services, including suppliers of insurance and advertising

- Interest paid

- Income taxes paid

- Other operating cash payments, if any (SFAS 95, par. 27)

Because the direct method shows only cash receipts and payments, no adjustments are necessary for noncash expenses such as depreciation or deferred income taxes. The following illustrates how cash flows from operating activities would be presented using the direct method:

CASH FLOWS FROM OPERATING ACTIVITIES

Cash received from customers	$ 435,000
Interest received	2,450
	437,450
Cash paid to suppliers and employees	274,000
Cash paid to settle lawsuit	15,000
Interest paid	3,475
Income taxes paid	12,000
	304,475
NET CASH PROVIDED BY OPERATING ACTIVITIES	132,975

4.213   If the direct method is used, a reconciliation of net income to cash flows from operating activities is required to be presented in a separate schedule showing all major classes of operating items, including, at a minimum, changes in receivables and payables related to operating activities and changes in inventory. (SFAS 95, par. 29)

Practical Consideration. Proponents of the direct method believe it is preferable because it shows the actual sources and uses of cash from operations. In addition, some accountants believe the statement of cash flows is easier to understand because there is no need to adjust for noncash items such as depreciation. The direct method may be preferable to the indirect method in the following circumstances:

- Information required for the direct method is readily available or can be obtained without significant cost.

Practical Consideration (Continued).

- There are numerous reconciling items between net income and cash flows from operations making the indirect presentation cluttered and cumbersome to analyze.

- Management or banks with which the company obtains financing find the relationship of specific cash receipts and payments to cash flows from operations useful for making decisions.

The authors believe that it generally will take more time to prepare a statement using the direct method than using the indirect method. Additional time is necessary because a separate reconciliation of net income to operating cash flows is required, thus presenting operating cash flows both directly and indirectly.

4.214 **Indirect Method.** The indirect method starts with net income and adjusts for (a) noncash items such as depreciation and deferred income taxes and (b) changes during the period in operating current assets and liabilities. The reconciliation should show all major classes of operating items, including, at a minimum, changes in receivables and payables related to operating activities and changes in inventory. Changes in current assets and liabilities arising from investing or financing activities (for example, short-term loans or notes receivable or payable not related to sales of goods or services) should be shown as investing or financing activities, as appropriate, however. In addition, accounts payable may have aspects of financing or investing activities, for example, dividends payable or equipment purchased on account. In such cases, it would not be appropriate to include the net change in payables as an adjustment in arriving at cash flows from operations. (SFAS 95, par. 28)

Practical Consideration. Although GAAP literally requires presenting changes in receivables, payables, and inventory separately in the reconciliation, some firms believe that amounts could be combined if they would affect a single line item under the direct method, such as increase in accounts payable and accrued expenses.

4.215 Items reconciling net income to net cash flows from operating activities may be presented in the statement of cash flows or in a separate schedule. The following illustrates presenting the reconciliation in the statement of cash flows:

CASH FLOWS FROM OPERATING ACTIVITIES

Net income	$ 223,000
Adjustments to reconcile net income to net cash	
provided by operating activities	
Depreciation	29,400
Gain on sale of equipment	(6,700)
(Increase) decrease in:	
Trade accounts receivable	(10,200)
Inventories	26,450
Prepaid expenses	4,100
Increase (decrease) in:	
Trade accounts payable	37,250
Accrued liabilities	(9,500)
Income taxes payable	4,300
NET CASH PROVIDED BY	
OPERATING ACTIVITIES	298,100

4.216   If the reconciling items were presented in a separate schedule, the cash flow statement would show a single line item for cash flows from operations such as the following:

Net cash flows from operating activities $ 298,100

4.217   **Agency Transactions.** Changes in certain current assets and liabilities do not flow through net income and, therefore, theoretically do not affect cash provided from operations. For example, some companies collect funds such as sales tax from third parties and remit them to a separate entity or otherwise hold or disburse cash on behalf of a customer. Operating activities include all transactions and events not defined as investing and financing activities, however, and are not limited to the cash effects of transactions that are reported in the income statement. Thus, the cash effects of agency transactions are operating activities. It is generally acceptable to report only the net changes in those assets and liabilities because knowledge of gross amounts generally is not essential to understanding the company's operating, investing, and financing activities. (SFAS 95, par. 12)

Extraordinary Items, Cumulative Accounting Adjustments, and Discontinued Operations

4.218   Extraordinary items, cumulative accounting adjustments, or discontinued operations need not be separately disclosed in cash flow statements. Thus, the criteria for classifying transactions and events as operating, investing, or financing also would apply to extraordinary items, cumulative accounting adjustments, and discontinued operations. (SFAS 95, par. 26)

Practical Consideration. The following are the authors' recommendations for presenting extraordinary items, cumulative accounting adjustments, and discontinued operations in the statement of cash flows:

- *Extraordinary items.* Cash flows related to extraordinary items should be appropriately classified as operating, investing, or financing activities. Thus, for example, cash payments to settle a lawsuit probably would be classified as an operating activity, while cash received from disposing assets following a pooling of interests probably would be classified as an investing activity, and cash paid to extinguish debt probably would be classified as a financing activity. Noncash extraordinary items should be treated in the same manner as other noncash items. That is, noncash extraordinary items would not be presented under the direct method of reporting cash flows from operations since cash flows from operations consist only of cash receipts and payments. Under the indirect method, however, net income should be adjusted to arrive at the cash effects of operating activities by adding the noncash elements of extraordinary losses to net income and subtracting the noncash elements of extraordinary gains from net income.

- *Cumulative accounting adjustments.* Most cumulative accounting adjustments are noncash items. Accordingly, under the direct method of reporting cash flows from operations, which only presents cash receipts and payments, cumulative accounting adjustments would be excluded. When the indirect method is used, however, net income should be adjusted to arrive at cash flows from operations by adding the noncash elements of expense amounts to net income and subtracting the noncash elements of income amounts from net income.

  Like extraordinary items, cumulative accounting adjustments need not be presented separately in the statement of cash flows. The authors recommend the adjustment be classified according to the nature of the change. For example, the gross amount of a cumulative effect of the change in depreciation methods would be combined with depreciation expense and shown as a single amount in the operating activities section of the cash flows statement.

Practical Consideration (Continued).

- *Discontinued operations.* Net operating cash flows from discontinued operations need not be reported separately as a single line item within the operations section of the cash flow statement. However, that information could be disclosed in the statement itself or in a separate schedule if it is considered relevant. When separate disclosure is made, the disclosures should be presented for all periods affected, including periods that may be affected long after the sale or liquidation of the operation.

  Although not required, cash flows from investing and financing activities may be allocated to continuing and discontinued operations if that information is relevant. The information may be presented (a) in a separate schedule, (b) on the face of the cash flow statement under captions such as "Continuing operations" and "Discontinued operations," or (c) on the face of the cash flow statement identified by a caption such as "Proceeds from disposal of property and equipment—discontinued operations."

Other Adjustments to Arrive at Net Cash Flows from Operating Activities

4.219   Other adjustments to arrive at net cash flows from operating activities are necessary when the indirect method is used to present cash flows from operations. The objective of the adjustments is to present net cash flows generated by operating activities by adding noncash expenses to and subtracting noncash revenues from net income. (SFAS 95, par. 28) Examples of those adjustments include—

a. Noncash entries to current operating assets and liabilities, such as recording a provision for bad debts or providing a reserve for inventory obsolescence

b. Amortization of intangible assets or deferred charges such as goodwill, copyrights, and trademarks

c. Increases in the cash value of life insurance, net of any premiums paid

d. Deferred income taxes

e. Deferred revenue

4.219

    f. Depletion

    g. Depreciation

    h. Gains or losses associated with the disposal of noncurrent assets

    i. Operating items purchased with a business (Such items should be shown as cash outflows from investing activities.)

    j. Long-term installment sale receivables

    k. Earnings on long-term investments in common stock accounted for under the equity method

    l. Unrealized gains and losses on marketable securities

The adjustments should be reflected either in the statement itself or in a separate schedule. When the direct method is used, the items should be excluded from the statement of cash flows because the direct approach only reflects cash receipts and payments. However, the items would be shown in the reconciliation of net income to net cash provided by operating activities. (SFAS 95, paras. 29–30)

CASH FLOWS FROM INVESTING ACTIVITIES

4.220   Investing activities include the following: (SFAS 95, par. 15)

- Lending money and collecting on loans

- Acquiring and selling or disposing of available-for-sale or held-to-maturity securities (Trading securities are classified as operating activities.)

- Acquiring and selling or disposing of productive assets that are expected to generate revenue over a long period of time

EXHIBIT 4-1 on page 4-5 lists examples of cash flows provided by and used in investing activities. The following paragraphs discuss how to handle cash flows from investing activities in the statement of cash flows.

Noncash Investing Activities

4.221   Certain investing activities, such as acquiring assets by assuming liabilities or exchanging assets, are noncash transactions that do not involve cash receipts or payments. Nevertheless, GAAP requires investing activities that do not involve cash to be reported separately so that information is provided on all investing activities. (SFAS 95, par. 32) Noncash investing activities are discussed in Paragraphs 4.239–.244.

Capital Expenditures

4.222 **Purchases.** Cash outlays for acquiring long-lived assets (including capitalized interest, if any) should be reported as a cash outflow from investing activities. The amount to be reported in a statement of cash flows generally should consist of (a) assets purchased for cash and (b) down payments for assets purchased by assuming liabilities. Payments of liabilities, including capital lease obligations, and trade-in allowance and other noncash aspects of the transaction should be excluded from the amounts reported as investing activities. (SFAS 95, par. 17)

> **Practical Consideration.** Purchase and sale or disposal of long-lived assets generally are classified as investing activities. However, sometimes it may be appropriate to classify such transactions as operating activities (for example, when long-lived assets are acquired or produced to be a direct source of a company's revenues, such as assets rented to others for a short period of time and then sold).

4.223   Investing cash flows only should include advance payments, the down payment, or other amounts paid at the time productive assets are purchased or shortly before or after. Subsequent principal payments on an installment loan should be classified as financing activities. (SFAS 95, par. 17) The noncash aspects of the transaction (equipment acquired by assuming liabilities, net of the trade-in allowance) should be disclosed separately as discussed in Paragraph 4.240.

4.224   **Sales.** Proceeds from sales of long-lived assets should be shown as cash inflows from investing activities. (SFAS 95, par. 16)

Investments

4.225   **Short-term Investments vs. Cash Equivalents.** If a company has amounts that do not meet the definition of cash, it must decide whether to account for them as cash equivalents or as other short-term investments. [As discussed in Paragraph 4.203, cash equivalents are defined as short-term, highly liquid investments that (a) are readily convertible to known amounts of cash and (b) are so near to their maturity that they present an insignificant risk of changes in value because of changes in interest rates.] GAAP allows a company to establish policies concerning which short-term, highly liquid investments with original maturities of three months or less are considered cash equivalents and which are to be reported as short-term investments. (As discussed in Paragraph 4.500, a company should disclose its policy in its financial statements.) Once established, the policy should be consistently followed. A change in the type of investments that are classified as cash equivalents is a change in accounting principle that requires prior-period financial statements presented for comparative purposes to be restated. (SFAS 95, par. 10) (See Chapter 1.)

4.226   Purchases and sales of investments that are classified as cash equivalents are part of a company's cash management rather than part of its operating, investing, and financing activities. Thus, the net change in cash equivalents should be included in the net change in cash and cash equivalents shown in the statement of cash flows, but purchases and sales of cash equivalents need not be reported separately. (SFAS 95, par. 9)

4.227   **Investments That Are Not Cash Equivalents.** Purchases and sales of investments in debt or equity securities that are not cash equivalents should be classified as operating or investing activities as follows:

a. Purchases and sales of trading securities should be shown as operating activities in cash flow statements. (SFAS 102, par. 8)

b. Purchases and sales of available-for-sale securities and held-to-maturity securities should be shown as investing activities. (SFAS 115, par. 132)

4.228   **Interest and Dividend Income.** As discussed in Paragraph 4.209, receipts from interest and dividends should be classified as cash flows from operating activities rather than cash flows from investing activities. (SFAS 95, par. 22)

Making Loans

4.229   Making loans (notes and loans receivable) is an investment activity. Accordingly, the principal amount of the loan should be shown as cash used for investing activities, and principal collected on the loans should be shown as cash provided by investing activities. (SFAS 102, par. 9) Interest collected on the loans should be shown as an operating activity. Cash flows relating to investments or loans receivable with original maturities of three months or less may be reported net. (SFAS 95, par. 13)

Purchase (Sale) of a Business

4.230   When a company is purchased or sold and is accounted for as a purchase (rather than a pooling), cash flow statements should report the cash paid to acquire the company (or cash proceeds from sale) as an investing activity. (SFAS 95, par. 17) For example, if a company pays $90,000 to acquire another business with working capital (other than cash) of $30,000 and net noncurrent assets of $60,000, cash flows from investing activities would be presented as follows:

CASH FLOWS FROM INVESTING ACTIVITIES
Acquisition of ABC Company
(net of cash acquired)   90,000

The fair values of assets obtained and liabilities assumed should be disclosed as noncash investing and financing activities. (See Paragraph 4.244.)

4.231   When a business combination is accounted for as a pooling of interests, APB Opinion No. 16, *Business Combinations,* requires the financial statements of the separate companies to be restated on a combined basis for all periods presented. (APB 16, par. 57)

CASH FLOWS FROM FINANCING ACTIVITIES

4.232   Financing activities include the following:

- Obtaining resources from owners and providing them with a return on, and a return of, their investment

- Borrowing money and repaying amounts borrowed, or otherwise settling the obligation

- Obtaining and paying for other resources from creditors on long-term credit (SFAS 95, par. 18)

EXHIBIT 4-1 on page 4-5 lists examples of cash flows provided by financing activities. The following paragraphs discuss how to handle cash flows from financing activities in the statement of cash flows.

Noncash Financing Activities

4.233   Certain financing activities do not involve cash receipts or payments (for example, issuing stock in exchange for noncash consideration such as property and equipment). Financing activities that do not involve cash should be reported separately so that information is provided on all financing activities. (SFAS 95, par. 32) Noncash financing activities are discussed in Paragraphs 4.239–.244.

Cash Dividends

4.234   Financing activities include providing owners with a return on their investment, and, thus, cash dividends paid should be shown as a cash outflow from financing activities. (SFAS 95, par. 20) Dividends declared but not paid and stock dividends are noncash transactions. Accordingly, they should not be shown in the cash flow statement itself. Rather, they should be disclosed as noncash investing and financing activities as discussed in Paragraph 4.243.

Issuing Stock

4.235   Proceeds from issuing stock should be reported as cash inflows from financing activities. (SFAS 95, par. 19)

> **Practical Consideration.** Although cash flows generally are required to be reported on a gross basis, the authors believe that it would be acceptable to show proceeds from issuing stock, net of stock issue costs, as cash received from financing activities provided the amount of stock issue cost is disclosed.

4.236   The following transactions relating to issuing stock do not affect cash flows and should be disclosed as noncash investing and financing activities:

- Stock issued for receivables or other noncash consideration such as property and equipment

- Stock issued to settle debt

- Stock issue costs that have not been paid in cash during the period

Short-term and Long-term Debt

4.237   Cash receipts from both short-term and long-term borrowings should be shown as cash inflows from financing activities. The reduction of short-term and long-term obligations should be reported as a separate cash outflow from financing activities, except for cash flows related to loans with original maturities of three months or less, which may be reported net. (SFAS 95, paras. 13 and 19–20)

Practical Consideration. The following are the authors' recommendations for presenting short-term and long-term debt in the statement of cash flows:

- *Debt issue costs.* The authors believe bank fees and other costs incurred in obtaining financing or refinancing should be offset against the debt and charged to interest expense over the life of the debt, generally using the interest method. All of the costs are therefore accounted for as discount on the debt. Accordingly, the amounts reported as a financing activity are the proceeds (the face amount of the debt less the bank fees and other costs incurred) and repayment of that amount (the reduction in the net liability reported in the financial statements). No adjustment is needed to reconcile net income with net cash provided by operating activities.

- *Life insurance policies.* Loans against life insurance policies should be treated as long-term borrowings if the loans will be repaid. If the loans are considered to be permanent, however, the authors recommend treating them as distributions rather than loans.

Treasury Stock

4.238   The cash paid to acquire a company's own stock should be reported as a cash outflow from financing activities. Subsequent reissuance of treasury stock for cash should be reported as a cash inflow from financing activities, similar to the treatment for issuing stock. (SFAS 95, paras. 19–20)

NONCASH INVESTING AND FINANCING ACTIVITIES

4.239   Investing and financing activities that do not involve cash receipts and payments during the period should be excluded from the cash flow statement and reported separately. That can either be done in a supplemental schedule on the face of the cash flows statement (usually at the bottom of the statement) or in the notes to the financial statements. (SFAS 95, par. 32)

Practical Consideration. The authors believe that all noncash investing and financing transactions should be disclosed either totally in a separate schedule or totally in the notes to the financial statements. In other words, they recommend against disclosing some noncash transactions in a separate schedule and other noncash transactions in the notes.

Assets Acquired by Assuming Liabilities

4.240   Assets acquired by assuming liabilities, including capital lease obligations, are noncash transactions that should be disclosed separately. Seller financing, as well as third-party financing, is considered a noncash transaction that must be disclosed. (SFAS 95, par. 32)

Practical Consideration. The traditional form of this transaction is for the lender to send a check to the seller or for the buyer to assume debt. In some situations, the form of the transaction is such that the buyer actually receives the proceeds of the borrowing and then sends those proceeds to the seller. The following are common examples:

- The lender deposits the proceeds of the loan into the company's checking account, and the company drafts a check to the vendor.

- The company drafts restricted cash accounts to pay the vendor, for example, cash restricted under the terms of an industrial development bond or cash restricted under a construction draw arrangement.

- The company draws against a pre-established line of credit to pay the vendor.

The substance of each of those situations is the same; the company acquires an asset by incurring a liability. The company is in the same position as if the lender sent a check to the vendor. Accordingly, the authors believe each should be reported as a noncash investing and financing activity.

Converting Debt to Equity

4.241   Converting debt to equity is a financing transaction since long-term financing is capitalized; however, the transaction does not involve cash. Thus, the debt reduction should be disclosed in the financial statements in a separate schedule or otherwise. (SFAS 95, par. 32)

Converting Stock

4.242   Converting one class of stock to another, such as preferred to common, is treated in a manner similar to converting debt to equity. An amount equal to the par value of the preferred stock and any related additional paid-in capital that is converted should be disclosed as a noncash financing transaction.

Noncash Dividends

4.243   GAAP requires the fair value of property that is distributed as a dividend to be charged to retained earnings. At the date property dividends are declared, the company should recognize a gain or loss for the difference between the carrying value and the fair value of the assets that are distributed. (APB 29, paras. 18 and 23) For example, if property with a cost of $85,000 and a fair value of $150,000 is distributed as a dividend, the company would recognize a gain of $65,000 ($150,000 − $85,000) when the dividend is declared. The gain would be subtracted from net income to arrive at cash flows from operations, and the transaction would be shown in the schedule of noncash investing and financing activities as follows:

Property dividends	
Fair value of property distributed as dividends	$ 150,000
Cost	(85,000)
Gain on distribution	$ 65,000

Practical Consideration. If a sufficient number of shares were issued so that the transaction would be classified as a stock split, the authors believe that whether the transaction should be separately disclosed as a noncash transaction would depend on the legal requirements of the company's state of incorporation. For example, some states require an amount equal to the par value of the shares issued to be capitalized to retained earnings. In those circumstances, the authors believe that the stock split should be disclosed as described in the preceding paragraph. However, if state regulations require the transaction to be accounted for by increasing the number of shares outstanding and decreasing the par value per share, there would be no formal entry to record the transaction, and, thus, the authors believe it would not need to be disclosed as a noncash transaction. (The transaction probably would be disclosed in the notes to the financial statements, however.)

Purchase (Sale) of a Business

4.244   As discussed in Paragraph 4.230, when a company is purchased or sold, the cash paid to acquire the company (or cash proceeds from sale of the company) should be shown as cash used (or provided) by investing activities. The fair value of assets acquired and the fair value of liabilities assumed should be disclosed as a noncash transaction. For example, the fair value of assets acquired and liabilities assumed may be reported in a schedule of noncash investing activities as follows:

Acquisition of ABC Company

Working capital other than cash	$ 17,000
Equipment and leasehold improvements	120,000
Intangibles and other assets	30,000
Long-term debt assumed	(90,000)
Cash paid to acquire ABC Company	$ 77,000

CASH FLOW PER SHARE

4.245   Because the FASB believes cash flow per share data is susceptible to misinterpretation (for example, it may imply that cash flow is equivalent or superior to earnings as a measure of performance or that an amount representing cash flow per share is available for distribution to stockholders), cash flow per share should not be presented. (SFAS 95, par. 33)

EXAMPLE STATEMENT OF CASH FLOWS

4.246   EXHIBIT 4-2 presents example balance sheets and an income statement and illustrates how a related statement of cash flows may be presented using the direct and indirect methods.

EXHIBIT 4-2

ILLUSTRATIVE CASH FLOW STATEMENT

ACE MANUFACTURING, INC.
BALANCE SHEETS
December 31

	19X6	19X5
ASSETS		
CURRENT ASSETS		
Cash	$ 32,450	$ 56,250
Accounts receivable	112,800	121,600
Notes receivable—stockholder	27,800	11,400
Accrued interest receivable	1,450	800
Inventory	149,500	183,300
TOTAL CURRENT ASSETS	324,000	373,350
PROPERTY AND EQUIPMENT		
Land	60,000	60,000
Building	320,000	320,000
Shop equipment	55,000	40,000
Furniture	18,500	18,500
Autos and trucks	11,000	23,500
	464,500	462,000
Accumulated depreciation	(195,850)	(185,000)
	268,650	277,000
OTHER ASSETS		
Cash value of life insurance	22,950	19,350
Organization costs	1,350	2,700
	24,300	22,050
TOTAL ASSETS	$ 616,950	$ 672,400

EXHIBIT 4-2 (Continued)

LIABILITIES AND STOCKHOLDERS' EQUITY

CURRENT LIABILITIES		
Notes payable	$ 40,000	$ 50,000
Current portion of long-term debt	72,000	67,500
Accounts payable	170,850	179,400
Accrued expenses		
Compensation	11,000	8,150
Interest	1,850	1,400
Payroll taxes	1,300	950
Income taxes	4,350	2,250
TOTAL CURRENT LIABILITIES	301,350	309,650
LONG-TERM DEBT, less current portion	180,500	242,500
STOCKHOLDERS' EQUITY		
Common stock	20,000	20,000
Retained earnings	115,100	100,250
TOTAL STOCKHOLDERS' EQUITY	135,100	120,250
TOTAL LIABILITIES AND STOCKHOLDERS' EQUITY	$ 616,950	$ 672,400

EXHIBIT 4-2 (Continued)

ACE MANUFACTURING, INC.
STATEMENT OF INCOME
Year Ended December 31, 19X6

REVENUE		
Sales		$ 737,200
Gain on sale of truck		250
Interest income		2,400
		739,850
COST OF SALES		
Raw materials		315,200
Direct labor		32,900
Freight		16,700
		364,800
	GROSS PROFIT	375,050
SELLING AND ADMINISTRATIVE EXPENSES		
Officers' salaries		89,600
Sales salaries		48,400
Office salaries		51,600
Payroll taxes		18,650
Rent		25,850
Office expense		10,800
Officers' life insurance		4,200
Professional fees		5,900
Telephone		4,700
Utilities		9,350
Repairs and maintenance		6,700
Insurance		14,300
Provision for bad debts		20,000
Depreciation		18,850
Amortization		1,350
Other taxes		3,200
Interest expense		14,650
		348,100
	INCOME BEFORE INCOME TAXES	26,950

EXHIBIT 4-2 (Continued)

INCOME TAXES	8,100
NET INCOME	18,850
BEGINNING RETAINED EARNINGS	100,250
Dividends paid	(4,000)
ENDING RETAINED EARNINGS	$ 115,100

ADDITIONAL FINANCIAL INFORMATION FOR ACE MANUFACTURING, INC.

- The company's principal stockholder repaid $3,600 of his $11,400 receivable during the year. At December 31, 19X6, the stockholder borrowed an additional $20,000.

- The company purchased machinery in exchange for a $5,000 down payment and a $10,000 equipment note. The first payment on the equipment note is due in 19X7.

- A truck with an original cost of $12,500 and accumulated depreciation of $8,000 was sold for $4,750.

- Notes payable shown as a current liability have original maturities of three months or less.

EXHIBIT 4-2 (Continued)

STATEMENT OF CASH FLOWS—INDIRECT METHOD

CASH FLOWS FROM OPERATING ACTIVITIES	
Net income	$ 18,850[a]
Adjustments to reconcile net income to net cash provided by operating activities	
Depreciation and amortization	20,200[b]
Gain on sale of truck	(250)[c]
Cash value of officers' life insurance	(3,600)[d]
Provision for bad debts	20,000[e]
(Increase) decrease in:	
Trade accounts receivable	(11,200)[e]
Interest receivable	(650)[f]
Inventories	33,800[f]
Increase (decrease) in:	
Trade accounts payable	(8,550)[f]
Accrued liabilities	5,750[f]
NET CASH PROVIDED BY OPERATING ACTIVITIES	74,350
CASH FLOWS FROM INVESTING ACTIVITIES	
Purchase of equipment	(5,000)[g]
Proceeds from sale of equipment	4,750[h]
Loans made	(20,000)[i]
Collection of loans	3,600[j]
NET CASH USED BY INVESTING ACTIVITIES	(16,650)
CASH FLOWS FROM FINANCING ACTIVITIES	
Debt reduction:	
Short-term	(10,000)[k]
Long-term	(67,500)[l]
Dividends paid	(4,000)[m]
NET CASH USED BY FINANCING ACTIVITIES	(81,500)
NET DECREASE IN CASH	(23,800)
CASH AT BEGINNING OF YEAR	56,250
CASH AT END OF YEAR	$ 32,450

EXHIBIT 4-2 (Continued)

SUPPLEMENTAL DISCLOSURES[n]
Operating activities reflect interest paid of $14,200 and income taxes paid of $6,000.

Noncash investing and financing transactions:		
Acquisition of equipment		
Cost of equipment	$	15,000
Equipment loan		(10,000)
Cash down payment for equipment	$	5,000

---

[a] When the indirect method is used to prepare the statement of cash flows, cash flows from operating activities begin with net income of $18,850, as reported in the income statement.

[b] Depreciation and amortization ($18,850 + $1,350) are noncash expenses. Thus, they are added back to net income in arriving at cash flows from operations.

[c] Gain on the sale of the truck (amounting to $250) is subtracted from net income to arrive at cash flows from operating activities. Proceeds from sales of noncurrent assets are shown as investing activities.

[d] Increases in cash value of life insurance ($22,950 − $19,350) that are allowed to accumulate are included in net income as a reduction of insurance expense. Since the increases do not provide cash, however, they should be subtracted from net income in arriving at cash flows from operations.

[e] The net change in trade accounts receivable should be adjusted for the provision for bad debts that is presented separately in the statement of cash flows. The change in accounts receivable is determined as follows:

Net decrease in accounts receivable	$	(8,800)
Add back provision for bad debts		20,000
Net increase attributable to cash amounts	$	11,200

[f] When cash flows from operations are presented using the indirect method, net income should be adjusted for changes during the period in operating current assets and liabilities to approximate actual cash receipts and payments attributed to operations. If there are no material noncash entries posted to operating current assets and liabilities, the net change would be as follows:

EXHIBIT 4-2 (Continued)

	19X6	19X5	Net Change
Interest receivable	$ 1,450	$ 800	$ 650
Inventories	149,500	183,300	(33,800)
Trade payables	(170,850)	(179,400)	8,550
Accrued expenses	(18,500)	(12,750)	(5,750)
Total	$ (38,400)	$ (8,050)	$ (30,350)

g A cash down payment for equipment amounting to $5,000 is shown as cash used by investing activities.

h Proceeds from the sale of the truck are shown as cash flows from investing activities.

i An additional stockholder loan in the amount of $20,000 is shown as cash used by investing activities.

j Cash collections of a stockholder loan are shown as cash flows from investing activities.

k Repayment of notes payable ($50,000 – $40,000) is shown as cash used by financing activities. (The net change is shown because the original maturities of the notes are three months or less.)

l Payment of the current portion of long-term debt is shown as cash used by financing activities.

m Dividends paid are shown as cash used by financing activities.

n Alternatively, the supplemental disclosures could be made in the notes to the financial statements rather than on the face of the cash flow statement.

EXHIBIT 4-2 (Continued)

STATEMENT OF CASH FLOWS—DIRECT METHOD

CASH FLOWS FROM OPERATING ACTIVITIES

Collections from customers	$ 726,000[a]
Interest collected	1,750[a]
Cash paid to suppliers and employees	(633,200)[a]
Interest paid	(14,200)[a]
Income taxes paid	(6,000)[a]
NET CASH PROVIDED BY OPERATING ACTIVITIES	74,350[b]

CASH FLOWS FROM INVESTING ACTIVITIES[c]

Purchase of equipment	(5,000)
Proceeds from sale of equipment	4,750
Loans made	(20,000)
Collection of loans	3,600
NET CASH USED BY INVESTING ACTIVITIES	(16,650)

CASH FLOWS FROM FINANCING ACTIVITIES[c]

Debt reduction:	
Short-term	(10,000)
Long-term	(67,500)
Dividends paid	(4,000)
NET CASH USED BY FINANCING ACTIVITIES	(81,500)
NET DECREASE IN CASH	(23,800)
CASH AT BEGINNING OF YEAR	56,250
CASH AT END OF YEAR	$ 32,450

EXHIBIT 4-2 (Continued)

SUPPLEMENTAL DISCLOSURES[c]

Noncash investing and financing transactions:
Acquisition of equipment

Cost of equipment	$ 15,000
Equipment loan	(10,000)
Cash down payment for equipment	$ 5,000

---

[a] Under the direct method, revenues and expenses presented in the income statement are adjusted for accrued amounts at the beginning and ending of the period and are grouped into categories. Noncash revenues and expenses are excluded. Amounts for Ace Manufacturing, Inc. are calculated as follows:

- Collections from customers:

Sales per income statement	$ 737,200
Increase in accounts receivable	(11,200)
	$ 726,000

- Interest collected:

Interest income	$ 2,400
Increase in accrued interest receivable	(650)
	$ 1,750

- Cash paid to suppliers and employees:

Cost of sales	$ 364,800
Selling and administrative expenses	348,100
Less interest expense presented separately	(14,650)
Less noncash items:	
Depreciation	(18,850)
Amortization	(1,350)
Increase in cash value of life insurance	3,600
Bad debt provision	(20,000)
Decrease in inventory	(33,800)
Decrease in trade payables	8,550
Increase in accrued compensation and payroll taxes	(3,200)
	$ 633,200

EXHIBIT 4-2 (Continued)

- Interest paid:

Interest expense per income statement	$	14,650
Increase in accrued interest payable		(450)
	$	14,200

- Income taxes paid:

Income tax provision per income statement	$	8,100
Increase in accrued income taxes payable		(2,100)
	$	6,000

b If Ace Manufacturing, Inc., prepared its cash flow statement using the direct method, it also would be required to present a separate schedule that reconciles net income to net cash provided by operating activities, such as the following:

RECONCILIATION OF NET INCOME TO NET CASH
PROVIDED BY OPERATING ACTIVITIES

Net income	$	18,850
Adjustments to reconcile net income to net cash provided by operating activities		
Depreciation and amortization		20,200
Gain on sale of truck		(250)
Cash value of officers' life insurance		(3,600)
Provision for bad debts		20,000
(Increase) decrease in:		
Trade accounts receivable		(11,200)
Interest receivable		(650)
Inventories		33,800
Increase (decrease) in:		
Trade accounts payable		(8,550)
Accrued liabilities		5,750
NET CASH PROVIDED BY OPERATING ACTIVITIES	$	74,350

c Cash flows from investing activities, cash flows from financing activities, and the schedule of noncash investing and financing activities are presented in the same manner as under the indirect method.

DISCLOSURE REQUIREMENTS

4.500   The following are required disclosures related to statements of cash flows: (Many of the requirements listed are presentation rather than disclosure requirements and are discussed in the Accounting Requirements section of this chapter. Presentation requirements have been summarized and repeated in this section, however, so that the primary considerations for statements of cash flows may be quickly identified. Numerical references following presentation requirements refer to paragraphs in this chapter that discuss the topic in more detail.)

    a. Descriptive terms such as *cash* or *cash and cash equivalents* should be used rather than terms such as *funds*. (SFAS 95, par. 7)

    b. Cash receipts and cash payments should be classified by operating, investing, and financing activities. (4.205)

    c. Cash inflows and outflows from investing and financing activities should be reported separately (for example, outlays for acquisitions should be reported separately from sales or other dispositions of property and equipment). Cash receipts and payments pertaining to investments (other than cash equivalents), loans receivable, and debt with original maturity of three months or less may be reported net, however. (4.206–.208)

    d. The net effect of cash flows on cash and cash equivalents during the period should be shown in a manner that reconciles beginning and ending cash and cash equivalents. (SFAS 95, par. 7)

    e. A reconciliation of net income and net cash flows from operating activities that reports all major classes of reconciling items separately, including, at a minimum, changes during the period in receivables and payables pertaining to operating activities and in inventory, should be presented. (If the indirect method is used, the reconciliation may be presented in a separate schedule or in the statement itself.) (4.214–.217)

    f. The following classes of operating cash receipts and payments should be shown separately when the direct method is used: (4.212)

        (1) Cash collected from customers, including lessees, licensees, and the like

(2) Interest and dividends received

(3) Other operating cash receipts

(4) Cash paid to employees and other suppliers of goods or services, including suppliers of insurance, advertising, and the like

(5) Interest paid

(6) Income taxes paid

(7) Other operating cash payments

g. The total amount of cash and cash equivalents at the beginning and end of the period shown in the statement of cash flows should be the same as similarly titled line items or subtotals in the balance sheet. (SFAS 95, par. 7)

h. The accounting policy for determining which items are treated as cash and cash equivalents should be disclosed. (SFAS 95, par. 10)

i. Noncash investing and financing transactions should be disclosed either in narrative form or summarized in a schedule. (4.239)

j. If the indirect method of reporting cash flows from operating activities is used, the amounts of interest paid (net of amounts capitalized) and income taxes paid during the period should be disclosed. (SFAS 95, par. 29) (The disclosures may be made on the face of the cash flows statement or in the notes. When included in the notes, they may be added to the existing long-term debt and income tax notes or disclosed in a separate note of supplemental cash flow disclosures.)

Practical Consideration. The authors offer the following suggestions for making the disclosures on interest and taxes paid:

- The objective of the disclosure is to allow financial statement users to consider interest paid (which is classified as an operating activity) as a financing cash outflow if that better suits their purposes. Thus, the amount to be disclosed is the amount of interest reflected in operating cash outflows. If interest is capitalized as part of the cost of property and equipment, the amount capitalized should be subtracted from total interest paid when calculating the interest payments to disclose. Total interest payments need not be reduced for interest amounts capitalized into inventory, however, since those amounts would be included in operating cash flows.

- The disclosure of income taxes paid should include all taxes that are included in the company's income tax provision. Since financial statements for partnerships and, generally, S corporations do not include income tax provisions, no disclosure is usually required for those entities. Accordingly, tax deposits paid by partnerships or S corporations to retain a fiscal year under IRC Section 444 should not be disclosed as income taxes paid.

- Authoritative literature does not address how income tax refunds affect disclosure of income taxes paid. The authors believe that the amount disclosed should be net of receipts of income tax refunds. In some years, that might result in disclosing net receipts. Furthermore, the authors believe it is unnecessary to disclose either the gross amounts of receipts and payments or that a net amount is presented.

AUTHORITATIVE LITERATURE AND RELATED TOPICS

AUTHORITATIVE LITERATURE

SFAS No. 95, *Statement of Cash Flows*

SFAS No. 102, *Statement of Cash Flows—Exemption of Certain Enterprises and Classification of Cash Flows from Certain Securities Acquired for Resale*

SFAS No. 104, *Statement of Cash Flows—Net Reporting of Certain Cash Receipts and Cash Payments and Classification of Cash Flows from Hedging Transactions*

RELATED PRONOUNCEMENTS

EITF Issue No. 95-13, *Classification of Debt Issue Costs in the Statement of Cash Flows*

RELATED TOPICS

Chapter 6—Comparative Financial Statements

CHANGING PRICES: REPORTING THEIR EFFECTS

Table of Contents

CHANGING PRICES: REPORTING THEIR EFFECTS

OVERVIEW

5.100   Generally, GAAP financial statements are based on historical costs. In periods of changing prices, however, historical costs may not always present an accurate picture of an entity's financial position or results of operations. For example, $1,000 received 10 years ago would still be carried in today's financial statements as $1,000 even though, due to inflation, its purchasing power is less than it was 10 years ago. Historical costs of nonmonetary assets such as inventory and equipment may be even less accurate since they are affected by increases or decreases in fair value as well as by the change in the value of the dollar. Consequently, the FASB issued SFAS No. 89, *Financial Reporting and Changing Prices,* to encourage financial statement preparers to present information about the effects of changing prices.

5.101   SFAS No. 89 encourages companies to present selected summarized financial information for each of the five most recent years as supplementary information to their primary financial statements. If presented, the amounts should be based on current, rather than historical, costs and adjusted for the effects of inflation. Additional disclosures about the current year are encouraged if certain of the amounts disclosed differ significantly from those reported in the primary financial statements.

DISCLOSURE REQUIREMENTS

SUGGESTED MINIMUM DISCLOSURES

5.500   SFAS No. 89 encourages, but does not require, a company to disclose certain supplementary information for each of its five most recent years. The information should be based on current costs (see Paragraphs 5.504–.507) and presented in (a) average-for-the-year or end-of-the-year units of constant purchasing power or (b) dollars that have a purchasing power equal to that of dollars of the base period used by the Bureau of Labor Statistics in calculating the Consumer Price Index for All Urban Consumers (CPI-U). The following summarizes the suggested disclosures and provides general information for computing the amounts to be disclosed: (EXHIBIT 5-1 illustrates a format that may be used to present the disclosures.)

a. *Net sales and other operating revenues*—Net sales and other operating revenues reported in the primary financial statements on a historical cost basis should be restated in units of constant purchasing power. (SFAS 89, paras. 7–8)

b. *Income from continuing operations on a current cost basis*—Income from continuing operations on a current cost basis equals income from continuing operations on a historical cost basis, except for the following: (SFAS 89, par. 32)

   (1) Cost of goods sold should be measured at the lower of current cost or recoverable amount at the sale date. (An asset's recoverable amount is the current worth of the net amount of cash expected to be received from the asset's sale or use.)

   (2) Depreciation, depletion, and amortization expense related to property, plant, and equipment should be based on the lower of the assets' recoverable amounts during the periods of use or the average current cost of acquiring the assets' same service potential.

   (3) Income tax expense should not be restated for the effects of temporary differences that may arise as a result of the adjustments in items (1) and (2). (SFAS 89, par. 33 and SFAS 109, par. 287)

   Income from continuing operations on a current cost basis should be restated in units of constant purchasing power. (SFAS 89, par. 12)

c. *Purchasing power gain or loss on net monetary items*—The purchasing power gain or loss on net monetary items is the net gain or loss determined by restating in units of constant purchasing power the beginning and ending balances of, and transactions in, monetary assets and monetary liabilities. (SFAS 89, par. 40)

d. *Increase or decrease in the lower of current cost or recoverable amount of inventory and property, plant, and equipment, net of inflation*—The increase or decrease in the current cost amounts of inventory and property, plant, and equipment is the difference between the current costs of the assets at their entry dates and exit dates for the year. (An asset's entry date for the year is the beginning of the year or the date it was acquired, whichever is applicable. Similarly, an asset's exit date is the end of the year or the date it was used or sold.) In the five-year summary, the increase or decrease in current cost amounts should be reported after eliminating the effects of inflation. For the current year, however, the increase or decrease should be reported both before and after eliminating the effects of inflation. (SFAS 89, paras. 34–35)

e. *Aggregate foreign currency translation adjustment on a current cost basis, if applicable*—For operations measured in a foreign functional currency, the effects of inflation on current costs are measured either by (1) translating amounts from the foreign currency to the U.S. dollar and restating the translated amounts based on the CPI-U (referred to as the "translate-restate" method) or (2) restating foreign currency amounts based on the functional currency's general price level index and translating the restated amounts to U.S. dollars (referred to as the "restate-translate" method). (SFAS 89, paras. 36–39 and 44)

f. *Net assets at year-end on a current cost basis*—If a company presents the minimum information required by SFAS No. 89 (that is, items a. through k.), net assets at the end of the year on a current cost basis should be the same as net assets on a historical cost basis, except that inventory and property, plant, and equipment are stated at the lower of current costs or recoverable amounts. If the company presents comprehensive current cost/constant purchasing power financial statements as supplementary information, however, net assets on a current cost basis should be the same as net assets reported in the supplementary balance sheet. (SFAS 89, paras. 27–28)

g. *Income per common share from continuing operations on a current cost basis*—Generally, this disclosure is computed by dividing income from continuing operations on a current cost basis, restated in units of constant purchasing power, as discussed in item b. by the outstanding number of shares of common stock.

h. *Cash dividends declared per common share*—The amount disclosed is cash dividends declared per common share restated in units of constant purchasing power.

i. *Market price per common share at year-end*—The amount disclosed is the market price per common share restated in units of constant purchasing power.

j. *Consumer Price Index for All Urban Consumers (CPI-U) used for each year's current cost/constant purchasing power calculations*—The CPI-U is updated monthly and may be obtained from the Department of Labor. If the CPI-U has not been published in time to prepare the disclosures, it may be estimated by referring to published economic forecasts or extrapolated based on recently reported changes in the index. (SFAS 89, par. 8)

k. *If the business has a significant foreign operation that it measures in a functional currency other than the U.S. dollar, whether adjustments of current cost information to reflect the effects of general inflation are based on the U.S. general price level index or on a functional currency general price level index*—As discussed in item e., companies with foreign operations may measure the effects of inflation on current costs using either the translate-restate method or the restate-translate method. If the translate-restate method is used, the U.S. general price level index (i.e., the CPI-U) would be used to measure the effects of inflation. On the other hand, if the restate-translate method is used, the effects of inflation would be measured based on the general price level index of the functional currency. (SFAS 89, par. 9)

To help financial statement users understand the supplemental information, companies also are encouraged to explain each disclosure and discuss its significance to their own unique circumstances. (SFAS 89, par. 10)

ADDITIONAL DISCLOSURES ABOUT THE CURRENT YEAR

5.501   If income from continuing operations on a current cost/constant purchasing power basis differs significantly from the income from continuing operations reported in the primary financial statements, the following additional information should be disclosed: (SFAS 89, paras. 11–13)

a. *Components of income from continuing operations for the current year on a current cost/constant purchasing power basis*—The information may be presented (1) in a statement that discloses revenues, expenses, gains, and losses, (2) in a reconciliation that shows the adjustments to income from continuing operations presented in the primary financial statements, or (3) in notes to the five-year summary described in Paragraph 5.500. Regardless of the format used, the presentation should disclose or allow the user to determine the difference between the amounts reported in the primary financial statements and the amounts on a current cost/constant purchasing power basis for cost of goods sold and depreciation, depletion, and amortization. (If depreciation is allocated to various expense categories, the total amount of depreciation on a current cost basis should be disclosed.)

EXHIBIT 5-1

FIVE-YEAR COMPARISON OF SELECTED FINANCIAL DATA ADJUSTED FOR THE EFFECTS OF CHANGING PRICES

(In average 19X6 dollars)

	Year Ended December 31,				
	19X6	19X5	19X4	19X3	19X2
Net sales and other operating revenues	$ 357,500	$ 334,600	$ 328,200	$ 320,900	$ 331,700
Income (loss) from continuing operations	15,600	6,600	(1,200)	(3,800)	4,200
Gain from decline in purchasing power of net amounts owed	5,400	8,900	3,700	1,500	6,400
Excess of increase in specific prices of inventory and property, plant, and equipment over increase in the general price level	16,800	19,300	11,000	14,100	4,700
Foreign currency translation adjustment	(900)	(500)	(400)	(300)	(700)
Net assets at end of year	110,700	81,300	54,500	46,400	39,900
Per share information:					
Income (loss) from continuing operations	$ 1.56	$ .66	$ (.12)	$ (.38)	$ .42
Cash dividends declared	.75	.75	.50	.50	.60
Market price at end of year	40	36	34	32	35
Average consumer price index	298.4	289.1	272.4	246.8	217.4

b. *Separate amounts for the lower of current cost or recoverable amount at the end of the current year of inventory and property, plant, and equipment*

c. *Increase or decrease during the current year in the lower of current cost or recoverable amount of inventory and property, plant, and equipment both before and after adjusting for the effects of inflation*

d. *Principal types of information used to calculate the current cost of inventory; property, plant, and equipment; cost of goods sold; and depreciation, depletion, and amortization expense*

e. *Any differences between (1) the depreciation methods, estimates of useful lives, and salvage values of assets used to calculate current cost/constant purchasing power depreciation and (2) the methods and estimates used to calculate depreciation in the primary financial statements*

ADDITIONAL DISCLOSURES FOR BUSINESSES WITH MINERAL RESOURCE ASSETS

5.502   As discussed in Paragraph 5.505, determining the current cost of mineral resource assets, such as metal ores, coal, salt, sand, gravel, etc., may be difficult because of the assets' unique nature. Thus, SFAS No. 89 encourages additional disclosures about mineral reserves other than oil and gas. The disclosures, which should be presented for each of the five most recent years, are as follows: (SFAS 89, par. 14)

a. *Estimates of significant quantities of proved mineral reserves or proved and probable mineral reserves (whichever is used for cost amortization purposes) at the end of the year or at the most recent date during the year for which estimates can be made—* Proved reserves are those that, based on geological, geophysical, and engineering data, can be recovered in the future with a reasonably high degree of certainty from known mineral deposits. Probable reserves are those that can be commercially recovered, but with a lower degree of certainty than proved reserves.

b. *If the mineral reserves in item a. include deposits containing one or more significant mineral products, the estimated quantity, expressed in physical units or in percentages of reserves, of each mineral product that is recoverable in significant commercial quantities*

c. *Quantities of each significant mineral produced during the year*—If the mineral reserves in item a. are milled or similarly processed, the business also should disclose the quantity of each significant mineral product produced by the milling or similar process.

d. *Quantity of significant proved, or proved and probable, mineral reserves purchased or sold in place during the year*

e. *The average market price of each significant mineral product*—If mineral products are transferred within the business, the equivalent market price prior to its further use should be disclosed.

5.503   When determining the quantities of mineral reserves to be reported in the preceding disclosures—

- if consolidated financial statements are issued, all of the quantities attributable to the parent and subsidiaries should be included, regardless of whether a subsidiary is wholly owned.

- if an investment is proportionately consolidated, the quantities reported should include the business's proportionate share of the investee's quantities.

- if the equity method is used to account for an investment, the investee's quantities should not be included in the quantities reported. (They should be reported separately if significant, however.) (SFAS 89, par. 15)

DETERMINING CURRENT COSTS

5.504   The current cost of inventory is the current cost to purchase or produce the goods. The current cost of property, plant, and equipment is the current cost to acquire the assets' same service potential. Various types of information may be used to determine those amounts. For example, current costs may be measured based on current invoice prices or using externally or internally generated price indexes for the class of goods or services being measured. The information used and the method of applying it should be appropriate under the circumstances, however. (SFAS 89, paras. 17–19)

Specialized Assets

5.505   Because mineral resource assets, timberlands and growing timber, income-producing real estate, and motion picture films have unique features, determining their current costs may be difficult. Consequently, SFAS No. 89

provides more flexible rules for determining the current costs of those specialized assets.

5.506 **Timberlands and Growing Timber, Income-producing Real Estate, and Motion Picture Films.** The current costs of timberlands and growing timber, income-producing real estate, and motion picture films may be determined by adjusting historical costs by an externally generated index of general purchasing power. If that method is used to determine the current cost of harvested timber and growing timber, the historical costs of those assets may include (a) only costs that are capitalized in the primary financial statements or (b) all costs directly related to reforestation and forest management, regardless of whether those costs are capitalized in the primary financial statements. (Examples of reforestation and forest management costs include planting, fertilization, fire protection, property taxes, and nursery stock.) (SFAS 89, paras. 25–26)

5.507 **Mineral Resource Assets.** There is no generally accepted approach for measuring the current cost of finding mineral reserves. Thus, SFAS No. 89 allows current costs to be determined by (a) applying specific price indexes to historical costs, (b) using direct information about market buying prices, or (c) using other statistical evidence about the cost of acquisitions. (SFAS 89, par. 23)

AUTHORITATIVE LITERATURE AND RELATED TOPICS

AUTHORITATIVE LITERATURE

SFAS No. 89, *Financial Reporting and Changing Prices*

RELATED PRONOUNCEMENTS

EITF Issue No. 93-9, *Application of FASB Statement 109 in Foreign Financial Statements Restated for General Price-Level Changes*

RELATED TOPICS

Chapter 22—Foreign Operations and Currency Translation

COMPARATIVE FINANCIAL STATEMENTS

Table of Contents

COMPARATIVE FINANCIAL STATEMENTS

OVERVIEW

6.100 Comparative presentations enhance the usefulness of financial statements. Therefore, although not required, it ordinarily is desirable for financial statement presentations to include the financial statements of two or more years.

ACCOUNTING REQUIREMENTS

6.200 Current year financial statements are presumed to be more useful if financial statements for one or more prior years are presented with them for comparative purposes. Although GAAP does not require such presentations, comparative financial statements often help readers more clearly understand the nature and trends of current changes affecting an entity. Furthermore, they help emphasize that the business is an ongoing entity and the current period is just one of a number of periods in its history. (ARB 43, Ch. 2A, par. 1)

6.201 Normally, it is preferable to present a balance sheet, income statement, and statement of changes in owners' equity for one or more prior years when current year financial statements are presented. (If both a balance sheet and income statement are presented, the presentation also should include a statement of cash flows for each year for which an income statement is presented. See Chapter 4.) To the extent they continue to be significant, notes to prior year financial statements should be repeated, or at least referred to, in the comparative presentation. (ARB 43, Ch. 2A, par. 2)

Practical Consideration. Although the issue is not addressed by authoritative literature, the authors believe it is acceptable to present comparative information in one statement but not another. For example, it would be acceptable to present a balance sheet for the current year and comparative income statements for the current and prior year.

DISCLOSURE REQUIREMENTS

6.500   Reclassifications or other changes may cause items for two or more periods to no longer be comparable. Changes affecting comparability should be disclosed. (ARB 43, Ch. 2A, par. 3)

Practical Consideration. As discussed further in Chapter 1, prior period financial statements are not always restated when current period financial statements include a change in accounting principle (for example, a change to the LIFO method of valuing inventory). However, the authors believe that prior period financial statements may be restated to conform to changes in the way amounts are *classified* in current year financial statements (for example, to present interest income as a separate line item rather than as a part of other income). In such cases, the fact that prior year amounts have been reclassified should be disclosed.

AUTHORITATIVE LITERATURE AND RELATED TOPICS

AUTHORITATIVE LITERATURE

ARB No. 43, *Restatement and Revision of Accounting Research Bulletins* (Chapter 2A—Comparative Financial Statements)

RELATED TOPICS

Chapter 1—Accounting Changes

COMPENSATED ABSENCES

Table of Contents

COMPENSATED ABSENCES

OVERVIEW

7.100   An employer generally is required to accrue a liability for employees' rights to receive compensation for future absences and postemployment benefits if—

    a. the rights relate to services already performed;

    b. the rights vest or accumulate;

    c. it is probable that the compensation will be paid; and

    d. the amount of the compensation is reasonably estimable.

An exception to that rule applies to sick pay benefits, which generally need not be accrued until employees are absent.

ACCOUNTING REQUIREMENTS

7.200   Employees often are paid for absences due to vacations, illnesses, and holidays. A liability for future compensated absences should be accrued if all of the following conditions are met: (SFAS 43, par. 6)

    a. *The employee's right to be paid for future absences is attributable to services he or she has already performed.* Individual facts and circumstances should be considered when determining whether a right relates to services already performed. For example, compensation for a leave of absence granted to allow an employee to perform public services that will enhance the reputation or otherwise benefit the employer does not relate to services already performed. A leave granted to allow an employee time off to attend to personal matters with no requirement that the employee return to work generally would relate to services already performed, however.

    b. *The employee's right to be paid for future absences vests or accumulates.* An employee's rights to be paid for future absences are vested if they are not contingent on the employee's performance of future services. An employer has an obligation to pay vested rights even if the employee leaves. An employee's rights accumulate if they may be carried forward to succeeding years, thereby increasing the benefits that would otherwise be available in those years. Accumulating rights may be vesting or nonvesting.

c. *It is probable that the compensation will be paid.*

d. *The amount that will be paid is reasonably estimable.*

7.201   Because it is difficult to estimate when an employee will be sick and the amounts paid are seldom material, SFAS No. 43, *Accounting for Compensated Absences,* excludes nonvesting accumulating sick pay benefits from the general accrual requirements. Those benefits need not be accrued even if they meet all of the criteria in Paragraph 7.200. (SFAS 43, par. 7) The employer's actual practices should be considered when determining whether benefits are actually sick pay benefits, however. For example, unused accumulated "sick pay" benefits that customarily are paid to employees who are not ill are not sick pay benefits and should be accrued. (SFAS 43, par. 15)

Practical Consideration. The accrual requirements discussed in the preceding paragraphs generally apply to postemployment benefits as well as compensated absences. The requirements do not apply to the following, however:

- Postemployment benefits provided through a pension or post-retirement benefit plan (See Chapters 40 and 41.)

- Deferred compensation arrangements (See Chapter 17.)

- Severance or termination benefits (See Chapters 39 and 41.)

- Stock or stock options issued to employees (See Chapter 50.)

DISCLOSURE REQUIREMENTS

7.500   If an employee's right to receive compensation for future absences meets conditions a.–c. in Paragraph 7.200 but does not meet condition d. (and thus is not accrued), that fact should be disclosed. (SFAS 43, par. 6)

AUTHORITATIVE LITERATURE AND RELATED TOPICS

AUTHORITATIVE LITERATURE

SFAS No. 43, *Accounting for Compensated Absences*
SFAS No. 112, *Employers' Accounting for Postemployment Benefits*

RELATED TOPICS

Chapter 39—Pension Plans: Accounting by Employers
Chapter 40—Postemployment Benefits
Chapter 41—Postretirement Benefits Other Than Pensions

COMPREHENSIVE INCOME

Table of Contents

COMPREHENSIVE INCOME

OVERVIEW

8.100 Comprehensive income is the change in an entity's equity during a period from transactions and events other than those resulting from investments by and distributions to owners. Comprehensive income and its components are required to be reported when an entity presents a full set of general-purpose financial statements. All items that are recognized as comprehensive income are required to be reported in a financial statement that is displayed with the same prominence as other financial statements (such as the balance sheet, income statement, and statement of cash flows). However, a separate statement of comprehensive income is not required.

8.101 An entity is required to (a) classify components of comprehensive income by their nature in a financial statement and (b) display the accumulated balance of other comprehensive income separately from retained earnings and additional paid-in-capital in the equity section of the balance sheet.

ACCOUNTING REQUIREMENTS

Practical Consideration. The guidance in this chapter is based on SFAS No. 130, *Reporting Comprehensive Income.* SFAS No. 130 is effective for fiscal years beginning after December 15, 1997. Earlier application is permitted. If comparative financial statements are provided for earlier periods, those financial statements should be reclassified to comply with SFAS No. 130. (The requirements for reclassification adjustments discussed in Paragraph 8.203 are encouraged, but not required in comparative financial statements for earlier periods, however). SFAS No. 130 should be adopted as of the beginning of the entity's fiscal year. For example, a nonpublic company with a calendar year end that prepares monthly financial statements would be required to apply SFAS No. 130 in its January 1998 interim financial statements. Consequently, if SFAS No. 130 is adopted prior to the effective date and during an interim period other than the first interim period, all prior interim periods should be reclassified.

WHAT IS COMPREHENSIVE INCOME?

8.200 Comprehensive income is the change in an entity's equity during a period from transactions and events other than those resulting from investments by and distributions to owners. (SFAS No. 130, par. 8) Comprehensive income includes net income and other changes in assets and liabilities not reported in net income, but instead reported as a separate component of stockholders' equity (referred to as other comprehensive income). Under current accounting standards, comprehensive income includes the following: (SFAS No. 130, paras. 17 and 39)

Foreign currency items (Chapter 22 discusses foreign operations and foreign currency transactions.)

- Foreign currency translation adjustments

- Gains and losses on foreign currency transactions designated as (and effective as) hedges of a net investment in a foreign entity

- Gains and losses on intercompany foreign currency transactions whose settlement is not planned or anticipated in the foreseeable future, when the entities involved in the transactions are reported in the financial statements through consolidation, combination, or the equity method

Unrealized gains and losses on investments (Chapter 35 discusses accounting for investments.)

- Changes in the market value of a futures contract that qualifies as a hedge of an asset reported at fair value

- Unrealized holding gains and losses on available-for-sale securities (or debt securities transferred from the held-to-maturity category to the available-for-sale category)

- Temporary increases or decreases in the fair value of available-for-sale securities that occur after the securities were written down as impaired

Minimum pension liability adjustments (Chapter 39 discusses minimum pension liability adjustments.)

- Net loss recognized under SFAS No. 87 as an additional pension liability but not yet recognized as net periodic pension cost

8.201   Comprehensive income does *not* include the following items, even though current GAAP requires them to be recorded directly to equity and they do not always appear to result from transactions with owners:

a. *Deferred compensation expense and unearned ESOP shares.* GAAP requires unearned compensation expense and unearned ESOP shares to be recorded as a reduction of stockholders' equity. (See Chapter 50.) While such transactions have equity characteristics, it could be argued that they should be included in comprehensive income since they will eventually be recognized as compensation expense. The FASB will consider the issues as part of its broad-scope project on comprehensive income. Until then, the Board has decided to treat reductions in equity due to deferred compensation and unearned ESOP shares as equity transactions and exclude them from comprehensive income. (SFAS No. 130, paras. 109–112)

b. *Taxes not payable in cash.* A reorganized entity may pay minimal amounts of income taxes as a result of operating losses incurred prior to reorganization. Nevertheless, GAAP requires the entity to report a "full tax rate" on its pretax income and record the portion of taxes that will not be paid in cash as an increase to paid-in capital rather than as a liability. Although the taxes not payable in cash is not a transaction with an owner, the credit to paid-in capital is necessary to adjust equity transactions recorded upon reorganization—it does not result from the current-period debit to income tax expense. Consequently, taxes not payable in cash should not be included in comprehensive income. (SFAS No. 130, paras. 113–115)

c. *Other transactions affecting paid-in capital.* GAAP may require transactions other than those listed in the preceding paragraphs to be recorded as direct adjustments of paid-in capital or other nonincome equity accounts. Such transactions should not be included in comprehensive income. (SFAS No. 130, par. 119)

Practical Consideration. The term *comprehensive income* is used to refer to all components of comprehensive income, including net income. The term *other comprehensive income* refers to revenues, expenses, gains and losses that, under GAAP, are included in comprehensive income, but excluded from net income. Although GAAP does not require an entity to use the terms comprehensive income and other comprehensive income in its financial statements, the authors believe the terms will be commonly used in practice.

REPORTING COMPREHENSIVE INCOME

8.202   An entity (other than a nonprofit entity following SFAS No. 117, *Financial Statements of Not-for-Profit Organizations*) must report comprehensive income and its components when it (a) has items of other comprehensive income and (b) presents a full set of financial statements that report financial position, results of operations, and cash flows. Investment companies, defined benefit pension plans, and other employee benefit plans that are exempt from the requirement to provide a statement of cash flows are *not* exempt from the requirement to report comprehensive income. (SFAS No. 130, par. 6)

8.203   When required to be reported, comprehensive income and its components must be presented in a financial statement that is displayed with the same prominence as the other financial statements. That does not mean that a separate statement of comprehensive income must be presented, however. Comprehensive income may be reported in a single statement of income and comprehensive income, in a separate statement of comprehensive income, or in a statement of changes in equity that includes comprehensive income. Regardless of the method used, the statement displaying comprehensive income must include net income, the components of other comprehensive income, and a total comprehensive income amount. (SFAS No. 130, paras. 14 and 22) The following are additional considerations for reporting comprehensive income:

    a. Items included in other comprehensive income must be classified according to their nature. For example, under current accounting standards, other comprehensive income should be classified as unrealized gains and losses on certain investments in debt and equity securities, foreign currency items, or minimum pension liability adjustments. (SFAS No. 130, par. 17)

    b. Reclassification adjustments may be necessary to avoid double counting items displayed in the current period's net income that previously were reported as other comprehensive income. For example, realized gains and losses on available-for-sale marketable securities reported in current year net income may have been reported previously in other comprehensive income as unrealized holding gains or losses. Reclassification adjustments should be calculated for each classification of other comprehensive income, except minimum pension liability adjustments, and reported on the face of the financial statement that reports comprehensive income or in the notes to the financial statements. (Reclassification adjustments related to foreign currency translation adjustments are not required unless the translation gains and

losses were realized upon the sale or substantially complete liquidation of the investment in the foreign entity.) Thus, an entity may
either—

(1) display the gross amount of each component of other comprehensive income on the face of the financial statement and
add or subtract any related reclassification adjustment for
that component; or

(2) display each component of other comprehensive income net
of related reclassification adjustments and disclose the gross
change in the notes to the financial statements. (SFAS No.
130, paras. 18–21)

EXHIBIT 8-1 and EXHIBIT 8-2 illustrate how reclassification
adjustments are calculated.

c. Components of comprehensive income may be presented net of
related tax effects or before related tax effects with one amount
displayed for the aggregate income tax expense or benefit
related to total other comprehensive income. Regardless, the
amount of income tax expense or benefit allocated to each component of comprehensive income (and related reclassification
adjustments) must be disclosed either on the face of the financial
statements or in the notes to the financial statements. (SFAS
No. 130, paras. 24–25)

EXHIBIT 8-3 to EXHIBIT 8-5 illustrate alternatives for reporting comprehensive
income.

Practical Consideration. Although GAAP does not require a specific format
for presenting comprehensive income and its components, it encourages entities to display the information on the income statement, below net income. The
authors believe presenting comprehensive income in the statement of
changes in stockholders' equity may be the preferable alternative, however.
That presentation avoids cluttering the income statement and does not require
presenting a separate statement of comprehensive income that may be unfa-
miliar to users.

EXHIBIT 8-1

COMPUTATION OF RECLASSIFICATION ADJUSTMENT
FOR REALIZED GAINS ON AN INVESTMENT IN
AVAILABLE-FOR-SALE EQUITY SECURITIES

Facts:

1. On December 31, 19X7, ABC Company, Inc. purchased 1,000 shares of equity securities at $50 per share.

2. The fair value of the securities at December 31, 19X8, and June 30, 19X9, was $75 and $65 per share, respectively.

3. No dividends were declared on the securities, which were sold on June 30, 19X9.

4. Assumed tax rate is 40%.

Computation of Holding Gain (Loss)

	Before Tax	Income Tax (Benefit)	Net of Tax
Holding gains (losses) recognized in other comprehensive income:			
Year ended December 31, 19X8	$ 25,000	$ 10,000	$ 15,000
Year ended December 31, 19X9	(10,000)	(4,000)	(6,000)
Total gain	$ 15,000	$ 6,000	$ 9,000

EXHIBIT 8-1 (Continued)

Amounts Reported in Net Income and Other Comprehensive Income for the Years Ended December 31, 19X8 And December 31, 19X9

	19X8	19X9
Net income:		
Gain on sale of securities	—	$ 15,000
Income tax expense	—	(6,000)
Net realized gain	—	9,000
Other comprehensive income:		
Holding gain (loss) arising during the period, net of tax	$ 15,000	(6,000)
Reclassification adjustment, net of tax	—	(9,000)
Net gain (loss) recognized in other comprehensive income	15,000	(15,000)
Total impact on comprehensive income	$ 15,000	($6,000)

EXHIBIT 8-2

COMPUTATION OF RECLASSIFICATION ADJUSTMENT FOR REALIZED LOSSES ON AN INVESTMENT IN AVAILABLE-FOR-SALE DEBT SECURITIES

Facts:

1. On December 31, 19X7, ABC Company, Inc. purchased $1,500,000 (face value) of 8% bonds for $1,609,500 (6.5% effective yield) and classified them as available-for-sale.

2. The fair value of the bonds on December 31, 19X8 and December 31, 19X9 was $1,441,500 and $1,383,000 respectively.

3. ABC Company, Inc. sold the bonds on December 31, 19X9.

4. Assumed tax rate is 40%.

Computation of Cost-based Carrying Amount, Interest Income, and Premium Amortization

Year	(a) Beginning Carrying Value	(b) Cash Interest Received [8% × par]	(c) Interest Income [(a) × 6.5%]	(d) Premium Amortiza-tion [(b) − (c)]	(e) Ending Carrying Value [(a) − (d)]
19X7					$1,609,500
19X8	$ 1,609,500	$ 120,000	$ 104,618	$ 15,382	1,594,118
19X9	1,594,118	120,000	103,618	16,382	1,577,736

Computation of Holding Loss (Before Tax)

Year	(a) Ending Carrying Value	(b) Ending Fair Value	(c) Change in Fair Value	(d) Premium Amortiza-tion	(e) Holding Loss [(c) + (d)]
19X7	$ 1,609,500	$ 1,609,500	$ —	$ —	$ —
19X8	1,594,118	1,441,500	(168,000)	15,382	(152,618)
19X7	1,577,736	1,383,000	(58,500)	16,382	(42,118)

EXHIBIT 8-2 (Continued)

Net-of-tax Holding Losses

	Before Tax	Income Tax (Benefit)	Net of Tax
Holding losses recognized in other comprehensive income:			
Year ended December 31, 19X8	$(152,618)	$ (61,047)	$ (91,571)
Year ended December 31, 19X9	(42,118)	(16,847)	(25,271)
Total loss	$(194,736)	$ (77,894)	$(116,842)

Amounts Reported in Net Income and Other Comprehensive Income for the Years Ended December 31, 19X8 And December 31, 19X9

	19X8	19X9
Net income:		
Loss on sale of securities	$ —	$ (194,736)
Income tax expense (benefit)	—	(77,894)
Net realized loss	—	(116,842)
Other comprehensive income:		
Holding loss arising during period, net of tax	(91,571)	(25,271)
Reclassification adjustment, net of tax	—	116,842
Net gain (loss) recognized in other comprehensive income	(91,571)	91,571
Total impact on comprehensive income	$ (91,571)	$ (25,271)

EXHIBIT 8-3

SINGLE STATEMENT OF INCOME AND COMPREHENSIVE INCOME

DEF INCORPORATED
STATEMENT OF INCOME AND COMPREHENSIVE INCOME
Year Ended December 31, 19X8

SALES	$ 11,000,000
COST OF SALES	6,000,000
GROSS PROFIT	5,000,000
SELLING, GENERAL AND ADMINISTRATIVE	3,000,000
OTHER OPERATING EXPENSES	750,000
OPERATING INCOME	1,250,000
OTHER INCOME (EXPENSE)	
Interest income	10,000
Interest expense	(250,000)
Gain on sale of securities	50,000
Other, net	(25,000)
	(215,000)
INCOME BEFORE TAXES	1,035,000
INCOME TAX EXPENSE	414,000
NET INCOME	621,000

EXHIBIT 8-3 (Continued)

OTHER COMPREHENSIVE INCOME[a]

Foreign currency translation adjustments		100,000
Unrealized gains on securities:		
Unrealized holding gains arising during the period[b]	$ 250,000	
Less: reclassification adjustment for gains included in net income	(50,000)	200,000
Minimum pension liability adjustment		(25,000)
		275,000
Income tax expense related to other comprehensive income		(110,000)
OTHER COMPREHENSIVE INCOME		165,000
TOTAL COMPREHENSIVE INCOME		$ 786,000

---

[a]   EXHIBIT 8-3 demonstrates presenting components of comprehensive income before tax with one amount shown for aggregate income tax expense. Alternatively, they could be displayed net of tax, as in EXHIBIT 8-4. In either case, the tax effects applicable to each component of other comprehensive income should be disclosed either parenthetically on the face of the financial statements or in the notes to the financial statements.

[b]   Alternatively, the entity could display the components of other comprehensive income net of reclassification adjustments on the face of the financial statements as long as the gross amount and the reclassification adjustments are disclosed in the notes to the financial statements.

EXHIBIT 8-4

SEPARATE STATEMENT OF COMPREHENSIVE INCOME

DEF INCORPORATED
STATEMENT OF COMPREHENSIVE INCOME
Year Ended December 31, 19X8

NET INCOME		$ 621,000
OTHER COMPREHENSIVE INCOME, NET OF TAX:[a]		
Foreign currency translation adjustments		60,000
Unrealized gains on securities:		
Unrealized holding gains arising during the period[b]	$ 150,000	
Less: reclassification adjustment for gains included in net income	(30,000)	120,000
Minimum pension liability adjustment		(15,000)
OTHER COMPREHENSIVE INCOME		165,000
TOTAL COMPREHENSIVE INCOME		$ 786,000

[a] EXHIBIT 8-4 demonstrates presenting components of comprehensive income net of tax. Alternatively, they could be displayed before tax with one amount shown for aggregate income tax expense as in EXHIBIT 8-3. In either case, the tax effects applicable to each component of other comprehensive income should be disclosed either parenthetically on the face of the financial statements or in the notes to the financial statements.

[b] Alternatively, the entity could display the components of other comprehensive income net of reclassification adjustments on the face of the financial statements so long as the gross amount and the reclassification adjustments are disclosed in the notes to the financial statements.

EXHIBIT 8-5
STATEMENT OF CHANGES IN EQUITY

DEF INCORPORATED
Statement of Changes in Equity
Year Ended December 31, 19X8

	Common Stock	Additional Paid-in Capital	Retained Earnings	Accumulated Other Comprehensive Income	Total
BALANCE AT BEGINNING OF YEAR	$ 1,000,000	$ 2,000,000	$ 4,250,000	$ 675,000	$ 7,925,000
COMPREHENSIVE INCOME					
Net income			621,000		621,000
Other comprehensive income, net of tax:[a]					
Foreign currency translation adjustments					60,000
Unrealized gains on securities:					
Unrealized holding gains arising during the period					150,000
Less: reclassification adjustment					(30,000)
Minimum pension liability adjustment					(15,000)
				165,000	165,000
TOTAL COMPREHENSIVE INCOME					786,000
ISSUANCE OF COMMON STOCK	250,000	500,000			750,000
DIVIDENDS DECLARED			(250,000)		(250,000)
BALANCE AT END OF YEAR	$ 1,250,000	$ 2,500,000	$ 4,621,000	$ 840,000	$ 9,211,000

[a] The tax effects applicable to each component of other comprehensive income should be disclosed either parenthetically on the face of the financial statements or in the notes to the financial statements.

Interim Reporting

8.204　Public companies that report condensed interim financial information to shareholders also should report total comprehensive income at interim dates. (SFAS No. 130, par. 27) (Chapter 29 discusses interim financial reporting further.)

> **Practical Consideration.** Although a public company's condensed interim financial information must report only total comprehensive income, the authors recommend disclosing the components of comprehensive income to help users understand the difference between net income and comprehensive income.
>
> Nonpublic companies that issue interim financial statements must report comprehensive income in accordance with the requirements discussed in this chapter.

REPORTING ACCUMULATED COMPREHENSIVE INCOME IN THE BALANCE SHEET

8.205　The accumulated balance of other comprehensive income should be reported as a component of equity, separate from retained earnings and additional paid-in-capital, and labeled with a descriptive title such as *accumulated other comprehensive income.* Accumulated balances for each component of other comprehensive income should be displayed on the face of the balance sheet, the statement of changes in stockholders' equity, or disclosed in the notes to the financial statements. The classifications of accumulated other comprehensive income should correspond to the classifications for components of other comprehensive income used elsewhere in the financial statements. (SFAS No. 130, par. 26)

> **Practical Consideration.** The following illustrates presenting accumulated other comprehensive income in the equity section of the balance sheet when accumulated balances of each component are disclosed in the notes:
>
> STOCKHOLDERS' EQUITY:
>
> | | |
> |---|---:|
> | Common stock | 1,250,000 |
> | Paid-in capital | 2,500,000 |
> | Retained earnings | 4,621,000 |
> | Accumulated other comprehensive income | 840,000 |
> | | 9,211,000 |

Practical Consideration (Continued).

Alternatively, the accumulated balances of each component could be presented in the equity section of the balance sheet in a manner similar to the following:

STOCKHOLDERS' EQUITY:

Common stock	1,250,000
Paid-in capital	2,500,000
Retained earnings	4,621,000
Accumulated other comprehensive income:	
Foreign currency translation adjustments	305,000
Unrealized gains on securities	611,000
Minimum pension liability adjustment	(76,000)
	840,000
	9,211,000

DISCLOSURE REQUIREMENTS

8.500 The following are required disclosures related to comprehensive income:

a. If not displayed on the face of the financial statement in which comprehensive income is presented, reclassification adjustments (discussed in Paragraph 8.203) should be disclosed in the notes to the financial statements. (SFAS No. 130, par. 20)

b. If not disclosed on the face of the financial statements, the amount of income tax expense or benefit allocated to each component of comprehensive income (including reclassification adjustments) should be disclosed in the notes to the financial statements. (SFAS No. 130, par. 25)

c. If not disclosed in the balance sheet or a statement of changes in equity, the accumulated balance for each classification of accumulated comprehensive income (discussed in Paragraph 8.205) should be disclosed in the notes to the financial statements. (SFAS No. 130, par. 26)

AUTHORITATIVE LITERATURE AND RELATED TOPICS

AUTHORITATIVE LITERATURE

SFAS No. 130, *Reporting Comprehensive Income*

RELATED PRONOUNCEMENTS

APB Opinion No. 28, *Interim Financial Reporting*
SFAS No. 52, *Foreign Currency Translation*
SFAS No. 80, *Accounting for Futures Contracts*
SFAS No. 87, *Employers' Accounting for Pensions*
SFAS No. 109, *Accounting for Income Taxes*
SFAS No. 115, *Accounting for Certain Investments in Debt and Equity Securities*

RELATED TOPICS

Chapter 22—Foreign Operations and Currency Translation
Chapter 24—Income Taxes
Chapter 29—Interim Financial Reporting
Chapter 35—Marketable Securities
Chapter 39—Pension Plans: Accounting by Employers

CONSOLIDATED FINANCIAL STATEMENTS

Table of Contents

CONSOLIDATED FINANCIAL STATEMENTS

OVERVIEW

9.100   Consolidated financial statements should be issued as the primary financial statements whenever a company owns a controlling financial interest in the voting stock of another company. Generally, a company has a controlling financial interest in another company if it owns more than fifty percent of the outstanding shares of the other company.

9.101   Consolidated financial statements present the results of operations, financial position, and cash flows of two or more companies as if they were a single company. They are prepared by combining all parent and subsidiary accounts and eliminating intercompany balances and transactions. (All intercompany profits should be eliminated in consolidation. The existence of a minority interest in a subsidiary does not affect the amount of intercompany profits that should be eliminated.)

ACCOUNTING REQUIREMENTS

9.200   In substance, a single economic or accounting entity exists when one company (investor) owns a controlling interest in the voting stock of another company (investee). (ARB 51, par. 1) In such cases, consolidated financial statements are presumed to be more meaningful than separate financial statements, and an investor should issue consolidated, rather than parent company financial statements, as its primary financial statements. (SFAS 94, par. 61)

9.201   Usually, a controlling financial interest is evidenced by ownership of a majority voting interest. Thus, as a general rule, when a company directly or indirectly owns more than fifty percent of the outstanding voting shares of another company, it should account for its investment through consolidation unless—

a. control is likely to be temporary

b. control does not rest with the majority owners (for example, if a subsidiary is in legal reorganization or operates under foreign exchange or governmental restrictions so severe that they cast significant doubt on the owners' ability to control the subsidiary) (SFAS 94, par. 13), or

c. minority shareholder(s) have certain approval or veto rights that allow the minority shareholder(s) to participate in significant decisions related to the investee's ordinary course of business. (EITF 96-16, par. 16)

Practical Consideration. Although an investor's ability to control an investee company may depend on a variety of factors, authoritative literature generally looks at the percentage ownership in the investee to determine whether, and to what extent, control exists. Consequently, the method used to account for an investment in another company normally is determined as follows:

% of Other Company Owned	Accounting Method Usually Required
Less than 20%	Fair value method if the fair value of the securities is readily determinable, otherwise recorded at cost
20% to 50%	Equity method
More than 50%	Consolidation

As discussed in the preceding paragraph, however, a majority-owned subsidiary may not be consolidated in all cases. A majority-owned subsidiary that is not consolidated should be accounted for using the equity method if the parent has the ability to exercise significant influence over the subsidiary. If it does not have that influence, the cost method should be used.

This chapter discusses the consolidation method of accounting. The equity method is discussed in Chapter 20, and the fair value method is discussed in Chapter 35.

CONSOLIDATION PROCEDURES

9.202   Consolidated statements are based on the assumption that they present the financial position and results of operations of a single entity. Thus, preparing consolidated financial statements consists of combining all parent and subsidiary accounts and eliminating all intercompany balances and transactions. For example, all gains and losses on transactions between the parent and subsidiaries (or between subsidiaries) should be eliminated. Similarly, all intercompany investments, payables, and receivables should be eliminated. (ARB 51, par. 6) EXHIBIT 9-1 illustrates how typical intercompany transactions would be eliminated in consolidation.

EXHIBIT 9-1

EXAMPLE CONSOLIDATION

Facts:

- On January 1, 19X5, Parent Company paid $140,000 for 80% of the outstanding common stock of Sub Co. On that date, Sub Co. had common stock of $100,000 and retained earnings of $50,000. The fair values of its identifiable assets and liabilities were the same as their book values.

- Sub Co. reported earnings of $30,000 and declared and paid dividends of $10,000 during 19X5. Parent Company uses the cost method to account for its investment in Sub Co.

- Sub Co. sold inventory to Parent Company during 19X1 and recorded a $15,000 gain on the sale. The inventory, which was carried on Sub Co.'s books at $55,000, had not been sold or used by Parent Company as of December 31, 19X5.

- Sub Co.'s accounts payable to Parent Company totaled $36,000 at December 31, 19X5.

- Sub Co. purchased equipment from Parent Company during 19X5 for $20,000. Prior to the sale, the carrying amount of the equipment on Parent Company's books was $15,000. Consequently, the transaction resulted in a gain to Parent Company of $5,000.

- Sub Co. is depreciating the equipment over five years using the straight-line method. It recorded a full year's depreciation ($4,000) in 19X5.

- For simplicity, the effects of income taxes are not considered.

Elimination entries:

a.   Common stock—Sub Co.   100,000
      Retained earnings—Sub Co.   50,000
      Goodwill [$140,000 × ($150,000   80%)]   20,000
          Investment in Sub Co.   140,000
          Minority interests in Sub Co.
             ($150,000 × 20%)   30,000

To eliminate the beginning investment account balance.

EXHIBIT 9-1 (Continued)

b.   Minority interests in Sub Co.'s earnings
     ($30,000 × 20%)   6,000
        Minority interests in Sub Co.   6,000

To record minority interest in Sub Co.'s earnings.

c.   Investment in Sub Co. ($10,000 × 80%)   8,000
    Minority interests in Sub Co. ($10,000 × 20%)   2,000
        Retained earnings—Sub Co.   10,000

To eliminate Sub Co. dividends.

d.   Amortization expense ($20,000 × 1/40)   500
        Goodwill   500

To amortize goodwill.

e.   Sales   70,000
    Minority interests in Sub Co. ($15,000 × 20%)   3,000
        Cost of sales   55,000
        Inventory   15,000
        Minority interests in Sub Co.'s earnings   3,000

To eliminate gain on sale of inventory to Parent
    Company.

f.   Accounts payable to Parent Company   36,000
        Accounts receivable from Sub Co.   36,000

To eliminate intercompany payables and receivables.

g.   Gain on sale of equipment   5,000
    Accumulated depreciation ($5,000 ÷ 5)   1,000
    Minority interest in Sub Co.'s earnings
       ($1,000 × 20%)   200
        Equipment   5,000
        Depreciation expense   1,000
        Minority interests in Sub Co.   200

To eliminate gain on sale of equipment to Sub Co. and adjust
    depreciation expense.

EXHIBIT 9-1 (Continued)

Consolidating worksheet for 19X5:

	Parent Company	Sub Co.		Eliminations	Consolidated
ASSETS					
Cash	14,000	8,000		—	22,000
Accounts receivable from Sub Co.	36,000	—	(f)	(36,000)	—
Inventory	240,000	65,000	(e)	(15,000)	290,000
Property and equipment:					
Cost	370,000	180,000	(g)	(5,000)	545,000
Accumulated depreciation	(95,000)	(26,000)	(g)	1,000	(120,000)
Investment in Sub Co.	132,000	—	(a)	(140,000)	—
			(c)	8,000	
Goodwill	—	—	(a)	20,000	19,500
			(d)	(500)	
	697,000	227,000		(167,500)	756,500
LIABILITIES					
Trade accounts payable	43,000	21,000			64,000
Accounts payable to Parent Company	—	36,000	(f)	(36,000)	—
STOCKHOLDERS' EQUITY					
Common stock	100,000	100,000	(a)	(100,000)	100,000
Retained earnings	554,000	70,000	(a)	(50,000)	561,300
			(c)	10,000	
				(22,700)	
	654,000	170,000		(162,700)	661,300
Minority interests in Sub Co.	—	—	(a)	30,000	31,200
			(b)	6,000	
			(c)	(2,000)	
			(e)	(3,000)	
			(g)	200	
	654,000	170,000		(131,500)	692,500
	697,000	227,000		(167,500)	756,500

EXHIBIT 9-1 (Continued)

	Parent Company	Sub Co.		Eliminations	Consolidated
EARNINGS					
Sales	643,000	395,000	(e)	(70,000)	968,000
Cost of sales	(421,000)	(305,000)	(e)	55,000	(671,000)
General and administrative expenses	(187,000)	(60,000)	(d)	(500)	(246,500)
			(g)	1,000	
Gain on sale of equipment	5,000	—	(g)	(5,000)	—
	40,000	30,000		(19,500)	50,500
Minority interests in Sub Co.'s earnings	—		(b)	(6,000)	(3,200)
			(e)	3,000	
			(g)	(200)	
	40,000	30,000		(22,700)	47,300

Income Taxes on Intercompany Profits

9.203　**Consolidated Tax Return.** If the affiliated group files a consolidated tax return (and there are no temporary differences between book and tax basis), consolidated income is the basis for determining the income tax expense reported on the financial statements and on the tax return. Since all intercompany profits and losses are eliminated to arrive at consolidated income, there is no need to make further adjustments for the tax effect of intercompany transactions. That is, the tax effects of intercompany transactions may be ignored if a consolidated tax return is filed.

9.204　Consolidated income tax expense may be recorded on the parent company's books or allocated among the affiliated entities so that each affiliate records its share of consolidated income tax expense on its own books. (Consolidated income tax expense must be allocated among affiliated companies if they issue separate financial statements in addition to consolidated financial statements.) Although GAAP does not require a specific allocation method to be used, it does require that the method used be systematic, rational, and consistent with the broad principles established by SFAS No. 109, *Accounting for Income Taxes.* An example of a method that meets those criteria would be to allocate current and deferred taxes to members of the affiliated group by applying SFAS No. 109 to each member as if it were a separate taxpayer. The following methods would not be acceptable, however: (SFAS 109, par. 40)

- A method that allocates only current taxes payable to a member of the group that has taxable temporary differences

- A method that allocates deferred taxes to a member of the group using a method fundamentally different from the method prescribed by SFAS No. 109

- A method that allocates no current or deferred income tax expense to a member of the group that has taxable income because the consolidated group has no current or deferred tax expense

EXHIBIT 9-2 illustrates acceptable methods of allocating consolidated income tax expense to members of an affiliated group. Chapter 24 discusses accounting for income taxes in further detail.

EXHIBIT 9-2

ALLOCATING CONSOLIDATED INCOME TAX EXPENSE TO AFFILIATES

Assume the following:

- During 19X5, Parent Company and its wholly owned subsidiary, Sub Co., had pretax income of $250,000 and $100,000, respectively.

- The companies had no deferred tax assets or liabilities at the beginning or end of 19X5.

- On December 31, 19X5, Parent Company has inventory on hand that it purchased in 19X5 from Sub Co. at a profit to Sub Co. of $20,000.

- Parent Company and Sub Co. file a consolidated tax return.

Assuming a tax rate of 30%, consolidated income tax expense would be computed as follows:

Reported income from operations before income taxes:	
Parent Company	$ 250,000
Sub Co.	100,000
	350,000
Less intercompany profit in ending inventory	20,000
Consolidated income before income taxes	$ 330,000
Consolidated income tax expense ($330,000 × 30%)	$ 99,000

The following methods of allocating consolidated income tax expense to Parent Company and Sub Co. would be acceptable: (Other methods that meet the criteria in Paragraph 9.204 would also be acceptable.)

EXHIBIT 9-2 (Continued)

Example Allocation A

An acceptable method would be to allocate current and deferred income taxes to members of the group by applying SFAS No. 109 to each member as if it were a separate taxpayer. Under that approach, Parent Company and Sub Co. would record the following amounts of income tax expense on their books:

Parent Company ($250,000 × 30%)	$ 75,000
Sub Co. ($100,000 × 30%)	30,000
	$ 105,000

The difference between the total amounts recorded by the affiliates ($105,000) and consolidated income tax expense ($99,000) relates to the tax effect of intercompany profits eliminated in consolidation and would be eliminated by the following entry:

Income taxes payable	6,000	
Income tax expense		6,000

To eliminate income taxes on intercompany profit.

Example Allocation B

Another acceptable method would be to apportion the $99,000 consolidated tax provision in the ratio of the income taxes computed separately for each affiliate as follows:

	Taxes Computed Separately	Percent of Total	Allocated Tax Amount
Parent Company	$ 75,000	71.4%	$ 70,686
Sub Co.	30,000	28.6	28,314
	$ 105,000	100.0%	$ 99,000

9.205 **Separate Tax Returns.** When a parent and subsidiary file separate tax returns rather than a consolidated tax return, the parent or subsidiary's accounts may include income taxes that were paid on intercompany profits. In such cases, the income taxes should be deferred, or the intercompany profits eliminated in consolidation should be appropriately reduced. (ARB 51, par. 17) For example, assume (a) a subsidiary sells inventory costing $400,000 to its parent and recognizes a $100,000 profit on the transaction and (b) the subsidiary files a separate return from its parent and pays $30,000 in income taxes as a result of the transaction. If consolidated financial statements were prepared, the following consolidating entries would be necessary:

a.	Sales	500,000	
	Cost of goods sold		400,000
	Inventory		100,000

To eliminate profits on intercompany sales of inventory

b.	Deferred income tax asset	30,000	
	Income tax expense		30,000

To defer the tax expense related to intercompany profits eliminated in consolidation

Acquisition of Subsidiary during the Year

9.206 Chapter 3 provides detailed guidance on accounting for the acquisition of a subsidiary. The following paragraphs discuss preparing the combined entity's consolidated financial statements for the year the business combination occurs.

9.207 **Combination Accounted for as a Pooling of Interests.** When a business combination is accounted for as a pooling of interests, all pre-affiliation intercompany profits should be eliminated to the extent possible. (APB 16, par. 56) (As discussed in Chapter 3, the effects of intercompany transactions involving long-term assets and liabilities need not be eliminated, however.) The underlying reason is that pooling of interests are reported on a retroactive basis as if the combination took place as of the beginning of the earliest period presented. Accordingly, all transactions, pre-affiliation as well as post-affiliation, between the combining companies are intercompany transactions and should be eliminated for consolidated financial statement purposes.

9.208 **Combination Accounted for as a Purchase.** When a subsidiary is acquired in a combination accounted for as a purchase, consolidated income and retained earnings should only include the subsidiary's earnings since the acquisition date. (APB 16, par. 94) All intercompany profits and transactions occurring on or after the acquisition date should be eliminated in consolidation, while those occurring before the acquisition date should not. For example, if a subsidiary is acquired on June 1, 19X5, only its earnings from June 1, 19X5 to December 31, 19X5, would be included in consolidated income for the year ended December 31, 19X5. In addition, intercompany profits occurring on or after June 1, 19X5, would be eliminated in consolidation while those occurring prior to June 1, 19X5, would not.

9.209   If a subsidiary is acquired in several purchases, the subsidiary's income and retained earnings generally should be included in consolidated income and retained earnings as determined on a step-by-step basis. (If small purchases are made followed by a purchase that results in control of the subsidiary, the date of the latest purchase may be used as the acquisition date for convenience, however.) As a result, consolidated income for the year in which control is acquired generally should include postacquisition income for the year, and consolidated retained earnings should include postacquisition income of prior years related to each block of stock acquired. (In some cases, prior year postacquisition income may already be included in retained earnings because the investment was accounted for under the equity method.) (ARB 51, par. 10) For example, assume that ABC Company acquired 15% of DEF Company's common stock on July 1, 19X4, and another 45% on October 1, 19X5. Consolidated income for the year ended December 31, 19X5 should include—

- 15% of DEF Company's earnings for the nine months ended September 30, 19X5 and

- 60% of DEF Company's earnings for the three months ended December 31, 19X5.

In addition, consolidated retained earnings should include 15% of DEF Company's undistributed earnings for the six months ended December 31, 19X4. (If the 15% investment was accounted for under the equity method in 19X4, consolidated retained earnings would already include those undistributed earnings. If the equity method was not used in 19X4, however, an entry would be needed in 19X5 to credit consolidated retained earnings for 15% of DEF Company's undistributed earnings for the six months ended December 31, 19X4.)

9.210   When a subsidiary is purchased during the year, either of the following methods may be used to show the subsidiary's results of operations in the consolidated income statement: (ARB 51, par. 11)

a. *Include the subsidiary's revenues and expenses for the entire year in consolidated amounts as if the acquisition occurred at the beginning of the year and deduct preacquisition earnings from the bottom of the income statement.* (This method is preferred because it presents results that are more indicative of the group's current status and facilitates comparisons with future years.)

b. *Prorate the subsidiary's results of operations so that only its revenues and expenses subsequent to the date of acquisition are included in consolidated amounts.*

Disposition of Subsidiary during the Year

9.211   If an investment in a subsidiary is sold during the year, the parent's income statement should include its portion of the subsidiary's earnings through the date of disposal as well as any gain or loss on the sale. (ARB 51, par. 12) The requirements for measuring and presenting the gain or loss on disposal and presenting the subsidiary's results of operations vary depending on whether the sale constitutes a disposal of a segment of a business or a disposal of only a portion of a line of business. (Chapter 23 discusses accounting for a disposal of a segment of a business and for the disposal of an activity that is less than a segment of a business.)

Fiscal Years of Parent and Subsidiaries Differ

9.212   If a parent and subsidiary's fiscal years differ by no more than about three months, it ordinarily is acceptable to consolidate the subsidiary using the subsidiary's financial statements for its fiscal year. In such cases, intervening events that materially affect results of operations or financial position should be disclosed or otherwise recognized. (ARB 51, par. 4)

Practical Consideration. GAAP provides little additional guidance about the issues that may arise when consolidated financial statements are prepared for companies with different fiscal years. Some of those issues and the authors' recommendations follow:

- *Classifying receivables and payables.* Questions may arise about the appropriate classification of receivables and payables when a consolidated subsidiary with a different fiscal year than its parent has a payable or receivable to an outside entity. For example, even though a subsidiary's September 30, 19X5, balance sheet reports debt to a bank due November 30, 19X6, as a noncurrent liability, should the December 31, 19X5, consolidated balance sheet report the debt as a current liability? In the authors' opinion, yes. Because the authors believe that the primary objective in accounting for intervening transactions is to fairly present the consolidated financial statements, they recommend a subsidiary's receivables and payables generally be classified based on the date of the consolidated balance sheet.

- *Eliminating intercompany transactions.* When a parent and its subsidiaries have different fiscal years, intercompany transactions may occur during the period between the year ends that do not eliminate in consolidation. For example, a subsidiary's payable to its parent at September 30 may not equal the parent's receivable from the subsidiary at December 31 due to intercompany transactions occurring between September 30 and December 31. In such cases, the authors recommend that, if material, the intervening transactions be reversed through consolidating entries. Material intercompany sales and purchases made during the period between the respective year ends should be treated in a similar manner.

Although the authors believe that the accounting recommendations above are preferable because they result in consolidated financial statements that include all transactions that have occurred as of the consolidated year end, intervening transactions may be disclosed in the consolidated financial statements rather than recognized by adjusting the financial statements.

Minority Interests

9.213   Minority interests refer to the investment in the voting stock of a subsidiary that is not held by the parent company. The existence of a minority interest does not affect the amount of intercompany profit that should be eliminated in consolidation. That is, the entire intercompany profit should be eliminated, not just the portion related to the controlling interest. (ARB 51, par. 14) The amounts to be reported in consolidated financial statements as the minority interest are determined as follows:

a. In the consolidated balance sheet, the minority interest is determined by multiplying the subsidiary's total realized stockholders' equity by the percentage of the subsidiary's stock that is owned by the minority interest. The subsidiary's realized stockholders' equity is its reported stockholders' equity adjusted for any unrealized intercompany profit or loss still residing in the retained earnings of the subsidiary.

b. In the consolidated income statement, the minority interest is determined by multiplying the subsidiary's income or loss (after intercompany profits are eliminated) by the percentage of the subsidiary's stock that is owned by the minority interest. If the minority interest's share of losses exceed its interest in the subsidiary's equity capital, the excess loss (and any further losses) should be charged against the *majority* interest since the minority interest has no obligation to cover the losses. However, any future earnings should be credited to the majority interest to the extent it has been charged for the minority interest's portion of losses. (ARB 51, par. 15)

Practical Consideration. GAAP provides little guidance for presenting minority interests in consolidated financial statements. Some accountants present minority interests as a separate line item between liabilities and equity. (That presentation is required in filings with the Securities and Exchange Commission.) Generally, however, the authors recommend presenting minority interests in the consolidated balance sheet as a part of equity, segregated from the equity of the controlling interest. (That presentation is consistent with positions taken in Statement of Financial Accounting Concepts No. 6, *Elements of Financial Statements*, and the FASB's proposed Statement of Financial Accounting Standards, *Consolidated Financial Statements: Policy and Procedures*.) For example:

STOCKHOLDERS' EQUITY

Controlling interests	
Common stock	40,000
Retained earnings	354,000
	394,000
Minority interests	60,000
	454,000

Practical Consideration (Continued).

The authors recommend showing the minority interests' share of earnings, if material, as a separate line item after the caption for income taxes, but before extraordinary items and the cumulative effects of accounting changes. In addition, because the allocation of income to minority interests does not use cash, the statement of cash flows should add that amount back to consolidated net income to arrive at cash provided by operations.

Shares of Parent Held by Subsidiary

9.214   The consolidated balance sheet should not treat shares of a parent owned by a subsidiary as outstanding stock. Instead, the stock should be treated as treasury stock and subtracted from consolidated stockholders' equity. (ARB 51, par. 13)

COMBINED FINANCIAL STATEMENTS

9.215   In some cases, combined financial statements (as distinguished from consolidated financial statements) may be useful or even necessary. For example, combined financial statements may be more meaningful than separate statements for (a) two or more companies that are related in their operations and are controlled by the same individual, (b) a group of unconsolidated subsidiaries, or (c) companies under common management. Combined financial statements are not limited to particular forms of entities. The principle prerequisites for preparing combined financial statements are—

   a. the entities to be combined are under common control or common management and

   b. combined financial statements are more meaningful than separate statements. (ARB 51, paras. 22–23)

Thus, combined financial statements may be appropriate for a combination of a partnership and a corporation that are commonly owned.

9.216   The procedures that apply to preparing combined financial statements are similar to those that apply to preparing consolidated financial statements. That is, intercompany profits and transactions should be eliminated and minority interests, foreign operations, differences resulting from different fiscal periods, and income taxes should be treated in the same manner as in consolidated financial statements. (ARB 51, par. 23)

> **Practical Consideration.** The principal difference between consolidated and combined financial statements is that, because none of the companies included in combined financial statements has an investment in the common stock of the other companies, the equity accounts of the various companies are combined rather than offset against the investment in subsidiaries held by the parent company. Unfortunately, GAAP does not state how to present the stockholders' equity section of a combined balance sheet. An AICPA technical practice aid at TIS 1400.06 provides limited guidance, however. It indicates that appropriate disclosure depends on the circumstances and suggests that the number of shares of stock authorized and outstanding and the par value of those shares for each company be disclosed either on the face of the balance sheet or in the notes.

PARENT COMPANY STATEMENTS

9.217   GAAP recognizes that parent company only financial statements may be needed in addition to consolidated financial statements in some cases. (ARB 51, par. 24) However, as discussed in Paragraph 9.200, it prohibits parent company financial statements to be issued to stockholders as the financial statements of the primary reporting entity. Thus, the authors believe that parent company financial statements may be issued in addition to consolidated financial statements provided (a) they do not purport to be the financial statements of the primary reporting entity and (b) there is a valid business reason for doing so.

9.218   Subsidiaries in parent company only financial statements should be accounted for under either the cost, fair value, or equity method as discussed in Paragraph 9.201.

DISCLOSURE REQUIREMENTS

9.500   Consolidated financial statements should include the following disclosures:

a. The consolidation policy used (for example, the companies consolidated, that all material intercompany transactions have been eliminated, etc.) (ARB 51, par. 5)

b. If the financial reporting periods of subsidiaries differ from that of the parent, the effect of intervening events that materially affect financial position or results of operations (ARB 51, par. 4) (Disclosure in the notes is not necessary if the effects are otherwise recognized in the consolidated financial statements. See Paragraph 9.212)

9.217

9.501   In addition, a company that is a member of a group that files a consolidated tax return should disclose the following in its separate financial statements: (SFAS 109, par. 49)

    a. Aggregate amount of current and deferred tax expense for each statement of earnings presented

    b. Amount of any tax-related balances due to or from affiliates as of the date of each balance sheet presented

    c. Method used to allocate consolidated current and deferred tax expense to members of the group and the nature and effect of any changes in that method (and in determining related balances to or from affiliates) during the years for which the disclosures in a. and b. are presented

AUTHORITATIVE LITERATURE AND RELATED TOPICS

AUTHORITATIVE LITERATURE

ARB No. 51, *Consolidated Financial Statements*
APB Opinion No. 16, *Business Combinations*
SFAS No. 94, *Consolidation of All Majority-Owned Subsidiaries*
SFAS No. 109, *Accounting for Income Taxes*
EITF Issue No. 96-16, *Investor's Accounting for an Investee when the Investor Owns a Majority of the Voting Stock but the Minority Shareholder or Shareholders Have Certain Approval or Veto Rights*

RELATED PRONOUNCEMENTS

EITF Issue No. 84-23, *Leveraged Buyout Holding Company Debt*
EITF Issue No. 84-30, *Sales of Loans to Special-Purpose Entities*
EITF Issue No. 84-41, *Consolidation of Subsidiary after Instantaneous In-Substance Defeasance*
EITF Issue No. 84-42, *Push-Down of Parent Company Debt to a Subsidiary*
EITF Issue No. 85-12, *Retention of Specialized Accounting for Investments in Consolidation*
EITF Issue No. 85-21, *Changes of Ownership Resulting in a New Basis of Accounting*
EITF Issue No. 85-28, *Consolidation Issues Relating to Collateralized Mortgage Obligations*
EITF Issue No. 87-21, *Change of Accounting Basis in Master Limited Partnership Transactions*
EITF Issue No. 88-15, *Classification of Subsidiary's Loan Payable in Consolidated Balance Sheet When Subsidiary's and Parent's Fiscal Years Differ*

EITF Issue No. 90-5, *Exchanges of Ownership Interests between Entities under Common Control*

EITF Issue No. 94-2, *Treatment of Minority Interests in Certain Real Estate Investment Trusts*

EITF Issue No. 95-7, *Implementation Issues Related to the Treatment of Minority Interests in Certain Real Estate Investment Trusts*

EITF Issue No. 95-20, *Measurement in the Consolidated Financial Statements of a Parent of the Tax Effects Related to the Operations of a Foreign Subsidiary That Receives Tax Credits Related to Dividend Payments*

EITF Issue No. 96-20, *Impact of FASB Statement No. 125 on Consolidation of Special-Purpose Entities*

EITF Issue No. 97-6, *Application of EITF Issue No. 96-20, 'Impact of FASB Statement No. 125, "Accounting for Transfers and Servicing of Financial Assets and Extinguishments of Liabilities," on Consolidation of Special-Purpose Entities,' to Qualifying SPEs Receiving Transferred Financial Assets Prior to the Effective Date of Statement 125*

RELATED TOPICS

Chapter 3—Business Combinations
Chapter 20—Equity Method Investments
Chapter 24—Income Taxes
Chapter 35—Marketable Securities

CONTINGENCIES

Table of Contents

CONTINGENCIES

OVERVIEW

10.100   An estimated loss from a loss contingency should be accrued through a charge to income and disclosed if (a) it is probable that a loss has been incurred at the financial statement date and (b) the amount of the loss can be reasonably estimated. Loss contingencies that do not meet those conditions should be disclosed if there is a reasonable possibility that a loss may have been incurred. A loss contingency that involves a guarantee also should be disclosed, even if the likelihood of loss is remote.

10.101   Gains from gain contingencies should not be accrued since doing so might recognize revenue before it is realized.

ACCOUNTING REQUIREMENTS

10.200   A contingency is an existing condition, situation, or set of circumstances involving an uncertainty that, when resolved, may result in a gain or loss. Contingencies that may result in the loss or impairment of an asset or the incurrence of a liability are called "loss contingencies" while those that may result in the acquisition of an asset or the reduction of a liability are called "gain contingencies." (SFAS 5, par. 1) The following paragraphs discuss accounting for both types.

Practical Consideration. Not all uncertainties inherent in the accounting process give rise to contingencies. For example, the possibility of a change in tax laws in the future is not a contingency. Also, the fact that estimates are used to record depreciation does not make depreciation a contingency. Similarly, amounts owed for services, such as advertising or utilities, are not contingencies even though the accrued amounts are estimates. Generally, only uncertainties about whether a liability has been incurred or reduced or an asset acquired or impaired give rise to contingencies.

Practical Consideration (Continued).

The guidance in this chapter generally does not apply to—

- pension costs,

- vacation pay, or

- deferred compensation contracts and stock issued to employees.

LOSS CONTINGENCIES

10.201   A loss contingency will not develop into an actual loss until a particular future event occurs. Thus, accounting for a loss contingency is based on whether the likelihood of the future event occurring is probable (likely to occur), reasonably possible (more than slight but less than likely) or remote (slight). (SFAS 5, par. 3) Depending on whether it is probable, reasonably possible, or remote, a loss contingency may be required to be accrued, disclosed, or neither.

10.202   The estimated loss from a loss contingency should be accrued through a charge to income and disclosed when both of the following conditions are met: (SFAS 5, par. 8)

    a. Information available prior to issuing the financial statements indicates that it is probable that a loss has been incurred at the financial statement date.

    b. The amount of loss can be reasonably estimated. (A loss that is not accrued in the period it becomes probable because its amount cannot be reasonably estimated should be accrued in the period its amount can be reasonably estimated. Prior periods should not be adjusted.) (SFAS 16, par. 37)

If a loss is probable but only a range of loss can be reasonably estimated, conditions a. and b. are still met and a loss should be accrued. In such cases, the minimum amount of the range should be accrued unless another amount is a better estimate. If it is reasonably possible that the actual loss will exceed the amount accrued, the additional exposure to loss should be disclosed. (FASBI 14, par. 4) Adjustment in subsequent periods of the amount accrued is a change in estimate. (See Chapter 1.)

> **Practical Consideration.** Contingencies that should be accrued are those that are material to the financial statements. In practice, for uncertainties that tend to more closely relate to financial position rather than to recurring operations, such as those regarding the recoverability of the cost of an asset or antitrust litigation, materiality judgments are based on a comparison of the potential effect to stockholders' equity or other relevant balance sheet components (e.g., total assets, total liabilities, or working capital). Other uncertainties, such as litigation over royalties or licensing fees, more closely relate to normal recurring operations. In evaluating the materiality of those types of uncertainties, it is more appropriate to compare the potential effect to the income statement.

10.203   A loss contingency should be disclosed, but not accrued, if—

     a. it is probable that a loss has occurred but the amount of the loss cannot be reasonably estimated or

     b. it is reasonably possible (but not probable) that a loss has occurred. (SFAS 5, par. 10)

In addition, a loss contingency should be disclosed if it involves a guarantee, even if the likelihood of loss is remote. Examples of such contingencies include the direct or indirect guarantee of indebtedness of others, obligations of commercial banks under standby letters of credit, and guarantees to repurchase receivables that have been sold or otherwise assigned. (SFAS 5, par. 12)

10.204   Required disclosures are discussed further in Paragraphs 10.500–.501. EXHIBIT 10-1 summarizes the accounting requirements for loss contingencies.

EXHIBIT 10-1

ACCOUNTING FOR LOSS CONTINGENCIES

Likelihood of Loss	Loss Can Be Reasonably Estimated	Loss Cannot Be Reasonably Estimated
Probable	Accrue the loss and disclose the contingency.	Do not accrue the loss but disclose the contingency.
Reasonably possible	Do not accrue the loss but disclose the contingency.	Do not accrue the loss but disclose the contingency.
Remote	Do not accrue the loss. Disclose the contingency if it involves the guarantee of indebtedness. Otherwise, disclosure is permitted, but not required.	Do not accrue the loss. Disclose the contingency if it involves the guarantee of indebtedness. Otherwise, disclosure is permitted, but not required.

Appropriating Retained Earnings

10.205   Some companies classify a portion of retained earnings as appropriated for loss contingencies. That practice is allowed so long as the following criteria are met: (SFAS 5, par. 15)

a. Appropriated retained earnings must be clearly identified and shown within the stockholders' equity section of the balance sheet.

b. Losses should not be charged to appropriated retained earnings. Furthermore, no part of appropriated retained earnings may be transferred to income or used in any way to affect the determination of net income.

Contingencies Arising after the Financial Statement Date

10.206   A loss contingency may arise after the financial statement date but before the financial statements are issued. Because the contingency arose after the financial statement date, a loss should not be accrued. However, the contingency may need to be disclosed to keep the financial statements from being misleading. (See Paragraph 10.500.) (SFAS 5, par. 11)

Applying the Rules to Specific Loss Contingencies

10.207   The following paragraphs discuss considerations for applying the accrual requirements to specific contingencies. In addition, EXHIBIT 10-2 illustrates applying the measurement and disclosure requirements to specific situations.

10.208   **Uncollectible Receivables.** There usually exists some degree of uncertainty about whether receivables will be collected. An allowance for uncollectible receivables should be recorded if both of the conditions in Paragraph 10.202 are met. That is—

     a. it is probable that receivables recorded at the financial statement date will not be collected and

     b. the uncollectible amount can be reasonably estimated.

The allowance should be recorded even if specific uncollectible receivables cannot be identified. (SFAS 5, par. 22)

10.209   A company may base its estimate of uncollectible receivables on its own experience, the experience of other companies in the same business, the debtor's ability to pay, or an appraisal of current economic conditions. A company's inability to reasonably estimate uncollectible receivables precludes it from recording an allowance and may suggest that it should use the installment method, cost recovery method, or other method to recognize revenues. (SFAS 5, par. 23) (See Chapter 48.)

10.210   **Product Warranty Obligations.** A warranty is an obligation arising in connection with the sale of goods or services that may require further performance by the seller after the sale takes place. Product or service warranty obligations are contingencies because of the potential claims that may result. Losses from warranty obligations should be accrued if (a) it is probable that claims will be paid under the warranty obligations and (b) the amount of the claims that will be paid can be reasonably estimated. In such cases, losses should be accrued even if the specific parties that will make the claims cannot be identified. (SFAS 5, par. 24)

EXHIBIT 10-2

EXAMPLES OF APPLYING THE LOSS CONTINGENCY MEASUREMENT AND DISCLOSURE REQUIREMENTS IN SPECIFIC SITUATIONS

Facts	Measurement	Disclosure
After the date of the financial statements but before they are issued, a fire destroys a company's operating facilities, which results in a substantial loss because the facilities were underinsured.	No. The assets were underinsured at the financial statement date, but the event that impaired them did not occur until after the financial statement date.	Yes. A loss occurred, and disclosure is required to keep the financial statements from being misleading. Disclosure should include an estimate of the possible loss or range of loss (or a statement that an estimate cannot be made) and, if applicable, an indication that it is at least reasonably possible that a change in estimate will occur in the near term.
After the date of the financial statements but before they are issued, a fire destroys a company's operating facilities. Their replacement was fully insured.	No. The assets were not impaired at the financial statement date, and there was no loss.	No. There was no loss.
A company is sued prior to the financial statement date. Before the financial statements are issued, the suit is settled at a material loss to the company.	Yes. A liability was incurred at the financial statement date, and the amount of the liability is known.	Yes, if disclosure is required to keep the financial statements from being misleading.
A company is sued after the financial statement date and settles at a material loss before the financial statements are issued. The event that caused the suit occurred after the financial statement date.	No. The liability was not incurred at the financial statement date.	Yes. A loss occurred, and disclosure is required to keep the financial statements from being misleading.

EXHIBIT 10-2 (Continued)

Facts	Measurement	Disclosure
Before year end, a company's truck driver is involved in a wreck. Although the driver did not cause it, one of the injured passengers in a separate vehicle is suing everyone involved. The company is sued for $1 million, but its driver is not charged by the police, and the company's lawyers say that the plaintiff has no chance of winning damages.	No. The chance of loss is remote.	No. the chance of loss is remote.
Before year end, a company is sued for $250,000. Any settlement would be covered by its $1 million liability policy, and the $10,000 deductible under the policy is not material. Although settlement has not been reached before the financial statements are issued, the company believes that it will eventually have to settle on the suit.	No. Any loss under the suit would not be material.	No. The loss would not be material.
Before year end, a company is assessed $170,000 in additional taxes as a result of an IRS audit. The company believes that a settlement with the IRS can be reached for $90,000. Settlement has not been reached before the financial statements are issued.	Yes. It is probable that a loss has been incurred at the financial statement date and the amount of loss can be reasonably estimated. The amount of loss to be accrued should be at least $90,000 unless a better estimate is available.	Yes. If disclosure is required to keep the financial statements from being misleading.

EXHIBIT 10-2 (Continued)

Facts	Measurement	Disclosure
At the financial statement date, trade receivables include a large account that is substantially overdue. A copy of that customer's most recent financial statements shows that it is in serious financial trouble. Before the financial statements are issued, the customer declares bankruptcy, and the company receives no settlement on the account because it is unsecured.	Yes. The asset was impaired at the financial statement date because of the customer's financial condition, and the loss is known. Declaring bankruptcy was only an extension of the condition that existed.	Yes, disclosure is required to keep the financial statements from being misleading.
Year-end receivables include a large balance due from a customer who has historically paid its accounts. Subsequent to the balance sheet date, the customer's operating facilities are destroyed by a flood. The loss is uninsured, and before the company issues its financial statements, the customer declares bankruptcy. The company receives no settlement on the account because it is unsecured.	No. The asset was not impaired at the financial statement date.	Yes. A loss occurred, and disclosure is required to keep the financial statements from being misleading.

10.211   A company may estimate losses from warranty obligations based on its own experience, the experience of other companies in the same business, or other relevant factors. A company's inability to reasonably estimate the amount of a warranty obligation precludes it from accruing the loss. In addition, it may raise questions about whether a sale should be recorded prior to the expiration of the warranty period. (SFAS 5, par. 25) (Revenue recognition is discussed further in Chapter 48.)

> **Practical Consideration.** The inability of management to make reasonable estimates (see Paragraphs 10.209 and 10.211) may raise questions about the appropriateness of accounting principles used. Using inappropriate accounting principles constitutes a GAAP departure. In those circumstances, even if the uncertainty were disclosed, accountants reporting on the financial statements would be required to modify their report for the departure.

10.212   **Uninsured Risks.** The fact that a company is not adequately insured against losses that may result from damage to its property, injury to others, or interruption of its business operations is a contingency. The absence of adequate insurance does not mean that an asset has been impaired or a liability has been incurred at the financial statement date, however. Losses from uninsured risks are probable only when future events occur, such as a fire or explosion, and thus relate to the future period in which the events occur rather than the current period. Consequently, contingencies arising from uninsured or underinsured risks should not be accrued. In addition, they generally do not need to be disclosed unless (a) an event that would make the likelihood of loss probable occurs subsequent to the financial statement date but before the financial statements are issued and (b) disclosure is necessary to prevent the financial statements from being misleading. (SFAS 5, paras. 27–28) (See Paragraph 10.206.)

10.213   **Expropriation of Assets.** The threat that a government will expropriate a company's assets is a contingency. Consequently, a loss should be accrued if (a) expropriation is imminent and a loss is expected and (b) the amount of the loss can be reasonably estimated. An expropriation's imminence may be indicated by a government's public or private declarations of intent or its actual expropriation of another company's assets. (SFAS 5, par. 32)

10.214   **Litigation, Claims, and Assessments.** A loss due to pending or threatened litigation or actual or possible claims and assessments should be accrued if all of the following conditions are met:

     a. *The underlying cause of the litigation, claim, or assessment occurred on or before the financial statement date.* The condition is met even if the company does not become aware of the existence or possibility of the litigation, claim, or assessment until after the financial statement date. (SFAS 5, paras. 33–35)

b. *The likelihood of an unfavorable outcome is probable.* Factors that should be considered include the nature of the litigation, claim, or assessment; the progress of the case (including its progress after the financial statement date but before the financial statements are issued); the opinions of legal counsel; similar experiences; and the company's intended response to the litigation, claim, or assessment. (SFAS 5, par. 36)

c. *The amount of the loss can be reasonably estimated.* If the estimated loss is expressed in a range, the lowest amount in the range should be accrued unless another amount within the range is a better estimate. If it is reasonably possible that the actual loss will exceed the amount accrued, the additional exposure to loss should be disclosed. (SFAS 5, par. 39)

10.215   When a claim or assessment is *unasserted* (for example, because either the claimant is unaware of its existence or has elected not to assert it), the criteria for disclosing or accruing the contingency differ slightly. In such cases, the company must first determine whether it is probable that a suit will be filed or a claim or assessment asserted. Based on its assessment of that probability, the following applies: (SFAS 5, par. 38)

a. No disclosure or accrual is required unless it is probable that a claim will be asserted.

b. Accrual and disclosure are required if (1) it is probable that a claim will be asserted, (2) it is probable that the outcome will be unfavorable, and (3) the amount of loss can be reasonably estimated.

c. Disclosure (but not accrual) is required if (1) it is probable that a claim will be asserted and it is probable that its outcome will be unfavorable but the amount of loss cannot be reasonably estimated or (2) it is probable that a claim will be asserted and reasonably possible (but not probable) that the outcome will be unfavorable.

10.216   **Catastrophe Losses of Insurance Companies.** When a property and casualty insurance company issues a policy, a contingency arises. The contingency is the risk of loss from catastrophes that may occur during the term of the policy. The loss contingency should not be accrued, however, unless the following conditions are met: (SFAS 5, paras. 40–41)

a. It is probable that a catastrophe loss has been incurred as of the financial statement date (even if the policy holder has not filed a claim as of that date).

b. The amount of the loss can be reasonably estimated.

In addition, unless the preceding criteria are met, premium income should not be deferred beyond the term of the policy since that, in substance, is the same as accruing catastrophe losses prematurely. (SFAS 5, par. 42)

10.217 **Preacquisition Contingencies.** A business may have contingent assets, contingent liabilities, or contingent impairments of assets on the date it is acquired in a business combination. Under the purchase method of accounting, a portion of the cost of acquiring the company should be allocated to the contingencies if the following conditions are met: (SFAS 38, paras. 4–5)

a. Information prior to the end of the allocation period indicates that it is probable that the contingent item existed on the consummation date of the business combination. (The allocation period is the period required to identify and quantify the assets acquired and the liabilities assumed. The existence of a preacquisition contingency that cannot be estimated does not extend the allocation period.)

b. The fair value of the preacquisition contingency can be reasonably estimated.

Chapter 3 discusses accounting for business combinations in further detail.

10.218 **Claims-made Insurance Policies.** An increasing number of liability insurance policies written are claims-made policies rather than the typical occurrence policies. The claims-made coverage insures only those claims that are reported to the insurance company during the policy period. (In contrast, occurrence policies insure claims arising from events that occur during the policy period regardless of when the claim is made.) Accordingly, with claims-made coverage, companies have a liability for any losses incurred during the policy period that have not been reported to the insurance company.

10.219 Companies should record a liability for probable losses from claims incurred but not reported during the policy period if the losses are both probable and reasonably estimable. Losses that are reasonably possible or probable but cannot be reasonably estimated should be disclosed. (EITF 86-12)

10.220 **Environmental Remediation Liabilities.** Environmental remediation liabilities should be accrued on a site-by-site basis when it is probable that a loss has been incurred at the financial statement date and the amount of the loss can be reasonably estimated. The following summarizes the accounting requirements for environmental remediation liabilities:

When to Accrue a Liability

An entity has incurred an environmental liability when the following two elements are met on or before the date the financial statements are issued: (SOP 96-1, par. 5.5)

a. It has been asserted or it is probable that it will be asserted (through litigation, claim, or regulatory assessment) that the entity is responsible for participating in an environmental remediation process as a result of a past event (which occurred on or before the balance sheet date).

Practical Consideration. GAAP does not specifically address accounting for costs associated with *voluntary* environmental remediation activities undertaken at the sole discretion of the entity and not as the result of threatened litigation, claims, or assessments. The authors believe such voluntary costs should be recognized when they have been incurred.

---

b. It is probable that the result of the litigation, claim, or assessment will be unfavorable and the entity will be held responsible.

Practical Consideration. Under SOP 96-1, the fact that particular components of the overall environmental remediation liability may not be reasonably estimated during the early stages of the remediation process should not preclude recognizing a liability. In addition, uncertainties regarding the share of an environmental liability should not preclude the entity from recognizing its best estimate of its share of the liability. The following benchmarks should be applied in determining when an environmental remediation liability meets SFAS No. 5's accrual criteria:

- *Identification and verification of the entity as a potentially responsible party (PRP).* If the entity determines that it is associated with a Superfund or RCRA site, it is probable a liability has been incurred, and the liability should be accrued when all or a portion of it is reasonably estimable.

Practical Consideration (Continued).

- *Receipt of order or mandates to take interim corrective measures.* For example, the entity might receive a unilateral administrative order from the EPA requiring it to take a "response action" or risk substantial penalties. In those situations, the cost of performing the required work generally is estimable within a range, and the entity should not delay accruing a liability for costs of removal actions beyond this point.

- *Participation as a PRP in a remedial investigation or feasibility study.* At this stage, the entity generally has agreed to pay the costs of a study to investigate the environmental impact of the contamination and identify remediation alternatives for the site. The cost of the investigation generally can be estimated within a reasonable range. As the investigation proceeds, the entity's estimate of its share of the total cost of the investigation can be refined.

- *Completion of feasibility or corrective measures study.* When the feasibility or corrective measures study is substantially complete, the entity generally will be able to reasonably estimate both a minimum remediation liability and the entity's allocated share of the liability.

- *Issuance of Record of Decision (ROD) or approval for corrective measures study.* At this stage, the EPA has issued its decision specifying a preferred remedy, and the entity can refine its estimated liability based on the specified remedy and a preliminary allocation of total remediation costs.

- *Remedial design and implementation of corrective measures.* During the design phase of the remediation, engineers develop a better estimate of the work to be performed and can provide more precise estimates of the total remediation costs. The entity should continue to refine and recognize its best estimate of its share of the liability as additional information becomes available throughout the operation and maintenance of the remedial action plan.

The preceding benchmarks should be considered when evaluating the probability that a loss has been incurred and the extent to which the loss is reasonably estimable. However, SOP 96-1's benchmarks should not be applied in a way that would delay recognizing an environmental remediation liability beyond the point at which a liability would be recognized under SFAS No. 5.

Estimating Environmental Remediation Costs

The following costs should be considered when estimating an entity's environmental remediation liability: (SOP 96-1, par. 6.5)

a. Incremental direct costs

b. Costs of compensation and benefits for employees who devote significant time to remediation activities

If the entity cannot estimate a single loss amount, a range of loss should be defined and an amount within that range should be accrued. (If no amount in the range is a better estimate than any other amount, the lowest amount in the range should be accrued.) (See Paragraph 10.202.)

Practical Consideration. Costs related to routine environmental compliance matters and legal costs associated with potential recoveries should not be included in remediation costs. In addition, when estimating the amount of environmental remediation liabilities, the accrual should be based on:

- *Enacted laws and adopted regulations.* Anticipated changes in those laws and regulations should not be considered. The impact of changes in laws and regulations should be recognized when those changes are enacted or adopted.

- *Remediation technology and methods expected to be approved to clean up the site.* When measuring the liability, the entity should consider anticipated advances in technology only to the extent that the entity has a reasonable basis to expect a remediation technology will be approved.

- *Productivity improvements.* The accrual should be based on the entity's estimated costs to perform each phase of the remediation effort at the time the phase is expected to be performed, considering factors such as productivity improvements due to experience with similar sites and similar remedial action plans.

Discounting Environmental Liabilities

Environmental liabilities may be discounted (but are not required to be discounted) only if both of the following are fixed or reliably determinable for each specific clean-up site:

a. Aggregate amount of the obligation

b. Amount and timing of cash payments

If only a range of loss can be estimated and no amount within the range is a better estimate of the liability than other amounts, discounting is not appropriate because the aggregate obligation is not fixed or reliably determinable. (SOP 96-1, par. 6.13)

Allocating Shared Costs among Responsible Parties

To record an environmental remediation liability, an entity must determine its share of the total remediation liability. That is a subjective estimate based on many factors, including the following:

- *Who are the PRPs for the site?* Generally, the EPA will notify the entity that it is a PRP, along with other PRPs identified by the EPA. However, depending on the available information, the EPA may not be aware of all PRPs. In that case, the entity, along with other identified PRPs, should consider investigating to find other parties who may be liable for a portion of the remediation costs. (SOP 96-1, par. 6.14)

- *What is the percentage of the total liability that will be allocated to the entity?* Several factors can be considered in allocating liability among PRPs, such as volume measures, the type of waste, whether the PRP was a site operator or owner, the degree of care exercised by the PRP, and any statutory or regulatory limitations on contributions from some PRPs. As a practical matter, the allocation often is determined by agreement among the parties, by hiring an allocation consultant, or by requesting that the EPA determine an allocation. The percentage for the entire remediation effort, not just a portion, should be used to determine the entity's allocable share of the total remediation liability. (SOP 96-1, paras. 6.17–.19)

- *What is the likelihood the other PRPs will pay their full share of the liability?* The entity should assess the likelihood that the other PRPs will pay their allocable portion of the total remediation liability. That assessment generally is based on the financial condition of the other PRPs and must be monitored as the remediation progresses. Any amounts that will not be paid by other PRPs must be allocated among the remaining PRPs and included in the remaining PRPs' liabilities. (SOP 96-1, par. 6.20)

Claims for Recovery

The amount of an environmental remediation liability should be determined independently from any potential claim for recovery. Furthermore, an asset related to a potential claim for recovery should be recognized only when realization of the claim is considered probable. (If a claim for recovery is being litigated, realization of the claim generally is not considered probable.) A potential claim for recovery should be measured at its fair value, considering both the costs related to the recovery and the time value of money. (However, the time value of money should not be considered if the related liability is not discounted and timing of the recovery depends on the timing of paying the liability.) In most cases, a legal right of offset does not exist for environmental liabilities and related claims for recovery. Thus, presentation of the gross liability and related claim for recovery in the balance sheet generally is appropriate. (SOP 96-1, paras. 6.21–.22)

GAIN CONTINGENCIES

10.221   Contingencies that might result in gains should not be accrued since doing so might recognize revenue before it is realized. Gain contingencies should be adequately disclosed in the notes to the financial statements, however. (SFAS 5, par. 17) (See Paragraph 10.500.)

DISCLOSURE REQUIREMENTS

CONTINGENCIES

10.500   When disclosures about loss contingencies are required (see Paragraphs 10.202–.203 and .206), the following information should be presented: (SFAS 5, paras. 9–10)

   a. The nature of the contingency

   b. An estimate of the possible loss or range of loss (or a statement that such an estimate cannot be made)

   c. Amount and nature of adjustments resulting from preacquisition contingencies that are reported other than as discussed in Paragraph 10.217

Similar disclosures should be made about gain contingencies, although care should be taken to avoid misleading implications about the likelihood of their

10.221

realization. (SFAS 5, par. 17) In some cases, contingencies arising after the financial statement date (see Paragraph 10.206) may best be disclosed by supplementing the financial statements with pro forma information that reports the loss as if it occurred at the financial statement date. (SFAS 5, par. 11)

Practical Consideration. The following are examples of contingency disclosures that meet the preceding requirements:

> The Company maintains a self-insurance program for its employees' health care costs. The Company is liable for losses on claims up to $25,000 per claim and $250,000 in total for the year. The Company has third-party insurance coverage for any losses in excess of such amounts. Self-insurance costs are accrued based on claims reported as of the balance sheet date as well as an estimated liability for claims incurred but not reported. The total accrued liability for self-insurance costs was $64,000 and $10,000 as of December 31, 19X4 and 19X5, respectively.

> The Company has guaranteed debt of XYZ Inc. totaling approximately $175,000 at December 31, 19X5, and $225,000 at December 31, 19X4. The fee for the guarantee was capitalized and is being amortized over the life of the loan using the interest method, which results in charges that are generally in proportion to principal reduction. Significant losses are not anticipated and will be charged to earnings when realized.

The following types of losses that occur after the date of the financial statements typically are disclosed:

     a. Settlement of litigation when the event giving rise to the claim took place after the financial statement date

     b. Loss of plant or inventories as a result of fire or flood

     c. Losses on recoveries resulting from conditions such as a customer's major casualty arising after the date of the financial statements

---

10.501 In addition to the disclosures in the preceding paragraphs, GAAP specifically requires the following risks and uncertainties to be disclosed: (SFAS 5, par. 18)

    a. Unused letters of credit

    b. Long-term leases

   c. Assets pledged as security for loans

   d. Pension plans

   e. Cumulative preferred stock dividends in arrears

   f. Commitments for plant acquisition or obligations to reduce debt, maintain working capital, or restrict dividends

Disclosures Related to Environmental Remediation Liabilities

10.502 An entity should make the following specific disclosures related to environmental remediation liabilities:

Accounting Policies (SOP 96-1, par. 7.11)

Whether environmental remediation liabilities are measured on a discounted basis

Accrued Liabilities (SOP 96-1, par. 7.20)

   a. The nature and the amount of the accrual (if necessary for the financial statements not to be misleading)

   b. If any part of the accrued obligation is discounted, the discount rate used and the undiscounted amount of the obligation

   c. An indication that it is at least reasonably possible that the estimate of the accrued obligation (or any related third-party receivables) will change in the near term if the criteria of SOP 94-6 for significant estimates are met (See Paragraph 10.503.)

Unaccrued Contingencies

For reasonably possible loss contingencies (including losses in excess of accrued amounts), the following disclosures should be made: (SOP 96-1, par. 7.21)

   a. A description of the contingency and an estimate of the possible loss (or the fact that such an estimate cannot be made)

   b. An indication that it is at least reasonably possible that the estimate will change in the near term if the criteria of SOP 94-6 for certain significant estimates are met (See Paragraph 10.503.)

For probable but not reasonably estimable loss contingencies that may be material, the following disclosures should be made: (SOP 96-1, par. 7.25)

a. A description of the remediation obligation

b. The fact that a reasonable estimate cannot currently be made

Unasserted Claims (SOP 96-1, par. 7.27)

If assertion of a claim is probable or if existing laws require the entity to report the release of hazardous substances and begin a remediation study, a loss contingency should be disclosed.

Practical Consideration. SOP 96-1 also encourages, but does not require, entities to disclose the following related to environmental remediation liabilities:

a. The event, situation, or set of circumstances that generally triggers recognition of loss contingencies resulting from environmental remediation-related obligations

b. The policy concerning the timing of recognition of recoveries

c. The estimated time frame for making environmental remediation disbursements (if expenditures are expected to occur over a long period)

d. The estimated time frame for realizing recognized recoveries (if realization is not expected in the near term)

e. The factors that cause the estimate of accrued environmental remediation liabilities, unaccrued contingencies, or third-party receivables to be sensitive to change if the criteria of SOP 94-6 are met

f. The reasons why an estimate of the loss (or range of the loss) cannot be made for probable or reasonably possible losses

g. The estimated time frame for resolving the uncertainty as to the amount of a probable but not reasonably estimable loss

h. The following information related to an individual site, if relevant to an understanding of the entity's financial position, cash flows, or results of operations:

   • Total environmental remediation liability accrued for the site

---

Practical Consideration (Continued).

- Nature and estimated amount of any reasonably possible loss contingency

- Involvement of other potentially responsible parties

- Status of regulatory proceedings

- Estimated time frame for resolving the contingency

i. The amount recognized in the income statement for environmental remediation loss contingencies in each period

j. The amount of any third-party recovery credited against environmental remediation costs in the income statement each period

k. The income statement caption that includes environmental remediation costs and related recoveries

l. A conclusion about whether the total unrecorded exposure to environmental remediation obligations is material to the financial statements

m. A description of the general applicability and impact of environmental laws and regulations on the entity's business and how those laws and regulations may result in loss contingencies for future remediation

---

OTHER RISKS AND UNCERTAINTIES

10.503   AICPA Statement of Position 94-6, *Disclosure of Certain Significant Risks and Uncertainties,* requires a business to include the following disclosures in its financial statements:

a. A description of its major products or services, including its principal markets and the locations of those markets

b. If the company operates in one or more businesses, the relative importance of each business and the basis for determining relative importance (for example, based on assets, revenues, net income, etc.) (SOP 94-6, par.10)

c. An explanation that preparing financial statements in conformity with generally accepted accounting principles involves the use of management's estimates (SOP 94-6, par. 11)

> **Practical Consideration.** Typically, the disclosure is based on standardized language such as the following:
>
>> The preparation of financial statements in conformity with generally accepted accounting principles requires management to make estimates and assumptions that affect the reported amounts of assets and liabilities and disclosure of contingent assets and liabilities at the date of the financial statements and the reported amounts of revenues and expenses during the reporting period. Actual results could differ from those estimates.

   d. When an estimate is used to determine the carrying amount of an asset or liability or in the disclosure of a gain or loss contingency and it is at least reasonably possible that the estimate will change in the near term and the effect of the change would be material to the financial statements: (SOP 94-6, paras. 12–14)

      (1) the nature of the estimate and

      (2) an indication that it is at least reasonably possible that a change in the estimate will occur in the near term

      (*Near term* is defined as a period of time not to exceed one year from the financial statement date.)

> **Practical Consideration.** The following is an example of a disclosure that meets the preceding requirements:
>
>> As a result of recent changes in the Company's market for certain products, carrying amounts for those inventories have been reduced by approximately $60,000 due to quantities in excess of current requirements. Management believes that this reduces inventory to its lower of cost or market, and no additional loss will be incurred upon disposition of the excess quantities. While it is at least reasonably possible that the estimate will change materially in the near term, no estimate can be made of the range of additional loss that is at least reasonably possible.

   e. The general nature of the risk associated with the following concentrations that exist at the financial statement date and make the business vulnerable to the risk of a severe near-term impact if it is at least reasonably possible that the events that could cause the severe impact will occur in the near term: (SOP 94-6, paras. 21–22)

(1) Concentrations in the volume of business transacted with a particular customer, supplier, lender, grantor, or contributor

(2) Concentrations in revenue from particular products, services, or fund-raising events

(3) Concentrations in the available sources of supply of materials, labor, or services, or of licenses or other rights used in the business's operations [For labor subject to collective bargaining agreements, the disclosure should include both the percentage of the labor force covered by the collective bargaining agreement and the percentage of the labor force covered by a collective bargaining agreement that will expire within one year. (SOP 94-6, par. 24)]

(4) Concentrations in the market or geographic area in which the business conducts its operations (For operations located outside the business's home country, the disclosure should include the carrying amounts of net assets and the geographic areas in which they are located.) (SOP 94-6, par. 24)

Practical Consideration. The following is an example of a disclosure that meets the preceding requirements:

> Helena Corporation has exclusive rights to produce and sell in the United States hair dryers bearing the name of a well-known personality in the hair care industry. Approximately 85% of Helena's revenues are derived from sales of those hair dryers.

GOING CONCERN CONTINGENCIES

10.504   Uncertainty about a company's ability to continue as a going concern relates to its inability to continue to meet its obligations as they become due without substantial disposition of assets outside the ordinary course of business, restructuring of debt, externally forced revisions of its operations, or similar actions. Thus, it is more than an evaluation of whether recorded assets and liabilities are recoverable and properly classified. If there is substantial doubt about a company's ability to continue as a going concern for a period of time not to exceed one year beyond the balance sheet date, the following information should be disclosed:

a. Pertinent conditions and events giving rise to the assessment of substantial doubt about the company's ability to continue as a going concern for a period of time not to exceed one year from the balance sheet date

b. Possible effects of the conditions and events

c. Management's evaluation of the significance of those conditions and events and any mitigating factors

d. Possible discontinuance of operations

e. Management's plans, including relevant prospective financial information

f. Information about the recoverability or classification of recorded asset amounts or the amounts or classification of liabilities (AU Section 341.10)

10.505   If the substantial doubt about the company's ability to continue as a going concern is alleviated, the following information should be disclosed:

a. Conditions and events that initially caused the substantial doubt

b. Possible effects of the conditions and events

c. Mitigating factors, including management's plans (AU Section 341.11)

AUTHORITATIVE LITERATURE AND RELATED TOPICS

AUTHORITATIVE LITERATURE

SFAS No. 5, *Accounting for Contingencies*
SFAS No. 16, *Prior Period Adjustments*
SFAS No. 38, *Accounting for Preacquisition Contingencies of Purchased Enterprises*
FASB Interpretation No. 14, *Reasonable Estimation of the Amount of a Loss*
FASB Interpretation No. 34, *Disclosure of Indirect Guarantees of Indebtedness of Others*
SAS 59, *The Auditor's Consideration of an Entity's Ability to Continue as a Going Concern*
SOP 94-6, *Disclosure of Certain Significant Risks and Uncertainties*
SOP 96-1, *Environmental Remediation Liabilities*
EITF Issue No. 86-12, *Accounting by Insureds for Claims-Made Insurance Policies*

RELATED PRONOUNCEMENTS

FASB Technical Bulletin 90-1, *Accounting for Separately Priced Extended Warranty and Product Maintenance Contracts*
EITF Issue No. 84-21, *Sale of a Loan with a Partial Participation Retained*
EITF Issue No. 85-20, *Recognition of Fees for Guaranteeing a Loan*
EITF Issue No. 86-2, *Retroactive Wage Adjustments Affecting Medicare Payments*
EITF Issue No. 87-22, *Prepayments to the Secondary Reserve of the FSLIC*
EITF Issue No. 95-5, *Determination of What Risks and Rewards, If Any, Can Be Retained and Whether Any Unresolved Contingencies May Exist in a Sale of Mortgage Loan Servicing Rights*
Practice Bulletin 5, *Income Recognition on Loans to Financially Troubled Countries*
Practice Bulletin 11, *Accounting for Preconfirmation Contingencies in Fresh-Start Reporting*

RELATED TOPICS

Chapter 3—Business Combinations
Chapter 48—Revenue Recognition

CONTRIBUTIONS

Table of Contents

CONTRIBUTIONS

OVERVIEW

11.100   Generally, contributions received and unconditional promises to give should be recognized as revenues when they are received. Similarly, contributions made, including unconditional promises to give, should be recorded as expenses in the period they are made. Conditional promises to give, whether received or made, should be recognized when the conditions to which they are subject are met. When recognized, contributions received and contributions made should be recorded at their fair values.

11.101   In addition, the following apply to contributed services and assets contributed to collections:

a. Contributed services should be recognized only if they (1) create or enhance nonfinancial assets or (2) require specialized skills, provided by individuals possessing those skills, and would ordinarily need to be purchased if not donated.

b. Contributed works of art, historical treasures, and similar assets need not be recorded when received if they are added to collections that meet certain criteria.

11.102   Certain disclosures about contributed services, promises to give, and collections not capitalized are required.

ACCOUNTING REQUIREMENTS

11.200   Contributions are voluntary, unconditional transfers of assets to an entity (or voluntary, unconditional cancellations of an entity's liabilities) by another entity acting other than as an owner. Their primary characteristic is that they are nonreciprocal—that is, one entity gives an asset or cancels a liability without directly receiving any value in exchange. Contributions include transfers of cash, nonmonetary assets, services, or unconditional promises to give those items in the future. (SFAS 116, par. 5)

Practical Consideration. The guidance in this chapter applies to contributions made or received by for-profit as well as not-for-profit entities. It does not apply to transfers in which the reporting entity is an agent rather than a donor or donee, however. An agent is an intermediary between a donor and donee and has little or no discretion in determining how contributions will be used. It does not make or receive contributions. Rather, it merely receives assets and distributes them as directed by the donor.

In addition, the guidance in this chapter does not apply to tax abatements or transfers from governments to businesses.

CONTRIBUTIONS RECEIVED

11.201   Unconditional contributions received should be measured at fair value and recognized immediately as revenues or gains, even if the donor has restricted their use. Generally, fair value should be based on quoted market prices. If quoted market prices are not available, fair value may be based on quoted market prices for similar assets, independent appraisals, or valuation techniques, such as the present value of estimated future cash flows. (SFAS 116, paras. 8 and 19)

Practical Consideration. SFAS No. 116, *Accounting for Contributions Received and Contributions Made,* distinguishes between donor-imposed *restrictions* and donor-imposed *conditions*. A donor-imposed restriction limits the way in which the contribution may be used (for example, to build a library for a private school) but does not restrict the donee's right to the donated assets. Thus, donor imposed restrictions generally do not delay the recognition of revenue or expense from contributions. A donor-imposed condition, however, requires a certain event to occur before the donee has unconditional rights to the donated asset. (For example, an entity may be required to raise a specified amount from other sources before a donor will make a sizable contribution.) As discussed further in Paragraph 11.205, a donor-imposed condition delays recognition of the contribution until the condition is met.

11.202   A not-for-profit organization that receives transferred assets will be considered a donee and donor (instead of an agent, trustee, or intermediary) if the original donor has (a) directed the not-for-profit organization to distribute the transferred assets (or income from the transferred assets) to a third-party beneficiary *and* (b) explicitly granted the not-for-profit organization the power to distribute the transferred assets (or income) to any third-party beneficiary at the organization's own discretion. (FASBI 42, par. 2)

Contributed Services

11.203   The value of contributed services received should be recognized if they (a) create or enhance a nonfinancial asset or (b) require specialized skills, provided by individuals possessing those skills, that would be purchased if they were not donated. For example, donated services (both skilled and unskilled) used to construct a building should be capitalized as a cost of construction because they are used to create a nonfinancial asset. Similarly, if a donor receives legal services (a specialized skill) at a reduced rate, the difference between the reduced fee and the fee that would have been charged in an arm's length transaction should be recognized as a donation. Donated services requiring specialized skills include those provided by accountants, architects, carpenters, doctors, electricians, lawyers, nurses, plumbers, teachers, and other professionals and craftsmen. (SFAS 116, par. 9)

11.204   Generally, the value of contributed services should be based on quoted market prices of the services. Alternatively, the fair value of services that create or enhance nonfinancial assets may be estimated by referring to the fair value of the resulting asset or asset enhancement. (SFAS 116, paras. 8 and 19)

Promises to Give

11.205   Donors may make promises to give contributions in the future (for example, a pledge to pay $1,000 over the next 12 months). Accounting for promises to give depends on whether they are unconditional or conditional.

   a. *Unconditional promises to give.* A promise is unconditional if its receipt depends only on the passage of time or demand by the donee and the donor has no right to have the donated assets returned. Unconditional promises to give should be recognized immediately. (SFAS 116, par. 22)

Practical Consideration. Sometimes it is difficult to distinguish between an unconditional promise to give and an intention to give. If an unconditional intention to give is legally enforceable, even if it does not clearly indicate that it is a promise, it is considered to be an unconditional promise to give and should be recorded. An unconditional promise does not have to be legally enforceable, however, to be required to be recorded under SFAS No. 116. Factors that may help to distinguish an unconditional promise from an intention include the written evidence and words used to communicate the intention (i.e., "promise to give" versus "plan to give"), whether a payment schedule exists, whether any partial payments have been made, and whether the donee has publicly announced the donation and has taken any action to rely on the promise.

---

b. *Conditional promises to give.* A conditional promise to give generally depends on a future event occurring before the donor is bound by the promise. A conditional promise should be recorded when the conditions on which it depends are substantially met. (For example, if a corporation agrees to match the donations of its employees, the corporation's promise to give is conditional. It should be recognized only as donations are received from the corporation's employees.) A conditional promise to give should be treated as an unconditional promise to give if there is only a remote possibility that the condition on which it depends will not be met. (SFAS 116, par. 22)

In practice, it may be difficult to determine whether a promise is conditional or unconditional. If the promise contains vague stipulations that do not clearly indicate an unconditional promise to give, it should be treated as a conditional promise to give (for example, a corporation promises to give $50,000, depending on its operating results). (SFAS 116, par. 23)

Practical Consideration. A promise to give may be written or oral. Verifiable documentation of the promise must exist before amounts may be recognized in the financial statements, however. The authors believe that sufficient documentation of an oral promise normally should include the following:

- Donor's name, address, and telephone number

- Amount of the promise

- Date of the promise and date it is due

- Name of the individual to whom the promise was made

11.206   When recorded, promises to give should be measured at their fair value. In many cases, net realizable value is a reasonable estimate of fair value. However, for unconditional promises to give cash in the future (particularly those that are not expected to be collected within one year), fair value is best measured by the present value of estimated future cash flows. When that method is used, subsequent accruals of interest should be accounted for as contribution income rather than interest income. (SFAS 116, paras. 8 and 20–21)

> **Practical Consideration.** As discussed in Chapter 10, losses from uncollectible receivables should be accrued if they are probable and can be reasonably estimated. Although SFAS No. 116 does not provide specific guidance on developing an allowance for uncollectible promises, the authors believe the following factors should be considered:
>
> - Entity's collection policy and past collection experience
>
> - Length of time the receivable has been outstanding
>
> - Credit standing of the individual making the promise
>
> - Other relevant economic factors

Contributions to Collections

11.207 Recording contributions of works of art, historical treasures, and similar assets is optional if the items are added to collections that are—

a. held for public exhibition, education, or research in furtherance of public service rather than financial gain;

b. protected, kept unencumbered, cared for, and preserved; and

c. subject to an organizational policy that requires the proceeds from sales of collection items to be used to acquire other items for collections.

If collections are capitalized, contributed collection items should be recorded as revenues or gains and as assets. If collections are not capitalized, certain disclosures must be made. (See Paragraph 11.501.) (SFAS 116, paras. 11 and 13)

CONTRIBUTIONS MADE

11.208 Contributions made should be recognized as expenses and as decreases to assets (or increases to liabilities, if applicable) when they are made. For example, a contribution of inventory should be recorded at the time of donation by reducing inventories and recording contribution expense. An unconditional promise to give cash should be recorded at the time it is promised by increasing a liability and recording contribution expense. The fair values of the assets transferred (or liabilities canceled) should be used to record contributions made. If an asset's or liability's fair value differs from its

DISCLOSURE REQUIREMENTS

11.500　Recipients of contributions should include the following disclosures in their financial statements:

Contributed Services

a. The programs or activities for which contributed services were used (The disclosure should describe the nature and extent of contributed services received during the period, including the amount recognized as revenues. Entities are encouraged to disclose the fair value of services received but not recognized as revenues if it is practicable to do so.) (SFAS 116, par. 10)

Unconditional Promises to Give

b. The amounts of unconditional promises receivable in less than one year, in one to five years, and in more than five years

c. The amount of the allowance for uncollectible unconditional promises receivable (SFAS 116, par. 24)

Conditional Promises to Give

d. The total of the amounts promised

e. A description and amount for each group of promises having similar characteristics, such as amounts of promises conditioned on establishing new programs, completing a new building, or raising matching gifts by a specified date (SFAS 116, par. 25)

11.501　In addition, an entity should disclose the following about its collections:

a. If collections are not capitalized, the following, reported on the face of its statement of activities (or income statement) separately from revenues, expenses, gains, and losses:

(1) Costs of collection items purchased (The amount should be reported as a decrease in the appropriate class of net assets or equity.)

(1) Costs of collection items purchased (The amount should be reported as a decrease in the appropriate class of net assets or equity.)

(2) Proceeds from sale of collection items (The amounts should be reported as an increase in the appropriate class of net assets or equity. If collections are capitalized prospectively after adopting SFAS No. 116, the amounts related to collection items not capitalized should be reported.)

(3) Proceeds from insurance recoveries of lost or destroyed collection items (The amounts should be reported as an increase in the appropriate class of net assets or equity. If collections are capitalized prospectively after adopting SFAS No. 116, the amounts related to collection items not capitalized should be reported.) (SFAS 116, par. 26)

b. If collections are not capitalized or are capitalized prospectively after adopting SFAS No. 116, a description of the collections, including their relative significance and the entity's accounting and stewardship policies for collections (SFAS 116, par. 27)

c. If collection items not capitalized are deaccessed during the period, (a) a description of the items given away, damaged, destroyed, lost, or otherwise deaccessed during the period or (b) the fair value of such items (SFAS 116, par. 27)

The statement of financial position should include a line item that refers to the disclosures in b. and c. If collections are capitalized prospectively after adopting SFAS No. 116, the line item should be dated, for example, Collections acquired since January 1, 19X5 (Note X). (SFAS 116, par. 27)

AUTHORITATIVE LITERATURE AND RELATED TOPICS

AUTHORITATIVE LITERATURE

SFAS No. 116, *Accounting for Contributions Received and Contributions Made*
FASB Interpretation No. 42, *Accounting for Transfers of Assets in Which a Not-for-Profit Organization is Granted Variance Power*

RELATED TOPICS

Chapter 10—Contingencies

CURRENT ASSETS AND CURRENT LIABILITIES

Table of Contents

CURRENT ASSETS AND CURRENT LIABILITIES

OVERVIEW

12.100   Classified balance sheets should present current assets and current liabilities separately from other assets and liabilities. Current assets are those that will be realized in cash, sold, or used within one year (or operating cycle, if longer). Current liabilities are obligations that will be liquidated by using current assets or creating other current liabilities. Current liabilities also include the following:

- Noncurrent obligations that, by their terms, are due on demand or will be due on demand within one year (or operating cycle, if longer) from the balance sheet date, even if their liquidation is not expected within that period

- Noncurrent obligations that are callable by the creditor because (a) the debtor is in violation of a provision of the debt agreement at the balance sheet date or (b) a violation has occurred at the balance sheet date that, if not cured within a specified grace period, will make the obligation callable (Callable obligations may be classified as noncurrent if certain conditions are met, however.)

12.101   A current liability that is expected to be refinanced on a long-term basis may be classified as noncurrent if the debtor intends to refinance the liability on a long-term basis and has demonstrated the ability to do so.

ACCOUNTING REQUIREMENTS

12.200   Classified balance sheets distinguish current assets and current liabilities from other assets and liabilities. They are presumed to be more useful than unclassified balance sheets because they present information that owners, lenders, and investors frequently use to measure a company's liquidity. For example, to assess a company's ability to meet obligations when they are due, financial statement users often compute a company's working capital (current assets less current liabilities), current ratio (current assets divided by current liabilities), and quick ratio (cash and assets convertible into cash divided by current liabilities).

> **Practical Consideration.** Classified balance sheets are useful for manufacturing, trading, and some service entities. However, in some industries, for example, savings and loan associations and real estate, presenting an unclassified balance sheet is accepted practice because the working capital distinction is not relevant. The authors recommend presenting a classified balance sheet unless an unclassified presentation is accepted industry practice or is specifically permitted by an industry accounting or audit guide.

CURRENT ASSETS

12.201 Current assets are cash and those assets that are reasonably expected to be realized in cash or sold or consumed within one year or within a business's normal operating cycle if it is longer. (A business whose operating cycle is not clearly defined should classify assets as current based on a one year time period.) A business's normal operating cycle is the time needed to convert cash first into materials and services, then into products, then by sale into receivables, and finally by collection back into cash. For most businesses, that period is less than one year or not recognizable. For some businesses, however, such as shipbuilders, distillers, logging companies, and others with extended production processes, the operating cycle may be longer than one year.

12.202 Generally, current assets include the following:

- Cash and cash equivalents available for current operations

- Marketable securities representing the investment of cash available for current operations, including investments in debt and equity securities classified as trading securities

- Inventories

- Trade accounts receivable

- Notes and other receivables that are expected to be collected within one year (or operating cycle, if longer)

- Prepaid expenses such as insurance, interest, rents, taxes, etc. (Although prepaid expenses will not be converted into cash, they are considered current assets because they would have required the use of current assets had they not been paid in advance.) (ARB 43, Ch. 3A, paras. 2–4 and SFAS 115, par. 125)

The following are *not* current assets, however, since they generally are not expected to be converted into cash within one year (or operating cycle, if longer):

- Cash restricted for special purposes (Restricted cash may be classified as a current asset if it is considered to offset maturing debt that has been properly classified as a current liability, however.)

- Long-term investments

- Receivables not expected to be collected within one year (or operating cycle, if longer)

- Cash surrender value of life insurance policies

- Land and other natural resources

- Depreciable assets

- Prepayments or deferred charges that will not be charged to operations within one year (or operating cycle, if longer) (ARB 43, Ch. 3A, Par. 6)

CURRENT LIABILITIES

12.203   Current liabilities are obligations whose liquidation is reasonably expected to require (a) the use of current assets or (b) the creation of other current liabilities. Current liabilities include the following:

- Payables for materials and supplies

- Amounts collected before goods or services are delivered

- Accruals for wages, salaries, commissions, rents, royalties, and taxes

- Other obligations, including portions of long-term obligations, that are expected to be liquidated within one year (or operating cycle, if longer) (ARB 43, Ch. 3A, par. 7)

Current liabilities do *not* include long-term notes, bonds, and obligations that will not be paid out of current assets.

> **Practical Consideration.** In some cases, authoritative literature specifically states how certain assets and liabilities are to be classified. For example, SFAS No. 109, *Accounting for Income Taxes,* provides specific guidance for classifying deferred tax assets and liabilities (see Chapter 24), and SFAS No. 115, *Accounting for Certain Investments in Debt and Equity Securities,* specifies how investments in debt and equity securities are to be classified (see Chapter 35).

Callable Obligations

12.204   An obligation that, by its terms, is due on demand at the balance sheet date is a current liability. Factors such as an assessment of whether the creditor will actually call the note do not affect the classification decision. In addition, if violations of a long-term debt agreement exist that make the debt callable within one year from the balance sheet date (or callable within one year from the balance sheet date if the violation is not cured within a specified grace period), the long-term debt should be classified as a current liability unless—

- the creditor has specifically waived the right to demand payment for more than one year from the balance sheet date,

- the violation is cured after the balance sheet date but before financial statements are issued, or

- the company demonstrates that it is probable it will be able to cure the violation within the grace period. (SFAS 78, par. 5)

12.205   **Subjective Acceleration Clauses.** A loan agreement may contain a subjective acceleration clause allowing the creditor to accelerate the maturity of long-term debt based on subjective criteria such as "occurrence of material adverse changes" or "failure to maintain satisfactory operations." In such cases, all facts and circumstances should be evaluated to determine whether (a) the long-term debt should be classified as current, (b) the subjective acceleration clause should be disclosed, or (c) neither disclosure nor reclassification is necessary because the company is in good financial condition. (FTB 79-3, par. 3)

Practical Consideration. Questions have been raised about whether long-term debt should be classified as current when a covenant violation has not occurred at the balance sheet date but it is probable that covenant violations will occur within the next year (or operating cycle, if longer). In Issue No. 86-30, the FASB's Emerging Issues Task Force concluded that such long-term obligations should be classified as noncurrent unless both of the following conditions exist:

    a. A covenant violation occurred at the balance sheet date or would have occurred absent a modification.

    b. It is probable that the borrower will not be able to cure the default (or comply with the covenant) at measurement dates that are within the next year (or operating cycle, if longer).

Obligations Expected to Be Refinanced

12.206 Obligations scheduled to mature within one year (or operating cycle, if longer) normally must be included in current liabilities. They may be included in noncurrent liabilities, however, if *both* of the following conditions are met:

    a. *The company intends to refinance the obligation on a long-term basis.*

    b. *The company has the ability to consummate the refinancing.* The company's ability may be demonstrated in either of the following ways:

        (1) After the balance sheet date but before the financial statements are issued, a long-term obligation or equity securities have been issued for the refinancing.

        (2) Before the financial statements are issued, the company enters into a financing agreement that clearly permits refinancing on terms that are readily determinable, and *all* of the following conditions are met:

            (a) The agreement does not expire within one year (or operating cycle, if longer) from the balance sheet date and the agreement is not cancelable or callable by the lender except for violation of a provision with which compliance is objectively determinable or measurable.

(b) No violation of any provision in the agreement exists at the balance sheet date, and no available information indicates that a violation has occurred prior to the issuance of the financial statements. (If there has been a violation, this condition is met if an unconditional waiver of the lender's right to cancel or call the agreement has been obtained.)

(c) The lender is expected to be financially capable of honoring the agreement. (SFAS 6, paras. 9–11)

12.207   Replacing a short-term obligation with another short-term obligation does not, by itself, demonstrate the company's ability to refinance the obligation on a long-term basis. Thus, for example, replacing a short-term obligation under the terms of a revolving credit agreement would not allow the company to classify the short-term obligation as noncurrent unless the revolving credit agreement meets the conditions in Paragraph 12.206. (SFAS 6, par. 14)

DISCLOSURE REQUIREMENTS

12.500   Classified balance sheets should contain totals for current assets and current liabilities. Furthermore, the notes to the financial statements should contain the following disclosures:

- If a short-term obligation is classified as a noncurrent liability because it will be refinanced on a long-term basis (see Paragraphs 12.206–.207), a general description of the financing agreement and the terms of any new obligation incurred or expected to be incurred or equity securities issued or expected to be issued as a result of the refinancing (SFAS 6, par. 15)

- If a debtor is in violation of a provision of a debt agreement at the balance sheet date but classifies the obligation as noncurrent because it is probable that the violation will be cured within the specified grace period, a description of the circumstances (SFAS 78, par. 5)

12.501   In addition, any allowance (such as those for uncollectible receivables or depreciation) should be deducted from the related asset and disclosed. (APB 12, par. 3)

AUTHORITATIVE LITERATURE AND RELATED TOPICS

AUTHORITATIVE LITERATURE

ARB No. 43, *Restatement and Revision of Accounting Research Bulletins* (Chapter 3A—Current Assets and Current Liabilities)

APB Opinion No. 12, *Omnibus Opinion—1967*

SFAS No. 6, *Classification of Short-Term Obligations Expected to Be Refinanced*

SFAS No. 78, *Classification of Obligations That Are Callable by the Creditor*

SFAS No. 115, *Accounting for Certain Investments in Debt and Equity Securities*

FASB Technical Bulletin 79-3, *Subjective Acceleration Clauses in Long-Term Debt Agreements*

FASB Interpretation No. 8, *Classification of Short-Term Obligation Repaid Prior to Being Replaced by a Long-Term Security*

RELATED PRONOUNCEMENTS

EITF Issue No. 84-11, *Offsetting Installment Note Receivables and Bank Debt ("Note Monetization")*

EITF Issue No. 86-5, *Classifying Demand Notes with Repayment Terms*

EITF Issue No. 86-30, *Classification of Obligations When a Violation Is Waived by the Creditor*

EITF Issue No. 95-22, *Balance Sheet Classification of Borrowings Outstanding under Revolving Credit Agreements That Include both a Subjective Acceleration Clause and a Lock-Box Arrangement*

RELATED TOPICS

Chapter 37—Offsetting Assets and Liabilities

DEBT: CONVERTIBLE DEBT

Table of Contents

DEBT: CONVERTIBLE DEBT

OVERVIEW

13.100   When convertible debt is issued, no value should be assigned to the conversion feature because it generally is inseparable from the debt. Consequently, the transaction should be recorded entirely as the issuance of debt. When debt is issued with detachable stock purchase warrants, however, a portion of the proceeds should be allocated to the warrants and recorded as additional paid-in capital since the warrants and debt are viewed as separate securities.

13.101   No gain or loss should be recognized when debt is converted into shares of the issuer's stock so long as the conversion is made in accordance with the original conversion terms. Consequently, the conversion of convertible debt should be recorded by eliminating the debt obligation and unamortized premium or discount and recording the issued shares as outstanding stock and additional paid-in capital as appropriate. If the original conversion terms are changed to induce holders to convert, however, an ordinary expense equal to the fair value of the additional consideration given to induce conversion should be recognized.

ACCOUNTING REQUIREMENTS

13.200   Debt may be issued with a conversion feature that gives the holder the option of being repaid with cash or with a specified number of shares of the issuer's stock. Such debt, referred to as convertible debt, typically has the following characteristics: (APB 14, paras. 3–4)

  a. Its interest rate is lower than for nonconvertible debt since investors derive some value from the conversion feature.

  b. At the time of issuance, the face amount of the debt is greater than the market value of the shares that could be received in conversion.

  c. It is subordinate to nonconvertible debt. (That is, in the case of insolvency, nonconvertible debt will be paid before convertible debt.)

    d. It may be called by the issuer to force conversion when the aggregate price of the stock to be issued in conversion is greater than the call price of the debt.

13.201   Convertible debt offers advantages to both the issuer and the holder. To the issuer, convertible debt provides financing at a lower rate than nonconvertible debt. Also, because it is expected to be repaid with stock rather than cash, it provides a means of securing equity financing. To the holder, convertible debt offers the option of receiving the face amount of the debt at maturity or converting to shares of the issuer's stock. Thus, the holder is guaranteed a rate of interest until conversion or maturity and has the opportunity to realize some of the benefits of any appreciation in the value of the issuer's stock.

ISSUANCE OF CONVERTIBLE DEBT

13.202   The conversion feature of convertible debt generally is not viewed separately from the debt. Therefore, when convertible debt is issued, no value is assigned to the conversion feature; the transaction is recorded entirely as the issuance of debt. (APB 14, par. 12) For example, assume that a company issues 6% convertible bonds with a face value of $1,000,000 for $975,000. Assume further that each $1,000 bond is convertible, at the holder's option, to 10 shares of the company's common stock. The company would record the transaction through the following journal entry:

Cash	975,000	
Discount on bonds payable	25,000	
Bonds payable		1,000,000

CONVERSION OF CONVERTIBLE DEBT

13.203   Normally, when the market value of the shares into which the debt can be converted exceeds the face amount of the debt, either (a) the holder will exercise its option to convert the debt to shares of the issuer's stock or (b) the issuer will call the debt to force conversion. When convertible debt is converted into shares of the issuer's stock in accordance with the debt's original terms, no gain or loss should be recognized. (SFAS 84, par. 23) The issuer simply retires the debt and issues shares of its stock. To illustrate, assume (a) all of the bonds issued in the example in Paragraph 13.202 were subsequently converted into 10,000 shares of the company's $50 par value common stock and (b) the unamortized discount on the bonds at the time of conversion was $15,000. The conversion would be recorded by the following entry:

Bonds payable	1,000,000	
Discount on bonds payable		15,000
Common stock (10,000 × $50)		500,000
Additional paid-in capital		485,000

Practical Consideration. Some accountants believe the market value method is an acceptable alternative to the book value method of accounting for debt conversions illustrated in the preceding paragraph. Under the market value method, a gain or loss is recorded for the difference between the book value and the market value of the debt at conversion (or the market value of the stock issued at conversion, if that is more readily determinable) with an off-setting entry to additional paid-in capital. The market value is seldom used in practice and usually is not an option for nonpublic companies since neither the market value of debt or stock is readily determinable. Furthermore, the authors believe Accounting Interpretation No. 1 of APB Opinion No. 26 essentially precludes using the market value method. It states that, upon conversion, the carrying amount of the debt is credited to the capital accounts and *no gain or loss is recognized.*

Inducements to Convert

13.204   In some cases, an issuer may change the conversion terms to induce holders to convert to equity securities. For example, an issuer might increase the number of shares to be issued on conversion, issue warrants or other securities, or pay cash or other consideration. The following rules apply when accounting for conversions that (a) are induced by changes in conversion terms that are exercisable for only a limited period of time and (b) include the issuance of at least as many shares as would have been required under the original conversion terms for each debt instrument converted: (SFAS 84, par. 2)

- No gain or loss should be recognized on the issuance of shares under the original conversion terms. (SFAS 84, par. 22)

- The fair value of any additional consideration paid should be recognized as an ordinary expense. (Fair value should be measured as of the date the inducement offer is accepted.) (SFAS 84, par. 3)

13.205   To illustrate, assume the following:

- On April 1, 19X3, ABC Company issued $750,000 of 6% bonds. Each $1,000 bond may be converted into 10 shares of the company's $5 par value common stock at any time after April 1, 19X5.

- To induce bondholders to convert, ABC Company makes an offer on June 1, 19X5, to increase the conversion rate to 20 shares per $1,000 bond. The offer expires September 1, 19X5.

- A holder of one $1,000 bond accepts the offer on July 15, 19X5. On that date, the market value of the ABC Company's common stock was $65 per share.

The additional consideration paid of 10 shares per $1,000 bond has a fair value of $650 on July 15, 19X5 (10 shares × $65 per share). The conversion should be recorded by the following entry:

Bonds payable	1,000	
Debt conversion expense	650	
Common stock (20 × $5)		100
Additional paid-in capital		1,550

DEBT WITH DETACHABLE STOCK PURCHASE WARRANTS

13.206   Debt is sometimes issued with detachable warrants to purchase stock. In such cases, the debt is expected to be paid when it matures and the warrants often are traded separately from the debt. Unlike convertible debt, which is considered a single instrument with inseparable debt and conversion features, debt and detachable stock purchase warrants are viewed as separate securities. Consequently, a holder may become a stockholder by surrendering its warrants and still remain a bondholder. (APB 14, par. 13)

Issuance of Debt with Detachable Stock Purchase Warrants

13.207   When debt with detachable stock purchase warrants is issued, a portion of the proceeds should be allocated to the warrants and recorded as additional paid-in capital. The amount allocated should be based on the relative fair values of the two securities at the time they are issued. (APB 14, paras. 16–17) To illustrate, assume that a company receives $196,000 from the issuance of 2,000 $100 par value, 6% convertible bonds. Each bond has a detachable stock purchase warrant that allows its holder to purchase 50 shares of the company's $5 par value common stock for $750. On the issue date, the quoted market prices of a single bond and warrant were $96 and $2, respectively. The transaction would be recorded through the following entry:

Cash	196,000	
Discount on bonds payable	8,000	
Bonds payable		200,000
Additional paid-in capital		
(2,000 warrants × $2)		4,000

> **Practical Consideration.** If a stock purchase warrant is not detachable (that is, both the debt and warrant must be surrendered to exercise the warrant), the warrant and debt are essentially the same as convertible debt and should be accounted for as such.

Conversion of Detachable Stock Purchase Warrants

13.208 Accounting for the conversion of detachable stock purchase warrants follows the principles discussed in Paragraphs 13.203–.205 for accounting for the conversion of convertible debt. That is, no gain or loss should be recognized on the transaction if a detachable stock purchase warrant is exercised in accordance with its original conversion terms. Thus, in the example in the preceding paragraph, if a single warrant were surrendered, the following entry would be made:

Cash	750	
Additional paid-in capital (warrants)	2	
Common stock (50 × $5)		250
Additional paid-in capital		
(common stock)		502

DISCLOSURE REQUIREMENTS

13.500 There are no disclosure requirements unique to debt with conversion features or detachable stock purchase warrants. Consequently, the disclosure requirements for convertible debt and debt issued with detachable stock purchase warrants are the same as for other long-term obligations. Those disclosures are discussed in Chapter 34.

> **Practical Consideration.** Although not specifically required, most financial statements disclose the conversion features of convertible debt.

AUTHORITATIVE LITERATURE AND RELATED TOPICS

AUTHORITATIVE LITERATURE

APB Opinion No. 14, *Accounting for Convertible Debt and Debt Issued with Stock Purchase Warrants*
SFAS No. 84, *Induced Conversions of Convertible Debt*

RELATED PRONOUNCEMENTS

EITF Issue No. 85-9, *Revenue Recognition on Options to Purchase Stock of Another Entity*

EITF Issue No. 85-17, *Accrued Interest upon Conversion of Convertible Debt*

EITF Issue No. 85-29, *Convertible Bonds with a "Premium Put"*

EITF Issue No. 87-25, *Sale of Convertible, Adjustable-Rate Mortgages with Contingent Repayment Agreement*

EITF Issue No. 90-19, *Convertible Bonds with Issuer Option to Settle for Cash upon Conversion*

EITF Issue No. 96-13, *Accounting for Derivative Financial Instruments Indexed to, and Potentially Settled in, a Company's Own Stock*

RELATED TOPICS

Chapter 14—Debt Extinguishments
Chapter 19—Earnings per Share
Chapter 34—Long-term Obligation Disclosures
Chapter 51—Stockholders' Equity

DEBT EXTINGUISHMENTS

Table of Contents

DEBT EXTINGUISHMENTS

OVERVIEW

14.100   When debt is extinguished, whether early or not, a gain or loss may occur equal to the difference between the amount paid to extinguish the debt and the net carrying amount of the debt. A gain or loss on extinguishment should be recognized in the period the extinguishment occurs rather than amortized to future periods. In addition, the gain or loss, if material, should be classified as an extraordinary item and presented net of related income tax effects.

ACCOUNTING REQUIREMENTS

14.200   A liability is considered to be extinguished for financial accounting purposes if either of the following conditions is met: (SFAS 125, par. 16)

- The debtor pays the creditor and is relieved of its obligation for the liability.

- The debtor is legally released from primary obligation under the liability.

14.201   If a creditor releases a debtor from primary obligation on the condition that a third party assumes the debt and the original debtor becomes secondarily liable, the release extinguishes the original debtor's liability. In that case, however, the original debtor becomes a guarantor, and should recognize a guarantee obligation at fair value if it is likely the third party will not pay the debt. The guarantee obligation reduces the debtor's gain (or increases the loss) recognized on the extinguishment of the debt. (SFAS 125, par. 84) Recognition of gain or loss is discussed further in Paragraphs 14.202–.203.

> **Practical Consideration.** The guidance in this chapter applies to all extinguishments, whether early or not, except for those accomplished through a troubled debt restructuring or by converting convertible debt to equity securities. Chapter 16 discusses accounting for debt restructurings, and Chapter 13 discusses accounting for convertible debt.

14.202   All debt extinguishments are fundamentally alike and produce the same result—the debtor is relieved of its obligations under the debt.

Consequently, accounting for debt extinguishments is the same regardless of the manner in which the extinguishment is achieved. An extinguishment is accounted for by recognizing a gain or loss in the period the extinguishment occurs equal to the difference between the following amounts: (APB 26, par. 20)

    a. *Net carrying amount.* The net carrying amount is the amount recorded for the debt in the financial statements. It represents the amount due at maturity, adjusted for any unamortized premium, discount, or issuance costs. (APB 26, par. 3)

    b. *Reacquisition price.* The debt's reacquisition price is the amount paid on extinguishment, including prepayment penalties and other miscellaneous reacquisition costs. If the debt is extinguished by exchanging new securities, the reacquisition price is the present value of the new securities. If nonconvertible debt is extinguished by issuing equity securities, the reacquisition price is the fair value of the equity securities or the debt, whichever is more clearly evident. (APB 26, par. 3)

14.203   Generally, a gain or loss from the extinguishment of debt should be classified as an extraordinary item and presented net of any related tax effects. (SFAS 4, par. 8) However, gains and losses from extinguishments of debt to satisfy sinking-fund requirements that the entity must meet within one year of the extinguishment should not be classified as extraordinary items. Instead, they should be included in income from continuing operations. (SFAS 64, par.4) For example, if a company is required each year to purchase a certain amount of its outstanding bonds before their scheduled maturity, the resulting gain or loss would be included in income from continuing operations rather than be presented as an extraordinary item.

DISCLOSURE REQUIREMENTS

14.500   As discussed in Paragraph 14.203, gains and losses on extinguishments of debt generally should be reported as an extraordinary item. In addition, the following should be disclosed on the face of the income statement or in the notes to the financial statements: (SFAS 4, par. 9)

    a. A description of the extinguishment transactions, including, if practicable, the sources of any funds used to extinguish the debt

    b. The income tax effect in the period of extinguishment

    c. For public companies, gain or loss per share, net of related income tax effects

If debt was extinguished prior to December 31, 1996 through an in-substance defeasance under the provisions of SFAS 76, *Extinguishment of Debt,* a general description of the transaction and the amount of debt that is considered extinguished at the end of the period should also be disclosed so long as the debt remains outstanding. (SFAS 125, par. 17)

Practical Consideration. Prior to SFAS No. 125, *Accounting for Transfers and Servicing of Financial Assets and Extinguishments of Liabilities* (which is effective for transactions occurring after December 31, 1996), debt was considered extinguished if assets meeting certain requirements were irrevocably placed in a trust to be used solely to make the debt's scheduled principle and interest payments. Such transactions, referred to as "in-substance defeasances," were considered debt extinguishments because the debtor, not legally but in substance, would not be required to make further payments on the debt. SFAS No. 125 changed the criteria for recognizing debt extinguishments, however. Thus, for transactions occurring after December 31, 1996, the criteria in Paragraph 14.200 must be met before debt is considered extinguished.

14.501   Gains and losses from extinguishments of debt to satisfy sinking-fund requirements that the entity must meet within one year of the extinguishment should not be classified as extraordinary items. Instead, they should be included in income from continuing operations and, if material, presented as a separate line item. (SFAS 4, par. 8)

14.502   If assets are set aside solely for satisfying scheduled payments of a specific debt, a description of the nature of restrictions placed on those assets should be disclosed. (SFAS 125, par. 17)

Practical Consideration. When an extinguishment occurs, the debtor is no longer primarily liable under the debt. In some cases, however, a debtor may remain contingently liable as a guarantor of the debt. In such situations, a contingent liability exists that must be disclosed. See Chapter 10.

AUTHORITATIVE LITERATURE AND RELATED TOPICS

AUTHORITATIVE LITERATURE

APB Opinion No. 26, *Early Extinguishment of Debt*
SFAS No. 4, *Reporting Gains and Losses from Extinguishment of Debt*
SFAS No. 22, *Changes in the Provisions of Lease Agreements Resulting from Refundings of Tax-Exempt Debt*

SFAS No. 64, *Extinguishments of Debt Made to Satisfy Sinking-Fund Requirements*

SFAS No. 125, *Accounting for Transfers and Servicing of Financial Assets and Extinguishments of Liabilities*

FASB Technical Bulletin 80-1, *Early Extinguishment of Debt through Exchange for Common or Preferred Stock*

RELATED PRONOUNCEMENTS

EITF Issue No. 84-19, *Mortgage Loan Payment Modifications*

EITF Issue No. 84-26, *Defeasance of Special-Purpose Borrowings*

EITF Issue No. 85-34, *Banker's Acceptances and Risk Participations*

EITF Issue No. 86-15, *Increasing-Rate Debt*

EITF Issue No. 86-36, *Invasion of a Defeasance Trust*

EITF Issue No. 95-15, *Recognition of Gain or Loss When a Binding Contract Requires a Debt Extinguishment to Occur at a Future Date for a Specified Amount*

EITF 96-19, *Debtor's Accounting for a Modification or Exchange of Debt Instruments*

Accounting Interpretations of APB Opinion No. 26, *Early Extinguishment of Debt*

RELATED TOPICS

DEBT: PRODUCT FINANCING ARRANGEMENTS

Table of Contents

DEBT: PRODUCT FINANCING ARRANGEMENTS

OVERVIEW

15.100   A product financing arrangement should be accounted for as a borrowing rather than a sale. Consequently, a sponsoring company that sells products to a financing company and, in a related transaction, agrees to repurchase the products over a specified period at a specified price, should (a) continue to carry the products in its balance sheet as assets and (b) record a liability for any amounts received from the financing company. Similarly, if a financing company purchases products on the sponsoring company's behalf and, in a related transaction, the sponsoring company agrees to purchase the products from the financing company, the sponsoring company should record an asset and liability for the products when the financing company purchases them.

15.101   A sponsoring company should record financing and holding costs as they are incurred by the financing company. The sponsoring company should account for the costs in accordance with its accounting policies for other financing and holding costs.

ACCOUNTING REQUIREMENTS

CHARACTERISTICS OF PRODUCT FINANCING ARRANGEMENTS

15.200   As its name implies, a product financing arrangement is a transaction in which one company (the sponsor) seeks to finance the purchase of products or inventory. Generally, a product financing arrangement requires one company to purchase inventory for the sponsor who, in a related transaction, agrees to purchase the inventory at specific prices over a specific period. The following are common examples of product financing arrangements: (SFAS 49, par. 3)

   a. A sponsor sells inventory to another company (the financing company) and, in a related transaction, agrees to repurchase the same or substantially identical inventory.

b. A sponsor arranges for the financing company to purchase the inventory and, in a related transaction, agrees to purchase the inventory from the financing company.

c. A sponsor controls the inventory of another company in accordance with the arrangements in a. or b. above.

15.201   All product financing arrangements exhibit a common characteristic—the sponsor agrees to purchase the inventory (or processed goods of which the inventory is a component) at specified prices over specified periods or guarantees the inventory's sale to third parties. (SFAS 49, par. 3) The following are other characteristics that may be present in some product financing arrangements: (SFAS 49, par. 4)

- The financing company is an existing trust, nonbusiness organization, credit grantor, or was established specifically to provide the financing arrangement.

- The majority of the product will be used or sold by the sponsor rather than sold directly to third parties.

- The products are stored on the sponsor's premises.

- The debt incurred by the financing company to purchase the inventory is guaranteed by the sponsor.

CRITERIA FOR TREATMENT AS A PRODUCT FINANCING ARRANGEMENT

15.202   A transaction is considered a product financing arrangement if it meets the following criteria: (SFAS 49, par. 5)

a. The arrangement requires the sponsor to purchase the inventory at specified prices that are not subject to change except for fluctuations due to finance and holding costs. That criteria is considered met in the following circumstances even though, in each case, the sponsor may not actually purchase the products:

(1) The specified prices are in the form of resale price guarantees under which the sponsor agrees to make up any difference between the specified price and the price received in sales to third parties.

(2) The sponsor is not required to purchase the product but has an option that, in substance, compels it to purchase the product.

(3) The sponsor is not required to purchase the product but the other company has an option under which it can require the sponsor to purchase the product.

b. Under the terms of the financing agreement, the amounts paid by the sponsor will be adjusted, if necessary, to cover substantially all costs incurred by the other company to purchase and hold the product.

Practical Consideration. SFAS No. 49, *Accounting for Product Financing Arrangements,* specifically states that unmined or unharvested natural resources and financial instruments are not considered products. Thus, the accounting requirements discussed in this chapter do not apply to those items. Also, the accounting in this chapter generally does not apply to purchase commitments or contractor-subcontractor relationships because they do not meet the criteria in the preceding paragraph.

ACCOUNTING FOR PRODUCT FINANCING ARRANGEMENTS

15.203   In a product financing arrangement, the sponsor is, in effect, the owner of the inventory or products; the arrangement is merely a means to finance the product's purchase or production. (SFAS 49, par. 22) Consequently, a sponsor should account for a product financing transaction as follows: (SFAS 49, par. 8)

a. If the sponsor sells product to another company and, in a related transaction, agrees to repurchase the product (or processed goods containing the product), no sale should be recorded. Instead, the sponsor should (1) continue to recognize the product as an asset and (2) record a liability for any proceeds it receives from the other company under the arrangement.

b. If another company purchases a product on the sponsor's behalf and, in a related transaction, the sponsor agrees to purchase the product from the company, the sponsor should record an asset and related liability when the other company purchases the product.

15.204   The difference between (a) the cost of the product under the product financing arrangement (excluding processing costs) and (b) the sponsor's original purchase or production cost (or the other company's purchase costs) represents financing and holding costs. The sponsor should account for those costs in accordance with its accounting policies for financing and holding costs as the costs are incurred by the other company. For example, if the sponsor's policy is to account for insurance as a period cost, insurance costs associated with the product financing arrangement should be expensed as they are incurred by the other company. (SFAS 49, par. 9)

Practical Consideration. Interest costs related to the product covered by the agreement should be identified and capitalized or expensed as appropriate. Chapter 27 discusses the requirements for capitalizing interest.

DISCLOSURE REQUIREMENTS

15.500   There are no disclosure requirements unique to product financing arrangements. Consequently, the disclosure requirements for product financing arrangements are the same as for other long-term obligations. Those disclosures are discussed in Chapter 34.

AUTHORITATIVE LITERATURE AND RELATED TOPICS

AUTHORITATIVE LITERATURE

SFAS No. 49, *Accounting for Product Financing Arrangements*

RELATED TOPICS

Chapter 27—Interest: Capitalized
Chapter 30—Inventory
Chapter 34—Long-term Obligation Disclosures

DEBT RESTRUCTURINGS

Table of Contents

DEBT RESTRUCTURINGS

OVERVIEW

16.100   How a debtor or creditor accounts for a troubled debt restructuring depends on the type of restructuring. The following are the primary types:

   a. *Transfer of assets (or equity interest) in full settlement of the debt.* Generally, the debtor should recognize an extraordinary gain on restructuring equal to the difference between the fair values of the assets transferred or equity interest granted and the carrying value of the debt. In addition, an ordinary gain or loss should be recognized for the difference between the transferred assets' fair values and carrying amounts.

   A creditor that receives assets (or an equity interest) in full settlement of debt should record the assets (or equity interest) received at their fair values and recognize an ordinary loss for the difference between its recorded investment in the receivable and the fair value of the assets (or equity interest) received. Subsequently, the assets received should be accounted for the same as if they were acquired for cash.

   b. *Modification of debt terms.* A restructuring that only involves the modification of terms generally should be accounted for prospectively. The debtor should not adjust the carrying amount of the debt unless it exceeds the future cash payments specified by the new debt terms. Interest should be determined by applying a constant effective interest rate to the outstanding debt.

   A creditor should account for a restructuring involving the modification of terms as it would an impaired loan.

16.101   If the restructuring involves a combination of the above types, the debtor and creditor generally should account for the transfer of assets or equity interest first and treat the remainder of the restructuring as a modification of terms. Thus, in a restructuring involving a combination of types, the debtor should (a) recognize a gain or loss by reducing the carrying amount of the debt by the fair value of the assets or equity interest transferred, and (b) account for the remainder of the restructuring as a modification of debt terms. Similarly, the creditor should reduce its recorded investment in the receivable by the fair value of the assets or equity interest received and account for the remainder of the restructuring as a modification of debt terms.

ACCOUNTING REQUIREMENTS

16.200   A troubled debt restructuring occurs when a creditor, for economic or legal reasons related to the debtor's financial difficulties, makes concessions to a debtor that it would not otherwise consider. The concessions may stem from an agreement between the two parties (e.g., a creditor might modify the debt's terms to reduce or defer required payments to help the debtor improve its financial condition and eventually repay the debt) or be imposed by law or a court. (SFAS 15, par. 2) In a troubled debt restructuring, either of the following occurs: (SFAS 15, par. 5)

a. Settlement of debt for less than its carrying value

   (1) The debtor transfers third-party receivables or other assets to the creditor to fully or partially satisfy the debt.

   (2) The creditor accepts an equity interest in the debtor to fully or partially satisfy the debt. (Converting convertible debt securities to equity securities is not a troubled debt restructuring, however. Accounting for convertible debt is discussed in Chapter 13.)

b. The creditor agrees to modify the debt terms. For example, the creditor might—

   (1) reduce the debt's stated interest rate.

   (2) extend the maturity date at a favorable interest rate.

   (3) reduce the debt's face or maturity amount.

   (4) reduce the interest accrued on the debt.

Whatever the concession, the creditor's primary objective is to increase its chances of collecting the debt. (SFAS 15, par. 3)

16.201   A debt restructuring is not necessarily a troubled debt restructuring merely because the debtor is in financial difficulty, however. For example, the following situations do not involve a troubled debt restructuring: (SFAS 15, par. 7)

- The fair value of the assets or equity interest accepted by the creditor in full satisfaction of its receivable is at least equal to (a) the creditor's recorded investment in the receivable or (b) the debtor's carrying amount of the payable.

- The creditor reduces the interest rate to reflect decreases in market rates.

- The debtor issues new marketable debt at current market rates in exchange for the old debt. (The fact that the debtor can obtain new financing at market rates indicates that the restructuring is not troubled.)

Debtors and creditors should individually apply the guidance in Paragraphs 16.200–.201 for troubled debt restructurings to their specific facts and circumstances to determine whether a troubled debt restructuring has occurred. It is possible for a debtor to have a troubled debt restructuring while the related creditor does not. (FTB 80-2, par. 3)

Practical Consideration. SFAS No. 15, *Accounting by Debtors and Creditors for Troubled Debt Restructurings,* states that the accounting requirements for troubled debt restructurings should not be applied to the following:

- Changes in lease agreements

- Changes in employment-related agreements

- Failures to pay trade accounts according to their terms

- Creditors' delays in taking legal action to collect overdue amounts of interest and principal (unless they involve an agreement between the debtor and creditor to restructure the debt)

In addition, the requirements do not apply to restructurings under the Federal Bankruptcy Act or other federal statutes if the debtor generally restates most of its liabilities, for example, in a quasi-reorganization, corporate readjustment, or similar situation. (Chapter 44 discusses accounting for quasi-reorganizations.) SFAS 15 would apply, however, to an isolated debt restructuring by a debtor involved in bankruptcy proceedings if such restructuring did not result in a general restatement of the debtor's liabilities.

16.202   Accounting for a troubled debt restructuring depends on its type, which generally is one of the following: (SFAS 15, par. 12)

    a. Transfer of assets in full settlement

    b. Grant of an equity interest in full settlement

    c. Modification of debt terms

    d. Combination of the above types

The following paragraphs discuss how creditors and debtors should account for each type of restructuring.

TRANSFERS OF ASSETS IN FULL SETTLEMENT

16.203   When assets are transferred in full settlement of debt, the debtor generally should recognize two gains (or a gain and a loss) as follows: (SFAS 15, paras. 13–14)

    a. A gain on the restructuring should be recognized equal to the difference between the fair value of the assets given up and the carrying amount of the debt. The gain should be included in current period net income and presented as an extraordinary item since it results from the extinguishment of debt.

    b. A gain or loss on transfer of assets should be recognized equal to the difference between the fair value and carrying amount of the assets given up. The gain or loss should be included in net income in the period the transfer occurs but should not be presented as an extraordinary item.

Practical Consideration. Fair value of the assets transferred is either (a) the amount the debtor could reasonably expect to receive for them in other than a forced sale or liquidation or (b) the fair value of the payable settled if it is more clearly evident. If the payable is only partially settled in the restructuring, however, the fair value of the assets transferred must be used. (That eliminates the need to allocate the payable's fair value between the portion settled and the portion still outstanding.)

The carrying amount of the debt is its face amount increased or decreased by accrued interest and unamortized premium or discount, finance charges, and issue costs.

16.202

16.204   The creditor should record the restructuring by (a) recording the assets received at their fair values and (b) recognizing a loss for the difference between the recorded investment in the receivable and the fair values of the assets received. The loss should be recognized in current period income to the extent it is not offset by an allowance for uncollectible accounts. The creditor should not present the loss from restructuring as an extraordinary item, however, since it was not the creditor's debt that was extinguished. (SFAS 121, par. 24)

> **Practical Consideration.** The creditor's recorded investment in the receivable is the receivable's face amount, increased or decreased by accrued interest, direct write-downs of the investment, and unamortized premium, discount, finance charges, or acquisition costs. It may differ from the carrying amount of the receivable since the carrying amount is net of any allowance for uncollectible amounts.

16.205   To illustrate, assume the following:

- A debtor owes a creditor $100,000, including interest.

- The carrying amount of the creditor's receivable is $85,000 since it previously recorded a $15,000 allowance for expected losses on the receivable.

- The creditor accepts real estate valued at $80,000 and carried on the debtor's books at $90,000 in full settlement of its receivable.

The debtor would recognize the following on settlement of the debt:

Extraordinary gain on extinguishment of debt:	
Carrying amount of the debt	$ 100,000
Fair value of assets given up	80,000
	$ 20,000
Ordinary loss on transfer of assets:	
Fair value of assets given up	$ 80,000
Carrying amount of the assets given up	90,000
	$ (10,000)

The creditor would record the real estate received at $80,000 and recognize a $20,000 loss on the restructuring ($100,000 recorded investment in the receivable less $80,000 fair value of real estate received). The loss would be recorded by reducing the $15,000 loss allowance to zero and including the remaining loss ($5,000) in current period income.

> **Practical Consideration.** According to the FASB staff during the discussion of EITF Issue No. 91-2, *Debtor's Accounting for Forfeiture of Real Estate Subject to a Nonrecourse Mortgage,* the requirements in Paragraphs 16.203–.204 also would apply when a borrower transfers real estate to a lender in full satisfaction of a nonrecourse mortgage.

GRANT OF EQUITY INTEREST IN FULL SETTLEMENT

16.206   A debtor that settles its debt by granting an equity interest to the creditor should recognize a gain equal to the difference between the carrying amount of the debt and the fair value of the equity interest. The gain should be reported as an extraordinary item from extinguishment of debt. (SFAS 15, par. 15)

> **Practical Consideration.** The equity interest's fair value is its market value or the fair value of the payable if it is more clearly evident. If the debt is only partially settled in the restructuring, however, fair value of the equity interest must be used.
>
> The carrying amount of the debt is its face amount increased or decreased by accrued interest and unamortized premium or discount, finance charges, and issue costs.

16.207   A creditor should record the receipt of an equity interest as it would record the receipt of any asset. That is, it should record the investment at its fair value and recognize a loss equal to the difference between the fair value of the equity interest and the recorded investment in the receivable. (SFAS 121, par. 24)

> **Practical Consideration.** The creditor's recorded investment in the receivable is the receivable's face amount, increased or decreased by accrued interest, direct write-downs of the investment, and unamortized premium, discount, finance charges, or acquisition costs. It may differ from the carrying amount of the receivable since the carrying amount is net of any allowance for uncollectible amounts.

16.208   To illustrate accounting for a debt restructuring that involves the granting of an equity interest, assume that a debtor settles a $15,000 debt by issuing 1,000 shares of its $10 par value stock. If the fair value of the stock is $13,000, the debtor would—

a. record the issued stock at $13,000 ($10,000 par value plus $3,000 additional paid-in capital) and

b. recognize an extraordinary gain of $2,000 on the restructuring ($15,000 carrying amount of the debt less $13,000 fair value of the equity interest issued).

The creditor would record an investment of $13,000 for the equity interest it received and recognize a $2,000 loss on the transaction ($15,000 recorded investment in the receivable less $13,000 fair value of the equity interest received).

Practical Consideration. In all troubled debt restructurings involving full settlement of debt for less than its carrying amount—

- the debtor recognizes an extraordinary gain as a result of the restructuring, and

- the creditor recognizes an ordinary loss as a result of the restructuring.

MODIFICATION OF TERMS

16.209   A troubled debt restructuring may involve the modification of debt terms rather than the transfer of assets or granting of an equity interest. In such cases, the debtor generally should account for the restructuring as follows: (SFAS 15, paras. 16–17)

a. The restructuring should be accounted for prospectively. The carrying amount of the debt should not be changed unless it exceeds the future cash payments specified by the new debt terms. (See item c.) Future cash payments include all payments of principal and interest, including any accrued interest at the time of restructuring that will be paid under the new debt terms. Estimates of future cash payments should assume that all indeterminate or contingent payments will be paid and the debt will be outstanding for the maximum number of periods possible under the new debt terms.

b. Interest expense should be determined by applying a constant effective interest rate to the outstanding debt. The effective interest rate is the discount rate at which the present value of future cash payments is equal to the carrying amount of the debt. (That method of computing interest expense, commonly referred to as the interest method, is discussed further in Chapter 28.)

c. If the total future cash payments specified by the new debt terms (including indeterminate or contingent payments) are less than the carrying amount of the debt, the debtor should (1) reduce the carrying amount of the debt to an amount equal to the total future cash payments and (2) recognize the reduction as an extraordinary gain. Thereafter, all payments made should be accounted for as a reduction of the carrying amount of the debt, and no interest expense should be recorded.

Future interest payments may be expected to fluctuate (for example, because they are tied to the prime interest rate). In such cases, estimates of future payments should be based on the interest rate in effect at the time of restructuring. Subsequent changes in interest payments should be accounted for as a change in accounting estimate. If subsequent declines in interest rates result in expected future cash flows that are less than the carrying amount of the debt, no gain should be immediately recognized, however. (To do so might result in the premature recognition of a gain since the gain might be offset by future increases in interest payments.) Instead, actual cash payments should reduce the carrying amount of the debt, and any carrying amount remaining after the debt has been satisfied should be recognized as a gain. (SFAS 15, par. 23)

16.210 A creditor should account for a troubled debt restructuring that involves the modification of debt terms as it would an impaired loan. That is, it generally should—

a. measure the loan based on the present value of expected future cash flows specified by the new contractual terms at the loan's effective interest rate (or, if more practical, the loan's market price or the fair value of the collateral) and

b. record a loss and allowance for loan losses equal to the difference between the carrying amount of the loan and its measured amount. (SFAS 114, par. 22)

Chapter 32 provides further guidance on a creditor's accounting for impaired loans.

16.211   To illustrate, assume that a debtor owes $15,400 of principal and interest to a creditor. As a result of a troubled debt restructuring, the debt's terms were modified so that the future cash payments of principal and interest will be $13,000. At the time of the restructuring, the present value of the future cash payments was $12,000. The debtor and creditor should account for the restructuring as follows:

     a. Since the total future cash payments are less than the carrying amount of the debt, the debtor should reduce the debt's carrying amount to $13,000 and recognize an extraordinary gain of $2,400 ($15,400 – $13,000) on the restructuring. Thereafter, the debtor should record all payments as a reduction of the debt's carrying amount. No portion of the payments should be recorded as interest expense.

     b. The creditor should record an allowance for loan losses of $3,400 ($15,400 – $12,000).

COMBINATION OF TYPES

16.212   A restructuring may involve a combination of asset or equity transfers and the modification of debt terms. In such cases, the debtor should (a) reduce the carrying amount of the debt by the fair value of the assets or equity interest transferred, (b) recognize a gain or loss equal to the difference between the carrying amount of the assets or equity interest transferred and their fair values, and (c) account for the remainder of the restructuring as a modification of debt terms as discussed in Paragraph 16.209 (SFAS 15, par. 19) Similarly, the creditor should reduce its recorded investment in the receivable by the fair value of the assets or equity interest received and account for the remainder of the restructuring as a modification of debt terms as discussed in Paragraph 16.210. (SFAS 15, par. 33)

RELATED ISSUES

Restructuring Costs

16.213   A debtor should record legal fees and other direct costs it incurs in granting an equity interest by reducing the amount it otherwise records for the equity interest. Other costs incurred should reduce the gain on restructuring or be included in expense for the period if no gain on restructuring is realized. (SFAS 15, par. 24)

16.214   A creditor should expense legal fees and other direct costs related to a restructuring as they are incurred. (SFAS 15, par. 38)

Contingently Payable Amounts

16.215 Amounts contingently payable in future periods should be accounted for similarly to other contingencies. That is, they should be accrued and recorded as interest expense when they are reasonably estimable and it is probable that they must be paid. When a liability for contingent payments is accrued, contingent amounts that were included in estimated future cash payments at the time of the restructuring should be deducted from the carrying amount of the debt to the extent they prevented recognizing a gain at that time. (SFAS 15, par. 22)

16.216 For example, assume a debtor owes $100,000 of principal and interest and enters into a troubled debt restructuring agreement to extend the debt's repayment period. As part of the restructuring agreement, the debtor agrees to make future cash payments of $90,000 and, if certain conditions are met, additional payments of $15,000. As discussed in Paragraph 16.209 the carrying amount of the debt should not be changed since it is less than the expected future cash payments including contingent payments. When it becomes probable that the $15,000 contingent payments must be made, the debtor should accrue the additional payments by—

     a. reducing the carrying amount of the debt by $10,000 (i.e., the portion of the contingent payments that prevented a gain on restructuring from being recorded);

     b. accruing a $15,000 liability for the additional payments; and

     c. recognizing interest expense of $5,000 (i.e., the portion of the contingent payments that did not prevent a gain on restructuring from being recorded).

16.217 Accounting by creditors for amounts contingently receivable is discussed in Chapter 32.

DISCLOSURE REQUIREMENTS

16.500 Debtors should disclose the following information about troubled debt restructurings that occur during the period: (SFAS 15, par. 25)

     a. Description of the principal changes in terms, major features of settlement, or both for each restructuring (Separate restructurings within a fiscal period for the same categories of payable may be grouped.)

b. Aggregate gain on restructuring of payables and the related income tax effect

c. Aggregate net gain or loss on transfers of assets

d. For public companies, per share amount of the aggregate gain on restructuring payables, net of related income tax effect

Debtors also should disclose the extent to which contingently payable amounts are included in the carrying amount of the restructured debt. In addition, if it is at least reasonably possible that contingent amounts will be required to be paid, the total contingently payable amounts and the conditions under which they would become payable or would be forgiven should be disclosed. (SFAS 15, par. 26)

16.501   A creditor should disclose the amount of any commitment to lend additional funds to a debtor owing a receivable whose terms have been modified in a troubled debt restructuring. (SFAS 15, par. 40) Additional disclosures about impaired loans also may be required. Those disclosures are discussed in Chapter 32.

Practical Consideration. Additional disclosures also may be required by SOP 94-6, *Disclosure of Certain Significant Risks and Uncertainties,* if it is reasonably possible that estimates may change in the near term (e.g., estimates relating to contingently payable amounts), and the effect of the change would be material to the financial statements. (See Chapter 10.)

AUTHORITATIVE LITERATURE AND RELATED TOPICS

AUTHORITATIVE LITERATURE

SFAS No. 15, *Accounting by Debtors and Creditors for Troubled Debt Restructurings*
SFAS No. 114, *Accounting by Creditors for Impairment of a Loan*
FASB Technical Bulletin 80-2, *Classification of Debt Restructurings by Debtors and Creditors*
FASB Technical Bulletin 81-6, *Applicability of Statement 15 to Debtors in Bankruptcy Situations*

RELATED PRONOUNCEMENTS

SFAS No. 125, *Accounting for Transfers and Servicing of Financial Assets and Extinguishments of Liabilities.*

SOP 92-3, *Accounting for Foreclosed Assets*

EITF Issue No. 86-18, *Debtor's Accounting for a Modification of Debt Terms*

EITF Issue No. 87-18, *Use of Zero Coupon Bonds in a Troubled Debt Restructuring*

EITF Issue No. 87-19, *Substituted Debtors in a Troubled Debt Restructuring*

EITF Issue No. 89-14, *Valuation of Repossessed Real Estate*

EITF Issue No. 89-15, *Accounting for a Modification of Debt Terms When the Debtor Is Experiencing Financial Difficulties*

EITF Issue No. 91-2, *Debtor's Accounting for Forfeiture of Real Estate Subject to a Nonrecourse Mortgage*

EITF Issue No. 94-8, *Accounting for Conversion of a Loan into a Debt Security in a Debt Restructuring*

EITF Issue No 96-19, *Debtor's Accounting for a Modification or Exchange of Debt Instruments*

EITF Issue No. 96-22, *Applicability of the Disclosures Required by FASB Statement No. 114, "Accounting by Creditors for Impairment of a Loan," When a Loan is Restructured in a Troubled Debt Restructuring into Two (or More) Loans*

RELATED TOPICS

DEFERRED COMPENSATION ARRANGEMENTS

Table of Contents

DEFERRED COMPENSATION ARRANGEMENTS

OVERVIEW

17.100   Benefits expected to be paid under a deferred compensation agreement should be accrued and charged to earnings as the related service is rendered. At the time the employee has rendered all the services necessary to earn the right to receive the deferred compensation, the amount that should be accrued should be the then present value of the benefits expected to be paid to the employee.

ACCOUNTING REQUIREMENTS

17.200   The guidance in this section does not apply to (a) individual arrangements that, when taken together, are in substance a retirement plan nor to (b) deferred compensation contracts with individual employees that, when taken together, are in substance a postretirement benefit plan. (Chapter 39 applies if the arrangements constitute a pension plan while Chapter 41 applies if the arrangements constitute a postretirement benefit plan.)

> **Practical Consideration.** Authoritative literature does not provide guidance on distinguishing between deferred compensation arrangements and pension plans or postretirement benefit plans. The authors believe that similar monetary arrangements for two or more employees normally constitute a retirement plan, while an arrangement with an individual employee or differing arrangements with two or more employees generally do not. Likewise, similar arrangements with two or more employees to provide postretirement health and welfare benefits generally constitute a postretirement benefit plan, while an arrangement with an individual employee or differing arrangements with two or more employees generally do not.

17.201   A deferred compensation agreement should be accounted for on an accrual basis in accordance with its underlying terms. If the agreement attributes benefits to a specific year of the employee's service, the cost of the benefits should be recognized in that year. If the agreement attributes the expected benefits to more than one year of the employee's service, the cost of the benefits should be recognized over those years in a systematic and rational manner. In other words, an employer should accrue deferred compensation costs in accordance with the terms of the agreement so that—

a. the costs are recognized in the period the related services are performed and

b. the costs accrued at the end of the employee's service period equal the then present value of the benefits expected to be paid to the employee. [The employee's service period ends when he or she has rendered all the services necessary to earn the right to receive all of the benefits expected to be paid under the agreement. (SFAS 106, par. 13) Estimates of benefits expected to be paid to the employee or his or her beneficiaries should be based on the life expectancy of the individual concerned using either recent mortality tables or the estimated cost of an annuity contract. Estimated benefits should not be based on the minimum payable in the event of early death. (APB 12, par. 7)].

Practical Consideration. Authoritative literature does not require a specific method of measuring the deferred compensation liability. In practice, however, the sinking fund approach or the benefit/years-of-service approach are often used. Both approaches yield the same liability at the date of retirement.

The liability under the sinking fund approach is determined as follows:

a. Calculate the present value at the date of retirement of payments to be made.

b. Determine the present value of an annuity of one for the number of years until retirement using either an annuity table or the following formula:

$$\frac{1 - (1 + \text{discount rate})^{-\text{years to retirement}}}{\text{discount rate}}$$

c. Divide 1 by the result of step b.

d. Subtract the interest rate from the result of step c.

e. Multiply the results of steps a. and d. to derive the level annual service cost.

f. Each year, calculate the interest cost by multiplying the interest rate by the beginning liability.

Practical Consideration (Continued).

The liability under the benefit/years of service approach is calculated as follows:

a. Calculate the present value at the date of retirement of payments to be made.

b. Divide the present value determined in step a. by the number of years until retirement to determine an average annual amount needed to accumulate the present value at the date of retirement.

c. Each year, the average accumulation amount is multiplied by $(1 + \text{the discount rate})^{-\text{years to retirement}}$ to determine the service cost; the sum of the beginning liability and the current year's service cost is multiplied by the discount rate to determine the interest expense; and the two are totaled to determine the addition to the liability.

EXHIBIT 17-1 illustrates calculating a deferred compensation liability under both approaches. (Methods other than the sinking fund or benefit/years of services approach are also acceptable, however, provided they meet the criteria in Paragraph 17.201.)

DISCLOSURE REQUIREMENTS

17.500 Authoritative literature requires no specific disclosures about deferred compensation agreements. (Required pension plan disclosures are discussed in Chapter 39, and required disclosures for postretirement benefits other than pensions are discussed in Chapter 41.)

Practical Consideration. Although no disclosures are required for deferred compensation agreements, the authors believe disclosures similar to those for pension plans should be provided.

EXHIBIT 17-1

EXAMPLE DEFERRED COMPENSATION LIABILITY CALCULATION

Assumptions:

- If a key employee remains with the company for the next five years (and then retires), he or his estate will receive payments of $8,500 at the end of each of the six years following retirement.

- The annual discount rate is 8%.

Sinking fund approach:

Annual service cost

Present value of payments at retirement date		$ 39,294
1 ÷ the present value of an annuity of one for the number of years until retirement	.250456	
Less discount rate	.080000	× .170456
Annual service cost		$ 6,698

Summary of annual results

Year	Service Cost	Interest Cost	Total Cost	Benefit	Ending Liability
1	$ 6,698	$ —	$ 6,698	$ —	$ 6,698
2	6,698	536	7,234	—	13,932
3	6,698	1,115	7,813	—	21,745
4	6,698	1,739	8,437	—	30,182
5	6,698	2,414	9,112	—	39,294
6	—	3,144	3,144	(8,500)	33,938
7	—	2,715	2,715	(8,500)	28,153
8	—	2,252	2,252	(8,500)	21,905
9	—	1,752	1,752	(8,500)	15,157
10	—	1,213	1,213	(8,500)	7,870
11	—	630	630	(8,500)	—

EXHIBIT 17-1 (Continued)

Benefit/years-of-service approach:

Annual service cost

Present value of payments at retirement date	$	39,294
Number of years to retirement	÷	5
Average amount needed to accumulate the present value at the date of retirement	$	7,859

Each year, the annual service cost is computed by multiplying $7,859 by $1.08^{-\text{years to retirement}}$

Summary of annual results

Year	Service Cost	Interest Cost	Total Cost	Benefit	Ending Liability
1	$ 5,349	$ 428	$ 5,777	$ —	$ 5,777
2	5,777	924	6,701	—	12,478
3	6,239	1,497	7,736	—	20,214
4	6,738	2,156	8,894	—	29,108
5	7,276	2,910	10,186	—	39,294
6	—	3,144	3,144	(8,500)	33,938
7	—	2,715	2,715	(8,500)	28,153
8	—	2,252	2,252	(8,500)	21,905
9	—	1,752	1,752	(8,500)	15,157
10	—	1,213	1,213	(8,500)	7,870
11	—	630	630	(8,500)	—

AUTHORITATIVE LITERATURE AND RELATED TOPICS

AUTHORITATIVE LITERATURE

APB Opinion No. 12, *Omnibus Opinion—1967*
SFAS No. 106, *Employers' Accounting for Postretirement Benefits Other Than Pensions*

RELATED TOPICS

Chapter 39—Pension Plans: Accounting by Employers
Chapter 40—Postemployment Benefits
Chapter 41—Postretirement Benefits Other Than Pensions

DEVELOPMENT STAGE ENTERPRISES

Table of Contents

DEVELOPMENT STAGE ENTERPRISES

OVERVIEW

18.100   The nature of the transaction, rather than the maturity of the company, governs how a company should account for revenues and costs. Thus, development stage companies must apply the same generally accepted accounting principles as established companies when determining whether revenues should be recognized or costs expensed, capitalized, or deferred.

18.101   A development stage company's financial statements should be identified as those of a development stage company. In addition, they should contain certain disclosures, including cumulative amounts of revenues, expenses, and cash flows from the company's inception.

ACCOUNTING REQUIREMENTS

WHAT IS A DEVELOPMENT STAGE COMPANY?

18.200   A business is a development stage company if it is devoting substantially all of its efforts to establishing a new business and its planned principal operations either (a) have not commenced or (b) have commenced, but have not produced any significant revenue. Consequently, a development stage company typically devotes substantially all of its efforts to activities such as the following: (SFAS 7, paras. 8–9)

- Financial planning and budgeting

- Raising capital

- Exploring for and developing natural resources

- Research and development activities

- Establishing sources of supply

- Acquiring or constructing property, plant, equipment, or other operating assets

- Recruiting and training personnel

- Developing markets

- Starting up production

Practical Consideration. Many of the preceding activities could apply to an already established company. Unless the established company is starting a new business, however, it would not be classified as a development stage enterprise. For example, none of the following would be considered a development stage enterprise:

- Established operating companies that are expanding their already existing business even if they are starting a new line of business, such as a computer company that begins publishing books

- Established operating companies in the extractive industry that are conducting exploration and development activities

- Established operating companies in the real estate industry that are developing properties

---

18.201   Once a company begins its planned operations and generates significant revenues, it ceases to be in the development stage. The point at which that occurs is a matter of judgment and must be evaluated on a case by case basis. (SFAS 7, par. 29)

ACCOUNTING FOR DEVELOPMENT STAGE COMPANIES

18.202   Financial statements issued by development stage companies must be in conformity with generally accepted accounting principles for established companies, both for recognizing revenue and for determining whether costs incurred should be charged to current-period expense, capitalized, or deferred. (SFAS 7, par. 10)

Practical Consideration. A common tendency may be to defer substantial costs while the company is in the development stage. Accounting literature prohibits deferring costs that would not be deferred under generally accepted accounting principles for established companies, however. Although accounting literature does not provide criteria for determining when costs should be charged to expense, capitalized, or deferred, the authors believe that costs should be charged to expense when—

- they provide no discernible future benefits or

- allocating costs either on the basis of association with revenue or among several accounting periods serves no useful purpose.

18.201

Practical Consideration (Continued).

The following are the authors' recommendations for accounting for certain costs common to development stage companies:

   a. *Research and development costs.* As discussed further in Chapter 47, research and development costs should be expensed as incurred. In addition, costs incurred internally to create a computer software product should be expensed as research and development costs until technological feasibility has been established for the product. -

   b. *Start-up costs.* Start-up costs generally are incurred after a company completes its research and development efforts and decides to begin operations. The authors recommend expensing start-up costs when incurred because it is usually doubtful that the costs are assets with future economic benefits. In addition, the AICPA has issued an exposure draft of an SOP that would require start-up costs to be expensed when incurred.

DISCLOSURE REQUIREMENTS

18.500   Financial statements issued by a development stage company must be identified as those of a development stage company. In addition, they should include the following information: (SFAS 7, par. 11)

   a. *Balance sheet.* Cumulative net losses, if any, should be reported with a descriptive caption such as "deficit accumulated in the development stage" in the stockholders' equity section.

   b. *Income statement.* Revenues and expenses for each period covered by the income statement should be shown. In addition, cumulative revenue and expense amounts from the company's inception should be shown.

   c. *Statement of cash flows.* A statement of cash flows should be presented for each period for which an income statement is presented. In addition, cumulative cash flows from operating, investing, and financing activities from the company's inception should be shown. (SFAS 95, par. 151)

   d. *Statement of stockholders' equity.* The statement should show the following from the company's inception: (SFAS 7, par. 11)

(1) For each issuance, the date and number of shares of stock, warrants, rights, or other equity securities issued for cash and for other consideration

(2) For each issuance, the dollar amounts (per share or other equity unit and in total) assigned to the consideration received for shares of stock, warrants, rights, or other equity securities (Dollar amounts should be assigned to any non-cash consideration received.)

(3) For each issuance involving noncash consideration, the nature of noncash consideration and the basis for assigning amounts

> **Practical Consideration.** Typically, the cumulative information described in items b. and c. is presented in an additional column alongside the financial statements for the period being presented. Alternatively, the cumulative information may be presented in the notes to the financial statements.

18.501   The notes to the financial statements should describe the development stage activities. For the first year the company is no longer in the development stage, the notes should disclose that the company had been in the development stage in prior years. If comparative financial statements presenting results during and after the development stage are issued, only the fact that the company was in the development stage in prior years must be disclosed; the disclosures in Paragraph 18.500 are not required. (SFAS 7, paras. 12–13)

> **Practical Consideration.** The requirements in the preceding paragraphs do not preclude development stage companies from presenting less than a full set of financial statements. Like established companies, they may present, for example, only a balance sheet. (Chapter 4 discusses when companies are required to present a statement of cash flows, however.)

AUTHORITATIVE LITERATURE AND RELATED TOPICS

AUTHORITATIVE LITERATURE

SFAS No. 7, *Accounting and Reporting by Development Stage Enterprises*
FASB Interpretation No. 7, *Applying FASB Statement No. 7 in Financial Statements of Established Operating Enterprises*

RELATED PRONOUNCEMENTS

SOP 93-7, *Reporting on Advertising Costs*

RELATED TOPICS

Chapter 47—Research and Development Costs

EARNINGS PER SHARE

Table of Contents

EARNINGS PER SHARE

OVERVIEW

19.100   Generally, all public companies must disclose earnings per share information whenever an income statement or summary of earnings is presented. Per-share information related to income from continuing operations and net income should be shown on the face of the income statement for all periods presented. Entities that report a discontinued operation, an extraordinary item, or the cumulative effect of an accounting change should present per-share information for those items either on the face of the income statement or in the notes to the financial statements.

19.101   Companies with simple capital structures (that is, those with only common stock or no potentially dilutive securities) should make a single earnings per share presentation (referred to as basic earnings per share) based on the weighted average number of shares of common stock outstanding during the period.

19.102   Companies with complex capital structures should make two earnings per share presentations—one showing basic earnings per share and another showing diluted earnings per share. Diluted earnings per share should be based on the weighted average number of shares of common stock and all other potential common stock outstanding during the period. Potential common stock consists of securities such as options, warrants, convertible securities, or contingent stock agreements.

19.103   Call options and warrants (and their equivalents) are incorporated into the diluted earnings per share calculation under the treasury stock method. Under that method, stock options and warrants are assumed to have been exercised at the beginning of the period (or when they were issued, if later). Contracts that require the entity to repurchase its own stock (such as written put options and forward purchase contracts) are incorporated into the diluted earnings per share calculation under the reverse treasury stock method.

19.104   Convertible securities are included in earnings per share calculations under the if-converted method. Under that method, the securities are assumed to have been converted into common stock at the beginning of the period (or when they were issued, if later). In addition, income available for common stockholders is determined by adjusting income to remove interest payments on the converted debt (and other nondiscretionary adjustments based on income), net of taxes, and dividends on the converted preferred stock.

ACCOUNTING REQUIREMENTS

> **Practical Consideration.** The guidance in this chapter is based on SFAS No. 128, *Earnings Per Share,* which is effective for financial statements for both interim and annual periods ending after December 15, 1997. Early application is not permitted, although proforma earnings per share information computed in accordance with SFAS No. 128 may be disclosed in the notes to the financial statements. After adopting SFAS No. 128, all prior period earnings per share information must be restated to conform with its provisions.
>
> SFAS No. 128 supersedes APB Opinion No. 15, *Earnings Per Share,* and is intended to simplify earnings per share calculations for companies with complex capital structures. It replaces primary earnings per share (based on common stock and common stock equivalents) with a basic earnings per share calculation based solely on common stock outstanding. Guidance on computing earnings per share under APB Opinion No. 15 can be found in the 1997 edition of *Guide to GAAP.*

19.200   Earnings per share is a measure of the income available to common shareholders. It must be presented in financial statements of all entities that issue common stock or potential common stock (such as options, warrants, convertible securities, or contingent stock agreements) if those securities are traded in a public market. (A public market is a domestic or foreign stock exchange or over-the-counter market, including local or regional markets.) In addition, entities that have made a filing or are in the process of making a filing with a regulatory agency to prepare for the sale of securities in a public market must also present earnings per share. Earnings per share need not be included in the financial statements of investment companies that comply with the requirements of the AICPA's *Audits of Investment Companies* or wholly owned subsidiaries. If an entity is not required to present earnings per share information but elects to do so anyway, the information should be presented following the requirements discussed in this chapter. (SFAS 128, par. 6)

> **Practical Consideration.** Most nonpublic entities are not required to present earnings per share in their financial statements unless they have made a filing to offer common stock or potential common stock that will be traded in the public market.

19.201   Companies with simple capital structures (that is, companies with only common stock outstanding) must present basic earnings per share, while companies with more complex capital structures must present both basic and diluted earnings per share. Per share amounts must be reported for net income and income from continuing operations and, if applicable, discontinued operations, extraordinary items, and the cumulative effect of an accounting change. (SFAS 128 paras. 36–37)

19.202   A company may disclose other per-share information, such as the per-share gain on the sale of real estate. While not required to be disclosed, such other per-share information, if presented, should be computed based on the guidance in this chapter. (SFAS 128, par. 37) Cash flow per share should not be reported, however.(SFAS 95, par. 33)

BASIC EARNINGS PER SHARE

19.203   Basic earnings per share is computed by dividing available earnings by the weighted average number of shares of common stock outstanding during the period. When making that calculation, the following should be considered:

    a. Income available to common stockholders is income less claims of preferred stockholders on income. Thus, dividends declared on *noncumulative* preferred stock (whether or not paid) should be deducted from income before computing earnings per share, and dividends on *cumulative* preferred stock should be deducted even if they have not been declared. (Preferred dividends that are cumulative only if earned should be deducted only to the extent they are earned, however.) (SFAS 128, par. 9)

    b. Stock dividends and stock splits should be recognized on a retroactive basis. That is, they should be treated as though they occurred on the first day of the earliest period presented. Also, if stock dividends and stock splits occur after the balance sheet date but before the financial statements are issued, earnings per share calculations should be based on the new number of shares since financial statement users are primarily concerned with earnings per share based on the corporation's current capitalization. (SFAS 128, par. 54)

    c. If shares are issued to acquire a company in a business combination and—

        (1) the combination is accounted for by the purchase method, the earnings per share calculation should treat the new shares as outstanding only from the date they were issued.

        (2) the combination is accounted for as a pooling of interests, the earnings per share calculation should be based on the

aggregate weighted average outstanding shares of the combining corporations, adjusted to equivalent shares of the surviving corporation, for all periods presented. (SFAS 128, par. 59)

d. Shares to be issued for little or no cash when certain specified conditions are met (i.e. contingently issuable shares) should be considered outstanding on the date all the necessary conditions were satisfied. Contingently returnable shares should be treated in same manner as contingently issuable shares. (Contingent shares are discussed further in Paragraphs 19.223–.226.) (SFAS 128, par. 10)

e. If the corporation has issued rights whose exercise price is less than the fair value of the stock, the rights issue contains a bonus element similar to a stock dividend. If the rights issue including the bonus element is offered to all existing shareholders, basic earnings per share should be retroactively adjusted for the bonus element for all periods presented. However, if the ability to exercise the rights is contingent on an event other than the passage of time, basic earnings per share should not be adjusted for the bonus element until that contingency is resolved. (SFAS 128, par. 55)

To restate basic earnings per share for the bonus element, the number of shares used in the calculation should be the number of shares outstanding prior to the rights issue multiplied by the following factor:

$$\frac{\text{Fair value per share immediately prior to exercise of the rights}}{\text{Theoretical ex-rights fair value per share}}$$

Theoretical ex-rights fair value is computed as—

$$\frac{\text{Aggregate fair value of shares immediately prior to the rights exercise plus the proceeds expected from the exercise of the rights}}{\text{Number shares outstanding after exercise of the rights}}$$

If the rights themselves will be publicly traded separate from the shares prior to their exercise, fair value should be determined as of the last day the shares and rights traded together. (SFAS 128, par. 56)

f. The entity may have issued common stock that is partially paid and entitled to dividends in proportion to the amount paid. In such cases, the common share equivalent of the partially paid shares should be reflected in the denominator of the basic earnings per share calculation to the extent the shares were entitled to participate in dividends. (SFAS 128, par. 64)

19.204   EXHIBIT 19-1 illustrates computing basic earnings per share.

DILUTED EARNINGS PER SHARE

General Rules

19.205   Corporations that issue dilutive potential common stock generally must disclose diluted earnings per share in addition to basic earnings per share. Potential common stock consists of securities such as options, warrants, convertible securities and contingent stock agreements that allow the holder to obtain common stock during or after the end of the period.

19.206   The diluted earnings per share calculation is similar to the calculation of basic earnings per share—it divides available income by the weighted average number of shares outstanding. Unlike the computation of basic earnings per share, however, diluted earnings per share is calculated by acting as if certain dilutive potential common stock had been issued. The denominator is adjusted to reflect the issuance of potential common stock, and the numerator is adjusted to add back:

  a. any dividends on convertible preferred stock;

  b. interest expense (net of tax) on convertible debt recognized during the period; and

  c. any other changes in net income resulting from the assumed conversion of potential common stock. (SFAS 128, par. 11)

> **Practical Consideration.** For example, if the corporation has bonus or profit sharing plans based on net income, the numerator should be adjusted for the effect on profit sharing or bonus expense from adding back interest (net of tax) on convertible debt.

19.207   Diluted earnings per share should be calculated using the most advantageous conversion rate or exercise price from the standpoint of the security holder. In addition, previously reported diluted earnings per share should not be restated for subsequent conversions or changes in the stock's market price. (SFAS 128, par. 12)

EXHIBIT 19-1

COMPUTING BASIC EARNINGS PER SHARE

Facts:

1. At the beginning of the year, ABC Company had 100,000 shares of common stock and 2,000 shares of noncumulative, nonconvertible preferred stock issued and outstanding.

2. An additional 25,000 shares of common stock were issued on June 30, 19X6.

3. On September 5, 19X6, the company declared a 2-for-1 stock split for common stockholders effective September 30, 19X6.

4. ABC Company purchased 24,000 shares of treasury stock on December 1, 19X6.

5. ABC Company reported net income of $750,000 for 19X6 and declared and paid dividends totaling $100,000 to preferred stockholders.

Weighted average number of shares of common stock outstanding during 19X6:

	Shares Originally Outstanding	Effect of 2-for-1 Stock Split	Adjusted Shares Outstanding	Months Outstanding	Weighted Average Shares
Beginning balance	100,000	2	200,000	12/12	200,000
Stock issue	25,000	2	50,000	6/12	25,000
Treasury purchase	24,000	1	24,000	1/12	(2,000)
					223,000

Earnings per share calculation:

Income available to common stockholders	
($750,000 − 100,000)	$ 650,000
Weighted average number of common shares outstanding	÷ 223,000
Earnings per share	$ 2.92

19.208   **No Antidilution.** Securities that have an antidilutive effect on earnings per share should not be included in the computation of diluted earnings per share. When determining whether a security is dilutive or antidilutive, each issue or series of issues of potential common stock should be considered individually (rather than in the aggregate). (SFAS 128, par. 13) Because some convertible securities may be dilutive on their own, but antidilutive when included with other potential common stock, each issue (or series of issues) should be considered in sequence from the most dilutive to the least dilutive to reflect maximum dilution. (That is, dilutive potential common stock with the lowest earnings per incremental share should be included in diluted earnings per share before those with higher earnings per incremental share). (SFAS 128, par. 14) EXHIBIT 19-2 illustrates sequencing issues of potential common stock to determine whether they are dilutive or antidilutive.

19.209   If the company reports a discontinued operation, an extraordinary item, or the cumulative effect of an accounting change during the period, income from continuing operations (adjusted for preferred dividends as discussed in Paragraph 19.203) should be used as the control number to determine whether potential common shares are dilutive or antidilutive. In other words, the number of potential common shares used to compute diluted earnings per share for continuing operations should be used to compute all other per-share amounts even if those amounts would be antidilutive to their respective basic per-share amounts. (SFAS 128, par. 15)

Practical Consideration. For example, assume ABC Company has income from continuing operations of $10,000, a loss from discontinued operation of ($15,000), a net loss of ($5,000), and 5,000 common shares and 1,000 potential common shares outstanding. Basic per-share amounts would be $2.00 for continuing operations, ($3.00) for discontinued operations, and ($1.00) for the net loss. The 1,000 potential common shares should be included in the denominator for determining diluted per-share results from continuing operations because the resulting $1.67 per-share amount is dilutive. The 1,000 potential common shares also should be included when determining the per-share amounts for loss from discontinued operations and net loss even though the resulting per share amounts [($2.50) for loss from discontinued operations and ($.83) for net loss)] are antidilutive when compared to the comparable basic per-share amounts.

EXHIBIT 19-2

DETERMINING WHETHER POTENTIAL COMMON STOCK IS ANTIDILUTIVE

Facts:

1. ABC Company has income available to common stockholders of $1,000,000 for the year 19X7.

2. 500,000 shares of common stock were outstanding the entire year 19X7.

3. If converted, ABC Company's potential common shares outstanding during the 19X7 would have had the following effect on income and common shares:

	Increase in Income	Increase in Number of Common Shares	Earnings per Incremental Share
Options	—	3,000	—
Convertible preferred stock	$ 400,000	160,000	$ 2.50
Convertible debentures	$ 300,000	200,000	$ 1.50

Computing Diluted Earnings per Share:

	Income Available	Common Shares	Per Share	
Basic earnings per share	$ 1,000,000	500,000	$ 2.00	
Options	—	3,000		
		503,000	$ 1.99	Dilutive
Convertible debentures	300,000	200,000		
	1,300,000	703,000	$ 1.85	Dilutive
Convertible preferred stock	400,000	160,000		
	$ 1,700,000	863,000	$ 1.97	Antidilutive

Based on the preceding analysis, only options and convertible debentures would be included in the diluted earnings per share calculation. Convertible preferred stock would not because its effect is antidilutive.

19.210   Including potential common shares in the denominator when computing the per-share amount for continuing operations is always antidilutive if the
company reports a loss for continuing operations. If the company has a loss
from continuing operations, no potential common shares should be included
in the denominator when computing any per-share amounts, even if the company reports net income. (SFAS 128, par. 16)

> **Practical Consideration.** A company may report income from continuing
> operations but have a loss from continuing operations available to common
> stockholders (for example, as a result of deducting preferred dividends as dis-
> cussed in Paragraph 19.203). In such cases, no potential common shares
> should be included in any per-share computations because they would be
> antidilutive to the per-share amount reported for continuing operations.
>
> In addition, if the company has income for the current quarter, but a year-to-
> date loss, potential common shares should be included in the per-share com-
> putations for the quarter, but not for year-to-date because they would be
> antidilutive to the year-to-date amounts.

Options, Warrants and Their Equivalents

19.211   Generally, stock options, warrants, and their equivalents (such as
nonvested stock granted to employees, stock purchase contracts, and partially paid stock subscriptions) that have a dilutive effect should be reflected in
diluted earnings per share using the treasury stock method. (See Paragraph 19.215, however.) Under the treasury stock method, earnings per share
is computed as if—

   a. the options or warrants were converted to common shares at the
      beginning of the period (or at the time they were issued, if later),

   b. proceeds that would have been received were used to purchase
      common stock at the average market price during the period,
      and

   c. shares that could not be purchased on the open market (because
      the assumed proceeds would have been insufficient) were
      issued from previously unissued shares.

In other words, under the treasury stock method, the incremental number of
shares issued (that is, the difference between the number of shares assumed
to be issued and the number of shares assumed to be purchased) is included
in the denominator when computing diluted earnings per share. (SFAS 128,
par. 17) Under the treasury stock method, options and warrants are dilutive only
when the average market price of common stock during the period is greater

than the exercise price of the options and warrants. The company should not restate previously reported earnings per share information as a result of changes in the market price of the common stock. (SFAS 128, par. 18)

Practical Consideration. To illustrate using the treasury stock method, assume ACE Company (a) has 1,000 warrants outstanding that may be exercised at $25 per share and (b) the average market price of the company's common stock during the period was $40. If the 1,000 warrants were exercised, the company would receive $25,000 (1,000 × $25), which would be sufficient to buy 625 shares of its stock on the open market ($25,000 ÷ $40). The company would then have to issue 375 additional shares of common stock (1,000 − 625) to convert all of the outstanding warrants. Thus, 375 shares should be added to outstanding common shares when computing diluted earnings per share.

19.212   When computing the number of incremental shares for quarterly earnings per share, the average market price of the company's stock for the three months included in the reporting period should be used. When computing year-to-date diluted earnings per share, the company should use a year-to-date weighted average of the incremental number of shares included in each quarterly diluted earnings per share calculation. (SFAS 128, par. 46)

Practical Consideration. Using a simple average of weekly or monthly closing prices usually is adequate when computing the average market price of a company's stock. However, if prices fluctuate widely, an average of the high and low prices for the period would result in a more representative price. Regardless, the method used should be applied consistently from period to period unless it is no longer representative due to changed conditions.

When computing average shares outstanding, the most precise average would be the sum of shares determined on a daily basis divided by the number of days in the reporting period. However, less precise methods (such as an average of the shares outstanding at each month end in the reporting period) are acceptable as long as they are reasonable.

19.213   Some option or warrant contracts may require that any proceeds received from exercise be used to retire debt or other securities issued by the company. In such cases, diluted earnings per share should be computed assuming the proceeds were used to purchase the debt (or other securities) at its average market price instead of to purchase common stock under the treasury stock method. (The treasury stock method should be applied to any excess proceeds, however.) The numerator should be adjusted to add back any interest (net of tax) on the debt assumed to be purchased. In addition, the numerator should be adjusted for any other nondiscretionary adjustments (net of tax). (See Paragraph 19.219.) (SFAS 128, par. 52)

19.214   Dilutive options or warrants issued, canceled, or exercised during the period should be reflected in the calculation of diluted earnings per share for the period they were outstanding. Common shares issued when options or warrants are exercised should be included in the denominator subsequent to the exercise date. (SFAS 128, par. 19)

19.215   **Written Put Options.** Written put options and forward purchase contracts are agreements that require the corporation to repurchase its own stock, and should be included in the determination of dilutive earnings per share if they are dilutive. If their exercise price is above the average market price for the period, the potential dilutive effect should be computed using the reverse treasury stock method. The reverse treasury method assumes—(SFAS 128, par. 24)

   a. the corporation issued a sufficient number of shares at the beginning of the period (at the average market price for the period) to raise enough cash proceeds to satisfy the contract, and

   b. the proceeds were used to satisfy the contract (i.e. repurchase the number of shares specified in the contract).

Thus, the incremental number of shares (shares assumed issued minus shares repurchased) should be included in the denominator in the diluted earnings per share calculation.

19.216   **Purchased Options.** Purchased put options and purchased call options (options held by the corporation on its own stock) should not be included when computing diluted earnings per share because their effect would be antidilutive. (SFAS 128, par. 25)

19.217   **Options and Warrants to Purchase Convertible Securities.** When computing diluted earnings per share, the company should assume options or warrants to purchase convertible securities were exercised whenever the average price of *both* the convertible security and the common stock obtainable upon conversion are above the option price of the options or warrants. Their exercise should not be assumed, however, unless it is assumed that similar convertible securities already outstanding were exercised. The incremental number of shares should be calculated using the treasury stock method. (SFAS 128, par. 49)

> **Practical Consideration.** It is not necessary to impute interest or dividends on the convertible securities assumed to be obtained through exercise of the options because any imputed amount would be reversed when applying the if-converted method for the convertible securities. (See Paragraphs 19.219–.221)

19.218   Debt or Other Securities Tendered as Payment of Option Price. Some options or warrants may permit (or require) the security holder to pay all or a portion of the option price by tendering debt or other securities issued by the company. When computing diluted earnings per share, the debt or other securities should be assumed to be tendered unless the contract permits the tendering of cash and doing so would be more advantageous to the option holder. (In that case, the treasury stock method should be applied.) If debt is assumed to have been tendered, interest (net of tax) should be added back to the numerator. The numerator also should be adjusted for any other non-discretionary adjustments to income (net of tax) that would have resulted from the conversion (for example, an adjustment of bonus expense based on net income). The treasury stock method should be applied for any cash proceeds assumed to be received. (SFAS 128, par. 51)

Convertible Debt and Convertible Preferred Stock

19.219   The calculation of diluted earnings per share should take into account the dilutive effect of convertible debt and convertible preferred stock using the if-converted method. Under the if-converted method: (SFAS 128, par. 26)

   a. dividends applicable to convertible preferred stock should be added back to the numerator.

   b. interest expense (net of tax) applicable to convertible debt outstanding should be added back to net income. In addition, the numerator should be adjusted for any other changes in net income (net of tax) resulting from assumed conversion (such as bonus expense that is based on net income).

   c. the denominator should be adjusted as if the convertible preferred stock or convertible debt was converted as of the beginning of the period (or when the convertible security was issued, if later).

19.220   If conversion options lapse, convertible preferred stock is redeemed, convertible debt is extinguished, or convertible securities were converted during the period, the dilutive effect of the convertible securities should be included in the denominator for the period they were outstanding. Common shares issued upon conversion of the securities should be included in the denominator subsequent to the exercise date. (SFAS 128, par. 28)

19.221   Convertible securities that permit or require the payment of cash at conversion should be treated as warrants. (See Paragraphs 19.211–.214.) When computing diluted earnings per share, the treasury stock method should be applied to any cash proceeds assumed to be received and the if-converted method should be applied to the convertible security. (SFAS 128, par. 53)

Contracts That May Be Settled in Stock or Cash

19.222   A company may issue a contract that can be settled in stock or cash at the election of the company or the holder. Generally, it should be assumed that the contract will be settled in common stock and the resulting potential common shares should be included in diluted earnings per share if the effect is more dilutive. However, if past experience or stated policy provides a reasonable basis to assume the contract will be settled partially or wholly in cash, the presumption that the contract will be settled in common stock may be overcome. If it is assumed the contract will be settled in common stock, an adjustment to the numerator may be necessary for any changes in net income or loss that would result if the contract had been treated as an equity instrument instead of an asset or liability (similar to the adjustment for convertible debt discussed in Paragraph 19.219). (SFAS 128, par. 29)

Contingently Issuable Shares

19.223   An agreement may call for the company to issue additional shares of common stock if certain conditions are met. Generally, the effects of such agreements should be considered in earnings per share calculations (basic and diluted) if the conditions for issuing the additional stock have been met and issuance of the stock depends solely on the passage of time. If all contingencies have not been satisfied by the end of the period, however, the number of contingently issuable shares included in diluted earnings per share should be based on the number of shares (if any) that would be issuable if the end of the reporting period were the end of the contingency period (for example, the number of shares that would be issuable based on current-period earnings or the end-of-period market price) and that would have a dilutive effect on the calculation. For interim earnings per share computations, the shares should be included in the denominator at the beginning of the period (or the date of the contingent stock agreement, if later). For year-to-date computations, the contingent shares should be weighted for the interim periods in which they were included in the diluted earnings per share computations. (SFAS 128, par. 30) Further considerations follow.

a. *Shares that must be issued if a specified level of earnings is met or maintained.* If the specified level of earnings has been attained, the additional shares should be included in the calculation of diluted earnings per share. The calculation of diluted earnings per share should include those shares that would be issued assuming that the current amount of earnings will remain unchanged until the end of the agreement (however, only if the effect would be dilutive). Basic earnings per share should not reflect such contingently issuable shares because all conditions for issuance have not been satisfied due to the fact earnings may change in future periods. (SFAS 128, par. 31)

b. *Shares that must be issued if the stock's market price reaches a specified amount.* Earnings per share calculations should consider the number of shares that would be issuable based on the stock's market price at the end of the period. If the contract is based on an average market price over some time period, the average for that time period should be used. Basic earnings per share should not reflect such contingently issuable shares because all conditions for issuance have not been satisfied due to the fact the market price may change in future periods. (SFAS 128, par. 32)

c. *Shares contingently issuable based on future earnings and on the stock's future market price.* Only shares that are issuable based on conditions existing at the end of the period should be reflected in diluted earnings per share. Thus, such contingently issuable shares would be included in diluted earnings per share calculations only if *both* conditions are met at the end of the reporting period and the effect of including them is dilutive. (SFAS 128, par. 33)

In some cases, shares may be issued contingent on conditions other than earnings or market price of the company's stock (for example, based on opening a certain number of retail locations by a certain date). In such cases, the contingently issuable shares should be included in diluted earnings per share computations based on the assumption that the current status of the condition will remain unchanged until the end of the contingency period. (SFAS 128, par. 34)

19.224 The conditions in the preceding paragraph also should be considered when determining whether contingently issuable potential common shares (such as contingently issuable options or warrants) should be included in diluted earnings per share. If the company determines the potential common shares should be included, computation of diluted earnings per share, the relevant guidance in Paragraphs 19.211–.218 (for options and warrants),

Paragraphs 19.219–.221 (for convertible securities), or Paragraph 19.222 (for contracts that may be settled in stock or cash) should be followed. In any event, exercise or conversion of contingently issuable potential common stock should not be assumed unless exercise or conversion of similar outstanding potential common shares is also assumed. (SFAS 128, par. 35)

Practical Consideration. For example, if the company has entered into contracts that require the issuance of stock options when certain specified conditions are met, those contingently issuable potential common shares should not be included in the computation of diluted earnings per share unless similar outstanding options are also assumed to be exercised.

19.225   EXHIBIT 19-3 illustrates the computation of earnings per share when a company has entered into contracts for contingently issuable shares.

EXHIBIT 19-3

EFFECT OF CONTINGENTLY ISSUABLE SHARES ON EARNINGS PER SHARE COMPUTATIONS

Facts:

1. ABC Company, Inc. had 1,000,000 shares of common stock outstanding during the year ended December 31, 19X8.

2. In connection with the acquisition of a subsidiary, ABC Company entered into a contingent stock agreement on January 1, 19X8. The terms are as follows:

   • 20,000 common shares must be issued for each new long-term contract entered into exceeding $1,000,000 in annual revenues.

   • 500 additional common shares must be issued for each $1,000 of consolidated net income (after tax) in excess of $1,000,000 for the year ended December 31, 19X8.

3. ABC Company was awarded two new long-term contracts exceeding $1,000,000 in annual revenues during 19X8—one on May 1, 19X8 and one on August 1, 19X8.

4. ABC Company's consolidated, year-to-date net income (after tax) was:

   • $750,000 as of March 31, 19X8.

   • $1,250,000 as of June 30, 19X8.

   • $900,000 as of September 30, 19X8.

   • $1,500,000 as of December 31, 19X8.

EXHIBIT 19-3 (Continued)

Computing Basic Earning per Share:

	First Quarter	Second Quarter	Third Quarter	Fourth Quarter	Full Year
Numerator	$ 750,000	$ 500,000	$ (350,000)	$ 600,000	$ 1,500,000
Denominator:					
Common shares outstanding	1,000,000	1,000,000	1,000,000	1,000,000	1,000,000
Contract contingency	—	13,333[a]	33,333[b]	40,000	21,666[c]
Earnings contingency[d]	—	—	—	—	—
Total shares	1,000,000	1,013,333	1,033,333	1,040,000	1,021,666
Basic earnings per share	$ .75	$ .49	$ (.34)	$ .58	$ 1.47

---

[a] 20,000 shares related to the May contract outstanding for two-thirds of the quarter (20,000 × 2/3)

[b] 20,000 shares related to the May contract + 20,000 shares related to the August contract that were outstanding for two-thirds of the quarter)

[c] 20,000 shares outstanding since May 1, 19X8 (20,000 × 8/12) + 20,000 shares outstanding since August 1, 19X8 (20,000 shares × 5/12)

[d] No effect on basic earnings per share because it is not certain the contingency has been satisfied until the end of the year.

EXHIBIT 19-3 (Continued)

Computing Diluted Earnings per Share:

	First Quarter	Second Quarter	Third Quarter	Fourth Quarter	Full Year
Numerator	$ 750,000	$ 500,000	$ (350,000)	$ 600,000	$1,500,000
Denominator:					
Common shares outstanding	1,000,000	1,000,000	1,000,000	1,000,000	1,000,000
Contract contingency	—	20,000[e]	40,000[e]	40,000[e]	25,000[f]
Earnings contingency	—	125,000[g]	—	250,000[h]	93,750[f]
Total shares	1,000,000	1,145,000	1,040,000	1,290,000	1,118,750
Diluted earnings per share	$ .75	.44	$ (.34)[i]	$ .47	$ 1.34

---

[e]   Contingent shares are included as of the beginning of the period when computing diluted earnings per share for interim periods.

[f]   When computing year-to-date diluted earnings per share, contingent shares are included on a weighted-average basis. In this example, the weighted average number of shares outstanding is determined by totalling the shares outstanding each quarter and dividing that total by four.

[g]   [($1,250,000 − $1,000,000) ÷ $1,000] × 500 shares

[h]   [($1,500,000 − $1,000,000) ÷ $1,000] × 500 shares

[i]   In the example, loss for the quarter is assumed to be due to discontinued operations, therefore, the antidilution rules discussed in Paragraphs 19.208–.210 do not apply.

19.226 **Contingently Returnable Shares.** Contingently returnable shares should be treated in the same manner as contingently issuable shares. (SFAS 128, par. 10)

Practical Consideration. Contingently returnable shares include shares issued or placed in escrow that must be returned in total or in part if specified conditions are not met.

Rights Issues

19.227 If the corporation has issued rights whose exercise price is less than the fair value of the stock, the rights issue contains a bonus element that is similar to a stock dividend. If the rights issue including the bonus element is offered to all existing shareholders, diluted earnings per share should be retroactively adjusted for the bonus element for all periods presented. If the ability to exercise the rights is contingent on an event other than the passage of time, however, diluted earnings per share should not be adjusted for the bonus element until the contingency is resolved. (SFAS 128, par. 55)

19.228 When restating earnings per share as a result of a rights issue, the number of shares used in computing basic and diluted earnings per share is the number of shares outstanding prior to the rights issue multiplied by the following factor:

$$\frac{\text{Fair value per share immediately prior to exercise of the rights}}{\text{Theoretical ex-rights fair value per share}}$$

Theoretical ex-rights fair value is computed as follows:

$$\frac{\text{Aggregate fair value of shares immediately prior to the rights exercise plus the proceeds expected from the exercise of the rights}}{\text{Number shares outstanding after exercise of the rights}}$$

If the rights themselves will be publicly traded (separate from the shares) prior to their exercise, fair value should be determined as of the last day that the shares and rights trade together. (SFAS 128, par. 56)

Stock-based Compensation Plans

19.229 Fixed awards and nonvested stock (defined in SFAS No. 123, *Accounting for Stock-Based Compensation,* see Chapter 50) issued to an employee in accordance with a stock-based compensation plan (or stock-based awards issued to a nonemployee in exchange for goods or services) should be treated as options when computing diluted earnings per share. Stock-based awards should be considered to be outstanding at the grant date (even though the holder may not be able to exercise them until they are vested) and included in the diluted earnings per share calculation if they have a dilutive effect (even though the employee may not receive or be able to sell the stock until some future date). The treasury stock method (discussed in Paragraph 19.211) should be used to determine the dilutive effect of stock-based compensation awards. (SFAS 128, par. 20) In addition—

a. when applying the treasury stock method, the proceeds from exercising the stock awards is the sum of (1) the amount the employee must pay, (2) compensation related to future services and not yet charged to expense, and (3) the amount of any tax benefit to be credited to capital. Assumed proceeds should not include amounts considered compensation for past services. (SFAS 128, par. 21)

b. generally, if a stock-based compensation agreement allows the employee or corporation to elect whether payment is in stock or cash, it should be presumed that the contract will be settled in common stock and the resulting potential common shares should be included in the diluted earnings per share calculation if the effect is more dilutive. If past experience or stated policy provides a reasonable basis to assume the contract will be settled wholly or partially in cash, however, the presumption that the contract will be settled in stock may be overcome. (SFAS 128, par. 22 and par. 29)

c. if the corporation has tandem stock plans (discussed in Chapter 50) that allow the entity or employee to make an election that involves two or more types of instruments, diluted earnings per share for the period should be computed based on the terms used to compute compensation for the period. (SFAS 128, par. 22)

d. if the corporation has issued performance awards and targeted stock price options (discussed in Chapter 50), the contingent share provisions discussed in Paragraphs 19.223–.226 should be followed when determining whether they are included in diluted earnings per share. (SFAS 128, par. 23)

> **Practical Consideration.** The preceding provisions also should be followed when determining how to consider junior stock plans in diluted earnings per share. (Junior stock plans are discussed further in Chapter 50.)

Example Calculation

19.230   EXHIBIT 19-4 illustrates calculating diluted earnings per share.

19.230

EXHIBIT 19-4

COMPUTING DILUTED EARNINGS PER SHARE

Facts:

1. ABC Company, Inc. had income from continuing operations of $2,000,000 (net of tax) and a loss from discontinued operations of ($500,000) (net of tax) for the year ended December 31, 19X8.

2. At January 1, 19X8, the company had 1,500,000 shares outstanding. An additional 250,000 shares were issued for cash on February 28, 19X8.

3. Three-percent convertible bonds with a principal amount of $10,000,000 were sold for cash (at par) during the fourth quarter of 19X7. Each $1,000 bond is convertible into 25 shares of common stock. No bonds were converted during 19X8.

4. 100,000 shares of convertible preferred stock were issued in 19X7. Each share of preferred stock is entitled to a cumulative dividend of $2 per share and is convertible to three shares of common stock. No preferred stock was converted during 19X8.

5. Options to buy 150,000 shares of common stock at $50 per share for a period of 10 years were issued on July 1, 19X3. All options were exercised on June 30, 19X8. The average market price of the stock between January 1, 19X8 and June 30, 19X8 was $65 per share.

6. Warrants to buy 100,000 shares of common stock at $55 per share were outstanding during all of 19X8. Average stock price for the year was $70 per share.

7. ABC Company's effective tax rate was 40% in 19X8.

EXHIBIT 19-4 (Continued)

Computation of Weighted Average Shares Outstanding:

Dates Outstanding	Shares Outstanding	Fraction of Period	Weighted Average Shares
January 1–February 28	1,500,000	$2/12$	250,000
Issuance of common stock on February 28	250,000		
	1,750,000	$4/12$	583,333
Exercise of options on June 30	150,000		
	1,900,000	$6/12$	950,000
Weighted-average shares			1,783,333

Computation of Basic Earnings per Share:

Income from continuing operations	$ 2,000,000
Less: Preferred dividends	(200,000)
Income available to common shareholders	$ 1,800,000
Loss from discontinued operations	$ (500,000)
Net income available to common share-holders	$ 1,300,000

Basic earnings per share:

Income from continuing operations ($1,800,000 ÷ 1,783,333)	$	1.01
Loss from discontinued operations ($500,000 ÷ 1,783,333)	$	(.28)
Net income ($1,300,000 ÷ 1,783,333)	$	.73

Computation of Diluted Earnings per Share:

Income available to common shareholders		$ 1,800,000
Add impact of assumed conversion:		
Preferred stock dividends	$ 200,000	
Interest on convertible bonds (net of tax)	180,000	380,000
Income from continuing operations available to common shareholders plus assumed conversions		2,180,000
Loss from discontinued operations		(500,000)
Net income available to common shareholders plus assumed conversions		$ 1,680,000

EXHIBIT 19-4 (Continued)

Weighted average shares		1,783,333
Add incremental shares from assumed conversion:		
Convertible preferred stock	300,000	
Options	17,308[a]	
Warrants	21,429[b]	
3% convertible bonds	250,000	
Dilutive potential common shares		588,737
Adjusted weighted average shares		2,372,070

Diluted earnings per share:

Income from continuing operations ($2,180,000 ÷ 2,372,070)	$	.92
Loss from discontinued operations ($500,000 ÷ 2,372,070)	$	(.21)
Net income ($1,680,000 ÷ 2,372,070)	$	.71

---

[a] $[(\$65 - \$50)/\$65] \times 150{,}000 \times {}^{6}/_{12}$

[b] $[(\$70 - \$55)/\$70] \times 100{,}000$

Other Considerations

19.231   **Participating Securities and Two-class Common Stock.** A corporation may issue securities that participate in dividends with common stockholders or a class of common stock with different dividend rates from another
class of common stock. If the effect of their conversion would be dilutive, the
"if-converted" method (discussed in Paragraphs 19.219–.221) should be used
for those securities that are convertible into common stock. For securities not
convertible into common stock, the two-class method should be used to calculate earnings per share. Under the two-class method—(SFAS 128, paras.
60–61)

a. dividends declared in the current period for each class of stock
and unpaid cumulative dividends (or contractual interest on participating bonds) should be deducted from income from continuing operations (or net income). The remaining earnings
(undistributed earnings) should be allocated to common stock
and the participating securities to the extent that each security
may share in earnings.

b. for each security, the undistributed earnings allocated in step a.
should be added to the amount allocated to the security for dividends to determine the total earnings allocated to each security.

c. The amount in b. should be divided by the total outstanding
shares for each security to which earnings were allocated to
arrive at earnings per share for the security.

Basic and diluted earnings per share should be presented for each class of
common stock.

> **Practical Consideration.** In essence, the two-class method determines
> earnings per share for each class of common stock and participating security
> using an allocation formula based on dividends declared (or accumulated)
> and participation rights in undistributed earnings.

19.232   EXHIBIT 19-5 illustrates the computation of basic earnings per share
under the two-class method.

EXHIBIT 19-5

COMPUTING EARNINGS PER SHARE
UNDER THE TWO-CLASS METHOD

Facts:

1. ABC Company had 1,000,000 shares of common stock and 500,000 shares of nonconvertible preferred stock outstanding as of December 31, 19X8.

2. The preferred stock is entitled to a $3 per share noncumulative dividend before any dividends are paid on common stock.

3. After common stock is paid a dividend of $1 per share, the preferred stock participates in any additional dividends paid on a 25:75 per share ratio with common shareholders.

4. Net income for 19X8 was $10,000,000.

5. Preferred shareholders were paid $1,625,000 ($3.25 per share) in 19X8.

6. Common shareholders were paid $1,750,000 ($1.75 per share) in 19X8.

Computation of Undistributed Earnings:

Net income		$ 10,000,000	
Less dividends paid:			
Preferred	$ 1,625,000		
Common	1,750,000	3,375,000	
Undistributed earnings		$ 6,625,000	

	(A) Shares Outstanding	(B) Dividend Sharing Ratio	(A) × (B) Equivalent Shares	Undistributed Earnings Allocation[a]
Preferred	500,000	25%	125,000	$ 946,429
Common	1,000,000	75%	750,000	5,678,571
		100%	875,000	$ 6,625,000

EXHIBIT 19-5 (Continued)

Total allocated earnings:

	Distributed Earnings	Undis- tributed Earnings	Total
Preferred	$ 1,625,000	$ 946,429	$ 2,571,429
Common	1,750,000	5,678,571	7,428,571
	$ 3,375,000	$ 6,625,000	$ 10,000,000

Basic earnings per share:

Preferred ($2,571,429 ÷ 500,000)	$	5.14
Common ($7,428,571 ÷ 1,000,000)	$	7.43

---

a Undistributed earnings are allocated based on the percentage of each class of stock's equivalent shares to total equivalent shares.

19.233   **Securities of Subsidiaries.** A subsidiary may issue options, warrants, or convertible securities that allow holders to obtain common stock of the subsidiary or the parent company. The following guidelines should be applied when computing consolidated diluted earnings per share of a company with subsidiaries that have issued common stock or potential common stock to parties other than the parent: (SFAS 128, par. 62)

    a. If the subsidiary issues securities enabling holders to obtain common stock of the subsidiary, those securities should be included in the subsidiary's diluted earnings per share computation. The subsidiary's resulting per share earnings should then be included in the consolidated company's earnings per share computation based on the consolidated group's holding of the subsidiary's securities.

    b. Securities issued (or held) by the subsidiary that allow the holder to obtain the parent's common stock should be considered potential common shares when computing the parent's diluted earnings per share.

> **Practical Consideration.** The provisions in Paragraph 19.233 should also be applied to investments in common stock of corporate joint ventures and investments in companies accounted for under the equity method discussed in Chapter 20.

19.234   If the parent company issues shares that are convertible into common stock of the subsidiary or an equity method investee, the if-converted method should be used to determine the effect on earnings per share. Under that method, the numerator of the earnings per share calculation should be adjusted so that it equals the parent's earnings that would have been reported if the securities had been converted to the subsidiary's common stock. (That includes the parent's portion of adjustments to the subsidiary's earnings resulting from the assumed conversion.) No adjustments to the denominator are necessary, however, because the number of parent company shares outstanding would not change from the assumed conversion. (SFAS 128, par. 63)

19.235   **Prior Period Adjustments.** GAAP may require the results of operations of a prior period to be restated. In such cases, earnings per share data for the prior period (or periods) also should be restated. Earnings per share should be computed following the provisions of this chapter as if the restated income or loss had been originally reported for the prior period or periods. The effect of the restatement (in per share terms) should be disclosed in the period of restatement. (SFAS 128, paras. 57–58)

DISCLOSURE REQUIREMENTS

19.500 Public companies with simple capital structures must present basic earnings per share while those with complex capital structures must present basic and diluted earnings per share. Earnings per share data should be presented for all periods for which an income statement or summary of earnings is presented. Companies required to present diluted earnings per share must do so for all periods presented—even if it equals basic earnings per share. (If they are the same, however, basic and fully diluted earnings per share may be reported as one line item on the income statement.)

> **Practical Consideration.** Companies are not required to use the terms "basic earnings per share" and "diluted earnings per share." Other descriptive terms, such as "earnings per common share" and "earnings per common share assuming dilution," are acceptable.

19.501 Per-share amounts for net income and income from continuing operations should be presented on the face of the income statement. Per-share amounts for discontinued operations, extraordinary items, or the cumulative effect of an accounting change (when those items are present) may be reported on the face of the income statement or disclosed in the notes to the financial statements. (SFAS 128, paras. 36–37) In addition, the financial statements should include the following disclosures for each period for which an income statement is presented:

a. A reconciliation of the numerators and denominators of the basic and diluted earnings per share computations for income from continuing operations. (Income and share amounts for all securities that affect earnings per share should be provided in the reconciliation.)

b. The effect of preferred dividends on the income available to common shareholders amount used in the basic earnings per share calculation.

c. Any securities (including those that could be issued under contingent stock agreements) that could potentially dilute basic earnings per share, but were not included in the diluted earnings per share computation because their effect was antidilutive for the periods presented.

d. Any transactions occurring after the end of the period, but before issuance of the financial statements, that would have a material effect on the number of common shares or potential common shares outstanding at the end of the period. (For example, issuance or purchase of common shares, issuance of options, warrants, or convertible securities, the resolution of a contingency specified in a contingent stock agreement, and the conversion or exercise of potential common shares outstanding at the end of the period.) (SFAS 128, paras. 40–41)

e. If applicable, the fact that per share amounts have been adjusted as a result of stock dividends, stock splits, or reverse stock splits. (See Paragraph 19.203.) (SFAS 128, par. 54)

f. If earnings per share amounts have been restated as the result of a prior period adjustment, the effects of the restatement (in per share amounts). (SFAS 128, par. 57)

g. If per share amounts other than those required to be presented are disclosed, whether the per share amounts are net of tax. (SFAS 128, par. 37)

Practical Consideration. Note that GAAP prohibits presenting cash flow per share.

EXHIBIT 19-6 illustrates how the more common disclosures could be presented in the notes to the financial statements.

EXHIBIT 19-6

EXAMPLE DISCLOSURE OF RECONCILIATION OF NUMERATORS AND DENOMINATORS FOR BASIC AND DILUTED EARNINGS PER SHARE COMPUTATIONS

NOTE H—EARNINGS PER SHARE

Basic earnings per share are computed by dividing earnings available to common stockholders by the weighted average number of common share outstanding during the period. Diluted earnings per share reflect per share amounts that would have resulted if dilutive potential common stock had been converted to common stock. The following reconciles amounts reported in the financial statements:

	For the Year Ended 19X8		
	Income (Numerator)	Shares (Denominator)	Per-share Amount
Income from continuing operations	$ 2,000,000		
Less preferred stock dividends	(400,000)		
Income available to common stock-holders—basic earnings per share	1,600,000	500,000	$ 3.20
Effect of dilutive securities			
Options	—	3,000	
5% convertible debentures	300,000	200,000	
Income available to common stock-holders—diluted earnings per share	$ 1,900,000	703,000	$ 2.70

During 19X8, the corporation had 80,000 shares of convertible preferred stock (entitled to a $5 per share cumulative dividend) outstanding. Each share of preferred stock is convertible into one share of common stock. The convertible preferred stock was not included in the computation of diluted earnings per share because the effect of conversion would be antidilutive. The convertible preferred stock was still outstanding at December 31, 19X8.

AUTHORITATIVE LITERATURE AND RELATED TOPICS

AUTHORITATIVE LITERATURE

APB Opinion No. 30, *Reporting the Results of Operations-Reporting the Effects of Disposal of a Segment of a Business, and Extraordinary, Unusual and Infrequently Occurring Events and Transactions*
SFAS No. 95, *Statement of Cash Flows*
SFAS No. 128, *Earnings Per Share*
FASB Interpretation No. 28, *Accounting for Stock Appreciation Rights and Other Variable Stock Option or Award Plans*
FASB Interpretation No. 38, *Determining the Measurement Date for Stock Option, Purchase, and Award Plans Involving Junior Stock*

RELATED PRONOUNCEMENTS

APB Opinion No. 18, *The Equity Method of Accounting for Investments in Common Stock*
APB Opinion No. 28, *Interim Financial Reporting*
SFAS No. 123, *Accounting for Stock-Based Compensation*
EITF Issue No. 84-22, *Prior Years' Earnings per Share following a Savings and Loan Association Conversion and Pooling*
EITF Issue No. 85-18, *Earnings-per-Share Effect of Equity Commitment Notes*
EITF Issue No. 90-19, *Convertible Bonds with Issuer Option to Settle for Cash upon Conversion*
EITF Issue No. 92-3, *Earnings-per-Share Treatment of Tax Benefits for Dividends on Unallocated Stock Held by an Employee Stock Ownership Plan*
SOP 93-6, *Employers' Accounting for Stock Ownership Plans*

RELATED TOPICS

Chapter 1—Accounting Changes
Chapter 3—Business Combinations
Chapter 12—Debt: Convertible Debt
Chapter 22—Income Statement
Chapter 50—Stockholders' Equity

EQUITY METHOD INVESTMENTS

Table of Contents

EQUITY METHOD INVESTMENTS

OVERVIEW

20.100   The equity method is used to account for an investment if the investor has the ability to significantly influence the investee's financial and operating policies. Under the equity method, an investment is initially recorded at cost. Thereafter, the carrying amount of the investment is (a) increased for the investor's proportionate share of the investee's earnings and (b) decreased for the investor's proportionate share of the investee's losses or for dividends received from the investee. Other adjustments similar to those made in consolidated financial statements are also made, such as the elimination of intercompany gains and losses and amortization of the difference between the purchase price of the investment and the underlying equity in the investee's net assets. The investment generally is shown in the investor's balance sheet as a single amount and earnings and losses from the investment are shown in the investor's income statement as a single amount. Because the investor's net income and equity at the end of the period are generally the same as if the investment had been consolidated, the equity method is sometimes referred to as a "one-line consolidation."

ACCOUNTING REQUIREMENTS

CRITERIA FOR USING THE EQUITY METHOD

20.200   An investor should use the equity method to account for an investment when it has the ability to significantly influence the investee's operating and financial policies. *Absent evidence to the contrary,* an investor is presumed to have the ability to significantly influence an investee if it owns (directly or indirectly) 20% or more of the investee's voting stock. (APB 18, par. 17) In addition, an investor should use the equity method to account for an investment in a corporate joint venture. (SFAS 94, par. 15)

Practical Consideration. Authoritative literature generally looks at the percentage ownership in the investee to determine the extent of an investor's ability to influence an investee. Consequently, the method used to account for an investment in another company generally is determined as follows:

% of Other Company Owned	Accounting Method Usually Required
Less than 20%	Cost method (See Chapter 35.)
20% to 50%	Equity method
More than 50%	Consolidation (See Chapter 9.)

The 20% ownership criteria is intended to provide a degree of uniformity in applying the equity method rather than absolutely require its use. An investor's ability to significantly influence an investee depends on a variety of factors, and determining whether there is significant influence requires an evaluation of all the facts and circumstances. For example, even if an investor does not own 20% of a company's voting stock, it may have significant influence if it is represented on the investee's board of directors, participates in the investee's policy making process, or exchanges management personnel. Significant influence may also exist if there are material intercompany transactions or the investee is technologically dependent on the investor. On the other hand, the following circumstances may indicate that an investor does not have significant influence, even if it owns 20% or more of an investee's voting stock:

a. The investee files a lawsuit or complaint against the investor.

b. The investor and investee execute an agreement restricting the investor's rights as a shareholder.

c. Majority ownership of the investee is concentrated among a small group of shareholders who operate the investee without regard to the views of the investor.

d. The investor seeks more financial information than is available to the investee's other shareholders and is unable to obtain that information.

e. The investor tries and fails to obtain representation on the investee's board of directors.

APPLYING THE EQUITY METHOD

20.201   Under the equity method, the investment is initially recorded at cost, then reduced by dividends and increased or decreased by the investor's proportionate share of the investee's net earnings or loss. The investment is shown in the investor's balance sheet as a single amount and the investor's share of earnings is reported in the investor's income statement as a single amount. (See item d., however.) Use of the equity method generally results in the investor's

20.201

stockholders' equity and net earnings being the same as if the investor and investee were consolidated. The following are additional considerations for applying the equity method: (APB 18, par. 19)

a. At acquisition, any difference between the cost of the investment and the investor's proportionate equity in the investee's net assets should be accounted for as if the investee were a consolidated subsidiary. That is, the difference should be related to the investee's tangible and intangible assets based on their fair values. Any difference that cannot be related to specific assets should be considered to be goodwill. Thereafter, the investment account and investment earnings should be adjusted by an amount that represents the additional depreciation or amortization related to the difference as if it were actually recorded by the investee.

b. An investor's equity in the operating results of the investee should be based on the shares of common stock held. Common stock equivalents should not be considered.

c. Intercompany profits and losses should be eliminated until realized as if the investee were consolidated.

Practical Consideration. AICPA Interpretation No. 1 of APB Opinion No. 18 offers the following guidance on eliminating intercompany profits and losses under the equity method:

a. Only intercompany profits and losses included in assets remaining on the investor or investee's books need be eliminated.

b. If the investor controls the investee through majority ownership and the transaction is not arm's length, no intercompany profit should be recognized. Otherwise—

    (1) when the investor purchases an asset from the investee (i.e., upstream sale), the investor should eliminate its proportionate share of the intercompany profit or loss (net of tax) from its equity in the investee's earnings. The eliminated profit or loss should be recorded in a deferred income or loss account or as an adjustment to the investment account and amortized over the life of the purchased asset. (Any remaining deferred income or loss should be recognized in full if the investor subsequently sells the asset.)

    (2) when the investor sells an asset to the investee (i.e., downstream sale), the investor should eliminate from its net income its proportionate share of the intercompany profit or loss. The eliminated profit or loss should be recorded in a deferred income or loss account and recognized as the investee depreciates or sells the asset.

---

d. An investor should report its share of an investee's extraordinary item (or prior period adjustment) as an extraordinary item (or prior period adjustment) unless the amount is immaterial. Similarly, if an investee has items of other comprehensive income, such as unrealized holding gains and losses on investments in debt and equity securities classified as available-for-sale (see Chapter 35), the investor should adjust its investment in the investee by its share of the items and include those amounts in other comprehensive income. (The format used by an investee to display other comprehensive income does not affect how the investor shows its proportionate share of those amounts. Thus, regardless of the format the investee uses to display other comprehensive income, the investor may combine its proportionate share of those amounts with its own other comprehensive income items and display the total of those amounts in a separate statement of comprehensive income, a single statement of income and comprehensive income, or in the statement of changes in equity.) (See Chapter 8.) (SFAS No. 130, paras. 120–122)

Practical Consideration. Although the subject is not specifically addressed by authoritative literature, the authors believe an investor also should report its share of an investee's cumulative accounting adjustments or discontinued operations separately.

---

e. Capital transactions of the investee that affect the investor's share of the investee's stockholders' equity should be accounted for as if the investee were a consolidated subsidiary.

f. An investor should recognize a gain or loss on the sale of its investment equal to the difference between the selling price and the carrying amount of the investment at the time of sale.

g. An investor should recognize a loss for declines in an investment's value that are other than temporary.

h. An investor ordinarily should discontinue applying the equity method when its share of the investee's losses reduces the investment in and advances to the investee to zero. Thereafter, the investor should not provide for additional losses unless it has guaranteed obligations of the investee or is otherwise committed to provide further financial support for the investee. If the investee subsequently reports net income, the investor should resume applying the equity method only after its share of net income equals the share of net losses not recognized during the period the equity method was suspended.

i. Dividends on the investee's cumulative preferred stock should be deducted when computing the investor's share of earnings, regardless of whether they have been declared.

EXHIBIT 20-1 illustrates accounting for an investment under the equity method.

EXHIBIT 20-1

EXAMPLE EQUITY METHOD CALCULATIONS

Facts:

- On June 30, 19X5, ABC, Inc. purchased 40% of XYZ Company for $55,000. On that date, XYZ Company had a total net book value of $100,000. The difference between the amount paid and 40% of XYZ Company's net book value is attributable to goodwill and is amortized over 15 years using the straight-line method.

- XYZ Company reported earnings of $20,000 for the six months ended December 31, 19X5, and $45,000 for the year ended December 31, 19X6. In addition, XYZ Company declared and paid dividends totaling $10,000 during 19X6.

- During 19X6, XYZ Company recognized a profit of $10,000 on the sale of inventory to ABC, Inc. The inventory is included in ABC, Inc.'s assets at December 31, 19X6.

- XYZ Company's effective tax rate is 30%.

Accounting for the investment on ABC, Inc.'s books:

	Investment in XYZ Co.		Equity in XYZ Co.'s Earnings	
Acquisition of 40% of XYZ Company	$	55,000	$	—
Amortization of goodwill included in the purchase price [$1/2$ of annual amortization of $1,000 ([$55,000 − ($100,000 × 40%)] ÷ 15)]		(500)		(500)
Proportionate share of XYZ Company's earnings for the six months ended December 31, 19X5 ($20,000 × 40%)		8,000		8,000
December 31, 19X5 balances		62,500	$	7,500
Proportionate share of XYZ Company's earnings for the year ended December 31, 19X6 ($45,000 × 40%)		18,000	$	18,000
Amortization of goodwill included in the purchase price		(1,000)		(1,000)
Dividends received ($10,000 × 40%)		(4,000)		—
Deferral of XYZ Company's profits on sale of inventory to ABC, Inc., net of related income taxes incurred by XYZ Company [($10,000 − [$10,000 × 30%]) × 40%]		(2,800)		(2,800)
December 31, 19X6 balances	$	72,700	$	14,200

Differences in Fiscal Years

20.202   An investor may recognize its share of the investee's earnings or losses based on the most recent available financial statements of the investee so long as the time lag in reporting periods is consistent from year to year. (APB 18, par. 19) Thus, for example, if an investor and investee have different fiscal year ends, the investor generally may compute its share of the investee's earnings or losses based on the investee's financial statements for its fiscal year.

> **Practical Consideration.** Authoritative literature does not address how to apply the equity method to transactions occurring during the intervening period between the investor and investee's year ends. ARB No. 51, *Consolidated Financial Statements,* discusses a similar situation in the consolidated financial statements of a parent and subsidiary, however. It states that intervening transactions that materially affect financial position or results of operations should be reflected in the financial statements or disclosed. The authors recommend that intervening transactions be accounted for similarly under the equity method.

Income Taxes

20.203   Accounting for an investment under the equity method may cause temporary differences between amounts reported for financial and tax reporting. (SFAS 109, par. 288) Recording the tax effects of such temporary differences is discussed in Chapter 24.

Changing to or from the Equity Method

20.204   Changes in its ability to significantly influence an investee's financial and operating policies may require an investor to change to or from the equity method. For example, an investor (or others) might buy or sell shares of the investee's stock, changing the investor's ownership percentage and ability to influence. In such cases, the following apply: (APB 18, par. 19)

a. When an investor loses its ability to significantly influence the investee, it should stop accruing its share of the investee's earnings or losses and begin accounting for the investment under the cost method. The investment's cost is its carrying amount on the date that it no longer qualifies for equity method accounting.

b. When an investment previously accounted for under the cost method becomes eligible for equity method accounting, an investor should retroactively adjust its investment, results of operations, and retained earnings in a manner consistent with the step-by-step acquisition of a subsidiary. For example, if ABC Company purchased 10% of DEF Company's voting stock on January 1, 19X4, and another 15% on October 1, 19X5, its earnings for 19X5 would include (1) 10% of DEF Company's earnings for the nine months ended September 30, 19X5, and (2) 25% of DEF Company's earnings for the three months ended December 31, 19X5. ABC Company would also restate its retained earnings to include 10% of DEF Company's undistributed earnings for the year ended December 31, 19X4. In addition, ABC Company should compare the cost of each purchase with the underlying net assets of DEF Company and account for any differences as discussed in Paragraph 21.501, item a.

DISCLOSURE REQUIREMENTS

20.500   An investor's financial statements should include the following disclosures about an investment accounted for under the equity method: (APB 18, par. 20)

   a. Name of the investee

   b. Percentage ownership of the investee's common stock

   c. Investor's accounting policies with respect to investments in common stock (If an investee is 20% or more owned but not accounted for under the equity method, the disclosure should include the name of the investee and the reasons why the equity method is not appropriate. Conversely, if an investee is less than 20% owned but accounted for under the equity method, the disclosure should include the name of the investee and the reasons why the equity method is being used.)

   d. Difference, if any, between the carrying amount of the investment and the underlying equity in net assets, and the accounting treatment of the difference

   e. If a quoted market price for the investment is available, the aggregate value of the investment based on the quoted price. (This disclosure is not required for investments in subsidiaries.)

   f. If equity method investments are, in the aggregate, material to the investor's financial position or results of operations, summarized information about the investees' assets, liabilities, and results of operations

g. Material effects on the investor of possible conversions of the investee's outstanding convertible securities

When determining the extent of the disclosures, the investment's significance to the investor's financial position and results of operations should be considered.

AUTHORITATIVE LITERATURE AND RELATED TOPICS

AUTHORITATIVE LITERATURE

APB Opinion No. 18, *The Equity Method of Accounting for Investments in Common Stock*
SFAS No. 94, *Consolidation of All Majority-Owned Subsidiaries*
SFAS No. 130, *Reporting Comprehensive Income*
FASB Technical Bulletin 79-19, *Investor's Accounting for Unrealized Losses on Marketable Securities Owned by an Equity Method Investee*
FASB Interpretation No. 35, *Criteria for Applying the Equity Method of Accounting for Investments in Common Stock*

RELATED PRONOUNCEMENTS

EITF Issue No. 89-7, *Exchange of Assets or Interest in a Subsidiary for a Noncontrolling Equity Interest in a New Entity*
EITF Issue No. 96-16, *Investor's Accounting for an Investee When the Investor Owns a Majority of the Voting Stock but the Minority Shareholder or Shareholders Have Certain Approval or Veto Rights*
Accounting Interpretations of APB Opinion No. 18, *The Equity Method of Accounting for Investments in Common Stock*

RELATED TOPICS

Chapter 3—Business Combinations
Chapter 8—Comprehensive Income
Chapter 9—Consolidated Financial Statements
Chapter 24—Income Taxes

FINANCIAL INSTRUMENT DISCLOSURES

Table of Contents

FINANCIAL INSTRUMENT DISCLOSURES

OVERVIEW

21.100 All entities are required to disclose certain information about their financial instruments. The disclosures, which generally should distinguish between financial instruments held or issued for trading purposes and financial instruments held or issued for purposes other than trading, include the following:

Financial instruments with off-balance-sheet risk

- Face, contract, or notional principal amount

- Nature and terms of the instrument, including a discussion of its credit and market risks, its cash requirements, and related accounting policies

- Accounting loss that would be incurred if a party to the financial instrument failed completely to perform according to the terms of the contract and the collateral or other security, if any, proved to be worthless

- Policy for requiring collateral or other security on financial instruments and a description of collateral on financial instruments presently held

All financial instruments

- Concentrations of credit risk

- Entities, except for certain nonpublic entities, also are required to disclose the fair value of financial instruments for which it is practicable to estimate fair value

Additional information is required to be disclosed about derivative financial instruments.

21.101 The accounting and financial statement disclosure for financial instruments is an emerging area of GAAP due to the increased use and complexity of financial instruments. This chapter discusses disclosure issues related to financial instruments. Accounting for transfers and servicing of financial assets is discussed in Chapter 52.

DISCLOSURE REQUIREMENTS

WHAT ARE FINANCIAL INSTRUMENTS?

21.500   A financial instrument is cash, evidence of ownership in an entity, or a contract that—

    a. imposes on one entity an obligation to (1) deliver cash or a financial instrument to another entity or (2) exchange financial instruments on potentially unfavorable terms with another entity, and

    b. conveys to the other entity the right to (1) receive cash or another financial instrument from the first entity or (2) exchange other financial instruments on potentially favorable terms with the first entity. (SFAS 105, par. 6)

Practical Consideration. The definition is necessarily broad so that it covers the variety of financial instruments used today or expected to be used in the future. Based on the definition, financial instruments include the following:

    a. *Cash.* The authors believe cash for this purpose is the same as discussed in Chapter 4 in connection with the statement of cash flows. Therefore, it includes currency on hand, demand deposits, and other accounts that have the general characteristics of demand deposits in that the customer may deposit or withdraw additional funds at any time. Although cash equivalents are not cash, they usually are financial instruments because they are contracts with the characteristics described in the preceding paragraph.

    b. *Evidence of ownership in an entity.* Common stock, preferred stock, partnership agreements, certificates of interest or participation, and warrants and options to subscribe to or purchase stock from the issuing entity are examples of financial instruments that provide evidence of ownership in an entity.

    c. *Contracts requiring the exchange of cash or other financial instruments.* Contracts that meet this criteria and are considered financial instruments include the following:

Practical Consideration (Continued).

(1) Conditional and unconditional receivable-payable contracts such as trade and notes receivable, short-term and
long-term notes payable, and accrued receivables and
payables (Contracts that will not be settled through the
transfer of a financial instrument are not financial instruments, however. For example, a loan to a stockholder is not
a financial instrument if it will be settled through a charge to
compensation or a dividend because it does not involve the
transfer of a financial instrument.)

(2) Financial option contracts such as fixed-rate loan commitments, mortgage loans with prepayment rights, and
convertible debt (A financial option contract is a financial
instrument only if it is potentially unfavorable to the option
writer, however.)

(3) Financial guarantees or other conditional exchanges such
as a guarantee of third-party indebtedness (Such contracts
are financial instruments only if the event causing the transfer is outside of the control of both parties, however.)

(4) Financial forward contracts such as a contract under which
a corporation agrees to buy back a prescribed number of
its shares at a price that will be determined based on the
value of the company at the purchase date (If the contract
is not limited to the exchange of financial instruments, however, it is not a financial instrument. For example, a commitment to acquire inventory at a fixed price is not a financial
instrument because it requires an exchange of cash for
inventory instead of for a financial instrument.)

DISCLOSING RISK OF ACCOUNTING LOSS

21.501   Accounting loss is essentially the charge to earnings that would result
from losing the contractual right or settling the contractual obligation of a financial instrument. An accounting loss may result from credit or market risks.
(SFAS 105, par. 7)

   a. Credit risk is the possibility that a loss may occur from the failure
      of another party to perform according to the terms of a contract.

b. Market risk is the possibility that future changes in market prices may make a financial instrument less valuable or more onerous.

Practical Consideration. The following illustrate the concepts of credit and market risk:

- The contractual right to cash deposits is subject to the credit risk that the financial institution will not pay when the cash is requested.

- A contractual right under a financial guarantee is subject to the credit risk that the issuer of the guarantee will not pay in the event of a default. A contractual obligation under a financial guarantee is subject to the credit risk that the party whose debt is guaranteed will default.

- The holder of an ownership interest is subject to the market risk of a loss from a decrease in value, for example, because of a decline that is other than temporary or from the sale of the interest. The issuer of the ownership interest does not recognize a loss from a decrease in value and, therefore, is not subject to market risk.

21.502   In some cases, the accounting risk related to a financial instrument is already reflected in the balance sheet. For example, the maximum risk of accounting loss associated with accounts receivable is the receivable's face amount less the allowance for doubtful accounts. (SFAS 105, par. 8) In other cases, however, the risk exceeds the amount recorded—that is, there is "off-balance-sheet risk." For example, a financial instrument that is not recorded on the balance sheet, such as a guarantee of another entity's debt or receivables sold with recourse, has off-balance-sheet risk. (SFAS 105, paras. 9–11)

Required Disclosures

21.503   SFAS No. 105, *Disclosure of Information about Financial Instruments with Off-Balance-Sheet Risk and Financial Instruments with Concentrations of Credit Risk,* requires certain disclosures about the credit and market risks associated with financial instruments. The requirements apply to all entities regardless of whether they are for-profit or not-for-profit organizations and to all periods presented in comparative financial statements. (See Paragraphs 21.507–.508 for a listing of financial instruments excluded from the disclosure requirements, however.)

21.504   Off-balance-sheet Credit or Market Risk. If a financial instrument has off-balance-sheet credit or market risk, the following must be disclosed by category of financial instrument: (SFAS 105, par. 17)

    a. The amount of risk (that is, the face or contract amount, or notional amount if there is no contract or face amount)

    b. The nature and terms of the instrument, including, at a minimum, a discussion of the instrument's credit and market risk, its cash requirements, and the related accounting policy

In addition, the preceding disclosures should distinguish between financial instruments with off-balance-sheet risk held or issued for trading purposes and financial instruments with off-balance-sheet risk held or issued for purposes other than trading. (SFAS 119, par. 14)

> **Practical Consideration.** Category of financial instrument refers to the group-ings used to manage the instruments. A category may be based on class, business activity, risk, etc. Class refers to how the financial instruments are grouped in the balance sheet or notes to the financial statements. If financial instrument categories used are other than by class, the classes of financial instruments included in each category should be disclosed.

21.505   Off-balance-sheet Credit Risk. An entity should disclose the follow-ing about each category of financial instruments with off-balance-sheet credit risk: (SFAS 105, par. 18)

    a. The amount of accounting loss that would be incurred if a party to the instrument failed completely to perform according to the terms of the contract and the collateral or other security, if any, for the amount due proved to be of no value

    b. Its policy of requiring collateral or other security to support finan-cial instruments subject to credit risk, information about its access to that collateral or other security, and the nature and a brief description of the collateral or other security supporting those financial instruments

21.506   Concentrations of Credit Risk. Concentrations of credit risk of financial instruments occur if their holders would be similarly affected by changes in economic or other conditions in meeting their contractual obliga-tions. For example, a concentration of financial instruments with credit risk would exist if an entity generates a significant number of credit sales and most of its customers are in the same geographical region. Similarly, a concentration would exist if an entity has a significant amount of receivables from entities in a particular industry (for example, from defense contractors).The following must be disclosed about each significant concentration of financial instruments with credit risk, regardless of whether the risk is off-balance-sheet: (SFAS 105, par. 20)

a. Information about the activity, region, or economic characteristic that identifies the concentration

b. The amount of the accounting loss due to credit risk the entity would incur if parties to the financial instruments that make up the concentration failed completely to perform according to the terms of the contracts and the collateral or other security, if any, for the amount due proved to be of no value

c. The entity's policy of requiring collateral or other security to support financial instruments subject to credit risk, information about the entity's access to that collateral or other security, and the nature and a brief description of the collateral or other security supporting those financial instruments

---

Practical Consideration. Cash deposits with banks, broker-dealers, and other financial entities are financial instruments with credit risk. Significant concentrations of credit risk can result when cash is deposited in a single financial entity or in two or more financial entities located in the same geographic region. In such cases, the authors believe the amount of credit risk that should be disclosed is the cash balance reported by the financial entity (i.e., the bank statement balance). The objective of the disclosure requirement is to disclose concentrations of credit risk that result from maintaining cash deposits in financial entities. Thus, the amount that is at risk is the amount for which the financial entity is responsible, which generally does not include deposits in transit or outstanding checks.

SFAS No. 105 does not address whether the amount of credit risk for cash deposits that is disclosed can be reduced by deposit insurance such as that provided by the Federal Deposit Insurance Corporation or the Securities Investor Protection Corporation. Some accountants argue that it should not. They believe that insurance merely decreases the likelihood of loss, but has no effect on the overall amount of credit risk. (In other words, there is still a risk that the insurance may not be collected.) While that may be conceptually correct, the authors believe that credit risk for cash deposits should be reduced by amounts that are federally insured. Federal insurance will fail only in the event of a national financial catastrophe, and such a negligible risk should be ignored for purposes of disclosing concentrations of credit risk.

21.507 Financial Instruments Excluded from the Disclosure Requirements. The following financial instruments are excluded from all of the disclosure requirements discussed in Paragraphs 21.504–.506: (SFAS 105, par. 14)

- Insurance contracts

- Unconditional purchase obligations subject to the disclosure requirements of SFAS No. 47, *Disclosure of Long-term Obligations* (SFAS No. 47's requirements generally only apply to non-cancelable agreements negotiated in connection with arranging financing for the facilities that will provide the contracted goods or services.)

- Employers' and plans' obligations for pension benefits, postretirement health care and life insurance benefits, employee stock option and stock purchase plans, and other forms of deferred compensation arrangements

- Financial instruments of a pension plan, including plan assets, when subject to the accounting and reporting requirements of SFAS No. 87, *Employers' Accounting for Pensions* (SFAS No. 87's requirements are discussed in Chapter 39.)

- Substantively extinguished debt subject to the disclosure requirements of SFAS No. 125, *Accounting for Transfers and Servicing of Financial Assets and Extinguishments of Liabilities.* (Extinguishments of debt are discussed in Chapter 14.)

21.508 In addition, the following financial instruments are excluded from the requirement to disclose information about financial instruments with off-balance-sheet risk discussed in Paragraphs 21.504–.505: (The financial instruments are still subject to the requirement discussed in Paragraph 21.506 to disclose information about concentrations of credit risk, however.) (SFAS 105, par. 15)

a. Lease contracts

b. Accounts payable, notes payable, and other financial instrument obligations that result in accruals or other amounts denominated in foreign currencies and included at translated or remeasured amounts in the statement of financial position in accordance with SFAS No. 52, *Foreign Currency Translation,* except (1) obligations under financial instruments that have off-balance-sheet risk from other risks in addition to foreign exchange risk and (2) obligations under foreign currency exchange contracts

FAIR VALUE DISCLOSURES

21.509   An entity must disclose the fair values of its financial instruments if it—

a. is publicly held;

b. has total assets on the financial statement date of $100 million or more; or

c. has held or issued derivative financial instruments during the reporting period. (SFAS No. 126, par. 2)

The disclosure, which may be made in the body of the financial statements or in the notes, also should include the methods and significant assumptions used to estimate fair value. (SFAS 107, par. 10) (See Paragraph 21.513, however, for a listing of financial instruments specifically excluded from the fair value disclosure requirement.) In addition, the following considerations apply when preparing the disclosures: (SFAS 119, par. 15)

- If the information is disclosed in more than one note, one of the notes must include a summary table that includes the fair value and related carrying amounts of all financial instruments. The table also should include cross-references to the other fair value disclosures.

- Fair value disclosures should be presented in a manner that makes it clear whether the reported amounts represent assets or liabilities and how the carrying amounts relate to what is reported in the balance sheet.

- The disclosures should distinguish between financial instruments held or issued for trading purposes and financial instruments held or issued for purposes other than trading.

- Fair values of nonderivative financial instruments should not be combined, aggregated, or netted with fair values of derivative financial instruments except where netting is allowed under FASB Interpretation No. 39, *Offsetting of Amounts Related to Certain Contracts.* (Offsetting amounts under FASB Interpretation No. 39 is discussed in Chapter 37.)

21.510   When it is not practicable to estimate the fair value of a financial instrument (or class of financial instruments), fair value need not be disclosed. (It is practicable to estimate fair value if the estimate can be made without incurring excessive costs.) Instead, information pertinent to estimating fair value, such as the financial instrument's carrying amount, effective interest rate, and maturity, should be disclosed. In addition, the entity should disclose the reasons why it is not practicable to estimate fair value. (SFAS 107, par. 14)

Determining Fair Value

21.511   **Financial Instruments with Quoted Market Prices.** The fair value of a financial instrument is the amount at which the instrument could be exchanged in a current transaction between willing parties, other than in a forced or liquidation sale. Quoted market prices are the best evidence of the fair value of financial instruments. If a price is quoted for a financial instrument on a number of markets, the price in the most active market should be used. (SFAS 107, paras. 11 and 20)

21.512   **Financial Instruments without Quoted Market Prices.** When a quoted market price is not available, fair market value should be estimated based on either (a) the quoted market price of a financial instrument with similar characteristics or (b) the results of a valuation technique, such as the present value of estimated future cash flows using a discount rate commensurate with the risks involved, current replacement cost, or pricing models. (SFAS 107, par. 11)

Financial Instruments Excluded from Fair Value Disclosure Requirements

21.513   The following financial instruments are specifically excluded from the fair value disclosure requirements discussed in Paragraphs 21.509–.510: (SFAS 107, par. 8)

- Employers' and plans' obligations for pension benefits, other postretirement benefits including health care and life insurance benefits, employee stock option and stock purchase plans, and other forms of deferred compensation arrangements

- Substantively extinguished debt subject to the disclosure requirements of SFAS 125, *Accounting for Transfers and Servicing of Financial Assets and Extinguishment of Liabilities*. (Extinguishment of debt is discussed in Chapter 14.)

- Insurance contracts

- Lease contracts

- Warranty obligations and rights

- Unconditional purchase obligations subject to the disclosure requirements of SFAS No. 47, *Disclosure of Long-Term Obligations* (SFAS No. 47's requirements generally only apply to non-cancelable agreements negotiated in connection with arranging financing for the facilities that will provide the contracted goods or services.)

- Investments accounted for under the equity method in accordance with the requirements of APB Opinion No. 18, *The Equity Method of Accounting for Investments in Common Stock* (Equity method investments are discussed in Chapter 20.)

- Minority interests in consolidated subsidiaries

- Equity investments in consolidated subsidiaries

- Equity instruments issued by the entity and classified in stockholders' equity in the balance sheet

In addition, the fair value disclosures do not apply to trade receivables and payables unless their carrying values do not approximate fair value.

DISCLOSURES ABOUT DERIVATIVE FINANCIAL INSTRUMENTS

What Are Derivative Financial Instruments?

21.514   Simply put, a derivative financial instrument is a financial agreement whose value is linked to, or derived from, the performance of an underlying asset. The underlying asset can be currencies, commodities, interest rates, stocks, or any combination. Changes in the underlying asset indirectly affect the value of the derivative. Authoritative literature defines a derivative financial instrument as a futures, forward, swap, or option contract, or other financial instrument with similar characteristics. (SFAS 119, par. 5) Based on that definition, a derivative financial instrument is one of the following types:

a. *Options.* Options give buyers the right, but not the obligation, to buy or sell an asset at a specified price for a given period of time. The value of an option is usually a small percentage of the underlying asset's value.

b. *Forward-type contracts.* These contracts commit the buyer and seller to trade a given asset at a set price on a future date. The agreements include forwards, futures, or swaps and usually commit the buyer to the same risks as actually owning the asset. Generally, however, no money changes hands until the delivery date, and the contract value is settled in cash without actually exchanging the asset.

Examples of derivative financial instruments include interest rate caps, floors, and swaps; fixed-rate loan commitments; interest rate collars; purchase commitments for securities; and forward interest rate and foreign currency agreements. (SFAS 119, par. 6)

21.515   The definition of derivatives excludes on-balance-sheet receivables and payables, including those that derive their values or required cash flows from the price of another security or index, such as mortgage-backed securities, interest-only and principal-only obligations, and indexed debt instruments. It also excludes optional features embedded within an on-balance sheet receivable or payable, such as the conversion feature of convertible bonds. (SFAS 119, par. 7)

Required Disclosures

21.516   The following information should be disclosed about each category of derivative financial instruments:

All derivative financial instruments (SFAS 119, paras. 8–9)

a. Face or contract amount, including a description of leverage features, if applicable

b. Nature and terms, including, at a minimum, the instrument's credit and market risks, its cash requirements, and the related accounting policy

c. Whether the instruments are held or issued for trading purposes or for purposes other than trading

---

Practical Consideration. Entities already must disclose information about the nature, amount, and terms of derivative financial instruments with off-balance-sheet risk. (See Paragraph 21.502.) Thus, the preceding disclosures primarily are directed towards options and other derivative financial instruments held that do not have off-balance-sheet risk of accounting loss.

Derivatives held or issued for trading purposes (SFAS 119, par. 10)

d. Average for the period and end-of-period fair value amounts, distinguishing between assets and liabilities

e. Net gains or losses from trading activities during the period, disaggregated by class, business activity, risk, or other category consistent with the management of those activities (The disclosure also should indicate where the net trading gains or losses are reported in the income statement. In addition, if the net gain or loss disclosure is disaggregated other than by class, the classes of derivative financial instruments, other financial instruments, and nonfinancial assets and liabilities from which the net gains and losses arose should be disclosed.)

Practical Consideration. Category of financial instrument refers to the groupings used to manage the instruments. A category may be based on class, business activity, risk, etc. Class refers to how the financial instruments are grouped in the balance sheet or notes to the financial statements.

Derivatives held or issued for purposes other than trading (SFAS 119, par. 11)

f. Description of the entity's objectives for holding or issuing the derivative financial instruments, the context needed to understand those objectives, and its strategies for achieving those objectives

g. Description of how each class of derivative financial instruments is reported in the financial statements including the following:

(1) Policies for recognizing and measuring the derivative financial instruments held or issued

(2) When recognized, where the instruments and related gains and losses are reported in the financial statements

h. For derivative financial instruments held or issued to hedge anticipated transactions:

(1) Description of the anticipated transaction whose risks are hedged, including the period of time until the anticipated transaction is expected to occur

(2) Description of the classes of derivative financial instruments used to hedge the anticipated transactions

(3) Amount of hedging gains and losses explicitly deferred

(4) Description of the transactions or other events that result in the recognition of gains or losses deferred by hedge accounting

21.517   In addition, GAAP encourages, but does not require, entities to disclose quantitative information about interest rate, foreign exchange, commodity price, or other market risks of derivative financial instruments. The disclosed information should be consistent with the way the risks are managed or adjusted and should be useful for comparing the results of applying the entity's strategies to its objectives for holding or issuing the instruments. The disclosure is likely to be more useful if similar information is disclosed about the risks of other financial instruments or nonfinancial assets and liabilities related to the derivative financial instruments by risk management or other strategy. Appropriate ways of reporting the information include disclosing—

a. more details about current positions and activity during the period.

b. the hypothetical effects on equity or annual income of possible changes in market prices.

c. a gap analysis of interest rate repricing or maturity dates.

d. the duration of the financial instruments.

e. the entity's value at risk from derivative financial instruments and from other positions at the end of the reporting period and the average value at risk during the year. (SFAS 119, paras. 12–13)

AUTHORITATIVE LITERATURE AND RELATED TOPICS

AUTHORITATIVE LITERATURE

SFAS No. 105, *Disclosure of Information about Financial Instruments with Off-Balance-Sheet Risk and Financial Instruments with Concentrations of Credit Risk*
SFAS No. 107, *Disclosures about Fair Value of Financial Instruments*

SFAS No. 119, *Disclosure about Derivative Financial Instruments and Fair Value of Financial Instruments*

SFAS No. 126, *Exemption from Certain Required Disclosures about Financial Instruments for Certain Nonpublic Entities*

RELATED PRONOUNCEMENTS

SFAS No. 125, *Accounting for Transfers and Servicing of Financial Assets and Extinguishments of Liabilities*

EITF Issue No. 84-5, *Sale of Marketable Securities with a Put Option*

EITF Issue No. 84-7, *Termination of Interest Rate Swaps*

EITF Issue No. 84-8, *Variable Stock Purchase Warrants Given by Suppliers to Customers*

EITF Issue No. 84-14, *Deferred Interest Rate Setting*

EITF Issue No. 84-36, *Interest Rate Swap Transactions*

EITF Issue No. 85-6, *Futures Implementation Questions*

EITF Issue No. 85-9, *Revenue Recognition on Options to Purchase Stock of Another Entity*

EITF Issue No. 85-30, *Sale of Marketable Securities at a Gain with a Put Option*

EITF Issue No. 86-15, *Increasing-Rate Debt*

EITF Issue No. 86-26, *Using Forward Commitments as a Surrogate for Deferred Rate Setting*

EITF Issue No. 86-28, *Accounting Implications of Indexed Debt Instruments*

EITF Issue No. 86-34, *Futures Contracts Used as Hedges of Anticipated Reverse Repurchase Transactions*

EITF Issue No. 87-1, *Deferral Accounting for Cash Securities That Are Used to Hedge Rate or Price Risk*

EITF Issue No. 87-26, *Hedging of Foreign Currency Exposure with a Tandem Currency*

EITF Issue No. 87-31, *Sale of Put Options on Issuer's Stock*

EITF Issue No. 88-8, *Mortgage Swaps*

EITF Issue No. 88-9, *Put Warrants*

EITF Issue No. 88-18, *Sales of Future Revenues*

EITF Issue No. 89-4, *Accounting for a Purchased Investment in a Collateralized Mortgage Obligation Instrument or in a Mortgage-Backed Interest-Only Certificate*

EITF Issue No. 94-7, *Accounting for Financial Instruments Indexed to, and Potentially Settled in, a Company's Own Stock*

EITF Issue No. 95-11, *Accounting for Derivative Instruments Containing Both a Written Option-Based Component and a Forward-Based Component*

EITF Issue No. 96-1, *Sale of Put Options on Issuer's Stock That Require or Permit Cash Settlements*

EITF Issue No. 96-3, *Accounting for Equity Instruments That Are Issued for Consideration Other Than Employee Services under FASB Statement No. 123*

EITF Issue No. 96-13, *Accounting for Derivative Financial Instruments Indexed to, and Potentially Settled in, a Company's Own Stock*

RELATED TOPICS

Chapter 2—Accounting Policies, Nature of Operations, and Use of Estimates Disclosures
Chapter 10—Contingencies
Chapter 20—Equity Method Investments
Chapter 35—Marketable Securities
Chapter 52—Transfers and Servicing of Financial Assets

FOREIGN OPERATIONS AND CURRENCY TRANSLATION

Table of Contents

FOREIGN OPERATIONS AND CURRENCY TRANSLATION

OVERVIEW

22.100   GAAP primarily addresses two issues that entities with foreign activities must deal with when preparing their financial statements:

a. Translating foreign currency statements to the reporting currency so that the foreign operations may be consolidated, combined, or accounted for on the equity method

b. Accounting for and reporting foreign currency transactions

> **Practical Consideration.** GAAP does not address translating financial statements from one currency to another for purposes other than consolidation, combination, or the equity method. Consequently, the guidance in this chapter does not apply to, for example, translating an entity's financial statements from its reporting currency to another currency for the convenience of readers familiar with the other currency.

22.101   Translating foreign currency statements to the reporting currency involves (a) adjusting the foreign currency statements to conform to U.S. generally accepted accounting principles, (b) remeasuring the amounts presented in the foreign currency statement into functional currency amounts, if necessary, and (c) translating functional currency amounts into reporting currency amounts. Exchange gains and losses that result from *remeasuring* foreign currency amounts into functional currency amounts are included in net income. On the other hand, exchange gains and losses that result from *translating* functional currency amounts into reporting currency amounts are not included in net income. Instead, they are reported as other comprehensive income.

22.102   A foreign currency transaction is one that must be settled in a currency other than the reporting entity's functional currency. If the foreign currency's exchange rate changes after the sale or purchase is recorded, but before payment is made, an exchange gain or loss results. Generally, an exchange gain or loss should be included in the reporting entity's net income in the period the exchange rates change unless the transaction (a) hedges a foreign currency commitment or net investment in a foreign entity or (b) is an intercompany transaction of a long-term investment nature.

ACCOUNTING REQUIREMENTS

GENERAL CONSIDERATIONS FOR REPORTING FOREIGN OPERATIONS

22.200   Because they can be influenced by wars, currency devaluations, government restrictions, etc., foreign operations should be carefully considered before they are included in financial statements of U.S. companies. Generally, a U.S. company should include earnings from foreign operations in its financial statements only to the extent that it receives funds in the United States or has unrestricted funds available to be transmitted to the United States. An appropriate provision should be made for known losses. Similarly, accounting for assets held in foreign countries should consider the fact that the ultimate realization of most foreign assets is in some degree of jeopardy. (ARB 43, Ch. 12, paras. 1–6)

OBJECTIVES

22.201   The primary objective in translating foreign currency statements and transactions is to preserve the financial results and relationships measured in the foreign currency. That is accomplished by measuring assets, liabilities, and operations in the foreign entity's functional currency and, if necessary, translating the functional currency to the reporting currency. (SFAS 52, par. 4)

Functional Currency

22.202   An entity's functional currency is the currency of the primary economic environment in which it generates and expends cash. In many cases, the functional currency is the currency of the country in which the entity is located. In other cases, it may be the currency of another country. (SFAS 52, par. 5) For example, if a foreign subsidiary's operations are (a) relatively self-contained, (b) located within a single country, and (c) not dependent on the parent's economic environment, the subsidiary's functional currency is the currency of the country in which it is located. On the other hand, if a foreign subsidiary's operations are a direct and integral component of the parent's operations (for example, if significant assets are acquired from or sold to the parent, financing primarily is supplied by the parent, etc.), its daily operations are dependent on the parent's economic environment and its functional currency is the parent's functional currency. (SFAS 52, paras. 80–81)

22.203   Often, the facts will clearly identify an entity's functional currency. If they do not (SFAS 52, par. 39) (for example, because the entity conducts significant amounts of business in two or more currencies) (SFAS 52, par. 8), management's judgment should be used to determine the functional currency. Typically, the following are some of the factors that should be considered when determining an entity's functional currency: (SFAS 52, paras. 41–42)

22.200

a. *Cash flow indicators.* A foreign entity's functional currency is the foreign currency if the entity's cash flows do not directly impact the parent's cash flows. If the foreign entity's cash flows directly impact the parent's cash flows and are readily available for remittance to the parent, the entity's functional currency is the parent's currency.

b. *Sales price indicators.* A foreign entity's functional currency is the foreign currency if its products' sales prices primarily are determined (on a short-term basis) by local competition or local government regulation rather than exchange rates. If exchange rates directly influence (on a short-term basis) product prices, the foreign entity's functional currency is the parent's currency.

c. *Sales market indicators.* A foreign entity's functional currency is the foreign currency if there is an active local market for its products (although there also may be significant amounts of exports). If sales are mostly in the parent's country or denominated in the parent's currency, the foreign entity's functional currency is the parent's currency.

d. *Expense indicators.* A foreign entity's functional currency is the foreign currency if the cost of its products or services (for example, labor, materials, etc.) primarily are local costs (although there also may be imports from other countries). If the entity's product or service costs, on a continuing basis, primarily are costs for components obtained from the parent's country, its functional currency is the parent's currency.

e. *Financing indicators.* A foreign entity's functional currency is the foreign currency if financing primarily is denominated in the foreign currency and the entity's operations are sufficient to service current and normally expected debt obligations. The functional currency is the parent's currency, however, if (1) financing primarily is from the parent or other obligations denominated in the parent's currency or (2) the entity cannot service its debt obligations without funds from the parent.

f. *Intercompany transactions.* A foreign entity's functional currency is the foreign currency if there are few intercompany transactions and little interrelationship between the parent's and foreign entity's operations. Otherwise, the functional currency is the parent's currency.

> **Practical Consideration.** An entity may have more than one distinct and separable operation, such as a division or branch. If conducted in different economic environments, each operation may have a different functional currency.

22.204   Changing the Functional Currency. Once a foreign entity's functional currency has been determined, it should be used consistently unless facts and circumstances clearly indicate that the functional currency has changed. Changes in the functional currency should be accounted for as a change in an accounting estimate. Thus, the change should be accounted for in the year of the change and prior period financial statements should not be restated. In addition—

    a. *if the functional currency changes from a foreign currency to the reporting currency,* translation adjustments for prior periods should remain in equity. The translated amounts for nonmonetary assets at the end of the period prior to the change become the assets' new bases for subsequent periods.

    b. *if the functional currency changes from the reporting currency to a foreign currency,* the adjustment needed to translate nonmonetary assets as of the date of the change should be reported in the cumulative translation adjustments component of equity. (SFAS 52, paras. 45–46)

Translation adjustments are discussed in Paragraph 22.210.

TRANSLATING FOREIGN CURRENCY STATEMENTS

22.205   Translating foreign currency statements to the reporting currency may involve the following steps:

    a. *Adjust the foreign currency financial statements to conform to U.S. generally accepted accounting principles.* Foreign currency financial statements must be presented in accordance with U.S. generally accepted accounting principles before they are translated to the functional or reporting currency.

    b. *Remeasure the amounts presented in the foreign currency statements into functional currency amounts.* If the foreign entity maintains its books of record in a currency other than the functional or reporting currency, its assets, liabilities, revenues, expenses, gains, and losses must be remeasured into the functional currency before translating amounts to the reporting currency. For example, assume a company presenting its financial statements in U.S. dollars owns a foreign subsidiary whose functional currency is Swiss francs. If some or all of the foreign subsidiary's records are maintained in German marks, its financial statements must be remeasured into Swiss francs before they may be translated into U.S. dollars. (SFAS 52, par. 10)

c. *Translate functional currency amounts into reporting currency amounts.* If the entity's functional currency is the reporting currency, further conversion is not needed. If a foreign entity's functional currency differs from the reporting currency, however, the functional currency amounts must be translated into reporting currency amounts before the entity can be consolidated, combined, or accounted for on the equity method. (SFAS 52, par. 13)

22.206   The following paragraphs discuss remeasuring amounts into the functional currency and translating functional currency amounts into the reporting currency.

Remeasuring the Books of Record into the Functional Currency

22.207   The process of remeasuring foreign currency amounts into functional currency amounts is intended to produce the same results as if the entity had kept its books of record in the functional currency. (SFAS 52, par. 10) To accomplish that, balance sheet and income statement items are remeasured into the functional currency based on historical or current exchange rates between the functional currency and the other currency as follows: (SFAS 52, paras. 47–48)

- Nonmonetary assets and liabilities should be remeasured into the functional currency using historical exchange rates (i.e., the rates in effect when the transactions occurred). EXHIBIT 22-1 lists common nonmonetary items that should be remeasured using historical rates.

- Monetary assets and liabilities, such as cash, marketable securities carried at market, inventory carried at other than cost, and most liabilities, should be remeasured based on current exchange rates.

- Revenues and expenses related to nonmonetary items, such as cost of goods sold, depreciation, and amortization of intangible assets, should be remeasured using the historical exchange rates that apply to the related assets while those related to monetary items should be remeasured using current exchange rates. Because it may be impractical to determine the exchange rate in effect on the date each revenue and expense is recognized, however, an appropriate average exchange rate may be used. Thus, for example, an average annual exchange rate might be used if revenues and expenses are recognized evenly throughout the year, or average monthly or quarterly rates might be used if significant revenues and expenses are recognized during certain periods of the year.

- Exchange gains and losses that result from remeasuring balance sheet and income statement items into the functional currency should be recognized as income or loss in the functional currency financial statements.

EXHIBIT 22-1

EXAMPLES OF AMOUNTS TO BE REMEASURED INTO THE FUNCTIONAL CURRENCY USING HISTORICAL EXCHANGE RATES

Balance sheet items:

Marketable securities, at cost
Inventories, at cost
Prepaid expenses such as insurance, advertising, and rent
Property, plant, and equipment
Accumulated depreciation on property, plant, and equipment
Patents, trademarks, licenses, and formulas
Goodwill
Other intangible assets
Deferred charges and credits, except policy acquisition costs for life insurance enterprises
Deferred income
Common stock
Preferred stock carried at issuance price

Income statement items:

Cost of goods sold
Depreciation of property, plant, and equipment
Amortization of intangible items such as goodwill, patents, and licenses
Amortization of deferred charges or credits, except policy acquisition costs for life insurance enterprises

---

22.208   EXHIBIT 22-2 illustrates remeasuring books of record into functional currency amounts.

22.209   **Applying Lower of Cost or Market Rules to Remeasured Inventory.** As discussed in Chapter 30, inventories should be recorded at the lower of cost or market. Thus, when remeasuring inventories into the functional currency, *remeasured* cost should be compared to *remeasured* market and the lower amount should be used. Applying the rule may result in a write-down to market in the functional currency statements even though no write-down may have been made in the books of record maintained in the other currency.

Similarly, a write-down to market in the books of record may have to be reversed prior to remeasuring the inventory into the functional currency if remeasured market exceeds remeasured cost. A similar procedure should be followed when assets other than inventory are required to be written down from historical cost. (SFAS 52, par. 49)

EXHIBIT 22-2

REMEASURING THE BOOKS OF RECORD INTO THE FUNCTIONAL CURRENCY

Although Foreign Company's functional currency is the U.S. dollar, it maintains its books of record in Swiss francs. During 19X6, the exchange rates between the Swiss franc and U.S. dollar were as follows:

Exchange rate at December 31, 19X6	1 SFr = $.82
Exchange rate at January 1, 19X6, when common stock was issued and land, machinery and equipment was purchased	1 SFr = $.70
Weighted average exchange rate during 19X6	1 SFr = $.75
Exchange rate when inventories were purchased	1 SFr = $.80

Foreign Company's financial statements at December 31, 19X6, remeasured from Swiss francs to U.S. dollars, are presented below:

	SFr	Exchange Rate	U.S. Dollars
ASSETS			
Cash	8,000	.82	$ 6,560
Trade accounts receivable	18,500	.82	15,170
Inventories, at cost	46,300	.80	37,040[a]
Land	150,000	.70	105,000
Machinery and equipment, net of accumulated depreciation	65,000	.70	45,500
	287,800		$ 209,270
LIABILITIES AND STOCKHOLDERS' EQUITY			
Accounts payable	3,700	.82	$ 3,034
Notes payable	20,400	.82	16,728
Common stock	1,000	.70	700
Additional paid-in capital	249,000	.70	174,300
Retained earnings	13,700		14,508
	287,800		$ 209,270

EXHIBIT 22-2 (Continued)

	SFr	Exchange Rate	U.S. Dollars
SALES	335,200	.75	$ 251,400
COST OF GOODS SOLD	235,000	.80	188,000
GROSS PROFIT	100,200		63,400
EXPENSES			
(excluding depreciation)	73,500	.75	55,125
DEPRECIATION	13,000	.70	9,100
REMEASUREMENT GAIN	—		(15,333)b
NET INCOME	13,700		14,508
RETAINED EARNINGS,			
BEGINNING OF THE YEAR	—		—
RETAINED EARNINGS,			
END OF THE YEAR	13,700		$ 14,508

a The market value of inventory in U.S. dollars is assumed to exceed remeasured inventory at cost.

b The remeasurement gain is determined as follows:

	U.S. Dollars
Cash	$ 6,560
Trade accounts receivable	15,170
Inventories, at cost	37,040
Land	105,000
Machinery and equipment	45,500
Accounts payable	(3,034)
Notes payable	(16,728)
Common stock	(700)
Additional paid-in capital	(174,300)
Sales	(251,400)
Cost of goods sold	188,000
Expenses	55,125
Depreciation	9,100
Remeasurement gain	$ 15,333

Translating Foreign Currency Statements into the Reporting Currency

22.210   Before an investor can account for a foreign entity through consolidation, combination, or the equity method, the foreign entity's financial statements must be stated in the investor's reporting currency. If the foreign entity's functional currency is the reporting currency, that poses no problem. If the foreign entity's functional currency differs from the reporting currency, however, the foreign entity's financial statements must be translated to the reporting currency as follows: (SFAS 52, par. 4)

- Assets and liabilities should be translated using the current exchange rate (i.e., the exchange rate at the foreign entity's balance sheet date). (SFAS 52, par. 12) If a current exchange rate is not available, the first exchange rate available after the balance sheet date should be used. (An investor should consider whether it is appropriate to account for a foreign entity by consolidating, combining, or applying the equity method if its inability to obtain an exchange rate is other than temporary.) (SFAS 52, par. 26)

- Revenues and expenses, including accounting allocations such as depreciation, amortization, and cost of sales, should be translated using the exchange rate in effect on the date they are included in net income. Since it may be impractical to separately translate each transaction, an appropriate weighted-average exchange rate may be used. (SFAS 52, paras. 12 and 99)

- Capital accounts should be translated using the exchange rate in effect when the foreign entity's capital stock was acquired or issued.

- Cash flows reported on the foreign entity's statement of cash flows should be translated using the exchange rates in effect at the time of the cash flows. (An appropriate weighted-average exchange rate may be used if it produces similar results, however.) The effect of exchange rate changes should be presented as a separate part of the statement of cash flows. (SFAS 95, par. 25)

- Gains or losses on translating the functional currency into the reporting currency should not be included in net income. Instead, they should be reported as other comprehensive income. (SFAS 52, par. 13) (See Chapter 8.) If all or part of the investment in the foreign entity is sold or liquidated, however, a prorata portion of the accumulated translation gain or loss should be included in the gain or loss on sale or liquidation. (SFAS 52, par. 14 and FASBI 37, par. 2)

22.211   EXHIBIT 22-3 illustrates translating a foreign entity's functional currency statements to the reporting currency.

EXHIBIT 22-3

TRANSLATING FUNCTIONAL CURRENCY FINANCIAL STATEMENTS INTO THE REPORTING CURRENCY

Assume the following about USA Company's wholly-owned German subsidiary:

- The subsidiary's functional currency is the Deutsche mark (DM). During 19X5, the exchange rates between the DM and USA Company's reporting currency (the U.S. dollar) were as follows:

Exchange rate at January 1, 19X5	1 DM = $.63
Exchange rate at December 31, 19X5	1 DM = $.68
Weighted average exchange rate during 19X5	1 DM = $.65

- The subsidiary commenced operations on March 1, 19X3, when it issued 10,000 shares of common stock to USA Company for 500,000 DM. On that date, the exchange rate between the DM and U.S. dollar was 1 DM = $.55.

- During April 19X5, the subsidiary made building improvements totaling 40,000 DM. The subsidiary paid for the improvements by borrowing 30,000 DM from a German bank and paying 10,000 DM in cash. The exchange rate between the DM and U.S. dollar at that time was 1 DM = $.64.

- On November 1, 19X5, the subsidiary declared a dividend of 1.5 DM per share. On that date, the exchange rate between the DM and U.S. dollar was 1 DM = $.66.

The subsidiary's financial statements at December 31, 19X5, translated from DMs to U.S. dollars, follow:

22.211

EXHIBIT 22-3 (Continued)

	DM	Exchange Rate	U.S. Dollars
ASSETS			
Cash	11,000	.68	$ 7,480
Trade accounts receivable	25,400	.68	17,272
Land	175,000	.68	119,000
Building and improvements, net of accumulated depreciation	455,000	.68	309,400
	666,400		$ 453,152
LIABILITIES AND STOCKHOLDERS' EQUITY			
Accounts payable	15,100	.68	$ 10,268
Notes payable	25,000	.68	17,000
Common stock	10,000	.55	5,500
Additional paid-in capital	490,000	.55	269,500
Retained earnings	126,300		78,270
Translation adjustments	—		72,614[a]
	666,400		$ 453,152
REVENUES	364,600	.65	$ 236,990
OPERATING EXPENSES	296,800	.65	192,920
NET INCOME	67,800		44,070
RETAINED EARNINGS, BEGINNING OF THE YEAR (assumed)	73,500		44,100
DIVIDENDS	(15,000)	.66	(9,900)
RETAINED EARNINGS, END OF THE YEAR	126,300		$ 78,270
CASH FLOWS FROM OPERATING ACTIVITIES			
Net income	67,800	.65	$ 44,070
Adjustments to reconcile net income to net cash provided by operating activities:			

EXHIBIT 22-3 (Continued)

	DM	Exchange Rate	U.S. Dollars
Depreciation	3,000	.65	1,950
Increase in trade accounts receivable	(15,500)	.65	(10,075)
Decrease in accounts payable	(17,300)	.65	(11,245)
NET CASH PROVIDED BY OPERATING ACTIVITIES	38,000		24,700
CASH FLOWS FROM INVESTING ACTIVITIES			
Purchase of building improvements	(10,000)	.64	(6,400)
NET CASH USED BY INVESTING ACTIVITIES	(10,000)		(6,400)
CASH FLOWS FROM FINANCING ACTIVITIES			
Payments made on notes payable	(5,000)	.64	(3,200)
Dividends paid	(15,000)	.66	(9,900)
NET CASH USED BY FINANCING ACTIVITIES	(20,000)		(13,100)
EFFECT OF EXCHANGE RATE CHANGES ON CASH	—		390
NET INCREASE IN CASH	8,000		5,590
CASH AT BEGINNING OF YEAR	3,000	.63	1,890
CASH AT END OF YEAR	11,000	.68	$ 7,480

EXHIBIT 22-3 (Continued)

If USA Company were accounting for its investment in the German subsidiary under the equity method of accounting, the following entries would be needed in 19X5:

a. Investment in German subsidiary   44,070
     Equity in earnings of
        subsidiary   44,070

     To record the subsidiary's 19X5 earnings.

b. Cash   9,900
     Investment in German
        subsidiary   9,900

     To record dividends received in 19X5.

c. Investment in German subsidiary   43,939
     Translation adjustments   43,939[a]

     To record foreign currency translation adjustments.

---

[a] Translation adjustments are determined as follows:

	U.S. Dollars
Cash	$ 7,480
Trade accounts receivable	17,272
Land	119,000
Building and improvements	309,400
Accounts payable	(10,268)
Notes payable	(17,000)
Common stock	(5,500)
Additional paid-in capital	(269,500)
Retained earnings	(78,270)
Cumulative translation adjustment at end of year	72,614
Cumulative translation adjustment at beginning of year (assumed)	28,675
Current year translation adjustment	$ 43,939

Foreign Entities in Highly Inflationary Economies

22.212   A highly inflationary economy is one whose cumulative inflation over a three-year period is 100% or more. The functional currency of a foreign entity in a highly inflationary economy is considered to be the investor's reporting currency. Consequently, if the financial statements of a foreign entity in a highly inflationary economy are stated in any currency other than the reporting currency, they must be *remeasured* into the reporting currency (i.e., the functional currency) following the guidance in Paragraphs 22.207–.209. (SFAS 52, par. 11) (The subsequent translation discussed in Paragraphs 22.210–.211 is not necessary since the remeasured functional currency financial statements will already be expressed in the reporting currency.) As a result of that process, gain and losses from converting foreign currency financial statements into reporting currency financial statements are recognized in net income rather than reported in stockholders' equity.

FOREIGN CURRENCY TRANSACTIONS

22.213   A foreign currency transaction is one that must be settled in a currency other than the reporting entity's functional currency. If the exchange rate between the foreign currency and functional currency changes after a purchase or sale is recorded but before payment is made, a foreign currency transaction gain or loss results. (SFAS 52, par. 15) For example, assume that a U.S. business purchased inventory on account from a British company for 100,000 pounds when the exchange rate between the British pound and U.S. dollar was 1 pound = $1.55. The U.S. business would record the purchase by debiting inventory and crediting account payable for $155,000 (100,000 pounds × 1.55). If the account payable was paid when the exchange rate was 1 pound = $1.65, the U.S. business would realize a $10,000 exchange loss [$155,000 − (100,000 pounds × 1.65)].

22.214   Generally, foreign currency transaction gains and losses should be included in net income in the period the exchange rate changes as follows: (SFAS 52, paras. 15–16)

     a. At the date a transaction is recognized, each asset, liability, revenue, expense, gain, or loss arising from the transaction should be measured and recorded in the reporting entity's functional currency using the exchange rate in effect at that time.

     b. At each balance sheet date, balances that will be settled in a foreign currency should be adjusted to reflect the current exchange rate.

Exceptions to the general rule apply to certain transactions, however, as discussed in Paragraphs 22.217–.218.

Forward Exchange Contracts

22.215   A forward exchange contract is a foreign currency transaction in which entities agree to exchange different currencies at a specified date and rate. Determining the gain or loss on a forward exchange contract varies depending on whether the contract is entered into for speculation or as a hedge. (SFAS 52, paras. 17–19)

   a. *Hedge contract.* The gain or loss on a forward exchange contract entered into as a hedge is (1) the difference between the spot exchange rate at the balance sheet date and the spot exchange rate at the inception of the contract (or the rate used to measure the contract at the end of the prior period) multiplied by (2) the principal amount of the foreign currency. The discount or premium on the contract is the difference between the contracted exchange rate and the spot rate at the inception of the contract, multiplied by the principal amount of the foreign currency.

   b. *Speculative contract.* The gain or loss on a speculative forward exchange contract is (1) the difference between the forward exchange rate available for the remaining maturity of the contract and the contracted forward rate (or the forward rate last used to measure the gain or loss for an earlier period) multiplied by (2) the foreign currency amount of the contract. A separate discount or premium is not recognized on a speculative forward exchange contract.

22.216   Generally, the gain or loss on a forward exchange contract should be included in net income in the period the exchange rate changes, and the discount or premium on a hedge contract should be amortized to income over the contract's life. See Paragraphs 22.217–.218 for exceptions to that rule, however. (SFAS 52, paras. 17–18)

Transaction Gains and Losses to Be Excluded from Net Income

22.217   Gains and losses on the following foreign currency transactions should be excluded from net income and reported as other comprehensive income: (SFAS 52, par. 20)

   a. *Foreign currency transactions that are designated and effective economic hedges of a net investment in a foreign entity.* For example, a U.S. company with an investment in a French subsidiary may borrow French francs in an amount equal to its investment (in French francs) in the subsidiary and designate the borrowing as an economic hedge of its investment. By doing so, it protects itself from changes in exchange rates since any decline in the investment due to changing exchange rates will be offset by a decline in the dollars needed to settle the foreign currency loan.

Practical Consideration. GAAP requires the translation adjustments related to the investment in the foreign subsidiary and foreign currency transaction to be included in the reporting entity's other comprehensive income only to the extent the adjustments offset. Consequently, any excess of the translation adjustment related to the foreign currency transaction (after taxes, if any) over the translation adjustment related to the investment in the foreign subsidiary, must be included in the reporting entity's net income rather than its other comprehensive income.

If the gain or loss related to a forward exchange contract is accounted for as a hedge of a net investment in a foreign entity (and thus reported as other comprehensive income), any discount or premium on the forward contract may be either—

(1) separately accounted for and amortized to income over the contract's life as discussed in Paragraph 22.216 or

(2) included with translation adjustments as other comprehensive income. (SFAS 52, par. 18)

b. *Intercompany foreign currency transactions whose settlement is not anticipated in the foreseeable future.* The entities involved in the transaction must be consolidated, combined, or accounted for by the equity method in the reporting entity's financial statements. (SFAS 52, par. 20)

22.218   In addition, a gain or loss on a forward exchange contract (or other foreign currency transaction) that is intended to hedge an identifiable foreign currency commitment should be deferred until the related foreign currency commitment is settled. A transaction is considered a hedge of an identifiable foreign currency commitment if (a) the transaction is designated and effective as a hedge of a foreign currency commitment and (b) the foreign currency commitment is firm. (For example, a U.S. company might commit to purchase inventory from a Japanese company at a later date and, at the time of delivery, pay 500,000 yen. To protect itself from declining exchange rates, the U.S.

company could purchase a forward exchange contract to purchase 500,000 yen at the exchange rate in effect on the date the commitment to purchase the inventory was made.) When deferring the gain or loss on such transactions, the following should be considered: (SFAS 52, par. 21)

a. The gain or loss related to the forward exchange contract generally should be deferred only to the extent the contract does not exceed the firm, identifiable commitment. However, the gain or loss related to any excess amount over the commitment also should be deferred to the extent the contract provides a hedge on an after-tax basis. (Such deferred gains and losses should be offset against the related tax effects in the period the taxes are recognized.)

b. If the hedging transaction is terminated before the commitment's transaction date, any deferred gain or loss should continue to be deferred until the related commitment is settled.

c. A loss should not be deferred if it is estimated that it will be recognized in later periods.

d. If a gain or loss related to the hedge of an identifiable foreign currency commitment is deferred, the discount or premium on the forward contract may be either—

(1) separately accounted for and amortized to net income over the contract's life as discussed in Paragraph 22.216 or

(2) deferred and included in the basis of the related foreign currency transaction when it is recorded.

INCOME TAX CONSIDERATIONS

22.219   Deferred taxes generally must be provided for the future tax effects of taxable foreign currency transactions and taxable translation adjustments. In such cases, the portion of total income tax expense attributable to amounts reported as other comprehensive income should be allocated to other comprehensive income. (SFAS 52, par. 135)

Practical Consideration. As discussed further in Chapter 24, deferred taxes should not be provided on unremitted earnings of a subsidiary in certain instances. In those instances, deferred taxes also should not be provided on related translation adjustments.

ELIMINATION OF INTERCOMPANY PROFITS

22.220   When eliminating intercompany profits, the exchange rate in effect at the date of the intercompany transaction should be used. An average or approximate rate may be used, however, if it is reasonable. (SFAS 52, par. 25)

DISCLOSURE REQUIREMENTS

22.500   Foreign operations should be fully disclosed to the extent they are significant. Foreign earnings reported beyond amounts received in the United States (or available for unrestricted transmittal to the United States) should be disclosed. (ARB 43, Ch. 12, paras. 5–6) In addition, the following information should be disclosed about foreign currency translations: (SFAS 52, paras. 30–32)

    a. *Aggregate foreign currency transaction gain or loss included in net income.* For purposes of this disclosure, gains and losses on forward exchange contracts are considered transaction gains or losses. (Dealers in foreign exchange may disclose transaction gains and losses as dealer gains and losses, however.)

    b. *Analysis of the changes during the period in accumulated other comprehensive income for cumulative translation adjustments.* The disclosure may be presented in a separate financial statement, in notes to the financial statements, or as part of the statement of changes in equity. Regardless, the analysis should include the following at a minimum:

        (1) Beginning and ending amount of cumulative translation adjustments

        (2) Aggregate adjustment for the period resulting from translation adjustments and gains and losses from hedges of a net investment in a foreign entity and long-term intercompany foreign currency transactions

        (3) Amount of income taxes for the period allocated to translation adjustments

        (4) Amounts transferred from cumulative translation adjustments and included in net income as a result of the sale or liquidation of an investment in a foreign entity

c. *Exchange rate changes occurring after the balance sheet date, including their effects on unsettled foreign currency transactions.* The disclosure is not required if the effects of the subsequent rate changes are immaterial. If it is not practicable to determine the effect of the rate changes, that fact should be stated.

22.501 The reporting entity is encouraged to supplement the preceding disclosures with an analysis of the effects of rate changes on the reported results of operations. The analysis might include, for example, the effect of translating revenues and expenses at exchange rates that are different from the prior year or the effects of exchange rate changes on selling prices, sales volume, and costs. (SFAS 52, par. 144)

AUTHORITATIVE LITERATURE AND RELATED TOPICS

AUTHORITATIVE LITERATURE

ARB No. 43, *Restatement and Revision of Accounting Research Bulletins* (Chapter 13—Foreign Operations and Foreign Exchange)
SFAS No. 52, *Foreign Currency Translation*
SFAS No. 130, *Reporting Other Comprehensive Income*
FASB Interpretation No. 37, *Accounting for Translation Adjustments upon Sale of Part of an Investment in a Foreign Entity*

RELATED PRONOUNCEMENTS

SOP 93-4, *Foreign Currency Accounting and Financial Statement Presentation for Investment Companies*
EITF Issue No. 87-2, *Net Present Value Method of Valuing Speculative Foreign Exchange Contracts*
EITF Issue No. 87-12, *Foreign Debt-for-Equity Swaps*
EITF Issue No. 87-26, *Hedging of Foreign Currency Exposure with a Tandem Currency*
EITF Issue No. 90-17, *Hedging Foreign Currency Risks with Purchased Options*
EITF Issue No. 91-1, *Hedging Intercompany Foreign Currency Risks*
EITF Issue No. 92-4, *Accounting for a Change in Functional Currency When an Economy Ceases to Be Considered Highly Inflationary*
EITF Issue No. 92-8, *Accounting for the Income Tax Effects under FASB Statement No. 109 of a Change in Functional Currency When an Economy Ceases to Be Considered Highly Inflationary*
EITF Issue No. 93-10, *Accounting for Dual Currency Bonds*
EITF Issue No. 95-2, *Determination of What Constitutes a Firm Commitment for Foreign Currency Transactions Not Involving a Third Party*

EITF Issue No. 96-15, *Accounting for the Effects of Changes in Foreign Currency Exchange Rates on Foreign-Currency-Denominated Available-for-Sale Debt Securities*

EITF Issue No. 97-7, *Accounting for Hedges of Foreign Currency Risk Inherent in an Available-for-Sale Marketable Equity Security*

Practice Bulletin 4, *Accounting for Foreign Debt/Equity Swaps*

RELATED TOPICS

INCOME STATEMENT

Table of Contents

INCOME STATEMENT

OVERVIEW

23.100   The income statement is one of the basic financial statements necessary to present a company's financial position and results of operations in conformity with generally accepted accounting principles. APB Opinion No. 9, *Reporting the Results of Operations,* states that the statement of income and the statement of retained earnings (separately or combined) are designed to reflect, in a broad sense, results of operations.

23.101   Each income statement item may be categorized as either a revenue, expense, gain, or loss. Although there are few strict rules for presenting those items in the income statement, generally accepted accounting principles require the following to be presented separately:

- Extraordinary items

- Unusual or infrequent items

- Discontinued operations of a business segment

- Cumulative effects of accounting changes (See Chapter 1.)

- Equity in operations of investees (See Chapter 20.)

23.102   Those items should be presented in the income statement in the following order:

a. Income from continuing operations, including, if applicable, unusual or infrequently occurring items and equity in operations of investees

b. Discontinued operations of a segment of a business

c. Extraordinary items

d. Cumulative effects of accounting changes

23.103   Companies may also report other comprehensive income in a combined statement of income and comprehensive income. Chapter 8 discusses reporting comprehensive income further.

ACCOUNTING REQUIREMENTS

COMPONENTS OF NET INCOME AND BASIC PRINCIPLES

23.200   According to Statement of Financial Accounting Concepts (SFAC) No. 6, *Elements of Financial Statements,* each item presented in the income statement may be categorized according to one of the following four components of net income:

- *Revenues*—actual or expected cash inflows (or the equivalent) that have occurred or will eventuate as a result of an entity's major or central operations

- *Expenses*—outflows or other using up of assets or incurrences of liabilities (or a combination of both) from delivering or producing goods, rendering services, or carrying out other activities that constitute the entity's ongoing major or central operations

- *Gains*—increases in equity (net assets) from peripheral or incidental transactions of an entity and from all other transactions and other events and circumstances affecting the entity except those that result from revenues or investments by owners

- *Losses*—decreases in equity (net assets) from peripheral or incidental transactions of an entity and from all other transactions and other events and circumstances affecting the entity except those that result from expenses or distributions to owners

23.201   Classifying amounts as revenues, expenses, gains, or losses varies among companies depending on the nature of each company's operations. Events or circumstances that are sources of revenues for one company may be gains for another. The primary differences between revenues and gains and between expenses and losses are that (a) revenues and expenses result from an entity's ongoing major or central operations such as producing or delivering goods or rendering services, while gains and losses result from incidental or peripheral events or circumstances and (b) revenues and expenses usually are recorded at their gross amounts while gains and losses usually are recorded at net amounts.

Recognizing Revenues, Expenses, Gains, and Losses

23.202   **Revenues.** SFAC No. 5, *Recognition and Measurement in Financial Statements of Business Enterprises,* states that revenue is recorded in financial statements when the following conditions are met:

23.200

a. Amounts are realized or realizable, i.e., converted or convertible into cash or claims to cash.

b. Amounts are earned, i.e., activities that are prerequisite to obtaining benefits have been completed.

Thus, as a general rule, revenue from selling products is recognized at the date of sale, and revenue from rendering services is recognized when the services have been performed and are billable.

23.203   SFAC No. 5 provides the following additional guidelines on recognizing revenue:

- If sale or cash receipt (or both) precedes production and delivery (for example, magazine subscriptions), revenues may be recognized as earned by production and delivery.

- If product is contracted for before production, revenues may be recognized by a percentage-of-completion method as earned—as production takes place—provided reasonable estimates of results at completion and reliable measures of progress are available.

- If services are rendered or rights to use assets extend continuously over time (for example, interest or rent), reliable measures based on contractual prices established in advance are commonly available, and revenues may be recognized as earned as time passes.

- If products or other assets are readily realizable because they are salable at reliably determinable prices without significant effort (for example, certain agricultural products, precious metals, and marketable securities), revenues and some gains or losses may be recognized at completion of production or when prices of the assets change.

- If product, services, or other assets are exchanged for nonmonetary assets that are not readily convertible into cash, revenues or gains or losses may be recognized on the basis that they have been earned and the transaction is completed. Recognition in both kinds of transactions depends on the provision that the fair values involved can be determined within reasonable limits.

- If collectibility of assets received for product, services, or other assets is doubtful, revenues . . . may be recognized on the basis of cash received.

23.204 Various pronouncements provide specific guidance on revenue recognition for certain transactions or in certain industries. Chapter 48 discusses revenue recognition principles in further detail.

23.205 **Expenses.** The term "matching" sometimes is used to describe the process of recognizing expenses in the same accounting period as the revenues associated with those costs. SFAC No. 5 describes the following broad expense recognition principles:

- Costs and revenues that result directly and jointly from the same transaction or event are recognized in the same accounting period, such as sales revenue, cost of goods sold, and certain selling expenses.

- Costs that are incurred to obtain benefits that are exhausted in the period in which the costs are incurred are recognized in that period, for example, salesmen's monthly salaries and utilities.

- Costs that provide benefits over several periods are allocated to those periods, for example, prepaid insurance and depreciation. Costs are generally allocated to accounting periods when no direct relationship between revenues and costs exists, and the costs cannot be identified with a particular accounting period.

23.206 **Gains and Losses.** SFAC No. 6 indicates that gains and losses generally result from one of the following events or circumstances:

a. Netting costs and proceeds of incidental transactions, such as sales of investments in marketable securities or equipment

b. Nonreciprocal transfers other than those between the company and its owners, for example, donations, winning a lawsuit, or thefts

c. Holding assets or liabilities while their values change, for example, causing inventory to be written down from cost to market

d. Environmental factors, such as damage or destruction of property by fire or flood

EXTRAORDINARY ITEMS

23.207   Extraordinary items are events or transactions that meet *both* of the following criteria: (APB 30, par. 20)

    a. *Unusual nature.* The underlying event or transaction should possess a high degree of abnormality and be of a type clearly unrelated to, or only incidentally related to, the ordinary and typical activities of the entity, taking into account the environment in which the entity operates. (An event or transaction is not considered to be unusual merely because it is beyond the control of management.)

    b. *Infrequency of occurrence.* The underlying event or transaction should be of a type that would not reasonably be expected to recur in the foreseeable future, taking into account the environment in which the entity operates.

23.208   An event or transaction should be classified as extraordinary only in rare circumstances. A presumption underlying the definition of extraordinary items is that an event or transaction should be considered ordinary and usual unless evidence clearly supports its classification as extraordinary. (APB 30, par. 19) The environment in which a company operates, including the characteristics of its industry, the geographical location of its operations, and the nature and extent of governmental regulation, should be a primary consideration when determining whether an event or transaction is extraordinary. Thus, as a general rule, particular events or transactions do not, of themselves, require classification as extraordinary items, and an event or transaction considered an extraordinary item for one company may not be considered an extraordinary item for another. (APB 30, par. 21)

23.209   The materiality of an event or transaction should be considered when deciding whether to present it as an extraordinary item. Materiality should be considered as it relates to individual items, except that the effects of a series of related transactions from a single specific and identifiable event or plan of action should be considered in the aggregate. (APB 30, par. 24)

Examples of Items That Are Not Extraordinary Items

23.210   Some events or transactions may either be unusual in nature or occur infrequently but not both, and thus do not meet the criteria for classification as extraordinary items. Examples of such items generally include the following: (APB 30, par. 23)

- Writedown or writeoff of receivables, inventories, equipment leased to others, or intangible assets

- Gains or losses from sale or abandonment of property, plant, or equipment used in the business

- Gains or losses from exchange or translation of foreign currencies including those relating to major devaluations and revaluations

- Effects of a strike, including those against competitors and major suppliers

- Adjustments of accruals on long-term contracts

- Disposals of part of a line of business

- Proceeds from life insurance on an officer

Paragraphs 23.214–.221 discuss presenting items that are unusual or occur infrequently in further detail.

> **Practical Consideration.** The preceding items could be considered extraordinary items, however, if they are part of a transaction or event that meets criteria in Paragraph 23.207. For example, a gain or loss from the abandonment of equipment used in the business could be included in extraordinary items if it is a direct result of an expropriation by a foreign government.

Examples of Extraordinary Items

23.211   The following events and transactions have been designated by authoritative pronouncements as extraordinary items even though they may not meet the criteria in Paragraph 23.207:

- Profit or loss on disposition of assets following a pooling of interests provided (1) the profit or loss is material in relation to the net income of the combined corporation and (2) the disposition is within two years after the combination is consummated (APB 16, par. 60)

- Material net gains or losses from extinguishment of debt whether extinguishment is early, at scheduled maturity date, or later (except gains or losses from extinguishments of debt made to satisfy sinking-fund requirements that a company must meet within one year of the extinguishment) (SFAS 4, par. 8)

- Material gains on restructuring payables in troubled debt restructurings (SFAS 15, par. 21)

- Material write-offs of interstate operating rights of motor carriers (SFAS 44, par. 6)

- Receipt of Federal Home Loan Mortgage Corporation participating preferred stock (FTB 85-1, par. 2)

- The net effect of the adjustments required when a company no longer meets the criteria for applying SFAS No. 71, *Accounting for the Effects of Certain Types of Regulation* (SFAS 101, par. 6)

Practical Consideration. The frequency of catastrophic events and natural disasters, such as earthquakes and floods, have brought into question whether they generally meet the criteria to be classified as extraordinary items in the income statement. An AICPA General Audit Risk Alert addressed that question and concluded that only in rare instances do catastrophic events meet the criteria for extraordinary item treatment, since they rarely meet the infrequency criterion. However, professional judgment is necessary in determining the appropriate classification of catastrophic events. The authors believe that there will be times when it is appropriate to classify the gains and losses that are a direct result of such events as extraordinary items. That treatment will usually be appropriate when the particular event is not reasonably expected to recur in the foreseeable future in the environment in which the entity operates.

Income Statement Presentation

23.212   Extraordinary items should be separately presented in the income statement, net of any related income tax effect. (Allocating income taxes to extraordinary items is discussed in Chapter 24.) Individual extraordinary items should be presented using descriptive captions and follow income from continuing operations. If the income statement includes discontinued operations or the cumulative effect of accounting changes, extraordinary items should be presented following discontinued operations and preceding the cumulative effect of accounting changes. (APB 30, par. 11) (Per-share amounts may be presented on the face of the income statement or in the related notes. See Chapter 19.) EXHIBIT 23-1 illustrates presenting extraordinary items in the income statement.

EXHIBIT 23-1

EXAMPLE INCOME STATEMENT PRESENTATION OF
EXTRAORDINARY ITEMS AND DISCONTINUED OPERATIONS

INCOME FROM CONTINUING OPERATIONS	437,000
DISCONTINUED OPERATIONS	
Income from operations of discontinued division	
(less applicable income taxes of $14,000)	33,000
Loss on disposal of division (less applicable	
income taxes of $21,000)	(49,000)
	(16,000)
INCOME BEFORE EXTRAORDINARY ITEM	
AND CUMULATIVE EFFECT OF A	
CHANGE IN ACCOUNTING PRINCIPLE	421,000
EXTRAORDINARY ITEM—Loss on early	
extinguishment of debt (less applicable	
income tax benefit of $12,600)	(29,400)
CUMULATIVE EFFECT ON PRIOR YEARS	
OF ACCOUNTING CHANGE (less applicable	
income taxes of $5,000)	12,000
NET INCOME	$ 403,600

Adjustment of Prior-period Extraordinary Items

23.213   In many circumstances, amounts reported as extraordinary items are based on estimates and require adjustments in subsequent periods. In those cases, unless the adjustments meet the criteria for prior period adjustments, they also should be reported as extraordinary items. (APB 30, par. 25) (Prior period adjustments are discussed in Chapter 42.)

UNUSUAL OR INFREQUENT ITEMS

23.214   Events or transactions that are either unusual or infrequent, but not both (and therefore, do not meet the criteria for extraordinary items), should be presented in the income statement as separate elements of income from continuing operations. The income statement presentation should not imply that the amounts are extraordinary items; for example, they should not be presented net of tax as separate line items following income from continuing operations. The nature and effects of the events or transactions should be disclosed on the face of the income statement or in the notes to the financial statements. (APB 30, par. 26)

23.215   Examples of items that may be considered unusual or infrequent, but not both, are listed in Paragraph 23.210. Captions such as "Nonrecurring items" or "Unusual items" may be used if the unusual or infrequent event or transaction is disclosed in the notes to the financial statements.

Practical Consideration. The following income statement presentation illus-trates an unusual or infrequent item. The example assumes that the warehouse closing represents discontinued operations of part of a line of business rather than of a segment of a business.

NET SALES	$350,000
COSTS AND EXPENSES	
Cost of sales	165,000
Selling and administrative	95,000
Closing of Eastern warehouse	83,000
	343,000
INCOME BEFORE INCOME TAXES	7,000

Disposal of an Activity That Is Less Than a Segment of a Business

23.216   As discussed in Paragraph 23.223, disposing of or discontinuing an activity may not always constitute the disposal of an entire segment of a busi-ness. In such cases, the event or transaction should not be reported as discontinued operations. Instead, it should be included in results of continuing operations and, if significant, reported as an unusual or infrequently occurring item. EITF Issue No. 94-3, *Liability Recognition for Certain Employee Termina-tion Benefits and Other Costs to Exit an Activity (including Certain Costs Incurred in a Restructuring),* provides guidance on reporting such transactions by discussing how employee termination benefits and other costs to exit an activity should be accounted for.

23.217   **Employee Termination Benefits.** A liability should be recorded for employee termination benefits in the period that management approves a plan of termination if all of the following conditions are met: (EITF 94-3)

     a. Prior to the financial statement date, management commits to the plan of termination and determines the actual benefits that termi-nated employees will receive.

b. The benefit arrangement is communicated to employees prior to financial statement issuance in sufficient detail to allow them to determine the benefits they will receive if they are terminated.

c. The termination plan specifically indicates the number of employees to be terminated, their job classifications, and their locations.

d. The time to complete the termination plan is short enough so that significant changes to the plan are not likely.

23.218   A termination plan may include voluntary and involuntary terminations. For example, a company might ask employees to volunteer for termination in return for higher termination benefits. If the necessary number of employees do not volunteer, additional employees would be selected for involuntary termination at lower benefit amounts. In such cases, the liability for termination benefits should be based on (a) the total number of employees to be terminated (both voluntarily and involuntarily) and (b) the benefits to be paid to employees who are involuntarily terminated. Additional benefits related to voluntary terminations should be accrued as each employee accepts the termination offer. (EITF 94-3)

23.219   A termination plan that meets the requirements in Paragraph 23.217 may require employees to continue working until they are involuntarily terminated. If so, the individual facts and circumstances should be evaluated to determine whether a portion of the termination benefits relates to future services to be performed by the employees. Any portion that relates to future services should be accounted for prospectively rather than recognized currently. (EITF 94-3)

Practical Consideration. The preceding guidance does not apply to benefits that are (a) part of a disposal of a segment of a business, (b) paid in accordance with the terms of a preexisting or ongoing employee benefit plan, or (c) paid under an individual deferred compensation plan. Paragraphs 23.222–.228 discuss disposing of a segment of a business. Accounting for termination benefits paid under an existing employee benefit plan or deferred compensation plan is discussed in Chapters 39 and 41.

23.220   **Other Costs to Exit an Activity.** A company may incur costs other than for employee termination benefits when exiting an activity. A liability for such costs should be recorded at the commitment date. That date occurs when all of the following conditions are met: (EITF 94-3)

     a. Prior to the financial statement date, management commits to an exit plan.

     b. The exit plan specifically identifies—

         (1) all significant actions that will be taken to complete the plan;

         (2) the activities that will not be continued, including the location of the activities and the disposition methods; and

         (3) the expected completion date of the exit plan.

     c. Actions will begin as soon as possible after the commitment date, and the time to complete the plan is sufficiently short so that significant changes to the plan are not likely.

The liability should include all exit costs that can be reasonably estimated at the commitment date. Other exit costs should be recognized when they can be reasonably estimated. (EITF 94-3)

23.221   An exit cost is one that meets the following two criteria: (EITF 94-3)

     a. The cost was not incurred prior to the commitment date and will be incurred as a direct result of the exit plan.

     b. The cost was incurred under a contractual obligation prior to the commitment date and will either continue after the activity is stopped with no economic benefit or will result in a cancellation penalty when cancelled.

Examples of exit costs include a cancellation penalty for a lease related to a facility that will no longer be used and relocation costs incurred from moving the operations of a facility that will be closed to another facility. Exit costs do *not* include—

     • the results of operations resulting from activities that will not be continued and that occur after the commitment date.

- costs to sell assets being disposed of as part of the plan to exit an activity (including environmental contamination treatment costs).

- expected gains from assets being disposed of. (Expected gains should be recognized when realized rather than offset against exit costs.) (EITF 94-3)

DISCONTINUED OPERATIONS OF A SEGMENT OF A BUSINESS

23.222   The results of continuing operations must be reported separately from discontinued operations of a segment. A segment of a business may be based on geographic location, line of business, or type of customer. Its assets, liabilities, profits and losses should be separately identifiable from other assets, liabilities, profits and losses of the entity for financial reporting purposes. A segment is routinely a subsidiary, division, department, joint venture or other nonsubsidiary investee of an entity. If the results of operations for the discontinued segment are not separately identifiable, the transaction should probably not be reported as a disposal of a segment of a business. (APB 30, par. 13)

23.223   In practice, determining whether an event or transaction constitutes disposal of a segment of a business is not always clear-cut. The following events and transactions, however, are not considered to be disposals of a segment of a business (although they may qualify as unusual or infrequent items as discussed in Paragraphs 23.214–.221): (APB 30, par. 13)

a. Disposal of part of a segment, a product line, or part of a line of a business, even if the operations disposed of are distinguishable such as by geographic location or physical facilities

b. Shifting production or marketing activities for a particular line of business from one location to another

c. Phasing out a product line or class of service and other changes as a result of technological improvements

d. Disposal of two or more unrelated assets that individually do not constitute a segment of a business

Practical Consideration. The authors believe disposal of a separate line of business that is not significant in relation to a company's total operations (and, therefore, does not constitute a separate major line of business) should not be reported as discontinued operations of a segment of a business even if gain or loss on disposal is material.

To illustrate determining whether an event or transaction constitutes a disposal of a segment, assume that a company manufactures men's and women's clothing and accessories through separate divisions and distributes them through manufacturers' representatives and through company-owned retail stores. The company would not be considered to have disposed of a segment in any of the following circumstances:

     a. The company closes all of its retail stores in the state of Oklahoma.

     b. The company discontinues the manufacture and sale of men's clothing.

     c. The company discontinues distributing through marketing representatives.

If the company were to shut down its clothing division and only sell accessories, however, reporting income or loss from discontinued operations would be appropriate. (Although they do not qualify as a disposal of a segment of a business, the preceding situations may warrant disclosure in the statement of income as unusual or infrequently occurring items. See Paragraphs 23.214–.221.)

Determining Income (Loss) from Discontinued Operations

23.224   Before a company reports the sale or abandonment of a segment of a business as discontinued operations, its management should commit to a formal plan to dispose of the segment. The date such a plan is adopted is referred to as the "measurement date," which is the date as of which gain or loss on disposal is estimated. Management's plan to dispose of a segment should include the following: (APB 30, par. 14)

     a. Identification of the major assets to be disposed of

     b. Expected method of disposal

     c. Period expected to be required for completion of the disposal

     d. An active program to find a buyer if disposal is to be by sale

e. Estimated results of operations of the segment from the measurement date to the disposal date (the date of closing the sale or the
date operations cease)

f. Estimated proceeds or salvage to be realized by disposal

Practical Consideration. The authors believe that the measurement date
should be the date when management is able to determine all, or virtually all,
of the preceding matters. (In other words, management should not formally
adopt a plan to dispose of a segment until it is able to determine the matters
above with reasonable accuracy.) In addition, accounting for the discontinued
operations will be facilitated if the plan of disposal designates a month-end or
quarter-end date as the measurement date.

Many small nonpublic companies do not operate in a formal manner and ordinarily would not adopt a formal plan to dispose of a segment. The authors
believe that formal action is not required, however. Formal action simply facilitates the determination of the measurement date. When formal action is not
taken, the company must use its judgment in determining the appropriate
measurement date based on the factors discussed in the preceding paragraphs.

23.225 Discontinued operations of a segment include the following
components: (APB 30, par. 15)

a. Income or loss of the segment from the beginning of the reporting
period to the measurement date

b. The gain or loss on disposal

Prior-period financial statements presented for comparative purposes that
include results of operations before the measurement date (for example, the
19X1 financial statements if a plan to dispose of a segment is adopted in 19X2)
also should be restated to present earnings or losses of the segment as a separate line item, net of tax, for those periods. (APB 30, par. 13)

> **Practical Consideration.** Authoritative literature does not mention specific items that should be included in determining income or loss of the segment prior to the measurement date. The authors believe that it should include amounts that can be specifically associated with the segment being discontinued, such as revenues and costs from products sold, operating, selling, and administrative expenses normally charged to the segment, depreciation and adjustments to value inventory at the lower of cost or market, and other similar types of adjustments that would be recognized on a going concern basis. The authors believe that indirect costs such as allocated overhead expenses should not be allocated to results of operations of the segment before disposal unless they also will be reduced as a result of the disposal of the segment.

23.226   The estimated gain or loss on disposal should be calculated as of the measurement date. The following elements, to the extent applicable, should be considered when calculating the gain or loss: (APB 30, paras. 15–16)

     a. Amounts to adjust net assets of the segment to net realizable value that are a direct result of the decision to dispose of the segment (Amounts that would have been recognized on a going concern basis should be included in results of operations of the segment prior to the measurement date.)

     b. Proceeds received or receivable, for example, from sales of assets or insurance claims, less net realizable value of assets disposed

     c. Accruals for estimated costs and expenses directly associated with the disposal, such as closing costs, costs related to relocating equipment or reassigning employees, future rentals on long-term leases that are not offset by sublease rentals, severance pay, and benefits for employees affected by the discontinued operations such as insurance and pension benefits (SFAS No. 88, *Employers' Accounting for Settlements and Curtailments of Defined Benefit Pension Plans and for Termination Benefits,* requires specific actuarial computations for pension plan settlements and curtailments arising in connection with discontinuing a segment. See Chapter 39.)

     d. Either (1) estimated loss from operations from the measurement date to the disposal date or (2) estimated income from operations from the measurement date to the disposal date not exceeding items a., b., and c. (Income in excess of the total of items a., b., and c. should be recorded only when realized.)

If a loss on disposal of a segment is expected, it should be recorded as of the measurement date. Expected gains should not be recorded as income until realized.

> **Practical Consideration.** Generally, if the measurement date occurs after the balance sheet date but before the financial statements are issued, the authors believe that costs directly associated with the disposal and the estimated loss on disposal should be accrued as of the balance sheet date as a "type 1" subsequent event. (Type 1 subsequent events are events that provide additional evidence about conditions existing at the balance sheet date and thus affect estimates inherent in preparing financial statements. If material, they require adjustment of the financial statements.)

Income Statement Presentation

23.227 Discontinued operations of a segment should be separately presented in the income statement, net of any related tax effect. (Allocating income taxes to extraordinary items is discussed in Chapter 24.) They should be presented after results from continuing operations but before extraordinary items and cumulative effects of accounting changes. (APB 30, par. 8) EXHIBIT 23-1 illustrates presenting discontinued operations of a segment in the income statement.

> **Practical Consideration.** The FASB's Emerging Issues Task Force (EITF) has studied various practice questions related to discontinued operations and provides the following additional guidance:
>
> - If there is reasonable assurance that the disposal of a segment will generate a net gain, estimated losses from operations should be deferred until the disposal date. (That conclusion assumes that the company has the ability to provide prospective information with reasonable accuracy and to carry out the plan of disposal within a period of one year.)
>
> - Gains and losses from the disposition of two or more segments may be netted, provided (1) a net gain is expected, (2) the disposals are part of the same formal plan, and (3) the dispositions satisfy all other related requirements of APB Opinion No. 30. However, netting would not be appropriate for disposals of a portion of a line of business that is not a segment of a business or for disposals of unrelated assets.

> **Practical Consideration (Continued).**
>
> - In the year a company decides to retain a segment previously reported as discontinued (1) any accrued loss on disposal at the beginning of the year should be reversed through a credit to continuing operations and (2) the segment's results of operations for the entire year should be included with the results of other continuing operations.

Adjustment of Prior-period Discontinued Operations

23.228   Because estimates are involved in calculating the gain or loss on disposal, adjustments of amounts originally reported may be necessary in subsequent periods. (APB 30, par. 25) In such cases, unless the adjustments meet the criteria for prior-period adjustments, they should be presented in the income statement of the subsequent period in the same manner as the original gain or loss. (SFAS 16, par. 16) (Prior-period adjustments are discussed in Chapter 42.) As discussed in Paragraph 23.503, revised estimates of income or loss from operations and proceeds from disposal compared with prior estimates also should be disclosed.

DISCLOSURE REQUIREMENTS

23.500   The following paragraphs describe the required disclosures for extraordinary items, unusual or infrequent items, and discontinued operations of a segment of a business.

EXTRAORDINARY ITEMS

23.501   In addition to the presentation requirements discussed in Paragraph 23.212, the following disclosures about extraordinary items are required:

- The nature of the event or transaction and the principal items entering into determination of the extraordinary gain or loss (APB 30, par. 11)

- The year of origin and nature of each adjustment in the current period of an element of an extraordinary item that was reported in a prior period (The adjustment should be presented separately in the current period income statement as an extraordinary item. See Paragraph 23.213.) (SFAS 16, par. 16)

UNUSUAL OR INFREQUENT ITEMS

23.502   As discussed in Paragraph 23.214, the gain or loss from events or transactions that are either unusual or infrequent, but not both should be presented as a separate component of income from continuing operations. In addition, the nature and financial effects of each event should be disclosed. Furthermore, the following disclosures should be made when a material liability is recognized for employee termination benefits or other costs to exit an activity:

Employee termination benefits (EITF 94-3)

a. The amount of the termination benefits accrued and charged to expense and the classification of those costs in the income statement

b. The number of employees to be terminated

c. A description of the employee group(s) to be terminated

d. The amount of actual termination benefits paid and charged against the liability and the number of employees actually terminated as a result of the plan to terminate employees

e. The amount of any adjustments to the liability

Other costs to exit an activity (EITF 94-3)

a. A description of the major actions comprising the exit plan, activities that will not be continued (including the method of disposition), and the anticipated date of completion

b. A description of the type and amount of exit costs recognized as liabilities and the classification of those costs in the income statement

c. A description of the type and amount of exit costs paid and charged against the liability

d. The amount of any adjustments to the liability

e. For all periods presented, the revenue and net operating income or losses from activities that will not be continued if those activities have separately identifiable operations

DISCONTINUED OPERATIONS OF A SEGMENT OF A BUSINESS

23.503   For discontinued operations of a segment of a business, the following disclosures are required for periods subsequent to the measurement date and including the period of disposal:

- Income or loss of the discontinued segment (net of applicable income taxes) reported separately from income from continuing operations (before extraordinary items and cumulative effects of accounting changes)

- Gain or loss from disposal of the discontinued segment (net of applicable income taxes) reported separately from income from continuing operations (If the gain or loss on disposal cannot be reasonably estimated, that fact should be disclosed.)

- Amounts of income taxes applicable to income from discontinued operations and the gain or loss on disposal

- Revenues applicable to the discontinued operations

- The identity of the segment of business that has been or will be discontinued

- The expected disposal date, if known

- The expected manner of disposal

- A description of the remaining assets and liabilities of the segment at the balance sheet date (may be disclosed by segregation of assets and liabilities on the balance sheet)

- Income or loss from discontinued operations and any proceeds from disposal of the segment during the period from the measurement date to the balance sheet date, and for periods subsequent to the measurement date including the period of disposal, along with comparisons of those amounts to previously disclosed estimates (APB 30, paras. 8 and 18)

- The year of origin and nature of each adjustment in the current period of a gain or loss on disposal of a business segment reported in a prior period (As discussed in Paragraph 23.228, the adjustment should be shown separately in the income statement in the same manner as as the original gain or loss.) (APB 30, par. 25 and SFAS 16, par. 16)

AUTHORITATIVE LITERATURE AND RELATED TOPICS

AUTHORITATIVE LITERATURE

APB Opinion No. 9, *Reporting the Results of Operations*

APB Opinion No. 13, *Amending Paragraph 6 of APB Opinion No. 9, Application to Commercial Banks*

APB Opinion No. 30, *Reporting the Results of Operations—Reporting the Effects of Disposal of a Segment of a Business, and Extraordinary, Unusual and Infrequently Occurring Events and Transactions*

EITF Issue No. 94-3, *Liability Recognition for Certain Employee Termination Benefits and Other Costs to Exit an Activity (including Certain Costs Incurred in a Restructuring)*

RELATED PRONOUNCEMENTS

SOP 93-2, *Determination, Disclosure, and Financial Statement Presentation of Income, Capital Gain, and Return of Capital Distributions by Investment Companies*

EITF Issue No. 85-36, *Discontinued Operations with Expected Gain and Interim Operating Losses*

EITF Issue No. 86-22, *Display of Business Restructuring Provisions in the Income Statement*

EITF Issue No. 87-4, *Restructuring of Operations: Implications of SEC Staff Accounting Bulletin No. 67*

EITF Issue No. 87-24, *Allocation of Interest to Discontinued Operations*

EITF Issue No. 90-16, *Accounting for Discontinued Operations Subsequently Retained*

EITF Issue No. 93-17, *Recognition of Deferred Tax Assets for a Parent Company's Excess Tax Basis in the Stock of a Subsidiary That Is Accounted for as a Discontinued Operation*

EITF Issue No. 95-18, *Accounting and Reporting for a Discontinued Business Segment When the Measurement Date Occurs after the Balance Sheet Date but before the Issuance of Financial Statements*

EITF Issue No. 96-9, *Classification of Inventory Markdowns and Other Costs Associated with a Restructuring*

EITF Issue No. 96-14, *Accounting for Costs Associated with Modifying Computer Software for the Year 2000*

Accounting Interpretations of APB Opinion No. 9, *Reporting the Results of Operations*

Accounting Interpretations of APB Opinion No. 30, *Reporting the Results of Operations*

RELATED TOPICS

INCOME TAXES

Table of Contents

INCOME TAXES

Table of Contents (Continued)

INCOME TAXES

OVERVIEW

24.100   The primary objective of accounting for income taxes is to record the tax effects of events that ultimately will affect both pretax accounting income and taxable income in the period the events occur. Authoritative literature accomplishes that objective by requiring an asset and liability approach for accounting for income taxes. That approach, commonly called the liability method, focuses on the balance sheet and on calculating current and deferred tax assets and liabilities at the balance sheet date. As a result, the tax provision under the liability method is essentially a residual amount calculated as the difference between deferred tax balance sheet amounts at the beginning and end of the year plus the current tax provision.

24.101   The following broad principles govern the requirements for accounting for income taxes:

- A current tax liability or asset should be recognized for the amount of taxes that are payable or refundable for the year.

- A deferred tax liability or asset should be recognized for the future tax effects of temporary differences and carryforwards.

- Current and deferred tax liabilities and assets should be measured based on enacted tax laws.

- Deferred tax assets should be reduced by the amount of tax benefits that are not expected to be realized.

Practical Consideration. The guidance in this chapter applies to all federal, foreign, state, and local taxes based on income. The authors consider an income tax to be any tax based on an excess of revenues and gains over expenses and losses. Consequently, the guidance in this chapter should be applied to, for example, the income based portion of franchise taxes but not to sales taxes or property taxes.

ACCOUNTING REQUIREMENTS

24.200   The basic tax provision calculation consists of the following steps:

a. Identify the taxable and deductible temporary differences and loss carryforwards available for tax reporting at the end of the year.

b. Calculate the deferred tax liability by multiplying total taxable differences by the applicable tax rate.

c. Calculate the deferred tax asset by multiplying total deductible differences and loss carryforwards by the applicable tax rate.

d. Identify the tax credit carryforwards available for tax reporting at the end of the year and record a deferred tax asset for the total of the carryforwards.

e. Provide a valuation allowance for the portion of the deferred tax asset for which there is not more than a 50% chance that the benefit of the deductible differences and carryforwards will be realized.

f. Subtract the net deferred tax asset or liability at the end of the year from the net amount at the beginning of the year to determine the deferred tax benefit or expense for the year. (The net deferred tax asset or liability is the difference between the deferred tax liability and the deferred tax asset net of the related valuation allowance.)

g. Add the deferred tax provision to the current tax provision to determine the total tax provision for the year. (The current tax provision represents the income taxes for the year as reported in the tax returns.)

The flowchart in EXHIBIT 24-1 summarizes the preceding steps.

EXHIBIT 24-1

COMPUTATION OF ANNUAL
TAX PROVISION

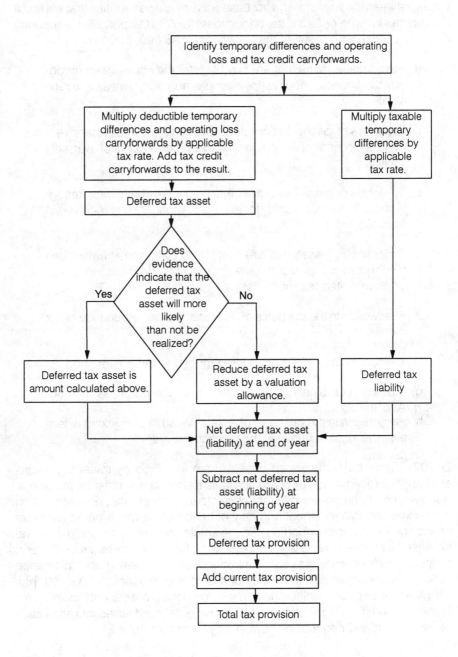

IDENTIFYING TEMPORARY DIFFERENCES

24.201   Temporary differences are differences between income tax and financial reporting that have future tax consequences. Specifically, they are differences between the financial and tax bases of assets and liabilities that will result in future tax income or future tax deductions. (SFAS 109, par. 289) Temporary differences arise as a result of the following: (SFAS 109, par. 11)

a. Revenues or gains that are taxable after they have been recognized in financial income (for example, an installment sale receivable)

b. Expenses or losses that are deductible after they have been recognized in financial income (for example, a product warranty liability)

c. Revenues or gains that are taxable before they have been recognized in financial income (for example, subscriptions received in advance)

d. Expenses or losses that are deductible before they have been recognized in financial income (for example, depreciation based on accelerated tax methods)

e. A reduction in the tax basis of depreciable assets because of tax credits

f. Investment tax credits accounted for by the deferral method

g. Business combinations accounted for by the purchase method

h. An increase in the tax basis of assets because of indexing whenever the local currency is the functional currency

24.202   Temporary differences generally are identified by reviewing assets and liabilities for financial reporting and isolating those with different tax bases. However, some temporary differences relate to amounts that only appear on the income tax balance sheet and cannot be identified with a particular asset or liability for financial reporting. For example, organization costs may be expensed for financial reporting but capitalized for tax purposes. Nevertheless, temporary differences are still determined by calculating the difference between the financial and tax bases of assets and liabilities. (SFAS 109, par. 15) (Whether temporary differences relate to specific assets and liabilities for financial reporting is significant when classifying deferred tax assets and liabilities as current and noncurrent, however. See Paragraph 24.219.)

24.201

24.203   EXHIBIT 24-2 lists examples of some of the more common temporary differences.

Practical Consideration. There are exceptions to the concept that differences between the bases of assets and liabilities for financial and tax reporting constitute temporary differences for which deferred taxes should be provided. Deferred taxes should not be provided for differences related to the following:

     a. Goodwill for which amortization is not deductible for tax purposes (Deferred taxes should be provided for temporary differences related to goodwill that is deductible for tax purposes, however.)

     b. Differences between the tax and financial bases of an investment in a leveraged lease

     c. Excess of the tax bases of assets in the buyer's tax jurisdiction over the financial bases of the assets as reported in the consolidated financial statements

     d. Differences between the tax and financial bases of assets and liabilities that will be recovered or settled in a tax-free transaction (For example, deferred taxes should not be provided for the difference between the tax and financial basis of an investment in a subsidiary if the tax law provides a means of recovering the investment tax-free and the company expects that it will use that means. Also, deferred taxes should not be provided for the excess of cash surrender value of life insurance over premiums paid if the company intends to hold the policy until the death of the insured since, under current federal tax law, such benefits are not taxable. Deferred taxes should be provided for the excess, however, if management does not intend to hold the policy until the death of the insured.)

     e. Differences between the tax and financial bases of assets and liabilities that, under SFAS No. 52, *Foreign Currency Translation,* are remeasured from the local currency into the functional currency using historical exchange rates and that result from changes in exchange rates or indexing for tax purposes

---

EXHIBIT 24-2

EXAMPLES OF TEMPORARY DIFFERENCES

The following table lists various examples of temporary differences based on current accounting and tax requirements. Specific temporary differences may change as changes to generally accepted accounting principles or income tax rules either create additional differences between the financial and tax bases of assets or liabilities or eliminate existing differences.

Marketable Securities

Unrealized gains and losses on securities that are reported as an adjustment to income in the financial statements based on the market value of the securities at the balance sheet date but are not reported in the tax return until the securities are sold

Unrealized gains and losses on securities that are reported as other comprehensive income for financial reporting but are not recorded in the tax return until the securities are sold

Receivables

Bad debts that are recognized using the allowance method for financial reporting and the direct charge-off method for tax reporting

Gross profit on sales that is recognized in different periods for financial and tax reporting:

- Gross profit recognized in the year of sale for financial reporting and on the installment method for tax reporting

- Gross profit recognized on the cost recovery or deposit method for financial reporting and installment method for tax reporting

Sales returns and allowances that are accrued for financial reporting but are not reported in the tax return until the goods actually are returned

Imputed interest for financial reporting that differs from amounts for tax reporting

Long-term Construction Contracts

Revenues on long-term construction contracts that are accounted for differently for financial and tax reporting:

EXHIBIT 24-2 (Continued)

- Percentage-of-completion method for financial reporting and completed-contract method for tax reporting

- Percentage of completion based on physical completion for financial reporting and on estimated total completed costs for tax reporting

- Percentage-of-completion method for financial reporting and cash or accrual method for tax reporting

Inventories

Inventories that are recorded at the lower of cost or market for financial reporting and at cost for tax reporting

Reserves for obsolete inventory that are expensed for financial reporting and are not deductible for tax reporting unless the inventory is actually scrapped or offered for sale at a reduced value

Inventory-related costs for manufacturers, wholesalers, and retailers that are expensed for financial reporting and capitalized for tax reporting

Investments

Investments that are accounted for by the equity method for financial reporting and the cost method for tax reporting

The excess of cash surrender value of life insurance over cumulative premiums paid, which is taxable if the insurance is terminated for reasons other than death

Property and Equipment

Depreciation for financial reporting determined using estimated useful lives or methods that differ from tax reporting

Interest income that is offset against capitalized interest for financial reporting and recognized as income for tax reporting

Assets that are recorded at fair market value for financial reporting and at a different basis for tax reporting

Gains and losses on depreciable assets that are recognized for financial reporting and deferred for tax reporting because the assets are traded in on similar assets

EXHIBIT 24-2 (Continued)

Gains on the appreciation of assets distributed as part of a liquidation that are recognized when liquidation is imminent for financial reporting and on distribution for tax reporting

Leases that are capitalized for financial reporting and reported as operating leases for tax reporting

Amortizing capitalized leases over different periods for financial and tax reporting

Depletion that is based on the historical cost of the asset (cost depletion) for financial reporting and on statutory rates (statutory depletion) for tax reporting

Intangible Assets

Intangible drilling costs that are capitalized for financial reporting and expensed for tax reporting

Amortization of intangible assets for financial reporting determined using periods or methods that differ from tax reporting

Organization costs that are expensed for financial reporting and capitalized for tax reporting

Liabilities

Debt issue costs that are amortized using the interest method for financial reporting and the straight-line method for tax reporting

Expenses that are accrued for financial reporting but deductible for tax reporting only when actually paid (for example, vacation pay, certain loss contingencies, and losses on discontinued operations)

Imputed interest for financial reporting that differs from amounts for tax reporting

Deferred Revenues

Revenues received in advance that are deferred for financial reporting and recognized as income for tax reporting (for example, subscription revenue)

Taxable vs. Deductible Temporary Differences

24.204 GAAP refers to temporary differences that will result in taxable amounts in future years as "taxable temporary differences" (or taxable differences). Taxable differences create deferred tax liabilities and generally represent expenses that have been deducted in the tax returns but that will be expensed in future financial statements, such as depreciation deducted over shorter lives for tax purposes than permitted by GAAP. They also may represent income recognized in the financial statements that will be taxable in future tax returns, such as use of the percentage-of-completion method of accounting by a small contractor for financial reporting and the completed-contract method for tax reporting. (SFAS 109, par. 13)

24.205 Similarly, temporary differences that will result in deductions in future years are referred to a "deductible temporary differences" (or deductible differences). Deductible differences give rise to deferred tax assets. Generally, they represent either (a) expenses that have been recognized in the financial statements but that will be deducted in future tax returns, such as a provision for warranty costs, or (b) income recognized in the tax returns but deferred for financial statement reporting, such as subscriptions received in advance. (SFAS 109, par. 13)

MEASURING DEFERRED TAX ASSETS AND LIABILITIES

24.206 As discussed in Paragraph 24.200, a deferred tax asset or liability should be recognized at the end of each year for all taxable and deductible temporary differences, operating loss carryforwards for tax reporting purposes, and tax credit carryforwards. The deferred tax liability is computed by multiplying taxable temporary differences by the applicable tax rate. The deferred tax asset is computed by multiplying deductible temporary differences and tax operating loss carryforwards by the applicable tax rate and adding tax credit carryforwards. The deferred tax asset should then be reduced by a valuation allowance if there is more than a 50% chance that all or a portion of it will not be realized. (SFAS 109, paras. 16–17)

Selecting a Tax Rate

24.207 A strict application of the asset and liability approach to measuring deferred taxes would require estimating the incremental effect of temporary differences. That is, deferred taxes would be determined by (a) computing the amount of taxes that will be payable or refundable in future years including carryforwards and reversing temporary differences and (b) subtracting the amount of taxes that would be payable or refundable in future years excluding carryforwards and reversing temporary differences. That method would be difficult, however, except in the simplest situations. As a practical alternative, authoritative literature requires deferred taxes to be measured using the enacted tax rate expected to apply to taxable income in the periods in which the temporary differences are expected to reverse. (SFAS 109, paras. 17–18)

24.208   Current federal tax law imposes a graduated rate structure. Corporations with taxable income between $335,000 and $10 million are taxed at a flat rate of 34%. Personal service corporations and corporations with taxable income over $18,333,333 are taxed at a flat rate of 35%. Other corporations are subject to a graduated rate structure that imposes rates ranging from 15% to 39% on various levels of taxable income. GAAP requires deferred federal taxes to be measured using the flat tax rate (currently 34% or 35%) unless (a) the effect of the graduated rate structure is significant or (b) special rates apply to the temporary difference. (SFAS 109, par. 18)

24.209   **Selecting a Tax Rate When Graduated Rates Are a Significant Factor.** In some situations, using a flat tax rate to measure deferred taxes may produce significantly different results than if graduated tax rates had been used. In those situations, deferred taxes should be computed using the average tax rate that will apply to estimated taxable income of the years in which the temporary differences are expected to reverse. The average graduated tax rate is calculated by dividing the tax on taxable income by taxable income. To illustrate, assume that currently enacted tax laws require the first $50,000 of income to be taxed at 15%, the next $25,000 to be taxed at 25%, and income above $75,000 to be taxed at 34%. A company expecting its taxable income in year 2 to be $100,000 can expect to pay taxes of $22,250 in that year. Thus, its expected average graduated tax rate in year 2 is 22% ($22,250 ÷ $100,000).

24.210   Different average graduated tax rates may apply in different years. In most cases, however, a different average graduated tax rate need not be computed for each year in which temporary differences and carryforwards are expected to reverse. Since the calculation is based on expected taxable income, which is no more than an estimate, determining a different average graduated tax rate for each future year in the reversal period is usually not necessary. Using a single average graduated tax rate based on average estimated annual taxable income during the reversal period usually will provide sufficient precision. To illustrate how the average graduated tax rate is computed based on average expected taxable income, assume that a company has a taxable temporary difference of $200,000. The difference is expected to reverse $150,000 in year 1 and $50,000 in year 2. In addition, the company expects $60,000 of taxable income from other sources in each year. Based on those assumptions, the company's expected taxable income will be $210,000 in year 1 ($150,000 + $60,000) and $110,000 in year 2 ($50,000 + $60,000), and the average taxable income per year during the reversal period will be $160,000 [($210,000 + $110,000) ÷ 2]. The company should use an average graduated tax rate based on estimated annual taxable income of $160,000. Using the method described in Paragraph 24.209, that rate would be 27%. Judgment may be used to deal with unusual situations, however. Thus, in some cases, a company may determine that more than one average graduated tax rate should be used during the reversal period (for example, if an unusually large temporary difference will reverse in a single future year or if an abnormal level of taxable income is expected for a single future year). (SFAS 109, par. 236)

24.211 **Selecting a Tax Rate When Special Rates Apply.** Certain types of taxable income may be taxed at different rates. For example, prior to the Tax Reform Act of 1986, federal tax law imposed a maximum tax rate of 28% on excess net long-term capital gains. If special tax rates apply and they differ significantly from the regular rate that would ordinarily be used, the deferred tax effect of temporary differences that will not be taxed as ordinary income should be measured using the special rates. (SFAS 109, par. 18)

24.212 **Special Considerations When Tax Losses Are Expected during the Reversal Period.** Future taxable losses cannot be considered to avoid providing a deferred tax liability for existing taxable differences. Taxable differences that reverse in a year in which a tax loss is expected reduce the tax loss. Similarly, deductible differences that reverse in a year in which a tax loss is expected increase the tax loss. As a result, they reduce (or increase) the tax benefits that will be received from the carryback or carryforward of the tax loss. The deferred tax liability or asset is measured using the tax rate that is expected to apply to the loss carryforward or carryback. If the loss carryforward or carryback is not expected to be realized, deferred tax assets and liabilities should be measured using the lowest graduated tax rate rather than an estimated average graduated tax rate of zero. (SFAS 109, paras. 233–235)

24.213 **Should Federal Alternative Minimum Tax Rates Be Considered?** Current federal income tax law requires corporations to compute taxes under the regular and alternative minimum tax (AMT) systems. The larger of the two calculations is the tax due for the year. When the AMT exceeds the regular tax, the excess (referred to as the AMT credit) may be carried forward indefinitely to offset the excess of the regular tax over the AMT in future years. The FASB views the AMT as having only a temporary effect. AMT will almost always be recovered through the use of AMT credit carryforwards. Therefore, over the entire life of an entity, cumulative income will be taxed under the regular tax system. Consequently, deferred taxes should be measured using regular tax rates, and AMT tax rates should not be considered. (SFAS 109, paras. 238–239) AMT credit carryforwards are considered in calculating deferred tax assets as discussed in Paragraph 24.200.

24.214   **Changes in Future Tax Rates.** Deferred taxes should be measured using the tax rate expected to apply to estimated taxable income in the periods in which temporary differences are expected to reverse. Thus, deferred tax calculations should consider future changes in tax rates. The calculations should only consider those changes prescribed by tax laws that are enacted at the balance sheet date, however. Changes in tax rates that are enacted subsequent to the balance sheet date should not be considered. As a result, the effects of changes in tax rates are recognized in the year the changes in tax law are enacted. (SFAS 109, paras. 18 and 27)

Practical Consideration. To illustrate selecting the appropriate tax rate when changes in future tax rates are expected, consider the following examples about a company with a taxable difference at December 31, 19X5, that is expected to reverse in 19X8:

  a. On December 31, 19X5, the President signs a tax law that raises the tax rate from 30% to 40%. The increase is effective January 1, 19X8. The company should compute its deferred tax liability at December 31, 19X5, using the newly enacted tax rate of 40%.

  b. After December 31, 19X5, but before the financial statements are issued, the President signs a tax law that raises the tax rate from 30% to 40%. The increase is effective January 1, 19X8. The company should compute its deferred tax liability at December 31, 19X5, using a 30% tax rate since that is the tax rate expected to be in effect in 19X8 based on tax laws that were enacted at the balance sheet date. (If considered material, the effect of the rate change should be disclosed in the December 31, 19X5, financial statements as a subsequent event, however.) At December 31, 19X6, the company should compute its deferred tax liability using the newly enacted tax rate of 40%.

Considering the Need for a Deferred Tax Asset Valuation Allowance

24.215   As discussed in Paragraph 24.200, the deferred tax asset should be reduced by a valuation allowance if it is likely that all or a portion of it will not be realized. In other words, a deferred tax asset should be recognized only if there is more than a 50% chance that it will be realized. (SFAS 109, par. 17) The need for a valuation allowance should be reevaluated each year based on current circumstances. Changes in the valuation allowance from year-to-year should be included in the deferred tax provision in the year of the change. (SFAS 109, paras. 26 and 35)

24.216   Whether a deferred tax asset will be realized requires considerable judgment. The potential effects of both positive and negative evidence should be weighed. If negative evidence exists, it may be difficult to conclude that a valuation allowance is not needed for at least a portion of the deferred tax asset. The existence of negative evidence does not always indicate that a valuation allowance is needed, however. In some cases, positive evidence may exist that outweighs the negative evidence, and a conclusion can be reached that a valuation allowance is not necessary. (SFAS 109, par. 25) The following are examples of negative and positive evidence that should be considered (the list is not all-inclusive): (SFAS 109, paras. 23–24)

Negative evidence

- Cumulative losses in recent years

- A history of operating loss or tax credit carryforwards expiring unused

- Losses expected in early future years by a presently profitable entity

- Unsettled circumstances that, if unfavorably resolved, would adversely affect future operations and profit levels on a continuing basis in future years

- A carryback, carryforward period that is so brief that it would limit realization of tax benefits if (a) a significant deductible temporary difference is expected to reverse in a single year or (b) the enterprise operates in a traditionally cyclical business

Positive evidence

- Existing contracts or firm sales backlog that will produce more than enough taxable income to realize the deferred tax asset based on existing sales prices and cost structures

- An excess of appreciated asset value over the tax basis of the entity's net assets in an amount sufficient to realize the deferred tax asset

- A strong earnings history exclusive of the loss that created the future deductible amount (tax loss carryforward or deductible temporary difference) coupled with evidence indicating that the loss (for example, an unusual, infrequent, or extraordinary item) is an aberration rather than a continuing condition

24.217   Whether a deferred tax asset will be realized ultimately depends on whether there will be sufficient taxable income available within the carryback, carryforward period available under the tax law. The following sources of taxable income should be considered when determining the need for a valuation allowance: (SFAS 109, paras. 21–22)

a. *Future reversals of existing taxable temporary differences* (Future reversals of taxable differences for which a deferred tax liability has not been recognized should not be considered, however.)

b. *Future taxable income exclusive of reversing temporary differences and carryforwards* (Future distributions of future earnings of a subsidiary or corporate joint venture should not be considered except to the extent that a deferred tax liability has been recognized for existing undistributed earnings or earnings have been remitted in the past.)

c. *Taxable income in prior carryback years if carryback is permitted under the tax law*

d. *Tax-planning strategies* (A tax-planning strategy should be considered as a source of future taxable income only if (1) it is prudent and feasible, (2) it is one that management ordinarily might not take, but would take to prevent an operating loss or tax credit carryforward from expiring unused, and (3) it would result in the realization of deferred tax assets.)

Practical Consideration. So long as management expects *taxable income* during each of the years that deductible differences are expected to reverse, a valuation allowance for the deferred tax effects of the deductible differences is not necessary. Since taxable income includes the effects of future reversals of current deductible differences, the fact that taxable income is expected to exist indicates that the deductible reversals will be offset by other sources of taxable income and their deferred tax effects will be realized.

Because taxable income does not include the effects of operating loss or tax credit carryforwards, however, the mere existence of taxable income during the carryforward period does not indicate that a valuation allowance for the deferred tax effects of those items is not needed. A company must still estimate the amount of future taxable income and consider whether there is more than a 50% chance that it will be sufficient to absorb the loss carryforward or that taxes on future taxable income will be sufficient to offset the tax credit carryforward.

CALCULATING THE INCOME TAX PROVISION

24.218   The income tax provision consists of the following components:

a. *Current tax expense or benefit.* The current income tax expense or benefit represents the income taxes payable or refundable for the year determined by applying the provisions of enacted tax law to taxable income. (SFAS 109, par. 289) Generally, it may be determined by aggregating the tax liabilities as reported in the tax returns for all tax jurisdictions, net of applicable tax credits, but before considering any estimated tax payments or prepayments.

b. *Deferred tax expense or benefit.* Under the liability method of accounting for income taxes, the deferred tax provision is a residual amount that equals the difference between deferred taxes payable or receivable at the beginning and end of the period. (SFAS 109, par. 16) Consequently, it is calculated as follows:

   (1) Aggregate the deferred tax assets and liabilities for all tax jurisdictions at the beginning of the year.

   (2) Aggregate the deferred tax assets and liabilities for all tax jurisdictions at the end of the year.

   (3) Record the difference between the amounts calculated in a. and b. as the deferred tax expense or benefit for the year.

EXHIBIT 24-3 presents a comprehensive example of calculating deferred tax assets, liabilities, and the deferred tax provision.

EXHIBIT 24-3

EXAMPLE TAX PROVISION CALCULATION

Facts:

- ACE Incorporated began operations in 19X5 and has reported the following amounts in its income statements and tax returns: (This exhibit uses the terms "pretax income" to refer to amounts reported in the company's income statements and "taxable income" to refer to amounts reported in its tax returns.)

	Pretax Income	Non-deductible Expenses	Taxable Income
Actual losses			
19X5	$ (299,900)	$ 5,000	$ (326,300)
19X6	(245,000)	2,500	(305,000)
Estimated future income			
19X7	24,400	3,000	4,900
19X8	20,500	4,000	7,000
19X9	15,600	3,500	34,300
19Y0	18,800	4,000	33,200
19Y1	22,000	2,500	29,900
19Y2–19Z1 (estimated amount per year)	37,600	3,400	49,700

- ACE Incorporated had the following temporary differences at the end of 19X5 and 19X6:

	GAAP Basis	Tax Basis	Deductible (Taxable) Difference	GAAP Expense Over (Under) Tax Expense
Accumulated depreciation				
19X5	$ 25,000	$ 71,400	$ (46,400)	$ (46,400)
19X6	75,000	193,900	(118,900)	(72,500)
Inventory				
19X5	$ 350,000	$ 365,000	$ 15,000	$ 15,000
19X6	370,000	395,000	25,000	10,000

EXHIBIT 24-3 (Continued)

- The company is subject only to federal income taxes. Current tax calculations assume that the regular tax exceeds the alternative minimum tax and are based on the following rate table:

If taxable income is:	The tax is:
$1 to $50,000	15% of taxable income
$50,001 to $75,000	$7,500 plus 25% of the amount over $50,000
$75,001 to $100,000	$13,750 plus 34% of the amount over $75,000
$100,001 to $335,000	$22,250 plus 39% of the amount over $100,000

There are no tax credits.

Graduated tax rates are not considered to have a significant effect on deferred tax calculations.

Tax Calculation for 19X6:

Current provision	
Pretax income (loss)	$ (245,000)
Nondeductible expenses	2,500
Temporary differences	
Depreciation	(72,500)
Inventory	10,000
Taxable income (loss)	(305,000)
Loss carryforward from 19X5	(326,300)
Loss carryforward available at end of 19X6	$ (631,300)

EXHIBIT 24-3 (Continued)

Deferred provision

	Deferred Tax Liability	Asset	Net
Net deferred tax asset at end of 19X5			
Depreciation	$ (46,400)	$ —	
Inventory	—	15,000	
Loss carryforward	—	326,300	
	(46,400)	341,300	
Tax rate	34%	34%	
Deferred tax asset (liability)	$ (15,776)	$ 116,042	$ 100,266
Deferred tax asset valuation allowance			— [a]
Net deferred tax asset at end of 19X5			$ 100,266
Net deferred tax asset at end of 19X6			
Depreciation	$ (118,900)	$ —	
Inventory	—	25,000	
Loss carryforward	—	631,300	
	(118,900)	656,300	
Tax rate	34%	34%	
Deferred tax asset (liability)	$ (40,426)	$ 223,142	$ 182,716
Deferred tax asset valuation allowance			(8,500)[a]
Net deferred tax asset at end of 19X6			174,216
Deferred tax asset at end of 19X5			100,266
Deferred benefit for 19X6			$ 73,950

EXHIBIT 24-3 (Continued)

Total provision

Current benefit	$ —
Deferred benefit	73,950
	$ 73,950

---

a The illustration assumes that a deferred tax asset valuation allowance was not considered necessary at the end of 19X5. A deferred tax asset valuation allowance is needed at the end of 19X6, however, since there is more than a 50% probability that ACE Incorporated will not realize the tax benefits of the deductible difference and operating loss carryforward. That conclusion was reached through the following analysis:

Estimated future taxable income during the carryforward period 19X7 through 19Z1 (Future taxable income includes the reversals of the existing taxable and deductible temporary differences)	$ 606,300
Operating loss carryforward	(631,300)
Operating loss carryforward in excess of future taxable income	(25,000)
	34%
	$ (8,500)

When determining the need for a valuation allowance, taxable income in prior carryback years and available tax-planning strategies that would generate future taxable income also should be considered. In this illustration, however, there is no available taxable income in prior carryback years and, for simplicity, it is assumed that there are no tax-planning strategies available to ACE Incorporated.

FINANCIAL STATEMENT PRESENTATION

Classifying Deferred Tax Assets and Liabilities

24.219   When classified balance sheets are presented, deferred tax assets and liabilities should be segregated into current and noncurrent components. The method used to classify deferred tax assets and liabilities depends on whether they relate to assets and liabilities for financial reporting as follows: (SFAS 109, par. 41)

   a. *Deferred tax assets and liabilities associated with particular assets and liabilities for financial reporting.* Deferred tax assets and liabilities that can be identified with particular assets and liabilities for financial reporting should be classified the same as those assets and liabilities. For example, a deferred tax asset related to trade accounts receivable would be classified as current since it relates to a current asset. On the other hand, a deferred tax asset related to property and equipment would be classified as noncurrent since it relates to a noncurrent asset.

   b. *Deferred tax assets and liabilities not associated with particular assets or liabilities for financial reporting.* As discussed in Paragraph 24.202, some temporary differences are associated with deferred taxable income or deductions and only appear on tax basis balance sheets. Those differences, as well as loss and tax credit carryforwards, cannot be easily identified with a particular asset or liability for financial reporting. Deferred tax assets or liabilities that are not associated with an asset or liability for financial reporting should be classified as current or noncurrent according to the reversal dates of the temporary differences or carryforwards. In other words, the portion of those deferred tax assets and liabilities that will reverse during the next year should be classified as current, and the portion that will reverse after the next year should be classified as noncurrent.

24.220   The deferred tax asset valuation allowance for a particular tax jurisdiction should be allocated ratably between current and noncurrent deferred tax assets for that jurisdiction. (SFAS 109, par. 41) Accordingly, if there is only one deferred tax asset, the valuation allowance would be classified the same as that asset. If there is more than one deferred tax asset, the valuation allowance would be allocated ratably between all deferred tax assets. For example, assume that a company has the following deductible temporary differences at the end of the year:

Accounts receivable	$	35,500
Investment in partnership		15,000
	$	50,500

Assume further that the company determines that a deferred tax asset valuation allowance of $8,500 is necessary at the end of the year. The valuation allowance would be allocated between current and noncurrent deferred tax assets as follows:

		% of Total	Allocated Amount
Current:			
Deferred tax asset related			
to accounts receivable			
($35,500 × 34%)	$ 12,070	70%	$ 5,950
Noncurrent:			
Deferred tax asset related			
to investment in partnership			
($15,000 × 34%)	5,100	30%	2,550
	$ 17,170	100%	$ 8,500

At the end of the year, the company's balance sheet would show a current deferred tax asset of $6,120 ($12,070 − $5,950) and a noncurrent deferred tax asset of $2,550 ($5,100 − $2,550).

24.221 Offsetting Assets and Liabilities. All current deferred tax assets and liabilities should be offset and presented as a single amount and all noncurrent deferred tax assets and liabilities should be offset and presented as a single amount. Income tax assets and liabilities should not be offset or netted unless a legal right of setoff exists, however. Thus, current tax assets and current tax liabilities or noncurrent tax assets and noncurrent tax liabilities should only be offset if they relate to the same tax jurisdictions (e.g., federal taxes) and to the same taxpaying entity (e.g.,the parent if a parent and subsidiary file separate tax returns). (SFAS 109, par. 42) For example, a tax asset for federal income taxes may not be offset against a tax liability for state or local income taxes.

Practical Consideration. Materiality should be considered in applying the preceding presentation principle, as it should in applying all accounting principles. Thus, the authors believe that tax assets and liabilities of different tax jurisdictions may be offset if doing so does not significantly distort the balance of assets or liabilities, working capital, or the current ratio.

Intraperiod Tax Allocation

24.222   Intraperiod tax allocation refers to the mechanics of allocating income taxes within a period to income from continuing operations and to other components of net income and other comprehensive income. Income taxes (tax benefits) for the year should be allocated to the following components: (SFAS 109, par. 35)

   a. Continuing operations

   b. Discontinued operations:

      (1) Income or loss from operations

      (2) Gain or loss on disposal

   c. Extraordinary items

   d. Other comprehensive income

24.223   The intraperiod tax allocation method focuses on continuing operations. Income tax expense is calculated on income from continuing operations and total pretax income to arrive at income tax attributable to continuing operations and total income tax expense for the period. The difference between those two amounts is allocated to income from sources other than continuing operations. The amount attributable to continuing operations is the tax effects of income or loss from continuing operations, plus or minus the following: (SFAS 109, par. 35)

   a. Changes in circumstances that cause a change in judgment about the realization of deferred tax assets in future years

   b. Changes in tax laws or rates

   c. Changes in tax status

   d. Tax-deductible dividends paid to shareholders (except for dividends paid on unallocated shares held by an employee stock ownership plan or any other stock compensation arrangement)

Practical Consideration. All categories of income or expense should be considered when determining the amount of taxes to allocate to continuing operations. To illustrate, assume that a company has a pretax loss from continuing operations of $305,500 and an extraordinary gain of $456,000 that is a capital gain for tax purposes. (Pretax income is the same for both financial and tax reporting.) Assume further that ordinary income is taxed at 35% and capital gains are taxed at 25%. For the three preceding years, the company paid income taxes of $148,750 based on taxable income of $425,000. Income tax expense allocated to continuing operations and extraordinary items under each method would be as follows:

Tax on taxable income ($150,500 × 25%)	$ 37,625
Tax on continuing operations ($305,500 × 25%)	(76,375)
Tax allocated to extraordinary gain	$ 114,000

The tax benefit allocated to continuing operations is based on the 25% capital gains rate rather than the 35% ordinary income rate because the effect of the loss from continuing operations is to offset a portion of the capital gain.

24.224 Certain tax effects should be charged or credited to other comprehensive income or equity rather than the components of net income, however, since they relate to items charged or credited directly to other comprehensive income or equity. Examples include the tax effects of the following: (SFAS 109, par. 36)

a. Gains and losses excluded from net income but included in other comprehensive income, such as the following:

(1) Changes in the market value of marketable securities classified as available for sale securities

(2) Adjustments from recognizing certain additional pension liabilities

(3) Foreign currency translation adjustments

b. Gains and losses excluded from net income, but charged or credited directly to equity, such as differences between the fair value and the cost of ESOP shares committed to be released

c. Prior-period adjustments

24.224

d. An increase or decrease in contributed capital (for example, deductible expenditures reported as a reduction of the proceeds from issuing capital stock)

e. An increase in the tax basis of assets acquired in a taxable business combination accounted for as a pooling-of-interests and for which a tax benefit is recognized at the date of the business combination

f. Expenses for employee stock options recognized differently for financial reporting and tax purposes

g. Dividends that are paid on unallocated shares held by an ESOP and that are charged to retained earnings

h. Deductible temporary differences and carryforwards that existed at the date of a quasi-reorganization

24.225   As discussed in Paragraph 24.223, amounts remaining after allocating the tax provision to continuing operations and stockholders' equity are allocated to the other components of net income. If there are two or more other components, the remaining tax provision should be allocated to each item in proportion to their individual effects on net income. The total of the separately calculated, individual effects of each item may not equal the amount of expense or benefit that remains after the allocation to continuing operations and equity, however. In those situations, the remaining amount should be allocated as follows: (SFAS 109, par. 38)

a. Determine the effect on income tax expense or benefit for the year of the total net loss for all net loss items.

b. Calculate the effect on income tax expense or benefit of each loss item, and apportion the tax benefit determined in a. ratably to each loss item in the following ratio:

$$\frac{\text{Tax benefit of each loss category}}{\text{Total tax benefit for all losses individually}}$$

c. Determine the amount that remains, that is, the difference between the amount to be allocated to all items other than continuing operations and the amount calculated in step a. to obtain the amount to be allocated to all net gain items.

d. Calculate the effect on income tax expense or benefit of each gain item, and apportion the tax expense determined in step c. ratably to each gain item in the following ratio:

$$\frac{\text{Tax effect of each gain category}}{\text{Total taxes for all gains individually}}$$

24.226 **Allocating the Tax Benefits of Loss Carrybacks and Carryforwards.** In most cases, the tax benefits of loss carryforwards or carrybacks should be reported in the same manner as the source of the income or loss in the current year rather than (a) the source of the operating loss carryforward or taxes paid in a prior year or (b) the source of expected future income that will result in realization of the loss carryforward's tax benefits. However, the following are exceptions to that general rule: (SFAS 109, par. 37)

a. The tax effects of deductible differences and operating losses that are recognized in a purchase business combination after the acquisition date should be applied first to reduce to zero any goodwill and other noncurrent intangible assets related to the acquisition as discussed in Paragraph 24.234.

b. The tax effects of deductible differences and carryforwards related to (1) contributed capital, (2) expenses for employee stock options, and (3) dividends paid on unallocated shares held by an ESOP that are charged to retained earnings should be allocated to the related components of equity as discussed in Paragraph 24.224.

c. Deductible differences and operating losses as of the date of a quasi-reorganization that are subsequently recognized generally are reported as an addition to contributed capital as discussed in Paragraph 24.227.

Practical Consideration. If no tax benefits were recognized in the year of the loss because the related deferred tax asset was offset by a valuation allowance, the tax benefits of the loss generally are characterized in the same manner as the income in the subsequent year that the tax benefits of the loss carryforward are realized. Thus, the tax benefit of an operating loss carryforward that (a) is first recognized in a company's financial statements during the current year and (b) resulted from an extraordinary loss in a prior year would be allocated to—

Practical Consideration (Continued).

    a. continuing operations if it offsets the current or deferred tax consequences of income from continuing operations,

    b. an extraordinary gain if it offsets the current or deferred tax consequences of the extraordinary gain, or

    c. continuing operations if it results from a change in circumstances that causes a change in judgment about the future realization of a tax benefit.

As discussed in Paragraph 24.223, however, adjustments of the beginning-of-the-year balance of a valuation allowance because of a change in circumstances that causes a change in judgment about the realizability of the related deferred tax asset always should be allocated to continuing operations.

24.227 Quasi-reorganizations. Generally, the tax benefits of deductible differences and carryforwards at the date of a quasi-reorganization are reported as a direct addition to contributed capital if they are recognized in subsequent years. An exception to that rule exists, however, if an entity has (a) previously adopted SFAS No. 96, *Accounting for Income Taxes,* and then (b) before adopting SFAS No. 109, *Accounting for Income Taxes,* affected a quasi-reorganization that involves only the elimination of a deficit in retained earnings by a noncurrent reduction in contributed capital. Such an entity should include the tax benefits of the prior deductible differences and carryforwards in net income when they are subsequently realized and then reclassify them from retained earnings to contributed capital. (SFAS 109, par. 39)

SPECIAL AREAS

Change in Tax Status

24.228 A change in a company's tax status generally occurs when (a) a corporation elects or terminates S corporation status, (b) a proprietorship or partnership incorporates, or (c) a corporation converts to a partnership or a proprietorship. If an entity's tax status changes from taxable to nontaxable, existing deferred tax assets and liabilities should be eliminated through a charge or credit to income tax expense for the period. On the other hand, if an entity's tax status changes from nontaxable to taxable, deferred tax assets and liabilities should be recorded for the tax effects of any temporary differences that exist on the date of the change. The effects of a change in tax status should be recognized in the financial statements at the date the entity either becomes taxable or ceases to be taxable. A change in tax status resulting from a change in tax law should be recognized in the period the law is enacted. (For federal tax purposes, that is the date the President signs the law.) A voluntary change in tax status should be recognized on the date the change is approved by the taxing authority or on the date of filing the election for change if approval is not necessary. (SFAS 109, par. 28)

> **Practical Consideration.** The taxable entity should not record deferred tax assets for the nontaxable predecessor entity's unused losses or tax credits since losses and tax credits incurred by the nontaxable predecessor entity are passed through to the individual owners and cannot be carried forward to the C corporation. (In other words, the nontaxable predecessor entity has no carryforwards for tax purposes.) Similarly, when determining the need for a valuation allowance for a deferred tax asset, income from carryback years before the entity became taxable should not be considered as a source of future taxable income since the tax benefits cannot be realized through carryback against income of the predecessor nontaxable entity.

Multiple Tax Jurisdictions

24.229   Deferred taxes should be provided for the tax effects of all federal, state, local, and foreign income taxes to which the entity is subject. If state or local taxable income is based on taxable income for federal reporting, temporary differences generally are the same for each jurisdiction. Some state and local laws require taxable income to be determined differently than for federal tax reporting. For example, they may permit deductions for bad debts based on the allowance method or require depreciation to be computed differently than for federal reporting. In such cases, temporary differences and carryforwards may not be the same for each jurisdiction. If the differences are significant, separate deferred tax computations will be necessary. (SFAS 109, par. 19)

> **Practical Consideration.** If temporary differences and carryforwards are the same for federal and state reporting, a combined tax rate may be used to simplify the deferred tax calculation. The combined rate, which reflects the interaction of federal and state income taxes, can be determined by the following formula:
>
> combined tax rate = [federal tax rate × (100% − state tax rate)] + state tax rate

Discounting Deferred Taxes

24.230   Deferred taxes should not be discounted to reflect the time value of money. (APB 10, par. 6) (Discounting was specifically excluded from the scope of the authoritative literature on accounting for income taxes because it is part of a broad project currently underway at the FASB on present value based measurements in financial statements.)

Regulated Enterprises

24.231   Regulated enterprises are not exempt from the authoritative literature on accounting for income taxes. Specifically, they are—

    a. prohibited from accounting and reporting net-of-tax.

    b. required to recognize a deferred tax liability for (1) tax benefits that flow through to customers when temporary differences originate and (2) the equity component of the allowance for funds used during construction.

    c. required to adjust a deferred tax liability or asset for an enacted change in tax laws or rates.

24.232   If an action by a regulator makes it probable that the future increase or decrease in taxes payable for items b. and c. above will be recovered from or returned to customers through future rates, an asset or liability should be recognized for the probable future revenue (or reduction in future revenue) in accordance with SFAS No. 71, *Accounting for the Effects of Certain Types of Regulation.* That asset or liability is a temporary difference for which a deferred tax asset or liability should be recorded. (SFAS 109, par. 29)

Business Combinations

24.233   When the purchase method is used to account for a business combination, GAAP requires the purchase price to be allocated to assets and liabilities based on their fair values at the date of acquisition. (See Chapter 3.) If the combination is nontaxable, the tax basis of the acquired company generally becomes the tax basis of the acquirer, and the financial basis of the acquired assets and liabilities usually will differ from their tax bases. If the combination is taxable, the purchase price also is allocated to the acquired assets and liabilities for tax reporting, although differences between the financial and tax basis of the assets and liabilities may still arise. Differences between the financial and tax bases of assets and liabilities acquired in a business combination are temporary differences. Accordingly, the deferred tax effect of the differences should be determined at the acquisition date and a portion of the purchase price allocated to it. (SFAS 109, paras. 259 and 261)

24.234   If a valuation allowance is provided for a deferred tax asset for an acquired company's deductible differences or operating loss or tax credit carryforwards at the acquisition date, the tax benefits of those items that are later realized (i.e., through elimination of the valuation allowance) should be applied first to reduce goodwill to zero and then to reduce any other noncurrent intangible assets related to the acquisition. Any benefits remaining should be applied to reduce income tax expense. (SFAS 109, par. 261)

Temporary Differences Whose Reversal Is Indefinite

24.235   Deferred tax assets and liabilities should not be recognized for the following types of temporary differences unless it becomes apparent that they will reverse in the foreseeable future: (The exemptions should not be applied to analogous types of temporary differences.) (SFAS 109, par. 31)

  a. Temporary difference related to an investment in a foreign sub-sidiary or foreign corporate joint venture that is essentially permanent in duration

  b. Undistributed earnings of a domestic subsidiary or a domestic corporate joint venture that is essentially permanent in duration that arose in fiscal years beginning on or before December 15, 1992

  c. Bad debt reserves for tax purposes of U.S. savings and loan associations (and other qualified thrift lenders) that arose in tax years beginning before December 31, 1987

  d. Policyholders' surplus of stock life insurance companies that arose in fiscal years beginning on or before December 15, 1992

In addition, U.S. steamship companies should record deferred taxes related to deposits in statutory reserve funds on a prospective basis after SFAS No. 109, *Accounting for Income Taxes,* is adopted. That is, the tax effects of those temporary differences that arise after SFAS No. 109 is adopted should be recorded in the period that they arise. The tax effects of temporary differences that existed before the Statement is adopted should be recognized either as they reverse or in their entirety when the Statement is adopted. (SFAS 109, par. 32)

Separate Financial Statements of a Subsidiary

24.236   Consolidated income tax expense may be allocated among the affiliated entities so that each of the affiliates may record its share of the consolidated income tax expense on its own books. (The allocation is necessary if separate financial statements will be prepared for the affiliates.) The allocation method used should be systematic, rational, and consistent with the liability method of accounting for income taxes. Methods that are not consistent (and thus prohibited) include the following: (SFAS 109, par. 40)

a. A method that allocates only current taxes payable to a member of the group that has taxable temporary differences

b. A method that allocates deferred taxes to a member of the group using a method fundamentally different from the asset and liability method

c. A method that allocates no current or deferred tax expense to a member of the group that has taxable income because the consolidated group has no current or deferred tax expense

24.237　A method that allocates current and deferred taxes to members of the group by applying the liability method to each member as if it were a separate taxpayer is acceptable even though the sum of the individual tax provisions may not equal the consolidated amount. That is because the difference between the consolidated provision and the total of the amounts allocated to the separate entities is a result of consolidation and has no effect on the consolidated statements. (SFAS 109, par. 40)

Interim Period Financial Statements

24.238　The basic premise underlying GAAP for interim periods is that interim periods are an integral part of an annual period, and annual results should be allocated to interim periods. (Certain revenues and expenses directly related to a specific interim period, including items such as significant unusual or infrequently occurring items, extraordinary items, and discontinued operations, should be reported in the interim period in which they occur rather than prorated over the balance of the fiscal year, however.) Under that view, interim income tax provisions related to ordinary income or loss (that is, income or loss from continuing operations before income taxes, excluding unusual or infrequently occurring items) are determined using an estimated annual effective tax rate (or tax benefit rate) that is based on estimated annual results. And the tax effects of unusual or infrequently occurring items, extraordinary items, discontinued operations, and cumulative effects of accounting changes are recorded in the period they occur. Interim tax effects of ordinary income or loss are determined as follows: (FASBI 18, paras. 6–9)

a. Estimate ordinary income or loss for the year and calculate the related income tax provision.

b. Determine the estimated annual effective tax rate (or tax benefit rate) by dividing the estimated income tax provision for the year by estimated ordinary income or loss for the year.

c. Determine the year-to-date tax provision or benefit by multiplying year-to-date ordinary income or loss by the estimated annual effective tax rate.

d. Subtract the tax provision related to ordinary income or loss through the preceding interim period from the provision calculated in step c. to determine the tax effect to report in the current interim period.

24.239   Certain limitations apply when an ordinary loss is expected for the year, however. The following must be considered when calculating interim income taxes and an ordinary loss is expected for the year: (FASBI 18, paras. 12–13)

a. If there is year-to-date ordinary income, year-to-date taxes are calculated by multiplying the year-to-date ordinary income by the estimated annual tax benefit rate.

b. If there is a year-to-date ordinary loss that is less than the estimated ordinary loss for the year, a deferred tax asset should be recognized at the interim date if the tax benefits of the loss are expected to be recognizable as a deferred tax asset at the end of the year. That limitation is accomplished by reflecting the tax effect of the expected year-end valuation allowance in the effective tax rate.

c. If there is a year-to-date ordinary loss that exceeds the estimated ordinary loss for the year, the year-to-date tax benefit is the lesser of (1) the amount calculated by applying the estimated annual tax benefit rate to the year-to-date ordinary loss or (2) the tax benefit obtained by applying the estimated annual tax benefit rate to ordinary income for the remainder of the year that is more likely than not plus the tax benefit of the excess loss that can be carried back to taxable income of prior years and the tax benefit of any remaining excess loss that is recognizable as a deferred tax asset at the end of the year. That limitation is accomplished by substituting the year-to-date ordinary loss for the estimated annual ordinary loss.

Practical Consideration. GAAP does not discuss how to allocate or classify an interim income tax provision to components of current and noncurrent taxes payable. Since the objective is to allocate annual results to interim periods, the authors believe that the interim income tax provision should be apportioned between current and noncurrent income tax assets and liabilities based on estimated annual results.

Practical Consideration (Continued).

Following the steps in Paragraph 24.238 for calculating the interim tax provision will provide estimates of the total tax provision for the year and its current and deferred components. Generally, those two amounts will be added together in determining the estimated annual effective tax rate and may be used to allocate the year-to-date interim income tax provision to the appropriate income tax balance sheet accounts as follows:

a. Divide the estimated total current provision for the year by the estimated total provision for the year, and multiply the result by the year-to-date total tax provision to determine the total year-to-date current provision. The resulting amount is the adjustment to refundable or accrued income taxes, and the balance ordinarily is classified as current.

b. Subtract the result of step a. from the total year-to-date tax provision to determine the total year-to-date deferred tax provision.

c. Determine the current and noncurrent portions of the estimated deferred tax asset or liability at the end of the year, and calculate the estimated change in the current and noncurrent balances from the beginning of the year to the end of the year.

d. Divide the change in the current deferred tax asset or liability by the total estimated deferred tax provision for the year, and multiply the result by the total year-to-date deferred tax provision from step b. to determine the adjustment to the current deferred tax asset or liability.

e. Subtract the result of step d. from the total year-to-date deferred tax provision in step b. to determine the adjustment to the noncurrent deferred tax asset or liability.

24.240 **Changes in Tax Rates or New Tax Legislation.** Deferred tax assets and liabilities in both annual and interim financial statements should be adjusted for the effects of changes in tax laws or rates in the period that includes the enactment date, that is, for federal tax purposes, the period in which the President signs the legislation and it becomes law. (FASBI 18, paras. 23–24) (For example, the President signed the Revenue Reconciliation Act of 1993 on August 10, 1993. Although many provisions of the Act were effective retroactively to the beginning of 1993, deferred tax assets and liabilities should have been adjusted for the effects of the change in tax law during the period that included August 10, 1993.) Thus, in any interim period that includes a change, the tax provision or benefit generally should be computed by (a) recomputing the estimated annual effective tax rate based on the newly enacted laws, (b) computing the year-to-date tax provision or benefit based on the new estimated annual effective tax rate, and (c) subtracting the year-to-date tax provision or benefit from the provision or benefit reported through the end of the preceding interim period.

Accounting for Investment Tax Credits

24.241   Two methods of accounting for investment tax credits (ITC) are commonly used—the flow-through method, in which the benefits of ITC are recognized in income in the period the qualifying property is acquired, (APB 4, par. 10) and the deferral method, in which the benefits of ITC are amortized over the life of the qualifying property (APB 2, par. 13). Although the flow-through method is conceptually more consistent with GAAP for accounting for income taxes, either method may be used. Once a method of accounting for ITC has been chosen, however, it must be applied consistently from year to year. (APB 2, paras. 14–15 and APB 4, paras. 10–11)

> **Practical Consideration.** Generally, the investment tax credit is no longer available under current federal tax law. However, ITC carryforwards may still exist, and Congress may reinstate the investment tax credit at some future date.

DISCLOSURE REQUIREMENTS

24.500   The following information about income taxes should be disclosed:

Accounting policies

a. Types of temporary differences and carryforwards that result in significant portions of deferred tax assets or liabilities (Public companies must disclose the approximate tax effect, before allocation of valuation allowances, of each type.) (SFAS 109, par. 43)

b. For a public company not subject to income taxes because its income is taxed directly to its owners, that fact and the net difference between the tax and financial bases of its assets and liabilities (SFAS 109, par. 43)

c. Method of accounting for the investment tax credit (if applicable) (APB 4, par. 11)

> **Practical Consideration.** Although not specifically required, many companies also disclose the method used to account for income taxes. The authors believe a brief disclosure about how deferred taxes are calculated is helpful, particularly for users not familiar with the liability method of accounting for income taxes.

Deferred tax assets and liabilities (SFAS 109, paras. 43–44)

a. Total of all deferred tax liabilities

b. Total of all deferred tax assets

c. Total valuation allowance recognized for deferred tax assets

d. Net change during the year in the total valuation allowance

e. If a deferred tax liability is not recognized because of the exceptions discussed in Paragraph 24.235—

   (1) a description of the types of temporary differences for which a deferred tax liability has not been recognized and the types of events that would cause the temporary differences to become taxable

   (2) the cumulative amount of each type of temporary difference

   (3) the amount of the unrecognized deferred tax liability for temporary differences related to investments in foreign subsidiaries and foreign corporate joint ventures that are essentially permanent in duration if determination of that liability is practicable (or a statement that determination is not practicable)

   (4) the amount of the unrecognized deferred tax liability for temporary differences related to undistributed domestic earnings, the bad-debt reserve for tax purposes of a U.S. savings and loan association or other qualified thrift lender, the policyholders' surplus of a life insurance enterprise, and the statutory reserve funds of a U.S. steamship enterprise

Income tax expense (SFAS 109, paras. 45–47)

a. Significant components of income tax expense attributable to continuing operations for each year presented, including, for example—

   (1) current income tax expense or benefit

   (2) deferred tax expense or benefit (excluding the effects of other components listed below)

   (3) investment tax credits

   (4) government grants (to the extent recognized as a reduction of income tax expense)

   (5) benefits of operating loss carryforwards

   (6) tax expense that results from allocating certain tax benefits either directly to contributed capital or to reduce an acquired company's goodwill (or other noncurrent intangible asset)

   (7) adjustments of deferred tax assets or liabilities for enacted changes in tax laws or rates or a change in a company's tax status

   (8) adjustments of the beginning-of-the-year balance of a valuation allowance because of a change in circumstances that causes a change in judgment about the realizability of the related deferred tax asset in future years

---

Practical Consideration. The total of the components of tax expense should equal the tax expense related to continuing operations that is reported in the income statement.

---

b. For each year presented, income tax expense or benefit allocated to (1) continuing operations, (2) discontinued operations, (3) extraordinary items, (4) items charged or credited directly to stockholders' equity, and (5) prior-period adjustments

c. Significant reconciling items between income tax expense attributable to continuing operations for the year and the amount of income tax expense that would result from applying domestic federal statutory rates to pretax income from continuing operations (Public companies must present a numerical reconciliation using either percentages or dollar amounts.)

Other disclosures

a. Amounts and expiration dates of operating loss and tax credit carryforwards for tax purposes

b. Any portion of the valuation allowance for deferred tax assets for which subsequently recognized tax benefits will be allocated to reduce goodwill or other noncurrent intangible assets of an acquired company or directly to contributed capital

c. In the separately issued financial statements of an entity that is part of a group that files a consolidated tax return—

   (1) the aggregate amount of current and deferred tax expense for each income statement presented

   (2) the amount of any tax-related balances due to or from affiliates as of the date of each balance sheet presented

   (3) the principal provisions of the method by which the consolidated amount of current and deferred tax expense is allocated to members of the group

   (4) the nature and effect of any changes in the method of allocating current and deferred tax expense to members of the group and in determining the related balances due to or from affiliates during each year for which the disclosures in (1) and (2) are presented (SFAS 109, paras. 48–49)

d. Method of accounting for the sale or purchase of tax benefits through tax leases, including the methods used to recognize revenue and allocate income tax benefits and asset costs to current and future periods (FTB 82-1, par. 4)

e. If unusual or infrequent, the nature and financial effects of sales or purchases of tax benefits through tax leases (FTB 82-1, par. 6)

f. Significant contingencies existing with respect to sales or purchases of tax benefits through tax leases (FTB 82-1, par. 7)

g. Nature and effect of any other significant matters affecting comparability of information for all periods presented, if not otherwise apparent from the preceding disclosures (SFAS 109, par. 47)

24.500

> **Practical Consideration.** FASB Implementation Guide, *A Guide to Implementation of Statement 109, Accounting for Income Taxes,* requires a company to disclose a change in its tax status that becomes effective after year end but before the financial statements are issued.

24.501   In addition, the statement of cash flows should disclose the amount of income taxes paid during the period (a) as a separate class of operating cash payments if the direct method of reporting cash flows from operating activities is used or (b) as a separate item outside the statement if the indirect method of reporting cash flows from operating activities is used. (SFAS 95, paras. 27 and 29)

AUTHORITATIVE LITERATURE AND RELATED TOPICS

AUTHORITATIVE LITERATURE

APB Opinion No. 2, *Accounting for the "Investment Credit"*
APB Opinion No. 4, *Accounting for the "Investment Credit"*
APB Opinion No. 10, *Omnibus Opinion—1966* (Paragraph 6, Tax Allocation
    Accounts—Discounting)
APB Opinion No. 23, *Accounting for Income Taxes—Special Areas*
SFAS No. 37, *Balance Sheet Classification of Deferred Income Taxes*
SFAS No. 109, *Accounting for Income Taxes*
FASB Interpretation No. 18, *Accounting for Income Taxes in Interim Periods*
FASB Technical Bulletin 79-9, *Accounting in Interim Periods for Changes in
    Income Tax Rates*
FASB Technical Bulletin 82-1, *Disclosure of the Sale or Purchase of Tax Benefits
    through Tax Leases*

RELATED PRONOUNCEMENTS

EITF Issue No. 84-10, *LIFO Conformity of Companies Relying on Insilco Tax
    Court Decision*
EITF Issue No. 84-33, *Acquisition of a Tax Loss Carryforward—Temporary
    Parent-Subsidiary Relationship*
EITF Issue No. 85-31, *Comptroller of the Currency's Rule on Deferred Tax
    Debits*
EITF Issue No. 86-9, *IRC Section 338 and Push-Down Accounting*
EITF Issue No. 86-31, *Reporting the Tax Implications of a Pooling of a Bank and
    a Savings and Loan Association*
EITF Issue No. 87-8, *Tax Reform Act of 1986: Issues Related to the Alternative
    Minimum Tax*
EITF Issue No. 88-4, *Classification of Payment Made to IRS to Retain Fiscal Year*

EITF Issue No. 91-3, *Accounting for Income Tax Benefits from Bad Debts of a Savings and Loan Association*

EITF Issue No. 91-8, *Application of FASB Statement No. 96 to a State Tax Based on the Greater of a Franchise Tax or an Income Tax*

EITF Issue No. 92-8, *Accounting for the Income Tax Effects under FASB Statement No. 109 of a Change in Functional Currency When an Economy Ceases to Be Considered Highly Inflationary*

EITF Issue No. 93-9, *Application of FASB Statement No. 109 in Foreign Financial Statements Restated for General Price-Level Changes*

EITF Issue No. 93-12, *Recognition and Measurement of the Tax Benefit of Excess Tax-Deductible Goodwill Resulting from a Retroactive Change in Tax Law*

EITF Issue No. 93-13, *Effect of a Retroactive Change in Enacted Tax Rates That Is Included in Income from Continuing Operations*

EITF Issue No. 93-16, *Application of FASB Statement No. 109 to Basis Differences within Foreign Subsidiaries That Meet the Indefinite Reversal Criterion of APB Opinion No. 23*

EITF Issue No. 93-17, *Recognition of Deferred Tax Assets for a Parent Company's Excess Tax Basis in the Stock of a Subsidiary That is Accounted for as a Discontinued Operation*

EITF Issue No. 94-1, *Accounting for Tax Benefits Resulting from Investments in Affordable Housing Projects*

EITF Issue No. 94-10, *Accounting by a Company for the Income Tax Effects of Transactions among or with Its Shareholders under FASB Statement No. 109*

EITF Issue No. 95-9, *Accounting for Tax Effects of Dividends in France in Accordance with FASB Statement No. 109*

EITF Issue No. 95-10, *Accounting for Tax Credits Related to Dividend Payments in Accordance with FASB Statement No. 109*

EITF Issue No. 96-7, *Accounting for Deferred Taxes on In-Process Research and Development Activities Acquired in a Purchase Business Combination*

Accounting Interpretations of APB Opinion No. 4, *Accounting for the Investment Credit*

FASB Implementation Guide, *A Guide to Implementation of Statement 109, Accounting for Income Taxes*

RELATED TOPICS

INSURANCE COSTS

Table of Contents

INSURANCE COSTS

OVERVIEW

25.100 The authoritative literature on accounting for insurance costs offers the following guidance:

    a. Premium payments on insurance policies that do not transfer risk to the insurer should be treated as deposits.

    b. The cash surrender value of an investment in life insurance should be reported as an asset. Any change in the cash surrender value during the period should be reported as an adjustment to premiums paid.

ACCOUNTING REQUIREMENTS

GENERAL RULE

25.200 In some instances, the substance of an insurance or reinsurance contract is such that the risk of loss is not transferred to the insurer or reinsurer. In those cases, the insured or ceding enterprise should account for the premiums paid, less the portion of the premiums that will be kept by the insurer or reinsurer, as a deposit. Consequently, that amount should be reported as an asset rather than as insurance expense. (SFAS 5, par. 44)

25.201 A business in a high risk industry who is unable to purchase insurance at reasonable rates may pool its risks with other businesses by forming a mutual insurance enterprise. Each business pays premiums to the mutual insurance enterprise and also has an equity interest in the enterprise. In such cases, risk of loss may or may not be transferred to the insurance enterprise. Thus, whether premium payments should be treated as an expense or deposit depends on the individual facts and circumstances involved. (SFAS 5, par. 45)

LIFE INSURANCE

25.202 Under certain life insurance policies, a portion of premium payments go to the insurer for its assumption of risk while the other portion accumulates as cash value. The insured can receive the cash value of the policy by either

(a) borrowing money from the insurer and using the cash value as collateral or (b) surrendering the policy. The amount that can be received, referred to as the policy's "cash surrender value," is the policy's cash value reduced by policy loans and surrender charges. (FTB 85-4, par. 5)

25.203   When a company buys a cash value policy for itself, the amount that it could receive by surrendering the policy at the balance sheet date should be reported as an asset. Any change in the policy's cash surrender value during the period should be reported as an adjustment of premiums paid. (FTB 85-4, par. 2)

Practical Consideration. GAAP does not address the balance sheet presentation of cash value of life insurance. The authors' recommendations are as follows:

    a. The asset normally is classified as noncurrent unless the cash value is reasonably expected to be realized within the next year.

    b. Loans against a policy's cash value should be netted against the cash value in the balance sheet in accordance with FASB Interpretation No. 39, *Offsetting of Amounts Related to Certain Contracts,* since the amount that will be received will be net of outstanding policy loans.

    c. Unpaid interest on policy loans should be included with other accrued interest if management expects to repay it. Otherwise, unpaid interest should be included with policy loans.

AUTHORITATIVE LITERATURE

AUTHORITATIVE LITERATURE

SFAS No. 5, *Accounting for Contingencies*
FASB Technical Bulletin 85-4, *Accounting for Purchases of Life Insurance*

INTANGIBLE ASSETS

Table of Contents

INTANGIBLE ASSETS

OVERVIEW

26.100   Assets that have no physical substance but have economic value are referred to as intangible assets. Generally, the cost of intangible assets should be capitalized and amortized to income over their useful lives. Similar to the accounting for depreciable assets, the estimated useful lives used to amortize intangible assets should be continually reassessed and adjusted if necessary. In addition, if an intangible asset becomes impaired, an immediate write down of cost through a charge to income may be required.

26.101   Special accounting requirements exist for intangible assets that were acquired before November 1, 1970, and for the intangible assets of motor carriers.

ACCOUNTING REQUIREMENTS

WHAT ARE INTANGIBLE ASSETS?

26.200   Simply stated, an intangible asset is an asset that lacks physical substance but possesses economic value. It may be purchased, such as a franchise, or developed internally, such as a patent. In some cases, an intangible asset may be specifically identified. That is, it has a value and identity apart from the entity itself and thus can be sold. Often, however, an intangible asset is unidentifiable. It results from a number of factors and has no value apart from the entity itself (for example, goodwill). Examples of intangible assets include trademarks, patents, franchises, company name, covenants not to compete, customer lists, copyrights, and goodwill. (APB 17, par. 1)

26.201   Accounting for an intangible asset involves the same basic issues as for any other asset. That is, it involves:

- valuing and recording the asset when it is acquired; and

- amortizing the cost of the asset during its period of use.

The following paragraphs discuss those issues and present additional guidance for specific types of intangible assets.

VALUING INTANGIBLE ASSETS

26.202   Intangible assets should be recorded at cost. Determining cost varies depending on whether the asset was purchased from another entity or developed internally. (APB 17, paras. 25–26)

Purchased Intangibles

26.203   When a single intangible asset is purchased, determining its cost is relatively straightforward. Its cost is equal to either (a) the cash paid, (b) the fair value of other assets given up, (c) the present value of payments to be paid on liabilities incurred, or (d) the fair value of the intangible asset if the company's stock is issued to acquire it. (APB 17, par. 25)

26.204   When intangible assets are acquired as part of a group of assets (or as part of an entity that is acquired), their costs are determined by allocating a portion of the total purchase price to each asset acquired. Generally, that is accomplished as follows: (APB 17, par. 26)

  a. Identifiable intangible assets are allocated a portion of the total cost of the group of assets or business acquired. Generally, the allocation is based on the fair values of the individual assets within the group.

  b. Unidentifiable intangible assets (i.e., goodwill) are assigned a cost equal to the excess of the cost of the assets acquired over the sum of costs assigned to identifiable tangible and intangible assets minus liabilities assumed.

26.205   To illustrate, assume that Parent Company purchased Sub Company for $1,000,000. The costs of the individual assets acquired would be determined as follows:

Purchase price			$ 1,000,000
Assets acquired (at fair value):			
Tangible assets	$	950,000	
Identifiable intangible assets:			
Patent		25,000	
Franchise		60,000	
		1,035,000	
Liabilities assumed		(220,000)	815,000
Unidentifiable intangible assets		$	185,000

26.206   Occasionally, the values allocated to assets exceed the purchase price, and the deficiency is commonly referred to as "negative goodwill." Negative goodwill should be allocated proportionately to reduce noncurrent assets. Any amount that cannot be allocated, for example, because all noncurrent assets have been reduced to zero, should be reported as a deferred credit. (APB 16, par. 91)

26.207   Valuing individual assets and liabilities acquired in a purchase business combination is discussed further in Chapter 3.

Internally Developed Intangibles

26.208   In many cases, intangible assets are developed internally rather than purchased from another entity. For example, a company may patent a unique product that it develops or develop goodwill through excellent business practices and superior service. Expenses incurred to develop an *identifiable* intangible asset (such as a patent, copyright, or trademark) should be capitalized. (APB 17, par. 6) Research and development costs should not be capitalized, however. As discussed in Chapter 47, those costs should be expensed when incurred.

Practical Consideration. Typically, the only costs of an internally developed intangible asset that will be capitalized are the costs associated with registering the asset (such as legal fees, filing fees, costs of models or drawings, etc.). However, merely registering certain intangibles (such as patents, copyrights, or trademarks) does not guarantee ownership. Ownership of such assets is not conclusively proved until it is successfully defended in court. Thus, the authors believe that the costs of *successful* court defenses also should be capitalized as part of the cost of an intangible.

26.209   Generally, no value should be assigned to an unidentifiable internally developed intangible asset, such as goodwill. Such assets should only be recorded if they are purchased from another entity. Thus, the costs of developing, maintaining, or restoring such intangibles should be charged to expense when incurred. (APB 17, par. 24)

AMORTIZING INTANGIBLE ASSETS

26.210   The cost of an intangible asset should be amortized to income over the asset's estimated useful life. Determining an asset's useful life is based on a variety of factors, including the following: (APB 17, par. 27)

- Legal, regulatory, or contractual provisions

- Provisions for renewals or extensions

- Effects of the economy including obsolescence, demand, supply, competition

- Relationship to the service life expectancies of individuals or groups of employees

- Expected actions of competitors

26.211   Although GAAP sets no minimum amortization period, APB Opinion No. 17, *Intangible Assets,* does state that the amortization period should not exceed 40 years. It also states that the straight-line method of amortization should be used unless another method is more appropriate. (APB 17, paras. 29–30)

Reassessing the Amortization Period

26.212   Often, changing facts and circumstances result in increases or decreases in an asset's estimated useful life. A company should continually evaluate whether the estimated useful life used to amortize an intangible asset is appropriate. A change in an asset's estimated useful life should be recorded prospectively. That is, the asset's unamortized cost should be amortized over the remaining number of periods in the asset's revised useful life. (The asset's total amortization period should not exceed 40 years, however.) (APB 17, par. 31)

Accounting for the Impairment of Intangible Assets

26.213   In some cases, the carrying amount of long-lived intangible assets may exceed what a company will eventually recover from continuing to use the assets. Consequently, a company should continually assess whether an intangible asset (or group of intangible assets) is impaired and should be written off or adjusted. SFAS No. 121, *Accounting for the Impairment of Long-Lived Assets and for Long-Lived Assets to Be Disposed Of,* provides guidance on the accounting for impairment of (a) identifiable intangible assets (except for long-term customer relationships of financial institutions) and (b) goodwill (but only as it relates to assessing the impairment of the other long-term assets that were acquired in a business combination). It generally requires companies to take the following steps to determine whether such assets have been impaired: (SFAS 121, paras. 3–12)

     a. *Determine whether events or conditions indicate that the asset may be impaired.*

b. *Estimate the cash flows expected from continuing to use the asset.* Cash flows should be based on the best available information, using reasonable and supportable assumptions. Cash flows should not be discounted and should not include interest.

c. *Compare the estimated cash flows to the asset's carrying amount.* If the estimated cash flows resulting from continuing to use the asset exceed the carrying amount of the asset, an impairment adjustment is not necessary. However, if the carrying amount of the asset exceeds the estimated cash flows, an impairment loss should be recorded to adjust the asset to its fair value. (Any goodwill related to an asset should be included in the total carrying amount of that asset when performing this step. Goodwill related to both assets being evaluated and assets not being evaluated generally should be allocated on a pro rata basis between the assets. If an impairment loss is indicated, goodwill should be reduced to zero before adjusting the carrying amount of the impaired assets.)

26.214   Once the carrying amount of an impaired intangible asset has been written down to fair value, that becomes its new cost. Subsequent increases in fair value should not be recorded. (SFAS 121, par. 11) Accounting for the impairment of long-lived assets is discussed further in Chapter 33 of this *Guide.*

Disposal of Goodwill

26.215   Generally, goodwill cannot be sold apart from the entity itself. However, if a large segment or group of assets is discontinued or sold, all or a portion of unamortized goodwill should be included in the cost of the assets sold. (APB 17, par. 32) In addition, as discussed in Paragraph 26.213, goodwill related to an impaired asset should be reduced to zero before the carrying amount of the impaired asset is adjusted.

Special Rules for Assets Acquired Prior to November 1, 1970

26.216   Assets held on October 31, 1970 (the effective date of APB Opinion No. 17), may continue to be accounted for in accordance with ARB No. 43 rather than APB Opinion No. 17. Under ARB No. 43, intangible assets are classified in one of two categories: (ARB 43, Ch. 5, par. 2)

a. Those having a life that is limited by law, regulation, agreement, or by their nature (such as patents, copyrights, leases, licenses, etc.)

b. Those having an unlimited or indeterminate life (such as goodwill, trade names, organization costs, etc.)

26.217　An intangible asset that has a limited life (category a.) should be amortized in the same manner as described in Paragraphs 26.210–.212. (ARB 43, Ch. 5, par. 5) However, an intangible asset with an indeterminate life (category b.) need not be amortized unless it becomes reasonably evident that— (ARB 43, Ch. 5, paras. 6–8)

- *Its life has become limited.* At that time, the asset should be amortized to income over its estimated remaining life. If the remaining life is so short that it results in substantial amortization charges that might mislead income statement users, a partial write-down may be made in the year the asset's life becomes limited.

- *The asset may not continue to have value during the life of the company.* At that time, the asset should be amortized to income based on a reasonable plan of amortization.

- *The asset has become worthless.* At that time, the asset should be written off through a charge to income.

INTANGIBLE ASSETS OF MOTOR CARRIERS

26.218　The deregulation of the motor carrier industry by the Motor Carrier Act of 1980 permanently and substantially impaired the value of intangible assets related to interstate operating rights. Thus, questions were raised about whether the costs of acquired interstate operating rights should continue to be reported as intangible assets or charged to income. Consequently, the FASB issued SFAS No. 44, *Accounting for Intangible Assets of Motor Carriers,* to clarify the accounting requirements. The Statement requires motor carriers to (a) allocate the costs of acquired intangible assets to interstate operating rights, other identifiable intangible assets, and goodwill and (b) expense, rather than capitalize, the costs assigned to interstate operating rights. (Other identifiable intangible assets and goodwill should be accounted for as described in the preceding paragraphs.) (SFAS 44, paras. 3 and 6)

26.219　The guidance in Paragraphs 26.210–.207 should be followed when allocating costs to interstate operating rights and other intangibles. If a motor carrier cannot separately identify interstate operating rights, other intangibles, and goodwill (or finds that it is not practical to do so), it should allocate the cost of acquiring all intangibles to interstate operating rights. (SFAS 44, par. 5)

Practical Consideration. Operating rights are a motor carrier's permit, as granted by the Interstate Commerce Commission (ICC) or similar state agency, to transport specified goods along specified routes with limited competition. Rights granted by the ICC are referred to as *interstate* operating rights and those granted by state agencies are referred to as *intrastate* operating rights. GAAP specifically addresses *interstate* operating rights and requires motor carriers to expense the cost of acquiring them. Acquired *intrastate* operating rights should also be charged to income, however, if a state deregulates motor carriers with effects that are similar to the Motor Carrier Act of 1980.

DISCLOSURE REQUIREMENTS

26.500   The following disclosures about intangible assets are required:

a. The method and period of amortization (APB 17, par. 30)

b. The reasons for significant reductions, if applicable (APB 17, par. 31)

c. For an intangible asset that has been impaired: (SFAS 121, par. 14)

     (1) A description of the impaired intangible asset and the facts and circumstances leading to its impairment

     (2) The amount of the impairment loss and how fair value was determined

     (3) The caption in the income statement in which the impairment loss is aggregated, if that loss has not been presented as a separate caption or reported parenthetically on the face of the statement (Impairment losses should be included in income from continuing operations.)

     (4) The business segment(s) affected, if applicable

AUTHORITATIVE LITERATURE AND RELATED TOPICS

AUTHORITATIVE LITERATURE

APB Opinion No. 16, *Business Combinations*
APB Opinion No. 17, *Intangible Assets*
SFAS No. 44, *Accounting for Intangible Assets of Motor Carriers*

SFAS No. 121, *Accounting for the Impairment of Long-Lived Assets and for Long-Lived Assets to Be Disposed Of*

RELATED PRONOUNCEMENTS

EITF Issue No. 85-8, *Amortization of Thrift Intangibles*
EITF Issue No. 85-42, *Amortization of Goodwill Resulting from Recording Time Savings Deposits at Fair Values*
EITF Issue No. 89-19, *Accounting for a Change in Goodwill Amortization for Business Combinations Initiated Prior to the Effective Date of FASB Statement No. 72*
Accounting Interpretations of APB Opinion No. 17, *Intangible Assets*

RELATED TOPICS

Chapter 3—Business Combinations
Chapter 47—Research and Development Costs

INTEREST: CAPITALIZED

Table of Contents

INTEREST: CAPITALIZED

OVERVIEW

27.100   Interest costs, if incurred, should be capitalized as part of the cost of acquiring or constructing qualifying assets. A qualifying asset is one that requires a period of time to make ready for its intended use. Examples of qualifying assets include assets that a company constructs for its own use (such as a plant or warehouse) and assets intended for sale or lease that are constructed as discrete projects (such as a real estate development). Although conceptually any asset that requires a period of time to prepare for its intended use qualifies for interest capitalization, GAAP precludes interest capitalization on certain assets, such as inventories that are routinely manufactured on a repetitive basis and assets acquired with gifts or grants that the donor restricts to acquiring the assets.

27.101   The interest capitalization period begins when all of the following conditions are met:

    a. Expenditures have been made.

    b. Activities necessary to prepare the asset for its intended use are in progress.

    c. Interest cost is being incurred.

Interest capitalization stops when the asset is substantially complete and ready for its intended use.

27.102   The amount of interest capitalized is determined by applying a rate to average accumulated expenditures for the asset. The rate is determined as follows:

    a. If a specific borrowing is incurred to finance a qualifying asset, the interest rate of that borrowing is applied to average accumulated expenditures up to the debt amount.

    b. If average accumulated expenditures exceed directly associated debt, a weighted average of the rates applicable to other borrowings during the period should be applied to the average accumulated expenditures that exceed the directly associated debt.

Interest capitalized during a period cannot exceed interest costs actually incurred. Once interest cost is capitalized, it is depreciated the same as other costs of the asset.

27.103   GAAP requires special treatment for capitalizing interest costs on qualifying assets that are financed with the proceeds of externally restricted tax-exempt borrowings. In such cases, the amount of interest cost that should be capitalized includes the total interest cost of the tax-exempt borrowings less any interest earned by temporarily investing the proceeds of the borrowings.

ACCOUNTING REQUIREMENTS

WHY CAPITALIZE INTEREST COSTS?

27.200   The cost of acquiring or constructing an asset should include all costs necessary to prepare the asset for its intended use. Thus, if preparing an asset for its intended use requires time, the asset's cost should include any related interest costs incurred during the preparation period (also referred to as the "acquisition period"). (SFAS 34, par. 6) The following paragraphs provide guidance for determining (a) whether an asset qualifies for interest capitalization and (b) the amount of interest that should be capitalized.

QUALIFYING ASSETS

27.201   Interest should be capitalized for the following types of assets:

     a. Assets constructed or produced for an entity's internal use (for example, buildings or machinery), including those produced by others for which the entity has made deposits or progress payments

     b. Assets intended for sale or lease that are constructed or produced as discrete projects (for example, real estate developments) (SFAS 34, par. 9)

     c. Investments (including equity funds, loans, and advances) accounted for by the equity method while the investee has activities in progress necessary to commence its planned principal operations (provided the investee's activities include the use of funds to acquire qualifying assets for its operations) (SFAS 58, par. 5)

27.202   Conceptually, interest costs always should be capitalized when a period of time is needed to make an asset ready for its intended use and interest costs are incurred. In some instances, however, the benefit of capitalizing interest costs may not justify the accounting and administrative costs involved. Consequently, interest should not be capitalized for the following assets:

    a. Inventories that are routinely manufactured or otherwise produced on a repetitive basis in the ordinary course of business

    b. Assets currently in use or ready for use in the company's earning activities

    c. Assets that are not being used in the company's earning activities and that are not being prepared for use (SFAS 34, par. 10)

    d. Assets not included in the consolidated balance sheet of the parent company and consolidated subsidiaries

    e. Investments accounted for by the equity method after the investee's planned principal operations begin

    f. Investments in regulated investees that are capitalizing both the cost of debt and equity capital (SFAS 58, par. 6)

    g. Assets acquired with gifts and grants that have been restricted by the donor to acquire those assets provided that such funds are available from the gifts and grants (Interest earned on the temporary investment of those funds is considered an addition to the gift or grant.) (SFAS 62, par. 5)

Land

27.203   Land that is not being prepared for its intended use is not a qualifying asset and related interest costs should not be capitalized. Once activities to prepare the land for its intended use begin, however, the interest incurred during the preparation period related to buying and improving the land should be capitalized as part of the cost of the resulting asset. If the resulting asset is a building (for example, a shopping center), the capitalized interest should be included in the cost of the building. If the resulting asset is developed land (for example, residential lots), the capitalized interest should be included in the cost of the developed land. (SFAS 34, par. 11)

Oil and Gas Producing Operations

27.204   Oil and gas properties accounted for by the full cost method do not qualify for interest capitalization if they are currently being depreciated, depleted, or amortized. However, unproved properties or cost centers that have no production do qualify for interest capitalization if (a) they are not currently being depreciated, depleted, or amortized and (b) exploration and development activities are in progress on them. (FASBI 33, par. 2)

DETERMINING THE AMOUNT OF INTEREST COST TO CAPITALIZE

27.205   The capitalized interest calculation is based on the notion of "avoidable cost." That is, it attempts to determine the interest costs that could have been avoided if expenditures for the asset had not been made. Thus, it is possible that interest should be capitalized even though no specific borrowing was incurred to acquire an asset. For example, if a company uses its cash to construct a building, any interest on existing debt that could have been avoided (i.e., by using cash to reduce the debt rather than construct the building) should be capitalized as part of the cost of the building. Interest capitalized during a period should not exceed the interest costs actually incurred during the period, however. Consequently, if the company in the preceding example had no existing debt (and, thus, did not incur interest costs that could have been avoided), no interest would be capitalized as part of the cost of the building. (SFAS 34, par. 12)

27.206   Calculating the amount of interest costs to capitalize involves applying a capitalization rate to the average accumulated expenditures made for the asset during the capitalization period. (SFAS 34, par. 13) The following paragraphs discuss determining the capitalization period, capitalization rate, and average accumulated expenditures. EXHIBIT 27-1 presents an example capitalized interest calculation.

EXHIBIT 27-1

EXAMPLE CAPITALIZED INTEREST CALCULATION

Assume the following related to the construction of ABC Corp.'s new warehouse:

- The following costs were incurred during calendar year 19X1:

April 1 — Payment for architect fees and permits	$ 25,000
July 1 — Progress payment	125,000
September 1 — Progress payment	150,000
December 1 — Progress payment	180,000
	$ 480,000

- To help finance the construction, ABC Corp. borrowed $100,000 at 11% on April 1, 19X1.

- ABC Corp.'s other borrowings during 19X1 consisted of the following:

Borrowing Date	Amount	Annual Interest Rate
January 1, 19X1	$ 300,000	10%
July 1, 19X1	200,000	11%
October 1, 19X1	400,000	12%

- The warehouse was completed in April 19X2.

The interest that should be capitalized during the calendar year 19X1 is computed as follows:

EXHIBIT 27-1 (Continued)

Average accumulated expenditures

Payment Amount	Months from Payment to End of Year	Weighted Average Expenditure
$ 25,000	9 months (9/12)	$ 18,750
125,000	6 months (6/12)	62,500
150,000	4 months (4/12)	50,000
180,000	1 month (1/12)	15,000
		$ 146,250

Weighted average rate on borrowings other than the construction loan

Loan Amount	Months Outstanding	Weighted Average Loan Amount	Interest Rate	Annual Interest
$ 300,000	12 months (12/12)	$ 300,000	10%	$ 30,000
200,000	6 months (6/12)	100,000	11%	11,000
400,000	3 months (3/12)	100,000	12%	12,000
		$ 500,000		$ 53,000

Weighted average rate = 10.6% ($53,000 ÷ $500,000)

EXHIBIT 27-1 (Continued)

Capitalized interest calculation

	Average Accumulated Expenditures	Interest Rate	Annual Interest
Construction loan	$ 75,000[a]	11%	$ 8,250
Other borrowings	71,250	10.6%	7,553
	$146,250		$ 15,803

Since ABC Corp. actually incurred more than $15,803 in interest during 19X1, the full $15,803 should be capitalized as part of the cost of the warehouse.

---

[a] The construction loan rate is applied to average accumulated expenditures to the extent they do not exceed the *weighted average* construction loan amount. That amount is less than the total loan amount since the loan was outstanding for only nine months during 19X1 (computed as $100,000 × $9/12$).

Capitalization Period

27.207   The period during which interest should be capitalized (referred to as the "capitalization period") generally begins when all of the following conditions are met: (SFAS 34, par. 17)

     a. Expenditures have been made.

     b. Activities necessary to prepare the asset for its intended use are in progress. (The term "activities" involves more than physically constructing the asset; it involves all procedures necessary to prepare the asset for its intended use. Thus, for example, it includes administrative activities during the preconstruction phase and activities after construction has begun, such as those necessary to settle labor disputes, technical problems, or litigation. If the company voluntarily suspends substantially all activities related to acquiring the asset, interest capitalization should cease. Interest capitalization should not cease, however, if activities are externally interrupted briefly or because of delays that are inherent in acquiring the asset.)

  c. Interest cost is being incurred.

27.208 The capitalization period ends when the asset is substantially complete and ready for its intended use. If the asset is completed in parts and it is possible to use each part independently while work continues on other parts (for example, a condominium), interest capitalization should stop on a part when the part is substantially complete and ready for its intended use. If the asset cannot be used effectively until another asset has been completed (for example, an oil well that cannot begin producing until a pipeline has been constructed), interest capitalization should continue until the other asset is substantially complete and ready for use. (SFAS 34, par. 18)

27.209 **Asset Impairment.** Interest capitalization should continue until the asset is substantially complete and ready for its intended use even if the asset becomes impaired and must be reduced to a value less than its acquisition cost. In such cases, the loss allowance recorded to reduce the asset's value should be increased appropriately. (SFAS 34, par. 19) Asset impairment is discussed further in Chapter 33.

Capitalization Rate

27.210 The capitalization rate used should be based on rates that apply to outstanding borrowings during the period. If debt can be directly associated with a qualifying asset, the rate on that debt should be applied to average accumulated expenditures up to the debt amount. If average accumulated expenditures exceed directly associated debt, a weighted average of the rates applicable to other debt should be applied to the average accumulated expenditures that exceed the directly associated debt. When determining the debt to include in the weighted average rate, judgment should be used to ensure that the rate used reasonably reflects the interest cost that could have been avoided. (SFAS 34, paras. 13–14) Interest costs that should be considered include the following: (SFAS 34, par. 1)

- Interest recognized on obligations with a fixed interest rate (excluding interest relating to net periodic pension costs)

- Interest recognized on obligations with an imputed interest rate (See Chapter 28.)

- Interest recognized on capital lease obligations (See Chapter 31.)

Interest income should not be considered when determining the rate. (SFAS 62, par. 3) (See Paragraphs 27.213–.214 for a discussion of the treatment of interest earned by temporarily investing the proceeds of tax-exempt borrowings, however.)

Average Accumulated Expenditures

27.211 Average accumulated expenditures are a weighted average of the capital expenditures (net of progress payment collections) incurred for the asset. Expenditures should include those made by cash payments, transfers of assets, or incurring an interest-bearing liability (excluding such items as accounts payable, retainages, and accruals). (SFAS 34, par. 16)

Considerations for Consolidated Entities

27.212 As discussed in Paragraph 27.205, interest capitalized during a period should not exceed the total interest incurred during the period. If separate financial statements are prepared for a parent or consolidated subsidiary, a separate limitation applies to each entity. That is, the total interest capitalized during the period in a consolidated subsidiary's separate financial statements may not exceed the total interest incurred by the subsidiary during the period, including intercompany interest. In consolidated financial statements, however, the limitation applies at the consolidated level—total interest capitalized by the *consolidated* entity during a period may not exceed the total interest incurred by the *consolidated* entity during the period. (SFAS 34, par. 15) Thus, it is possible that the combined amounts of interest capitalized by the separate entities may not equal the interest that should be capitalized by the consolidated entity. In such cases, a consolidating entry may be needed to capitalize additional interest based on consolidated interest costs incurred.

FINANCING QUALIFYING ASSETS WITH TAX-EXEMPT BORROWINGS

27.213 When externally restricted tax-exempt borrowings, such as industrial revenue bonds (IRBs), are used to finance all or part of a project, a different procedure is used to determine the interest costs that should be capitalized. Under such arrangements, all of the interest costs related to the restricted borrowing should be capitalized as part of the cost of the qualifying asset. In addition, any interest income from temporarily investing the proceeds of the borrowings should be offset against costs capitalized. Thus, interest capitalization starts when the proceeds are received, rather than when activities begin. (The capitalization period should still end when the project is ready for its intended use, however.) If a project is financed entirely through tax-exempt borrowings, there is no need to compute a weighted average rate that considers other borrowings. If tax-exempt borrowings only provide partial financing, however, interest would be capitalized on the average accumulated

expenditures that exceed the tax-exempt borrowings using a weighted average rate of all other borrowings. (SFAS 62, par. 4)

Practical Consideration. The guidance in Paragraph 27.213 only applies
when an external party restricts use of the tax-exempt borrowings to acquiring
the qualifying asset or servicing related debt. In addition, only interest income
earned from investing the proceeds of the tax-exempt borrowings should be
offset against capitalized costs. Other interest income should not be offset.

An Example with Tax-exempt Borrowings

27.214   To illustrate capitalizing interest when qualifying assets are purchased with externally restricted tax-exempt borrowings, assume that XYZ
Partnership constructs an office building for $500,000 and funds 90% of the
costs through 6% industrial revenue bonds and the remainder through capital
contributions. (The partnership has no other debt.) Assume also that (a) the industrial revenue bonds were issued on January 1st, (b) construction takes one
year, (c) costs are incurred evenly during the year, and (d) the bond proceeds
are invested in a money market account and earned $14,400 during the year.
The cost of the building would be determined as follows:

Construction costs	$ 500,000
Interest cost on restricted borrowing	
($500,000 × 90% × 6%)	27,000
Interest earned	(14,400)
	$ 512,600

DISCLOSURE REQUIREMENTS

27.500   The following disclosures about interest costs should be included in
the financial statements or related notes: (SFAS 34, par. 21)

   a. The amount of interest costs incurred and charged to expense
      during the period

   b. The amount of interest costs capitalized during the period, if any

STATEMENT OF CASH FLOWS

27.501   SFAS No. 95, *Statement of Cash Flows,* requires that the amount of
interest paid, net of amounts capitalized, be disclosed. (SFAS 95, par. 29) The
objective of the disclosure is to allow financial statement users to determine the

27.214

amount of interest paid that is included in the operating activities section of the cash flows statement, so that they may consider the interest as a financing cash outflow if that better suits their purposes. Thus, the amount of interest paid that should be disclosed is the amount of interest reflected in operating cash flows. For example—

- Interest capitalized as part of the cost of property and equipment (which is included in the investing activities section of the cash flows statement) should be subtracted from total interest payments to determine the amount of interest to disclose.

- Interest paid and capitalized as part of inventory (which is included in operating cash flows) should not be subtracted from total interest payments to determine the amount of interest to disclose.

27.502   The disclosure may be made on the face of the cash flows statement or in the notes as follows:

Interest paid during 19X5 and 19X4 (net of capitalized interest of $3,500 in 19X4) amounted to $16,200 and $14,400, respectively.

AUTHORITATIVE LITERATURE AND RELATED TOPICS

AUTHORITATIVE LITERATURE

SFAS No. 34, *Capitalization of Interest Cost*
SFAS No. 42, *Determining Materiality for Capitalization of Interest Cost*
SFAS No. 58, *Capitalization of Interest Cost in Financial Statements That Include Investments Accounted for by the Equity Method*
SFAS No. 62, *Capitalization of Interest Cost in Situations Involving Certain Tax-Exempt Borrowings and Certain Gifts and Grants*
SFAS No. 95, *Statement of Cash Flows*
FASB Interpretation No. 33, *Applying FASB Statement No. 34 to Oil and Gas Producing Operations Accounted for by the Full Cost Method*

RELATED PRONOUNCEMENTS

SOP 97-1, *Accounting by Participating Mortgage Loan Brokers*

RELATED TOPICS

Chapter 20—Equity Method Investments
Chapter 33—Long-lived Assets, Depreciation, and Impairment

INTEREST: IMPUTED

Table of Contents

INTEREST: IMPUTED

OVERVIEW

28.100   When a note is exchanged for property, goods, or services, consideration should be given about whether the note's stated interest rate is reasonable in comparison to prevailing market conditions. If it is not, the exchange should be valued at the fair value of the note or property, goods, or services, whichever is more clearly determinable. If there is no established exchange price for the property, goods, or services or evidence of the note's fair value, the exchange should be valued at the present value of the note, determined by discounting future cash payments under the note by an appropriate interest rate.

28.101   The difference between the face amount of the note and its present value represents a discount or premium. A discount or premium should be amortized over the life of the note using the interest method (or a method that produces similar results).

ACCOUNTING REQUIREMENTS

28.200   When a note is exchanged for property, goods, or services in an arm's length transaction, it generally is assumed that the note's stated interest rate is fair and adequate. That assumption may not be true, however, if—

a. there is no stated interest rate,

b. the stated interest rate is unreasonable, or

c. the note's stated face amount materially differs from the current cash sales price for the same or similar items or from the note's market value at the date of the transaction (APB 21, par. 12)

28.201   In such instances, the transaction's substance, rather than its form, dictates how it should be recorded and the following applies: (APB 21, par. 12)

a. The property, goods, or services received should be recorded at the fair value of the items received or the market value of the note, whichever is more clearly determinable.

b. If there are no established prices for the items received and the market value of the note cannot be determined, the property, goods, or services received should be recorded at the present value of the future payments under the note, discounted using an appropriate interest rate.

c. Any difference between the note's face value and the recorded amount of the property, goods, or services received is a discount or premium that should be amortized over the life of the note as discussed in Paragraph 28.204.

d. The determination of whether a note's interest rate is fair and adequate should be made at the time the note is issued, assumed, or acquired. Subsequent changes in prevailing interest rates should be ignored.

Practical Consideration. Generally, the preceding guidance applies to all receivables and payables representing rights to receive or pay money at a fixed or determinable date. It does not apply to the following, however:

- Note exchanges solely for cash (The guidance does not apply since the present value of the principal and interest is presumed to equal the cash received.)

- Receivables and payables arising in the normal course of business that are due in approximately one year or less (for example, trade receivables and payables)

- Amounts that will be repaid by applying them to the purchase price of the property, goods, or services involved (for example, deposits or progress payments)

- Amounts intended to provide security for one party of the agreement (for example, security deposits or retainages)

- Receivables and payables arising from the normal lending activities or demand or savings deposit activities of a financial institution

- Receivables and payables whose interest rates are determined by a government agency (for example, industrial revenue bonds and tax-exempt bonds)

- Receivables and payables between a parent and its subsidiary or between subsidiaries of a common parent

---

Practical Consideration (Continued).

Also, the present value technique discussed in Paragraph 28.201 should not be applied to estimates of obligations assumed in connection with sales of property, goods, or services (for example, product warranty liabilities).

DETERMINING THE APPROPRIATE INTEREST RATE

28.202   The interest rate used to determine the present value of future payments should approximate the rate that an independent borrower and an independent lender would have negotiated in a similar transaction. Generally, the following should be considered when selecting a rate: (APB 21, par. 13)

     a. Issuer's credit standing

     b. Restrictive covenants, collateral, and other debt terms

     c. Prevailing market rates

     d. Tax consequences to buyer and seller (if appropriate)

     e. Rate at which the issuer could borrow funds

28.203   As discussed in Paragraph 28.201, the appropriate interest rate should be determined when the note is issued, and subsequent changes in prevailing interest rates should be ignored.

DISCOUNT AND PREMIUM

Amortization

28.204   If the present value of the note's future cash flows exceeds the face amount of the note, a premium exists. Conversely, a discount exists if the present value of the note's future cash flows is less than the face amount of the note. The discount or premium should be amortized as interest expense or income over the life of the note. Amortization should be computed using the interest method so that a constant and fair interest rate will be applied to the outstanding note balance during the period. (APB 21, par. 15)

> **Practical Consideration.** A method other than the interest method may be used to amortize a discount or premium so long as it produces similar results. A straight-line method normally would vary materially from the interest method. Some debt agreements provide for amortization using the "Rule of 78s" method. Under that method, amortization is based on the sum-of-the-years' digits method, which amortizes interest faster in the early periods. The results are normally not materially different from the interest method when the note's term is five years or less.

Financial Statement Presentation

28.205   A discount or premium has no value apart from the note that gives rise to it. Consequently, it should not be reported on the balance sheet as a separate asset or liability. Instead, it should be added to or subtracted from the related note balance. Amortization of a discount or premium should be reported as interest expense or income. (APB 21, par. 16)

28.206   Issue costs should be reported in the balance sheet as deferred charges. (APB 21, par. 16)

ILLUSTRATION

28.207   EXHIBIT 28-1 demonstrates how a note's discount or premium should be determined and amortized.

EXHIBIT 28-1

ILLUSTRATION OF IMPUTING INTEREST

Facts:

Assume that on December 31, 19X2, a company sells machinery for $1 million and accepts a noninterest bearing note receivable with the following terms:

- Annual payments of $100,000 are due on December 31 of each year beginning in 19X3.

- The appropriate interest rate is 8%.

EXHIBIT 28-1 (Continued)

Imputing interest and recording the transaction:

The manufacturer should record the note at its face amount but record the sale based on the note's present value. The difference represents the discount on the note. The present value of the note and related discount are determined as follows:

Present value of the $100,000 annuity as of December 31, 19X2 (Present value of 10 payments of $100,000 at 8%)	$ 671,008
Face amount of the note	1,000,000
Discount	$ (328,992)

Assuming the machinery was carried in inventory at $700,000, the following journal entry would be necessary at December 31, 19X2, to record the sale:

Note receivable	1,000,000	
Cost of sales	700,000	
Sales		671,008
Inventory		700,000
Discount on note receivable		328,992

Amortizing the discount:

The discount should be amortized by applying the 8% annual interest rate to the outstanding note balance. Thus, the discount would be amortized as follows:

	Beginning Note Balance	Annual Payment Applied to: Discount Amortization	Principal	Ending Note Balance
19X3	$ 671,008	$ 53,681	$ 46,319	$ 624,689
19X4	624,689	49,975	50,025	574,664
19X5	574,664	45,973	54,027	520,637
19X6	520,637	41,651	58,349	462,288
19X7	462,288	36,983	63,017	399,271
19X8	399,271	31,942	68,058	331,213
19X9	331,213	26,497	73,503	257,710
19Y0	257,710	20,617	79,383	178,327
19Y1	178,327	14,266	85,734	92,593
19Y2	92,593	7,407	92,593	—
		$ 328,992	$ 671,008	

DISCLOSURE REQUIREMENTS

28.500   The financial statements or notes to the financial statements should include a description of the note, including the effective interest rate and the face amount of the note. (APB 21, par. 16)

AUTHORITATIVE LITERATURE AND RELATED TOPICS

AUTHORITATIVE LITERATURE

APB Opinion No. 21, *Interest on Receivables and Payables*

RELATED PRONOUNCEMENTS

Accounting Interpretations of APB Opinion No. 21, *Interest on Receivables and Payables*
SOP 97-1, *Accounting by Participating Mortgage Loan Borrowers*

RELATED TOPICS

Chapter 27—Interest: Capitalized

INTERIM FINANCIAL REPORTING

Table of Contents

INTERIM FINANCIAL REPORTING

OVERVIEW

29.100   Because an interim period is an integral part of an annual period, its results should be based on the accounting principles used in annual financial statements. Certain accounting principles may require modification at interim dates, however, so that the interim period's results better relate to annual results. For example, inventories may be estimated at interim dates using the gross profit method when interim physical inventory counts are not taken. Similarly, income taxes may be estimated at interim dates by applying an estimated annual effective tax rate. Other modifications of accounting principles may be necessary to properly recognize revenues and expenses or account for changes in accounting principles.

29.101   With certain exceptions, disclosures required in interim financial statements generally are the same as those required in annual financial statements.

ACCOUNTING REQUIREMENTS

29.200   In general, each interim period should be viewed as an integral part of the annual period. The results of each interim period should be based on the accounting principles and practices used by a company in preparing its latest annual financial statements, unless a change in accounting practice or policy has been adopted during the current year. Consequently, most authoritative accounting pronouncements apply to both interim and annual financial statements. Some difficulties in applying GAAP in interim periods may arise, however, particularly in recording inventories and recognizing revenues and expenses. The following paragraphs discuss modifications to GAAP that are permitted or required for interim periods. (APB 28, paras. 9–10)

REVENUE AND EXPENSE RECOGNITION

29.201   The following are general guidelines for recognizing revenues and expenses during interim periods:

   a. Revenue should be recognized during interim periods on the same basis as followed for the full year. (APB 28, par. 11)

Adjustments should not be made to annualize seasonal revenue. (APB 28, par. 18)

b. Expenses directly associated with revenue, such as material costs, wages and salaries, manufacturing overhead, and fringe benefits, should be reported in the same period that the related revenue is recognized. (APB 28, par. 13)

c. Costs and expenses other than product costs should be charged to income in the interim period in which they are incurred or be allocated among interim periods based on an estimate of time expired, benefit received, or activity associated with the periods. Procedures adopted for assigning specific cost and expense items to an interim period should be consistent with the basis used to report annual results of operations. (APB 28, par. 12)

d. Some costs and expenses incurred in an interim period cannot be readily identified with the activities or benefits of other interim periods and should be charged to the interim period in which they are incurred. Such costs should not be arbitrarily assigned to an interim period.

e. Gains and losses that would not be deferred at year end should be recognized in the interim period in which they arise. They should not be deferred to later interim periods within the same fiscal year. (APB 28, par. 15)

f. Certain costs and expenses, such as depreciation, profit-sharing contributions, and year-end bonuses, frequently require adjustments at the end of the year even though they can be reasonably approximated at interim dates. Such adjustments should be estimated and the estimated costs and expenses assigned to interim periods so that the interim periods bear a reasonable portion of the anticipated annual amount. (APB 28, par. 17)

g. Material extraordinary items, unusual or infrequently occurring items, and gains and losses on disposal of a segment of a business should be recognized in the interim period in which they occur. They should not be prorated over the fiscal year. Materiality should be related to the full fiscal year. (APB 28, par. 21)

h. The effect of a change in estimate, including a change in the estimated effective annual tax rate, should be accounted for in the period of the change—prior interim periods should not be restated. (APB 28, par. 26)

INVENTORIES

29.202   Generally, the same inventory pricing methods used in annual financial statements, including write-downs to market, should be followed in interim periods. The following modifications are permitted or required in interim periods, however: (APB 28, par. 14)

a. The gross profit method (or other methods not used in annual statements) may be used to estimate inventories at interim dates when physical inventories are not taken. However, interim financial statements should disclose the method used to value inventory and any significant adjustments that result from reconciliation with the annual physical inventory.

b. Temporary declines in the market value of inventory to values below cost need not be recognized in interim financial statements if the market decline can reasonably be expected to be restored by the end of the fiscal year. If the decline cannot reasonably be expected to reverse by year end, however, inventory should be adjusted to market value at the interim date. A subsequent recovery in value before year end should be recognized in the interim period during which the recovery occurs. (Inventory should not be written up above its original cost, however.)

c. When there is a liquidation of a LIFO layer in an interim period, a determination must be made of whether the liquidation is temporary or permanent. If the liquidation is permanent, the interim period financial statements should disclose the effect on net income resulting from the liquidation. If the liquidation is temporary, the inventory at the interim reporting date should not give effect to the LIFO liquidation, and cost of sales should include the expected cost of replacement of the liquidated LIFO layer. The temporary nature of the liquidation should be disclosed in the financial statements.

d. When a standard cost system is used to value inventory, planned variances expected to be absorbed by the end of the fiscal year should ordinarily be deferred in interim financial statements. Unanticipated variances not expected to be absorbed should be reported in interim financial statements.

CHANGES IN ACCOUNTING PRINCIPLES

29.203   For interim financial statements, a change in an accounting principle occurs if an accounting principle or the method of applying a principle differs from that used in the preceding interim period, the prior annual period, or the comparable interim period of the prior year. (APB 28, par. 23)

29.204   Changes in accounting principles that are reported by including the cumulative effect of the change should be recognized in the first interim period regardless of when the change was actually made. The dollar effect of the change should be determined as of the end of the previous year. Thus, if a change in accounting principle is made in the second quarter, the cumulative effect of the change should be reported in the first quarter, not in the second quarter. Both quarters should be presented as if the accounting change was effective at the beginning of the year. (That is, net income before extraordinary items would be based on the new accounting principles.) (SFAS 3, paras. 9–10)

ADJUSTMENTS RELATED TO PRIOR INTERIM PERIODS

29.205   An item of profit or loss that occurs other than in the first interim period of the fiscal year and relates all or in part to prior interim periods of the fiscal year should be reported as follows: (SFAS 16, par. 14)

a. The portion that directly relates to activities during the current interim period should be included in the current interim period's net income.

b. Prior interim periods of the current fiscal year should be restated to include the portion that directly relates to activities during each prior interim period.

c. The portion that directly relates to activities during prior fiscal years should be included in net income of the first interim period of the current fiscal year.

Practical Consideration. An adjustment related to a prior interim period of the current fiscal year is defined as an adjustment or settlement of litigation or similar claims, renegotiation proceedings, or utility revenue under rate making processes that meets all of the following criteria:

a. The effect of the adjustment is material in relation to income from continuing operations of the current fiscal year or in relation to the trend of income from continuing operations or is material by another appropriate criteria.

b. All or part of the adjustment can be identified with and is directly related to business activities of specific prior interim periods of the current fiscal year. (This criteria is not met because of incidental effects such as interest on a settlement.)

Practical Consideration (Continued).

   c. The amount of the adjustment could not be reasonably esti-mated prior to the current interim period but became reason-ably estimable in the current interim period.

Consequently, normal recurring corrections and adjustments resulting from the use of estimates inherent in the accounting process should not be treated as adjustments of prior interim periods of the fiscal year. Similarly, changes in the provision for doubtful accounts are not adjustments of prior interim periods of the fiscal year even if the changes result from litigation or similar claims.

INCOME TAXES

29.206   Income taxes in interim periods generally should be determined by—

   a. applying an estimated annual effective tax rate (based on the current fiscal year's estimated annual results) to income or loss from continuing operations (excluding unusual or infrequently occurring items) and

   b. recording the tax effects of unusual or infrequently occurring items, extraordinary items, discontinued operations, and cumu-lative effects of accounting changes in the interim period in which they occur. (APB 28, par. 19)

Additional considerations for recording income taxes in interim periods are dis-cussed in Chapter 24.

DISCLOSURE REQUIREMENTS

29.500   Disclosure requirements for interim financial statements basically are the same as for annual financial statements with the following exceptions:

Practical Consideration. Generally, required disclosures need not be made in interim or annual financial statements if they relate to immaterial items. Mate-riality should be based on the financial statements being presented, however. In other words, an item that is not disclosed in annual financial statements because it is immaterial would still need to be disclosed in interim financial statements if it is material to the interim statements.

---

   a. Accounting policies need not be disclosed in interim statements unless an accounting policy has changed. (APB 22, par. 10)

> **Practical Consideration.** Most accountants disclose accounting policies when interim statements include notes to financial statements, however.

b. For entities with material seasonal variations in revenues and expenses, the seasonal nature of the activities should be disclosed. In addition, consideration should be given to supplementing interim reports with information for a twelve-month period ending with the interim date. (APB 28, par. 18)

c. Use of the gross profit method for interim inventory pricing should be disclosed. Adjustments needed to reconcile to the annual physical inventory also should be disclosed. (APB 28, par. 14)

d. Other unusual methods of accounting for interim inventories, such as LIFO estimations, should be disclosed. (APB 28, par. 14)

e. The nature and amount of material costs or expenses incurred in an interim period that cannot be readily identified with the activities or benefits of other interim periods should be disclosed. Generally, the disclosure may be made on the face of the income statement by showing the cost or expense as a single line item and providing an appropriate descriptive title. (APB 28, par. 15)

f. If an accounting principle used in an interim financial statement differs from that applied in (a) the preceding interim period, (b) the prior annual financial statements, or (c) the comparable interim period of the prior year, the change in accounting principle should be disclosed. (APB 28, par. 23)

g. The gross and net of tax effects of prior-period adjustments of net income should be disclosed in the interim period in which the adjustments are made. (APB 9, par. 26)

h. When adjustments related to prior interim periods of the current fiscal year are made, (a) the effect on net income from continuing operations and net income for each prior interim period and (b) restated income from continuing operations and net income of each prior interim period should be disclosed. (SFAS 16, par. 15)

i. The following should be disclosed about a cumulative effect-type accounting change: (SFAS 3, par. 11)

In the interim period in which the change is adopted:

(1) Nature of and justification for the change

(2) Effect of the change on income from continuing operations and net income and, for public companies, the effect of the change on related per share amounts (If the change occurs in a period other than the first interim period of the fiscal year, the effect of the change on income from continuing operations, net income, and related per share amounts for each prechange interim period of the fiscal year should be disclosed. In addition, the restated income from continuing operations, net income and related per share amounts for those prior interim periods should be disclosed.)

(3) Pro forma income from continuing operations and net income (and, for public companies, related per share amounts) for the interim period in which the change is made and any interim periods of prior fiscal years are presented (If no interim periods from prior fiscal years are presented, the actual and pro forma amounts of income from continuing operations, net income, and related per share amounts for the interim period of the immediately preceding fiscal year that corresponds to the interim period in which the changes are made should be disclosed.)

In year-to-date and last-12-months-to-date financial reports that include the interim period in which the new principle is adopted:

(4) The effect of the change on income from continuing operations and net income (and, for public companies, related per share amounts) for the interim period in which the change is made

(5) Pro forma income from continuing operations and net income (and, for public companies, related per share amounts) for the interim period in which the change is made and any interim periods of prior fiscal years that are presented (If no interim periods from prior fiscal years are presented, the actual and pro forma amounts of income from continuing operations, net income, and related per share amounts for the interim period of the immediately preceding fiscal year that corresponds to the interim period in which the changes are made should be disclosed.)

In financial reports for subsequent interim periods of the fiscal year:

(6) The effect of the change on income from continuing operations and net income (and for public companies, related per share amounts) for the postchange interim period

DISCLOSURES FOR PUBLIC COMPANIES

29.501   Publicly traded companies that report summarized financial information at interim dates should disclose the following: (APB 28, par. 30)

a. Gross revenues, provision for income taxes, extraordinary items, cumulative effect of a change in accounting principles, net income, and comprehensive income (See Chapter 8.)

b. Basic and diluted earnings per share data for each period presented (See Chapter 19.)

c. Seasonal revenue, costs, or expenses

d. Significant changes in estimates or provisions for income taxes

e. Disposal of a segment of a business and extraordinary, unusual, or infrequently occurring items

f. Contingent items

g. Changes in accounting principles or estimates

h. Significant changes in financial position

29.502   If summarized financial data is not presented separately for the fourth quarter, the annual financial statements should include disclosures about accounting changes, disposals of segments of a business, and extraordinary, unusual, or infrequently occurring items that were recognized in the fourth quarter. In addition, the aggregate effects of year-end adjustments that are material to the fourth quarter should be disclosed. (APB 28, par. 31)

AUTHORITATIVE LITERATURE AND RELATED TOPICS

AUTHORITATIVE LITERATURE

APB Opinion No. 22, *Disclosure of Accounting Policies*
APB Opinion No. 28, *Interim Financial Reporting*
SFAS No. 3, *Reporting Accounting Changes in Interim Financial Statements*
SFAS No. 16, *Prior Period Adjustments*

RELATED PRONOUNCEMENTS

EITF Issue No. 86-13, *Recognition of Inventory Market Declines at Interim Reporting Dates*

RELATED TOPICS

INVENTORY

Table of Contents

INVENTORY

OVERVIEW

30.100　Generally, inventory should be recorded at cost, which includes all direct and indirect costs incurred to prepare it for sale or use. However, in some cases, inventory should be stated at other than cost. For example, if its cost exceeds its market value, inventory should be written down to market value and an unrealized loss should be recognized in current period income. Also, inventory items may be stated above cost if certain conditions are met.

30.101　The primary objective when determining the sequence in which inventory costs are charged to cost of sales is to select the method that most accurately reflects periodic net income. GAAP essentially permits a company to use the following methods to account for inventory:

- Specific identification

- First-in, first-out

- Last-in, first-out

- Average cost

GAAP recognizes certain variations of the above methods and allows them to be used when appropriate. (For example, the retail method is a variation of the average cost method.) In addition, different methods may be used to account for different components of inventory so long as the methods are applied consistently.

ACCOUNTING REQUIREMENTS

DEFINITION

30.200　Inventory is defined as personal tangible property that is:

    a. held for sale in the ordinary course of business;

    b. in the process of production for sale; or

   c. consumed in the production of goods or services to be available for sale. (ARB 43, Ch. 4, par. 3)

Long-term assets that are subject to depreciation (or will be subject to depreciation when they are put into use) are specifically excluded from the definition of inventory. In addition, depreciable assets that are retired from use and held for sale are not considered inventory.

INVENTORY VALUATION

30.201   Except as discussed in Paragraphs 30.207–.210, inventories should be recorded at cost. Although that rule may seem relatively straightforward, applying it in practice may be difficult. It involves (a) identifying product costs (that is, the costs that should be charged to inventory rather than current period expenses) and (b) determining how costs will be charged to cost of sales as inventory is sold. (ARB 43, Ch. 4, par. 5)

Identifying Product Costs

30.202   An inventory item's product cost includes all direct and indirect costs incurred to prepare the item for sale. Thus, for a retail store, an item's product cost may include the purchase price, excise and sales taxes, freight, storage, insurance, etc. For a manufacturing company, inventory typically includes the cost of the following:

   a. Direct materials, including invoice cost, freight-in, and tooling charges from vendors

   b. Direct labor, including payroll costs of personnel whose efforts directly result in the manufacture of the product

   c. Indirect costs, including factory facility costs, utilities, and indirect manufacturing labor and related costs (Interest costs incurred to finance inventory and selling costs are not indirect product costs. Those costs should be expensed when incurred rather than included in inventory.)

30.203   Allocating indirect costs between inventory and period expense is a key factor in determining inventory cost. It often requires considerable judgment because items considered product costs at one company may be considered period expenses at another. (ARB 43, Ch. 4, par. 5) For example, costs that normally would be included in inventory, such as idle facility expense, excessive spoilage, double freight, and rehandling costs, may be immaterial or occur so infrequently that they are treated as period expenses. Conversely, general and administrative costs, which usually are considered period expenses, should be allocated to inventory if they relate to purchasing or producing products for sale. In no case, however, should all overhead be excluded from inventory.

Practical Consideration. As a result of the Tax Reform Act of 1986, certain indirect costs often are capitalized as inventory for tax reporting but not for GAAP. For example, manufacturing companies capitalize the following costs for tax purposes but generally do not for GAAP reporting:

- Warehousing costs such as rent or depreciation, insurance premiums, and property taxes attributable to a warehouse

- Cost of recruiting, hiring, relocating, assigning, and maintaining personnel records of employees whose labor costs are allocable to inventories

- Accounting and data services operations related to inventory activities, including cost accounting and accounts payable

In addition, retailers and wholesalers with average annual gross receipts of $10 million must capitalize costs such as the following for tax purposes even though they do not typically capitalize them for GAAP reporting:

- Costs incidental to the purchasing activity, such as wages of employees responsible for purchasing

- Handling, processing, repackaging, assembly, and similar costs, including labor costs attributable to unloading goods and loading goods for shipment to retail facilities (but not including labor costs attributable to loading goods for final shipment to customers)

- Cost of storing goods

- The portion of general and administrative functions allocable to the preceding functions

The nature of a company's operations and industry practice should be considered when determining whether a cost capitalized for tax reporting also should be capitalized for GAAP reporting. If a company determines that costs previously expensed for GAAP reporting should now be capitalized, it must assess whether the GAAP capitalization requirements are met because of a change in circumstances (for example, a change in the production process) or because generally accepted accounting principles were applied incorrectly in prior periods. A change in circumstances should be accounted for prospectively and does not require beginning inventories to be adjusted. Correcting an error, however, requires beginning inventories to be adjusted through a restatement of retained earnings. (See Chapter 42.)

Methods Used to Charge Inventory to Cost of Sales

30.204　The primary objective in determining how inventory will be charged to cost of sales is to select a method that most accurately reflects the company's income for the period. In some cases, it may be appropriate to apply one method to one portion of inventory and other methods to other portions of inventory. Generally accepted accounting principles essentially permit the following methods of determining the sequence of costs to be charged to cost of sales: (ARB 43, Ch. 4, par. 6)

　　a. *Specific identification.* Under the specific identification method, the cost of each inventory item is tracked from the time of purchase through the time of sale. When an item is sold, its specific cost is charged to cost of sales. Generally, companies use the specific identification method when there are small numbers of easily identifiable inventory items, such as jewelry, furniture, or large pieces of specialized equipment.

　　b. *First-in, first-out.* The first-in, first-out (FIFO) method assumes that items flow through inventory in the order they were purchased. That is, the first items purchased are the first items used or sold. The FIFO method produces an inventory balance sheet account that more closely approximates replacement costs since inventory consists of the items that were purchased most recently. The FIFO cost flow method may be preferred in industries where spoilage or obsolescence is a concern because it more closely corresponds to the physical flow of goods.

　　c. *Last-in, first-out.* The last-in, first-out (LIFO) method assumes that the most recently purchased inventory items are the first items to be sold or used. Because it results in the most recent purchases being charged to cost of sales, the LIFO method more closely matches current costs with current revenues. However, it also results in an inventory balance sheet account that consists of old costs, which may or may not reflect the current value of the assets.

　　d. *Average cost.* The average cost method values inventory based on the average cost of all similar items available during the period. Generally, average cost is determined using either the weighted-average method or the moving-average method.

　　　(1) Under the weighted-average method, average cost is computed at the end of a period by dividing the cost of all items available for sale during the period by the number of units

available for sale during the period. That result is multiplied by the number of items remaining in inventory to obtain the ending inventory's cost, and remaining product costs are charged to cost of sales.

(2) Under the moving-average method, a new average cost is computed after each purchase rather than at the end of the period. Thus, when an inventory item is sold, the average cost existing at that time is charged to cost of sales.

The weighted-average method generally is applied when a periodic inventory system is used, and the moving-average method is applied when a perpetual inventory system is used.

EXHIBIT 30-1 illustrates how inventory and cost of sales is calculated under the FIFO, LIFO, and average cost methods.

30.205   GAAP recognizes that in some cases, it may be preferable to use variations of the methods described in the preceding paragraph. (ARB 43, Ch. 4, par. 6) For example, a department store whose inventories consist of large numbers of low-dollar value items may find it preferable to use a reversed mark-up procedure of inventory pricing, such as the retail inventory method. The retail method is an average cost method designed to approximate the lower of FIFO cost or market. It requires determining inventory at the end of the retail period and converting it to cost using an average cost ratio as follows:

	Cost	Retail
Beginning inventory	$ 50,000	$ 62,500
Purchases	75,000	90,000
	$ 125,000	152,500
Sales		(100,000)
Ending inventory at retail		$ 52,500
Ratio of cost to retail ($125,000 ÷ $152,000)		82%
Ending inventory at cost ($52,500 × 82%)		$ 43,050

EXHIBIT 30-1

ILLUSTRATIVE CALCULATIONS UNDER THE FIFO, LIFO, AND AVERAGE COST INVENTORY METHODS

Assume that XYZ Company, which uses a periodic inventory system, made the following inventory purchases during the year:

	Units	Unit Cost	Total Cost
January 28	300	$ 1.00	$ 300
April 5	400	1.10	440
June 8	200	1.20	240
October 14	600	1.25	750
November 3	300	1.30	390
December 10	600	1.35	810
	2,400		$ 2,930

Assume further that XYZ Company's beginning inventory contained 1,000 units at $.90 per unit and its ending inventory contains 1,200 units.

First-in, First-out

Under the FIFO method, ending inventory contains the most recently purchased items. Thus, ending inventory and cost of sales would be computed as follows:

	Units	Unit Cost	Total Cost
Ending inventory:			
December 10 purchase	600	$ 1.35	$ 810
November 3 purchase	300	1.30	390
October 14 purchase	300	1.25	375
	1,200		$ 1,575
Cost of sales:			
Beginning inventory (1,000 × $.90)			$ 900
Purchases			2,930
			3,830
Ending inventory			(1,575)
			$ 2,255

EXHIBIT 30-1 (Continued)

Last-in, First-out

Under the LIFO method, the most recently purchased items are charged to cost of sales and inventory contains the oldest items. Thus, inventory and cost of sales would be computed as follows:

	Units	Unit Cost	Total Cost
Ending inventory:			
Beginning inventory	1,000	$ .90	$ 900
January 28 purchase	200	1.00	200
	1,200		$ 1,100
Cost of sales:			
Beginning inventory (1,000 × $.90)			$ 900
Purchases			2,930
			3,830
Ending inventory			(1,100)
			$ 2,730

Weighted Average Cost

Under the weighted average cost method, inventory and cost of sales is based on the average cost per unit as follows:

	Units	Unit Cost	Total Cost
Beginning inventory	1,000	$ .90	$ 900
Purchases	2,400		2,930
	3,400		$ 3,830
Average cost per unit ($3,830 ÷ 3,400)			$ 1.13
Ending inventory (1,200 × $1.13)			$ 1,356
Cost of sales:			
Beginning inventory (1,000 × $.90)			$ 900
Purchases			2,930
			3,830
Ending inventory			(1,356)
			$ 2,474

30.206   Manufacturing companies often use the standard cost method, which values inventory items based on predetermined unit costs for material, labor, and manufacturing overhead. The standard costs used approximate the ideal or expected costs based on past performance or other criteria. Differences between standard costs and actual costs are recorded in variance accounts and charged to current period expense rather than inventory. GAAP permits companies to use the standard cost method, but only if standard costs are adjusted periodically to reflect the approximate cost under one of the recognized inventory cost methods discussed in Paragraph 30.204. (ARB 43, Ch. 4, par. 6)

> **Practical Consideration.** The retail and standard cost methods are generally accepted conventions used to apply one of the four methods allowed by GAAP. Disclosing the use of those conventions is not required and, if disclosed, usually is included in the notes rather than on the face of the balance sheet.

Lower of Cost or Market Rule

30.207   Obsolescence, deterioration, damage, changing prices, or other factors may cause an inventory's recorded cost to exceed its market value. In such cases, GAAP requires inventory to be written down to market value and an unrealized loss to be recognized in current period income. Market value is considered to be current replacement cost, with the following limitations: (ARB 43, Ch. 4, paras. 8–9)

  a. Market value should not exceed the inventory's net realizable value, which is its estimated selling price less costs of completion and disposal. (In other words, net realizable value should be used to value inventory if it is lower than current replacement cost.)

  b. Market value should not be less than net realizable value reduced by an allowance for an approximately normal profit margin. (Thus, cost should be used to value inventory if net realizable value will provide for an approximately normal profit, even if current replacement cost is lower than historical cost.)

30.208   To illustrate, assume that an item costs $100, sells for $120 (which provides for a normal profit margin of $20) and its current replacement cost drops to $80.

  • If the selling price is unaffected by the drop in current replacement cost (perhaps because of firm sales commitments), the item would continue to be carried at $100 since the selling price will recover cost plus the normal profit margin.

- If the selling price drops to $100, the item would be carried at $80. The current period income statement would report a loss of $20 for the loss in value.

- If the item's net realizable value drops to $40, the item would be stated at $40.

30.209   Generally, the lower of cost or market rule should be applied to each item in inventory. However, it may be applied to each inventory item, total inventory, or the total of the components of each major category of inventory depending on the method that most fairly presents current period income. (ARB 43, Ch. 4, par. 11) For example, if the cost of a minor component of a finished product exceeds its current replacement cost but the cost of the finished product does not exceed market value, the cost of the component need not be reduced to market.

Stating Inventories above Cost

30.210   Precious metals that have a fixed monetary value with no substantial cost of marketing may be stated at that monetary value, even if it exceeds cost. Other inventory items may be stated above cost only if all of the following conditions are met:

- Appropriate approximate costs for the item cannot be determined.

- The item is immediately marketable at a quoted market price.

- The item is interchangeable.

In such cases, the items generally are stated at market price less disposal costs. Agricultural or mineral products are examples of inventories that may meet the preceding conditions. (ARB 43, Ch. 4, par. 16)

LOSSES ON FIRM PURCHASE COMMITMENTS

30.211   Expected losses on firm, noncancelable purchase commitments for inventory goods should be measured in the same manner as inventory losses (see Paragraph 30.207) and accrued through a charge to current period income. (ARB 43, Ch. 4, par. 17)

INTERIM FINANCIAL STATEMENTS

30.212   Although the same inventory accounting principles generally apply to both annual and interim financial statements, APB Opinion No. 28, *Interim Financial Reporting,* states that the following modifications to inventory accounting principles may be appropriate in interim periods:

   a. *Gross profit method.* Because physical inventories usually are not taken at interim dates, many companies use the gross profit method to estimate inventory and cost of goods sold in interim periods. Companies that use the gross profit method during interim periods (or another method that differs from the method used in annual financial statements) should disclose the method used and any significant adjustments that result from reconciliation with the annual physical inventory.

   b. *Market declines.* As discussed in Paragraph 30.207, inventory should be written down to market value when market value is lower than cost. In interim financial statements, such write-downs should be recorded in the interim period in which the decline in value occurs. A subsequent recovery in value before year end should be recognized in the interim period during which the recovery takes place. However, upward adjustments should not exceed write-downs made during the year's previous interim periods. In addition, inventory need not be adjusted to market in interim periods if the market decline is temporary (i.e., it is reasonably expected to be recovered by the end of the fiscal year).

   c. *Standard cost systems.* Planned purchase price or volume variances that are expected to be absorbed by the end of the fiscal year ordinarily should be deferred in interim financial statements. Unanticipated purchase price or volume variances should be reported in interim financial statements, however.

   d. *LIFO inventory liquidations.* Companies that use the LIFO method may encounter a liquidation of a LIFO layer in an interim period that is expected to be restored by the end of the fiscal year. Companies should not include the effect of such temporary liquidations in their interim period financial statements. Instead, cost of sales should reflect the expected cost of replacing the liquidated LIFO layer. (APB 28, par. 14)

Practical Consideration. Some companies compute LIFO inventory values only on an annual basis and use the FIFO method in interim financial statements. In such cases, the authors recommend the following:

- If the difference between LIFO and FIFO values as of the interim date is immaterial, the inventory basis may be identified as LIFO.

- If the difference between LIFO and FIFO is material and interim financial statements are issued with inventories on a FIFO basis, the statements are not in conformity with GAAP because they do not use the same method as used in the year-end statements.

- If the difference between LIFO and FIFO values is material, the company may want to approximate an adjustment to LIFO and present inventory in interim financial statements at estimated LIFO value. That approach parallels the use of gross profit percentages at interim dates as described in item a. The authors believe such an approach is proper and is not a departure from GAAP if the estimation method has a reasonable basis. Of course, the estimation method used to value the inventories should be disclosed.

VALUING INVENTORY IN A BUSINESS COMBINATION

30.213   When a company acquires inventory in a business combination accounted for under the purchase method of accounting, APB Opinion No. 16, *Business Combinations,* requires the inventory to be valued as follows:

- *Finished goods and merchandise*—estimated selling prices less the sum of costs of disposal and a reasonable profit allowance

- *Work in process*—estimated selling prices of finished goods less the sum of costs to complete, costs of disposal, and a reasonable profit allowance

- *Raw materials*—current replacement costs (APB 16, par. 88)

30.214   In a business combination accounted for under the pooling of interests method, the recorded assets and liabilities of each entity generally are combined and become the recorded assets and liabilities of the combined entity. (APB 16, par. 51) Thus, under the pooling of interests method, the recorded value of inventory should equal the combined book values of the combining entities' inventories.

CONSIGNED INVENTORIES

30.215 Generally accepted accounting principles do not specifically address consigned inventories. However, a basic accounting concept is that a company should not record an asset until it receives title to the asset, and it should not record a sale until title transfers to the customer. In traditional consignment arrangements, the consignor ships goods to the consignee but continues to own them until they are sold by the consignee. When the goods are sold, title passes directly from consignor to the purchaser—title never passes to the consignee. Under such arrangements, no entries are needed at the time of consignment. That is, consigned goods continue to be included in inventory in the consignor's financial statements and not in the consignee's financial statements. When the consigned goods are sold, however, an entry is needed on the consignor's books to record the sale and on the consignee's books to record commission income. (In some consignment arrangements, the consignee acquires title to the goods from the consignor at the time of the sale. In such cases, when the consigned inventory is sold, the consignee records the transaction as a sale to the purchaser rather than as commission income.)

DISCLOSURE REQUIREMENTS

30.500 A company should include the following disclosures about inventories in its financial statements: (ARB 43, Ch. 4, paras. 14–15)

a. Basis for stating inventories (for example, the cost basis)

b. Method of determining costs (for example, average cost, first-in, first-out, last-in, first-out, etc.)

Practical Consideration. It is common practice to disclose the inventory basis and method of determining cost within the balance sheet caption (for example, "Inventories, at the lower of first-in, first-out cost or market"). However, the disclosures may be made in the notes rather than on the face of the balance sheet as follows:

> Inventories are stated at the lower of cost or market value. Cost is determined using the last-in, first-out method for groceries and primarily the first-in, first-out method for all other inventories.

---

c. Unusual losses resulting from lower of cost or market adjustments or losses on firm purchase commitments (If material, the losses should be disclosed separately from cost of goods sold in the income statement.)

Practical Consideration. GAAP does not require a company to disclose the components or types of inventory. In practice, however, that disclosure is almost universal in the following situations:

a. Manufacturing inventories in various stages of completion

b. Inventories of distinct product lines

The following are examples of such disclosures, which may be made on the face of the balance sheet or in the notes:

	19X5	19X4
Inventories		
Raw materials	$ 55,000	$ 50,000
Work in process	15,000	20,000
Finished goods	40,000	30,000

	19X5	19X4
Inventories		
New materials	$ 100,000	$ 125,000
Used vehicles	150,000	175,000
Parts and accessories	50,000	40,000

AUTHORITATIVE LITERATURE AND RELATED TOPICS

AUTHORITATIVE LITERATURE

ARB No. 43, *Restatement and Revision of Accounting Research Bulletins* (Chapter 4—Inventory Pricing)
APB No. 16, *Business Combinations*
APB No. 28, *Interim Financial Reporting*

RELATED PRONOUNCEMENTS

EITF Issue No. 84-10, *LIFO Conformity of Companies Relying on Insilco Tax Court Decision*
EITF Issue No. 84-24, *LIFO Accounting Issues*
EITF Issue No. 86-13, *Recognition of Inventory Market Declines at Interim Reporting Dates*

EITF Issue No. 86-46, *Uniform Capitalization Rules for Inventory under The Tax Reform Act of 1986*

Practice Bulletin 2, *Elimination of Profits Resulting from Intercompany Transfers of LIFO Inventories*

RELATED TOPICS

LEASES

Table of Contents

LEASES

Table of Contents (Continued)

LEASES

Table of Contents (Continued)

LEASES

OVERVIEW

31.100   Accounting for leases is based on the notion that a lease transferring substantially all of the risks and rewards of ownership should be capitalized. That is, an asset and related obligation should be recorded by the lessee and a sale or financing should be recorded by the lessor. Other leases should be accounted for as the rental of property.

CLASSIFYING LEASES

31.101   A lessee should classify a lease as a capital lease if the lease meets *at least one* of the following criteria: (Otherwise, the lessee should classify the lease as an operating lease.)

   a. The lease passes title to the lessee by the end of the lease term.

   b. The lease contains a bargain purchase option.

   c. The lease term is at least 75% of the property's estimated remaining economic life.

   d. The present value of the minimum lease payments is at least 90% of the property's fair value.

The 75% and 90% tests do not apply if the lease term begins within the last 25% of the leased property's total estimated economic life, however.

31.102   Sales-type and direct financing leases are the lessor's equivalent of a capital lease. In a sales-type lease, the leased property's book value is different from its fair value, resulting in a gain or loss to the lessor. In a direct financing lease, the leased property's book value and fair value are the same and no gain or loss results. A lessor should classify a lease as a sales-type or direct financing lease if the lease meets *at least one* of the tests in the preceding paragraph and *both* of the following criteria: (Otherwise, the lessor should classify the lease as an operating lease.)

   a. Collectibility of the minimum lease payments is reasonably predictable.

b. There are no important uncertainties about additional unreimbursed costs the lessor will incur.

31.103   A leveraged lease is a type of direct financing lease that has the following additional characteristics:

a. It involves a lessee, a lessor, and a long-term creditor.

b. The financing provided by the long-term creditor is nonrecourse to the general credit of the lessor.

c. The amount of financing provided by the long-term creditor is substantial to the transaction.

d. The lessor's net investment in the lease declines in the early years of the lease and rises during the later years before it is finally eliminated.

e. Any investment tax credit retained by the lessor is deferred and allocated to income over the lease term.

31.104   Certain exceptions to the lessee and lessor classification criteria exist for leases involving real estate.

ACCOUNTING FOR LEASES—LESSEES

31.105   A lessee should account for a capital lease as if the leased asset were purchased and the entire purchase price were financed. As a result, the lessee should record a leased asset and lease obligation of the same amount. The amount recorded should be the lesser of the fair value of the leased asset at the inception of the lease or the present value of the minimum lease payments as of the beginning of the lease term. Once recorded, the leased asset should be depreciated like any owned asset, and the lease obligation should be accounted for under the interest method.

31.106   A lessee should account for an operating lease by charging the lease payments to expense. Generally, rent expense under an operating lease should be recognized on a straight-line basis over the lease term, however, even if payments are not made on a straight-line basis.

ACCOUNTING FOR LEASES—LESSORS

31.107   A lessor should account for a sales-type lease as follows:

a. The gross investment in the lease and the present value of the gross investment in the lease should be determined.

b. The present value of the gross investment should be recorded as a receivable and classified as current or noncurrent like any other receivable. The difference between the gross investment and its present value should be recorded as unearned income and amortized over the lease term using the interest method.

c. The present value of the minimum lease payments to be received should be recognized as income. The carrying amount of the leased property, plus any initial direct costs and less the present value of the unguaranteed residual value, should be charged against income.

31.108   A lessor should account for a direct financing lease as follows:

a. The gross investment in the lease should be determined.

b. The difference between the gross investment and the book value of the property represents unearned interest income. The unearned interest income and any initial direct costs should be amortized to income over the lease term using the interest method.

c. The net investment in the lease should be shown as a single line item on the balance sheet and classified as current and noncurrent like any other receivable. The net investment consists of the gross investment plus any unamortized initial direct costs minus the unearned interest income.

31.109   A lessor should record its net investment in a leveraged lease net of the nonrecourse debt. The total net income over the lease term, which should only be recognized in periods in which the net investment net of deferred taxes is positive, is determined by subtracting the original investment from total cash receipts.

31.110   When accounting for an operating lease, the lessor should continue to carry the leased asset in its balance sheet and depreciate it according to its normal depreciation policy. Rent income should be reported as it becomes receivable in the same way rent expense is reported by lessees. That is, it generally should be recognized on a straight-line basis.

OTHER LEASE TRANSACTIONS

31.111   Additional requirements (or variations of the preceding requirements) apply to subleases, leases involving real estate, leases with governmental entities, money-over-money leases, sale-leaseback transactions, and wrap leases.

ACCOUNTING REQUIREMENTS

31.200   In general terms, a lease is a contract that provides an entity the right to use property that it does not own in exchange for some consideration, usually for a specified period of time. Leases ordinarily involve two parties—a lessor (the one who owns the leased property and is paid rent) and a lessee (the one who pays rent). All agreements that meet the preceding definition are considered leases, including those not specifically referred to as leases and those that require the lessor to provide substantial services to operate or maintain the leased assets. However, for purposes of applying GAAP, leases do not include agreements that—

- concern the right to explore for or to exploit natural resources such as oil, gas, minerals, and timber.

- apply to licensing agreements for items such as motion picture films, plays, manuscripts, patents, and copyrights. (SFAS 13, par. 1)

TYPES OF LEASES

31.201   Accounting for leases varies depending on the type of lease. Under generally accepted accounting principles, leases are classified as one of the following types:

Lessees

- *Capital lease.* A capital lease transfers substantially all the benefits and risks of ownership to the lessee and is recorded as if the lessee borrowed money to purchase the leased property.

- *Operating lease.* Operating leases are those that are not classified as capital leases. They are treated as the rental of property by the lessee from the lessor, and their effects are recorded as consideration is paid. (SFAS 13, par. 6)

Lessors

- *Direct financing lease.* Direct financing leases and sales-type leases are the lessor's equivalent of a capital lease. In a direct financing lease, the fair value and book value of the leased asset are the same. Thus, there is no profit involved for the lessor, and the lease is accounted for as a financing. The difference between the total lease payments to be received and the book value of the property is assumed to be the equivalent of interest that would have been paid had the lessee borrowed the money from the lessor to purchase the property. (SFAS 13, par. 6)

- *Sales-type lease.* In a sales-type lease, the leased property's book value is different from its fair value. Consequently, the sale provides a profit (or loss) to the lessor. The basic accounting for sales-type leases involves recognizing both a profit element and a financing element. (SFAS 98, par. 22)

- *Operating lease.* An operating lease is one that does not meet the criteria for classification as a sales-type or direct financing lease by the lessor. Like operating leases of lessees, operating leases of lessors are similar to rentals of property and their effects are recorded as consideration is received. (SFAS 98, par. 22)

Classifying Leases—Lessees

31.202   From the lessee's perspective, a lease should be considered a capital lease if it meets at least one of the following criteria: (Otherwise, it should be considered an operating lease.) (SFAS 13, par. 7)

a. *Ownership transfer test.* The lease passes title to the lessee by the end of the lease term.

b. *Bargain purchase option test.* The lease contains a bargain purchase option.

c. *75% test.* The lease term is at least 75% of the property's estimated economic life.

d. *90% test.* The present value of the minimum lease payments is at least 90% of the property's fair value.

The 75% test and 90% test should not be considered if the lease term begins within the last 25% of the leased property's total estimated economic life, however. In addition, certain exceptions to the preceding criteria exist for real estate leases. (See Paragraphs 31.249–.257.) The flowchart in EXHIBIT 31-1 illustrates the basic lease classification criteria for a lessee.

31.203   **Ownership Transfer Test.** The basis for this test is fairly straightforward. If the lease transfers ownership of the property by the end of the lease term, it effectively transfers all the benefits and risks of ownership. The following definitions and issues should be considered when applying this test:

    a. *Lease term.* The lease term is defined as the fixed, noncancelable portion of the lease, plus all periods—(SFAS 98, par. 22)

        (1) covered by bargain renewal options.

        (2) for which failure to renew imposes enough of a penalty on the lessee that renewal is reasonably assured.

        (3) for which the lease can be renewed or extended at the option of the lessor.

        (4) covered by ordinary renewal options during which a guarantee by the lessee of the lessor's debt that is directly or indirectly related to the leased property is expected to be in effect or a loan from the lessee to the lessor directly or indirectly related to the leased property is expected to be outstanding. (It is assumed that the lessee will not terminate the lease if the lease payments are being used by the lessor to pay debt related to the leased property.)

        (5) covered by ordinary renewal options preceding the exercise date of a bargain purchase option. (It is assumed that the bargain purchase option will be exercised, so it is also assumed that all renewal options up to that date will be exercised.)

        (6) representing renewals or extensions of the lease at the lessor's option.

The lease term cannot extend past the date a bargain purchase option becomes exercisable, however, since it is assumed that the option will be exercised and the lease will end at that time. In addition, a lease term is considered noncancelable if it may be canceled only (1) on the occurrence of some remote contingency, (2) with the permission of the lessor, (3) if the lessee enters into a new lease with the same lessor, or (4) if cancellation imposes enough of a penalty on the lessee that continuation of the lease appears reasonably assured.

EXHIBIT 31-1

BASIC LEASE CLASSIFICATION—LESSEE

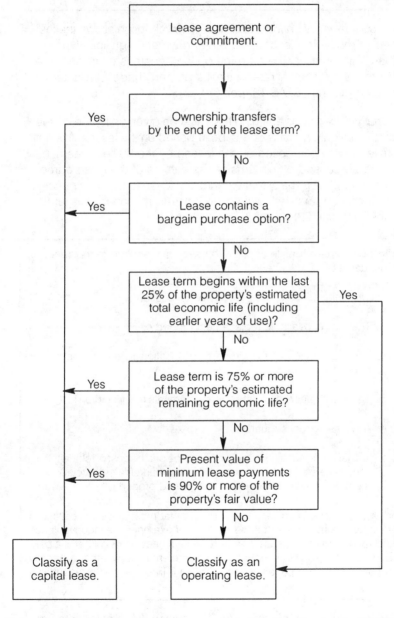

Note: Classification of real estate leases may differ. See Paragraphs 31.249–.257.

> **Practical Consideration.** Some leases provide for a noncancelable period followed by cancelable renewal periods (typically on a year-to-year basis). Only the noncancelable period should be considered when determining how to classify the lease.

  b. *Bargain renewal option.* A bargain renewal option allows the lessee to renew the lease for a rental payment significantly lower than "fair rental" at the date the option becomes exercisable. A fair rental is the rental rate for similar property under similar terms and conditions. (SFAS 13, par. 5)

  c. *Penalty.* A penalty is anything that must be given up by the lessee or any obligation that is or can be imposed on the lessee. It is not limited to items imposed on the lessee by the lease agreement. It can be caused by circumstances outside of the lease agreement as well. A penalty that extends the lease term is any penalty so significant that renewal of the lease is reasonably assured. (SFAS 98, par. 22)

> **Practical Consideration.** In addition to payments required for nonrenewal, penalties can exist due to the following:
>
>   a. The uniqueness of the property or its location
>
>   b. The lack of available replacement property
>
>   c. The importance of the property or location to the lessee's business
>
>   d. The significance of leasehold improvements that would be lost
>
>   e. Adverse tax consequences
>
>   f. The lessee's inability or unwillingness to bear the cost of relocation, lease equivalent property at current market rates, or tolerate a competitor moving into the vacated property
>
> Based on the above definition, it is apparent that most lease cancellations involve at least some penalty for the lessee. For example, the inconvenience and cost of moving from a leased property would meet the definition of a penalty. Thus, the difficult part is not necessarily determining whether a penalty exists, but whether the penalty is so significant that renewal is reasonably assured.

  d. *Timing of the ownership transfer.* The ownership transfer criterion is met if ownership is transferred at or shortly after the end of the lease term. That includes situations in which the lessee purchases the property at the end of the lease term for a nominal fee, such as $1. That often occurs when the lease is intended to transfer ownership, but state law requires that some consideration be given up in order to establish a valid contract. (SFAS 98, par. 22)

31.204 **Bargain Purchase Option Test.** A bargain purchase option is an option for the lessee to purchase the leased property at a price substantially below its expected fair value at the date the option is exercisable. In essence, the bargain purchase option test is similar to the ownership transfer test. That is, the existence of a bargain purchase option is assumed to virtually assure that ownership will be transferred. (SFAS 13, par. 5)

Practical Consideration. Deciding whether a purchase option is a bargain depends to a large extent on how closely the future value of the property can be estimated. For example, if the future value of the property can be estimated with relatively high precision, a purchase option of up to 90% of the property's expected fair value might be considered a bargain. In other cases, a purchase option of 80% may not be considered a bargain. Generally, the more subjective the estimate, the more difficult it is to conclude that the purchase option is a bargain. Management's plans for the property at the end of the lease term can provide evidence about whether management considers a purchase option to be a bargain. Also, management's estimate of the property's residual value at the end of the lease term should be the same as the fair value used to assess whether a bargain purchase option exists.

31.205 **The 75% Test.** The 75% test is met if the lease term (defined in Paragraph 31.203) is at least 75% of the estimated remaining economic life of the leased property. The estimated remaining economic life of the leased property is the remaining period during which the property is expected to be economically usable, with normal repairs and maintenance, for the purpose intended at the inception of the lease, regardless of the lease term.

31.206 When determining whether a lease is a capital lease, the 75% test should not be applied if the lease term begins within the last 25% of the leased property's total estimated economic life. The total estimated economic life of the leased property is similar to its estimated remaining economic life except that it includes periods of prior use. (SFAS 13, paras. 5 and 7)

31.207 **The 90% Test.** The 90% test is met if the present value at the beginning of the lease term of the minimum lease payments is at least 90% of the property's fair value to the lessor at the inception of the lease. (The 90% test should not be applied if the lease term begins within the last 25% of the leased property's total estimated economic life, however.) The following should be considered when applying this test: (SFAS 13, paras. 5 and 7)

a. When computing the present value of the minimum lease payments, a lessor should use the interest rate implicit in the lease. A lessee should use the lower of its incremental borrowing rate or the lessor's implicit rate, if known. (The lessee has no obligation to estimate the lessor's implicit rate if it does not know that rate.)

    (1) The lessee's incremental borrowing rate is the rate the lessee would have incurred if it had borrowed money to purchase the property rather than lease it. The lessee may use a secured borrowing rate as the incremental rate if it is determinable, reasonable, and consistent with the financing that would have been used if the property were purchased instead of leased.

    (2) The interest rate implicit in the lease is the rate that discounts the minimum lease payments and the unguaranteed residual value to the fair value of the property to the lessor at the inception of the lease. The fair value used in the calculation of the implicit rate should be reduced by any investment tax credit retained and to be used by the lessor.

b. The lessee's minimum lease payments consist of all rental payments called for during the lease term plus any residual value guaranteed by the lessee. It includes any payment the lessee must make for not renewing or extending the lease, including a requirement to purchase the property. The lessee's minimum lease payments do not include the following, however:

    (1) Any guarantee by the lessee of the lessor's debt

    (2) The lessee's obligation (separate from rental payments) to pay executory costs (for example, insurance, taxes, etc.) and any related profit on those costs

    (3) Any penalty for which the lease term has been extended

    (4) Contingent rentals (Increases in minimum lease payments occurring during the preacquisition or construction period that result from an escalation clause in the lease are not considered contingent rentals.)

If the lease contains a bargain purchase option, however, the above criteria are disregarded. In that case, minimum lease payments consist only of the rental payments to the date the option is exercisable (excluding executory costs and profit thereon) and the option amount.

Practical Consideration. The estimated residual value of the leased property is its estimated fair value (i.e., salvage value) at the end of the lease term. The guaranteed residual value is any part of the property's estimated residual value that is guaranteed by the lessee. (Guarantees by parties related to the lessee are considered to be guarantees by the lessee.) Thus, if the lessee agrees to purchase the property at the end of the lease term (i.e., the lessee has a purchase commitment, not a purchase option), the purchase price is treated as a residual value guarantee. On the other hand, if the lessee agrees to make up any shortfall at the end of the lease term, the amount included in the minimum lease payments is the amount guaranteed by the lessee, not the expected shortfall. (For example, if the lessee agrees to reimburse the lessor any shortfall in the property's residual value below $10,000, the amount included in minimum lease payments is $10,000, the lessee's maximum exposure).

FASB Interpretation No.19, *Lessee Guarantee of the Residual Value of Leased Property,* provides the following additional clarification of what should be included in minimum lease payments under certain types of residual value guarantees:

- If the lessee is required to make up a deficiency for damage, extraordinary wear, or excessive usage, the estimated cost is not considered a residual value guarantee (and is not included in minimum lease payments). The reasoning is that such costs are contingent on future events and are not determinable.

- If the lease contains a "first loss guarantee" by the lessee, the residual value guarantee included in the minimum lease payments is the lessee's maximum amount of loss. For example, if a lessee agrees to make up any shortfall in the property's residual value below $10,000 but the deficiency that the lessee must make up is limited to $6,000, only $6,000 would be considered a residual value guarantee and included in the minimum lease payments.

- If a lessee contracts with a third party to be responsible for all or part of the residual value guarantee (i.e., the lessee gets a guarantee of its guarantee), the lessee's minimum lease payments cannot be reduced for the amount of the guarantee that is transferred unless the lessee is explicitly released by the lessor from primary and secondary responsibility for the residual value guarantee.

---

c. The lessor's minimum lease payments are the same as the lessee's with one exception—they also include any guarantee of the
residual value or lease payments beyond the lease term by a third
party (provided the third party is financially capable of meeting
the obligation).

d. The fair value of the leased property is the price for which the
property can be exchanged between unrelated parties in an
arms-length transaction. When the lessor is a manufacturer or
dealer, the property's fair value is usually its normal selling price.
When the lessor is not a manufacturer or dealer, the property's fair
value is usually its cost. (Current market conditions must be considered, however, particularly when significant time has lapsed
since the construction or acquisition of the property.)

Classifying Leases—Lessors

31.208   A lessor should classify a lease as a sales-type lease or direct financing lease if it meets at least one of the four tests discussed in Paragraph 31.202
and *both* of the following criteria:

a. *Collectibility of the minimum lease payments must be reasonably
   predictable.* A lease meets this criteria even if it is believed that
   not all of the minimum lease payments will be collected so long
   as the uncollectible portion can be reasonably estimated based
   on experience with similar receivables. The minimum lease payments are not considered "reasonably predictable" when other
   than normal credit risks are involved, however. (SFAS 98, par. 22)

b. *There are no important uncertainties about additional unreimbursed costs the lessor will incur.* Important uncertainties might
   relate to such items as performance guarantees beyond a typical
   product warranty or commitments to replace the leased asset if
   it becomes obsolete. (SFAS 13, par. 8)

31.209   Certain exceptions to the preceding criteria exist for real estate
leases. (See Paragraphs 31.249–.257.) The flowchart in EXHIBIT 31-2 illustrates the basic lease classification criteria for a lessor.

EXHIBIT 31-2
BASIC LEASE CLASSIFICATION—LESSOR

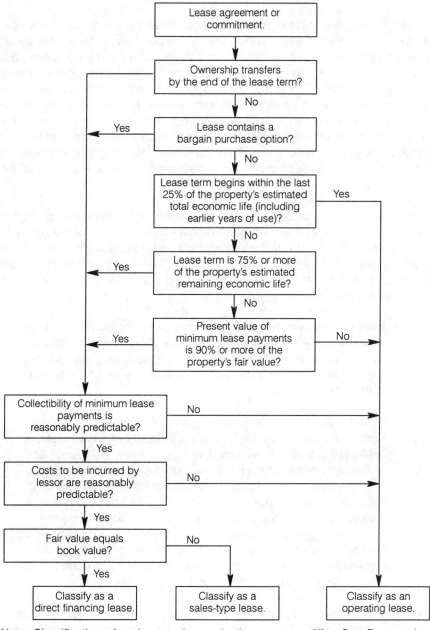

Note: Classification of real estate leases by lessors may differ. See Paragraphs 31.249–.257.

ACCOUNTING FOR LEASES—LESSEES

Capital Leases

31.210   When a lease is classified as a capital lease, it is accounted for as if the leased asset were purchased and the entire purchase price were financed. Consequently, the lessee should record a leased asset and a lease obligation of the same amount. The amount recorded should be the lesser of (a) the fair value of the leased asset at the inception of the lease or (b) the present value of the minimum lease payments (excluding executory costs to be paid by the lessor and related profit) as of the beginning of the lease term. The present value of the minimum lease payments should be discounted using the interest rate used to apply the 90% test. As discussed in Paragraph 31.207, that rate is the lower of the lessee's incremental borrowing rate or the lessor's implicit rate, if known. (SFAS 13, par. 10)

31.211   Once recorded, the leased asset should be depreciated like any owned asset. That is, it should be depreciated over its estimated useful life down to its expected value to the lessee at the end of the lease term. In a capital lease, however, the period over which the asset should be depreciated, and the value to which it should be depreciated, depends on why the lease was capitalized. (SFAS 13, par. 11)

   a. If the lease meets the transfer of ownership or bargain purchase option test, it is assumed that the lessee will own the property for its full economic life. Consequently, the asset should be depreciated over its estimated economic life down to its estimated residual value.

   b. If the lease does not meet the transfer of ownership or bargain purchase option tests (i.e., it was capitalized because it met the 75% or 90% test), it is assumed that the property will revert back to the lessor at the end of the lease term. Consequently, the asset should be depreciated over the lease term down to its expected value to the lessee. That will ordinarily be zero since the property reverts back to the lessor at the end of the lease term. However, if the lease agreement contains a residual value guarantee and the lessee gets no benefit from any value in excess of the guarantee, the expected value is the amount the lessee can realize from the property, up to the amount of the guarantee.

31.212   The lease obligation should be accounted for using the interest method of accounting. Consequently, a portion of each minimum lease payment should be allocated to interest expense, and the remainder applied to reduce the obligation, so that a constant rate of interest is produced on the out-standing liability. (SFAS 13, par. 12) (Applying the interest method is discussed further in Chapter 28.) Contingent rental payments should be recognized as expense in the periods they arise. (SFAS 29, par. 13)

Operating Leases

31.213   Generally, rent expense under an operating lease should be recognized on a straight-line basis over the lease term, even if payments are not made on a straight-line basis. (SFAS 13, par. 15)

Practical Consideration. To illustrate recognizing rent expense on a straight-line basis when lease payments vary, assume that a lessee is not required to make any payments during the first year of a five-year lease, but must make monthly payments of $550 thereafter during the lease term. Total rent expense under the lease would be $26,400 ($550 × 48 months) and the amount charged to expense each month during the lease term would be $440 (26,400 ÷ 60 months). The excess of expense over payments during the rent-free period would be credited to an accrued liability as expense is accrued each month during the first year. In subsequent months, the accrued liability would be reduced by the excess of the monthly payments over the monthly expense ($550 − $440).

31.214   Rent expense may be recognized using a method other than straight-line if the method is systematic, rational, and more representative of the time pattern in which the leased asset is used. Using factors such as the time value of money, anticipated inflation, or expected future revenues to allocate scheduled rent increases to expense is not appropriate because those factors do not relate to the time pattern of actually using the leased property. (FTB 85-3, par. 2)

31.215   **Contingent Rentals.** Rent increases or decreases based on future conditions, such as future sales volume, machine hours, interest rates, or price indexes, are considered contingent rentals. A contingent rental payment should be recognized as an expense in the period it arises. (SFAS 29, paras. 11 and 13)

31.216   **Right to Control the Use of the Asset Is Equivalent to Physical Use.** The right to control the use of the leased asset is considered the equivalent of physical use. Thus, whether the lessee actually uses the leased asset has no effect on rental expense or rental revenue. For example, if an entire manufacturing building with excess capacity is leased, and the lease agreement includes escalating rental payments in contemplation of the lessee's expected expansion and physical use of the excess capacity, the aggregate lease payments should be recognized on a straight-line basis over the lease term as discussed in Paragraph 31.213, regardless of whether the excess capacity is actually used. (FTB 88-1, par. 2)

31.217   On the other hand, if rents escalate as the lessee *gains* control of the additional leased property, the additional rental expense should be recognized as it is due, provided rental amounts are based on the relative fair value of the additional leased property at the inception of the lease. If escalating rental payments are not based on fair value, however, they should be reallocated between the original leased property and the additional leased property based on the relative fair value of the property at the inception of the lease. After the reallocation, the amount of rental expense or rental revenue attributable to the additional leased property should be proportionate to the relative fair value of the additional property, as determined at the inception of the lease, in the periods during which the lessee controls its use. (FTB 88-1, par. 2)

Practical Consideration. To illustrate accounting for rent escalations as the lessee gains control of additional leased property, assume a lessee signs a 10-year master lease agreement under which it will lease the first floor of a two-story office building during the first five years and the first and second floors during the last five years. (The second floor is currently under lease to another tenant and will not be available until the sixth year.) Rent for the first year is $50,000 with scheduled annual increases of 5% during the second through the fifth years. Rent for the sixth year is $90,000 with scheduled annual increases of 6%. At the inception of the lease, the market rental is $50,000 for the first floor and $80,000 for the entire building, resulting in a fair value for the first floor lease equal to 62.5% of the total fair value of the lease. Rental payments under the agreement should be recognized based on the fair values of the leased property as follows:

	First Floor	Second Floor	Total
Year 1	$ 50,000	$ —	$ 50,000
Year 2	52,500	—	52,500
Year 3	55,100	—	55,100
Year 4	57,900	—	57,900
Year 5	60,800	—	60,800
	276,300	—	276,300
Year 6	56,300	33,700	90,000
Year 7	59,600	35,800	95,400
Year 8	63,200	37,900	101,100
Year 9	67,000	40,200	107,200
Year 10	71,000	42,600	113,600
	$ 593,400	$ 190,200	$ 783,600

Practical Consideration (Continued).

Annual rent recognized on the first floor space would be $59,340 (that is, total rentals of $593,400 ÷ the 10-year lease term), and $38,040 would be recognized annually on the second floor space while it is leased (that is, total rentals of $190,200 ÷ the five-year lease term). As a result, the lessee would recognize annual rent expense of $59,340 during the first five years and $97,380 during the last five years (that is, $59,340 for the first floor plus $38,040 for the second floor).

31.218   **Lease Incentives.** Incentive payments include items such as up-front cash payments to the lessee to sign the lease, payments to reimburse the lessee for specific costs such as moving costs or abandoned leasehold improvements, and payments to third-parties on behalf of the lessee, such as for leasehold improvements. The lessee should amortize incentive payments against rental expense over the term of the lease. (FTB 88-1, par. 7) The lessee should record receipt of the payment through a debit to cash and a credit to a deferred lease incentive account. The deferred lease incentive account should be amortized through a credit to rent expense over the lease term using the straight-line method.

Practical Consideration. To illustrate, assume the lessor reimburses the lessee for $10,000 of its moving costs as an incentive to enter into a five-year non-cancelable lease requiring annual rentals of $50,000. The lessee would record receipt of the payment as a debit to cash and a credit to deferred lease incentive for $10,000. (Receipt of the payment has no effect on the lessee's accounting for the moving costs. Expenses or losses such as moving expenses, losses on subleases, or the write-off of abandoned leasehold improvements are charged to expense as incurred.) The $10,000 deferred lease incentive should be amortized over the five-year lease term through annual credits to rent expense of $2,000 calculated using the straight-line method. As a result, the lessee would make the following entry each year to record payment of the annual rentals:

Rent expense	48,000	
Deferred lease incentive	2,000	
Cash		50,000

Over the lease term, both the lessor and lessee would recognize rent of $240,000 (that is, annual rent of $48,000 × five years), which represents total minimum lease payments of $250,000 (that is, annual payments of $50,000 × five years) less the $10,000 incentive payment.

31.219   If a lessor assumes a lessee's pre-existing lease with a third party, the related loss incurred by the lessor is considered a rent incentive. The lessor and the lessee should independently estimate the loss incurred by the lessor. An

appropriate method for the lessee to estimate the lessor's loss is to base its estimate on a comparison of the new lease with the market rental rate available for
similar leased property or the market rental rate from the same lessor without
the lease assumption. (FTB 88-1, paras. 7–8)

Practical Consideration. To illustrate accounting for the lessor's assumption
of the lessee's pre-existing lease, assume that the lessee presently pays
annual rent of $32,000 on its office facilities and three years remain under that
lease. The lessee enters into a lease for new facilities that requires annual rentals of $50,000 over a noncancelable term of five years and the assumption of
its existing lease. The lessee believes the annual market rental for property
similar to its new facilities is $45,000. Thus, the lessee calculates the value of
the incentive as $25,000 [($50,000 – $45,000) × 5 years]. The lessee would
record a loss of $25,000 at inception. As lease payments are made, the
$25,000 would be amortized as a reduction of rent expense. The entries would
be as follows:

At inception:

Loss on sublease assumed by lessor	25,000	
Deferred lease incentive		25,000

Annually thereafter:

Rent expense	45,000	
Deferred lease incentive	5,000	
Cash		50,000

ACCOUNTING FOR LEASES—LESSORS

Sales-type Leases

31.220   As discussed in Paragraph 31.201, a lease is classified as a sales-
type lease when the transaction is, in essence, a sale of property to the lessee
that provides a profit or loss to the lessor. A lessor should account for a sales-
type lease as follows: (SFAS 13, par. 17)

    a. The gross investment in the lease should be determined. The les-
sor's gross investment is equal to (1) the total minimum lease payments to be received (net of any included executory costs and
related profits to be paid by the lessor) plus (2) any unguaranteed
residual value accruing to the benefit of the lessor (that is, the
unguaranteed fair value of the leased asset to which the lessor
is entitled at the end of the lease term.)

    b. The gross investment in the lease should be discounted to its
present value using the interest rate implicit in the lease. The

difference between the gross investment and its present value should be recorded as unearned income and amortized over the lease term using the interest method. (Other amortization methods may be used if they do not produce materially different results.) The present value of the gross investment, referred to as the net investment in the lease, should be recorded as a receivable and classified as current or noncurrent like any other receivable. (See Chapter 12.)

c. The present value of the minimum lease payments to be received (net of any included executory costs and related profits to be paid by the lessor) should be recognized as income. The carrying amount of the leased property, plus any initial direct costs (i.e., costs incurred by the lessor to negotiate and consummate the lease) and less the present value of the unguaranteed residual value, should be charged against income.

d. The present value of the unguaranteed residual value should be reviewed at least annually to determine whether a decline in value has occurred. If a decline that is other than temporary has occurred, the transaction should be revised using the new estimate. The resulting reduction in the net investment in the lease should be recognized as a loss in the period of the decline. An upward adjustment should not be made.

Practical Consideration. To illustrate accounting for a sales-type lease, assume that XYZ Company leases equipment to ABC Company under the following terms:

- The lease agreement is dated January 1, 19X5, and requires ABC Company to pay 20 annual rents of $47,154 beginning January 1, 19X5. ABC must also make an initial payment of $100,000 on January 1, 19X5.

- At the end of the lease term, ABC Company will purchase the equipment for $1.

- The interest rate implicit in the lease is 8%.

- The carrying amount of the equipment on XYZ Company's books is $500,000.

Practical Consideration (Continued).

On January 1, 19X5, the gross investment in the lease is $1,043,080 ($47,154 × 20 payments + $100,000) and the present value of the gross investment is $600,000 (the present value of 19 annual payments of $47,154 plus $147,154). The transaction initially would be recorded through the following entry:

Minimum lease payments receivable	1,043,080	
Equipment		500,000
Unearned interest income ($1,043,080 − $600,000)		443,080
Gain on sale of equipment		100,000

Direct Financing Leases

31.221   A lessor should account for a direct financing lease as follows:

a. The gross investment in the lease should be determined by adding (1) the total minimum lease payments to be received (net of any included executory costs and related profits to be paid by the lessor) and (2) any unguaranteed residual value accruing to the benefit of the lessor (that is, the unguaranteed fair value of the leased asset to which the lessor is entitled at the end of the lease term.)

b. The difference between the gross investment and the book value of the property represents unearned interest income. The net investment in the lease consists of the gross investment plus any unamortized initial direct costs minus the unearned interest income. The net investment should be shown as a single line item on the balance sheet and classified as current and noncurrent like any other receivable.

c. The unearned interest income and initial direct costs should be amortized to income over the lease term using the interest method or another method that produces similar results. (SFAS 98, par. 22) (Chapter 28 discusses the interest method.)

d. The unguaranteed residual value should be reviewed at least annually to determine whether a decline in value has occurred. If a decline that is other than temporary has occurred, the transaction should be revised using the new estimate. The resulting reduction in the net investment in the lease should be recognized as a loss in the period of the decline. An upward adjustment should not be made. (SFAS 13, par. 18)

31.222   Leveraged Leases. Basically, a leveraged lease is one that is structured primarily to provide certain tax benefits (and the temporary use of funds due to taxes saved in the early years of the lease) to the lessor without the lessor being entirely at risk for nonperformance by the lessee. Although technically not considered a direct financing lease, a leveraged lease must meet the criteria for classification as a direct financing lease (see Paragraphs 31.201 and 31.206) and also possess all of the following characteristics: (SFAS 13, par. 42)

   a. It involves at least three parties—a lessee, a lessor, and a long-term creditor.

   b. The financing provided by the long-term creditor is nonrecourse to the general credit of the lessor.

   c. The amount of financing provided by the long-term creditor gives the lessor "substantial leverage."

> **Practical Consideration.** "Substantial leverage" is commonly interpreted to mean that the financing is more than 50% of the lessor's cost of the property.

   d. The lessor's net investment in the lease declines in the early years of the lease and rises during the later years before it is finally eliminated (although decreases and increases in the net investment balance may occur more than once).

   e. Any investment tax credit is deferred and allocated to income over the lease term.

31.223   A lessor should include the following in its recorded net investment in a leveraged lease: (SFAS 13, par. 43)

   a. Rents receivable, net of the portion applicable to principal and interest on the nonrecourse debt

   b. A receivable for the investment tax credit to be realized on the transaction

   c. Estimated residual value of the leased asset

   d. Unearned and deferred income consisting of (1) the estimated pretax lease income or loss, after deducting initial direct costs, that remains to be allocated to income over the lease term and (2) the investment tax credit that remains to be allocated to income over the lease term

Based on its recorded net investment, less applicable deferred income taxes, and the projected cash receipts and disbursements during the term of the lease, the lessor should compute the rate of return on the net investment in the periods in which the net investment is positive. (The rate of return is the rate that, when applied to the net investment in the periods the net investment is positive, will distribute the net income to those periods.) The net investment balance is increased or decreased each period by the difference between the net cash flow and the amount of income recognized, if any. The amount of net income that should be recognized each year should consist of the following: (SFAS 13, paras. 43–44)

a. Pretax lease income or loss allocated from unearned income included in the net investment

b. Investment tax credit allocated from deferred income included in the net investment

c. The tax effect of the pretax lease income or loss recognized, which is included in tax expense for the period

31.224   If, at any time, projected cash receipts over the remaining term of the lease are less than the lessor's investment in the lease, a loss should be recognized immediately. In addition, all important assumptions affecting estimated net income from the leveraged lease should be reviewed at least annually. (SFAS 13, paras. 45–46)

Operating Leases

31.225   When accounting for an operating lease, the lessor should continue to carry the leased asset in its balance sheet and depreciate it according to its normal depreciation policy. Rent income should be reported as it becomes receivable in the same way rent expense is reported by lessees. (See Paragraphs 31.213–.219.) That is, it should be recognized on a straight-line basis unless another systematic and rational basis is more representative of the time pattern in which the lessor's benefits in the leased asset are depleted. Any initial direct costs (i.e., costs incurred by the lessor in negotiating and consummating the lease) should be deferred and allocated to income in proportion to the recognition of rental income. (SFAS 13, par. 19)

31.226   **Incentive Payments by Lessors.** Incentive payments include items such as up-front cash payments to the lessee to sign the lease and payments to reimburse the lessee for specific costs such as moving costs or abandoned leasehold improvements. The lessor should amortize incentive payments against rental income over the term of the lease. The lessor should record the payment as a debit to a deferred lease incentive account and a credit to cash. The deferred lease incentive account should be amortized against rent income over the lease term using the straight-line method. (FTB 88-1, par. 7)

> **Practical Consideration.** The preceding guidance also applies when an incentive arises from payments by the lessor to third parties on behalf of the lessee, such as payments for leasehold improvements or moving costs. A common example relating to leasehold improvements is an agreement under which the lessor makes all leasehold improvements requested by the lessee and bills the lessee for its cost less an allowance. In that situation, the authors believe that the lessor should record the allowance as a deferred lease incentive.

31.227   If a lessor assumes a lessee's pre-existing lease with a third party, the related loss incurred by the lessor is considered a rent incentive. The lessor and the lessee should independently estimate the loss incurred by the lessor. The lessor should estimate its loss based on the total remaining costs reduced by the expected benefits from the sublease or use of the assumed leased property. (FTB 88-1, par. 8)

31.228   **Contingent Rentals.** Rent increases or decreases based on future conditions, such as future sales volume, machine hours, interest rates, or price indexes, are considered contingent rentals. A lessor should accrue a contingent rental payment in the period it arises. (FTB 85-3, par. 12)

31.229   **Losses on Operating Leases.** If an operating lease involving real estate would have qualified as a sales-type lease except for the fact that it does not transfer ownership, and if the property's fair value is less than its book value, the property should be written down to its fair value and a loss recognized at the inception of the lease. (SFAS 98, par. 22)

CHANGES, EXTENSIONS, AND TERMINATIONS

31.230   After a lease has been classified and recorded, it is not unusual for changes to occur prior to the end of the lease term. Some of those changes require that adjustments be made to the amounts originally recorded under the lease, whereas others do not. This section discusses common types of changes and how to account for them.

Changes in Lease Provisions

31.231   When the provisions of a lease are changed (other than by renewing or extending the term), and the revised provisions would have resulted in a different classification had they existed at the inception of the lease, the revised lease should be treated as a new agreement over its remaining term and classified accordingly. As a result, all related accounts should be adjusted to what they would have been if the revised provisions had existed at inception. (SFAS 13, par. 9)

31.232   **Lessee Accounting.** For the lessee, if the provisions of a capital lease are changed, the accounting depends on whether (a) the revised lease would have been classified as an operating lease if the revised terms had existed at inception and (b) whether the revision changes the amount of remaining minimum lease payments.

     a. If the revised lease would have been an operating lease, the asset and obligation are written off and a gain or loss is recognized for the difference. The revised lease should be subsequently accounted for similar to any other operating lease.

     b. If the revised lease is still a capital lease, but the revision changes the remaining minimum lease payments, the lease obligation should be adjusted to the present value of the remaining minimum lease payments. The asset should be adjusted by the same amount, and no gain or loss should be recorded. The interest rate used to compute the present value of the remaining minimum lease payments should be the same rate used when the lease was initially recorded. (SFAS 13, par. 14)

An exception to the preceding guidance applies if the provisions of a lease are changed due to the refunding by the lessor of tax-exempt debt. In such cases, the change should be accounted for as follows:

     a. If the change results from a refunding that is accounted for as an early extinguishment of debt, the lessee should adjust the lease obligation to the present value of the revised future minimum lease payments using the effective interest rate applicable to the revised agreement. Any resulting gain or loss should be recognized currently as a gain or loss on early extinguishment of debt.

     b. If the change results from a refunding that is not accounted for as an early extinguishment of debt and the lessee is obligated to reimburse the lessor for costs related to the refunded debt (such as unamortized discount or issue costs or a call premium), the lessee should accrue the costs using the interest method over the period from the date of the advance refunding to the call date of the refunded debt. (SFAS 22, par. 12)

31.233   If the provisions of an operating lease are changed in a way that would have caused it to be classified as a capital lease had the revised terms existed at inception, the revised lease is treated as a new agreement. An asset and obligation equal to the present value of the future minimum lease payments should be recorded. (SFAS 13, par. 9)

31.234   **Lessor Accounting.** For the lessor, the lease changes that require accounting adjustments are essentially the same as for a lessee. If a sales-type or direct financing lease is revised, and the revised lease would have been an operating lease had the revised terms existed at inception, the following adjustments are required: (SFAS 13, par. 17)

   a. The net investment in the lease should be written off.

   b. The leased asset should be recorded on the lessor's books at the lower of its original cost, present fair value, or present carrying amount (that is, the amount of the net investment in the lease).

   c. Any difference in the net investment and the amount at which the asset is recorded on the lessor's books should be recognized as a loss in the period of the change. (No gain will result because the asset cannot be reestablished at more than the amount of the net investment.)

   d. The lease subsequently should be accounted for as any other operating lease.

31.235   If a sales-type or direct financing lease is revised, the revision changes the remaining minimum lease payments, and the revised lease would still have been a sales-type or direct financing lease had the revised terms existed at inception, the following adjustments are required: (SFAS 13, par. 17)

   a. The gross investment in the lease should be adjusted to reflect the new minimum lease payments receivable and the new estimated residual value, if affected (although the residual value estimate cannot exceed the amount estimated originally).

   b. The net adjustment should be charged or credited to unearned income.

Practical Consideration. Although not specifically stated by authoritative literature, the authors believe that the adjusted unearned income amount should be amortized over the remaining lease term to provide a level return on the net investment. That may require that a new rate be imputed, which can be done in the same way the lessor's implicit rate is determined, as discussed in Paragraph 31.207.

Also, an exception to the guidance in Paragraph 31.235 applies if the provisions of a lease are changed due to the refunding by the lessor of tax-exempt debt. In such cases, the change should be accounted for as follows:

a. If the change results from a refunding that is accounted for as an early extinguishment of debt, the lessor should adjust the balance of the minimum lease payments receivable and the estimated residual value based on the effective interest rate applicable to the revised agreement. Any resulting gain or loss should be recognized currently as a gain or loss on early extinguishment of debt.

b. If the change results from a refunding that is not accounted for as an early extinguishment of debt, the lessor should recognize as revenue any reimbursements from the lessee for costs related to the refunded debt (such as unamortized discount or issue costs or a call premium) over the period from the date of the advance refunding to the call date of the refunded debt.

31.236　If the provisions of an operating lease are changed in a way that would have caused it to be classified as a sales-type or direct financing lease had the revised terms existed at inception, the revised lease should be treated as a new agreement. (SFAS 13, par. 9)

Renewals and Extensions

31.237　Renewals and extensions are any actions that extend the lease beyond its original lease term. (SFAS 13, par. 6) Renewals, for example, often occur when renewal options (other than those already included in the lease term) are exercised. Renewals and extensions also include situations in which the same lessee continues to rent the same property under a new lease. Renewals and extensions of operating leases are treated as new agreements. Renewals and extensions of capital leases (as well as sales-type and direct financing leases) can be slightly more complex, however. Accounting for renewals and extensions of capital leases depends on (a) whether they render a guarantee or penalty inoperative and (b) if a guarantee or penalty is not rendered inoperative, whether the renewal or extension is classified as a capital or operating lease. (SFAS 13, paras. 9, 12 and 17)

31.238 **Original Lease Contains a Guarantee or Penalty.** If a lease contains a residual value guarantee or penalty for failure to renew (other than penalties so severe that the renewal period was included in the original lease term), the renewal or extension of the lease will nullify the guarantee or penalty. An example is the extension of a 10-year lease that would have required the lessee to purchase the property for $100,000 at the end of the original lease (which is considered a residual value guarantee). Another example is the extension or renewal of a lease that would have required the lessee to pay a penalty if it had not been renewed or extended (unless the penalty were so significant that, at inception, it was assumed that the lease would be renewed and, thus, the renewal period was included in the lease term). If a renewal or extension of a capital lease renders a guarantee or penalty inoperative, the accounting is the same as when lease provisions are revised to change the remaining minimum lease payments, but they do not create an operating lease. As discussed in Paragraphs 31.232 and 31.235, the accounting is as follows: (SFAS 13, paras. 12 and 17)

- The lessee should adjust the lease obligation to the present value of the remaining minimum lease payments. The asset should be adjusted by the same amount, and no gain or loss should be recorded. The interest rate used to compute the present value of the remaining minimum lease payments should be the rate used when the lease was initially recorded.

- The lessor should adjust the gross investment to reflect the new minimum lease payments receivable and the new estimated residual value, if affected (although the residual value estimate cannot exceed the amount originally estimated). The net adjustment should be charged or credited to unearned income.

31.239 **Original Lease Does Not Contain a Guarantee or Penalty.** If renewal or extension of a capital lease does not render a guarantee or penalty inoperative, the accounting for the renewal or extension depends on whether it is classified as an operating lease. If the renewal or extension is not classified as an operating lease, it should be accounted for as discussed in Paragraph 31.238. If it is classified as an operating lease, both the lessee and lessor should continue to account for the lease "as is" to the end of its original term. Subsequently, the lease should be accounted for as any other operating lease. (SFAS 13, paras. 14 and 17)

31.240 **Classifying Renewals or Extensions as Sales-type Leases.** Renewals or extensions of sales-type or direct financing leases may be classified as sales-type leases only if they meet the criteria for such leases and occur at or near the end of the lease term. ("At or near the end" is defined as "within the last few months.") Such renewals or extensions that do not occur at or near the end of the lease term must be classified as direct financing leases. (SFAS 27, par. 8)

Terminations

31.241 When a capital lease is terminated because the lessee purchases the leased asset from the lessor, the lessee should remove the lease obligation and record the difference between the purchase price and the obligation as an adjustment to the carrying amount of the asset. The asset would subsequently be presented and accounted for as any other owned asset. (FASBI 26, par. 5)

> **Practical Consideration.** Although GAAP does not specifically address the lessor's accounting, the authors believe the transaction should be accounted for the same as a sale to a third party. That is, unless recourse provisions are involved, the investment should be written off, and the difference between the purchase price and the net investment recorded as gain or loss.

31.242 When a capital lease is terminated other than due to the purchase of the leased asset by the lessee, the lessee should write off the leased asset and obligation and record any difference as a gain or loss. (SFAS 13, par. 14) The lessor should account for the termination in the same way as for a change in the provisions of a sales-type or direct financing lease. That is—

a. the net investment in the lease should be written off,

b. the leased asset should be recorded on the lessor's books at the lower of its original cost, present fair value, or present carrying amount, and

c. any difference in the net investment and the amount at which the asset is recorded on the lessor's books should be recorded as a loss in the period of the change. (No gain will result because the asset cannot be reestablished at more than the amount of the net investment.) (SFAS 13, par. 17)

> **Practical Consideration.** A lessee may enter into a new operating lease agreement prior to the expiration of its existing lease. In so doing, the lessee may incur costs such as moving expenses, losses on subleases, or the write-off of abandoned leasehold improvements. EITF Issue No. 88-10, *Costs Associated with Lease Modification or Termination,* addresses the accounting for those types of costs. The Task Force agreed that moving costs are ordinarily expensed as incurred. Other costs related to the old lease, such as rental

---

Practical Consideration (Continued).

payments, leasehold improvements, and costs incurred to terminate the lease, should be expensed when the property has no future use or benefit to the lessee. If the lease is not terminated and is not used by the lessee, the amount expensed would be the total remaining costs, including total future rental payments, reduced by actual or probable sublease income. The consensus view states that the loss recognized could be based on either actual or discounted amounts. The authors believe that actual amounts should be used, which is consistent with the recognition of losses on subleases under FASB Interpretation No. 27, *Accounting for a Loss on a Sublease,* and FASB Technical Bulletin 79-15, *Accounting for Loss on a Sublease Not Involving the Disposal of a Segment.*

Any of the preceding costs assumed by the new lessor are considered lease incentives. As discussed in Paragraphs 31.218–.219 and 31.226–.227, lease incentives are recognized by both the lessor and lessee over the term of the new lease as reductions of rent income and expense, respectively. However, the lessee still must expense the costs as indicated in EITF Issue No. 88-10.

Changes in Estimates or Circumstances

31.243   Changes in estimates, such as changes in the estimated economic life or residual value of leased assets, do not require the classification of the lease to be reconsidered. Likewise, changes in circumstances do not require that classification of the lease be reconsidered. (SFAS 13, par. 9) For example, assume that a lessee's financial condition unexpectedly improves so that a required payment for failing to exercise a renewal option is no longer considered a penalty. Had the situation existed at the inception of the lease, the lease term would have been defined differently and the lease would not have been classified as a capital lease. That (or any other) change in circumstances would not change the classification of the lease, however. The lease would continue to be accounted for as a capital lease over the originally determined lease term. If the lessee does not exercise the renewal option, the termination would be accounted for as discussed in Paragraphs 31.241–.242.

TRANSFER OR ASSIGNMENT OF LEASED PROPERTY, RENTAL PAYMENTS, OR RESIDUAL VALUE INTERESTS

Transfer of Leased Property or Rental Payments

31.244   **Sales-type or Direct Financing Leases.** After a lease is entered into, the lessor may transfer the lease or the property subject to the lease to a third party. In such a case, the original accounting for the lease should not be reversed. (SFAS 13, par. 20) Receivables related to sales-type and direct financing leases are made up of two components: minimum lease payments and residual values. Transfers of those receivables should be accounted for as follows:

a. *Transfers of unguaranteed residual values.* Unless the sale or assignment is to a related party, a transfer of *unguaranteed* residual values without recourse should be recognized as a sale. Accordingly, the difference between the sales price and the carrying amount of the unguaranteed residual values should be recognized at the time of the transaction as a gain or loss. (SFAS 13, par. 20) When selling or securitizing lease financing receivables, the lessor should allocate its gross investment in receivables between minimum lease payments and unguaranteed residual values using the individual carrying amounts of those components at the transfer date. (SFAS 125, par. 59)

> **Practical Consideration.** When assets are sold to a related party, the transaction should be accounted for based on its economic substance rather than its form.

b. *Transfers of minimum lease payments and guaranteed residual values.* A transfer of minimum lease payments receivable and guaranteed residual values in which the transferor surrenders control should be accounted for as a sale to the extent consideration (other than beneficial interests in the transferred assets) is received in exchange. Control over transferred assets has been surrendered when all of the following conditions are met: (SFAS 125, par. 9)

(1) The transferred assets have been isolated from the transferor (that is, put beyond the reach of the transferor and its creditors, even if the transferor is in bankruptcy or receivership).

(2) The transferee (or holders of beneficial interests in the transferee if it is a special-purpose entity) obtains the right (free of conditions that prevent it from taking advantage of that right) to pledge or exchange the transferred assets.

(3) Effective control over the transferred assets is not maintained by the transferor through an agreement that entitles and obligates the transferor to repurchase or redeem the assets before their maturity or that entitles the transferor to repurchase or redeem transferred assets that are not readily obtainable.

If the transfer meets the preceding conditions, the transferor should remove the assets sold from its balance sheet, record all proceeds received from the sale at fair value, and recognize any gain or loss. A transfer that does not meet the preceding criteria should be accounted for as a secured borrowing. (SFAS 125, par. 12) (Chapter 52 discusses accounting for secured borrowings.)

Practical Consideration. The lessor should recognize a servicing asset or liability if it continues to service the transferred assets. Accounting for servicing assets is discussed in Chapter 52.

31.245   **Operating Leases.** A sale of property subject to an operating lease should not be recorded as a sale if the seller (or any party related to the seller) retains substantial risks of ownership in the property. That can occur when the seller guarantees the recovery of the buyer's investment. For example, if the lessee defaults or terminates the lease, the seller may have a formal or informal agreement to purchase the leased property, substitute an existing lease, or secure a new lessee under a remarketing agreement. (A remarketing agreement does not disqualify accounting for the transaction as a sale, however, if the seller (a) receives a reasonable fee for its efforts in securing a replacement lessee and (b) is not required to give priority to re-leasing the property over similar property owned or produced by the seller.) (SFAS 13, par. 21)

31.246   If the seller retains substantial risks of ownership, the transaction should be accounted for as a borrowing rather than a sale. In essence, it is assumed that the sales proceeds are actually a borrowing by the "seller" from the "buyer," and the "loan" is to be repaid with the lease proceeds (even if the lease payments go directly to the buyer). Consequently, the "seller" should record the proceeds from the "sale" as a liability and, if necessary, record a portion of each payment as interest expense. (Imputing interest is discussed further in Chapter 28.) Rent receipts should continue to be recorded as revenue and the leased asset included in the "seller's" balance sheet as an asset. (The term over which the asset is depreciated should be limited to the estimated amortization period of the obligation, however.) (SFAS 13, par. 22)

31.247   The preceding guidance also applies if leased property is sold to a third party that leases, or intends to lease, the property to another party.

Accounting for Purchased Residual Value Interests

31.248   As discussed in Paragraph 31.207, the residual value of a leased asset is its value at the end of the lease. Although the residual value usually accrues to the lessor, sometimes it is owned by a nonlessor. For example a lease broker may receive an interest in the residual value of a leased asset as a fee for services, an interest in the residual value of a leased asset may be purchased directly from lessors, or a lessor may sell the minimum rental payments associated with a lease and retain an interest in the residual value of the leased asset. The following guidance applies to accounting for an interest in the *unguaranteed* residual value of a leased asset: (FTB 86-2, paras. 6 and 8)

    a. An asset should be recorded at the amount of cash disbursed, the fair value of other consideration given, or the present value of liabilities assumed at the date the right is acquired. However, the asset should be recorded at the fair value of the interest if that is more clearly evident than the fair value of assets surrendered, services rendered, or liabilities assumed.

    b. The asset should not be accreted. Thus, it should never be recorded at an amount greater than cost.

    c. The asset's recorded value should be written down to market through a charge to earnings if recorded value subsequently exceeds market value.

An interest in the *guaranteed* residual value of a leased asset also should be recorded as an asset. However, because guaranteed residual value interests are considered financial assets, any increase in the estimated residual value should be recognized over the remaining lease term. (SFAS 125, par. 59)

LEASES INVOLVING REAL ESTATE

31.249   Although the basic principles discussed in the preceding paragraphs apply to all leases, certain exceptions exist for leases involving real estate. Classifying real estate leases depends on whether they involve land only; land and buildings; land, buildings, and equipment; or only part of a building. (SFAS 13, par. 24)

Leases Involving Land Only

31.250   A *lessee* should consider only two of the capitalization tests discussed in Paragraph 31.202 when classifying leases of land—the transfer of ownership test and the bargain purchase option test. Thus, if a land lease does not transfer ownership by the end of the lease term or contain a bargain purchase option, a lessee should classify it as an operating lease rather than a capital lease. (SFAS 98, par. 22)

31.251   A *lessor* should classify a lease involving only land as follows: (SFAS 98, par. 22)

a. The lease should be classified as a sales-type lease if it provides a sales-type profit or loss and meets the transfer of ownership test.

b. The lease should be classified as a direct financing or leveraged lease, whichever is applicable, if it does not provide a sales-type profit or loss but meets the following criteria:

(1) The lease transfers ownership by the end of the lease term or contains a bargain purchase option.

(2) Collection of the minimum lease payments is reasonably predictable and there are no important uncertainties about additional unreimbursed costs the lessor will incur.

All other leases involving land only, including those that provide a sales-type profit but do not meet the transfer of ownership test, should be classified as operating leases.

Leases Involving Land and Buildings

31.252   Classifying the lease of a building and the underlying land depends on whether the lease transfers ownership or contains a bargain purchase option and, if not, whether the fair value of the land is less than 25% of the total fair value of the property.

31.253   **Lease Transfers Ownership or Contains a Bargain Purchase Option.** A *lessee* should classify a lease involving land and buildings as a capital lease if it transfers ownership by the end of the lease term or contains a bargain purchase option. In such cases, the land and building portions of the lease must be separated so that the building portion can be depreciated. The capitalized lease cost should be allocated between the land and building so that the cost associated with the building can be depreciated. That is accomplished by—

- allocating the present value of minimum lease payments based on the relative fair values of the land and building at the inception of the lease.

- recording two leased assets—one for the land and one for the building. (Only one lease obligation should be recorded, however.) (SFAS 13, par. 26)

> **Practical Consideration.** As discussed in Paragraph 31.210, if the present value of the minimum lease payments is greater than the property's fair value, the leased assets (that is, the land and building) should be recorded at their fair values and the underlying rate imputed. In that case, allocating lease payments based on the relative fair values of the land and building will be unnecessary.

31.254   A *lessor* should classify a lease involving land and buildings that transfers ownership by the end of the lease term and/or contains a bargain purchase option as follows: (SFAS 98, par. 22)

     a. If the lease transfers ownership by the end of the lease term and provides a sales-type profit or loss, the lessor should classify the lease as a sales-type lease. In that case, the lessor should treat the lease as a single unit, and need not allocate the lease payments received between the land and building.

     b. If the lease contains a bargain purchase option and provides a sales-type profit or loss, the lessor should classify the lease as an operating lease.

     c. If the lease transfers ownership by the end of the lease term (or contains a bargain purchase option) and does not provide a sales-type profit or loss, the lessor should classify the lease as—

         (1) a direct financing or leveraged lease if collectibility of the minimum lease payments is reasonably predictable and there are no important uncertainties about additional unreimbursed costs the lessor will incur.

         (2) an operating lease if collectibility of the minimum lease payments is not reasonably predictable or there are important uncertainties about additional unreimbursed costs the lessor will incur.

31.255   **Lease Does Not Transfer Ownership or Contain a Bargain Purchase Option.** If a land and building lease does not transfer ownership or contain a bargain purchase option, the lessor and lessee must determine whether the land portion of the lease is material.

     a. If the fair value of the land is less than 25% of the total fair value of the property at the inception of the lease, the land is considered immaterial. Consequently, the lessee and lessor should consider the lease to be a single unit for the purposes of applying the 75% and 90% tests and the estimated economic life of the building should be used when applying the 75% test. (The 75% and 90%

tests are discussed in Paragraphs 31.205–.207.) If the lease meets either the 75% test or the 90% test—

(1) the *lessee* should classify the lease as a capital lease. (Otherwise, it should classify the lease as a single operating lease.)

(2) the *lessor* should classify the lease as a direct financing or leveraged lease, as appropriate, if collectibility of the minimum lease payments is reasonably predictable and there are no important uncertainties about additional unreimbursed costs the lessor will incur. (If collectibility of the minimum lease payments is not reasonably predictable or there are important uncertainties about additional unreimbursed costs the lessor will incur, the lessor should classify the lease as an operating lease.) (SFAS 98, par. 22)

b. If the fair value of the land is greater than or equal to 25% of the total fair value of the property at the inception of the lease, the land is considered to be material. Consequently, the lessee and lessor should consider the land portion and the building portion of the lease as separate leases. To determine the portion of the minimum lease payments applicable to the land, the fair value of the land should be multiplied by the lessee's incremental borrowing rate. The remaining payments are attributed to the building. The lessee and lessor should account for the land and building portions of the lease as follows:

(1) The *lessee* should classify the land portion of the lease as an operating lease because the criteria for capitalizing leases of land only are not met. The 75% and 90% test should be applied to the building portion and, if either test is met, the building portion should be treated as a capital lease. If neither the 75% or 90% test is met, the lessee should consider the land and building as a single operating lease. (SFAS 13, par. 26)

(2) The *lessor* should classify the land portion of the lease as an operating lease because the criteria for capitalizing land only leases are not met. The 75% and 90% tests should be applied to the building portion of the lease. If the 75% test or the 90% test is met, and collectibility of the minimum lease payments is reasonably predictable and there are no important uncertainties about additional unreimbursed costs the lessor will incur, the lessor should classify the building portion as a direct financing lease. (SFAS 98, par. 22) If neither the

75% test nor the 90% test is met, or if collectibility of the minimum lease payments is not reasonably predictable or there are important uncertainties about additional unreimbursed costs the lessor will incur, the lessor should consider the land and building as a single operating lease. (SFAS 13, par. 26)

Practical Consideration. In a land and building lease in which the fair value of the land is 25% or more of the property's total fair value, the portion of the minimum lease payments applicable to the land is determined by multiplying the fair value of the land by the lessee's incremental borrowing rate. That is done under the assumption that, since land is assumed not to depreciate, the lessor only requires a return "on" its investment in the land—not a return "of" the investment in the land. The desired return on the investment in the land is estimated by applying the lessee's incremental borrowing rate to the fair value of the land. Since the lease is only providing a return "on" the land, and because the 90% test is not applied when deciding how to classify a lease of land only, any residual value guarantee is assumed to apply entirely to the building. That situation can create unusual results when a residual value guarantee exceeds the fair value of the building. The issue was referred to the FASB's Emerging Issues Task Force (EITF) as Issue No. 92-1, *Allocation of Residual Value or First-Loss Guarantee to Minimum Lease Payments in Leases Involving Land and Building(s)*. The EITF concluded that any residual value guarantee must be allocated entirely to the building, even if it exceeds the building's fair value at the inception of the lease. The portion of the minimum lease payments attributable to the land should be determined by multiplying the fair value of the land by the lessee's incremental borrowing rate. The remaining minimum lease payments, which include the entire residual value guarantee, should be attributed to the building.

Leases Involving Land, Buildings, and Equipment

31.256   Some real estate leases may provide for the lease of both real estate and equipment. The real estate portions and the equipment portions of such leases should be classified and accounted for separately based on the guidance in Paragraphs 31.202, 31.208, and 31.250–.255. If the lease agreement does not indicate how much of the minimum lease payments apply to real estate and how much apply to equipment, or if the allocation is unreasonable, the lease payments should be allocated by "whatever means are appropriate in the circumstances." (SFAS 13, par. 27)

Practical Consideration. GAAP does not provide guidance on allocation methods. The authors believe the following methods may be used:

- Determine the market rental amount for either the real estate or equipment and assign the difference between the rental payments and that amount to the other element. For example, if monthly lease payments are $10,000 and a market rental for the equipment is $1,000 per month, allocate $9,000 to the real estate.

- Determine the market rental amount for both the real estate and equipment, and allocate the rental payments proportionately. For example, if a separate lease of the equipment would require monthly payments of $2,000, and a separate lease of the real estate would require monthly payments of $12,000, allocate 14% ($2,000 ÷ $14,000) of the monthly payment to equipment and 86% to real estate.

- Allocate the rental payments based on the relative fair values of the equipment and real estate.

Choosing the appropriate method in a particular set of circumstances is a matter of judgment. The authors believe the allocation of any residual value guarantee should be done using the same method used to allocate rental payments. Also, leases of equipment and real estate may require an additional "allocation" of lease payments if the real estate portion of the lease involves land and building and the land portion is material as discussed in Paragraph 31.255.

Leases Involving Only Part of a Building

31.257   Many real estate leases involve only part of a building. Examples include leases of office space in office buildings and leases of retail space in shopping malls. The lessee and lessor's classification of those types of leases depends on whether the cost or fair value of the leased property is objectively determinable.

     a. If the *lessee* can objectively determine the fair value of the property, it should classify the lease as it would any other land and building lease, as discussed in Paragraphs 31.252–.255.

> **Practical Consideration.** Because it would be unusual for a lease of only part of a building to provide for ownership transfer or a bargain purchase option, the guidance in Paragraphs 31.253–.254 normally will not apply. Also, the land portion of such leases is usually immaterial. Consequently, a land and building lease normally will be considered a single unit and classified based on the 75% and 90% tests.

If the lessee cannot objectively determine the fair value of the property, it should apply only the 75% test to determine the lease's classification. When applying the test, the estimated economic life of the building in which the leased premises are located should be used rather than the estimated economic life of the leased premises. If the 75% test is met, the lessee should classify the lease as a capital lease. Otherwise, the lease should be considered a single operating lease.

b. If the *lessor* can objectively determine both the cost and fair value of the property, it should classify the lease as it would any other land and building lease, as discussed in Paragraphs 31.252–.255. If it cannot objectively determine either the cost or fair value of the property, the lessor should classify the lease as an operating lease. (SFAS 13, par. 28)

RELATED PARTY LEASES

31.258   Related parties in leasing transactions are defined as owners, parent companies, or investors who have significant influence over the other party to the lease. Two or more otherwise unrelated companies are considered related if they are subject to significant influence by a common entity, investors, officers, or directors (for example, brother/sister companies). (SFAS 13, par. 5)

31.259   In some leasing arrangements, it is clear that the terms of the transactions have been significantly affected by the fact that the parties are related. In those cases, the substance of the lease, rather than its form, should govern the accounting for the transaction. (SFAS 13, par. 29)

Practical Consideration. In some situations, a lease is designed to qualify as an operating lease using a special-purpose lessor that lacks economic substance. The FASB Emerging Issues Task Force was concerned that accounting for the lease as an operating lease by the lessor and lessee would not properly reflect the economic substance of the arrangement. EITF Issue No. 90-15, *Impact of Nonsubstantive Lessors, Residual Value Guarantees, and Other Provisions in Leasing Transactions,* states that, in those situations, the lessee should consolidate the financial position, results of operations, and cash flows of the lessor with its operations even though the lessee does not own the lessor. Consolidation is required if all of the following conditions are met:

    a. Substantially all of the activities of the lessor involve assets that are to be leased to a single lessee.

    b. The expected risks and rewards of the leased property and the related debt rest directly or indirectly with the lessee. Indicators of that include:

        (1) The lease agreement (or other contract) grants the lessee management and control of the leased property.

        (2) The lessee guarantees the property's residual value.

        (3) The lessee guarantees the lessor's debt on the property.

        (4) The lessee has an option to purchase the property at a fixed price or a defined price other than fair value (or receive any of the lessor's sales proceeds in excess of a specified amount).

    c. The owners of the lessor have not made an initial substantive residual equity capital investment that is at risk during the entire term of the lease.

EITF No. 90-15 does not require that all entities involved in related party leases be consolidated. However, the authors believe that the requirements of EITF No. 90-15 should be carefully considered if—

- a company leases real estate from a related entity that has no other purpose, and

- the nature of the transaction is such that it appears the lease was specifically designed to avoid capitalization, but the risk and rewards of ownership rest with the lessee.

Practical Consideration (Continued).

Furthermore, SFAS No. 13, *Accounting for Leases,* requires companies to consolidate subsidiaries whose principal business activity is leasing property or facilities to the parent or other affiliated entities.

Even if the criteria of EITF No. 90-15 or SFAS No. 13 are not met, the authors recommend that, when practical, combined financial statements be presented when a company leases property from a partnership (or other entity) whose sole business activity is leasing property to the company, and the two are commonly owned.

SUBLEASES AND SIMILAR TRANSACTIONS

31.260   The authoritative literature related to accounting for subleases and similar transactions addresses the following situations: (SFAS 13, par. 35)

- A new lessee is substituted for the original lessee under a new agreement, and the original lease agreement is terminated.

- A new lessee is substituted under the original lease agreement for the original lessee, and the new lessee is primarily obligated for the lease (the original lessee may or may not be secondarily obligated).

- The lessee releases the property and the original lease remains in effect (i.e., a sublease).

In each situation, the new lessee should classify and account for the lease as it would any other new lease. (SFAS 13, par. 40) Classification and accounting by the original lessor and the original lessee vary, however, depending on the circumstances as discussed in the following paragraphs.

New Lessee Substituted through a New Agreement

31.261   If a new lessee is substituted for the original lessee under a new agreement, and the original lease agreement is terminated, the accounting is relatively straightforward. The transaction is accounted for by both the original lessee and original lessor as a termination, as discussed in Paragraphs 31.241–.242. Accordingly, if the lessee recorded the original lease as a capital lease, the lessee should remove all accounts related to the lease and record a gain or loss for the difference. Any consideration paid or received should be included in the gain or loss. If the lessor recorded the original lease as a sales-type or direct financing lease, the lessor should remove the net investment in the lease and record the leased asset at the lower of its original cost, present fair value, or present carrying amount. (SFAS 13, paras. 36–38)

31.262   The lessor should classify and account for the new lease agreement as a new transaction. The lessor's "cost" for purposes of classifying and accounting for the new lease is the amount at which the property was recorded upon termination of the original lease (i.e., the lower of its original cost, present fair value, or present carrying amount). (SFAS 13, par. 37)

New Lessee Substituted under the Original Agreement

31.263   If a new lessee is substituted under the original lease agreement for the original lessee, and the new lessee is primarily obligated for the lease, the lessor's accounting for the original lease is unchanged. (SFAS 13, par. 36) The original lessee, on the other hand, should account for the transaction as a termination. Accordingly, if the lessee recorded the original lease as a capital lease, the lessee should remove all accounts related to the lease and record a gain or loss for the difference. Any consideration paid or received should be included in the gain or loss.

31.264   If the lessee remains secondarily liable for the lease, that contingency and related off-balance-sheet risk should be disclosed. (SFAS 13, par. 38) (See Chapters 10 and 21.)

Sublease

31.265   If the lessee releases the property and the original lease remains in effect (i.e., a sublease), the original lessor's and lessee's accounting for the original lease should not change. (SFAS 13, paras. 36 and 39) The original lessee (new sublessor) should classify and account for the sublease as a new agreement as discussed in the following paragraphs.

31.266   **Original Lease Was an Operating Lease.** If the original lease was an operating lease, the sublease should be accounted for as an operating lease. (SFAS 13, par. 39)

31.267   **Original Lease Was a Capital Lease.** If the original lease was a capital lease, accounting for the sublease depends on why the original lease was capitalized: (SFAS 13, par. 39)

    a. If the original lease was capitalized because the lease transferred ownership or contained a bargain purchase option, the sublease should be classified and accounted for as any other lease. The unamortized balance of the leased asset should be considered its cost.

b. If the original lease was capitalized because it met the 75% or 90% test, the new lease should be capitalized only if it meets the 75% test and collectibility of the minimum lease payments is reasonably predictable and there are no important uncertainties about additional unreimbursed costs the new lessor will incur.

Practical Consideration. An exception to the criteria in b. exists if the sublessor is only an intermediary between the original lessor and the sublessee. In that case, both the 75% and 90% tests should be applied as well as the additional criteria about collectibility of minimum lease payments and uncertainties about additional unreimbursed costs. The fair value that should be used when applying the 90% test is the fair value of the property to the original lessor at the inception of the original lease.

Losses on Subleases

31.268   Losses on subleases may be incurred by the lessee/sublessor. Generally, that occurs when—

- the original lease is a capital lease, the sublease is a sales-type lease, and the property's book value (i.e., the unamortized balance of the leased property) exceeds its fair value.

- the original lease is a capital lease, the sublease is a direct financing lease, and the property's book value exceeds the total rental payments and residual value to be received.

- the original lease is a capital lease, the sublease is an operating lease, and the property's book value plus executory costs to be incurred exceed the total rental payments to be received.

- the original lease and the sublease are operating leases, and the sublessor pays more under the original lease (in rental payments and executory costs) than it receives under the sublease.

Losses on subleases should be recognized when they occur. The amount of loss to be recognized is the amount by which costs to be incurred exceed revenues to be received over the term of the sublease. (FTB 79-15, par. 2)

BUSINESS COMBINATIONS

31.269   A business combination by itself does not affect a lease's classification. Consequently, so long as its terms are not changed as part of the combination, a lease classified as a capital lease prior to a business combination would continue to be classified as a capital lease after the business combination. (FASBI 21, par. 12) (As discussed in Paragraph 31.231, however, a lease should be classified and accounted for as a new lease if its terms are changed and the revised terms would have resulted in a different classification if they had been in effect at the inception of the lease.)

Practical Consideration. The acquiring company in a combination accounted for under the purchase method may assign a new value to a capitalized lease since it must allocate the purchase price to the individual assets and liabilities acquired. (See Chapter 3.) Nevertheless, a lease's classification remains the same as before the combination (so long as its terms are not modified), and the new lease value should be accounted for based on that classification.

31.270   A leveraged lease acquired in a business combination accounted for under the purchase method should be accounted for as follows: (FASBI 21, par. 16)

     a. The amount assigned to an investment in a leveraged lease at the date of the combination should be based on the lease's remaining future cash flows with appropriate recognition given to the estimated tax effects of those cash flows.

     b. Once assigned, the amount should be allocated to the lease's components (that is, net rentals receivable, estimated residual value, and unearned income) and accounted for as discussed in Paragraphs 31.222–.224.

LEASES WITH GOVERNMENTAL ENTITIES

31.271   **Fiscal Funding Clauses.** Some leases with governmental entities contain clauses referred to as fiscal funding clauses. Those clauses allow the governmental entity to cancel the lease if sufficient funds are not appropriated for it to fulfill its obligations under the lease. Questions arose as to whether fiscal funding clauses resulted in the leases being cancelable and, consequently, preclude them from being classified as capital leases. FASB Technical Bulletin No. 79-10, *Fiscal Funding Clauses in Lease Agreements,* states that the likelihood of cancellation should be assessed, and, if the likelihood is considered to be remote, the lease should be considered noncancelable. (FTB 79-10, paras. 2 and 5)

31.272   Property Owned by a Governmental Unit or Authority. Leases of terminal space or other airport facilities from governmental units or authorities normally are classified as operating leases because they do not transfer ownership or contain a bargain purchase option, the estimated life of the facility is not determinable (because the governmental unit can abandon the facility), and the concept of fair value is not applicable (because such property is not available for sale). Typically, other leases from governmental units or authorities (for example, leases of bus terminals) also are classified as operating leases because they possess similar characteristics. Leases involving governmental units or authorities should be classified as operating leases if all of the following conditions are met:

a. The leased property is owned by a governmental unit or authority.

b. The leased property is operated by or on behalf of the governmental unit or authority and is part of a larger facility, such as an airport.

c. The leased property cannot be moved to another location because it is a permanent structure or is part of a permanent structure. (SFAS 13, par. 28)

d. The governmental unit or authority has the right to terminate the lease at any time.

e. The lease does not transfer ownership to the lessee or allow the lessee to purchase or otherwise acquire the leased property.

f. Equivalent property in the service area cannot be purchased or leased from a nongovernmental unit or authority. (FASBI 23, par. 8)

MONEY-OVER-MONEY LEASE TRANSACTIONS

31.273   A money-over-money lease transaction is one in which a company manufactures or purchases an asset, leases the asset to the lessee, and obtains nonrecourse financing in excess of the asset's cost using the leased asset and future lease rentals as collateral. Such transactions should be accounted for as (a) the manufacture or purchase of an asset, (b) the leasing of the asset under an operating, direct financing, or sales-type lease, and (c) the borrowing of funds. (FTB 88-1, paras. 16–17) (Classification of the lease as an operating, direct financing, or sales-type lease should be based on the same criteria as for any other lease. See Paragraphs 31.208–.209.)

31.274   In a money-over-money lease, the company should not offset the asset (if the lease is classified as an operating lease) or the lease receivable (if the lease is classified as a direct financing or sales-type lease) and the non-recourse debt unless a right of setoff exists. (FTB 88-1, par. 17) (Chapter 37 discusses offsetting assets and liabilities in further detail.)

SALE-LEASEBACK TRANSACTIONS

31.275   A sale-leaseback transaction occurs when an owner sells property and then leases all or part of it back from the new owner. The seller is referred to as the seller-lessee and the buyer is referred to as the buyer-lessor. (SFAS 28, par. 2) Sale-leaseback transactions typically are entered into as a means of financing, for tax reasons, or both. In addition, if a property owner has accumulated significant equity in a property, a sale-leaseback transaction provides a way to realize the equity without giving up the use of the property.

Buyer-lessor Accounting

31.276   For the buyer-lessor, there is nothing very unique about accounting for a sale-leaseback transaction. The sale-leaseback should simply be treated as two separate transactions—the purchase of an asset and the lease of an asset. The asset purchase should be recorded at cost and accounted for like any other purchase, and the lease should be classified and accounted for like any other lease. The only exception is that the buyer-lessor may not classify the leaseback as a sales-type lease; it must classify the lease as either an operating or direct financing lease. (SFAS 13, par. 34)

Seller-lessee Accounting

31.277   The seller-lessee should account for the lease portion of a sale-leaseback as a capital lease if it meets the criteria in Paragraph 31.202. Otherwise, it should account for the lease as an operating lease. Any profit or loss on the sale of the asset should be deferred and amortized in proportion to the amortization of the leased asset (if the lease is classified as a capital lease) or in proportion to the gross rental charged to expense over the lease term (if the lease is classified as an operating lease) except in the following situations: (SFAS 28, par. 3)

   a. *The seller-lessee retains the rights to only a minor portion of the remaining use of the property sold.* In that event, the seller-lessee should account for the sale-leaseback as separate transactions based on their respective terms. The lease must provide for a reasonable amount of rent based on market conditions at the inception of the lease, however. If it does not, an appropriate amount of the profit or loss should be deferred and amortized as

31.277

described above so that the total rent for the leased property is a reasonable amount.

b. *The seller-lessee retains the rights to more than a minor portion but less than substantially all of the remaining use of the property sold.* In that event, the seller-lessee should recognize any excess profit determined at the sale date.

If the lease is classified as an operating lease, the amount that should be recognized is the profit in excess of the present value of minimum lease payments over the lease term. When computing that amount, the present value of the minimum lease payments should be determined using the interest rate used to apply the 90% test. (See Paragraph 31.207.)

If the lease is classified as a capital lease, the amount that should be recognized is the profit in excess of the recorded amount of the leased asset.

c. *The fair value of the property at the time of the transaction is less than its undepreciated cost.* In that event, a loss should be recognized equal to the difference between undepreciated cost and fair value.

31.278   The seller-lessee is presumed to have retained *only a minor portion* of the rights to the asset's remaining use if the present value of a reasonable amount of rental for the leaseback is 10% or less of the fair value of the asset sold. The seller-lessee is presumed to have retained *substantially all* of the rights to the asset's remaining use if the leaseback (a) covers the entire property sold and (b) meets the criteria for classification as a capital lease. (SFAS 28, par. 3)

> **Practical Consideration.** A reasonable rental is the rent that would be charged for similar property under similar lease terms and conditions. Fair value is the price for which the leased property could be sold between unrelated parties in an arm's length transaction.

31.279   **Sale-leaseback Transactions Involving Real Estate.** If a sale-leaseback transaction involves real estate, the seller-lessee should apply the sale-leaseback accounting described in the preceding paragraphs only if the transaction meets all of the following conditions: (SFAS 98, par. 7)

a. *The leaseback is a "normal leaseback."* A normal leaseback is defined as one in which the seller-lessee actively uses the property during the lease term in exchange for payment of rent, provided any subleasing of the property is minor, and provided there is no continuing involvement with the property on the part of the seller-lessee. When determining whether a leaseback is a normal leaseback, the following should be considered: (SFAS 98, par. 8)

   (1) To satisfy the active use requirement, the seller-lessee must occupy the property and use it in its trade or business. The active use requirement also is satisfied in situations in which the seller-lessee only provides services and the property is occupied occasionally or on a short-term basis generally transient or short-term and is integral to the services being provided. That provision allows sale-leaseback accounting for sale-leasebacks of properties such as hotels and golf courses.

   (2) For the leaseback to be considered a normal leaseback, any subleasing of the property must be minor. For that purpose, "minor" is determined in the same way a "minor leaseback" is determined. (See Paragraph 31.278.)

   (3) If the leaseback includes rental payments that are contingent on the future operations of the seller-lessee (for example, a percentage of the seller-lessee's gross sales), the leaseback is still considered to be a normal leaseback, and sale-lease-back accounting should be used. As discussed in item c., however, if the leaseback includes rental payments that are contingent on the future operations of the *buyer-lessor,* the seller-lessee is considered to have continuing involvement with the property, and sale-leaseback accounting is precluded.

b. *Payment terms and provisions adequately demonstrate the buyer-lessor's initial and continuing investments.* The buyer-lessor's initial and continuing investment in the property must be adequate as prescribed by SFAS No. 66, *Accounting for Sales of Real Estate.* (SFAS 66, paras. 8–12)

> **Practical Consideration.** To use sale-leaseback accounting, authoritative literature essentially requires that the sale portion of a sale-leaseback qualify for recognition as a sale. Failure to meet the initial and continuing investment requirements prescribed by SFAS No. 66 does not necessarily result in the sale not being recognized, however. For example, even though the sale cannot be recognized under the full accrual method if the initial and continuing investment requirements were not met, the sale could still be recognized under the installment or cost recovery methods. Only the use of the deposit method would preclude the transaction from qualifying as a sale. Consequently, the authors believe the initial and continuing investment requirements are a factor when determining whether sale-leaseback accounting is appropriate only when a failure to meet those requirements leads to the use of the deposit method. Because the deposit method is rarely used when the initial and continuing investment tests are not met, however, failure to meet the initial or continuing investment test rarely leads to sale-leaseback accounting being prohibited.

  c. *The sale has been completed and the seller-lessee has no continuing involvement with the property other than the leaseback.* Continuing involvement includes situations in which the seller-lessee has a repurchase obligation or option or the seller-lessee guarantees the buyer-lessor's investment or a specific return on that investment. The following are specific examples of continuing involvement that preclude sale-leaseback accounting: (SFAS 98, paras. 11–13)

    (1) The seller-lessee guarantees a specified residual value.

    (2) The seller-lessee provides nonrecourse financing to the buyer-lessor for any portion of the sales proceeds.

    (3) The seller-lessee provides recourse financing in which the only recourse is to the leased asset.

    (4) The seller-lessee remains obligated under any existing debt related to the property, including secondary liability.

    (5) The seller-lessee provides collateral on behalf of the buyer-lessor (other than the property directly involved in the sale-leaseback transaction).

    (6) The seller-lessee guarantees the buyer-lessor's debt.

    (7) A party related to the seller-lessee guarantees the buyer-lessor's debt.

(8) A party related to the seller-lessee guarantees a return of the buyer-lessor's investment.

(9) A party related to the seller-lessee guarantees a return on the buyer-lessor's investment.

(10) The seller-lessee's rental payment is contingent on future operations of the buyer-lessor.

(11) The seller-lessee does not sell or lease the underlying land to the buyer-lessor.

(12) A provision or circumstance allows the seller-lessee to participate in future appreciation of the property or future profits of the buyer-lessor.

31.280   Sale-leaseback transactions that do not qualify for sale-leaseback accounting should be accounted for by the deposit method or the financing method as follows: (SFAS 98, par. 10)

- Under the deposit method, the down payment and collections of principal and interest on the note should be credited to a deposit liability and lease payments should be charged to the liability. (SFAS 66, par. 65)

- Under the financing method, the down payment and collections of principal and interest on the note also should be credited to a liability. Lease payments, however, should be apportioned between interest expense and a reduction of the financing obligation. Interest expense should be calculated by applying the effective rate to the financing obligation outstanding. The effective interest rate is the rate that discounts lease payments to the value of the property at the inception of the lease. (SFAS 66, par. 25)

Under both the deposit method and financing method, the seller-lessee should convert to sale-leaseback accounting when the criteria for sale-leaseback accounting are met (for example, when continuing involvement ends). At that time, an adjustment to convert income to what it would have been if the sale had been initially recorded should be calculated, the profit should be deferred over the remaining lease term, and the sale and the lease should be recorded.

> **Practical Consideration.** SFAS No. 66, *Accounting for Sales of Real Estate,* requires the financing method to be used when certain types of continuing involvement exist. The authors believe that the financing method should be used in those situations, and the deposit method should be used for all other situations. In general terms, that means the financing method should be used if the continuing involvement requires a guarantee, requires the seller-lessee to buy the property, or permits the buyer-lessor to require the seller-lessee to buy the property. Those situations are generally significant enough that, in substance, the arrangement is a loan by the buyer-lessor to the seller-lessee. However, there are exceptions to that general rule. For example, if the seller-lessee guarantees a return on the buyer-lessor's investment for an extended period, the financing method should be used. If, however, the guarantee is for a limited period, the deposit method should be used. (Some accountants, as a rule of thumb, define an extended period as one that is longer than five years.)

WRAP LEASE TRANSACTIONS

31.281   A wrap lease transaction is one in which a company purchases an asset and leases it to a lessee, obtains nonrecourse financing using the lease rentals or the asset and lease rentals as collateral, sells the asset and nonrecourse debt to a third party, and leases the asset back while remaining the lessor on the original lease. A wrap lease transaction is essentially a sale-leaseback of property and should be accounted for as such. If the property involved in the transaction is real estate, the guidance in Paragraphs 31.279–.280 should be followed. Otherwise, the guidance in Paragraphs 31.275–.278 for sale-leaseback of other property should be followed. (FTB 88-1, paras. 21–22)

31.282   When presenting a wrap lease transaction in the balance sheet, the subleased asset and related nonrecourse debt should not be offset unless a legal right of setoff exists. (FTB 88-1, par. 22) (Offsetting assets and liabilities is discussed further in Chapter 37.)

DISCLOSURE REQUIREMENTS

GENERAL DISCLOSURES ABOUT LEASES

31.500   Authoritative literature requires the following information about leases to be disclosed:

Lessees:

   a. A general description of the leasing arrangements including, but not limited to, the following: (SFAS 13, par. 16)

    (1) Basis on which contingent rental payments are determined

    (2) Existence and terms of renewal or purchase options and escalation clauses

    (3) Restrictions imposed by lease agreements, such as those concerning dividends, additional debt, and further leasing

  b. Nature and extent of leasing transactions with related parties (SFAS 13, par. 29)

  c. For capital leases—

    (1) Gross amount of assets recorded under capital leases presented by major classes according to nature or function (The information should be disclosed as of the date of each balance sheet presented and may be combined with comparable information with owned assets.)

    (2) Future minimum lease payments as of the date of the latest balance sheet presented, in the aggregate and for each of the five succeeding fiscal years, with separate deductions from the total for the amount representing executory costs (including any related profit) included in the minimum lease payments and for the amount of the imputed interest necessary to reduce the net minimum lease payments to present value

    (3) Total minimum sublease rentals to be received in the future under noncancelable subleases as of the date of the latest balance sheet presented

    (4) Total contingent rentals actually incurred for each period for which an income statement is presented

    (5) Assets recorded under capital leases and related accumulated depreciation should be separately identified in the balance sheet or notes to the financial statements. Likewise, lease obligations should be separately identified in the balance sheet or notes to the financial statements as obligations under capital leases and classified as current or noncurrent like any other liability.

    (6) Unless depreciation expense related to assets recorded under capital leases is included with depreciation expense related to owned assets (and that fact is disclosed),

depreciation expense related to assets recorded under capital leases should be separately disclosed in the financial statements or notes to the financial statements. (SFAS 13, paras. 13 and 16)

d. For operating leases having initial or remaining noncancelable lease terms in excess of one year—

  (1) Future minimum rental payments required as of the date of the latest balance sheet presented, in the aggregate and for each of the five succeeding fiscal years

  (2) Total minimum rentals to be received in the future under non-cancelable subleases as of the date of the latest balance sheet presented

e. For all operating leases, rental expense for each period for which an income statement is presented, with separate amounts for minimum rentals, contingent rentals, and sublease rentals (Rental payments under leases with terms of a month or less that were not renewed need not be included.) (SFAS 13, par. 16)

Lessors:

a. General description of the leasing arrangements (SFAS 13, par. 23)

b. Nature and extent of leasing transactions with related parties (SFAS 13, par. 29)

c. For sales-type and direct financing leases—

  (1) Components of the net investment in sales-type and direct financing leases as of the date of each balance sheet presented (The components of the net investment include future minimum lease payments to be received, executory costs and related profit, accumulated allowance for uncollectible minimum lease payments receivable, unguaranteed residual values accruing to the benefit of the lessor, unearned income, and initial direct costs of direct financing leases.)

  (2) Future minimum lease payments receivable for each of the five fiscal years following the date of the latest balance sheet presented

  (3) Contingent rentals included in income for each income statement presented (SFAS 13, par. 23)

d. For operating leases—

(1) Cost and carrying amount of property leased to lessees or held for leasing (The information should be disclosed for each balance sheet presented and include the amounts for each major class of property and the amount of accumulated depreciation for all such assets in total.)

(2) Minimum future rentals on noncancelable leases as of the date of the latest balance sheet presented, in total and for each of the five succeeding fiscal years

(3) Total contingent rentals included in each income statement presented (SFAS 13, par. 23)

LEVERAGED LEASES

31.501   A lessor's balance sheet should report an investment in a leveraged lease separately from the related deferred taxes. If leveraged leasing activities comprise a significant part of the lessor's revenue, net income, or assets, the components of the net investment in leveraged leases should be disclosed. The components include the following: (SFAS 13, paras. 43 and 47)

a. Rentals receivable, net of the portion applicable to principal and interest on the nonrecourse debt

b. Receivable for investment tax credits to be received on the transaction

c. The leased asset's estimated residual value

d. Unearned and deferred income

SALE-LEASEBACK TRANSACTIONS

31.502   In addition to the lessee disclosures in Paragraph 31.500, a seller-lessee in a sale-leaseback transaction should describe the terms of the transaction, including any future commitments, obligations, provisions, or circumstances that require or result in the seller-lessee's continuing involvement. The seller-lessee also should disclose the following if it accounts for the transaction under the deposit method or as a financing: (SFAS 98, paras. 17–18)

a. Obligation for future minimum lease payments as of the date of the latest balance sheet presented

b. Total minimum sublease rentals to be received in the future under noncancelable subleases

Both of the preceding disclosures should be presented in the aggregate and for each of the five years succeeding the latest balance sheet date.

AUTHORITATIVE LITERATURE AND RELATED TOPICS

AUTHORITATIVE LITERATURE

SFAS No. 13, *Accounting for Leases*

SFAS No. 22, *Changes in the Provisions of Lease Agreements Resulting from Refundings of Tax-Exempt Debt*

SFAS No. 23, *Inception of the Lease*

SFAS No. 27, *Classification of Renewals or Extentions of Existing Sales-Type or Direct Financing Leases*

SFAS No. 28, *Accounting for Sales with Leasebacks*

SFAS No. 29, *Determining Contingent Rentals*

SFAS No. 91, *Accounting for Nonrefundable Fees and Costs Associated with Originating or Acquiring Loans and Initial Direct Costs of Leases*

SFAS No. 98, *Accounting for Leases:*
- *Sale-Leaseback Transactions Involving Real Estate*
- *Sales-Type Leases of Real Estate*
- *Definition of the Lease Term*
- *Initial Direct Costs of Direct Financing Leases*

SFAS No. 125, *Accounting for Transfers and Servicing of Financial Assets and Extinguishments of Liabilities*

FASB Technical Bulletin 79-10, *Fiscal Funding Clauses in Lease Agreements*

FASB Technical Bulletin 79-12, *Interest Rate Used in Calculating the Present Value of Minimum Lease Payments*

FASB Technical Bulletin 79-13, *Applicability of FASB Statement No. 13 to Current Value Financial Statements*

FASB Technical Bulletin 79-14, *Upward Adjustment of Guaranteed Residual Values*

FASB Technical Bulletin 79-15, *Accounting for Loss on a Sublease Not Involving the Disposal of a Segment*

FASB Technical Bulletin 79-16 (R), *Effect of a Change in Income Tax Rate on the Accounting for Leveraged Leases*

FASB Technical Bulletin 79-17, *Reporting Cumulative Effect Adjustment from Retroactive Application of FASB Statement No. 13*

FASB Technical Bulletin 79-18, *Transition Requirement of Certain FASB Amendments and Interpretations of FASB Statement No. 13*

FASB Technical Bulletin 85-3, *Accounting for Operating Leases with Scheduled Rent Increases*

FASB Technical Bulletin 86-2, *Accounting for an Interest in the Residual Value of a Leased Asset:*
- *Acquired by a Third Party or*
- *Retained by a Lessor That Sells the Related Minimum Rental Payments*

FASB Technical Bulletin 88-1, *Issues Relating to Accounting for Leases:*
- *Time Pattern of the Physical Use of the Property in an Operating Lease*
- *Lease Incentives in an Operating Lease*
- *Applicability of Leveraged Lease Accounting to Existing Assets of the Lessor*
- *Money-Over-Money Lease Transactions*
- *Wrap Lease Transactions*

FASB Interpretation No. 19, *Lessee Guarantee of the Residual Value of Leased Property*

FASB Interpretation No. 21, *Accounting for Leases in a Business Combination*

FASB Interpretation No. 23, *Leases of Certain Property Owned by a Governmental Unit or Authority*

FASB Interpretation No. 24, *Leases Involving Only Part of a Building*

FASB Interpretation No. 26, *Accounting for Purchase of a Leased Asset by the Lessee during the Term of the Lease*

FASB Interpretation No. 27, *Accounting for a Loss on a Sublease*

RELATED PRONOUNCEMENTS

EITF Issue No. 84-25, *Offsetting Nonrecourse Debt with Sales-Type or Direct Financing Lease Receivables*

EITF Issue No. 84-37, *Sale-Leaseback Transaction with Repurchase Option*

EITF Issue No. 85-16, *Leveraged Leases*
- *Real Estate Leases and Sale-Leaseback Transactions*
- *Delayed Equity Contributions by Lessors*

EITF Issue No. 86-17, *Deferred Profit on Sale-Leaseback Transaction with Lessee Guarantee of Residual Value*

EITF Issue No. 86-33, *Tax Indemnifications in Lease Agreements*

EITF Issue No. 86-43, *Effect of a Change in Tax Law or Rates on Leveraged Leases*

EITF Issue No. 86-44, *Effect of a Change in Tax Law on Investments in Safe Harbor Leases*

EITF Issue No. 87-7, *Sale of an Asset Subject to a Lease and Nonrecourse Financing: "Wrap Lease Transactions"*

EITF Issue No. 88-10, *Costs Associated with Lease Modification or Termination*

EITF Issue No. 88-21, *Accounting for the Sale of Property Subject to the Seller's Preexisting Lease*

EITF Issue No. 89-16, *Considerations of Executory Costs in Sale-Leaseback Transactions*

EITF Issue No. 89-20, *Accounting for Cross Border Tax Benefit Leases*

EITF Issue No. 90-14, *Unsecured Guarantee by Parent of Subsidiary's Lease Payments in a Sale-Leaseback Transaction*

EITF Issue No. 90-15, *Impact of Nonsubstantive Lessors, Residual Value Guarantees, and Other Provisions in Leasing Transactions*

EITF Issue No. 90-20, *Impact of an Uncollateralized Irrevocable Letter of Credit on a Real Estate Sale-Leaseback Transaction*

EITF Issue No. 92-1, *Allocation of Residual Value or First-Loss Guarantee to Minimum Lease Payments in Leases Involving Land and Building(s)*

EITF Issue No. 93-8, *Accounting for the Sale and Leaseback of an Asset That Is Leased to Another Party*

EITF Issue No. 95-4, *Revenue Recognition on Equipment Sold and Subsequently Repurchased Subject to an Operating Lease*

EITF Issue No. 95-17, *Accounting for Modifications to an Operating Lease That Do Not Change the Lease Classification*

EITF Issue No. 96-21, *Implementation Issues in Accounting for Leasing Transactions Involving Special-Purpose Entities*

EITF Issue No. 97-1, *Implementation Issues in Accounting for Lease Transactions, Including Those Involving Special-Purpose Entities*

RELATED TOPICS

Chapter 3—Business Combinations
Chapter 14—Debt Extinquishments
Chapter 34—Long-term Obligation Disclosures
Chapter 52—Transfers and Servicing of Financial Assets

LOAN IMPAIRMENT

Table of Contents

LOAN IMPAIRMENT

OVERVIEW

32.100   A loan is considered impaired if it is probable that at least some of the scheduled principal or interest payments will not be collected. An impaired loan should be measured based on the present value of expected future cash flows. (Expected future cash flows should be discounted using the loan's effective interest rate.) As a practical expedient, however, an impaired loan may be measured at its market value or the fair value of its collateral if it is collateral dependent.

32.101   If the measured value of the loan is less than the recorded investment in the loan, a loss should be recognized by recording a valuation allowance (or adjusting an existing valuation allowance for the impaired loan) and a corresponding charge to bad debt expense.

ACCOUNTING REQUIREMENTS

32.200   A loan is defined as the contractual right to receive money on demand or on fixed or determinable dates and is recorded as an asset in the creditor's balance sheet. Examples of loans include notes and accounts receivable with terms longer than one year. Notes and accounts receivable maturing within one year are *not* considered loans, however. (SFAS 114, par. 4)

Practical Consideration. The guidance in this chapter generally applies to all loans identified for collectibility evaluation except (a) those accounted for at fair value or the lower of cost or fair value, (b) large groups of smaller balance homogeneous loans that are collectively evaluated (such as consumer install-ment loans), (c) leases, and (d) debt securities. Although GAAP does not pro-vide specific guidance on how a creditor should identify loans for collectibility evaluation, it states that the creditor should apply its normal loan review proce-dures in making that judgment. Information such as the following may be help-ful in identifying loans for collectibility evaluation:

- Materiality of the loan

- Regulatory reports of examination

Practical Consideration (Continued).

- Internally generated reports such as "watch lists," past due reports, overdraft lists, lists of loans to insiders, and reports of total loan amounts by borrower

- Previous loss experience

- Loan files lacking current financial information on borrowers and guarantors

- Borrowers experiencing financial difficulties

- Loans secured by collateral that is not readily marketable or is susceptible to decline in value

- Loans to borrowers in economically unstable industries or countries

- Loan documentation and compliance exception reports

WHEN IS A LOAN IMPAIRED?

32.201   A loan is considered impaired if it is probable that the creditor will be unable to collect all amounts due under the contractual terms of the loan agreement. In other words, a loan is impaired if it is probable that at least some of the scheduled principal or interest payments will not be collected. (For a loan that has been restructured in a troubled debt restructuring, the "contractual terms of the loan agreement" refers to the terms of the original agreement, not the restructured agreement.) GAAP does not provide specific guidance on making that determination although it states that the judgment should be based on normal loan review procedures. GAAP does list the following events that do *not* cause a loan to be considered impaired, however: (SFAS 114, par. 8 and SFAS 118, par. 6)

- There are insignificant delays or shortfalls in payment amounts.

- There is a delay in payment, but the creditor expects to collect all amounts due plus accrued interest at the contractual rate for the period of the delay

Practical Consideration. Use of the term "probable" is consistent with its use in SFAS No. 5, *Accounting for Contingencies*. (See Chapter 10.) That is, it means more likely than not; it does not mean virtually certain. In addition, "all amounts due under the contractual terms of the loan agreement" means all of the principal and interest payments will be received as scheduled in the loan agreement (excluding insignificant delays or shortfalls in payments). The authors believe that if the loan agreement contains either (a) a demand clause, (b) provision for maturity or renewal, or (c) periodic review of the loan status, the period to be used in determining the amounts due under the terms of the loan agreement should be one of the following:

    a. The time period the loan would remain outstanding based on the original understanding between the borrower and creditor.

    b. The creditor's original estimate of the time period the loan would remain outstanding, if there was no such understanding between the borrower and creditor.

MEASURING IMPAIRMENT

32.202　If a loan is considered to be impaired, its value generally should be measured based on the present value of expected future cash flows discounted at the loan's effective interest rate. As a practical expedient, however, the loan's value may be based on (a) the loan's market price or (b) the fair value of the loan's collateral, less discounted estimated costs to sell, if the collateral is expected to be the sole source of repayment. (The fair value of the loan's collateral must be used to value the loan if foreclosure is probable.) The selection of the method used to value a loan may be made either on a loan-by-loan or aggregate basis. Once a method is selected for a loan, however, it should be applied consistently unless circumstances change. (SFAS 114, paras. 12–13)

32.203　If the value of the loan (as determined in the preceding paragraph) is less than the recorded investment in the loan, a loss should be recognized by recording a valuation allowance (or adjusting an existing valuation allowance for the impaired note) and a corresponding charge to bad debt expense. (SFAS 114, par. 13) As changes in the amount or timing of the expected future cash flows occur (thus affecting the net present value of the impaired loan), the valuation allowance should be adjusted accordingly. (SFAS 114, par. 16)

Using the Expected Cash Flows Method to Measure the Loan

32.204　Measuring the impaired loan based on expected future cash flows requires making subjective judgments about several uncertainties. For example, if the loan is past due (which probably is the case for most impaired loans), a judgment must be made about when the delinquent payments will be made.

The creditor should consider all available evidence, including estimated costs to sell if those costs are expected to reduce the cash flows available to satisfy the loan. The weight given to the evidence should be commensurate with the creditor's ability to objectively verify the evidence. (SFAS 114, par. 15)

32.205   Under the expected cash flows method, the loan's effective interest rate should be used to discount the expected future cash flows. The effective rate of the loan is the contractual rate, adjusted for any premiums, discounts, or deferred loan fees or costs existing at the loan origination date. In addition—

a. if the loan has a floating interest rate, the effective rate should be initially computed using the rate in effect at the date the loan is first considered impaired. When measuring the impaired loan thereafter, cash flows may be discounted using the effective interest rate at the recalculation date or the rate in effect at the date the allowance initially was provided. (SFAS 114, par. 14)

b. if the loan was restructured in a troubled debt restructuring, the effective interest rate should be based on the original contractual rate, not the rate specified in the restructuring agreement. (SFAS 118, par. 6)

RECOGNIZING INCOME ON IMPAIRED LOANS

32.206   GAAP does not prescribe how interest income from an impaired loan should be measured, recognized, or displayed. Some methods used to recognize income may result in the recorded investment in an impaired loan that is less than the measured value of the loan (for example, if interest is recognized using the cost-recovery method, cash-basis method, or a combination of those methods). In that case, even though the loan may meet the definition of an impaired loan, no additional impairment should be recognized. (SFAS 118, par. 6)

DISCLOSURE REQUIREMENTS

32.500   A creditor should disclose the following information about impaired loans:

a. As of the date of each balance sheet presented, the total recorded investment in impaired loans (as defined in Paragraph 32.201) and (1) the amount of the recorded investment for which there is a related valuation allowance determined in accordance with Paragraph 32.203 and the amount of the allowance and (2) the amount of the recorded investment for which there is no valuation allowance determined in accordance with Paragraph 32.203.

b. The creditor's policy for recognizing interest income on impaired loans, including how cash receipts are recorded

c. For each period for which an income statement is presented, the average recorded investment in impaired loans during the period, the related amount of interest income recognized during the time within that period that the loans were impaired, and, if practicable, the amount of interest income recognized using a cash-basis method of accounting during the time within the period the loans were impaired

The information in a. and c. need not be disclosed about an impaired loan that was restructured in a troubled debt restructuring involving a modification of debt terms in years after the restructuring if (a) the interest rate in the restructuring agreement is at least equal to the rate the creditor was willing to accept at the time of the restructuring for a new loan with comparable risk and (b) the loan is not impaired based on the terms of the restructuring agreement. (SFAS 118, par. 6)

32.501   For each period for which an income statement is presented, the creditor also should disclose the activity in the total valuation allowance related to loans, including the beginning and ending valuation allowance account balances, additions charged to operations, direct write-downs charged against the allowance, and recoveries of amounts previously charged off. (SFAS 118, par. 6)

AUTHORITATIVE LITERATURE AND RELATED TOPICS

AUTHORITATIVE LITERATURE

SFAS No. 114, *Accounting by Creditors for Impairment of a Loan*
SFAS No. 118, *Accounting by Creditors for Impairment of a Loan—Income Recognition and Disclosures*

RELATED PRONOUNCEMENTS

EITF Issue No. 85-44, *Differences between Loan Loss Allowances for GAAP and RAP*
EITF Issue No. 93-18, *Recognition of Impairment for an Investment in a Collateralized Mortgage Obligation Instrument or in a Mortgage-Backed Interest-Only Certificate*

EITF Issue No. 96-22, *Applicability of the Disclosures Required by FASB Statement No. 114 When a Loan is Restructured in a Troubled Debt Restructuring into Two (or More) Loans*

RELATED TOPICS

LONG-LIVED ASSETS, DEPRECIATION, AND IMPAIRMENT

Table of Contents

LONG-LIVED ASSETS, DEPRECIATION, AND IMPAIRMENT

OVERVIEW

33.100   A tangible capital asset should be recorded at cost. That cost, less salvage value, should be charged to expense (i.e., depreciated) over the asset's estimated useful life in a systematic and rational manner.

33.101   A long-lived asset to be disposed of (other than as part of a disposal of a business segment) should be reported at the lower of its carrying amount or fair value less costs to sell.

33.102   Long-lived assets to be held and used should be reviewed for impairment if events or changes in circumstances indicate that their carrying amounts may not be recoverable. A long-lived asset is considered impaired if the undiscounted estimated cash flows from continuing to use the asset are less than the asset's carrying amount. (For purposes of determining whether the asset has been impaired, its carrying amount should include any related goodwill.) If an asset is considered impaired, an impairment loss equal to the difference between the asset's carrying amount and fair value should be recognized by reducing the carrying amount of the impaired asset and charging current period net income. (Any related goodwill should be reduced to zero before reducing the asset's carrying amount, however.)

ACCOUNTING REQUIREMENTS

ASSET COST

33.200   Tangible long-lived assets include property and equipment and other assets held for investment or used in a company's operations that have an estimated useful life longer than one year. Under generally accepted accounting principles, an acquired long-lived asset should be stated at acquisition cost, including all costs necessary to bring the asset to its location in working condition. Thus, the cost of a long-lived asset should include the asset's purchase price, sales tax, freight, installation costs, and direct and indirect costs (including interest) incurred by an entity in constructing its own assets. It generally should not include routine repairs and maintenance costs that do not add to the utility of the asset. Long-lived assets should not be written up to reflect appraisal, market, or current values that are above cost. (APB 6, par. 17)

(An entity may adjust the carrying amounts of its assets to current value in a quasi-reorganization, however, as discussed in Chapter 44.)

Practical Consideration. Costs to remove, contain, neutralize, or prevent existing or future environmental contamination generally should not be capitalized, however. EITF Issue No. 90-8, *Capitalization of Costs to Treat Environmental Contamination,* states that those costs should be expensed when incurred unless one of the following conditions is met:

   a. The costs extend the life, increase the capacity, or improve the safety or efficiency of property owned by the company. In addition, the costs improve the property as compared to its condition when constructed or acquired.

   b. The costs mitigate or prevent environmental contamination that has not occurred but may have resulted otherwise from future operations or activities. In addition, the costs improve the property as compared to its condition when constructed or acquired.

   c. The costs prepare for sale property that is currently held for sale.

DEPRECIATION

33.201   Depreciation is a means of charging the cost of an asset used in a company's operations to expense over the periods benefited. It is not a valuation method, but rather a method of allocating cost. Its objective is to spread the asset's cost, less salvage value, over the asset's estimated useful life in a systematic and rational manner.

Estimated Useful Life

33.202   An asset's estimated useful life is the time the company intends to use the asset, and varies depending on factors such as the company's maintenance policy and obsolescence of the asset. (ARB 43, Ch. 9C, par. 5)

Practical Consideration. For example, some companies buy trucks with the intention of having minimal maintenance costs and trading them before repairs become a problem. Others buy them with the intention of holding them for a long time and consequently pay greater attention to maintenance. The estimated useful life for trucks would vary under each of those approaches. As another example, because computer technology advances so rapidly, computer hardware quickly becomes obsolete. Accordingly, the estimated useful life of computer equipment might be less than for other machinery or equipment.

33.203 The estimated useful life of some assets is so long that the benefit used up in a period is imperceptible (for example, land used as a building site). Depreciation need not be recorded for such assets. (SFAS 93, par. 34)

> **Practical Consideration.** Although land generally is not depreciated, the authors believe that the benefits derived from certain uses of land may be used up relatively quickly and, thus, depreciation should be recorded. Examples include land used as a site for toxic waste storage, as a source of gravel or ore, or for certain farming operations.

Salvage Value

33.204 Some assets have value at the end of their useful life that can be realized through sale or trade-in. By depreciating to salvage value, a company spreads the net cost (acquisition cost less salvage value) over the period it uses the assets. (If a company were to ignore salvage value and depreciate an asset to zero, there would be a gain when the salvage value is realized. However, the gain really would represent only a recovery of prior depreciation expense.) Salvage value often fluctuates with market conditions. For example, the salvage values of used vehicles may increase during recessionary periods because the market value for used vehicles may increase. On the other hand, for computers and other depreciable assets subject to rapid obsolescence, there may be no market for older assets and, thus, no salvage value.

> **Practical Consideration.** If salvage value is minor, the authors believe it need not be considered in depreciation calculations.

Depreciation Methods

33.205 Generally accepted accounting principles essentially recognize the following methods of computing depreciation:

    a. *Straight-line method* allocates cost less salvage value evenly over the asset's estimated useful life.

    b. *Accelerated methods* allocate cost disproportionately over the asset's useful life so that the early years are charged with most of the cost. There are a number of acceptable accelerated depreciation methods, including the following:

       (1) Sum-of-the-years' digits. Under this method, depreciation is determined by multiplying the asset's cost less salvage value by a fraction in which the sum-of-the-years' digits is the denominator and the number of years remaining in the

asset's life is the numerator. The sum-of-the-years' digits is determined by the following formula:

$$\text{Number of years in the asset's life} \times \left[\frac{\text{Number of years in the asset's life} + 1}{2}\right]$$

For example, the sum-of-the-years' digits for an asset with a five year life is 15 (i.e., 5 × [(5 + 1) ÷ 2]), and 5/15 of the asset's cost would be depreciated in the first year, 4/15 of the asset's cost would be depreciated in the second year, and so on.

(2) Declining balance. Under this method, a depreciation rate that is a multiple of the straight-line depreciation rate is applied to the asset's *net depreciable value*. (Although the asset's salvage value is ignored in the depreciation calcula-tion, the asset should not be depreciated below its salvage value.) For example, the straight-line rate for an asset whose useful life is 5 years would be 20% per year. Under the double declining balance method, the depreciation rate would be twice the straight-line rate or 40%. Similarly, under the 150% declining balance method, the depreciation rate would be 150% of the straight-line rate or 30%. Since the depreciation rate is applied to the asset's net depreciable value (i.e., cost less accumulated depreciation), declining balance methods do not depreciate to zero. Consequently, some companies adopt a policy of using a declining balance method until it drops below what straight-line would have been and then switch to the straight-line method.

(3) Units-of-production. Under this method, depreciation is a function of the asset's total estimated production capability during its estimated useful life and is based on the following formula:

$$\frac{\text{Cost less salvage value}}{\text{Estimated units}} = \text{Depreciation per unit}$$

For example, if a machine with a total estimated life of 25,000 hours were used for 4,000 hours during the year, 16% (4,000 ÷ 25,000) of the machine's cost less salvage value would be depreciated for the year.

> **Practical Consideration.** Accelerated depreciation methods permitted for tax purposes ignore salvage value and are based on prescribed asset lives that may differ from an asset's actual estimated useful life. Consequently, the authors believe tax depreciation methods are appropriate for GAAP reporting only if they do not distort depreciation expense or the asset's book value.

33.206 Although depreciation is not a valuation process, the depreciation method used typically should reflect the asset's decline in value. Thus, using an accelerated method to compute depreciation, rather than the straight-line method, would be appropriate if an asset's value declines faster in the early years than in the later years. [SFAS 109, par. 288(a)] Annuity methods of computing depreciation generally are not acceptable under generally accepted accounting principles, however. (SFAS 92, par. 37)

> **Practical Consideration.** Depreciation methods usually are selected for components of depreciable assets and all assets within that component are depreciated using the same method. For example, assume that a company's depreciable assets consist of a building, production machinery, and office equipment. It could use a different depreciation method for each component (e.g., the 150% declining balance method for the building, the sum-of-the-years' digits method for the production machinery, and the straight-line method for the office equipment). All items within a component, however, normally would be depreciated using the same method. (For example, all office equipment would be depreciated using the straight-line method.)

Changes in Estimated Useful Life, Salvage Value, and Depreciation Methods

33.207 Changes in estimated useful life and salvage value normally are changes in estimates caused by changing market conditions or better information about the asset. Prior period financial statements should not be adjusted for changes in estimates. Instead, the dollar amount of the change should be recorded entirely in current year earnings or current and future earnings if the change affects both. (APB 20, par. 31)

33.208 A change in the method used to depreciate previously recorded assets is a change in accounting principle. (Consistently applying a policy of changing from an accelerated method to a straight-line method at a specific point in the service life of an asset does not constitute a change in accounting principle, however.) (APB 20, par. 9) A change in accounting principle is recorded by including the cumulative effect of the change as of the beginning of the year of the change in current period earnings. (APB 20, par. 20)

33.209 Chapter 1 discusses accounting for changes in estimates and accounting principles in further detail.

> **Practical Consideration.** Some accountants question whether depreciation should be suspended or reduced during periods that productive assets are idle. SFAS No. 121, *Accounting for the Impairment of Long-Lived Assets and for Long-Lived Assets to Be Disposed of,* indicates that no depreciation should be taken if the company plans to dispose of the idle assets but provides no guidance on depreciating temporarily idle assets that will be used again in the future. The authors suggest continuing to depreciate temporarily idle assets. However, the fact that assets are idle may indicate that they have been impaired and an impairment loss is necessary. (See Paragraphs 33.212–.217.)

Not-for-profit Organizations

33.210   Similar to for-profit entities, not-for-profit organizations are required to depreciate long-lived tangible assets. Depreciation need not be recognized on individual works of art or historical treasures that have indefinite or extraordinarily long useful lives, however. Works of art or historical treasures have indefinite or extraordinarily long useful lives if they (a) have cultural, aesthetic, or historical value that is worth preserving perpetually and (b) are being preserved by a holder that has the technological and financial ability to do so (for example, by placing art in a protective environment and limiting its use solely to display). (SFAS 93, par. 36) Works of art or historical treasures do not have indefinite or extraordinarily long useful lives (and thus should be depreciated) if their cultural, aesthetic, or historical values can be preserved, if at all, only by periodically protecting, cleaning, and restoring them, usually at significant cost. (For example, the wear and tear of normal use, destructive effects of pollutants, vibrations, etc. may reduce the useful life of a monument or cathedral unless major preservation and restoration efforts periodically are made.) (SFAS 93, par. 35)

33.211   Capitalized costs of major preservation and restoration efforts should be depreciated, regardless of whether depreciation is recognized on the asset being protected or restored, if the efforts provide future economic benefits or service potential. (SFAS 93, par. 37)

IMPAIRMENT OF LONG-LIVED ASSETS

33.212   Sometimes changes in operating conditions raise doubts about a company's ability to fully recover the carrying value of a particular asset. When it is determined that the carrying value will not be fully recovered, the asset is considered impaired. Accounting for impaired assets differs depending on whether the company intends to continue to use the asset or dispose of it. (Idle assets that a company plans to dispose of in the future but for which it does not have a plan of liquidation should be classified as assets to be held and used.)

> **Practical Consideration.** The guidance in Paragraphs 33.212–.217 applies to all entities, including not-for-profit organizations. However, it does not apply to financial instruments, long-term customer relationships of a financial institution, mortgage and other servicing rights, deferred policy acquisition costs, deferred tax assets, or assets that are part of a disposal of a business segment.

Assets to Be Disposed of

33.213   Assets for which management has committed to a plan to sell or abandon (other than as part of the disposal of a business segment) should be stated at the lower of carrying value or fair value less costs to sell. (SFAS 121, par. 15)

> **Practical Consideration.** Assets related to a segment of a business to be disposed of, however, should be valued as described in APB Opinion No. 30. *Reporting the Results of Operations—Reporting the Effects of Disposal of a Segment of a Business, and Extraordinary, Unusual, and Infrequently Occurring Events and Transactions.* (See Chapter 23.)

Fair value less costs to sell should be determined as follows:

a. Fair value is the amount at which the asset could be bought or sold in a current transaction between willing parties, other than in a forced sale or liquidation. Fair value should be based on quoted market prices, if available. Otherwise, it should be estimated using the best available information. Techniques that may be used to estimate fair value include the following: (SFAS 121, par. 7)

   (1) Net present value of future cash flows (Cash flows should be discounted using a discount rate consistent with the risks involved.)

   (2) Option pricing models

   (3) Matrix pricing

   (4) Option-adjusted spread models

b. Selling costs include only the incremental direct costs of selling the asset, such as sales commissions, transfer fees, and other closing costs. Costs that are not directly related to the sale (for example, insurance and property taxes incurred while the asset is being sold and other holding costs) should be charged to operations as they are incurred. If fair value is estimated using discounted cash flows and the sale is expected to occur beyond one year, selling costs also should be discounted. (SFAS 121, par. 16)

33.214   The carrying amount of an asset to be disposed of should be adjusted (either up or down) for subsequent changes in fair value. It should never be adjusted above the asset's original carrying amount, however. (SFAS 121, par. 17) In addition, assets to be disposed of should not be depreciated or amortized while held for disposal. (SFAS 121, par. 16)

33.215   **Reporting Impairment Losses in Financial Statements.** Gains and losses on assets to be disposed of that do no qualify as a disposal of a segment should be reported in the income statement as components of income from continuing operations before income taxes. If a subtotal such as "Income (loss) from operations" is presented, any gains and losses must be included in the subtotal. (SFAS 121, par. 18)

Assets to Be Held and Used

33.216   A long-lived asset to be held and used in the company's operations should be reviewed for impairment if events or changes in circumstances indicate that its carrying amount may not be fully recoverable. The following may indicate that the recoverability of an asset's carrying amount should be assessed: (SFAS 121, par. 5)

   a. Significant decrease in the asset's market value

   b. Significant change in the asset's use

   c. Significant physical change in the asset

   d. Significant adverse changes in legal factors or business climate or an adverse action or assessment by a regulator

   e. Costs to acquire or construct an asset that significantly exceed original expectations

   f. Continuing losses associated with an asset used to produce revenue

33.217   If there is doubt about the recoverability of an asset, an assessment of whether the asset has been impaired should be made. To make that assessment, expected cash flows from continuing to use the asset and its eventual disposition (undiscounted and without interest) should be estimated using reasonable and supportable assumptions. In testing for and measuring impairment, if it is not possible to estimate cash flows from a specific asset, assets should be grouped at the lowest level from which there are identifiable cash flows (i.e., assets should be grouped together when they are used together to generate joint cash flows). If the expected undiscounted cash flows exceed the asset's carrying amount, the asset is not considered impaired and no further considerations are necessary. Otherwise, the asset is considered to be impaired and the following apply: (SFAS 121, par. 6)

a. An impairment loss should be recorded equal to the amount by which the asset's carrying amount exceeds its fair value. Fair value should be determined as discussed in Paragraph 33.213, item a. (SFAS 121, par. 7)

b. After an impairment has been recognized, the asset's reduced carrying amount becomes its new cost. Subsequent recoveries of the impairment loss due to increases in the asset's fair value should not be recognized. (SFAS 121, par. 11)

Practical Consideration. SFAS No. 121 acknowledges that, in some circumstances, expected cash flows from an asset's use may be the only information available for estimating fair value without undue cost. Note that the impaired asset is written down to its fair value, not its undiscounted estimated cash flows. The sole purpose of comparing the carrying amount and the undiscounted estimated cash flows is to determine whether an impairment loss should be recorded. The *amount* of the impairment loss should be derived from the fair value of the asset.

33.218   In limited circumstances, an asset being tested for impairment does not produce cash flows independently of other asset groupings (e.g., corporate headquarters). In that case, the asset should be accounted for as follows:

a. If the asset is not expected to provide any service potential to the company, it should be accounted for as if it were abandoned or held for disposal. (See Paragraphs 33.213–.215.)

b. If the asset is expected to provide service potential, an impairment loss should be recognized if the sum of the expected future cash flows (undiscounted and without interest) for the entity is less than the carrying amount of the entity's assets covered by SFAS No. 121.

33.219   **Considering Goodwill Related to an Asset Being Tested for Impairment.** If the asset being assessed for impairment was acquired in a purchase business combination, its carrying amount for purposes of the assessment should include any related goodwill. Goodwill that relates to both an asset being evaluated and assets not being evaluated should be allocated on a pro rata basis using the fair values of the assets at the original acquisition date (unless another allocation method is more appropriate). When recording an impairment loss, related goodwill should be reduced to zero before reducing the carrying amount of the impaired asset. (SFAS 121, par. 12) (Goodwill not identified with impaired assets should be accounted for as discussed in Chapter 26.)

Practical Consideration. Whether an impairment loss is recognized or the review of cash flows indicated that an impairment loss should not be recognized, it may be appropriate to review depreciation policies, including the depreciation method and estimated useful life and salvage values. (Chapter 1 describes accounting for changes in depreciation estimates.)

In addition, even if an impairment loss is not recognized, SOP 94-6, *Disclosure of Certain Significant Risks and Uncertainties,* may require disclosures because, according to the SOP, the events or changes in circumstances listed in Paragraph 33.215 may indicate that an estimate associated with the carrying amount of a long-lived asset may be particularly sensitive to change in the near term.

33.220 Reporting Impairment Losses in Financial Statements. An impairment loss on assets to be held and used should be reported in the income statement as a component of income from continuing operations before income taxes. If a subtotal such as "Income (loss) from operations" is presented, the impairment loss must be included in the subtotal. (SFAS 121, par. 13)

DISCLOSURE REQUIREMENTS

DEPRECIATION

33.500   GAAP basis financial statements should include the following disclosures about long-lived assets and depreciation: (APB 12, par. 5)

   a. Depreciation expense for the period

   b. Balances of major classes of depreciable assets, by nature or function, at the balance sheet date

   c. Accumulated depreciation, either by major classes of depreciable assets or in total, at the balance sheet date (Accumulated depreciation should be presented as a reduction of the related asset rather than as a liability.) (APB 12, par. 3)

   d. General description of the methods used to compute depreciation on each major class of depreciable assets

IMPAIRED LONG-LIVED ASSETS

33.501   Impairment losses related to long-lived assets (and subsequent gains related to assets held for disposal) should be reported as a component of income from continuing operations before income taxes. (SFAS 121, paras. 13 and 18)

Impaired Assets to Be Held and Used

33.502   If an impairment loss related to assets that are to be held and used has been recognized, the following disclosures should be made in financial statements that include the period of the write-down: (SFAS 121, par. 14)

   a. Description of the impaired assets and the facts and circumstances leading to the impairment

   b. Amount of the impairment loss and how fair value was determined

   c. Caption in the income statement (or statement of activities) in which the impairment loss is reported, unless the loss is presented as a separate caption or reported parenthetically on the face of the income statement

   d. Business segments affected, if applicable

Assets to Be Disposed of

33.503   The following information should be disclosed about assets to be disposed of in each period the assets are held: (SFAS 121, par. 19)

   a. Description of the assets to be disposed of, the facts and circumstances leading to the expected disposal, the expected disposal date, and the carrying amount of the assets

   b. Business segments that hold the assets to be disposed of, if applicable

   c. Loss, if any, resulting from writing down the asset to fair value less costs to sell

   d. Gain or loss, if any, resulting from subsequent changes in the carrying amounts of assets to be disposed of

   e. Caption in the income statement (or statement of activities) in which the gains and losses in c. and d. are reported, unless the gains and losses are presented as a separate caption or reported parenthetically on the face of the income statement

   f. Results of operations for assets to be disposed of to the extent the results are included in the company's results of operations for the period and can be identified

AUTHORITATIVE LITERATURE AND RELATED TOPICS

AUTHORITATIVE LITERATURE

ARB No. 43, *Restatement and Revision of Accounting Research Bulletins* (Chapter 9A—Depreciation and High Costs; Chapter 9C—Emergency Facilities—Depreciation, Amortization, and Income Taxes)
APB Opinion No. 6, *Status of Accounting Research Bulletins*
APB Opinion No. 12, *Omnibus Opinion—1967*
SFAS No. 92, *Regulated Enterprises—Accounting for Phase-in Plans*
SFAS No. 93, *Recognition of Depreciation by Not-for-Profit Organizations*
SFAS No. 109, *Accounting for Income Taxes*
SFAS No. 121, *Accounting for the Impairment of Long-Lived Assets and for Long-Lived Assets to Be Disposed Of*

RELATED PRONOUNCEMENTS

EITF Issue No. 84-28, *Impairment of Long-Lived Assets*
EITF Issue No. 89-13, *Accounting for the Cost of Asbestos Removal*
EITF Issue No. 90-8, *Capitalization of Costs to Treat Environmental Contamination*
EITF Issue No. 95-23, *The Treatment of Certain Site Restoration/Environmental Exit Costs When Testing a Long-Lived Asset for Impairment*
EITF Issue No. 96-2, *Impairment Recognition When a Nonmonetary Asset Is Exchanged or Is Distributed to Owners and Is Accounted for at the Asset's Recorded Amount*

RELATED TOPICS

Chapter 1—Accounting Changes
Chapter 26—Intangible Assets
Chapter 27—Interest: Capitalized
Chapter 31—Leases
Chapter 36—Nonmonetary Transactions

LONG-TERM OBLIGATION DISCLOSURES

Table of Contents

LONG-TERM OBLIGATION DISCLOSURES

OVERVIEW

34.100   A company should disclose certain information about its commitments under unconditional purchase obligations related to suppliers' financing arrangements. For unrecorded obligations, the disclosures include the nature of the obligations, the amount of the obligations that are determinable (for the latest balance sheet presented and for the next five years), a description of any variable portion of the obligations, and actual purchases under the contracts during the year. For recorded unconditional purchase commitments, the required payments for each of the next five years should be disclosed.

34.101   A company also should disclose, for each of the next five years, maturities and sinking fund requirements of long-term borrowings and redemption requirements of redeemable stock.

DISCLOSURE REQUIREMENTS

34.500   Generally accepted accounting principles require certain information about long-term obligations to be disclosed. Those disclosures include information about unrecorded unconditional purchase obligations, recorded unconditional purchase obligations, long-term borrowings, and redeemable debt.

UNCONDITIONAL PURCHASE OBLIGATIONS

34.501   An unconditional purchase obligation requires one party to transfer funds to another party in the future in return for specified quantities of goods and services at specified prices. Certain disclosures are required about unconditional purchase obligations that have the following characteristics: (SFAS 47, par. 6)

a. The obligation is noncancelable, or cancelable only—

(1) upon the occurrence of a remote contingency;

(2) with the other party's permission;

(3) if a replacement agreement is signed between the same parties; or

(4) upon payment of a penalty in an amount that reasonably assures that the agreement will be continued.

b. The obligation is associated with financing arrangements for (1) the facilities that will provide the specified goods or services or (2) the costs related to the goods or services (for example, carrying costs).

c. The obligation's remaining term is for more than one year.

Practical Consideration. Examples of unconditional purchase obligations include the following:

- *Take-or-pay contract.* A take-or-pay contract is one in which the purchaser is required to pay specified minimum amounts even if it does not take delivery of the specified goods or services.

- *Throughput contract.* In a throughput contract, one party (the shipper) agrees to pay to another party specified amounts to transport or process a product (for example, oil or natural gas). The contract requires the shipper to pay specified minimum amounts even if it does not provide the product for transporting or processing.

Each of the preceding contracts have one common element—they are unconditional. That is, the required specified payments must be made regardless of whether the specified goods or services are delivered.

34.502   Under current accounting practices, assets and liabilities created by purchase obligations may or may not be recorded. Often, unfulfilled purchase obligations are not recorded until at least part of the commitment is fulfilled. In issuing SFAS No. 47, *Disclosure of Long-Term Obligations,* the FASB did not address the issue of when purchase obligation assets and liabilities should be recorded. Instead, it merely required that the obligations be disclosed. The required disclosures vary depending on whether the unconditional purchase obligation is recorded or not. In addition, although obligations to pay future minimum lease payments under leases may possess all of the characteristics in Paragraph 34.501, lease obligations that are disclosed in accordance with SFAS No. 13, *Accounting for Leases* (see Chapter 31), are excluded from the unconditional purchase obligation disclosure requirements. (SFAS 47, par. 6)

Unrecorded Unconditional Purchase Obligations

34.503   The following information should be disclosed about unconditional purchase obligations that have not been recognized in the balance sheet:

     a. Nature and term of the obligations

     b. Total amount of the fixed and determinable portion of the obligations as of the date of the latest balance sheet presented and, if determinable, for each of the five succeeding fiscal years

     c. Nature of any variable components of the obligations

     d. Amounts actually purchased under the obligations for each period for which an income statement is presented

34.504   Disclosure of the *present value* of the fixed and determinable portion of the obligations (item b. in the preceding paragraph) is encouraged but not required. The discount rate used to compute the obligations' present value should be the initial effective interest rate of the borrowings used to finance the facilities that will provide the contracted goods or services. If that rate is not known, the purchaser's incremental borrowing rate should be used. (SFAS 47, par. 8) The purchaser's incremental borrowing rate is the rate the purchaser would have incurred at the inception of the unconditional purchase obligation to borrow funds, on similar terms, to discharge the obligation. (SFAS 47, par. 23)

Recorded Unconditional Purchase Obligations

34.505   If an unconditional purchase obligation has been recorded, the total payments required for each of the five years following the latest balance sheet date presented should be disclosed. (SFAS 47, par.10)

LONG-TERM BORROWINGS AND REDEEMABLE STOCK

34.506   The following information about long-term borrowings and redeemable stock should be disclosed for each of the five years following the latest balance sheet presented:

     a. Combined amount of maturities and sinking fund requirements for all long-term borrowings (SFAS 47, par. 10)

b. Total required redemption (separately or combined) for all classes of capital stock that are redeemable at determinable prices on determinable dates (SFAS 129, par. 8)

AUTHORITATIVE LITERATURE AND RELATED TOPICS

AUTHORITATIVE LITERATURE

SFAS No. 47, *Disclosure of Long-Term Obligations*
SFAS No. 129, *Disclosure of Information about Capital Structure*

RELATED TOPICS

Chapter 10—Contingencies
Chapter 13—Debt: Convertible Debt
Chapter 15—Debt: Product Financing Arrangements
Chapter 31—Leases

MARKETABLE SECURITIES

Table of Contents

MARKETABLE SECURITIES

OVERVIEW

DEBT AND EQUITY SECURITIES

35.100   Certain marketable equity securities and all debt securities should be classified as either held-to-maturity, trading, or available-for-sale. Debt securities classified as held-to-maturity should be reported in the balance sheet at amortized cost. Trading securities should be reported in the balance sheet at fair value with realized and unrealized gains and losses included in current period income. Available-for-sale securities also should be reported at fair value. However, only realized gains and losses from available-for-sale securities should be included in income. Unrealized gains and losses should be reported as other comprehensive income.

35.101   If the fair value of an available-for-sale or held-to-maturity security is less than its carrying amount and the decline is other than temporary, the carrying amount of the investment should be reduced to fair value through a charge to current period income.

FUTURES CONTRACTS

35.102   The deposit paid to the commodities broker for a futures contract should be recorded as an asset and the recorded amount increased or decreased as the market value of the contract changes. The changes should be recognized as a gain or loss in the period they occur unless the contract qualifies as a hedge of an exposure to price or interest rate risk. In that event, changes in the market value of a futures contract should not be recognized in income until the related change in the fair value of the hedged item is recognized in income.

ACCOUNTING REQUIREMENTS

DEBT AND EQUITY SECURITIES

35.200   Marketable securities include both debt and equity securities. Debt securities represent a creditor relationship with another entity. Examples include bonds, bankers acceptances, U.S. Treasury notes, convertible debt,

35.200

and preferred stock that must be redeemed. Equity securities represent an ownership interest in another entity (or the right to buy or sell an ownership interest at a determinable price). Examples of equity securities include common and preferred stock, warrants, calls, and puts.

Practical Consideration. The guidance in this chapter applies to all investments in equity securities that have readily determinable fair values and all investments in debt securities. The fair value of equity securities is readily determinable if they are traded on a securities exchange registered with the SEC or in the over-the-counter market, and sales prices or bid-and-asked quotations are currently available. Similarly, the fair value of a mutual fund is readily determinable if the fair value per share or unit is determined and published and is the basis for current transactions. The guidance in this chapter does not apply to the following investments:

- Equity securities accounted for under the equity method (See Chapter 20.)

- Investments in consolidated subsidiaries (See Chapter 9.)

- Entities whose specialized accounting practices include accounting for substantially all investments in debt and equity securities at market or fair value, with changes in value recognized in earnings or the change in net assets (e.g., securities brokers and dealers, defined benefit pension plans, and investment companies)

- Not-for-profit organizations (See Chapter 63.)

Classifying and Accounting for Marketable Securities

35.201 Accounting for marketable securities varies depending on (a) whether the security is a debt or equity security and (b) the entity's intent and ability to hold the security to maturity. Consequently, when a security is acquired, it should be classified as either held-to-maturity, trading, or available-for-sale. (SFAS 115, par. 6) The following paragraphs discuss each classification in further detail. EXHIBIT 35-1 summarizes the classification and reporting requirements.

EXHIBIT 35-1

ACCOUNTING FOR MARKETABLE SECURITIES

Category	Type of Investment	Amount Reported in the Balance Sheet	Reporting Gains and Losses
Held-to-maturity	Debt—Entity has positive intent and ability to hold to maturity	Amortized cost, reduced for nontemporary declines in fair value	Charge nontemporary losses to earnings; do not recognize other unrealized gains and losses
Trading	Debt and equity—Held principally for sale in the near term	Fair value	Include unrealized gains and losses in current period earnings
Available-for-sale	Debt and equity—Securities not classified as held-to-maturity or trading	Fair value	Charge realized gains and losses and nontemporary unrealized losses to earnings; report other unrealized gains and losses as other comprehensive income

---

Practical Consideration. Recording unrealized gains and losses results in a temporary difference between the GAAP and tax bases of debt and equity securities since, for tax reporting, gains and losses are not recognized until they are realized. As discussed further in Chapter 24, deferred taxes should be provided for such temporary differences.

35.202   Held-to-maturity Securities. A debt security for which the entity has both the positive intent and ability to hold to maturity should be classified as held-to-maturity and reported in the balance sheet at its amortized cost. (SFAS 115, par. 7) If, however, contract terms allow for the debt security to be prepaid or otherwise settled in such a way that results in the holder not recovering substantially all of its recorded investment, the security may not be classified as held-to-maturity. (SFAS 125, par. 233) In addition, debt securities should not be classified as held-to-maturity if the entity intends to hold them for only an indefinite period. Thus, for example, a debt security should not be classified as held-to-maturity if the entity expects that it would be available for sale in response to the following factors: (SFAS 115, par. 9)

a. Changes in market interest rates and related changes in the security's prepayment risk

b. Need for liquidity (for example, due to the withdrawal of deposits, increased demand for loans, surrender of insurance policies, or payment of insurance claims)

c. Changes in the availability of and the yield on alternative investments

d. Changes in funding sources and terms

e. Changes in foreign currency risk

35.203   Certain circumstances that are isolated, nonrecurring, and unusual that could not have been reasonably anticipated may cause an entity to change its intent to hold a security to maturity without calling into question its intent to hold other securities to maturity. Selling a security classified as held-to-maturity would not indicate that its original classification was incorrect if the decision to sell is a result of one of the following factors: (SFAS 115, par. 8)

• The issuer's creditworthiness significantly deteriorates.

• A change in tax law eliminates or reduces the tax-exempt status of interest on the debt security.

• A major business combination or disposition necessitates the sale or transfer of the security to maintain the entity's existing interest rate risk position or credit risk policy.

• A regulator significantly increases the industry's capital require-ments causing the entity to downsize by selling the security.

• The risk weights of debt securities used for regulatory risk-based capital purposes increase significantly.

- Events occur that could not be reasonably anticipated and are isolated, nonrecurring, and unusual for the entity.

> **Practical Consideration.** According to a FASB Special Report, *A Guide to Implementation of Statement 115 on Accounting for Certain Investments in Debt and Equity Securities,* the sale of a held to maturity security in response to a tender offer is not an isolated, nonrecurring, and unusual event and such a sale may call into question an entity's intent to hold other debt securities to maturity in the future.

In addition, the sale of a debt security classified as held-to-maturity is considered a maturity if (a) it occurs so near the maturity date (typically within three months) that changes in market interest rates would not have had an effect on the security's fair value or (b) the entity has already collected at least 85% of the principal that was outstanding when the security was acquired. (SFAS 115, par. 11)

> **Practical Consideration.** The authors believe that, as a practical matter, most debt securities will not meet the held-to-maturity criteria because they usually represent the investment of excess funds as part of an entity's cash management policies. Consequently, they could be sold to meet the entity's cash needs. SFAS No. 115, *Accounting for Certain Investments in Debt and Equity Securities,* does permit entities to designate a portion of their debt securities portfolio as unavailable to be sold as a part of their cash management policies, however. In that circumstance, those securities could be designated as held-to-maturity and accounted for at amortized cost.

35.204   **Trading Securities.** Debt and equity securities with readily determinable fair values should be classified as trading securities and reported in the balance sheet at fair value if they are purchased and held principally for the purpose of selling them in the near term. Trading securities generally are involved in active and frequent buying and selling with the objective of generating profits on short-term differences in price. Mortgage-backed securities held for sale in conjunction with mortgage banking activities should be classified as trading securities. (SFAS 115, par. 12)

35.205   **Available-for-sale Securities.** Investments not classified as held-to-maturity or trading should be classified as available-for-sale and reported in the balance sheet at fair value. (SFAS 115, par. 12)

Practical Consideration. Held–to–maturity securities are recorded as non-current assets and reclassified to current assets when maturity is within the next year. Available–for–sale securities are either (1) recorded as current assets because they represent an excess of available funds and, even though management has no current plans to dispose of them, it can sell them at any time at its option or (2) classified as current and noncurrent based on management's plans to dispose of them. Trading securities are classified as current assets.

Accounting for Changes in Fair Value

35.206   As discussed in the preceding paragraphs, investments in trading and available-for-sale securities should be recorded at fair value. Quoted market prices provide the most reliable measure of fair value. To determine the fair value of debt securities for which no market price is available, other pricing techniques, such as discounted cash flow analysis, matrix pricing, option-adjusted spread models, and fundamental analysis, may be used. (SFAS 115, par. 111)

35.207   Changes in fair value (i.e., unrealized holding gains and losses) should be accounted for as follows: (SFAS 115, par. 13 as amended by SFAS 130, par. 33)

a. *Trading securities.* Unrealized gains and losses should be included in earnings in the period they arise.

b. *Available-for-sale securities.* Unrealized gains and losses should be reported as other comprehensive income. (See Chapter 8.) Realized gains and losses should be included in income in the period they are realized.

Practical Consideration. SFAS No. 130, *Reporting Comprehensive Income* amended SFAS No. 115 to require unrealized holding gains and losses on securities classified as available-for-sale to be reported as other comprehensive income. SFAS No. 130 is effective for fiscal years beginning after December 15, 1997. (Chapter 8 discusses reporting comprehensive income.) Prior to adopting SFAS No. 130, such gains and losses are reported as a separate component of stockholders' equity.

35.208   Dividends and interest income related to trading, available-for-sale, and held-to-maturity securities should be included in income as they are earned. (SFAS 115, par. 14)

Impairment of Securities

35.209 If the fair value of an available-for-sale or held-to-maturity security is less than its carrying amount and the decline is other than temporary, the carrying amount of the investment should be reduced to fair value. The amount of the write-down should be included in earnings as if it was a realized loss.

Practical Consideration. Factors that management may consider in determining whether an other than temporary impairment condition exists are (1) whether a market decline is attributable to specific adverse conditions for a particular investment, (2) whether a market decline is attributable to general market conditions that reflect prospects of the economy as a whole or prospects of a particular industry, (3) the length of time and the extent to which fair value has been less than amortized cost, (4) the financial condition of the issuer, (5) the intent and ability of management to retain the investment for a period of time sufficient to allow for a prudent anticipation of a recovery in market value, and (7) whether dividends have been reduced or eliminated or scheduled interest payments on debt securities have not been made.

Subsequent increases in the fair value of an available-for-sale security should be included in other comprehensive income as discussed in Paragraph 35.207. Subsequent temporary decreases also should be included in other comprehensive income. (SFAS 115, par. 16 as amended by SFAS 130, par. 33)

Practical Consideration. According to a FASB staff announcement, when an entity has decided to sell an available-for-sale security whose fair value is less than its cost basis and the entity does not expect the fair value of the security to recover prior to the expected time of sale, a write down for other than temporary impairment should be recognized in the income statement in the period in which the decision to sell is made.

Transferring Securities between Categories

35.210 The appropriateness of a security's classification should be reassessed at each reporting date. (SFAS 115, par. 6) Changes in circumstances, such as an entity no longer having the ability to hold a debt security to maturity, may cause a security to be re-categorized. Security transfers between categories should be accounted for at fair value. The security's unrealized holding gain or loss at the transfer date should be accounted for as follows:

     a. *Securities transferred from the trading category.* The unrealized holding gain or loss at the transfer date has already been recognized in earnings and should not be reversed.

b. *Securities transferred to the trading category.* The unrealized holding gain or loss should be recognized in income immediately.

c. *Held-to-maturity securities transferred to the available-for-sale category.* The unrealized holding gain or loss at the transfer date should be recorded as other comprehensive income.

d. *Available-for-sale debt securities transferred to the held-to-maturity category.* The unrealized holding gain or loss at the transfer date should continue to be reported as accumulated other comprehensive income. (See Chapter 8.) It then should be amortized over the remaining life of the security as an adjustment of yield (similar to amortizing a premium or discount).

Transfers from held-to-maturity and into or out of the trading category should be rare due to the strict requirements for classifying investments into those categories. (SFAS 115, par. 15 as amended by SFAS 130, par. 33)

> **Practical Consideration.** Transition guidance in a FASB Special Report, *A Guide to Implementation of Statement 115 on Accounting for Certain Investments in Debt and Equity Securities,* permits an entity to reassess the appropriateness of the classifications of all securities held upon the initial adoption of the Special Report but no later than December 31, 1995. Any reclassifications from the held-to-maturity category resulting from that one-time reassessment would not call into question the intent of that entity to hold other debt securities to maturity in the future. However, any questions that may have been raised about prior sales or transfers are not affected by that transition guidance.

Unrealized Losses on Marketable Securities Owned by an Equity Method Investee

35.211   If an investee accounted for under the equity method of accounting includes unrealized holding gains and losses on debt and equity securities in its accumulated other comprehensive income, the investor should adjust its investment in the investee by its proportionate share of the unrealized gains and losses and include those unrealized gains and losses in accumulated other comprehensive income in its balance sheet. (FTB 79-19, par. 1 and SFAS 115, par. 135)

Financial Instruments Used to Hedge Investments at Fair Value

35.212   Similar to the reporting of unrealized gains and losses on trading securities, gains and losses on financial instruments used to hedge trading securities should be included in earnings as they arise. Gains and losses on instruments that hedge available-for-sale securities initially should be reported as other comprehensive income and then amortized as a yield adjustment. (See Paragraph 35.215.) (SFAS 115, par. 115)

Debt Securities Restructured in a Troubled Debt Restructuring

35.213   The guidance in Paragraphs 35.201–.212 applies to all loans that meet the definition of debt security. (See Paragraph 35.200.) Thus, it should be applied to a creditor's investment in a loan restructured in a troubled debt restructuring involving a modification of terms. (Chapter 16 discusses troubled debt restructurings in further detail.) (FTB 94-1. par. 3)

FUTURES CONTRACTS

35.214   In a futures contract, an investor agrees to purchase or sell specified amounts of a commodity on a specified future date at a specified price. Generally, the deposit paid to the commodities broker for the futures contract should be recorded as an asset and the recorded amount increased or decreased as the market value of the contract changes. The changes should be recognized as a gain or loss in the period they occur unless the contract qualifies as a hedge of an exposure to price or interest rate risk. (SFAS 80, par. 3) A futures contract qualifies as a hedge if all of the following criteria are met: (SFAS 80, par. 4)

   a. *The item to be hedged exposes the entity to price or interest rate risk.* This condition is not met if other assets, liabilities, firm commitments, or anticipated transactions already offset or reduce the entity's exposure. For example, inventory may be subject to price risk, but the risk may already be offset by firm, fixed-price sales commitments.

   b. *The contract reduces the entity's exposure.* The changes in the market value of the futures contract must highly correlate to the fair value of (or interest associated with) the hedged items. It also must be probable that the results of the contract will substantially offset the price or interest changes related to the hedged item. Consequently, the underlying commodity or financial instrument of a futures contract generally should be identical to the commodity or financial instrument being hedged. The underlying commodity or financial instrument may differ from the hedged item only if (1) there is a clear economic relationship between the prices of the two items and (2) high correlation is probable.

   c. *The contract is designated as a hedge.*

Accounting for Hedges

35.215   A change in the market value of a futures contract that qualifies as a hedge should not be recognized in income until the related change in the fair value of the hedged item is recognized in income. Thus, if a company includes unrealized gains and losses related to a hedged item in income as they occur, changes in the market value of the futures contract should be included in income as they occur. Similarly, if changes in the fair value of the hedged item are reported as other comprehensive income, changes in the fair value of the futures contract should be reported as other comprehensive income. (SFAS 80, par. 5 as amended by SFAS 130, par. 30)

35.216   A change in the market value of a futures contract that qualifies as a hedge of an existing asset or liability should be recognized as an adjustment of the carrying amount of the hedged item. If the contract hedges a firm commitment, the change should be included in the ultimate gain or loss on the transaction that satisfies the commitment. An adjustment of the carrying amount of a hedged interest-bearing financial instrument that is otherwise reported at amortized cost should be amortized to interest income or expense over the expected remaining life of the instrument. (Amortization should begin no later than the date the futures contract is closed out.) (SFAS 80, paras. 6–7)

35.217   If it is probable that the hedged item and futures contract will be retained to the delivery date specified in the futures contract, the premium or discount on a hedge contract may be recognized in income over the life of the contract. The premium or discount is determined at the inception of the contract by reference to the contracted futures price and the fair value of the hedged item. (SFAS 80, par. 6)

35.218   **Hedges of Anticipated Transactions.** A futures contract may hedge a transaction that the entity expects, but is not obligated, to enter into. A change in the market value of a futures contract that hedges such an antici-pated transaction should be included in the ultimate gain or loss on the hedged transaction if the contract meets the hedge criteria in Paragraph 35.214 and both of the following conditions are met: (SFAS 80, par. 9)

     a. The significant characteristics and expected terms of the antici-pated transaction are identified.

     b. It is probable that the anticipated transaction will occur.

35.219   If a gain or loss in the fair value of an asset or liability will be realized before the asset is acquired or liability issued, the gain or loss on the related futures contract should be recognized at the same time. If the futures contract is closed before the date of the anticipated transaction, the accumulated change in the market value of the contract should be carried forward and included in the measurement of the anticipated transaction. If it becomes probable that the quantity of the anticipated transaction will be less than the quantity originally hedged, a prorata portion of the changes in the market value of the futures contract should be recognized as a gain or loss and a pro rata portion should be included in the measurement of the anticipated transaction. (SFAS 80, par. 10)

35.220 **Ongoing Assessment of Correlation.** The entity should regularly assess the results of the futures contract designated as a hedge to determine whether the high correlation between the hedged item and the commodity or financial instrument underlying the futures contract is being achieved. If that assessment indicates that a high correlation has not occurred, the futures contract should no longer be accounted for as a hedge. Instead, the entity should recognize a gain or loss for the amount of the change in the contract's market value that has not been offset by the change in the fair value of the hedged item. (SFAS 80, par. 11)

DISCLOSURE REQUIREMENTS

DEBT AND EQUITY SECURITIES

35.500   The following information should be disclosed about marketable debt and equity securities:

   a. For all major security types classified as available-for-sale and held-to-maturity (separately and as of the date of each balance sheet presented)—

   (1) Aggregate fair value

   (2) Gross unrealized gains and losses

   (3) Amortized cost basis

The disclosures should be made as of each date for which a balance sheet is presented. Financial institutions should include the following major security types: (Additional types may be included as appropriate.)

   • Equity securities

   • Debt securities issued by the U.S. Treasury and other U.S. government corporations and agencies

- Debt securities issued by states of the United States and political subdivisions of the states

- Debt securities issued by foreign governments

- Corporate debt securities

- Mortgage-backed securities

- Other debt securities (SFAS 115, par. 19)

b. For all investments in debt securities classified as available-for-sale or classified as held-to-maturity (separately), information about the contractual maturities (The information should be disclosed as of the date of the most recent balance sheet presented and may be combined in appropriate groupings. Financial institutions should disclose the fair value and amortized cost of debt securities based on at least 4 maturity groupings—within 1 year, after 1 year through 5 years, after 5 years through 10 years, and after 10 years. Securities not due at a single maturity date may be disclosed separately rather than allocated over several groups. If allocated, the basis for allocation should be disclosed.) (SFAS 115, par. 20.)

c. For each period for which an income statement is presented—

(1) Proceeds from sales of available-for-sale securities and the gross realized gains and losses on those sales

(2) Basis on which cost was determined in computing realized gains and losses

(3) Gross gains and losses included in earnings as a result of transferring securities from the available-for-sale category to the trading category

(4) Change in net unrealized holding gain or loss on available-for-sale securities that has been included in other comprehensive income during the period

(5) Change in net unrealized holding gain or loss on trading securities that has been included in earnings for the period (SFAS 115, par. 21)

35.500

    d. For each period for which an income statement is presented, the following about sales of or transfers from securities classified as held-to-maturity—

      (1) Amortized cost of the sold or transferred security

      (2) Related realized or unrealized gain or loss

      (3) Circumstances leading to the decision to sell or transfer the security (SFAS 115, par. 22)

FUTURES CONTRACTS

35.501   The following information should be disclosed about futures contracts that have been accounted for as hedges: (SFAS 80, par. 12)

    a. Nature of the assets, liabilities, firm commitments, or anticipated transactions that are hedged with futures contracts

    b. Method of accounting for futures contracts (The disclosure should include a description of the events or transactions that cause changes in the contracts' value to be recognized in income.)

35.502   Generally, cash receipts and disbursements should be classified in the statement of cash flows without regard to whether they stem from an item intended as a hedge. For example, the proceeds of a borrowing should be considered a financing activity even though the debt is considered a hedge of an investment. However, cash flows from futures contracts, forward contracts, option contracts, or swap contracts that are accounted for as hedges of identifiable transactions or events, including anticipatory hedges, may be classified in the same category as the cash flows from the hedged items so long as that accounting policy is disclosed. (SFAS 104, par. 7)

AUTHORITATIVE LITERATURE AND RELATED TOPICS

AUTHORITATIVE LITERATURE

SFAS No. 80, *Accounting for Futures Contracts*

SFAS No. 104, *Statement of Cash Flows—Net Reporting of Certain Cash Receipts and Cash Payments and Classification of Cash Flows from Hedging Transactions*

SFAS No. 115, *Accounting for Certain Investments in Debt and Equity Securities*

SFAS No. 125, *Accounting for Transfers and Servicing of Financial Assets and Extinguishments of Liabilities*

SFAS No. 130, *Reporting Comprehensive Income*

FASB Technical Bulletin 79-19, *Investor's Accounting for Unrealized Losses on Marketable Securities Owned by an Equity Method Investee*

FASB Technical Bulletin 94-1, *Application of Statement 115 to Debt Securities Restructured in a Troubled Debt Restructuring*

RELATED PRONOUNCEMENTS

EITF Issue No. 84-5, *Sale of Marketable Securities with a Put Option*

EITF Issue No. 85-39, *Implications of SEC Staff Accounting Bulletin No. 59 on Noncurrent Marketable Equity Securities*

EITF Issue No. 86-40, *Investments in Open-End Mutual Funds That Invest in U.S. Government Securities*

EITF Issue No. 94-4, *Classification of an Investment in a Mortgage-Backed Interest-Only Certificate as Held-to-Maturity*

EITF Issue No. 96-10, *Impact of Certain Transactions on the Held-to-Maturity Classification under FASB Statement No. 115, "Accounting for Certain Investments in Debt and Equity Securities"*

EITF Issue No. 96-11, *Accounting for Forward Contracts and Purchased Options to Acquire Securities Covered by FASB Statement No. 115, "Accounting for Certain Investments in Debt and Equity Securities"*

EITF Issue No. 96-12, *Recognition of Interest Income and Balance Sheet Classification of Structured Notes*

EITF Issue No. 96-15, *Accounting for the Effects of Changes in Foreign Currency Exchange Rates on Foreign-Currency-Denominated Available-for-Sale Debt Securities*

EITF Issue No. 97-7, *Accounting for Hedges of Foreign Currency Risk Inherent in an Available-for-Sale Marketable Equity Security*

SOP 83-1, *Reporting by Banks of Investment Securities Gains or Losses*

SOP 90-3, *Definition of the Term "Substantially the Same" for Holders of Debt Instruments, as Used in Certain Audit Guides and a Statement of Position*

SOP 90-11, *Disclosure of Certain Information by Financial Institutions About Debt Securities Held as Assets*

SOP 93-1, *Financial Accounting and Reporting for High-Yield Debt Securities by Investment Companies*

FASB Special Report, *A Guide to Implementation of Statement 115 on Accounting for Certain Investments in Debt and Equity Securities*

RELATED TOPICS

Chapter 8—Comprehensive Income

Chapter 9—Consolidated Financial Statements

Chapter 12—Current Assets and Current Liabilities

Chapter 20—Equity Method Investments

Chapter 21—Financial Instrument Disclosures

Chapter 52—Transfers and Servicing of Financial Assets

NONMONETARY TRANSACTIONS

Table of Contents

NONMONETARY TRANSACTIONS

OVERVIEW

36.100   Generally, a nonmonetary transaction should be recorded based on the fair values of the assets or services involved, and any gain or loss should be recognized. Certain exceptions exist for exchanges involving similar assets, nonreciprocal transfers to owners, and exchanges in which fair value is not determinable.

ACCOUNTING REQUIREMENTS

36.200   Most business transactions are monetary transactions. That is, they involve the transfer of monetary assets and liabilities such as cash, accounts receivable, and accounts payable. Some transactions are nonmonetary, however. They involve the transfer of assets and liabilities whose amounts are not fixed in terms of currency (by contract or otherwise), such as property and equipment, investments in common stock, and inventories.

36.201   Nonmonetary transactions can be nonreciprocal or reciprocal. A nonreciprocal nonmonetary transaction is the one-way transfer of nonmonetary assets or services either (a) from an entity to its owners or another entity or (b) to an entity from its owners or another entity. Examples include the distribution of nonmonetary assets to stockholders as dividends or the donation of nonmonetary assets to charitable organizations. A reciprocal transfer (i.e., exchange) of nonmonetary assets is a transaction in which each party distributes or receives nonmonetary assets. Examples of nonmonetary exchanges include the exchange of inventory for other inventory and the exchange of services for inventory. (APB 29, paras. 5–7)

Practical Consideration. The guidance in this chapter does not apply to the following:

- Business combinations accounted for in accordance with the guidance in Chapter 3

- Transfers of nonmonetary assets solely between entities under common control, such as between a parent and its subsidiaries or subsidiaries of the same parent

---

ACCOUNTING FOR NONMONETARY TRANSACTIONS

36.202   As a general rule, nonmonetary transactions should be recorded the same as monetary transactions. That is, they should be based on the fair values of the assets or services involved. Consequently, the amount recorded for an asset received in a nonmonetary exchange should be the fair value of the asset given up (or the fair value of the asset received if it is more clearly evident), and a gain or loss should be recognized on the transaction. (APB 29, par. 18) (The gain or loss, if any, should be classified as part of continuing operations, extraordinary items, etc., depending on the circumstances surrounding the transaction. Chapter 23 discusses classifying transactions in the income statement in further detail.) For example, assume that a company exchanges machinery with a net book value of $25,000 for land appraised at $35,000 and that, because of the specialized nature of the machinery, there is no readily determinable market value for it. The exchange would be recorded through the following entry:

Land	35,000	
Machinery—net		25,000
Gain on exchange		10,000

36.203   Exceptions to the general rule exist related to like-kind exchanges, nonreciprocal transfers to owners, and exchanges in which neither the fair value of the asset given up nor the fair value of the asset received is determinable. Those exceptions are discussed in the following paragraphs.

Like-kind Exchanges

36.204   In a like-kind exchange, (a) products or property held for sale in the ordinary course of business is exchanged for products or property to be sold in the same line of business or (b) producing assets not held for sale in the ordinary course of business are exchanged for similar productive assets (or an equivalent interest in the same productive asset). Because a like-kind exchange generally does not result in the culmination of the earnings process, the following rules apply:

a. A like-kind exchange involving only nonmonetary assets should be based on recorded amounts and no gain or loss recognized. Thus, for example, if a truck with a book value of $20,000 were exchanged for another truck, the amount recorded for the new truck would be $20,000, and no gain or loss would be recognized.

b. If the exchange involves monetary consideration—

(1) the entity receiving the monetary consideration should recognize a portion of any gain on the transaction in the ratio of cash received to total consideration received (i.e., cash plus the fair value of the asset received);

(2) the entity paying the monetary consideration should not recognize any gain (i.e., the new asset should be recorded at the surrendered asset's book value plus the cash payment); and

(3) any losses on the exchange should be recognized by the entity receiving the monetary consideration. (APB 29, paras. 21–22)

Practical Consideration. To illustrate accounting for a like-kind exchange, assume that ACE Manufacturing acquired a truck with a fair value of $25,000 (book value $21,000) from Monroe Company in exchange for a truck with a fair value of $23,000 (net book value of $20,000) plus a cash payment of $2,000. The entries to record the trade would be as follows:

ACE Manufacturing

New truck	22,000	
Old truck—net		20,000
Cash		2,000

Monroe Company

Cash	2,000	
New truck	19,320	
Old truck—net		21,000
Gain [($25,000 − $21,000) × ($2,000 ÷ $25,000)]		320

Practical Consideration (Continued).

In EITF Issue 86-29, *Nonmonetary Transactions: Magnitude of Boot and the Exceptions to the Use of Fair Value,* the FASB Emerging Issues Task Force concluded that the decision about whether an exchange of nonmonetary assets is a like-kind exchange depends on whether the assets received will be sold or used in the same line of business as the assets given up. Thus, the following guidelines generally apply:

    a. An exchange is a like-kind exchange if products or properties held for sale are exchanged (or similar productive assets are exchanged) and the assets will be sold in the same line of business.

    b. An exchange is not a like-kind exchange if a product or property held for sale is exchanged for a productive asset not held for sale, even if both are used in the same line of business. Thus, the transaction should be recorded at fair value.

The EITF also reached the following conclusions:

- If an exchange of nonmonetary assets involves monetary consideration in excess of 25% of the fair value of the exchange, the transaction should be considered a *monetary* transaction. Consequently, both parties should record the transaction based on the exchanged assets' fair values.

- If a company acquires control of a subsidiary through an exchange of securities, the exchange should be accounted for as a business combination following the guidance of APB Opinion No. 16, *Business Combinations.* (See Chapter 3.)

Nonreciprocal Transfers to Owners

36.205   Generally, nonreciprocal transfers of nonmonetary assets to owners should be recorded at fair value if the fair value of the assets distributed are objectively measurable and could have been realized in an outright sale at or near the time of the distribution. However, distributions in a reorganization or liquidation (including spin-offs) or in a rescission of a prior business combination should be based on recorded amounts less any necessary reduction for impairment of value.

36.206   A prorata distribution to owners of the shares of a company that has been or is being consolidated or accounted for under the equity method is considered to be the equivalent of a spin-off. (APB 29, par. 23)

36.207   **Distributions of FHLMC Participating Preferred Stock.** In December 1984, each Federal Home Loan bank declared a dividend of Federal Home Loan Mortgage Corporation participating preferred stock. FASB Technical Bulletin 85-1, *Accounting for the Receipt of Federal Home Loan Mortgage Corporation Participating Preferred Stock,* states that members of the Federal Home Loan Banking System who received the stock should initially record it at its fair value as of December 31, 1984. (Thereafter, the stock should be accounted for the same as any other marketable security.) In addition, the Technical Bulletin requires the resulting gain on the nonmonetary transaction to be reported as an extraordinary item because the transaction is both unusual in nature and occurs infrequently. (FTB 85-1, par. 2)

Fair Value Not Determinable

36.208   The fair value of a nonmonetary asset should be based on sales of similar assets, quoted market prices, independent appraisals, estimated fair values of assets or services received, or other available evidence. If neither the fair value of the asset given up nor the fair value of the asset received can be determined within reasonable limits, the recorded amount of the asset transferred should be used to measure the transaction. (APB 29, par. 26)

INVOLUNTARY CONVERSIONS OF NONMONETARY ASSETS TO MONETARY ASSETS

36.209   A nonmonetary asset may involuntarily be converted to a monetary asset. (For example, a building may be totally or partially destroyed by fire or other disaster.) In such cases, the involuntary conversion should be considered a monetary transaction and a gain or loss recognized even if the entity reinvests in a similar nonmonetary asset. The gain or loss recognized on the conversion is the difference between the carrying amount of the nonmonetary asset and the monetary assets received, if any. (FASBI 30, paras. 1–2)

36.210   The preceding guidance does not apply to the involuntary conversion of a LIFO inventory layer at an interim reporting date (and thus a gain should not be recognized) if the proceeds are reinvested in replacement inventory by the end of the fiscal year. If the proceeds are not reinvested in replacement inventory by the end of the fiscal year, a gain still should not be recognized so long as no gain is recognized for tax reporting. (FASBI 30, paras. 2 and 11)

DISCLOSURE REQUIREMENTS

36.500   An entity should disclose the nature of any nonmonetary transactions that occur during the period, including the basis of accounting for the assets transferred and gains or losses recognized. (APB 29, par. 28)

AUTHORITATIVE LITERATURE AND RELATED TOPICS

AUTHORITATIVE LITERATURE

APB Opinion No. 29, *Accounting for Nonmonetary Transactions*
FASB Technical Bulletin 85-1, *Accounting for the Receipt of Federal Home Loan Mortgage Corporation Participating Preferred Stock*
FASB Interpretation No. 30, *Accounting for Involuntary Conversions of Nonmonetary Assets to Monetary Assets*

RELATED PRONOUNCEMENTS

EITF Issue No. 84-29, *Gain and Loss Recognition on Exchanges of Productive Assets and the Effect of Boot*
EITF Issue No. 84-39, *Transfers of Monetary and Nonmonetary Assets among Individuals and Entities under Common Control*
EITF Issue No. 86-29, *Nonmonetary Transactions: Magnitude of Boot and the Exceptions to the Use of Fair Value*
EITF Issue No. 87-29, *Exchange of Real Estate Involving Boot*
EITF Issue No. 91-5, *Nonmonetary Exchange of Cost-Method Investments*
EITF Issue No. 93-11, *Accounting for Barter Transactions Involving Barter Credits*
EITF Issue No. 96-4, *Accounting for Reorganizations Involving a Non-Pro Rata Split-off of Certain Nonmonetary Assets to Owners*

RELATED TOPICS

Chapter 23—Income Statement

OFFSETTING ASSETS AND LIABILITIES

Table of Contents

OFFSETTING ASSETS AND LIABILITIES

OVERVIEW

37.100   Related assets and liabilities may be offset and presented in the balance sheet as a net amount if a right of setoff exists. Generally, a right of setoff exists if four conditions, established by FASB Interpretation No. 39, *Offsetting of Amounts Related to Certain Contracts,* are met. FASB Interpretation No. 39 provides certain exceptions to that general rule, however, for fair value amounts of conditional or exchange contracts executed with the same counterparty under a master netting arrangement.

ACCOUNTING REQUIREMENTS

GENERAL RULE

37.200   Assets and liabilities should not be offset in a statement of financial position (i.e., reported at a net amount) unless a right of setoff exists. (APB 10, par. 7) FASB Interpretation No. 39, *Offsetting of Amounts Related to Certain Contracts,* defines the right of setoff as ". . . a debtor's legal right, by contract or otherwise, to discharge all or a portion of the debt owed to another party by applying against the debt an amount that the other party owes to the debtor. A right of setoff exists when all of the following conditions are met:

a. Each of *two* parties owes the other determinable amounts.

b. The reporting party has the right to set off the amount owed with the amount owed by the other party.

c. The reporting party intends to set off.

d. The right of setoff is enforceable at law." (FASBI 39, par. 5)

Practical Consideration. Insurance proceeds should not be offset against related litigation liabilities because the receivable and payable are not between the same two parties. Thus, the circumstance does not meet the criterion that each of two parties owe the other determinable amounts.

37.201   When determining whether assets and liabilities may be offset, accountants should note the following:

- The reporting party must actually intend to set off amounts owed. Thus, even though the ability to offset may exist, assets and liabilities should not be offset if the reporting party does not intend to set off.

- Because the right of setoff must be enforceable at law, situations involving state laws and the U.S. Bankruptcy Code, may modify or restrict the reporting party's right of setoff.

- Assets and liabilities need not be denominated in the same currency or bear interest at the same rates to be offset. If an asset and liability have different maturities, however, only the party with the earlier maturity may offset since the party with the longer maturity must settle in the manner the other party selects at the earlier maturity date.

> **Practical Consideration.** GAAP permits, but does not require, assets and liabilities to be offset when a right of setoff exists. Thus, in the authors' opinion, presenting accounts at their gross amounts would not be a GAAP departure even though the accounts qualify for offsetting.

OFFSETTING SECURITIES AGAINST TAXES PAYABLE

37.202   Generally, a government's securities should not be offset against taxes and other liabilities owed to it. The only exception to that rule is when it is clear that the security purchase is, in effect, an advance payment of taxes that will be owed in the near future (for example, if a government issues securities that it designates as acceptable for the payment of taxes). (APB 10, par. 7)

OFFSETTING FORWARD, INTEREST RATE SWAP, CURRENCY SWAP, OPTION, AND OTHER CONDITIONAL OR EXCHANGE CONTRACTS

37.203   Questions have been raised about offsetting conditional or exchange contracts that are measured at fair value rather than notational amounts or amounts to be exchanged. FASB Interpretation No. 39 clearly states that the carrying amount for such contracts is fair value. Thus, so long as the conditions in Paragraph 37.200 are met, the fair value of contracts in a loss position may be offset against the fair value of contracts in a gain position. (FASBI 39, par. 8)

Master Netting Arrangements

37.204   Under a master netting arrangement, individual contracts are effectively consolidated into a single agreement between the parties. Failure to make one payment under the master netting arrangement entitles the other party to terminate the entire arrangement and demand the net settlement of all contracts. Such arrangements typically do not meet the conditions for offsetting because the right to set off is conditional (i.e., a party must default). However, because the FASB believes that presenting aggregate fair values of the individual contracts does not provide information that is more useful than presenting net amounts, FASB Interpretation No. 39 makes an exception to the general rule. It allows an entity to offset the fair value amounts of forward, interest rate swap, currency swap, option, and other conditional or exchange contracts that are executed with the same counterparty under a master netting arrangement. (FASBI 39, par. 10)

37.205   The FASB Interpretation No. 39 exception applies only to *fair value amounts* recognized for conditional or exchange contracts executed with the same counterparty under a master netting arrangement. It does not apply to other contracts not recorded at fair value (for example, repurchase agreements and reverse repurchase agreements) that are executed under master netting arrangements. The FASB concluded that the gross amounts recorded for such assets and liabilities provide useful information about the timing and amount of future cash flows that would be lost if the amounts were offset. Thus, such contracts may not be offset solely because they are executed under a master netting arrangement; they may be offset only if they meet the conditions in Paragraph 37.200. (FASBI 39, par. 22)

OFFSETTING RECEIVABLES AND PAYABLES FROM REPURCHASE AND REVERSE REPURCHASE AGREEMENTS

37.206   Amounts recognized as payables under repurchase agreements may be offset against amounts recognized as receivables under reverse repurchase agreements if all of the following conditions are met:

     a. The repurchase and reverse repurchase agreements are executed with the same counterparty.

     b. The repurchase and reverse repurchase agreements have the same explicit settlement date specified at the inception of the agreement.

     c. The repurchase and reverse repurchase agreements are executed in accordance with a master netting arrangement. (See Paragraphs 37.204–.205.)

     d. The securities underlying the agreements exist in "book entry" form and can be transferred only by means of entries in the records of the transfer system operator or securities custodian.

e. The agreements will be settled on a securities transfer system that requires the security's owner of record to initiate the transfer by notifying its custodian to transfer the security. In addition, an associated banking arrangement is in place that requires each party to maintain available cash on deposit only for the amount of any net payable unless it fails to instruct its securities custodian to transfer securities to its counterparty. It must be probable that the associated banking arrangement will provide sufficient daylight overdraft or other intraday credit at the settlement date for each of the parties.

f. The reporting entity intends to use the same account at the clearing bank or other financial institution at the settlement date to transact both (1) the cash inflows from settlement of the reverse repurchase agreement and (2) the cash outflows from settlement of the offsetting repurchase agreement.

The reporting party may offset related receivables and payables regardless of whether it actually intends to set off the amounts. (FASBI 41, par. 3) Thus, the requirements provide an exception to the general rule discussed in Paragraph 37.200.

CIRCUMSTANCES NOT COVERED BY FASB INTERPRETATION NO. 39

37.207   FASB Interpretation No. 39 does not apply to offsetting cash balances on deposit in banks and other financial institutions because it states that amounts on deposit should not be considered to be amounts owed to the depositor. Accordingly, the condition in item a. in Paragraph 37.200 is not met.

37.208   The Interpretation also does not address derecognition or nonrecognition of assets or liabilities. Derecognition is the removal of a *recognized* asset or liability, for example, by sale of the asset or extinguishment of the liability, and generally results in a gain or loss. Nonrecognition, on the other hand, involves not recognizing assets or liabilities (commonly known as off-balance-sheet financing) and, therefore, results in no gain or loss. The Interpretation clarifies that offsetting relates solely to the display of a recognized asset or liability, in contrast to derecognition or nonrecognition, which relates to the *measurement* of assets or liabilities. (FASBI 39, par. 5)

37.209   FASB Interpretation No. 39 does not supersede or amend other pronouncements that require a particular accounting treatment in specific circumstances. (FASBI 39, par. 7)

AUTHORITATIVE LITERATURE AND RELATED TOPICS

AUTHORITATIVE LITERATURE

APB Opinion No. 10, *Omnibus Opinion—1966*
FASB Interpretation No. 39, *Offsetting of Amounts Related to Certain Contracts*
FASB Interpretation No. 41, *Offsetting of Amounts Related to Certain Repurchase and Reverse Repurchase Agreements*
FASB Technical Bulletin 86-2, *Accounting for an Interest in the Residual Value of a Leased Asset*

RELATED PRONOUNCEMENTS

EITF Issue No. 84-11, *Offsetting Installment Note Receivables and Bank Debt ("Note Monetization")*
EITF Issue No. 84-25, *Offsetting Nonrecourse Debt with Sales-Type or Direct Financing Lease Receivables*
EITF Issue No. 86-25, *Offsetting Foreign Currency Swaps*
EITF Issue No. 87-20, *Offsetting Certificates of Deposit against High-Coupon Debt*

RELATED TOPICS

PENSION PLAN FINANCIAL STATEMENTS

Table of Contents

PENSION PLAN FINANCIAL STATEMENTS

OVERVIEW

38.100   This chapter discusses the accounting, reporting, and disclosure requirements for defined benefit pension plans. A defined benefit pension plan is generally defined as a plan that promises to pay specified retirement benefits to its participants. Generally, the amount of benefits to be paid is based on factors such as each participant's years of service, compensation, and age.

38.101   GAAP does not require defined benefit plans to present financial statements. If presented, however, a plan's financial statements should include information about the following:

- Net assets available for benefits as of the period end

- Changes during the period in net assets available for benefits

- Actuarial present value of accumulated plan benefits

- Significant factors affecting the change during the year in the actuarial present value of accumulated plan benefits

In addition, the Statement requires certain disclosures about the plan and its accounting policies.

ACCOUNTING REQUIREMENTS

INTRODUCTION

38.200   A defined benefit plan provides a specified benefit to a participant upon retirement, death, disability, termination of employment, or the occurrence of another covered event. The benefit paid is based on the participant's length of service, compensation, age, or other factors. (SFAS 35, par. 280) This chapter discusses the unique accounting requirements that apply when preparing financial statements for defined benefit plans. (Other generally accepted accounting principles may apply to defined benefit pension plans. However, this chapter only discusses those that are unique to defined benefit pension plans or that differ from generally accepted accounting principles for other types of entities.) Accounting for the costs of defined benefit plans in an *employer's* financial statements is discussed in Chapter 39.

Practical Consideration. Unlike a defined benefit plan, a defined contribution plan does not promise participants a specific benefit. Instead, the plan maintains separate accounts for each participant, and participants receive benefits equal to the amounts accumulated in their individual accounts. Examples of defined contribution plans include profit sharing plans, money purchase plans, employee stock ownership plans, and 401(k) plans. The guidance in this chapter does not apply to defined contribution plans. Accountants should consult the AICPA's Industry Audit Guide, *Audits of Employee Benefit Plans,* for accounting and reporting guidance for those plans.

REQUIRED FINANCIAL STATEMENTS

38.201 The primary objective of a plan's financial statements is to provide financial information that will help users assess the plan's ability to pay benefits when due. Consequently, a pension plan's financial statements should include information about (a) the plan's resources, (b) the accumulated plan benefits of participants, (c) the results of transactions affecting the plan's resources and accumulated benefits, and (d) other factors, if necessary to make the financial statements understandable. (SFAS 35, par. 5)

38.202 Generally accepted accounting principles do not require defined benefit plans to prepare or distribute financial statements. (SFAS 35, par. 51) If annual financial statements are prepared, however, GAAP requires that they include the following: (SFAS 35, par. 6)

    a. Statement of net assets available for benefits as of the plan's year end

    b. Statement of changes during the year in net assets available for benefits

    c. Information about the actuarial present value of accumulated plan benefits as of either the beginning or end of the plan's year

    d. Information about significant factors affecting the change during the year in the actuarial present value of accumulated plan benefits

As discussed further in Paragraphs 38.215–.216, information about the actuarial present value of accumulated plan benefits (items c. and d.) may be presented in separate statements, on the face of other financial statements, or in the notes to the financial statements.

Comparative Financial Statements

38.203   As explained in Paragraph 38.217, comparative financial statements are required if a plan presents the actuarial present value of accumulated plan benefits as of the beginning of the plan year. Otherwise, comparative financial statements need not be presented. EXHIBIT 38-1 summarizes the requirements for presenting comparative financial statements.

> **Practical Consideration.** GAAP suggests that financial information about several plan years may be more helpful than information about a single plan year when assessing a plan's ability to pay benefits when they are due. Thus, comparative presentations may be preferable even if not required. In addition, Department of Labor regulations and IRS Forms 5500 and 5500C/R require comparative statements of net assets available for benefits.

Statement of Cash Flows

38.204   Defined benefit plans need not present a statement of cash flows. GAAP encourages a plan to present a statement of cash flows, however, if doing so would provide relevant information about its ability to meet future obligations (for example, when its assets are not highly liquid or when it obtains financing for investments). (SFAS 102, par. 5)

STATEMENT OF NET ASSETS AVAILABLE FOR BENEFITS

38.205   The primary purpose of the statement of net assets available for benefits is to identify, in reasonable detail, the resources that are available to pay benefits to plan participants. The statement, which should be prepared on the accrual basis of accounting, includes information about the plan's liabilities as well as its assets. (SFAS 35, paras. 9 and 86) EXHIBIT 38-2 illustrates a statement of net assets available for benefits. The following paragraphs discuss the significant categories that typically are included in the statement.

> **Practical Consideration.** The FASB has not resolved the issue of whether the actuarial present value of accumulated plan benefits (often referred to as the "benefit obligation") is a liability of the plan or an equity interest in the plan. Thus, to avoid any implication that the benefit obligation is a liability of the plan, it should not be included in liabilities on the statement of net assets available for benefits. Paragraphs 38.215–.217 discuss presenting information about the present value of accumulated plan benefits.

EXHIBIT 38-1

SUMMARY OF GAAP REQUIREMENTS FOR DEFINED BENEFIT PLAN FINANCIAL STATEMENTS

	Current Period	Prior Period
IF BENEFIT INFORMATION IS PREPARED AS OF THE END OF THE PERIOD:		
Statement of net assets available for benefits	Required	Not required (but required by DOL and IRS Form 5500)
Statement of changes in net assets available for benefits	Required	Not required
Information about the actuarial present value of accumulated plan benefits	Required (may be presented in a separate statement; on the statement of net assets available for benefits, if information is as of the same date; or in the notes)	Not required
Information about changes in the actuarial present value of accumulated plan benefits	Required (may be presented in a separate statement; on the statement of changes in net assets available for benefits, if information is for the same period; or in the notes)	Not required
IF BENEFIT INFORMATION IS PREPARED AS OF THE BEGINNING OF THE PERIOD:		
Statement of net assets available for benefits	Required	Required
Statement of changes in net assets available for benefits	Required	Required
Information about the actuarial present value of accumulated plan benefits	Not required	Required (may be presented in a separate statement; on the statement of net assets available for benefits, if information is as of the same date; or in the notes)
Information about changes in the actuarial present value of accumulated plan benefits	Not required	Required (may be presented in a separate statement; on the statement of changes in net assets available for benefits, if information is for the same period; or in the notes)

EXHIBIT 38-2

ILLUSTRATIVE STATEMENT OF ACCUMULATED PLAN BENEFITS AND NET ASSETS AVAILABLE FOR BENEFITS

September 30, 19X4

ACCUMULATED PLAN BENEFITS
    Actuarial present value of vested benefits:

Participants currently receiving payments	$ 4,100,000
Other participants	9,000,000
	13,100,000
Actuarial present value of nonvested benefits	2,000,000
TOTAL ACTUARIAL PRESENT VALUE OF ACCUMULATED PLAN BENEFITS	$ 15,100,000

NET ASSETS AVAILABLE FOR BENEFITS
    Investments, at fair value:

U.S. government securities	$ 1,000,000
Investment contracts	3,250,000
Corporate bonds and debentures	2,900,000
Common stock	300,000
Mortgages	150,000
Real estate	400,000
	8,000,000
Receivables:	
Employees' contributions	100,000
Accrued interest and dividends	125,000
Securities sold	700,000
	925,000
Cash	500,000
Total assets	9,425,000
Accounts payable	225,000
Accrued expenses	100,000
Total liabilities	325,000
NET ASSETS AVAILABLE FOR BENEFITS	$ 9,100,000
EXCESS OF ACTUARIAL PRESENT VALUE OF ACCUMULATED BENEFITS OVER NET ASSETS AVAILABLE FOR BENEFITS	$ 6,000,000

Contributions Receivable

38.206   Plans should record a contribution receivable as of the reporting date for amounts due from employers, participants, and others. Contributions receivable should include amounts that are formally committed to be paid to the plan as well as amounts that are legally or contractually due. The following may indicate that an employer has formally committed to make a contribution: (SFAS 35, par. 10)

- The employer's governing body approves a resolution to make a specified contribution.

- The employer has a history of consistently making payments after the plan's year end, and the payments are made under an established funding policy that attributes the payments to the preceding plan year.

- The employer deducts a contribution on its federal income tax return for periods ending on or before the reporting date.

- The employer records a contribution payable to the plan as of the reporting date. (The existence of an accrual in the employer's financial statements is not, by itself, sufficient to support the plan's recognition of a receivable, however. Pension cost reported in the employer's financial statements may differ from amounts that are formally committed to the plan and required to be funded. Similarly, the plan should not record receivables for the employer's unfunded prior service costs or excess benefit obligation over net assets available for benefits unless the employer has formally committed to pay those amounts.)

Investments

38.207   Employee benefit plans own various types of investments, including the following:

- Marketable debt or equity securities

- Securities that do not have a ready market, for example, restricted or unregistered securities

- Real estate, mortgages, or leases

- Units of participation in real estate investment pools or limited partnerships

- Units of participation in common or commingled trusts

- Repurchase or reverse repurchase agreements

- Futures and options

- Contracts with insurance companies that are an investment vehicle, such as separate or pooled accounts

38.208   Plan investments, except insurance contracts (SFAS 110, par. 7), should be presented at their fair value (that is, the amount that could be received in a sale, other than a forced or liquidation sale, to a willing buyer). If there is an active market for the investment, its fair value is its market price. If there is not an active market for the investment, its fair value may be estimated by (a) considering the selling prices of similar investments that are traded in an active market, (b) discounting expected cash flows using a rate appropriate for the risk involved, or (c) using independent experts qualified to estimate fair value. Significant brokerage commissions and other selling costs should be considered when estimating fair value. (SFAS 35, paras. 11 and 104)

38.209   Investment information should be presented in the statement of net assets in enough detail to identify the types of investments. The presentation should indicate the method used to determine an investment's fair value (for example, by using a quoted market price in an active market or another method). (SFAS 35, par. 13)

Practical Consideration. The AICPA Audit and Accounting Guide, *Audits of Employee Benefit Plans,* states that an interest in a master trust (a trust holding assets of several plans that are all sponsored by a single employer or by several employers under common control), should be reported as a single line item in the statement of net assets available for benefits.

Contracts with Insurance Companies

38.210   Contracts with insurance companies should be presented as follows: (SFAS 110, par. 4)

    a. *Insurance contracts* should be presented as required by ERISA (that is, at either contract value or fair value).

    b. *Investment contracts* should be presented at fair value.

Investment contracts are those that do not expose the insurance company to risks arising from the policyholders' mortality or morbidity. Mortality or morbidity risk exists when the insurance company is required to make payments or forego required premiums contingent upon the death or disability (in the case of life insurance contracts) or the continued survival (in the case of annuity contracts) of a specific individual or group of individuals. (SFAS 110, par. 6) A guaranteed interest contract, which typically provides for a specified return on principle invested over a specified period, is an example of an investment contract.

> **Practical Consideration.** Insurance contracts entered into by retirement plans may be broadly classified as allocated and unallocated. Under allocated contracts, payments to the insurance company are used to purchase insurance or annuity contracts for specific individual plan participants. Since they transfer the obligation to pay benefits to the insurance company, allocated contracts and the related benefit obligations should not be included in the plan's financial statements. Under unallocated contracts, payments to insurance companies are not allocated to specific participants, but are held in an undivided fund until they are used to pay benefits. Unallocated contracts are investment vehicles that do not transfer any benefit obligation or risk to the insurance company and, thus, should be recorded in the plan's financial statements.

38.211   Although investment contracts should be presented at fair value, deposit administration contracts and immediate participation guarantee contracts entered into before March 20, 1992, may continue to be presented at contract value. (SFAS 110, par. 8)

> **Practical Consideration.** The credit quality of the issuing insurance company should be considered when evaluating the value of a contract. If losses due to the insurer's poor credit may occur, those that are probable and estimable should be recorded and those that are possible (or probable but inestimable) should be disclosed. See Chapter 10.

Operating Assets

38.212   Plan operating assets such as buildings, furniture, equipment, and leasehold improvements should be reported at cost less accumulated depreciation and amortization. (SFAS 35, par. 14) Such assets that are held for investment, rather than used in the plan's operations, should be reported at fair value with other investments. (SFAS 35, par. 11)

Accrued Liabilities

38.213   As discussed in Paragraph 38.205, a defined benefit plan should not record the benefit obligation as a liability. Liabilities such as those for investment purchases, third-party administrative fees, trustee fees, etc., should be accrued, however.

STATEMENT OF CHANGES IN NET ASSETS AVAILABLE FOR BENEFITS

38.214   The statement of changes in net assets available for benefits should identify the significant changes and disclose the following: (SFAS 35, par. 15)

- *The net change (appreciation or depreciation) in fair value for each significant class of investments, segregated between investments with fair value measured by quoted prices in an active market and investments with otherwise determined fair value.* The net change must include realized gains and losses on investments that were both bought and sold during the year. Other realized gains and losses may, but need not, be included. (GAAP does not prohibit separate reporting of realized gains and losses.)

- *Investment income, excluding the separately reported net appreciation or depreciation in fair value.* GAAP does not explicitly require separate reporting of interest, dividends, and rents, but the illustrative financial statements present investment income in that manner. They also show investment expenses deducted from total investment income.

- *Contributions from the employer, segregated between cash and noncash contributions.* Noncash contributions should be reported at fair value and the nature of noncash contributions should be described parenthetically or in a note to the financial statements.

- *Contributions from participants, including those transmitted by the sponsor.*

- *Contributions from other identified sources.*

- *Benefits paid to participants.*

- *Payments to insurance companies to purchase contracts that are excluded from plan assets, for example, allocated contracts.* Dividend income related to such contracts may be netted against the payment amounts.

- *Administrative (operating) expenses.*

EXHIBIT 38-3 illustrates a statement of changes in net assets available for benefits. The exhibit also presents information about changes in accumulated plan benefits as discussed in Paragraphs 38.223–.224.

38.214

INFORMATION ABOUT THE ACTUARIAL PRESENT VALUE OF ACCUMULATED PLAN BENEFITS

Presentation Requirements

38.215   The following information about the actuarial present value of accumulated plan benefits (also called the "benefit obligation") should be presented: (SFAS 35, par. 22)

- Vested benefits (i.e., benefits that are not contingent on an employee's future services) of participants currently receiving payments, including benefits due and payable as of the benefit information date

- Other vested benefits

- Nonvested benefits

38.216   The benefit obligation information may be presented either as a separate statement, on the face of another statement (see EXHIBIT 38-2), or in the notes to the financial statements, as long as it is presented all in one place. It should not be included in liabilities on the statement of net assets available for benefits, however, nor should it be presented as supplementary information. Also, if the information is presented on the statement of net assets available for benefits, it must be determined as of the same date as the statement of net assets available for benefits. (SFAS 35, paras. 8 and 232)

38.217   GAAP states that it is preferable to present the benefit obligation information as of the end of the plan's year. However, because it may be difficult to obtain actuarial determinations made as of the plan's year-end in time to present timely financial statements, the Statement allows a plan to present the information as of the beginning of its year. (Presenting the information as of an interim date is not permitted.) A plan that presents benefit obligation information as of the beginning of its year must also present the following:

- Statement of net assets available for benefits as of the beginning of the plan year (in addition to the required year-end statement of net assets)

- Statement of changes in net assets available for benefits during the prior year (in addition to the required current year statement)

EXHIBIT 38-3

ILLUSTRATIVE STATEMENT OF CHANGES IN ACCUMULATED PLAN BENEFITS AND NET ASSETS AVAILABLE FOR BENEFITS

NET INCREASE IN ACTUARIAL PRESENT VALUE OF ACCUMULATED PLAN BENEFITS	
Increase (decrease) during the year attributable to:	
Plan amendment	$ 3,500,000
Change in actuarial assumptions	(1,500,000)
Benefits accumulated	1,200,000
Benefits paid	(1,400,000)
NET INCREASE	$ 1,800,000
NET INCREASE IN NET ASSETS AVAILABLE FOR BENEFITS	
Investment income:	
Net appreciation in fair value of investments	$ 500,000
Interest	400,000
Dividends	200,000
Rents	100,000
	1,200,000
Less: investment expenses	100,000
	1,100,000
Contributions:	
Employer	1,000,000
Employees	500,000
	1,500,000
Benefits paid directly to participants	(900,000)
Purchases of annuity contracts	(500,000)
Administrative expenses	(200,000)
NET INCREASE	$ 1,000,000
INCREASE IN EXCESS OF ACTUARIAL PRESENT VALUE OF ACCUMULATED PLAN BENEFITS OVER NET ASSETS AVAILABLE FOR BENEFITS	$ 800,000
EXCESS OF ACTUARIAL PRESENT VALUE OF ACCUMULATED PLAN BENEFITS OVER NET ASSETS AVAILABLE FOR BENEFITS:	
Beginning of year	5,200,000
End of year	$ 6,000,000

The additional statements are required because the FASB believes that it is important to present information about net assets available for plan benefits and the actuarial present value of accumulated plan benefits as of the same date, and to present information on changes in net assets available for benefits and changes in the actuarial present value of accumulated plan benefits as of the same date. (SFAS 35, paras. 7 and 208)

Determining the Actuarial Present Value of Accumulated Plan Benefits

38.218   The actuarial present value of accumulated plan benefits is the accumulated plan benefit adjusted to reflect the time value of money and probability of payment between the information date and the expected date of payment. Thus, determining the actuarial present value of accumulated plan benefits involves two parts: measuring the accumulated plan benefits and computing the present value of the accumulated benefits. (SFAS 35, par. 280)

38.219   Generally, accumulated plan benefits should be measured based on the history of employees' pay and service and other appropriate factors as of the benefit information date. In addition, the plan's provisions should be applied, to the extent possible. For example, assume that a plan provides for an annual benefit equal to 2% of a participant's average annual salary for the five years preceding retirement for each year of employment, up to a maximum of 30 years. The accumulated plan benefit for a participant who has been employed for 15 years and averaged $45,000 in annual salary for the last five years would be $13,500 ($45,000 × 2% × 15). The following should also be considered when measuring accumulated plan benefits: (SFAS 35, par. 18)

   a. Plan amendments adopted *after* the benefit information date should not be considered. Automatic benefit increases currently specified by the plan but expected to occur after the benefit information date, such as cost-of-living increases, should be considered, however.

   b. The benefit for each year of service for certain benefits may not be stated by the plan or may not clearly be determinable from its provisions. In such cases, the benefit should be considered to accumulate in proportion to:

      (1) the ratio of the number of years of service completed at the benefit information date to the number that will have been completed when the benefit first becomes fully vested, if the type of benefit is includable in vested benefits (for example, a supplemental early retirement benefit that is a vested benefit after a stated number of years) or

38.218

(2) the ratio of completed years of service to projected years of service upon anticipated separation from covered employment, if the benefit is not includable in vested benefits (for example, a death or disability benefit that is payable only if death or disability occurs during active service).

c. Projected years of service should only be considered when determining employees' expected eligibility for particular benefits, such as the following:

(1) Benefits that are increased provided a specified number of years of service are rendered (for example, a benefit that increases from $9 to $10 per month for each year of service if 20 or more years of service are rendered)

(2) Early retirement benefits

(3) Death benefits

(4) Disability benefits

d. It may be necessary to consider future pay to determine Social Security benefits in an integrated plan. If so, participants' pay as of the benefit information date should be presumed to remain unchanged during their assumed service. Also, no effect should be given to scheduled, or possible, future increases in the wage base or benefit level under the Social Security law.

e. Benefits that are to be provided by a contract that is excluded from the plan's financial statements, such as by an allocated insurance contract, should not be considered.

38.220   The present value of accumulated plan benefits is determined by applying actuarial assumptions to the accumulated plan benefit. Each individual assumption should reflect the plan's most likely expectations. In addition, the following is required for certain assumptions: (SFAS 35, par. 20)

- Assumed rates of return on plan assets should reflect expected rates of return during periods for which payment of benefits are deferred. The assumed rates of return should be consistent with returns that can be realistically achieved on the types of assets the plan holds and with the plan's investment policy.

- Expected inflation rates used in determining automatic benefit increases for plans with such provisions should be consistent with the assumed rates of return on plan assets.

- Administrative expenses the plan expects to pay (not those the plan sponsor assumes) that are associated with providing accumulated plan benefits should be reflected either by adjusting the assumed rates of return or by assigning the expenses to future periods and discounting them to the benefit information date.

Alternatively, the plan may use the assumptions that are inherent in the estimated cost at the benefit information date to obtain an insurance contract to provide the accumulated plan benefits. That approach may be particularly appropriate for a small plan because the assumptions would be tailored to the plan's specific size. Also, using insurance company premium rates may be a less expensive approach to making assumptions. (SFAS 35, paras. 21 and 203)

Practical Consideration. Typically, plan administrators engage actuaries to calculate the accumulated benefit obligation and its actuarial present value based on plan provisions and on salary, employment, and demographic data that the administrator supplies. The actuaries may advise the plan about the choice of a discount rate, but plan management is responsible for the reasonableness of the assumptions, particularly the assumed rates of return on plan assets.

38.221 Changes in actuarial assumptions are considered changes in accounting estimates. Thus, the effects of such changes should be accounted for in the year of change (and future years if the changes affect future years) rather than by restating prior period financial statements or by reporting pro forma amounts for prior years. (SFAS 35, par. 23) (Changes in accounting estimates are discussed in Chapter 1.)

38.222 EXHIBIT 38-4 presents an example calculation of the present value of accumulated plan benefits.

EXHIBIT 38-4

DETERMINING THE PRESENT VALUE OF AN ACCUMULATED PLAN BENEFIT

Plan Provisions:

Normal retirement age   65

Annual benefit equal to 2% of a participant's average annual salary for five years preceding retirement for each year of employment (up to a maximum of 30 years)

Participant Data at Benefit Information Date:

Age	40
Life expectancy	85
Years to retirement (64 − 40)	25
Expected years of retirement (85 − 65)	20
Years employed	15
Average salary for the last five years	$ 45,000
Accumulated plan benefit ($45,000 × 2% × 15)	$ 13,500 annually

Present Value Factors:

Assumed discount rate	10%
Discount factor for present value of annuity for 20 periods and 10% discount rate (from a present value table)	8.51356
Discount factor for present value of lump sum due after 25 years and 10% discount rate (from a present value table)	.0923

Present Value of Accumulated Plan Benefit at Benefit Information Date:

Present value of 20-year annuity starting in 25 years ($13,500 × 8.51356)	$ 114,933
Present value of $114,933 required in 25 years ($114,933 × .0923)	$ 10,608

NOTE: As discussed in Paragraph 38.218, the actuarial present value of accumulated plan benefits is computed by adjusting accumulated plan benefits for the time value of money and the probability of payment. For simplicity, the example calculation only shows the effect of the time value of money on the present value of an accumulated benefit obligation. In practice, the plan's actuary would also apply a discount factor that considers the probability of paying the accumulated benefit in the future.

INFORMATION ABOUT CHANGES IN THE ACTUARIAL PRESENT VALUE OF ACCUMULATED PLAN BENEFITS

38.223   Significant changes affecting the actuarial present value of accumulated plan benefits should be identified. Information about the changes may be presented as a separate statement, on the face of another statement (see EXHIBIT 38-3), or in notes to the financial statements, as long as it is presented all in one place. (The information may be presented on the statement of changes in net assets available for benefits only if the information is for the same period, however.) At a minimum, the significant effects of the following should be disclosed:

- Plan amendments

- Changes in the nature of the plan, for example, merger with another plan

- Changes in actuarial assumptions (If actuarial assumptions are determined based on assumptions inherent in the cost of an insurance contract, the effects of changes in actuarial assumptions due to changes in the insurance rates must be disclosed if it is practical to do so. If such disclosure is not practical, the effects should be included in the otherwise optional disclosure of benefits accumulated. See Paragraph 38.224.)

- Actuarial present value of accumulated plan benefits as of the preceding benefit information date, if the three preceding items are presented in other than a statement format

38.224   Factors other than those listed in the preceding paragraph may affect the actuarial present value of accumulated plan benefits. Thus, if information about the actuarial present value of accumulated plan benefits is presented in a statement that accounts for the change between two benefit information dates, an unidentified "other" category may need to be presented to reconcile the beginning and ending amounts. Plans are encouraged to disclose significant factors included in the "other" category. Such factors may include the following:

- Benefits accumulated, with actuarial experience gains or losses either included with the effects of additional benefits accumulated or separately disclosed

- The increase (for interest) as a result of the decrease in the discount period

- Benefits paid (This item should not include benefit payments made by an insurance company under a contract that is excluded from plan assets, that is, under an allocated contract. But, it should include payments the plan made to an insurance company under such a contract, including purchasing annuities with amounts allocated from existing contracts with the insurance company.) (SFAS 35, paras. 25–26)

DISCLOSURE REQUIREMENTS

38.500   In addition to the disclosures discussed in the preceding paragraphs that are typically made on the face of the financial statements, GAAP requires a defined benefit plan to disclose the following: (SFAS 35, paras. 27–28)

a. Its accounting policies regarding:

   (1) significant assumptions and methods used to determine the fair value of investments and the reported value of insurance contracts

   (2) significant assumptions and methods used to determine the actuarial present value of accumulated plan benefits, for example, the assumed rates of return, inflation rates, and retirement ages of plan participants (In addition, a plan's accounting policies disclosure should include a description of any significant changes of methods or assumptions for determining the actuarial present value of accumulated plan benefits made between benefit information dates.)

b. A brief description of the plan agreement including vesting and benefit provisions (Referring to a published source, such as the plan document furnished to participants, for that same information is also acceptable.)

c. A description of significant plan amendments adopted during the year ending on the latest benefit information date (If significant plan amendments were adopted between the latest benefit information date and the plan's year end, the plan should disclose the fact that the actuarial present value of accumulated plan benefits does not reflect those amendments.)

d. The order of priority for participants' claims to the plan's assets upon termination (The plan should also include a description of the benefits guaranteed by the Pension Benefit Guarantee Corporation (PBGC), including the application of the PBGC guaranty to any recent plan amendments. If material providing the information is published and made available to plan participants, the disclosures may be replaced by a reference to the other source of information and a disclosure similar to the following:

> "Should the plan terminate at some future time, its net assets generally will not be available on a pro rata basis to provide participants' benefits. Whether a particular participant's accumulated plan benefits will be paid depends on both the priority of those benefits and the level of benefits guaranteed by the PBGC at that time. Some benefits may be fully or partially provided for by the then existing assets and the PBGC guarantee while other benefits may not be provided for at all."

e. The plan's funding policy including any changes in the policy during the year (For a contributory plan, the disclosure should include the method of determining a participant's contributions. A plan subject to ERISA should disclose whether the minimum funding requirements have been met. If applicable, it should also disclose that a minimum funding waiver has been granted or is pending before the IRS.)

f. The fact that the employer absorbs significant costs of plan administration, if applicable

g. The plan's policy concerning the purchase of insurance contracts that are excluded from plan assets

h. The plan's federal income tax status if a favorable determination letter has not been obtained or maintained

i. Identification of investments that represent 5% of more plan net assets available for benefits

j. Any significant real estate or other transactions between the plan and the sponsor, employer, or the employee organization (for example, a union representing employees)

k. Unusual or infrequent events or transactions that occur subsequent to the latest benefit information date, but before the financial statements are issued, that may significantly affect the plan's present and future ability to pay benefits (If reasonably determinable, the plan should also disclose the effects of those events or transactions. If the effects are not quantified, the plan should disclose the reasons why the effects cannot be reasonably determined.)

AUTHORITATIVE LITERATURE AND RELATED TOPICS

AUTHORITATIVE LITERATURE

SFAS No. 35, *Accounting and Reporting by Defined Benefit Pension Plans*
SFAS No. 75, *Deferral of the Effective Date of Certain Accounting Requirements for Pension Plans of State and Local Governmental Units*
SFAS No. 102, *Statement of Cash Flows—Exemption of Certain Enterprises and Classification of Cash Flows from Certain Securities Acquired for Resale*
SFAS No. 110, *Reporting by Defined Benefit Pension Plans of Investment Contracts*

RELATED PRONOUNCEMENTS

EITF Issue No. 89-1, *Accounting by a Pension Plan for Bank Investment Contracts and Guaranteed Investment Contracts*
AICPA Industry Audit and Accounting Guide, *Audits of Employee Benefit Plans*
SOP 92-6, *Accounting and Reporting by Health and Welfare Benefit Plans*
SOP 94-4, *Reporting of Investment Contracts Held by Health and Welfare Benefit Plans and Defined Contribution Pension Plans*
Practice Bulletin 12, *Reporting Separate Investment Fund Option Information of Defined Contribution Pension Plans*

RELATED TOPICS

Chapter 39—Pension Plans: Accounting by Employers
Chapter 41—Postretirement Benefits Other Than Pensions

PENSION PLANS: ACCOUNTING BY EMPLOYERS

Table of Contents

PENSION PLANS: ACCOUNTING BY EMPLOYERS

Table of Contents (Continued)

PENSION PLANS: ACCOUNTING BY EMPLOYERS

OVERVIEW

39.100   A pension plan provides benefits to participants upon the occurrence of a covered event, such as retirement, death, disability, or termination of employment. A plan may be broadly classified as either a defined benefit plan or a defined contribution plan. As the names imply, a plan's classification depends on whether it specifies benefit payments or contribution amounts. That is, a defined benefit plan provides specified benefits to participants while a defined contribution plan provides an account for each participant and describes how contributions to the accounts are determined.

DEFINED BENEFIT PLANS

39.101   The employer's primary objectives when accounting for a defined benefit plan are to (a) charge pension costs to operations over the period employee services are rendered and (b) charge liabilities and credit assets when retirement benefits are paid. However, to reduce the volatility of pension costs in their financial statements, employers may amortize certain costs to operations in future periods rather than recognize them immediately. Those costs are actuarial gains and losses, the projected net asset or obligation at the time SFAS No. 87, *Employers' Accounting for Pensions,* was adopted, and benefits related to participants' services prior to a plan's adoption or amendment. Consequently, the annual pension cost of a defined benefit plan consists of the following components:

- a. Service cost

- b. Interest cost on the projected benefit obligation

- c. Actual return on plan assets

- d. Amortization of unrecognized prior service cost

- e. Amortization of unrecognized gains and losses

- f. Amortization of the unrecognized net asset or obligation for the plan at the time SFAS No. 87, *Employers' Accounting for Pensions,* was first adopted

39.102   Because of SFAS No. 87's amortization requirements, it is difficult to generalize about what the accrued pension liability or prepaid expense reported in an employer's balance sheet represents. However, if an employer does not amend its plan after adopting SFAS No. 87 and all of its net asset or obligation for the plan at the time SFAS No. 87 was adopted has been recognized, the accrued liability or prepaid expense will represent the funded status of the plan. That is, a prepaid asset would be recorded if plan contributions exceed prior charges to operations (indicating that the plan is over funded), and an accrued liability would be recorded if prior charges to operations exceed plan contributions (indicating that the plan is under funded).

39.103   Employers may be required to record unrecognized gains and losses, prior service costs, and the net asset or obligation that arose when SFAS No. 87 was adopted if a pension plan settlement or curtailment occurs. A plan settlement eliminates the employer's responsibility for its pension obligation. Examples of settlements include purchasing annuity contracts covering vested benefits or making lump sum distributions to participants in exchange for their rights to receive future pension benefits. A plan curtailment occurs when a portion of future pension benefits are reduced for current participants (for example, by suspending the plan).

39.104   Some employers pay benefits to employees when employment is terminated. The cost of the termination benefits is the total of any lump-sum payments made and the present value of any future payments. Termination benefits that are considered special termination benefits should be accrued when the amount of benefits can be reasonably estimated and the employee accepts the employer's offer to provide the benefits. Those that are considered contractual benefits should be accrued (a) when it is probable that employees will be entitled to benefits and (b) the amount of benefits can be reasonably estimated.

DEFINED CONTRIBUTION PLANS

39.105   Under a defined contribution plan, the employer and participants contribute amounts to accounts maintained by the plan for each participant. A participant receives benefits equal to (a) the amounts contributed to his or her account, (b) income earned on the investment of those amounts, and (c) forfeitures of amounts contributed to the accounts of other participants who terminated employment before vesting in the plan. The pension expense that should be recorded by the employer is the contribution that applies for the period, accounted for on the accrual basis.

ACCOUNTING REQUIREMENTS

TYPES OF PLANS

39.200 Pension plans provide benefits to participants upon retirement, death, disability, termination of employment, or the occurrence of another covered event. The following are the two basic types of pension plans:

    a. *Defined benefit plans.* A defined benefit plan provides specified benefits to plan participants. The benefits are based on a variety of factors including a participant's age, years of service, and compensation. (SFAS 87, par. 264) For example, a plan might provide a participant with an annual retirement benefit equal to 2% of the participant's annual salary for the five years preceding retirement for each year of employment, up to a maximum of 30 years.

    b. *Defined contribution plans.* A defined contribution plan provides an individual account for each participant and specifies how contributions to the individual's account are to be determined. Unlike defined benefit plans, defined contribution plans do not define specific benefit amounts that participants are to receive. Instead, they provide benefits based solely on (a) the amount contributed to a participant's account, (b) the returns earned on the investment of those contributions, and (c) forfeitures of other participants' benefits that may be allocated to the participant's account. (SFAS 87, par. 264) Examples of defined contribution plans include profit sharing plans, money purchase plans, employee stock ownership plans (see Chapter 50), and 401(k) plans.

39.201 Determining whether a plan is a defined contribution or a defined benefit plan is important because different measurement and disclosure requirements apply. As an example, the annual cost of a defined contribution plan usually is the contribution related to that year, but the cost charged against earnings for a defined benefit plan generally differs from the annual contribution. The substance of a plan, not its form, governs whether it is a defined contribution or a defined benefit plan. For example, a plan may provide prescribed benefits but base contributions on wages per hour. In that case, the plan should be considered a defined benefit plan.

> **Practical Consideration.** As a general rule, any plan that is not a defined contribution plan should be considered a defined benefit plan for purposes of applying the accounting standards.

ACCOUNTING FOR DEFINED BENEFIT PENSION PLANS

Recognizing Net Periodic Pension Cost

39.202   Over the life of a defined benefit pension plan, pension cost equals benefits paid less investment earnings. That net cost is charged to operations during the time a plan participant is employed. However, it is accomplished through a combination of current accruals and amortization of prior results that when considered together (a) charge the company's operations and credit its liabilities for the cost during the period employee services are rendered and (b) charge the company's liabilities and credit its assets as retirement benefits are paid. Specifically, the annual pension cost of a defined benefit pension plan consists of the following six components: (SFAS 87, par. 20)

Related primarily to employee service rendered during the period:

a. Service cost

b. Interest cost on the projected benefit obligation

c. Actual return on plan assets

Amortization of prior period results:

d. Amortization of unrecognized prior service cost

e. Amortization of unrecognized gains and losses

f. Amortization of the unrecognized net asset or net obligation for the plan at the time SFAS No. 87, *Employers' Accounting for Pensions,* was first adopted.

Practical Consideration. Usually, an actuary performs the complex calculations needed to determine an employer's net periodic pension cost. However, the employer is responsible for making assumptions about future events that ultimately will affect net periodic pension cost. Those assumptions include the following:

- *Assumed discount rates* should be based on comparable interest rates available to settle the plan's benefit obligation. Consequently, the rates should consider the length of time remaining until individual benefit payment dates. Assumed discount rates may be determined by considering annuity contract rates used by insurance companies or by referring to current rates of return on high-quality, fixed-income investments (for example, long-term bond yields). Assumed discount rates should be reevaluated each time the plan's benefit obligation is measured.

Practical Consideration (Continued).

- *The expected long-term rate of return on plan assets* generally should be based on the expected return of the plan's portfolio of investments. Consideration should also be given to the actual rates of return currently earned in the plan's investment portfolio and the rates expected to be earned when portfolio earnings are reinvested.

- *Future compensation levels* should be considered when calculating the service cost component of net periodic pension cost and the projected benefit obligation to the extent the plan's benefit formula considers future compensation levels. The estimate of future compensation should consider, for example, seniority, promotions, productivity, and the level of individual employees involved. Compensation assumptions also should be consistent with respect to future economic conditions, for example, estimated future rates of inflation.

39.203 Service Cost. Service cost relates only to employee service rendered during the year and is computed as the actuarial present value of benefits attributed by the pension benefit formula to employee service during the period. It requires assumptions about the attrition of present participants and future changes in their compensation and ignores participants that may be added to the plan in the future. (SFAS 87, par. 21)

39.204 In some instances, a plan's benefit formula may attribute all or a disproportionate share of total pension benefits to later years of service. For example, a plan may provide no benefits for the first 20 years of service and a $25,000 vested benefit at the beginning of year 21. (A vested benefit is one that an employee is entitled to receive and is not contingent on the employee's future service.) Because such a plan is substantially the same as a plan that provides $1,250 per year for the first 20 years of service and requires 20 years of service to become vested, the projected benefit should accumulate in proportion to the ratio of completed years of service to the number of years that will have been completed when the benefit first becomes fully vested. In other cases, a plan's benefit formula may not address how benefits relate to employee services provided. In such cases, the benefit should be assumed to accumulate as follows: (SFAS 87, par. 42)

     a. If the benefit is includable in vested benefits, the benefit amount should be included in proportion to the ratio of the completed years of service to the number of years that will be completed when the benefit becomes fully vested.

   b. If the benefit is not includable in vested benefits, the benefit amount should be included in proportion to the ratio of completed years of service to total projected years of service. (An example of a benefit that is not includable in vested benefits is a death or disability benefit that is payable only if the employee's death or disability occurs during active service.)

39.205   Service cost for the period should consider automatic benefit changes required by plan terms, such as cost-of-living increases, or that result from plan amendments already in effect. (SFAS 87, par. 48) In addition, employers that have a history of providing plan benefits that are greater than those defined in writing should base their pension accounting on the "substantive commitment" and disclose those commitments in their financial statements. (SFAS 87, par. 41)

39.206   **Interest Cost.** Interest cost reflects interest for the year on the plan's obligation to provide benefits. The information needed to compute interest cost is (a) the projected benefit obligation and (b) an assumed discount rate. The projected benefit obligation is the actuarial present value of benefits expected to be paid to current plan participants in the future. The projected benefit obligation requires assumptions about the attrition rates and future compensation levels for current participants but does not consider that additional employees will become plan participants in future years. (SFAS 87, paras. 17 and 22) As discussed in Paragraph 39.202, the discount rate is based on current market conditions and, therefore, may vary from year to year.

39.207   **Actual Return on Plan Assets.** Actual return on plan assets generally represents realized and unrealized investment gains and losses as well as any interest and dividends received. The actual return on plan assets is computed as the fair value of plan assets at the beginning of the year plus contributions during the year minus benefits paid during the year and minus the fair value of plan assets at the end of the year. (SFAS 87, par. 23) A net return on plan assets decreases pension cost for the period.

39.208   **Amortization of Unrecognized Prior Service Cost.** The cost of providing benefits related to services rendered before a plan was adopted or amended should be amortized over the remaining service lives of participants who are active at the date of the plan adoption or amendment. If most of the plan's participants are inactive, however, unrecognized prior service cost should be amortized over the expected remaining lives of the inactive participants. (SFAS 87, paras. 24–25)

39.209   So long as it is applied consistently, any one of a variety of amortization methods may be used—even if the method selected amortizes unrecognized prior service cost more rapidly than other methods. For example, to reduce the complexity of the amortization calculations, it may be preferable to amortize unrecognized prior service cost over the *average* remaining service period of all active participants using the straight-line method. Also, if the period that benefits are expected to be realized from a retroactive plan amendment is shorter than the remaining future service lives of active participants, unrecognized prior service cost should be amortized over the future periods expected to benefit from the amendment. (SFAS 87, paras. 26–27)

39.210   Plan amendments that decrease the cost of providing pension benefits also decrease the projected benefit obligation. Decreases in the projected benefit obligation should first be used to reduce any existing unrecognized prior service cost. The excess, if any, should be amortized on the same basis as increases in unrecognized prior service cost (that is, amortized over the remaining service period of employees expected to receive benefits). (SFAS 87, par. 28)

> **Practical Consideration.** The accounting treatment of unrecognized prior service costs applies to plan adoptions or amendments occurring after SFAS No. 87 was adopted. As discussed in Paragraph 39.214, unrecognized prior service costs at the date SFAS No. 87 was adopted are charged to future earnings through amortization of the net plan asset or liability.

39.211   **Gains and Losses.** Gains and losses arise when the following occur: (SFAS 87, paras. 29–30)

     a. *Assumptions used to compute the projected benefit obligation change.* The gain or loss is the difference between the projected value of the year-end pension obligation based on beginning-of-year assumptions and the actual year-end obligation based on end-of-year assumptions.

     b. *Actual results differ from the expected return on plan assets.* The gain or loss is the difference between the actual and expected return on plan assets. The following discuss how the actual and expected returns on plan assets are determined:

         (1) As discussed in Paragraph 39.207, the actual return on pension plan assets is computed as the difference between the fair value of plan assets at the beginning and end of the period, adjusted for contributions and benefit payments made during the period. Generally, fair value is the amount that would be paid between a willing buyer and a willing seller who are under no obligation to buy or sell.

(2) The expected return on plan assets is computed by multiplying the plan's expected long-term rate of return by the beginning of the year market-related value of plan assets. The market-related value of plan assets is determined by using either the fair value of plan assets or by computing a value that recognizes changes in the fair value of plan assets systematically over a period not to exceed five years. For example, rather than using fair value, a company may compute market-related value by recognizing changes in value over five years. Assuming market-related value at the beginning of the year is $1,200 and net asset gains and losses over the past five years are $580, the market-related value of plan assets at the end of the year would be computed as follows: (Expected long-term rate of return and amounts for contributions and benefit payments are assumed.)

Market-related value at beginning of year	$	1,200
Expected return on assets for the year ($1,200 × 10% expected long-term rate of return)		120
Net gain (loss) to be included in market-related value ($580 ÷ 5 years)		116
Employer contributions		400
Benefit payments		(200)
Market-related value at end of year	$	1,636

Market-related value may be computed differently for each class of plan assets; however, the method of computing market-related value for each class should be used consistently from year to year. For example, an employer may use the fair value for equity securities and a five-year moving average for bonds and other debt securities.

> **Practical Consideration.** When accounting for gains and losses, no distinction is made between the sources of gains and losses. Unrecognized gains and losses from all sources are netted.

39.212   Generally, the gains and losses discussed in the preceding paragraph (frequently referred to as actuarial gains and losses) are not required to be included in pension expense in the period they arise. Instead, they may be deferred until amortization is required in a future year. Amortization is required in any year in which the beginning of the year unrecognized net gain or loss exceeds the greater of 10% of the projected benefit obligation or the market-related value of plan assets. In such years, the amount of net gain or loss that must be included in net pension cost is the excess net gain or loss (i.e., amount greater than 10% of projected benefit obligation or market-related value) divided by the average remaining service lives of active employees (or, if substantially all plan participants are inactive, the average remaining lives of inactive participants). (SFAS 87, paras. 29 and 32)

> **Practical Consideration.** Net asset gains and losses not yet included in market-related value need not be amortized to pension expense. Thus, in the example in Paragraph 39.211, the net gain of $464 not included in market-related value (total net gain of $580 minus $116 included in market-related value) would not be included in the amount subject to amortization in the current year.

39.213   An alternative amortization method may be used so long as it (a) reduces the unamortized net gain or loss balance by an amount in excess of that resulting from the minimum amortization method, (b) is applied similarly to both gains and losses, (c) is systematic and used consistently, and (d) is disclosed in the financial statements. (SFAS 87, par. 33)

39.214   **Amortization of Unrecognized Net Obligation or Asset.** Rather than require an employer to immediately recognize the difference between the fair value of plan assets and the projected benefit obligation as of the date SFAS No. 87 was adopted, the Statement allows an employer to amortize the difference to earnings over future years. As it is amortized, the difference is charged or credited to pension cost and credited or charged to accrued pension cost (or to prepaid pension cost if there is no accrual). The difference should be amortized using the straight-line method, and the amortization period should be the average remaining service period of participants that were employed when SFAS No. 87 was adopted, except in the following circumstances: (SFAS 87, par. 77)

a. An employer may amortize the difference over 15 years if the remaining service period of plan participants is less than 15 years.

b. The difference should be amortized over the expected remaining lives of plan participants if substantially all of the participants were not employed when SFAS No. 87 was adopted.

Recording Accrued Pension Liabilities in the Balance Sheet

39.215   Pension costs recognized under GAAP may differ from amounts allowable as deductions under income tax regulations. Since plan contributions are often heavily influenced by their tax attributes, they may differ from costs charged against operations. Therefore, either an accrued liability or a prepaid expense will be recorded in the employer's balance sheet. Generalizations about what the recorded asset or liability represents are difficult because of the amortization requirements of SFAS No. 87. However, as a simplification, if a company's plan does not change after adopting SFAS No. 87, after the unrecognized net asset or obligation is fully amortized, the accrued liability or prepaid expense reflected in the company's balance sheet will represent the funded status of the plan. For example, a prepaid asset would be reported if contributions to the plan exceed prior charges to operations and would indicate that the plan was over funded so that the fair value of plan assets exceeds the present value of future obligations to present plan participants.

39.216   **Measurement Date.** Plan assets and pension obligations generally should be measured as of the employer's financial statement date or, if used consistently from year to year, as of a date not more than three months prior to the date of the financial statements. (SFAS 87, par. 52) Thus, for example, a calendar-year company using a year-end measurement date would determine its net periodic pension cost for the period beginning each January 1 and ending each December 31. The company may measure the plan's assets and its pension obligation as of September 30, however, if that date is used consistently from year to year. In that case, the company would determine net periodic pension cost for the period beginning October 1 of the prior calendar year to September 30 of the current calendar year.

> **Practical Consideration.** Companies that must issue financial statements soon after year-end often measure pension obligations and plan assets as of a date prior to year-end. Doing so allows them to obtain pension information before financial statements must be issued.

39.217   **Minimum Liability.** Although SFAS No. 87 attempts to phase in recognition of the funded status of the plan (see Paragraph 39.214), it requires early recognition of an additional liability if two conditions are met at the balance sheet date: (SFAS 87, par. 36)

a. *The fair value of plan assets is less than the accumulated benefit obligation.* The accumulated benefit obligation differs from the projected benefit obligation discussed in Paragraph 39.206 only in that future compensation changes are not considered. Thus, it represents the present value of benefits expected to be provided to present plan participants if their compensation does not change. It requires assumptions about attrition of present participants but does not consider participants that may enter the plan in the future.

b. *Any liability already recognized is less than the unfunded accumulated benefit obligation.* The unfunded accumulated benefit obligation is the excess of the accumulated benefit obligation over the fair value of plan assets.

39.218   If *both* of the preceding conditions are met, the employer should include the unfunded obligation liability in its balance sheet. However, the liability should not be recorded through a charge to earnings. Instead—

a. if the adjustment needed to recognize the liability is less than unrecognized prior service cost plus any remaining unrecognized net obligation, all of the adjustment should be charged to an intangible asset.

b. if the adjustment needed to recognize the liability exceeds unrecognized prior service cost plus any unrecognized net obligation, (1) an intangible asset equal to the amount of unrecognized prior service cost plus any unrecognized net obligation should be recognized and (2) the difference should be reported as other comprehensive income, net of any tax benefits. (SFAS 87, par. 37) Chapter 8 illustrates financial statement presentation of other comprehensive income.

39.219   As a result of the minimum liability requirement, the following amounts are recorded and revised annually:

a. An intangible asset that will not exceed the cost of covered prior service (including any remaining unrecognized net obligation) that has not yet been charged to operations

b. A liability at least equal to the unfunded liability for benefits to present plan participants assuming no future compensation changes

Note, however, that adjustments to recognize the unfunded status of the plan do not affect how cost is charged to earnings for the period. The guidance in Paragraphs 39.202–.214 still applies.

Practical Consideration. The value of assets held by the plan is important to the employer's accounting since it is one of the benchmarks for determining whether a minimum liability should be recorded. Measuring plan assets is discussed in detail in Chapter 38.

39.220 **Annuity Contracts.** Employers who sponsor defined benefit plans sometimes enter into irrevocable contracts with insurance companies to cover benefit obligations. The contracts, which are referred to as annuity or "allocated" contracts, transfer the risk of providing benefits from the employer and plan to the insurance company. (For purposes of applying the accounting requirements for pension plans, the definition of an annuity contract is not met if there is a reasonable doubt that the insurer will meet its obligation or if the contract is with a captive insurance company, that is, one that does business primarily with the employer and its related parties.) If a plan is funded through annuity contracts that cover all plan obligations, the insurance premium is the pension cost the employer should charge to earnings, and the company and the plan would have no plan assets or projected benefit obligation. If annuity contracts cover only a portion of the benefit obligation, however, the employer still has a responsibility to fund the uncovered obligation. In that case, the uncovered obligation would be accounted for following the guidance in the preceding paragraphs of this chapter. (SFAS 87, paras. 57–60)

Practical Consideration. Insurance contracts entered into by retirement plans may be broadly classified as allocated and unallocated. Under allocated contracts, payments to the insurance company are used to purchase insurance or annuity contracts for specific individual plan participants. Since they transfer the obligation to pay benefits to the insurance company, allocated contracts and the related benefit obligations should not be included in the plan's financial statements. Under unallocated contracts, payments to insurance companies are not allocated to specific participants, but are held in an undivided fund until they are used to pay benefits. Unallocated contracts are investment vehicles that do not transfer any benefit obligation or risk to the insurance company and, thus, should be recorded in the plan's financial statements. Accounting for insurance contracts in the *plan's* financial statements are discussed in further detail in Chapter 38.

39.221   Annuity contracts may be participating contracts. In a participating contract, the insurer pays to the purchaser a portion of the income it receives from investing the premiums. Usually, the payments are in the form of dividends and are used to reduce the plan's costs. Participating contracts generally cost more than nonparticipating contracts. The cost difference relates to the participation right and should be recorded as a plan asset. In subsequent years, the participation right should be measured at fair value. If fair value is not reasonably estimable, the asset should be recorded at cost and amortized over the dividend period under the contract. (SFAS 87, par. 61)

39.222   **Business Combinations.** When a defined benefit plan is acquired as part of a business combination accounted for under the purchase method, a liability should be recorded for any projected benefit obligation in excess of plan assets. Similarly, an excess of plan assets over the projected benefit obligation should be recorded as an asset. Recognizing a new pension asset or liability at the date of purchase results in the elimination of the following:

a. Unrecognized net gain or loss

b. Unrecognized prior service cost

c. Unrecognized net obligation or asset that existed when SFAS No. 87 was adopted

In subsequent years, the asset or liability recorded at the date of purchase is reduced by any differences between the acquiring company's net periodic pension cost and contributed amounts. However, the asset or liability is only reduced to the extent that items a.–c. were used in determining plan contributions. (SFAS 87, par. 261)

Employers with More Than One Defined Benefit Plan

39.223   Employers with more than one plan are required to separately determine net periodic pension cost, liabilities, and the fair value of assets for each plan sponsored. Thus, an employer may not offset a liability related to one plan with an asset related to another unless the employer has the right to use the assets of one plan to pay the liabilities and benefits of another. (SFAS 87, par. 55) Disclosures for all of an employer's single-employer defined benefit plans may be aggregated, however, with the following exceptions: (SFAS 87, par. 56)

- Certain disclosures about plans whose accumulated benefit obligations exceed the fair value of plan assets may not be aggregated with those of plans whose assets exceed the accumulated benefit obligations. (See Paragraph 39.500, item c.)

- Disclosures for plans located outside the U.S. should not be aggregated with those for U.S. plans unless the plans use similar economic assumptions.

Settlements and Curtailments of Defined Benefit Pension Plans

39.224   As discussed in Paragraphs 39.208–.214, SFAS No. 87 allows for the delayed recognition of net gains and losses, prior service costs, and the net asset or obligation that arose when the Statement was adopted. However, all or part of those unrecognized amounts may become recognized in a pension plan settlement or curtailment. (SFAS 88, par. 45)

a. A settlement essentially eliminates the plan's obligation for benefits. To be considered a settlement, SFAS No. 88, *Employers' Accounting for Settlements and Curtailments of Defined Benefit Pension Plans and for Termination Benefits,* requires that the transaction:

  (1) be an irrevocable action;

  (2) relieve the company (or the plan) of primary responsibility for a pension benefit obligation; and

  (3) eliminate significant risks related to the obligation and the assets used to effect the settlement.

   Examples of settlements are purchasing annuity contracts (see Paragraphs 39.220–.221) or making lump-sum cash payments to plan participants in exchange for their rights to receive specified pension benefits. (SFAS 88, par. 3)

b. A curtailment generally prevents the pension benefit obligation from growing for future services of present employees. Examples of a curtailment are (1) terminating employee services through closing a facility or discontinuing a segment and (2) terminating (or suspending) a plan. In both situations, the plan's obligation is not relieved, but generally will not increase. (SFAS 88, par. 6)

39.225   A settlement or curtailment may occur together or as separate transactions. For example, when the expected future years of service of certain employees are reduced due to a layoff but the plan continues to exist, a curtailment has occurred but not a settlement. If the employer's defined benefit pension plan is terminated without replacement, and settlement of the plan obligation occurs, a curtailment and settlement have resulted. Finally, when the employer settles all or a portion of its plan obligation and still provides defined benefits to employees for their future service, a settlement has taken place but not a curtailment. (SFAS 88, par. 7)

39.226 **Settlements.** Since plan settlements involve eliminating an obligation, a gain or loss should be recognized at the time of settlement. If the employer settles the entire pension obligation, the gain or loss can be viewed as the balancing entry needed to record any plan assets reverting back to the employer plus the adjustment needed to eliminate the prepaid asset or accrued liability recorded as a result of applying SFAS No. 87. In such cases, the maximum gain or loss on plan settlement should be recognized. That amount is based on balances measured as of the settlement date and equals the total of (a) any unrecognized net gain or loss (see Paragraphs 39.211–.213) and (b) any unrecognized net asset remaining from the adoption of SFAS No. 87 (see Paragraph 39.214). (SFAS 88, par. 9)

39.227   It is not uncommon for participants who are partially vested to withdraw from a plan because of voluntary or involuntary termination of employment, and then to be "cashed out" of the plan as of the withdrawal date. Also, some plans may purchase annuity contracts each year to cover the year's benefit accruals. In such cases, gain or loss on settlement should be determined as follows: (SFAS 88, paras. 9 and 11)

     a. If only a portion of the pension obligation is settled, the employer should recognize a pro rata portion of the maximum gain or loss. For example, if a settlement results in a 30% reduction of the projected benefit obligation, only 30% of the maximum gain or loss should be recognized.

     b. If the cost of all settlements in a year are less than or equal to the sum of the service cost and interest cost components of the year's net periodic pension cost, gain or loss may be recognized following the guidance in item a. (Gain or loss recognition is not required, however.) Once adopted, the accounting policy for small settlements should be used consistently.

     The cost of a settlement is the amount paid to relieve the employer of its obligation to provide benefit payments. For example, (1) the cost of a settlement paid in cash is the amount of cash paid to the employee, (2) the cost of a settlement made by purchasing a nonparticipating annuity contract is the cost of the contract, and (3) the cost of a settlement made by purchasing a participating annuity contract is the cost of the contract net of the amount paid for the participation right.

EXHIBIT 39-1 illustrates calculating the gain or loss on a partial plan settlement.

Practical Consideration. As discussed in Paragraph 39.220, purchasing an annuity contract does not relieve the employer of its pension obligation, and thus does *not* constitute a settlement, if either of the following conditions are met:

- The insurer is controlled by the employer.

- There is a reasonable doubt that the insurer will not meet its obligations under the annuity contract.

In addition, a participating annuity contract does not constitute a settlement if its terms are such that the employer remains subject to most of the risks connected with the benefit obligation. For example, if a participating annuity contract requires the purchaser to pay additional premiums if the insurer experiences investment losses, purchasing the annuity contract would not constitute a settlement.

EXHIBIT 39-1

CALCULATING THE GAIN OR LOSS ON PARTIAL SETTLEMENT

Assumptions:

1. On December 31, 19X5, ABC Incorporated purchased nonparticipating annuity contracts to cover the benefits of all retired participants.

2. On December 30, 19X5, the plan's projected benefit obligation was comprised of the following:

Cost of settling retirees' benefits (cost of purchasing nonparticipating annuities)	$ 50,000
Benefits not settled (active employees)	35,000
	$ 85,000

3. On December 30, 19X5, the company's balance sheet showed prepaid pension costs that consisted of the following:

EXHIBIT 39-1 (Continued)

Projected benefit obligation	$ (85,000)
Plan assets	100,000
Less unrecognized items:	
Prior service costs	12,000
Net loss	10,000
Net obligation at the time SFAS No. 87	
was adopted	(25,000)
Prepaid pension cost	$ 12,000

Maximum gain (loss) on settlement

Unrecognized net loss prior to settlement	$ (10,000)
Net obligation at the time SFAS No. 87	
was adopted	25,000
Maximum gain recognizable	$ 15,000

Reduction in the projected benefit obligation as a result of the settlement

$$\frac{\text{Projected benefit obligation settled}}{\text{Total projected benefit obligation}} = \frac{\$\,50,000}{\$\,85,000} = 58.8\%$$

Settlement gain

Maximum gain recognizable	$ 15,000
Reduction in projected benefit obligation	× 58.8%
Settlement gain	$ 8,820

39.228 Settlement gains and losses generally do not meet the criteria for treatment as extraordinary items. Consequently, they are reported in the income statement as an ordinary gain or loss. Chapter 23 discusses extraordinary items.

39.229 **Curtailments.** A curtailment generally prevents the projected benefit obligation from growing for all or a portion of the plan's participants. It may eliminate coverage for certain participants, eliminate future defined benefit accruals (e.g., freezing the plan), or both. The following two components comprise the effects of a plan curtailment: (SFAS 88, paras. 12–13)

a. *Decrease in unrecognized prior service cost.* For purposes of applying SFAS No. 88 to curtailments, prior service cost includes any unrecognized net obligation remaining from adopting SFAS No. 87 as well as any unrecognized prior service cost. Such costs should be written off in proportion to the reduction in the remaining future years of service at the date of the curtailment. For example, if a plan curtailment eliminates 30% of the estimated future years of service of active employees receiving prior service credit, the loss on curtailment related to prior service cost is 30% of the combined unrecognized prior service cost and remaining unrecognized net asset or obligation. Note that the amount of loss recognized on the decrease in unrecognized prior service cost is not part of the gain or loss on plan curtailment (see item b. below) but it is included in the total effects of a plan curtailment.

b. *Curtailment gain or loss.* Gains and losses should be recognized for changes in the projected benefit obligation that result from curtailments. If a curtailment causes a plan's projected benefit obligation to decrease (for example, because the effects of future salary increases are eliminated), a gain would result. Conversely, a loss results if a curtailment causes the projected benefit obligation to increase (for example, because a plan's benefit formula creates additional benefits for employees who retire early). To compute a curtailment gain or loss, the employer first should determine the decrease or increase in the projected benefit obligation resulting from the curtailment (excluding increases arising from termination benefits). The employer then should compare that amount to the total of any unrecognized net gain or loss plus any net asset or obligation remaining from adopting SFAS No. 87.

   (1) If the change in the projected benefit obligation is a decrease (gain) and an unrecognized net loss exists, a curtailment gain exists to the extent the decrease in the projected benefit obligation exceeds the unrecognized net loss.

   (2) If the change in the projected benefit obligation is a decrease (gain) and there is no unrecognized net loss, a curtailment gain exists equal to the entire decrease in the projected benefit obligation.

   (3) If the change in the projected benefit obligation is an increase (loss) and an unrecognized net gain exists, a curtailment loss

exists to the extent the increase in the projected benefit obligation exceeds the unrecognized net gain.

(4) If the change in the projected benefit obligation is an increase (loss) and there is no unrecognized net gain, a curtailment loss exists equal to the entire increase in the projected benefit obligation.

39.230   If the total effect of a pension plan curtailment (that is, the sum of items a. and b. in the preceding paragraph) results in a loss, the loss should be recognized when it is probable that the curtailment will occur and the effects of the curtailment can be reasonably estimated. If the total effect of a curtailment results in a gain, the gain should be recognized when the affected employees terminate or when the employer adopts the plan suspension or amendment. (SFAS 88, par. 14) Curtailment gains and losses are reported in the employer's income statement as ordinary gains and losses. EXHIBIT 39-2 presents several examples of computing a curtailment gain or loss based on the preceding measurement criteria.

Practical Consideration. Settlement or curtailment gains and losses that are recognized and that relate to the disposal of a business segment should be reported as part of the employer's discontinued operations. Chapter 23 of this *Guide* discusses accounting for discontinued operations

---

Termination Benefits

39.231   Employers sometimes provide benefits to employees when employment is terminated. Such termination benefits are often in the form of periodic future payments, lump-sum payments, or both. Furthermore, benefits may be paid from the employer's general corporate assets, an existing employee benefit plan, a newly formed plan, or a combination of all three. The cost of termination benefits that should be recognized by the employer is the lump-sum payments made and/or the present value of future payments. (SFAS 88, par. 15)

EXHIBIT 39-2

CALCULATING THE EFFECT OF CURTAILMENTS

Example 1

Decrease in unrecognized prior service cost as a result of the curtailment	$ (2,000)
Combined unrecognized gain (loss) at date of curtailment:	
Unrecognized net loss	$ (7,000)
Unrecognized net asset remaining from the time SFAS No. 87 was adopted	6,500
Combined loss	$ (500)
Increase (loss) in projected benefit obligation as a result of the curtailment	$ (6,000)

Because there is no unrecognized net gain, a curtailment loss exists equal to the entire $6,000 increase in the projected benefit obligation. The total effect of the curtailment is an $8,000 loss ($2,000 loss due to the decrease in prior service cost plus the $6,000 curtailment loss). The loss should be recognized when it is probable that the curtailment will occur.

Example 2

Decrease in unrecognized prior service cost as a result of the curtailment	$ (2,000)
Combined unrecognized gain at date of curtailment:	
Unrecognized net gain	$ 9,000
Unrecognized net asset remaining from the time SFAS No. 87 was adopted	6,500
Combined gain	$ 15,500
Increase (loss) in projected benefit obligation as a result of the curtailment	$ (6,000)

No curtailment loss exists because the combined unrecognized gain exceeds the increase in the projected benefit obligation. The total effect of the curtailment is a $2,000 loss (the $2,000 loss due to the decrease in prior service cost). The loss should be recognized when it is probable that the curtailment will occur.

EXHIBIT 39-2 (Continued)

Example 3

Decrease in unrecognized prior service cost as a result of the curtailment	$ (2,000)
Combined unrecognized gain at date of curtailment:	
Unrecognized net gain	$ 7,000
Unrecognized net asset remaining from the time SFAS No. 87 was adopted	6,500
Combined gain	$ 13,500
Decrease (gain) in projected benefit obligation as a result of the curtailment	$ 6,000

Because there is no unrecognized net loss, a curtailment gain exists equal to the entire $6,000 decrease in the projected benefit obligation. The total effect of the curtailment is a $4,000 gain ($2,000 loss due to the decrease in prior service cost plus the $6,000 curtailment gain). The gain should be recognized when the affected employees terminate or when the employer adopts the plan suspension or amendment.

Example 4

Decrease in unrecognized prior service cost as a result of the curtailment	$ (2,000)
Combined unrecognized gain (loss) at date of curtailment:	
Unrecognized net loss	$ (9,000)
Unrecognized net asset remaining from the time SFAS No. 87 was adopted	6,500
Combined loss	$ (2,500)
Decrease (gain) in projected benefit obligation as a result of the curtailment	$ 6,000

A curtailment gain exists since the decrease in the projected benefit obligation exceeds the combined unrecognized loss. The curtailment gain is equal to the excess of the decrease in the projected benefit obligation over the combined unrecognized loss or $3,500 ($6,000 − $2,500). The total effect of the curtailment is a $1,500 gain ($2,000 loss due to the decrease in prior service cost plus the $3,500 curtailment gain). The gain should be recognized when the affected employees terminate or when the employer adopts the plan suspension or amendment.

39.232　The date on which termination benefits should be accrued depends on whether the benefits are special or contractual termination benefits.

- *Special termination benefits.* Termination benefits that are offered for only a short period of time are referred to as "special termination benefits." Special termination benefits should be accrued when an employee accepts the employer's offer and the amount of benefits can be reasonably estimated.

- Contractual termination benefits. As its name implies, contractual termination benefits are those required by the terms of a separate agreement or the terms of an existing employee benefit plan. Contractual termination benefits are provided only as the result of a specified event. Examples of such events include the closing of a manufacturing plant or the early retirement of employees. Recognition of contractual termination benefits occurs in the employer's financial statements when (a) it is probable that employees will be entitled to benefits and (b) the amount of benefits to be provided can be reasonably estimated. (SFAS 88, par. 15)

Practical Consideration. Termination benefits that are recognized and that relate to the disposal of a business segment should be reported as part of the employer's discontinued operations. Chapter 23 of this *Guide* discusses accounting for discontinued operations. The chapter also discusses accounting for termination benefits that are paid as part of a restructuring.

ACCOUNTING FOR DEFINED CONTRIBUTION PLANS

39.233　As discussed in Paragraph 39.200, a defined contribution plan does not specify a defined benefit amount. Instead, it specifies how contributions to the plan are determined. The plan provides a separate account for each participant, which is increased by employer and/or participant contributions, returns earned on the investment of those amounts, and forfeitures of amounts contributed to the accounts of other participants who terminated employment before vesting in the plan. Defined contribution plan benefits are equal to the value of each individual participant's account balance. (SFAS 87, par. 63)

39.234　The pension cost to be recorded as expense normally should be the contribution that applies to that period accounted for on the accrual basis. (SFAS 87, par. 64) Therefore, a company preparing financial statements for the year ended December 31, 19X5 would report pension costs equal to the contribution allowable for 19X5 salaries, and the difference between that and deposits made to the plan during the year would be reflected in the company's

December 31, 19X5 balance sheet either as a prepaid expense or an accrued liability.

MULTIEMPLOYER PLANS

39.235 A multiemployer plan is a plan to which two or more unrelated employers make contributions, usually as the result of a collective-bargaining agreement. In a multiemployer plan, the assets contributed by one participating employer may be used to provide benefits to employees of other participating employers. Therefore, the assets contributed by an employer are not segregated in a separate account or restricted to pay benefits only to that employer's employees. An example of a multiemployer plan is a union contract that requires companies with union employees to contribute to the union's plan. The plan, in turn, assumes the liability for paying benefits to participants. Employers who participate in multiemployer plans should record net pension cost equal to the required contribution for the period. Any contributions due but not paid should be recognized as a liability. (SFAS 87, paras. 67–68)

39.236 An employer who withdraws from a multiemployer plan may have a liability for a portion of the plan's unfunded benefit obligation. If the withdrawal would give rise to an obligation that is either probable or reasonably possible, SFAS No. 5, *Accounting for Contingencies,* should be followed. (SFAS 87, par. 70) That is, if (a) it is probable that the employer will incur a liability by withdrawing from the plan and (b) the amount of the liability can be reasonably estimated, the employer should accrue a liability and record it as a loss. If one or both of those conditions are not met but it is reasonably possible that a liability has been incurred, the contingency should be disclosed. (Chapter 10 discusses accounting for contingencies in greater detail.)

MULTIPLE-EMPLOYER PLANS

39.237 Multiple-employer plans are similar to multiemployer plans in that they consist of two or more unrelated employers. However, multiple-employer plans are in substance an aggregation of single-employer plans that are combined to allow assets to be pooled for investment purposes and to reduce plan administration costs. Multiple-employer plans often permit participating employers to have different benefit formulas, allowing an employer's contributions to be based on the formula it selects. Each employer participating in the plan is required to account for its respective interest in the plan as if that interest were a separate plan. (SFAS 87, par. 71) An example of a multiple-employer plan is an association of car dealerships that contribute to a plan administered by the association. Each dealership retains the obligation for its own employees and assumes no responsibility for the obligation to employees of other dealerships.

FOREIGN PLANS

39.238   The guidance in this chapter applies to pension arrangements outside the U.S. that are similar in substance to U.S. plans. (GAAP does not place any additional accounting requirements on such plans.) In addition, in some countries it is customary to provide employee benefits upon voluntary or involuntary termination of employment. The guidance in this chapter also applies to those arrangements if they are in substance pension plans (for example, if benefits are paid for virtually all employee terminations). (SFAS 87, paras. 72–73)

DISCLOSURE REQUIREMENTS

DEFINED BENEFIT PENSION PLANS

39.500   The following disclosures are required for single-employer defined benefit plans: (The disclosures may be combined for all of a company's plans, or information about plans may be presented in groups, whichever is more useful. Disclosures for plans outside of the U.S. should not be combined with those for U.S. plans unless all plans use similar economic assumptions, however.) (SFAS 87, par. 54)

   a. A description of the plan including employee groups covered, type of benefit formula used, funding policy, types of assets held by the plan, significant liabilities other than plan benefits (for example, unsettled security purchases, unsecured borrowings, or borrowings secured by investments in real estate), and the nature and effect of significant matters affecting comparability of information disclosed for all periods presented

   b. The amount of net periodic pension cost for the period showing separately the service cost component, interest cost component, actual return on plan assets for the period, and the net total of the other components discussed in Paragraph 39.202

   c. A schedule reconciling the plan's funded status with amounts in the employer's balance sheet. The reconciliation should separately show the following: (Plans with assets in excess of the accumulated benefit obligation should not be combined with plans that have accumulated benefit obligations that exceed plan assets)

(1) Fair value of plan assets

(2) Projected benefit obligation, accumulated benefit obligation, and vested benefit obligation

(3) Unrecognized prior service cost

(4) Unrecognized net gain or loss, including asset gains and losses not yet included in market-related value

(5) Remaining unrecognized net obligation or net asset existing at the date of initial application of SFAS No. 87

(6) Additional minimum liability

(7) The net pension asset or liability that has been recorded in the balance sheet (which is the net result of combining the preceding six items).

d. Weighted-average assumed discount rate and, if applicable, the rate of compensation increase used to measure the projected benefit obligation and the weighted-average long-term rate of return on plan assets

e. Amounts and types of securities of related parties (including the employer) that are included in plan assets, and the approximate amount of annual benefits of employees and retirees covered by annuity contracts issued by the employer and related parties

f. If applicable, the alternative amortization method used for unrecognized prior service cost and the alternative amortization method used to reflect the substantive commitment of the employer to pay more benefits than its existing pension benefit formula may indicate

39.501   An employer should consider the following optional disclosures if it wants to disclose more information about its pension plan (for example, because the plan is material to its operations): (SFAS 87, paras. 223–224)

a. Ratio of net periodic pension cost to covered payroll

b. Separate amounts of amortization of unrecognized prior service and amortization of unrecognized net gain or loss

c. Information about the cash flows of the plan separately showing employer contributions, other contributions, and benefits paid during the period

d. Amounts of plan assets classified by major asset category

e. Amounts of vested benefit obligation owed to retirees and others

f. Change in the projected benefit obligation that would result from a one-percentage-point change in (1) the assumed discount rate and (2) the assumed rate of compensation increase

g. Change in the service cost and interest cost components of net periodic pension cost that would result from a one-percentage-point change in (1) the assumed discount rate and (2) the assumed rate of compensation increase

Settlements and Curtailments

39.502   If a gain or loss has been recognized as a result of the settlement or curtailment of a defined benefit plan or of termination benefits, the following should be disclosed: (SFAS 88, par. 17)

a. A description of the nature of the event(s)

b. The amount of gain or loss recognized

39.503   If a gain or loss from a settlement or curtailment has not been recognized in the current fiscal year and the employer's balance sheet or income statement would have been materially different had it been recognized, appropriate disclosures should be made.

DEFINED CONTRIBUTION PLANS

39.504   An employer that sponsors a defined contribution plan should disclose the following items separately from disclosures about its defined benefit pension plan: (SFAS 87, par. 65)

a. A description of the plan(s) including employee groups covered, the basis for determining contributions, and the nature and effect of significant matters affecting comparability of information for all periods presented

b. The amount of pension cost recognized during the period

MULTIEMPLOYER PLANS

39.505   For multiemployer plans, the following should be disclosed separately from the disclosures made for a single-employer plan: (SFAS 87, par. 69)

a. A description of the multiemployer plan(s) including the employee groups covered, the type of benefits provided (defined benefit or defined contribution), and the nature and effect of significant matters affecting comparability of information for all periods presented

b. The amount of pension cost recognized during the period

AUTHORITATIVE LITERATURE AND RELATED TOPICS

AUTHORITATIVE LITERATURE

APB Opinion No. 16, *Business Combinations*
SFAS No. 87, *Employers' Accounting for Pensions*
SFAS No. 88, *Employers' Accounting for Settlements and Curtailments of Defined Benefit Pension Plans and for Termination Benefits*
SFAS No. 106, *Employers' Accounting for Postretirement Benefits Other Than Pensions*

RELATED PRONOUNCEMENTS

AICPA Industry Audit and Accounting Guide, *Audits of Employee Benefit Plans*
SOP 92-6, *Accounting and Reporting by Health and Welfare Benefit Plans*
SOP 94-4, *Reporting of Investment Contracts Held by Health and Welfare Benefit Plans and Defined-Contribution Pension Plans*
EITF Issue No. 84-44, *Partial Termination of a Defined Benefit Pension Plan*
EITF Issue No. 86-27, *Measurement of Excess Contributions to a Defined Contribution Plan or Employee Stock Ownership Plan*
EITF Issue No. 87-13, *Amortization of Prior Service Cost for a Defined Benefit Plan When There Is a History of Plan Amendments*
EITF Issue No. 88-1, *Determination of Vested Benefit Obligation for a Defined Benefit Pension Plan*
EITF Issue No. 88-23, *Lump-Sum Payments under Union Contracts*
EITF Issue No. 90-3, *Accounting for Employers' Obligations for Future Contributions to a Multiemployer Pension Plan*
EITF Issue No. 91-7, *Accounting for Pension Benefits Paid by Employers after Insurance Companies Fail to Provide Annuity Benefits*
EITF Issue No. 96-5, *Recognition of Liabilities for Contractual Termination Benefits or Changing Benefit Plan Assumptions in Anticipation of a Business Combination*

Practice Bulletin 12, *Reporting Separate Investment Fund Option Information of Defined-Contribution Pension Plans*

FASB Implementation Guide, *A Guide to Implementation for Statement 87, Employers' Accounting for Pensions*

FASB Implementation Guide, *A Guide to Implementation for Statement 88, Employers' Accounting for Settlements and Curtailments of Defined Benefit Pension Plans and for Termination Benefits*

SOP 93-6, *Employers' Accounting for Employee Stock Ownership Plans*

RELATED TOPICS

POSTEMPLOYMENT BENEFITS

Table of Contents

POSTEMPLOYMENT BENEFITS

OVERVIEW

40.100   Postemployment benefits should be accrued if—

a. they relate to services already performed;

b. they vest or accumulate;

c. it is probable they will be paid; and

d. their amount is reasonably estimable.

Postemployment benefits that do not meet all of the preceding criteria should be accounted for as contingencies.

ACCOUNTING REQUIREMENTS

40.200   Companies often provide benefits to former or inactive employees, their beneficiaries, and covered dependents after employment but before retirement. Such postemployment benefits include cash or other consideration paid as a result of disability, layoff, death, or other specified events. The benefits frequently are paid immediately when the employee terminates employment; however, they may be paid over a specified period of time. (SFAS 112, par. 4)

Practical Consideration. Several chapters of this *Guide* discuss accounting for postemployment benefits. The guidance in this chapter does not apply to postemployment benefits covered by other chapters of this *Guide*. Consequently, it does not apply to—

- postemployment benefits provided through a pension or post-retirement benefit plan (Chapters 39 and 41);

- the individual deferred compensation arrangements addressed in Chapter 17;

40.200

> **Practical Consideration (Continued).**
>
> - the termination benefits covered in Chapters 39 and 41;
>
> - termination benefits incurred in a restructuring (Chapter 23); or
>
> - stock compensation plans (Chapter 50).

40.201   An employer should accrue a liability for postemployment benefits if all of the following conditions are met: (SFAS 112, par. 6)

   a. The employee's right to the benefits is attributable to services he or she already has performed.

   b. The employee's right to be paid postemployment benefits vests or accumulates.

   c. It is probable the benefits will be paid.

   d. The amount that will be paid is reasonably estimable.

40.202   Postemployment benefits that do not meet the preceding criteria should be accounted for as contingencies. (SFAS 112, par. 6) That is, they should be—

   a. accrued if (1) information available prior to issuing the financial statements indicates it is probable a liability has been incurred at the balance sheet date and (2) the amount of the liability can be reasonably estimated.

   b. disclosed, but not accrued, if (1) it is probable a liability exists but the amount of the liability cannot be reasonably estimated or (2) it is reasonably possible (but not probable) a liability exists.

Chapter 10 discusses accounting for contingencies in greater detail.

40.203   Authoritative literature does not specifically address how to measure the postemployment benefit obligation. It does state, however, that employers may refer to the guidance on measuring pension obligations (Chapter 39) and obligations for postretirement benefits other than pensions (Chapter 41) to the extent similar issues apply to the postemployment benefit plan. (SFAS 112, par. 23)

DISCLOSURE REQUIREMENTS

40.500   If a liability for postemployment benefits is not accrued only because the amount cannot be reasonably estimated, that fact should be disclosed. (SFAS 112, par. 7)

AUTHORITATIVE LITERATURE AND RELATED TOPICS

AUTHORITATIVE LITERATURE

SFAS No. 112, *Employers' Accounting for Postemployment Benefits*

RELATED PRONOUNCEMENTS

SFAS No. 106, *Employers' Accounting for Postretirement Benefits Other Than Pensions*

EITF Issue No. 92-12, *Accounting for OPEB Costs by Rate-Regulated Enterprises*

RELATED TOPICS

Chapter 10—Contingencies
Chapter 17—Deferred Compensation Arrangements
Chapter 39—Pension Plans: Accounting by Employers
Chapter 41—Postretirement Benefits Other Than Pensions

POSTRETIREMENT BENEFITS OTHER THAN PENSIONS

Table of Contents

POSTRETIREMENT BENEFITS OTHER THAN PENSIONS

Table of Contents (Continued)

POSTRETIREMENT BENEFITS OTHER THAN PENSIONS

OVERVIEW

41.100   Postretirement benefit plans provide a variety of health and welfare benefits to participants upon the occurrence of a covered event, such as retirement, death, disability, or termination of employment. A plan may be broadly classified as either a defined benefit plan or a defined contribution plan. As the names imply, a plan's classification depends on whether it specifies benefit payments or contribution amounts. That is, a defined benefit plan provides specified benefits to participants while a defined contribution plan provides an account for each participant and describes how contributions to the accounts are determined.

DEFINED BENEFIT PLANS

41.101   The employer's primary objectives when accounting for a defined benefit plan are to (a) charge postretirement benefit costs to operations over the period employee services are rendered and (b) charge liabilities and credit assets when retirement benefits are paid. However, to reduce the volatility of costs in their financial statements, employers may amortize certain costs to operations in future periods rather than recognize them immediately. Those costs are actuarial gains and losses, the accumulated postretirement benefit asset or obligation at the time SFAS No. 106, *Employers' Accounting for Postretirement Benefits Other Than Pensions,* was adopted, and benefits related to participants' services prior to a plan's adoption or amendment. Consequently, the annual cost of a defined benefit plan consists of the following components:

    a. Service cost

    b. Interest cost on the plan's obligation to provide benefits

    c. Actual return on plan assets

    d. Amortization of unrecognized prior service cost

    e. Amortization of unrecognized gains and losses

    f. Amortization of the unrecognized net asset or obligation for the plan at the time SFAS No. 106 was first adopted

41.102   Employers may be required to record unrecognized gains and losses, prior service costs, and the unrecognized net asset or obligation that arose when SFAS No. 106 was adopted if a plan settlement or curtailment occurs. A plan settlement eliminates the employer's responsibility for its postretirement benefit obligation. Examples of settlements include purchasing insurance contracts covering benefits accrued during the period or making lump-sum distributions to participants in exchange for their rights to receive future benefits. A plan curtailment occurs when a portion of future postretirement benefits are reduced for current participants (for example, by suspending the plan).

41.103   Some employers pay benefits to employees when employment is terminated. Termination benefits that are considered special termination benefits should be accrued when the amount of benefits can be reasonably estimated and the employee accepts the employer's offer to provide the benefits. Those that are considered contractual benefits should be accrued (a) when it is probable that employees will be entitled to benefits and (b) the amount of benefits can be reasonably estimated.

DEFINED CONTRIBUTION PLANS

41.104   Under a defined contribution plan, the employer and/or participants contribute amounts to accounts maintained by the plan for each participant. A participant receives benefits equal to (a) the amounts contributed to his or her account, (b) income earned on the investment of those amounts, and (c) forfeitures of amounts contributed to the accounts of other participants who terminated employment before vesting in the plan. The postretirement benefit expense that should be recorded by the employer is the contribution that applies for the period, accounted for on the accrual basis.

ACCOUNTING REQUIREMENTS

TYPES OF PLANS

41.200   A postretirement benefit plan is a mutually understood arrangement between an employer and its employees that provides employees specified benefits after retirement in exchange for services over a specified time period, upon reaching a specified age, or both. (SFAS 106, par. 7) Most commonly, postretirement benefit plans provide health care and life insurance benefits to retirees, their beneficiaries, and covered dependents. However, they may provide other benefits as well, such as tuition assistance, day care, legal services, or housing subsidies. The following are the two basic types of postretirement benefit plans:

41.102

a. *Defined benefit plans.* A defined benefit plan provides specified benefits stated in terms of (a) monetary amounts (for example, $100,000 of life insurance) or (b) benefit coverage (for example, 80% of the cost of certain medical procedures). (SFAS 106, par. 16) The benefits provided are based on a benefit formula that considers a variety of factors including the participant's age, years of service, and compensation. (SFAS 106, par. 18)

b. *Defined contribution plans.* A defined contribution plan provides an individual account for each participant and specifies how contributions to the individual's account are to be determined. Unlike defined benefit plans, defined contribution plans do not define specific benefit amounts that participants are to receive. Instead, they provide benefits based solely on (a) the amount contributed to a participant's account, (b) the returns earned on the investment of those contributions, and (c) forfeitures of other participants' benefits that may be allocated to the participant's account. For example, an employer may establish an individual postretirement health care plan for each employee. After retirement, an employee may use the amount in his or her account to purchase health insurance. (SFAS 106, par. 104)

41.201   Determining whether a plan is a defined contribution or defined benefit plan is important because different measurement and disclosure requirements apply. In some cases, a plan may possess many of the characteristics of a defined contribution plan but its substance is to provide a defined benefit (for example, a target benefit plan). In such cases, the substance of the plan, not its form, governs the accounting treatment. (SFAS 106, paras. 23 and 107)

Practical Consideration. Generally, accounting for postretirement benefits other than pensions follows the concepts discussed in Chapter 39 on accounting for pensions. There are some differences in accounting for defined benefit plans, however. The following is a brief summary of the differences:

Practical Consideration (Continued).

a. *Unrecognized prior service cost.* Unrecognized prior service cost relates to service rendered by plan participants prior to either the adoption of the plan or amendment of an existing plan. When accounting for a pension plan, the plan document should determine whether future benefits will consider employee services rendered prior to adoption or amendment of the plan. When accounting for postretirement benefits other than pensions, however, future benefits should always consider employee services rendered prior to adoption or amendment of the plan unless the plan document specifically states that the new benefits will be provided only in exchange for future services.

b. *Amortization of net plan asset or liability.* The pension plan asset or liability should be computed as of the date SFAS No. 87, *Employers' Accounting for Pensions,* is adopted. Similarly, the postretirement benefit plan asset or liability should be computed as of the date SFAS No. 106, *Employers' Accounting for Postretirement Benefits Other Than Pensions,* is adopted. In each case, the plan asset or liability generally should be amortized over the remaining service period of active plan participants. As an alternative, however, employers may choose to recognize the *postretirement benefit* plan asset or liability in operations immediately upon adopting SFAS No. 106 as a cumulative effect adjustment.

c. *Unfunded accumulated benefit obligation.* Employers should recognize an additional *pension* liability if (1) the fair value of plan assets is less than the accumulated benefit obligation and (2) any liability already recognized is less than the unfunded accumulated benefit obligation. Employers are not required to recognize a minimum liability for postretirement benefits other than pensions, however.

The following paragraphs discuss accounting for postretirement benefits other than pensions in further detail.

ACCOUNTING FOR DEFINED BENEFIT POSTRETIREMENT PLANS

Determining the Net Periodic Postretirement Benefit Cost and Obligation

41.202   The cost of providing postretirement benefits should be charged to operations during the period related employee services are rendered. That is accomplished through a combination of current accruals and amortization of prior results. Thus, the annual cost of a postretirement benefit plan consists of the following components: (SFAS 106, paras. 45–46)

Related primarily to employee service rendered during the period:

a. Service cost

b. Interest cost

c. Actual return on plan assets

Amortization of prior period results:

d. Amortization of unrecognized prior service cost

e. Amortization of unrecognized gains and losses

f. Amortization of the unrecognized net asset or net obligation for the plan at the time SFAS No. 106, *Employers' Accounting for Postretirement Benefits Other Than Pensions,* was first adopted

Retrospective adjustments

Practical Consideration. Usually, an actuary performs the complex calculations needed to determine an employer's net periodic postretirement benefit cost and obligation. However, the employer is responsible for making assumptions about future events that affect net periodic cost. Those assumptions include the following:

- *Discount rates* should be based on comparable interest rates available to settle the plan's benefit obligation. Consequently, the rates should consider the length of time remaining until individual benefit payment dates. Assumed discount rates may be determined by considering annuity contract rates used by insurance companies or by referring to current rates of return on high-quality, fixed-income investments whose cash flows match the timing and amount of expected benefit payments (for example, long-term bond yields). Assumed discount rates should be reevaluated each time the plan's benefit obligation is measured.

Practical Consideration (Continued).

- *The expected long-term rate of return on plan assets* generally should be based on the expected return of the plan's portfolio of investments. Consideration should also be given to the actual rates of return currently earned in the plan's investment portfolio and the rates expected to be earned when portfolio earnings are reinvested.

- *Future compensation levels* should be considered when calculating the service cost component of net periodic postretirement benefit cost and the accumulated benefit obligation to the extent the plan's benefit formula considers future compensation levels. The estimate of future compensation should consider, for example, seniority, promotions, productivity, and the level of individual employees involved. Compensation assumptions also should be consistent with respect to future economic conditions, for example, estimated future rates of inflation.

- *The assumed per capita claims cost* is the annual cost per participant to provide the benefits. Since benefits frequently are paid from retirement until death, the per capita claims cost is based, in part, on the life expectancy of the participant. In addition, it may be appropriate to consider factors such as sex, geographic location, information about current claims, or the experience of other employers when determining per capita claims cost.

- *Health care cost trend rates* represent the expected change in the cost of providing current postretirement health care benefits. When developing assumptions about health care cost trend rates, past or current trends that consider the effects of inflation, expected changes in health care utilization or delivery, technological advances, and changes in participants' health should be considered.

- *Medical coverage to be paid by others* includes claims covered by government programs, such as Medicaid, or other plans, such as a spouse's health plan. Assumptions about claims covered by others should be based on currently enacted law or the other health care provider's plan. Changes in laws or other health care plans that are expected, but not enacted, should not be anticipated.

41.203   Service Cost. Service cost relates only to employee service rendered during the year and is computed as the actuarial present value of benefits attributed by the postretirement benefit formula to employee service during the period. It requires assumptions about the attrition of present participants and future changes in their compensation and ignores participants that may be added to the plan in the future. (SFAS 106, par. 47)

41.204   Generally, an equal amount of a participant's expected postretirement benefit obligation should be attributed to each year in the attribution period. The attribution period typically begins on the employee's date of hire and ends when the employee has performed all of the services necessary to become fully eligible for benefits under the plan. In some cases, however, a plan's benefit formula may (a) require a participant to work for a specified period before benefits accrue or (b) attribute a disproportionate share of the expected benefit obligation to the participant's early years of service. In such cases, the estimated postretirement benefit obligation should be attributed to years of service in accordance with the plan's benefit formula. (SFAS 106, paras. 43–44)

41.205   Service cost for the period should consider automatic benefit changes required by plan terms, such as cost-of-living increases, or that result from plan amendments already in effect. In addition, employers that have a history of providing plan benefits greater than those defined in writing should base their accounting on the "substantive commitment" and disclose those commitments in their financial statements. (SFAS 106, paras. 26 and 28)

41.206   **Interest Cost.** Interest cost reflects interest for the year on the plan's obligation to provide benefits. The information needed to compute interest cost is (a) the accumulated benefit obligation and (b) an assumed discount rate. The accumulated benefit obligation is the actuarial present value of benefits expected to be paid to current plan participants in the future. The accumulated benefit obligation requires assumptions about the attrition rates and future compensation levels for current participants but does not consider that additional employees will become plan participants in future years. As discussed in Paragraph 41.202, the discount rate is based on current market conditions and, therefore, may vary from year to year. (SFAS 106, par. 48)

41.207   **Actual Return on Plan Assets.** Actual return on plan assets generally represents the after tax effects of realized and unrealized investment gains and losses and any interest or dividends received. The actual return on plan assets is computed as the fair value of plan assets at the beginning of the year plus contributions during the year minus (a) benefits paid during the year, (b) the fair value of plan assets at the end of the year, and (c) the tax effects of those amounts (if the fund holding the plan assets is subject to income taxes). A net return on plan assets decreases postretirement benefit cost for the period. (SFAS 106, par. 49)

41.208 **Amortization of Unrecognized Prior Service Cost.** The cost of providing benefits related to services rendered before a plan was adopted or amended should be amortized over the remaining service lives of participants who are active at the date of the plan adoption or amendment. If most of the plan's participants are inactive, however, unrecognized prior service cost should be amortized over the expected remaining lives of the inactive participants. (SFAS 106, par. 52)

41.209 So long as it is applied consistently, any one of a variety of amortization methods may be used— even if the method selected amortizes unrecognized prior service cost more rapidly than other methods. For example, to reduce the complexity of the amortization calculations, it may be preferable to amortize unrecognized prior service cost over the average remaining service period of all active participants using the straight-line method. Also, if the period that benefits are expected to be realized from a retroactive plan amendment is shorter than the remaining future service lives of active participants, unrecognized prior service cost should be amortized over the future periods expected to benefit from the amendment. (SFAS 106, par. 53)

41.210 Plan amendments that decrease the cost of providing postretirement benefits also decrease the accumulated benefit obligation. Decreases in the accumulated benefit obligation should first be used to reduce any existing unrecognized prior service cost. The excess, if any, should be amortized on the same basis as increases in unrecognized prior service cost (that is, amortized over the remaining service period of employees expected to receive benefits). (SFAS 106, par. 55)

Practical Consideration. The accounting treatment of unrecognized prior service costs applies to plan adoptions or amendments occurring after SFAS No. 106 was adopted. As discussed in Paragraph 41.214, unrecognized prior service costs at the date SFAS No. 106 was adopted should be charged (a) as a cumulative effect adjustment to earnings in the year the Statement was adopted or (b) to future earnings through amortization of the net plan asset or liability.

41.211 **Gains and Losses.** Gains and losses arise when the following occur: (SFAS 106, par. 56–58)

   a. *Assumptions used to compute the accumulated benefit obliga- tion change.* The gain or loss is the difference between the pro- jected value of the year-end postretirement benefit obligation based on beginning-of-year assumptions and the actual year- end obligation based on end-of-year assumptions.

41.208

b. *Actual results differ from the expected return on plan assets.* The gain or loss is the difference between the actual and expected return on plan assets. The following discuss how the actual and expected returns on plan assets are determined:

(1) As discussed in Paragraph 41.207, the actual return on plan assets is computed as the difference between the fair value of plan assets at the beginning and end of the period, adjusted for contributions and benefit payments made during the period. Generally, fair value is the amount that would be paid between a willing buyer and a willing seller who are under no obligation to buy or sell.

(2) The expected return on plan assets is computed by multiplying the plan's expected long-term rate of return by the beginning of the year market-related value of plan assets. The market-related value of plan assets is determined by using either the fair value of plan assets or by computing a value that recognizes changes in the fair value of plan assets systematically over a period not to exceed five years. For example, rather than using fair value, a company may compute market-related value by recognizing changes in value over five years. Assuming market-related value at the beginning of the year is $1,200 and net asset gains and losses over the past five years are $580, the market-related value of plan assets at the end of the year would be computed as follows: (Expected long-term rate of return and amounts for contributions and benefit payments are assumed.)

Market-related value at beginning of year	$ 1,200
Expected return on assets for the year ($1,200 × 10% expected long-term rate of return)	120
Net gain (loss) to be included in market-related value ($580 ÷ 5 years)	116
Employer contributions	400
Benefit payments	(200)
Market-related value at end of year	$ 1,636

Market-related value may be computed differently for each class of plan assets; however, the method of computing market-related value for each class should be used consistently from year to year. For example, an employer may use the fair value for equity securities and a five-year moving average for bonds and other debt securities.

Practical Consideration. When accounting for gains and losses, no distinction is made between the sources of gains and losses. Unrecognized gains and losses from all sources are netted.

41.212   Generally, the gains and losses discussed in the preceding paragraph (frequently referred to as actuarial gains and losses) are not required to be included in postretirement benefit expense in the period they arise. Instead, they may be deferred until amortization is required in a future year. Amortization is required in any year in which the beginning of the year unrecognized net gain or loss exceeds the greater of (a) 10% of the accumulated benefit obligation or (b) the market-related value of plan assets. In such years, the amount of net gain or loss that must be included in net postretirement benefit cost is the excess net gain or loss (i.e., amount greater than 10% of accumulated benefit obligation or market-related value) divided by the average remaining service lives of active employees (or, if substantially all plan participants are inactive, the average remaining lives of inactive participants). (SFAS 106, par. 59)

Practical Consideration. Net asset gains and losses not yet included in market-related value need not be amortized to postretirement benefit expense. Thus, in the example in Paragraph 41.211, the net gain of $464 not included in market-related value (total net gain of $580 minus $116 included in market-related value) would not be included in the amount subject to amortization in the current year.

41.213   An alternative amortization method may be used so long as it (a) reduces the unamortized net gain or loss balance by an amount in excess of that resulting from the minimum amortization method, (b) is applied similarly to both gains and losses, (c) is systematic and used consistently, and (d) is disclosed in the financial statements. (SFAS 106, par. 60)

41.214   **Amortization of Unrecognized Net Obligation or Asset.** Authoritative literature gives an employer the option of either (a) immediately recognizing the difference between the fair value of plan assets and the accumulated benefit obligation as of the date SFAS No. 106 was adopted as a cumulative effect adjustment or (b) amortizing the difference to earnings over future years. (SFAS 106, par. 110) If amortized, the difference should be charged or credited to postretirement benefit cost and credited or charged to accrued postretirement benefit cost (or to prepaid postretirement benefit cost if there is no accrual). The difference should be amortized using the straight-line method, and the amortization period should be the average remaining service period of participants that were employed when SFAS No. 106 was adopted, except in the following circumstances:

a. An employer may amortize the difference over 20 years if the remaining service period of plan participants is less than 20 years.

b. The difference should be amortized over the expected remaining lives of plan participants if substantially all of the participants were not employed when SFAS No. 106 was adopted.

c. Amortization of the difference should be accelerated if cumulative benefit payments after adopting SFAS No. 106 exceed cumulative postretirement benefit costs accrued after adopting SFAS No. 106. The additional amount that should be amortized is the excess cumulative benefit payments over cumulative benefit costs. When applying that requirement, cumulative benefit payments after adopting SFAS No. 106 should be reduced by any plan assets or any recognized postretirement benefit obligation at the date the Statement was adopted. In addition, payments made as part of a settlement should be included in the amount of cumulative benefits paid after adopting the Statement. (SFAS 106, par. 112)

41.215   **Retrospective Adjustments.** An employer may temporarily change a plan's cost-sharing provisions to increase or decrease its share of the benefit costs incurred in current or past periods. For example, a postretirement health-care plan may require retirees to pay, in the subsequent year, any shortfalls that result when current year benefit payments exceed current year employer cost and retiree contributions. If the shortfall in a single year is large, however, the employer may decide to deviate from the plan and absorb the shortfall so that retiree contributions do not increase significantly. When an employer temporarily changes a plan's cost-sharing provisions, the resulting gain or loss should be recognized immediately. (SFAS 106, par. 61)

Practical Consideration. An employer's continued deviation from the plan (for example, if it continues to absorb shortfalls) suggests that the plan has been, in substance, amended. In such cases, future deviations should be accounted for as plan amendments as discussed in Paragraphs 41.208–.210.

Measuring Plan Assets

41.216   Plan assets consist of stocks, bonds, and other investments that have been segregated (usually in a trust) and restricted to the payment of postretirement benefits. Assets not restricted solely to provide postretirement benefits are not plan assets, even though the employer may intend to use them to satisfy its postretirement benefit obligation. Furthermore, plan assets do not include contributions that have been accrued but not paid. (SFAS 106, paras. 63–64)

41.217   For disclosure purposes, plan investments should be measured at their fair values. Fair value is the amount that could be received in a sale between a willing buyer and willing seller (other than in a forced sale or liquidation). Generally, it should be based on market prices if the investment is traded in an active market. If no active market for the investment exists, market prices of similar investments that are sold in an active market may be used. If no market price is available, fair value may be determined based on the investment's discounted cash flows. (SFAS 106, par. 65)

41.218   Plan assets used in plan operations, such as buildings or equipment, should be measured at cost less accumulated depreciation or amortization. (SFAS 106, par. 66)

41.219   **Insurance Contracts.** Employers who sponsor defined benefit plans sometimes enter into irrevocable contracts with insurance companies to cover benefit obligations. The contracts transfer the risk of providing benefits from the employer and plan to the insurance company. Benefits covered by insurance contracts are not included in the accumulated postretirement benefit obligation. In addition, except for the cost of participation rights in a participating insurance contract (see Paragraph 41.220), the insurance contracts are not included in plan assets. For purposes of applying the accounting requirements for postretirement benefit plans, the definition of an insurance contract is not met if there is a reasonable doubt that the insurer will meet its obligation or if the contract is with a captive insurance company (that is, one that does business primarily with the employer and its related parties). (SFAS 106, par. 67)

> **Practical Consideration.** Contracts with insurance companies that do not legally obligate the insurer to pay the specified benefits are not considered insurance contracts. Such contracts should be accounted for as investments.

41.220   Insurance contracts may be participating contracts. In a participating contract, the insurer pays to the purchaser a portion of the income it receives from investing the premiums. Usually, the payments are in the form of dividends and are used to reduce the plan's costs. Participating contracts generally cost more than nonparticipating contracts. The cost difference relates to the participation right and should be recorded as a plan asset. In subsequent years, the participation right should be measured at fair value. If fair value is not reasonably estimable, the asset should be recorded at cost and amortized over the dividend period under the contract. (SFAS 106, paras. 68–69)

41.221   To the extent insurance contracts are purchased during the period to cover benefits attributed to service in the current period, the insurance premium is the postretirement benefit cost that should be charged to earnings for the period. If the insurance contracts cover only a portion of the benefit obligation, however, the employer still has a responsibility to fund the uncovered obligation. In that case, the uncovered obligation would be accounted for following the guidance in the preceding paragraphs of this chapter. (SFAS 106, par. 70)

41.222   **Measurement Date.** Plan assets and benefit obligations generally should be measured as of the employer's financial statement date or, if used consistently from year to year, as of a date not more than three months prior to the date of the financial statements. Thus, for example, a calendar-year company using a year-end measurement date would determine its net periodic benefit cost for the period beginning each January 1 and ending each December 31. The company may measure the plan's assets and its benefit obligation as of September 30, however, if that date is used consistently from year to year. In that case, the company would determine net periodic benefit cost for the period beginning October 1 of the prior calendar year to September 30 of the current calendar year. (SFAS 106, par. 72)

Practical Consideration. Companies that must issue financial statements soon after year-end often measure postretirement benefit obligations and plan assets as of a date prior to year-end. Doing so allows them to obtain the necessary information before financial statements must be issued.

Employers with More Than One Defined Benefit Postretirement Plan

41.223   Generally, an employer with more than one defined benefit postretirement plan should measure each plan separately. Postretirement health care plans may be aggregated and measured as one plan, however, if they meet the following criteria:

a. The plans are unfunded (i.e., they have no assets).

b. The plans provide different benefits to the same group of employees or the same benefits to different groups of employees.

Similarly, an employer may separately aggregate plans that provide postretirement benefits other than health care benefits if they meet the preceding criteria. (SFAS 106, paras. 75–76)

41.224   Disclosures for all of an employer's postretirement defined benefit plans may be aggregated, with the following exceptions: (SFAS 106, paras. 77–78)

    a. Certain disclosures about plans whose accumulated benefit obligations exceed the fair value of plan assets may not be aggregated with those of plans whose assets exceed the accumulated benefit obligations. (See Paragraph 41.500, item c.)

    b. Disclosures about postretirement health-care benefit plans should not be aggregated with those of plans that provide other postretirement welfare benefits unless the accumulated benefit obligation of the welfare benefit plans is insignificant to the accumulated postretirement benefit obligation of all of the plans.

    c. Disclosures for plans located outside the U.S. should not be aggregated with those for U.S. plans unless the accumulated postretirement benefit obligation of the foreign plans is insignificant to the accumulated postretirement benefit obligation of all of the plans.

Business Combinations

41.225   When a defined benefit plan is acquired as part of a business combination accounted for under the purchase method, a liability should be recorded for any accumulated benefit obligation in excess of plan assets. Similarly, an excess of plan assets over the accumulated benefit obligation should be recorded as an asset. Recognizing a new postretirement benefit asset or liability at the date of purchase results in the elimination of the following:

    a. Unrecognized net gain or loss

    b. Unrecognized prior service cost

    c. Unrecognized net obligation or asset that existed when SFAS No. 106 was adopted

In subsequent years, the asset or liability recorded at the date of purchase is reduced by any differences between the acquiring company's net periodic benefit cost and contributed amounts. However, the asset or liability is only reduced to the extent that items a.–c. were used in determining plan contributions. (SFAS 106, paras. 86–88)

Settlements and Curtailments of Defined Benefit Postretirement Plans

41.226   As discussed in Paragraphs 41.208–.214, SFAS No. 106 allows for the delayed recognition of net gains and losses, prior service costs, and the net asset or obligation that arose when the Statement was adopted. However, all or part of those unrecognized amounts may become recognized in a postretirement benefit plan settlement or curtailment.

     a. A settlement essentially eliminates the plan's obligation for benefits. To be considered a settlement, SFAS No. 106 requires that the transaction:

         (1) be an irrevocable action;

         (2) relieve the company (or the plan) of primary responsibility for a benefit obligation; and

         (3) eliminate significant risks related to the obligation and the assets used to effect the settlement.

         Examples of settlements are purchasing long-term nonparticipating insurance contracts (see Paragraphs 41.219–.221) or making lump-sum cash payments to plan participants in exchange for their rights to receive specified benefits. (SFAS 106, par. 90)

     b. A curtailment generally prevents the postretirement benefit obligation from growing for future services of present employees. Examples of a curtailment are (1) terminating employee services earlier than expected, possibly as a result of closing a facility or discontinuing a segment and (2) terminating (or suspending) a plan. In both situations, the plan's obligation is not relieved, but generally will not increase. (SFAS 106, par. 96)

41.227   A settlement or curtailment may occur together or as separate transactions. For example, when the expected future years of service of certain employees are reduced due to a layoff but the plan continues to exist, a curtailment has occurred but not a settlement. If the employer's defined benefit postretirement plan is terminated without replacement, and settlement of the plan obligation occurs, a curtailment and settlement have resulted. Finally, when the employer settles all or a portion of its plan obligation and still provides defined benefits to employees for their future service, a settlement has taken place but not a curtailment. (SFAS 106, par. 100)

41.228   **Settlements.** Since plan settlements involve eliminating an obligation, a gain or loss should be recognized at the time of settlement. If the
employer settles the entire benefit obligation, the gain or loss can be viewed
as the balancing entry needed to record any plan assets reverting back to the
employer plus the adjustment needed to eliminate the prepaid asset or
accrued liability recorded as a result of applying SFAS No. 106. In such cases,
the maximum gain or loss on plan settlement should be recognized. That
amount is based on balances measured as of the settlement date and equals
the total of (a) any unrecognized net gain or loss (see Paragraphs 41.211–.213)
and (b) any unrecognized net asset remaining from the adoption of SFAS
No. 106. (See Paragraph 41.214.) ((SFAS 106, par. 93)

41.229   It is not uncommon for some, but not all, participants to withdraw from
a plan because of voluntary or involuntary termination of employment. Also,
some plans may purchase insurance contracts each year to cover the year's
benefit accruals. In such cases, gain or loss on settlement should be determined as follows:

  a. If only a portion of the benefit obligation is settled, the employer
     should recognize a pro rata portion of the maximum gain or loss.
     For example, if a settlement results in a 30% reduction of the
     accumulated benefit obligation, only 30% of the maximum gain
     or loss should be recognized. (SFAS 106, par. 93)

  b. If participating insurance contracts are purchased to settle the
     obligation, the maximum gain (but not loss) should be reduced
     by the cost of the participation right. (SFAS 106, par. 94)

  c. If the cost of all settlements in a year are less than or equal to the
     sum of the service cost and interest cost components of the year's
     net periodic postretirement benefit cost, gain or loss may be rec-
     ognized. (Gain or loss recognition is not required, however.)
     Once adopted, the accounting policy for such settlements
     should be used consistently.

     The cost of a settlement is the amount paid to relieve the
     employer of its obligation to provide benefit payments. For exam-
     ple, (1) the cost of a settlement paid in cash is the amount of cash
     paid to the employee, (2) the cost of a settlement made by pur-
     chasing a nonparticipating insurance contract is the cost of the
     contract, and (3) the cost of a settlement made by purchasing a
     participating insurance contract is the cost of the contract net of
     the amount paid for the participation right. (SFAS 106, par. 95)

> **Practical Consideration.** As discussed in Paragraph 41.219, purchasing an insurance contract does not relieve the employer of its postretirement benefit obligation, and thus does not constitute a settlement, if either of the following conditions are met:
>
> - The insurer is controlled by the employer.
>
> - There is a reasonable doubt that the insurer will not meet its obligations under the insurance contract.
>
> In addition, a participating insurance contract does not constitute a settlement if its terms are such that the employer remains subject to most of the risks connected with the benefit obligation. For example, if a participating insurance contract requires the purchaser to pay additional premiums if the insurer experiences investment losses, purchasing the insurance contract would not constitute a settlement.

41.230   **Curtailments.** A curtailment generally prevents the accumulated benefit obligation from growing for all or a portion of the plan's participants. It may eliminate coverage for certain participants, eliminate future defined benefit accruals (e.g., freezing the plan), or both. The following two components comprise the effects of a plan curtailment:

a. *Decrease in unrecognized prior service cost.* For purposes of applying SFAS No. 106 to curtailments, prior service cost includes any unrecognized net obligation remaining from adopting SFAS No. 106 as well as any unrecognized prior service cost. Such costs should be written off in proportion to the reduction in the remaining future years of service at the date of the curtailment. For example, if a plan curtailment eliminates 30% of the estimated future years of service of active employees receiving prior service credit, the loss on curtailment related to prior service cost is 30% of the combined unrecognized prior service cost and remaining unrecognized net asset or obligation. Note that the amount of loss recognized on the decrease in unrecognized prior service cost is not part of the gain or loss on plan curtailment (see item b. below) but it is included in the total effects of a plan curtailment. (SFAS 106, par. 97)

b. *Curtailment gain or loss.* Gains and losses should be recognized for changes in the accumulated benefit obligation that result from curtailments. If a curtailment causes a plan's accumulated benefit obligation to decrease (for example, because the effects of future salary increases are eliminated), a gain would result.

Conversely, a loss results if a curtailment causes the accumulated benefit obligation to increase (for example, because a plan's benefit formula creates additional benefits for employees who retire early). To compute a curtailment gain or loss, the employer first should determine the decrease or increase in the accumulated benefit obligation resulting from the curtailment (excluding increases arising from termination benefits). The employer then should compare that amount to the total of any unrecognized net gain or loss plus any net asset or obligation remaining from adopting SFAS No. 106.

(1) If the change in the accumulated benefit obligation is a decrease (gain) and an unrecognized net loss exists, a curtailment gain exists to the extent the decrease in the accumulated benefit obligation exceeds the unrecognized net loss.

(2) If the change in the accumulated benefit obligation is a decrease (gain) and there is no unrecognized net loss, a curtailment gain exists equal to the entire decrease in the accumulated benefit obligation.

(3) If the change in the accumulated benefit obligation is an increase (loss) and an unrecognized net gain exists, a curtailment loss exists to the extent the increase in the accumulated benefit obligation exceeds the unrecognized net gain.

(4) If the change in the accumulated benefit obligation is an increase (loss) and there is no unrecognized net gain, a curtailment loss exists equal to the entire increase in the accumulated benefit obligation. (SFAS 106, par. 98)

41.231   If the total effect of a plan curtailment (that is, the sum of items a. and b. in the preceding paragraph) results in a loss, the loss should be recognized when it is probable that the curtailment will occur and the effects of the curtailment can be reasonably estimated. If the total effect of a curtailment results in a gain, the gain should be recognized when the affected employees terminate or when the employer adopts the plan suspension or amendment. (SFAS 106, par. 99)

> **Practical Consideration.** Settlement or curtailment gains and losses that are recognized and that relate to the disposal of a business segment should be reported as part of the employer's discontinued operations. Chapter 23 of this *Guide* discusses accounting for discontinued operations.

Termination Benefits

41.232   Employers sometimes provide benefits to employees when employment is terminated. The date on which termination benefits should be accrued depends on whether the benefits are special or contractual termination benefits. (SFAS 106, par. 101)

- *Special termination benefits.* Termination benefits that are offered for only a short period of time are referred to as "special termination benefits." Special termination benefits should be accrued when an employee accepts the employer's offer and the amount of benefits can be reasonably estimated.

- *Contractual termination benefits.* As its name implies, contractual termination benefits are those required by the terms of a separate agreement or the terms of an existing employee benefit plan. Contractual termination benefits are provided only as the result of a specified event. Examples of such events include the closing of a manufacturing plant or the early retirement of employees. Recognition of contractual termination benefits occurs in the employer's financial statements when (a) it is probable that employees will be entitled to benefits and (b) the amount of benefits to be provided can be reasonably estimated.

> **Practical Consideration.** Termination benefits that are recognized and that relate to the disposal of a business segment should be reported as part of the employer's discontinued operations. Chapter 23 of this *Guide* discusses accounting for discontinued operations. The chapter also discusses accounting for termination benefits that are paid as part of a restructuring.

ACCOUNTING FOR DEFINED CONTRIBUTION POSTRETIREMENT PLANS

41.233   As discussed in Paragraph 41.200, a defined contribution plan does not specify a defined benefit amount. Instead, it specifies how contributions to the plan are determined. The plan provides a separate account for each participant, which is increased by employer and/or participant contributions, returns earned on the investment of those amounts, and forfeitures of amounts contributed to the accounts of other participants who terminated employment before vesting in the plan. Defined contribution plan benefits are equal to the value of each individual participant's account balance. (SFAS 106, par. 104)

41.234   The postretirement benefit cost to be recorded as expense normally should be the contribution that applies to that period accounted for on the accrual basis. Therefore, a company preparing financial statements for the year ended December 31, 19X5 would report postretirement benefit costs equal to the contribution allowable for 19X5, and the difference between that and contributions made to the plan during the year would be reflected in the company's December 31, 19X5 balance sheet either as a prepaid expense or an accrued liability. Required contributions for periods after the employee retires or terminates should be estimated and accrued during the employee's service period. (SFAS 106, par. 105)

MULTIEMPLOYER PLANS

41.235   A multiemployer plan is a plan to which two or more unrelated employers make contributions, usually as the result of a collective-bargaining agreement. In a multiemployer plan, the assets contributed by one participating employer may be used to provide benefits to employees of other participating employers. Therefore, the assets contributed by an employer are not segregated in a separate account or restricted to pay benefits only to that employer's employees. An example of a multiemployer plan is a union contract that requires companies with union employees to contribute to the union's plan. The plan, in turn, assumes the liability for paying benefits to participants. Employers who participate in multiemployer plans should record net postretirement benefit cost equal to the required contribution for the period. Any contributions due but not paid should be recognized as a liability. (SFAS 106, paras. 79–81)

41.236   An employer who withdraws from a multiemployer plan may have a liability for a portion of the plan's unfunded benefit obligation. If it is probable or reasonably possible that (a) the employer will withdraw under circumstances that would give rise to an obligation or (b) the employer's contribution to the plan will be increased during the remaining contract period to make up for a shortfall in the funds necessary to maintain the negotiated level of benefit coverage, SFAS No. 5, *Accounting for Contingencies,* should be followed. That is, if (a) it is probable that the employer will incur a liability and (b) the amount of the liability can be reasonably estimated, the employer should accrue the liability and record it as a loss. If one or both of those conditions are not met but it is reasonably possible that a liability has been incurred, the contingency should be disclosed. (SFAS 106, par. 83) In those circumstances, SOP 94-6, *Disclosure of Certain Significant Risks and Uncertainties,* also may require disclosures. (Chapter 10 discusses accounting for contingencies in greater detail.)

MULTIPLE-EMPLOYER PLANS

41.237　Multiple-employer plans are similar to multiemployer plans in that they consist of two or more unrelated employers. However, multiple-employer plans are in substance an aggregation of single-employer plans that are combined to allow assets to be pooled for investment purposes and to reduce plan administration costs. Multiple-employer plans often permit participating employers to have different benefit formulas, allowing an employer's contributions to be based on the formula it selects. Each employer participating in the plan is required to account for its respective interest in the plan as if that interest were a separate plan. An example of a multiple-employer plan is an association of car dealerships that contribute to a plan administered by the association. Each dealership retains the obligation for its own employees and assumes no responsibility for the obligation to employees of other dealerships. (SFAS 106, par. 84)

FOREIGN PLANS

41.238　The guidance in this chapter applies to postretirement benefit arrangements outside the U.S. that are similar in substance to U.S. plans. GAAP does not place any additional accounting requirements on such plans. (SFAS 106, par. 85)

DISCLOSURE REQUIREMENTS

DEFINED BENEFIT POSTRETIREMENT PLANS

41.500　The following disclosures are required for single-employer defined benefit plans: (The disclosures may be combined for all of a company's plans, or information about plans may be presented in groups, whichever is more useful. However, disclosures for postretirement health care benefit plans should not be combined with disclosures for plans that provide other welfare benefits unless the accumulated benefit obligation of the other welfare benefit plans is insignificant to the accumulated benefit obligation of all plans. In addition, disclosures for plans outside of the U.S. should not be combined with those for U.S. plans unless the accumulated benefit obligation of the foreign plans is insignificant to the accumulated benefit obligation of all plans.) (SFAS 106, par. 74)

    a. A description of the plan (including the nature of the plan, any modifications of the existing cost-sharing provisions that are encompassed by the plan, employee groups covered, and the existence and nature of any commitment to increase monetary benefits provided by the plan), type of benefits provided, funding policy, types of assets held by the plan, significant liabilities other than plan benefits (for example, unsettled security purchases, unsecured borrowings, or borrowings secured by investments in real estate), and the nature and effect of significant matters affecting comparability of information disclosed for all periods presented

b. The amount of net periodic postretirement benefit cost for the period showing separately the service cost component, interest cost component, actual return on plan assets for the period, amortization of the unrecognized obligation or asset at the time SFAS No. 106 was adopted, and the net total of the other components discussed in Paragraph 41.202

c. A schedule reconciling the plan's funded status with amounts in the employer's balance sheet. The reconciliation should separately show the following: (Plans with assets in excess of the accumulated benefit obligation should not be combined with plans that have accumulated benefit obligations that exceed plan assets.)

  (1) Fair value of plan assets

  (2) Accumulated postretirement benefit obligation, identifying separately the portion attributable to retirees, other fully eligible plan participants, and other active participants

  (3) Unrecognized prior service cost

  (4) Unrecognized net gain or loss, including asset gains and losses not yet included in market-related value

  (5) Remaining unrecognized net obligation or net asset existing at the date SFAS No. 106 was initially applied

  (6) Net postretirement benefit asset or liability recorded in the balance sheet (That amount is the total of the preceding five items.)

d. Assumed health care cost trend rate used to measure the expected cost of benefits covered under the plan for the next year and a general description of the direction and pattern of change in the assumed trend rates thereafter, together with the ultimate trend rate and when that rate is expected to be achieved

e. Weighted-average assumed discount rate and, if applicable, the rate of compensation increase used to measure the accumulated benefit obligation and the weighted-average long-term rate of return on plan assets (For plans whose income is segregated from the employer's investment income for tax purposes, the estimated income tax rate included in the weighted-average long-term rate of return on plan assets also should be disclosed.)

f. Effect of a one-percentage-point increase in the assumed health care cost trend rates for each future year on—

    (1) the combined total of the service and interest cost components of net periodic postretirement health care benefits and

    (2) the accumulated postretirement benefit obligation for health care benefits

g. Amounts and types of securities of related parties (including the employer) that are included in plan assets, and the approximate amount of future annual benefits of plan participants covered by insurance contracts issued by the employer and related parties

h. If applicable, the alternative amortization method used for unrecognized prior service cost and the alternative amortization method used to reflect the substantive commitment of the employer to pay more benefits than its existing postretirement benefit formula may indicate

i. If a gain or loss has been recognized as a result of the settlement or curtailment of a defined benefit postretirement plan or of termination benefits, a description of the nature of the event(s) and the amount of gain or loss recognized

j. Cost of providing special or contractual termination benefits recognized during the period and a description of the nature of the event(s)

DEFINED CONTRIBUTION PLANS

41.501   An employer that sponsors a defined contribution plan should disclose the following items separately from disclosures about its defined benefit plan: (SFAS 106, par. 106)

     a. A description of the plan(s) including employee groups covered, the basis for determining contributions, and the nature and effect of significant matters affecting comparability of information for all periods presented

     b. The amount of cost recognized during the period

MULTIEMPLOYER PLANS

41.502   For multiemployer plans, the following should be disclosed separately from the disclosures made for a single-employer plan: (SFAS 106, par. 82)

     a. A description of the multiemployer plan(s) including the employee groups covered, the type of benefits provided (defined benefit or defined contribution), and the nature and effect of significant matters affecting comparability of information for all periods presented

     b. The amount of postretirement benefit cost recognized during the period, if available (Otherwise, the amount of the aggregate required contribution for the period to the plan that provides health and welfare benefits to both active employees and retirees should be disclosed.)

AUTHORITATIVE LITERATURE AND RELATED TOPICS

AUTHORITATIVE LITERATURE

SFAS No. 106, *Employers' Accounting for Postretirement Benefits Other Than Pensions*

RELATED PRONOUNCEMENTS

EITF Issue No. 92-12, *Accounting for OPEB Costs by Rate-Regulated Enterprises*

EITF Issue No. 92-13, *Accounting for Estimated Payments in Connection with the Coal Industry Retiree Health Benefit Act of 1992*

41.501

EITF Issue No. 93-3, *Plan Assets under FASB Statement No. 106*
EITF Issue No. 96-5, *Recognition of Liabilities for Contractual Termination Bene-
fits or Changing Benefit Plan Assumptions in Anticipation of a Business
Combination*
FASB Implementation Guide, *A Guide to Implementation of Statement 106,
Employers' Accounting for Postretirement Benefits Other Than Pensions*

RELATED TOPICS

Chapter 3—Business Combinations
Chapter 10—Contingencies
Chapter 17—Deferred Compensation Arrangements
Chapter 23—Income Statement
Chapter 39—Pension Plans: Accounting by Employers

PRIOR PERIOD ADJUSTMENTS

Table of Contents

PRIOR PERIOD ADJUSTMENTS

OVERVIEW

42.100   Generally, all revenues, expenses, gains, and losses recognized during the current period should be included in current period net income—beginning retained earnings or previously issued financial statements of a prior period should not be adjusted. Sometimes, however, an error may be discovered in previously issued prior period financial statements. In such cases, an adjustment to correct the error, referred to as a "prior period adjustment," may be necessary. In addition, although not within the definition of prior period adjustment, previously issued prior period financial statements may also require restatement if there is a:

  a. settlement or adjustment of certain items related to a prior interim period of the current fiscal year;

  b. change in reporting entity; or

  c. change in certain accounting principles.

Changes in reporting entity and changes in accounting principles are discussed further in Chapter 1.

42.101   The balance of retained earnings at the beginning of the period should be restated for the effects of prior period adjustments. In addition, if the financial statements of the affected prior periods are presented, the components of net income, retained earnings, and other affected accounts of those prior periods should be restated. Certain disclosures about the adjustments and their effects on prior period net income are required in the year in which the adjustments are made.

ACCOUNTING REQUIREMENTS

PRIOR PERIOD ADJUSTMENTS

42.200   Profits and losses related to the correction of an error in previously issued prior period financial statements should *not* be included in current-period net income. (SFAS 109, par. 288) Instead, the prior period's financial statements (and beginning retained earnings of the current period) should be adjusted to correct the error. (APB 9, par. 18) An error may result from any of the following: (APB 20, par. 13)

- *Making a mathematical mistake*

- *Using an accounting principle that is not in conformity with GAAP* (This differs from a change in accounting principle, which is a change from one *acceptable* principle to another or a change from one *acceptable* method of applying a principle to another *acceptable* method. A change in accounting principle is not considered an error. Changes in accounting principles are discussed in Chapter 1.)

- *Applying a GAAP principle incorrectly*

- *Disregarding or misusing facts that existed at the date the financial statements were prepared* (This differs from a change in accounting estimate, which results from new information or developments that did not exist at the time the financial statements were prepared. Changes in accounting estimates are discussed in Chapter 1.)

> **Practical Consideration.** Although authoritative literature is not explicit, the authors believe that a change to GAAP from a comprehensive basis of accounting other than GAAP also should be accounted for as a correction of an error.

42.201   A prior period adjustment is made by adjusting the current period's beginning retained earnings balance for the error's effect on prior years' earnings. (SFAS 16, par. 16) In addition, balance sheets and income statements of the affected prior periods, if presented, should be restated to show the correct amounts. (APB 9, par. 18)

42.202   To illustrate correcting an error in prior period financial statements, assume that a company determined in 19X2 that its inventories were understated by $190,000 at the end of 19X1 and $120,000 at the beginning of 19X1. As a result, 19X1 income before taxes was understated by $70,000 ($190,000 − $120,000), and net income after taxes (assuming a 30% tax rate) was understated by $49,000 [$70,000 − ($70,000 × 30%)]. The company would adjust its 19X1 balance sheet and income statement to reflect the proper balances of inventory, retained earnings, cost of sales, and income tax expense, and present a statement of retained earnings similar to the following:

42.201

	19X2	19X1
RETAINED EARNINGS AT BEGINNING OF YEAR		
As previously reported	$1,711,000	$1,374,000
Adjustment for understatement of inventories (net of applicable income taxes of $57,000 in 19X2 and $36,000 in 19X1)	133,000	84,000
Balance at beginning of year, as restated	1,844,000	1,458,000
Net income (as restated in 19X1)	419,000	386,000
RETAINED EARNINGS AT END OF YEAR	$2,263,000	$1,844,000

ADJUSTMENT RELATED TO PRIOR INTERIM PERIODS OF THE CURRENT FISCAL YEAR

42.203   GAAP requires prior interim periods of the current fiscal year to be restated for the adjustment or settlement of (a) litigation or similar claims, (b) income taxes (SFAS 16, par. 13) (excluding the effects of retroactive tax legislation) (SFAS 109, par. 288), (c) renegotiation proceedings, or (d) utility revenues subject to a rate-making process. Prior interim periods may only be adjusted for those items, however, if all of the following criteria are met:

- The settlement is material to income from continuing operations of the current fiscal year or is material as measured by other appropriate criteria.

- All or part of the settlement is specifically identifiable with prior interim periods of the current fiscal year. (This criterion is not met solely because of incidental effects such as interest on a settlement.)

- The settlement amount could not be reasonably estimated prior to the current interim period but becomes reasonably estimable in the current interim period. (This criterion normally is met by the occurrence of an event whose effects can be currently measured, such as a final decision on a rate order.)

Prior interim periods should not be restated for normal or recurring corrections that result from the use of estimates. Consequently, prior interim periods should not be restated for adjustments to the provision for doubtful accounts even if the adjustments result from litigation or similar claims. (SFAS 16, par. 13)

42.204   When adjusting interim periods of the current fiscal year, any settlement related to prior fiscal years should be included in the first interim period's income. Otherwise, the interim periods of the current fiscal year that are affected by the adjustment should be restated. (SFAS 16, par. 14) For example, net income of the second and third quarters of the current fiscal year would be restated if a settlement occurring in the fourth quarter relates to the business activities of the second and third quarters.

DISCLOSURE REQUIREMENTS

42.500   The following disclosures are required when previously issued prior-period financial statements are adjusted:

Correction of an Error

   a. Nature of the error

   b. Effect of the error in the period of correction on income before extraordinary items and net income (and for public companies, related per share amounts) (APB 20, par. 37)

   c. For single period financial statements, the effect of restatement (gross and net of tax) on beginning retained earnings and on net income of the preceding year

   d. The amount of income tax applicable to each prior period adjustment (APB 9, par. 26)

   e. If a restated historical financial summary (commonly 5 or 10 years) is presented, disclosure of the restatements in the first summary published after the restatements (APB 9, par. 27)

   f. For comparative financial statements, the adjusted net income and its components, retained earnings balances, and other affected balances for all periods presented to reflect retroactive application of the prior period adjustment (APB 9, par. 18)

Adjustment Related to a Prior Interim Period of the Current Fiscal Year

a. The effect on income from continuing operations and net income (and for public companies, related per share amounts) for each prior interim period of the current fiscal year

b. Income from continuing operations and net income (and for public companies, related per share amounts) for each restated prior interim period (SFAS 16, par. 15)

Generally, financial statements of periods subsequent to the period in which the adjustment occurred need not repeat the disclosures. (APB 20, par. 37)

AUTHORITATIVE LITERATURE AND RELATED TOPICS

AUTHORITATIVE LITERATURE

APB Opinion No. 9, *Reporting the Results of Operations*
APB Opinion No. 20, *Accounting Changes*
SFAS No. 16, *Prior Period Adjustments*
SFAS No. 109, *Accounting for Income Taxes*
SFAS No. 111, *Rescission of FASB Statement No. 32 and Technical Corrections*

RELATED TOPICS

Chapter 1—Accounting Changes
Chapter 29—Interim Financial Reporting

PROPERTY TAXES

Table of Contents

PROPERTY TAXES

OVERVIEW

43.100   Property taxes should be accrued monthly during the fiscal period of the related taxing authority. Generally, they should be charged to operations as they are accrued. In some instances, however, it may be appropriate to capitalize real estate taxes related to property being developed for internal use or sale.

ACCOUNTING REQUIREMENTS

43.200   Real and personal property taxes are based on the assessed value of tangible or intangible property at a given date. Consequently, an entity generally is legally liable for property taxes on a specified date rather than over a period of time. Depending on a particular tax jurisdiction's laws or court decisions, that date may be one of the following: (ARB 43, Ch. 10A, par. 2)

- Assessment date

- Beginning of the taxing authority's fiscal year

- End of taxing authority's fiscal year

- Date on which the tax becomes a lien on the property

- Date the tax is levied

- Date(s) the tax is payable

- Date the tax becomes delinquent

- Tax period appearing on the tax bill

> **Practical Consideration.** Although the date that an entity becomes legally liable for property taxes varies with each jurisdiction, most taxing authorities contend that the taxes accrue on the date they are assessed.

43.201   Regardless of the date it becomes legally liable to pay property taxes, an entity usually knows it will be required to pay tax on property owned at the assessment date. In fact, most agreements between buyers and sellers of real estate include adjustments to reflect a pro rata portion of the property taxes that will be owed on the assessment date. Consequently, the most appropriate basis for recording real and personal property taxes is to accrue them monthly over the fiscal period of the taxing authority. Doing so results in the appropriate liability or prepayment at any closing date. (ARB 43, Ch. 10A, par. 14)

43.202   Property taxes should be accrued as a current liability regardless of whether the exact amount owed can be determined. Accrued amounts subject to substantial uncertainties should be labeled as estimated, however. (ARB 43, Ch. 10A, par. 16) If the liability has been estimated, it may be necessary to adjust the provision for a prior year's taxes when the actual amounts due are determined. In such cases, the adjustment is a change in estimate and, accordingly, should be made to current year earnings, either as an increase or decrease to the current year provision or as a separate line item in the income statement. (ARB 43, Ch. 10A, par. 19)

Practical Consideration. To illustrate accounting for property taxes, assume that on October 1, 19X5, the city assessed ABC Company (a calendar-year end company) $120,000 in property taxes. The taxes cover the city's fiscal year of October 1, 19X5 through September 30, 19X6. ABC Company should record the assessed taxes on October 1, 19X5 through the following entry:

Deferred property taxes	120,000	
Property taxes payable		120,000

ABC Company should recognize a portion of the property taxes in income each month through the following entry:

Property tax expense ($120,000 ÷ 12)	10,000	
Deferred property taxes		10,000

43.203   Sometimes, it may be appropriate to capitalize real estate taxes related to property being developed for the entity's own use or for sale. Generally, however, property taxes should be considered a cost of doing business and either (a) charged to operating expenses, (b) shown as a separate deduction from income, or (c) allocated to other accounts, such as factory overhead, rent income, and selling and general expenses. They should not be combined with taxes on income, however. (ARB 43, Ch. 10A, paras. 17–18)

> **Practical Consideration.** Authoritative literature states that it may be appropriate to capitalize real estate taxes on property being developed, but provides no further guidance. The authors believe real estate taxes should be capitalized during the period interest would be capitalized. That is, they should be capitalized while activities necessary to prepare the property for its intended use are in progress. Real estate taxes incurred after that period should be charged to operations. (Chapter 27 discusses the period during which interest should be capitalized in further detail.)

AUTHORITATIVE LITERATURE AND RELATED TOPICS

AUTHORITATIVE LITERATURE

ARB No. 43, *Restatement and Revision of Accounting Research Bulletins* (Chapter 10A—Real and Personal Property Taxes)

RELATED TOPICS

Chapter 12—Current Assets and Current Liabilities
Chapter 27—Interest: Capitalized

QUASI-REORGANIZATIONS

Table of Contents

QUASI-REORGANIZATIONS

OVERVIEW

44.100   In a quasi-reorganization, an entity reduces the carrying amounts of its balance sheet accounts to fair value. The adjustments should be charged to retained earnings (to the extent there is retained earnings) and then charged to additional paid-in capital. A debit balance in retained earnings also should be charged to additional paid-in capital so that, after the quasi-reorganization, no deficit remains in any capital account.

ACCOUNTING REQUIREMENTS

44.200   A corporation with unrealistic carrying values for its assets may undergo a quasi-reorganization (also referred to as a corporate readjustment) when it appears that operations are turning around and profits are likely. Doing so allows the corporation to restate its assets and eliminate the accumulated deficit, which in turn may (a) make it possible for the corporation to pay dividends sooner and (b) improve the appearance of the financial statements so that a loan is easier to obtain.

> **Practical Consideration.** The fresh start accounting of a quasi-reorganization is similar in many ways to the accounting followed by entities emerging from Chapter 12 bankruptcy. However, a quasi-reorganization should not be confused with a formal reorganization under the bankruptcy code. In a quasi-reorganization, a formal plan to restructure liabilities to creditors is not adopted. SOP 90-7, *Financial Reporting by Entities in Reorganization Under the Bankruptcy Code,* provides guidance on accounting for entities involved in bankruptcy proceedings.

ACCOUNTING FOR A QUASI-REORGANIZATION

44.201   A corporation electing to restate its accounts through a quasi-reorganization should clearly report its intentions to its stockholders and obtain their approval. (ARB 43, Ch. 7A, par. 3) After doing so, it should record the following adjustments to accomplish the readjustment:

   a. Assets should be written down to their fair values. If an asset's fair value is not readily determinable, a conservative estimate should be made. Material subsequent adjustments of the estimate should be charged or credited to additional paid-in capital rather than net income. (ARB 43, Ch. 7A, par. 4)

b. Unknown losses incurred prior to the readjustment should be estimated and accrued. If the amounts estimated subsequently are found to be excessive or insufficient, the differences should be charged or credited to additional paid-in capital rather than net income. (ARB 43, Ch. 7A, par. 5)

c. The adjustments in a. and b. should be charged first to retained earnings to the extent there is retained earnings, and then to additional paid-in capital. Any deficit in retained earnings also should be charged to additional paid-in capital. (ARB 43, Ch. 7A, par. 6)

d. A corporation with subsidiaries should carefully follow the preceding procedures so that a credit balance in consolidated retained earnings does not exist when losses and deficits have been charged to additional paid-in capital. If the adjustments and deficits must be charged to additional paid-in capital rather than the credit balance of a subsidiary's retained earnings, the parent company should consider its interest in the subsidiary's retained earnings to be capitalized by the quasi-reorganization just as its interest in the subsidiary's retained earnings at the acquisition date was capitalized. (ARB 43, Ch. 7A, paras. 6–7)

Practical Consideration. Because no deficit should exist in any capital accounts after a quasi-reorganization, capital accounts (other than capital stock) must be sufficient to absorb the adjustments and any deficit in retained earnings. To provide more capital for that purpose, many corporations reduce the par value of stock in conjunction with the reorganization and transfer the amounts in excess of the new par value to additional paid-in capital.

44.202   The effective date of a quasi-reorganization should be as near as possible to the date the stockholders approved the readjustment and ordinarily should be at the beginning of a fiscal year. (ARB 43, Ch. 7A, par. 8)

ACCOUNTING FOR OPERATIONS AFTER A QUASI-REORGANIZATION

44.203   After a quasi-reorganization, a corporation should account for its operations as if it were a new company. Consequently, transactions should be capitalized or charged to current period income or expense following generally accepted accounting principles. Retained earnings should be "dated" in the financial statements, however, to show that the account was readjusted in a quasi-reorganization. (ARB 43, Ch. 7A, par. 10) For example:

Retained earnings after December 31, 19X5　　　　455,000

The entity should continue to date retained earnings until the effective date of the quasi-reorganization no longer has significance. Generally, the date of a quasi-reorganization would not be significant after a period of 10 years. Exceptional circumstances might justify a period of less than 10 years, however. (ARB 46, paras. 1–2)

ACCOUNTING FOR A TAX BENEFIT

44.204　The tax benefits of deductible temporary differences and carryforwards should be reported as a direct addition to additional paid-in capital if they are recognized in subsequent years. An exception to that rule exists, however, if an entity has (a) previously adopted SFAS No. 96, *Accounting for Income Taxes,* and then (b) before adopting SFAS No. 109, *Accounting for Income Taxes,* affected a quasi-reorganization involving only the elimination of a deficit in retained earnings by a concurrent reduction in contributed capital. In such cases, an entity should include the tax benefits of the prior deductible differences and carryforwards in net income when they are subsequently realized and then reclassify them from retained earnings to contributed capital. (SFAS 109, par. 39)

DISCLOSURE REQUIREMENTS

44.500　As discussed in Paragraph 44.203, retained earnings should be dated for a period of 10 years to show that it was readjusted in a quasi-reorganization. In addition, an entity that recognizes the tax benefits of prior deductible temporary differences and carryforwards in net income rather than contributed capital should disclose—

　　a. the date of the quasi-reorganization;

　　b. the manner of reporting the tax benefits and that it differs from present accounting requirements for other entities; and

　　c. the effect of the tax benefits on income from continuing operations, income before extraordinary items, and net income (and for public companies, related per share amounts). (SFAS 109, par. 39)

Practical Consideration. Although not specifically required by authoritative literature, the authors believe the nature and a description of the quasi-reorganization should be adequately disclosed in the financial statements.

AUTHORITATIVE LITERATURE AND RELATED TOPICS

AUTHORITATIVE LITERATURE

ARB No. 43, *Restatement and Revision of Accounting Research Bulletins* (Chapter 7A—Quasi-Reorganization or Corporate Readjustment)
ARB No. 46, *Discontinuance of Dating Earned Surplus*
SFAS No. 109, *Accounting for Income Taxes*

RELATED TOPICS

Chapter 24—Income Taxes
Chapter 51—Stockholders' Equity

REAL ESTATE TRANSACTIONS

Table of Contents

REAL ESTATE TRANSACTIONS

Table of Contents (Continued)

REAL ESTATE TRANSACTIONS

OVERVIEW

45.100   GAAP specifies the accounting methods that must be used to recognize profit on real estate sales. For sales other than retail land sales, the full accrual method (which recognizes all profits immediately) should be used if—

a. the sale has been completed,

b. the buyer's initial and continuing investments are sufficient,

c. the seller's receivable is not subject to future subordination, and

d. the seller has no continuing involvement with the property and all risks and rewards of ownership have been transferred.

If one of the preceding criteria is not met, either the deposit, installment, cost recovery, reduced profit, or percentage-of-completion method should be used depending on which criterion was not met.

45.101   Certain criteria also must be met before the full accrual method may be used to account for retail land sales. The full accrual method should be used to recognize revenues from retail land sales only if all of the following criteria are met:

a. The refund period has expired.

b. Cumulative payments are sufficient.

c. Receivables are collectible and generally are not subordinate to new loans on the property.

d. Development of the lots sold has been completed.

Otherwise, revenue should be recognized under the percentage-of-completion, installment, or deposit method.

45.102   GAAP also establishes standards for capitalizing costs associated with acquiring, developing, constructing, selling, and renting real estate projects and allocating costs to individual components of such projects.

ACCOUNTING REQUIREMENTS

REAL ESTATE SALES (OTHER THAN RETAIL LAND SALES)

Methods of Accounting

45.200   Sales of real estate (other than retail land sales) should be accounted for under one of six methods of accounting, each of which recognizes profit differently. Those methods include the full accrual method (which recognizes all profit at closing), the deposit method (which recognizes no profit at closing), the cost recovery, installment, and reduced profit methods (which recognize profit as the sales price is collected) and the percentage-of-completion method (which recognizes profit as development and construction progress).

45.201   **Full Accrual Method.** The full accrual method assumes that all conditions necessary for a sale have been met (i.e., the earnings process is complete). Thus, all profit is recognized. EXHIBIT 45-1 presents an example of the full accrual method of accounting for real estate transactions.

EXHIBIT 45-1

ILLUSTRATION OF THE FULL ACCRUAL METHOD

Assume a developer owns lots with land and development costs totaling $200,000 and enters into a contract to sell them to a builder for $300,000. The developer receives cash of $75,000 and a note for $225,000. The note is due in two equal installments of $125,000 plus interest at 10% and is secured by an irrevocable letter of credit. The following entry records the sale:

Cash	75,000	
Cost of lot sales	200,000	
Note receivable	225,000	
Capitalized costs		200,000
Revenue from lot sales		300,000

45.202   **Deposit Method.** Under the deposit method, the seller should not recognize any profit or notes receivable at the sale date. Instead, the seller should continue to report the property, any related existing debt (even debt assumed by the buyer), and depreciation in its financial statements. Cash received from the buyer (including the initial investment and subsequent principal and interest collections) should be recorded as a deposit on the contract. Forfeited deposits should be recognized as income if the sales contract is subsequently canceled. (SFAS 66, paras. 65–66)

45.203   Under the deposit method, the seller should recognize a loss when the sales contract is signed if the net carrying amount of the property exceeds the sum of the deposit received, the fair value of the seller's unrecorded note receivable, and the existing debt assumed by the buyer. If a buyer subsequently defaults or if subsequent events indicate that it is probable the buyer will default and the property will revert to the seller, the seller should consider whether the property's value has declined and a loss allowance is needed. (SFAS 66, par. 21)

45.204   EXHIBIT 45-2 illustrates the deposit method of accounting for real estate transactions.

EXHIBIT 45-2

ILLUSTRATION OF THE DEPOSIT METHOD

Assume that on 1/1/X1 Seller (S) sells raw land with a book value of $300,000 to Buyer (B) for $505,000. B makes a token down payment of $5,000. B also assumes existing debt of $150,000, but S remains liable on the debt. S finances the remaining sales value of $350,000 with a second lien mortgage. Payment terms on the assumed debt are $15,000 per year plus interest at 8%. Terms on the sellers receivable are interest only at 10% for nine years with a balloon payment of $350,000 plus interest at the end of the 10th year. Recovery of the seller's investment is uncertain, and the deposit method is determined to be the most appropriate accounting method.

Under the deposit method, the sale is not recognized, the seller's receivable is not recorded, and both the property and existing debt remain on S's books. S should make the following journal entry on the date of sale:

Cash	5,000	
Deposit liability		5,000

Assuming that, on 1/1/X2, B makes payments of $27,000 (including interest of $12,000) on the assumed debt and $35,000 (interest) on the seller's receivable, S would need to make the following entries on that date:

EXHIBIT 45-2 (Continued)

Assumed debt payment

Liability on property sold	15,000	
Deposit liability		15,000

Seller's receivable payment

Cash	35,000	
Deposit liability		35,000

Note that no entry is made for the $12,000 of interest paid on the assumed debt. Under GAAP, the seller only records the principal payments on assumed debt.

45.205　**Cost Recovery Method.** Under the cost recovery method, the seller defers all profit until the buyer's total payments (including principal and interest on debt due to the seller and on existing debt assumed by the buyer) exceed the seller's cost of the property sold. The buyer's payments are considered first to be a recovery of cost, then a recovery of profit. Until the seller recovers the book value of the property, the principal payments received reduce the seller's receivable and the interest payments received increase the deferred profit. After the property's book value has been recovered, deferred profit is recognized as each of the remaining principal payments is received and the interest payments are recognized as interest income. (SFAS 66, paras. 62–63)

45.206　EXHIBIT 45-3 illustrates accounting for a real estate sale under the cost recovery method.

EXHIBIT 45-3

ILLUSTRATION OF THE COST RECOVERY METHOD

To illustrate the cost recovery method, assume lots with land and development costs totaling $450,000 are sold for $500,000. The developers receive $125,000 in cash and an unsecured note for $375,000 payable in three annual installments of $125,000 plus interest at 12%. The following summarizes scheduled collections:

	Principal Outstanding	Interest Income	Cumulative Payments
Inception	$ 375,000	—	$ 125,000
Year 1	250,000	$ 45,000	295,000
Year 2	125,000	30,000	450,000
Year 3	—	15,000	590,000
		$ 90,000	

Under the cost recovery method, all of the gain of $50,000 (calculated as the sales price of $500,000 less capitalized costs of $450,000) is deferred. Until cumulative payments (including both principal and interest) exceed cost, none of the deferred gross profit is recognized, and the interest collected is added to deferred gain. At the end of Year 2, the deferred gain is $125,000, consisting of the initial deferred gain of $50,000 plus interest income of $45,000 for Year 1 and $30,000 for Year 2. All of the deferred gain would be recognized in Year 3. The following entries would be made:

Inception

Cash	125,000	
Note receivable	375,000	
Cost of lot sales	450,000	
Capitalized project costs		450,000
Deferred gain		50,000
Revenue from lot sales		450,000

Year 1

Cash	170,000	
Note receivable		125,000
Deferred gain		45,000

EXHIBIT 45-3 (Continued)

Year 2

Cash	155,000	
Note receivable		125,000
Deferred gain		30,000

Year 3

Cash	140,000	
Deferred gain	125,000	
Note receivable		125,000
Revenue from lot sales		125,000
Interest income		15,000

45.207   **Installment Method.** Under the installment method, the seller recognizes profit proportionately as the sales value is collected. A profit percentage (total profit on the sale divided by the sales value) is normally calculated as of the sale date and that percentage is applied to the principal payments received to calculate the profit to be recognized each period. The difference between the principal payments and the profit recognized represents recovery of cost. If the receivable's stated interest rate is less than or equal to the market rate, the receivable should not be reduced to its present value. (SFAS 66, paras. 56–57)

45.208   EXHIBIT 45-4 illustrates the installment method of accounting for real estate transactions.

EXHIBIT 45-4

ILLUSTRATION OF THE INSTALLMENT METHOD

To illustrate the installment method, assume the following facts:

    a. Lots with land and development costs totaling $400,000 are sold for $500,000.

    b. The developer receives:

      (1) $50,000 in cash,

      (2) A note for $300,000 that is secured by the lots and payable in three annual installments of $100,000 plus interest at 12%, and

      (3) The buyer assumes a note of the developer for $150,000 that is payable in three annual installments of $50,000 plus interest at 10%.

Gain on the sale is $100,000 (calculated as the excess of the selling price of $500,000 over costs of $400,000) and is 20% of the selling price. Under the installment method, 20% of each dollar of the selling price that is collected is considered to be a recovery of the gain. The following summarizes scheduled collections:

	Inception	Year 1	Year 2	Year 3
Cash collected:				
Down payment	$ 50,000	$ —	$ —	$ —
Principal reduction				
Buyer's note	—	100,000	100,000	100,000
Seller's note assumed	—	50,000	50,000	50,000
	50,000	150,000	150,000	150,000
Gain recognized	10,000	30,000	30,000	30,000
Buyer's note				
Principal	300,000	200,000	100,000	—
Interest income	—	36,000	24,000	12,000

EXHIBIT 45-4 (Continued)

The following entries would be made:

Inception

Cash	50,000	
Note receivable	300,000	
Note payable	150,000	
Cost of lot sales	400,000	
Capitalized project costs		400,000
Deferred gain		90,000
Revenue from lot sales		410,000

Year 1

Cash	136,000	
Deferred gain	30,000	
Note receivable		100,000
Gain on sale		30,000
Interest income		36,000

Year 2

Cash	124,000	
Deferred gain	30,000	
Note receivable		100,000
Gain on sale		30,000
Interest income		24,000

Year 3

Cash	112,000	
Deferred gain	30,000	
Note receivable		100,000
Gain on sale		30,000
Interest income		12,000

45.209   **Reduced Profit Method.** Under the reduced profit method, the seller determines a reduced profit by discounting the receivable from the buyer to the present value of the minimum annual payments due under the sales contract over 20 years for land debt or over the normal loan term for other real estate. The profit recognized at the sale date is the total profit on the sale less the discount. The seller defers the portion of the profit equal to the discount. None of the deferred profit (i.e., the discount) is recognized until the end of the period used in the present value calculation. After that time, the deferred profit is recognized as payments are collected. (SFAS 66, par. 68)

45.210   EXHIBIT 45-5 illustrates using the reduced profit method to account for sales of real estate.

EXHIBIT 45-5

ILLUSTRATION OF REDUCED PROFIT METHOD

To illustrate the reduced profit method, assume the following:

    a. Commercial developers build an office building on a part of the tract, fully lease it with five- and ten-year leases, and sell the building for $3,000,000.

    b. The developers have allocated land and development costs of $1,500,000 and building costs of $800,000, resulting in a profit of $700,000.

    c. As consideration for the sale, the developers accept a cash down payment of $500,000 and a note of $2,500,000. The note is secured by the land and building and due over 25 years in annual installments of $363,700, including interest at 14%.

    d. Lenders within the area would issue a maximum first mortgage of $2,500,000 over 20 years with interest at 12% resulting in payments of $334,700.

Discounting the payments required under the note of $363,700 at 14% over 20 years yields a present value of $2,408,800. Gain deferred in the year of sale is $91,200 ($2,500,000 − $2,408,800). Gain recognized in the year of sale is $608,800 (calculated as $3,000,000 less costs of $2,300,000 less deferred gain of $91,200). Deferred gain should be recognized as payments are received over the last five years in proportion to principal reduction.

Total payments on the note in the last five years of $1,818,500 (calculated as 5 × $363,700) are allocated $1,248,600 to principal reduction and $569,900 to interest income. Gain is recognized as follows: (All amounts are rounded to the nearest hundred dollars.)

EXHIBIT 45-5 (Continued)

	Principal Outstanding	Principal Reduction	Interest Income	Profit Recognized
End of Year 20	$ 1,248,600			
Year 21	1,059,700	$ 188,900	$ 174,800	$ 13,800
Year 22	844,400	215,300	148,400	15,800
Year 23	598,900	245,500	118,200	17,900
Year 24	319,000	279,900	83,800	20,400
Year 25	—	319,000	44,700	23,300
		$ 1,248,600	$ 569,900	$ 91,200

Thus, none of the deferred gain (i.e., discount) is recognized until the end of the period used in the present value calculation. After that, the deferred gain is recognized as payments are collected. Although not addressed in SFAS No. 66, the authors believe the deferred gain should be recognized in proportion to the principal reduction.

45.211 **Percentage-of-completion Method.** Under the percentage of completion method, profit recognized is calculated based on the percentage of costs incurred to the total costs expected to be incurred. Profit is allocated to the sale of the land and the later development or construction based on the estimated cost of each activity, with the same rate of profit attributed to each activity. If future development costs and profit cannot be reasonably estimated, no profit should be recognized at the time of sale. (SFAS 66, paras. 41–42).

45.212   EXHIBIT 45-6 illustrates the percentage-of-completion method of accounting for real estate transactions.

EXHIBIT 45-6

ILLUSTRATION OF THE PERCENTAGE-OF-COMPLETION METHOD

To illustrate the percentage-of-completion method, assume the following:

a. A tract of land is acquired for $5,600,000 and is expected to be developed into 140 lots for additional costs totaling $4,900,000.

b. Total estimated costs per lot are $75,000, consisting of land costs of $40,000 and development costs of $35,000.

c. The developers expect to sell each lot for $130,000.

d. When development costs of $2,800,000 have been incurred (that is, approximately 57% of the estimated total development costs of $4,900,000), a builder buys 20 lots for cash of $2,400,000 (that is, $120,000 per lot).

The gain recognized at closing would be calculated as follows:

Costs incurred		
Land acquisition—$40,000 × 20	$	800,000
Development—($2,800,000 ÷ 140 = $20,000) × 20		400,000
	$	1,200,000
Estimated cost at completion—$75,000 × 20	$	1,500,000
% of completion—$1,200,000 ÷ $1,500,000		80%
Revenues—$2,400,000 × 80%	$	1,920,000
Costs		1,200,000
Gain	$	720,000

Gain of $36,000 would be recognized for each of the 20 lots sold (calculated as $720,000 ÷ 20 or 80% of the total gross profit of $45,000 estimated on each of the lots). The following entry would be made to report the sale:

Cash	2,400,000	
Cost of lot sales	1,200,000	
Capitalized costs		1,200,000
Deferred revenue		480,000
Revenue from lot sales		1,920,000

EXHIBIT 45-6 (Continued)

Assuming development is completed in the following year for costs totaling $400,000, the following entry should be made:

Cost of lot sales	400,000	
Deferred revenue	480,000	
Cash		400,000
Revenue from lot sales		480,000

Determining the Appropriate Method of Accounting

45.213   Determining the appropriate method to use to account for sales of real estate depends on the answers to the following questions:

    a. *Has the sale been consummated?* A sale is consummated when all of the following conditions are met: (SFAS 66, par. 6)

        (1) The parties are bound by the terms of a contract.

        (2) All consideration has been exchanged.

        (3) Any permanent financing for which the seller is responsible has been arranged.

        (4) All conditions needed to close the sale (e.g., title policy, surveys, inspections) have been met.

    The preceding conditions are usually met at or after closing, not when an agreement to sell is signed or at a preclosing.

    b. *Has the buyer made a sufficient initial investment?* The buyer's initial investment in the property is one indicator of the buyer's commitment to pay for the property. The buyer's initial investment should include—(SFAS 66, par. 9)

        (1) cash paid as a down payment.

        (2) the buyer's notes payable to the seller backed by irrevocable letters of credit from an independent established lending institution.

45.213

(3) the buyer's payments to third parties to reduce existing debt on the property.

(4) additional cash proceeds paid by the buyer as part of the sales value (e.g., points, prepaid interest).

(5) other consideration that has been sold or otherwise converted to cash without recourse to the seller.

The initial investment should not include the buyer's payments to third parties for property improvements; a permanent loan commitment by an independent third party to replace a loan made by the seller; any funds that have been or will be loaned, refunded, or otherwise provided to the buyer by the seller; or loans guaranteed or collateralized by the seller for the buyer. (SFAS 66, par. 10)

The buyer's initial investment is considered significant (and this criterion is met) if it is at least equal to the downpayment an independent financial institution usually would require for a loan on the same type of property at the same sales value. (SFAS 66, paras. 8 and 11) A table presenting minimum initial investment percentages (SFAS 66, par. 54) is presented in EXHIBIT 45-7.

Practical Consideration. GAAP states that sales value is determined by adding to the stated price the proceeds from the issuance of a real estate option that is exercised and any other payments that are in substance additional sales proceeds (for example, management fees, points, prepaid interest or fees maintained in an advance status to be applied to amounts due the seller at a later date) and subtracting (a) an amount to reduce the receivable to its present value and (b) the net present value of services the seller has committed to perform without compensation or the net present value of the services the seller will perform in excess of compensation that will be received.

Sometimes sales contracts (especially land sales) contain release provisions that require the seller to release the lien on a portion of the property after receiving specified payments from the buyer. The seller will normally release its lien only if it has recovered a sufficient amount to indicate that its risk on remaining financing is acceptable. In this situation, the buyer's initial investment is considered sufficient for the property as a whole if it is adequate to cover the release prices on property released at the date of sale and is an adequate initial investment on property not released. (SFAS 66, par. 13) If the amounts applied to unreleased portions do not meet the initial and continuing investment criteria, each release should be treated as a separate sale. (SFAS 66, par. 15)

Practical Consideration. The following are examples of release provisions:

- If raw land is sold for development as residential lots, liens on the land will need to be released before the developed lots can be sold. In that arrangement, the payments often are stipulated as a percentage of the sales value of the developed lots, and they are often designed so that the seller is fully paid before the development is sold out.

- If raw land is sold to a partnership through a syndication, the seller may agree to release the lien on a portion of the land in exchange for a special payment, often within a relatively short period of time after closing, or the seller may apply substantially all of the release payments first to the land for which the lien will be released. The advantage to the buyer is that it effectively owns land that is unencumbered and can be pledged for other financing.

---

c. *Does the buyer have a sufficient continuing investment?* The buyer has a continuing investment in the real estate if the buyer is contractually required to pay an annual amount at least equal to the annual principal and interest payment needed to pay the total debt for the purchase price of the property within (a) 20 years for land debt and (b) the normal term of a first mortgage loan by an independent lending institution for other real estate. Funds to be provided by the seller generally should be subtracted from the buyer's contractually required payments in determining whether the continuing investment is adequate. (SFAS 66, par. 12) Any excess of the initial investment over the required minimum can be considered part of the buyer's continuing investment. (SFAS 66, par. 16)

Practical Consideration. Collections of the sales value not only include receipts of principal on the buyer's note to the seller, but also principal payments by the buyer on any of the seller's existing notes that the buyer assumed. However, according to EITF 88-24, *Effect of Various Forms of Financing under FASB Statement No. 66,* those payments should not include funds obtained from (a) the seller or (b) loans that are secured by the property, even if those loans are provided from third parties.

The adequacy of a buyer's initial and continuing investments should be tested cumulatively when the sale is consummated and annually thereafter. (SFAS 66, par. 16)

d. *Is the sale subject to future subordination?* The seller should have a superior lien to all other debt on the property, except (a) a loan (first mortgage) existing at the sale date or (b) a future loan provided for in the sales agreement if the loan proceeds will be applied first to pay the seller's receivable. (SFAS 66, par. 17)

e. *Does the sale transfer the risks and rewards of ownership without continuing seller involvement?* The seller's continuing involvement in the property after it has been sold may indicate that the risks and rewards of ownership have not been transferred. (SFAS 66, par. 18) For example, the seller may have an obligation to repurchase the property or may have guaranteed a return on the buyer's investment.

EXHIBIT 45-7

TABLE OF MINIMUM INITIAL INVESTMENT

Type of Property	Percentage of Sales Value (See Paragraph 45.213)
LAND to be developed beginning:	
Within 2 years from sale date.	20%
After 2 years.	25
SINGLE FAMILY HOMES, CONDOMINIUM UNITS, TOWN-HOMES, AND 1–4 FAMILY RESIDENCES [1,2]	
Buyer's primary residence.	5
Buyer's secondary or recreational residence.	10
MULTI-FAMILY RESIDENTIAL PROPERTY	
Primary residence:	
Current cash flow is adequate to cover all debt payments.	10
Cash flow is not adequate (including start-up situations).	15
Secondary or recreational residence:	
Current cash flow is adequate to cover all debt payments.	15
Cash flow is not adequate (including start-up situations).	25
OFFICE BUILDINGS, SHOPPING CENTERS, INDUSTRIAL BUILDINGS, AND SIMILAR PROPERTIES	
Current cash flow is adequate to cover all debt payments; property is subject to long-term leases to parties with good credit ratings.	10
Single-tenant properties sold to a buyer with a good credit rating.	15
All other.	20
HOTELS, MOBILE-HOME PARKS, MARINAS, AND OTHER INCOME-PRODUCING PROPERTIES	
Current cash flow is adequate to cover all debt payments.	15
Cash flow is not adequate (including start-up situations).	25

---

[1]　If the sale is financed under an FHA or VA insured program, the normal down payment requirement can be used to determine the required initial investment.

[2]　If the remaining portion of the sales value is financed by the seller and collectibility of the seller's receivable cannot be supported by reliable evidence of collection experience, then the minimum initial investment must be at least 60% of the difference between the sales value and the maximum amount of financing available through FHA or VA insured programs or through independent financial institutions.

45.214   **All Criteria for Revenue Recognition Have Been Met.** The full accrual method should be used to account for a real estate sale when the answers to all of the preceding questions are yes. (SFAS 66, par. 5) Otherwise, the method of accounting depends on which of the criteria have not been met. The flowchart in EXHIBIT 45-8 illustrates determining the appropriate method of accounting for real estate sales.

45.215   **Sale Has Not Been Consummated.** If the sale has not been consummated, the seller should use the deposit method of accounting. An exception to that general rule exists when constructing office buildings, apartments, condominiums, shopping centers and similar structures. Because of their relatively long construction period, the percentage-of-completion method, rather than the deposit method, may be used to record revenues related to sale proceeds received during the construction period.(SFAS 66, par. 20)

45.216   **Initial Investment Does Not Qualify.** If the buyer's initial investment is not sufficient but recovery of the property's cost is reasonably assured if the buyer defaults, the sale should be accounted for under the installment method. If the buyer's initial investment is not sufficient and recovery of the property's cost is uncertain (or costs have already been recovered and collection of the rest of the sales value is uncertain) the cost recovery or the deposit method should be used. (SFAS 66, par. 22)

45.217   The seller may change to the full accrual method of recognizing profit if a transaction accounted for under the installment or cost recovery method subsequently meets the requirements for the full accrual method. The remaining profit that had not been recognized under the installment or cost recovery method should be recognized in income at that time. (SFAS 66, paras. 61 and 64)

45.218   **Continuing Investment Does Not Qualify.** If the buyer's initial investment meets the criteria for the full accrual method, but the continuing investment is not sufficient to recognize profit under that method, the seller should use the reduced profit, installment, or cost recovery method. The reduced profit method should be used if the buyer's annual payments will be sufficient to cover both: (SFAS 66, par. 23)

     a. principal and interest on the maximum first mortgage loan that could be obtained on the property and

     b. interest, at market rates, on the excess of the actual total debt on the property over such a maximum first mortgage loan.

EXHIBIT 45-8
A PRACTICAL APPROACH FOR SELECTING ACCOUNTING METHODS FOR SALES OF REAL ESTATE

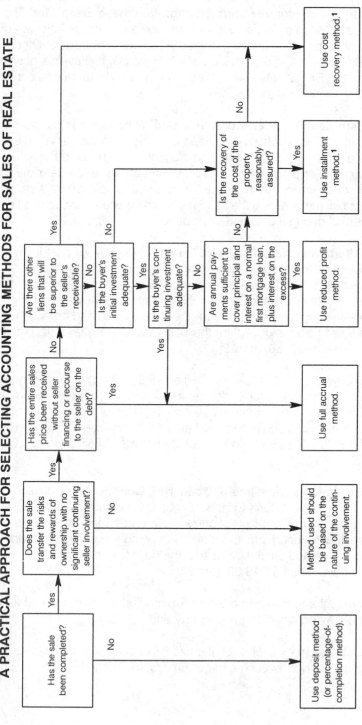

1 According to SFAS No. 66, the cost recovery method may be used anytime the installment method is appropriate, and the deposit method can be used either (a) if recovery of the seller's investment is uncertain if the buyer defaults or (b) if the seller recovers its investment at closing, but collection of additional amounts is uncertain. Those alternative methods are rarely used in practice, however.

If both of the criteria for using the reduced profit method are not met, the seller may recognize profit by the installment method or the cost recovery method. (SFAS 66, par. 23)

Practical Consideration. GAAP does not specify whether the installment or cost recovery method should be used when the reduced profit method is not appropriate. The authors recommend using the installment method if recovery of the seller's investment in the property is reasonably assured and the cost recovery method if either recovery of the seller's investment is uncertain or the seller's investment has already been recovered but recovery of the rest of the sales value is uncertain.

45.219 **Receivable Subject to Future Subordination.** Recoverability of the seller's investment in the property is not assured if the seller's receivable is subject to future subordination since the seller would not have the first right to the property if the buyer defaults. Consequently, the seller should recognize profit by the cost recovery method when its lien is not superior to all other debt on the property except (a) a first mortgage loan existing at the sale date or (b) a future loan provided for in the sales agreement if the loan proceeds will be applied first to pay the seller's receivable. (SFAS 66, paras. 17 and 24)

45.220 **Seller Has Continuing Involvement.** If the seller's continuing involvement with a property after it is sold does not result in the transfer of substantial risks or rewards of ownership to the buyer, the full accrual method generally should not be used. (SFAS 66, par. 18) Profit may be recognized at the time of sale, however, if the amount of the seller's loss of profit (because of continued involvement with the property) is limited by the terms of the sales contract. Any profit so recognized should be reduced by the seller's maximum exposure to loss. Otherwise, if the seller has some other form of continuing involvement with the property, the transaction should be accounted for according to the nature of the seller's involvement (such as a profit-sharing, financing, or leasing arrangement), rather than as a sale. (SFAS 66, par. 25)

45.221 The following summarizes the appropriate method of accounting for some of the more common forms of continuing involvement: (EXHIBIT 45-9 also lists examples of various forms of continuing involvement and the accounting methods that should be used.)

    a. *The seller is obligated to repurchase the property or the contract terms allow the buyer to require the seller or give an option to the seller to repurchase the property.* The transaction should be accounted for as either a financing, leasing, or profit-sharing arrangement rather than as a sale. (SFAS 66, par. 26)

b. *A limited partnership in which the seller is a general partner acquires an interest in the property and the seller holds a receivable from the buyer for a significant portion of the sales price.* The transaction should be accounted for as either a financing, leasing, or profit-sharing arrangement rather than as a sale. (SFAS 66, par. 27)

c. *The seller guarantees a return of the buyer's investment in the property or guarantees a return on that investment for an extended period of time.* The transaction should be accounted for as either a financing, leasing, or profit-sharing arrangement rather than as a sale. (If the guarantee of investment return is for a limited period of time, however, the deposit method of accounting should be used until operations of the property cover all operating expenses, debt service and contractual payments. Subsequently, profit should be recognized when required services are performed.) (SFAS 66, par. 28)

d. *The seller is required to initiate or support the operations of the property.* If the seller is required to initiate or support operations for an *extended* period of time, the transaction should be accounted for as either a financing, leasing, or profit-sharing arrangement rather than a sale. On the other hand, if the seller is required to initiate or support operations for only a limited time, profit on the sale should be recognized on the basis of performance of the services required. Performance of services is measured based on the costs incurred and to be incurred over the period that services will be performed. However, before any profit can be recognized, there should be a reasonable assurance that the future receipts will be sufficient to cover operating expenses, debt payments (including payments on the seller's receivable) and other contractual obligations. (SFAS 66, par. 29)

If the sales contract does not specify the support period, support is presumed for at least two years beyond the date rental operations begin and revenue should be recognized on the basis of performance of services. However, if actual rental receipts become sufficient to cover operating expenses, debt service, and other contractual payments before the two year period ends, profit may be recognized at the earlier date. (SFAS 66, par. 30)

If the sales contract requires the seller to manage the property without compensation or at less than market rates for the services required (or at terms not usual for the services rendered), compensation should be imputed when the sale is recognized and recognized in income as the services are performed over the contract term. (SFAS 66, par. 31)

e. *The seller leases back all or any part of the property for its remaining economic life.* The transaction should be accounted for as either a financing, leasing, or profit-sharing arrangement rather than as a sale. (SFAS 98, par. 23)

f. *The buyer merely has an option to buy the property.* Some sales agreements are structured as sales, but in effect, only give the buyer an option to buy the property. For example, the buyer may only make a token down payment and is not required to make more payments until certain contingencies are resolved (such as, zoning changes are made or building permits are obtained). Such transactions generally should be accounted for using the deposit method, and accordingly, the proceeds of the sale should be recorded as a liability and recognized in income either when the option is exercised or when it expires. (SFAS 66, par. 32)

For subsequent sale of options by option holders, the accounting method used should be either (a) the full accrual method, if the buyer's initial and continuing investments are adequate or (b) the cost recovery method, if the buyer's investments are not adequate. In applying the initial and continuing investment tests, the sales value is the total of the exercise price of the option and the sales price of the option. (SFAS 66, par. 32)

g. *The seller has made a partial sale.* Partial sales are those in which the seller keeps an ownership interest in the property or has an ownership interest in the buyer. Profit should be recognized at the date of the sale if:

(1) the buyer and seller are independent,

(2) it is reasonably assured the sales price is collectible, and

(3) the seller is not obligated to support the operations of the property (or its related obligations) to an extent greater than its proportionate interest. (SFAS 66, par. 33)

If the seller owns a noncontrolling interest in the buyer, the seller should recognize profit in proportion to the outside ownership of the buyer. If the seller owns a controlling interest in the buyer, no profit should be recognized until it is realized through either (a) sale to an independent party or (b) profits from continuing operations. (SFAS 66, par. 34)

If the seller is not reasonably assured that the sales price is collectible, the cost recovery or installment method should be used to recognize profit. (SFAS 66, par. 35)

If the seller has continuing support obligations and the transaction is in substance a sale, the seller should recognize profit to the extent that proceeds from the sale (including receivables from the buyer) exceed all of the seller's cost related to the entire property. (SFAS 66, par. 36)

h. *Sales of condominium projects or time-sharing interests.* Profit should be recognized on the percentage-of-completion method on the sale of individual condominium units or time-sharing interests if all of the following conditions are met: (SFAS 66, par. 37)

   (1) Construction is beyond the preliminary stage.

   (2) The buyer can no longer require a refund (except for nondelivery of the unit or interest).

   (3) Sufficient units have been sold to assure that the entire project will not revert to rental property.

   (4) Sales prices are considered to be collectible.

   (5) Total sales proceeds and costs can be reasonably estimated.

   If any of the above conditions are not met, the deposit method should be used until all of the conditions are met.

i. *Seller sells property improvements and leases the underlying land to buyer.* If the seller sells building improvements and leases the land underlying the improvements to the buyer, the entire transaction should be accounted for as a lease if the land lease does not cover the entire economic life of the improvements or is not for a substantial period (for example, greater than 20 years). If both of those conditions are met, profit recognized on the sale of the improvements at the time of sale is (1) the present value of lease rental payments (not in excess of the cost of the land) plus

(2) the sales value of the improvements less (3) the carrying value of the improvements and the land.

The seller may recognize profit on the buyer's rental payments on the land to the extent they exceed the land's cost and rent received after the primary debt on the improvements is paid off. The profit should be recognized when (1) the land is sold or (2) the rents in excess of the seller's cost of the land are earned under the lease. (SFAS 66, par. 39)

j. *Seller participates in future profits of the property without risk of loss.* If the seller participates in future profits of the property without risk of loss and the sale otherwise qualifies for full accrual accounting, the transfer of risks and rewards of ownership and the absence of continuing involvement criteria are considered to be met. The contingent future profit is recognized when the profits are realized. All costs of the sale are recognized at the time of sale (that is, no costs are deferred to periods when the contingent profits are realized). (SFAS 66, par. 43)

k. *The seller is obligated to develop the property in the future.* The percentage-of-completion (or performance-of-services) method is commonly used when the seller is obligated to develop property or build additional facilities as a condition of the sale. (SFAS 66, par. 41)

EXHIBIT 45-9

EXAMPLES OF ACCOUNTING FOR CONTINUING SELLER INVOLVEMENT

Financing, Leasing, or Profit-sharing Arrangement	Percentage-of-completion or Performance-of-services	Deposit Method or Other Methods
• Seller guarantees a return of the buyer's investment or a return on that investment for an *extended* period.	• Seller guarantees a return on the buyer's investment for a *limited* period, and current operations cover all expenses and other payments.	• Seller guarantees a return on the buyer's investment for a *limited* period, and current operations do *not* cover all expenses and other payments.
• Seller is required to support operations of the property for an *extended* period.	• Seller is required to support operations of the property for a *limited* period.	• Seller, in substance, issues an option.
• Seller has option or obligation to repurchase property.	• Seller is required to develop the property or build facilities or amenities, and development costs can be reasonably estimated.	• Seller is required to develop the property, etc., but development costs cannot be estimated.
• Buyer has an option to force seller to repurchase the property.		
• Seller is a general partner in a partnership that buys the property, and the seller holds a significant receivable.		

RETAIL LAND SALES

45.222   Retail land sales generally are characterized as volume sales of residential lots that are subdivisions of large tracts of land. Using concentrated marketing efforts, the developer usually provides the buyer with financing terms that require a lower down payment than financial institutions would require. Typically, the terms are such that financial institutions will not purchase the buyer's note without a substantial discount. In addition, the developer is often required by law to provide a refund period during which the buyer can rescind the sale and receive a refund of all payments made under the contract.

Recognizing Profits from Retail Land Sales

45.223   The following paragraphs discuss the various methods used to recognize profits from retail land sales and when they are appropriate. The flowchart in EXHIBIT 45-10 also may be used to determine the appropriate method of accounting for retail land sales.

45.224   **Full Accrual Method.** The full accrual method of accounting should be applied to a retail land sale project if all of the following conditions are met: (SFAS 66, par. 45)

a. *Expiration of refund period.* The buyer has made the down payment and each required subsequent payment until the refund period has expired.

b. *Sufficient cumulative payments.* The cumulative payments of principal and interest equal at least 10% of the contract sales price.

c. *Collectibility of receivables.* This criterion is met if a down payment of at least 20% is received. Otherwise, the seller's collection experience should indicate that at least 90% of the contracts from the current project will be collected in full if they are not canceled within six months following the date the sales contract is recorded.

d. *Nonsubordination of receivables.* The receivable from the sale should not be subordinate to new loans on the property, except that it can be subordinate to a home construction loan obtained by the buyer if the collection experience on such "subordinated receivables" is the same or better than on other receivables.

EXHIBIT 45-10

SELECTING ACCOUNTING METHODS FOR RETAIL LAND SALES

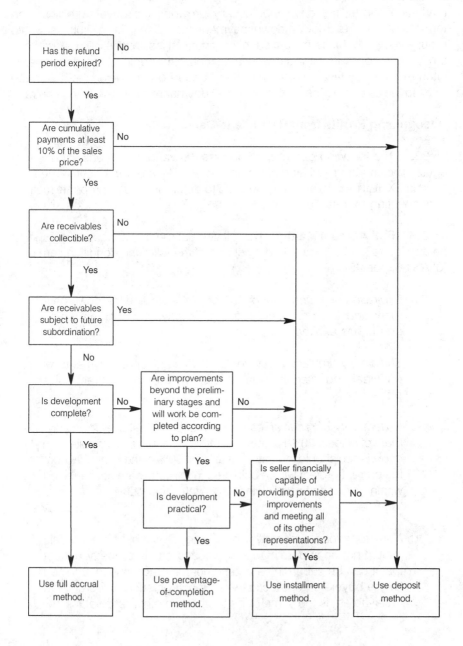

e. *Completion of development.* The seller has met its obligations to complete improvements of lots sold or to construct amenities or other facilities applicable to lots sold.

45.225   Under the full accrual method for retail land sales, (a) sales are recorded at the contract amount; (b) an allowance is provided for receivables not expected to be collected due to cancellation in subsequent periods; (c) the cost of retail lot sales (net of those sales expected to be canceled in the future) is transferred from the inventory accounts; and (d) a provision for discounts is recorded to reduce the contracts receivable to the present value of the required payments. At the end of each reporting period, earned discounts are recognized in income; and canceled contracts are charged in their entirety to the allowance for contract cancellations. (SFAS 66, par. 70)

45.226   To record an allowance for receivables not expected to be collected due to cancellation, a historical cancellation percentage must be computed. That is accomplished by accumulating and evaluating historical collection data obtained from a representative sample of previous contracts whose collection period covers an adequate period of time to provide reasonable evidence of collectibility. Generally, receivables are considered uncollectible if they exceed the following delinquency periods:

When the Percent of the Total Contract Price Collected Is—	And the Delinquency Period Is at Least—
Less than 25%	90 days (3 months)
25% but less than 50%	120 days (4 months)
50% or over	150 days (5 months)

The delinquency periods can be extended if the seller's recent collection experience has been better or the buyer as accepted (or is willing to accept) personal liability for the debt and the buyer's ability to make payments has been determined. (SFAS 66, par. 71)

Practical Consideration. Most retail land projects maintain cancellation data on a cumulative basis from inception of each project. Consequently, sampling is usually not required.

45.227   If the seller has programs (or expects to initiate programs) that offer incentives (such as a reduction of the principal amount due) to accelerate collection of receivables, profit recognized at the date of the sale should be reduced by charges to income for the anticipated discounts. Discounts granted sporadically should be charged to income in the period they are granted. (SFAS 66, par. 72)

45.228   Percentage-of-completion Method. A retail land sale that meets all of the criteria for full accrual except the completion of development condition should be accounted for under the percentage-of-completion method if both of the following criteria are met: (SFAS 66, par. 46)

a. *The project's improvements have progressed beyond prelimi-nary stages and there are indications that the work will be com-pleted according to plan.* To meet this condition, there should be no indication of significant delaying factors, and estimates of costs to complete and extent of progress toward completion should be reasonably dependable.

b. *There is a reasonable expectation that the land can be devel-oped for the purposes represented and the properties will be useful for those purposes at the end of the normal payment period.*

45.229   Under the percentage-of-completion method, revenue should be rec-ognized by (a) calculating the ratio of costs already incurred to total estimated costs to be incurred (including selling costs) and (b) multiplying that ratio by the net sales amount (gross sales less cancellation provisions). Deferred reve-nue is recognized as the costs of completing the improvements related to lots sold are incurred. (SFAS 66, par. 73)

45.230   The costs already incurred and total costs to be incurred include land cost, costs previously charged to expense (such as interest and project carry-ing costs incurred prior to sale), and selling costs directly associated with a project. The estimates for future improvement costs should be based on costs generally expected in the local construction industry, and unrecoverable costs of off-site improvements, utilities, and amenities should be provided for. Esti-mates of future improvement costs should be reviewed at least annually. When cost estimates are revised, the percentage-of-completion should be recalcu-lated on a cumulative basis to determine future income recognition as perfor-mance takes place. (SFAS 66, paras. 74–75)

45.231   Installment Method. A retail land sale whose refund period has expired and whose cumulative payments equal at least 10% of the contract sales price, but that does not meet any of the other criteria for the full accrual or percentage-of-completion methods, should be accounted for under the installment method if the seller is financially capable of (a) providing both land improvements and off-site facilities promised in the contract and (b) meeting all other representations it has made, including funding or bonding the planned improvements in the project when required. (SFAS 66, par. 47)

45.232   If a retail land sale project originally reported by the installment method subsequently satisfies the criteria for using the percentage-of-completion method, the seller may adopt that method for the entire project (current and prior sales) and account for the effect as a change in accounting estimate. (SFAS 66, par. 49)

45.233   **Deposit Method.** A retail land sale that does not meet the criteria for the full accrual, percentage-of-completion, or installment methods should be accounted for under the deposit method. (SFAS 66, par. 48)

REAL ESTATE ACQUISITION, DEVELOPMENT, AND CONSTRUCTION COSTS

45.234   Prior to the sale or rental of real estate projects, developers incur costs for land development and construction. Land development involves acquiring land for the project and developing the land into lots for sale or rental.

Preacquisition Costs

45.235   Preacquisition costs relate to the purchase of the land and are incurred before the land is acquired. They include payments for surveying, zoning or traffic studies, or obtaining an option on the property. Payments to obtain an option to acquire real property should be capitalized as incurred. The developer should capitalize other preacquisition costs if all of the following conditions are met: (SFAS 67, par. 4)

     a. The costs are directly identifiable with the specific property.

     b. The costs would be capitalized if the property were already acquired.

     c. Acquisition of the property or of an option to acquire the property is probable.

45.236   Capitalized preacquisition costs should be reclassified as project costs when the property is acquired or charged to expense (to the extent the costs are not recoverable through sale of options, plans, etc.) when it is probable that the property will not be acquired. Costs that do not meet the capitalization criteria should be expensed as incurred. (SFAS 67, par. 5)

Property Taxes and Insurance

45.237   The developer should only capitalize real estate property taxes and insurance as property costs when activities necessary to get the property ready for its intended use are in progress. After the property is substantially complete and ready for its intended use, such costs should be expensed as incurred. (SFAS 67, par.6)

Project Costs

45.238   Project costs directly associated with the acquisition, development, and construction of a real estate project should be capitalized as a cost of the project. Indirect project costs incurred after the acquisition of the property and that clearly relate to projects under development or construction should also be capitalized. Indirect costs may include the costs associated with a field office at a project site and the office's administrative personnel, legal fees, and office costs for cost accounting, design, and other departments providing services that are clearly related to real estate projects. Indirect project costs relating to several projects should be capitalized and allocated to the related projects. Indirect costs not clearly relating to projects under development or construction, including general and administrative expenses, should be expensed as incurred. (SFAS 67, par. 7)

Amenities

45.239   Amenities include golf courses, utility plants, clubhouses, swimming pools, tennis courts, indoor recreational facilities, and parking facilities. The developer's plans for the amenities determines the accounting for their costs, as follows: (SFAS 67, par. 8)

   a. If the developer intends to sell or transfer the amenity in connection with the sale of individual units, the amenity's costs in excess of anticipated proceeds should be allocated as common costs of the project. Common costs relate to multiple units within the project and include expected future operating costs to be borne by the developer until they are assumed by buyers of units in a project.

   b. If the developer intends to sell the amenity to a third party or retain and operate it, the amenity's capitalizable costs in excess of its estimated fair value at its expected completion date should be allocated as common costs.

45.240 Costs of amenities should be allocated as common costs among the benefited units for which development is probable. (SFAS 67, par. 8) The developer should include the amenity's operating revenues and expenses in common costs until the amenity is substantially complete and available for use. After completing an amenity that is to be sold separately or retained by the developer, the amenity's current operating income and expenses should be included in current operating results. (SFAS 67, par. 9)

Incidental Operations

45.241 Incidental operations are revenue-producing activities engaged in during the holding or development period to reduce the cost of developing the property for its intended use (e.g., selling timber, top soil, and other material removed from the land during development). Incidental operations result in incremental revenues and costs that would not be produced or incurred except in relation to those operations. Incremental revenues that exceed incremental costs should be offset against capitalized project costs. Incremental costs that exceed incremental revenues should be expensed as incurred. (SFAS 67, par. 10)

ALLOCATION OF CAPITALIZED COSTS

45.242 The developer should allocate the capitalized costs of real estate projects to each individual component of the project based on specific identification. If specific identification is not practicable, capitalized costs should be allocated based on relative values as follows: (SFAS 67, par. 11)

     a. Land cost and all other common costs (prior to construction) should be allocated to each land parcel benefited, based on the relative fair value of each parcel before construction.

     b. Construction costs should be allocated to individual units in the phase on the basis of relative sales value of each unit.

If allocation based on relative value also is impracticable, capitalized costs should be allocated based on other appropriate methods (such as square footage).

REVISIONS OF ESTIMATES

45.243 The developer should review estimates and cost allocations at the end of each financial reporting period until a project is substantially complete and available for sale. Costs should be revised and reallocated as necessary for material changes on the basis of current estimates. Changes in estimates should be accounted for prospectively. That is, their effects should be recorded in the period of the change and in any future periods that are affected. (SFAS 67, par. 12)

ABANDONMENTS AND CHANGES IN USE

45.244   The capitalized costs associated with abandoned real estate should be written off. The costs of an abandoned property that is only part of a project should not be allocated to the rest of the project or to other projects. (SFAS 67, par. 13) Real estate donated to municipalities or other governmental agencies for uses that will benefit the project are not abandonments and should be allocated as a common cost of the project. (SFAS 67, par. 14)

45.245   Developers occasionally decide not to follow the original plan for a project, and some or all of the land may be put to a different use. If development has begun on the property and its use is later changed, some of the project's costs may need to be written down. If a formal plan supporting the change in use shows that the change is expected to result in higher profits on the project, the development and construction costs should only be written down to the amount that is recoverable. The recoverable amount is the amount by which the capitalized costs incurred and to be incurred exceed the estimated value of the revised project when it is substantially complete and ready for its intended use. (SFAS 67, par. 15)

SELLING COSTS

45.246   Selling costs related to a real estate project should be capitalized if they are reasonably expected to be recovered from the project's sale or from incidental operations and are incurred for (a) tangible assets that are used directly during the selling period to aid in the sale of the project or (b) services that have been performed to obtain regulatory approval of sales. Examples include model units and their furnishings, sales facilities, legal fees for preparing prospectuses, and semipermanent signs. (SFAS 67, par. 17)

45.247   Developers should capitalize sales commissions and other selling costs directly related to a specific sale as prepaid costs if the costs are expected to be recovered from sales not accounted for by the full accrual method. Otherwise, the selling costs should be expensed as incurred. Capitalized selling costs should be charged to expense when the related revenue is recognized. When a sales contract is canceled or the related receivable is written off as uncollectible, the developer should charge related unrecoverable capitalized selling costs to expense or an allowance previously established for that purpose. (SFAS 67, paras. 18–19)

RENTAL COSTS

45.248   Costs incurred to rent real estate projects (other than initial direct costs) under operating leases should be capitalized if the costs relate to future rental operations and recovery of the costs is reasonably expected from those operations. Examples include model units and their furnishings, rental facilities, semipermanent signs, "grand openings," and unused rental brochures. Costs that do not meet the capitalization criteria should be expensed as incurred. (SFAS 67, par. 20)

45.249   The developer should amortize capitalized rental costs directly related to revenue from a specific operating lease over the lease term. Capitalized rental costs not directly related to revenue from a specific operating lease should be amortized over the period of expected benefit. The amortization period should begin when the project is substantially complete and available for occupancy. Estimated unrecoverable amounts of unamortized capitalized rental costs related to a lease should be charged to expense when it becomes probable that the lease will be terminated. (SFAS 67, par. 21)

Initial Rental Operations

45.250   When a real estate project is substantially complete and available for occupancy, the developer should recognize rental revenues and operating costs in income and expense as they accrue. All carrying costs (such as real estate taxes) should be charged to expense when incurred; depreciation on the cost of the project should be recorded; and costs to rent the project should be amortized. A real estate project should be considered substantially complete and available for occupancy when the developer completes tenant improvements, but no later than one year after major construction activity has ended. (SFAS 67, par. 22)

45.251   Portions of a rental project that are substantially complete and occupied by tenants or available for occupancy should be accounted for as a separate project from other portions that have not yet reached that state. The developer should allocate incurred costs between the portions under construction and the portions substantially complete and available for occupancy. (SFAS 67, par. 23)

RECOVERABILITY

45.252   A real estate project (or parts thereof) that is substantially complete and ready for its intended use should be accounted for at the lower of carrying amount or fair value less cost to sell. The provisions of SFAS No. 121, *Accounting for the Impairment of Long-Lived Assets and for Long-Lived Assets to Be*

Disposed Of, should be applied to determine whether an impairment loss should be recognized for real estate held for development and sale (including property to be developed in the future as well as property currently under development). (Assessing long-lived assets for impairment is discussed in Chapter 33.) Determining whether the carrying amounts of real estate projects require write-downs should be based on an evaluation of individual projects. (SFAS 67, par. 31)

Practical Consideration. If a real estate project is composed of separate components (for example, a single-family home tract, an apartment complex, and a retail center), each component should be evaluated separately. However, components that are relatively homogenous and part of a single project (such as individual lots in a single-family home tract) can be evaluated for recoverability as a group.

BORROWER'S ACCOUNTING FOR PARTICIPATING MORTGAGE LOANS

45.253   Real estate transactions may result in the mortgage lender participating in the appreciation in the market value of the mortgaged property, the results of operations of the mortgaged real estate project, or both.

Practical Consideration. The guidance in Paragraphs 45.254–.256 is based on SOP 97-1, *Accounting By Participating Mortgage Loan Borrowers.* The SOP is effective for fiscal years beginning after June 30, 1997, and for interim statements of such years. Restatement of previously issued financial statements is not permitted. Early adoption is encouraged; however, if adopted for a fiscal year beginning on or before June 30, 1997, previously issued financial statements for interim periods of that year should be restated.

Initial application of SOP 97-1 should be reported as a cumulative effect of a change in accounting principle (see Chapter 1). For participation loans with variable rates, the cumulative effect should be determined using the interest rate in effect at the origination of the participating mortgage loan. (The initial rate should be treated as a fixed rate for the purposes of this calculation.)

Accounting for Participation in the Mortgaged Asset's Appreciation

45.254   If the loan agreement allows the lender to participate in the appreciation of the mortgaged real estate's market value, the borrower should determine the fair value of the participation feature and record a participation liability for that amount at the loan's origination. The offsetting debit to a debt discount account should be amortized under the interest method using the effective interest rate. (SOP 97-1, par. 10) At the end of each period, the current fair value of the participation feature should be estimated and the participation liability

45.253

account should be adjusted accordingly. The offsetting debit or credit should be recorded to the debt discount, with the resulting balance in the debt discount account amortized prospectively under the interest method. (SOP 97-1, par. 15)

Interest Expense

45.255 The borrower's interest expense on a participating mortgage loan consists of: (SOP 97-1, paras. 11–14)

     a. *Interest stated in the mortgage agreement.* Such amounts should be charged to interest expense in the period the interest is incurred.

     b. *Amounts related to the lender's participation in the results of operations of the real estate project.* Such amounts should be charged to interest expense (in the borrower's corresponding financial reporting period) with an offsetting credit to the participation liability.

     c. *Amortization of the debt discount related to the lender's participation in the appreciation of the mortgaged real estate.* (See Paragraph 45.254.)

Extinguishment of Participating Mortgage Loans

45.256 The difference between the recorded amount of the debt (including any unamortized debt discount and the participation liability) and the amount exchanged to extinguish the debt for a participating mortgage loan extinguished prior to its due date should be treated as a debt extinguishment gain or loss. (See Chapter 14.) (SOP 97-1, par. 17)

DISCLOSURE REQUIREMENTS

REAL ESTATE TRANSACTIONS (OTHER THAN RETAIL LAND SALES)

Installment Method

45.500 When the installment method is used to recognize revenue for real estate transactions other than retail land sales, the income statement (or related notes) for the period of the sale should present the sales value, the gross profit that has not yet been recognized, and the total cost of the sale. Revenue and cost of sales should be presented as separate items on the income statement or should be disclosed in the notes when profit is recognized as earned. (SFAS 66, par. 59)

Cost Recovery Method

45.501   Under the cost recovery method, the income statement for the period including the sale date should present the sales value, the gross profit that has not yet been recognized, and the total cost of the sale. Deferred gross profit should be offset against the related receivable on the balance sheet. Gross profit should be presented as a separate revenue item on the income statement when it is recognized as earned. (SFAS 66, par. 63)

Deposit Method

45.502   Under the deposit method, nonrecourse debt assumed by the buyer should be reported as a liability in the seller's balance sheet (that is, not offset against the related asset). (SFAS 66, par. 67)

RETAIL LAND SALES

45.503   The following disclosures are required for entities with retail land sales operations: (SFAS 66, par. 50)

   a. Maturities of accounts receivable for each of the five years following the date of the financial statements

   b. The balance of delinquent accounts receivable and the method for determining delinquency

   c. The range and weighted average of stated interest rates of receivables

   d. Estimated total costs and estimated dates of expenditures for improvements for major areas from which sales are being made for each of the five years after the balance sheet date

   e. Recorded obligations for improvements

Practical Consideration. SOP 78-9, *Accounting for Investments in Real Estate Ventures,* also requires the following disclosures for entities with investments in real estate joint ventures: (SOP 78-9, par. 12)

- Investee's name and percentage of ownership

- Legal form of venture

- For limited partnership interests of less than 20%, an explanation of why the equity method is used

- Material differences at the balance sheet date between the book value of the investment and the underlying equity in net assets, and the manner of accounting for those differences

- Summary financial information about the assets, liabilities, and results of operations of material investments

- Effects of contingent issuances or provisions of the venture agreement that, if exercised, would materially affect the investor's share of venture profits and losses

- Market value of the investment, if a quoted market price is available

- For limited partnerships interests of 20% or more that are accounted for by the cost method, the investee's name, percentage of ownership, and an explanation of why the cost method is used

PARTICIPATING MORTGAGE LOAN BORROWERS

45.504   For fiscal years beginning after June 30, 1997, participating mortgage loan borrowers should disclose the following: (SOP 97-1, par. 17)

a. The total amount of participating mortgage loan obligations, with separate disclosure of the total participation liabilities and related debt discounts

b. Terms of the lender's participation in either the appreciation of the mortgage property's market value or the mortgage property's results of operations, or both

AUTHORITATIVE LITERATURE AND RELATED TOPICS

AUTHORITATIVE LITERATURE

SFAS No. 66, *Accounting for Sales of Real Estate*
SFAS No. 67, *Accounting for Costs and Initial Rental Operations of Real Estate Projects*
SFAS No. 98, *Accounting for Leases*
- *Sale-Leaseback Transactions Involving Real Estate*
- *Sales-Type Leases of Real Estate*
- *Definition of the Lease Term*
- *Initial Direct Costs of Direct Financing Leases*

SFAS No. 121, *Accounting for the Impairment of Long-Lived Assets and for Long-Lived Assets to Be Disposed Of*
SOP 97-1, *Accounting by Participating Mortgage Loan Borrowers*

RELATED PRONOUNCEMENTS

AICPA Audit and Accounting Guide, *Common Interest Realty Associations*
SOP 75-2, *Accounting Practices of Real Estate Investment Trusts*
SOP 78-2, *Accounting Practices of Real Estate Investment Trusts*
SOP 78-9, *Accounting for Investments in Real Estate Ventures*
SOP 92-1, *Accounting for Real Estate Syndication Income*
EITF Issue No. 84-17, *Profit Recognition on Sales of Real Estate with Graduated Payment Mortgages or Insured Mortgages*
EITF Issue No. 85-16, *Leveraged Leases*
- *Real Estate Leases and Sale-Leaseback Transactions*
- *Delayed Equity Contributions by Lessors*

EITF Issue No. 85-37, *Recognition of Note Received for Real Estate Syndication Activities*
EITF Issue No. 86-6, *Antispeculation Clauses in Real Estate Sales Contracts*
EITF Issue No. 86-7, *Recognition by Homebuilders of Profit from Sales of Land and Related Construction Contracts*
EITF Issue No. 87-9, *Profit Recognition on Sales of Real Estate with Insured Mortgages or Surety Bonds*
EITF Issue No. 87-29, *Exchange of Real Estate Involving Boot*
EITF Issue No. 88-12, *Transfer of Ownership Interest as Part of Down Payment under FASB Statement No 66*
EITF Issue No. 88-24, *Effect of Various Forms of Financing under FASB Statement No. 66*
EITF Issue No. 89-14, *Valuation of Repossessed Real Estate*
EITF Issue No. 90-20, *Impact of an Uncollateralized Irrevocable Letter of Credit on a Real Estate Sale-Leaseback Transaction*

EITF Issue No. 91-2, *Debtor's Accounting for Forfeiture of Real Estate Subject to a Nonrecourse Mortgage*

EITF Issue No. 94-2, *Treatment of Minority Interests in Certain Real Estate Investment Trusts*

EITF Issue No. 95-6, *Accounting by a Real Estate Investment Trust for an Investment in a Service Corporation*

EITF Issue No. 95-7, *Implementation Issues Related to the Treatment of Minority Interests in Certain Real Estate Investment Trusts*

RELATED TOPICS

Chapter 1—Accounting Changes
Chapter 14—Debt Extinguishments
Chapter 31—Leases
Chapter 33—Long-lived Assets, Depreciation, and Impairment
Chapter 48—Revenue Recognition

RELATED PARTY DISCLOSURES

Table of Contents

RELATED PARTY DISCLOSURES

OVERVIEW

46.100 Material related party transactions (other than compensation arrangements, expense allowances, and similar items occurring in the normal course of business) should be disclosed. Generally, the disclosures include the nature of the relationships, a description of the transactions and their amounts, and the terms and manner of settling the transactions.

46.101 Common control relationships also should be disclosed, even if no related party transactions occurred, if the relationships could significantly affect the reporting entity's financial position or results of operations.

DISCLOSURE REQUIREMENTS

DEFINITION OF A RELATED PARTY

46.500 A related party is an entity that can control or significantly influence the management or operating policies of another entity to the extent one of the entities may be prevented from pursuing its own interests. A related party may be any party the entity deals with that can exercise that control. Examples of related parties include (a) affiliates, (b) investments accounted for under the equity method, (c) trusts for the benefit of employees (for example, pension or profit-sharing trusts), and (d) principal owners and members of management and their immediate families. (SFAS 57, par. 24)

46.501 Transactions between related parties should be recorded in the same manner as transactions between unrelated parties. That is, their substance, rather than their form, generally should govern the accounting. The following are examples of common related party transactions: (SFAS 57, par. 1)

- Sales, purchases, and transfers of property

- Services provided or received

- Property and equipment leases

- Loans or guarantees

- Maintenance of compensating bank balances for the benefit of a related party

- Allocations of common costs

- Filing consolidated tax returns

Common related party transactions include (a) officer or stockholder loans to or from the company, (b) purchases and sales among affiliated companies, (c) leases between stockholders and the company, and (d) guarantees or pledged personal assets of a stockholder.

> **Practical Consideration.** A related party relationship does not exist simply because a company is economically dependent on another party (for example, a sole or major customer, supplier, franchisor, or distributor).

DISCLOSURES

46.502　The following information about material related party transactions (other than compensation arrangements, expense allowances, and similar items occurring in the normal course of business) should be disclosed: (The disclosures apply to the separate financial statements of each combined or consolidated entity as well as to the combined or consolidated financial statements. However, separate financial statements that are presented with the combined or consolidated financial statements need not duplicate the disclosures. Also, consolidated or combined financial statements need not disclose related party transactions that were eliminated in consolidation or combination.)

    a. Nature of the relationship involved (If necessary to an understanding of the relationship, the name of the related party also should be disclosed.)

    b. Description of the transactions, including those for which no or nominal amounts were recorded, for each period for which an income statement is presented (The disclosure should include any other information necessary to understand the transactions' financial statement effects.)

    c. Dollar amounts of the transactions for each period for which an income statement is presented (The disclosure also should include the effects of any change in terms from the terms used in the prior period.)

    d. Amounts due from or to related parties as of the date of each balance sheet presented and, if not otherwise apparent, the terms and manner of settlement (SFAS 57, par. 2) (Receivables from officers, employees, or affiliates should be shown separately rather than presented under a general heading such as notes receivable or accounts receivable.) (ARB 43, Ch. 1A, par. 5)

Practical Consideration. Disclosure of the relationship and amounts often may be conveniently provided through balance sheet captions. The authors generally interpret "nature of the relationship" to mean position rather than an individual's name. Accordingly, captions usually may refer to "stockholders," "officers," or "affiliates." A related party may need to be identified by name, however, if that is necessary to understand the effects of the transaction on the financial statements.

---

e. For an entity that is part of a group that files a consolidated tax return, the following in its separately issued financial statements: (SFAS 109, paras. 49)

   (1) Aggregate amount of current and deferred tax expense for each income statement presented

   (2) Amount of any tax-related balances due to or from affiliates as of the date of each balance sheet presented

   (3) Principal provisions of the method by which the consolidated amount of current and deferred tax expense is allocated to members of the group

   (4) Nature and effect of any changes in the method of allocating current and deferred tax expense to members of the group and in determining the related balances due to or from affiliates during each year for which the disclosures in a. and b. are presented

If results of operations or financial position could change significantly as a result of common ownership or management control of the reporting entity and other entities, the nature of the ownership or management control also should be disclosed, even if there are no transactions between the entities. (SFAS 57, par. 4)

Practical Consideration. Authoritative literature does not require economic dependence to be disclosed. However, SOP 94-6, *Disclosure of Certain Significant Risks and Uncertainties,* does require concentrations in the volume of business transacted with particular customers to be disclosed if loss of the relationship could cause a severe impact to the company. (Chapter 10.)

46.503   Because related party transactions cannot be presumed to be conducted under competitive, free-market conditions, the preceding disclosures should not imply that the transactions were made on an arm's-length basis unless that representation can be substantiated. (SFAS 57, par. 3)

Practical Consideration. Thus, for example, if a company represents in its financial statements that transactions with a related party were consummated on terms no less favorable than would have been obtained from an unrelated party, accountants must be satisfied that such a representation is appropriate. If management is unable to substantiate that representation, accountants reporting on the company's financial statements are required to modify their report for a departure from GAAP.

AUTHORITATIVE LITERATURE AND RELATED TOPICS

AUTHORITATIVE LITERATURE

ARB No. 43, *Restatement and Revision of Accounting Research Bulletins* (Chapter 1A—Rules Adopted by Membership)
SFAS No. 57, *Related Party Disclosures*
SFAS No. 109, *Accounting for Income Taxes*

RELATED PRONOUNCEMENTS

EITF Issue No. 84-15, *Grantor Trusts Consolidation*

RELATED TOPICS

Chapter 9—Consolidated Financial Statements
Chapter 20—Equity Method Investments
Chapter 31—Leases
Chapter 36—Nonmonetary Transactions

RESEARCH AND DEVELOPMENT COSTS

Table of Contents

RESEARCH AND DEVELOPMENT COSTS

OVERVIEW

47.100   Research and development costs should be charged to expense when incurred. If an entity obtains funding for its research and development through arrangements with others, the nature of its obligation under the arrangement determines the accounting. To the extent the entity is obligated to repay the other parties, it should record a liability for its obligation to repay and charge research and development costs to expense as they are incurred. If the entity is not obligated to repay the other parties, regardless of the results of the research and development, its obligation under the arrangement should be accounted for as a contract to provide research and development services for others.

ACCOUNTING REQUIREMENTS

DEFINITION OF RESEARCH AND DEVELOPMENT ACTIVITIES

47.200   *Research* is defined as an entity's efforts to discover information that will be useful in developing a new product, service, process, or technique or in significantly improving an existing product or process. *Development* involves converting research into a plan to create or significantly improve a product, service, process, or technique. Development activities include conceptualizing, designing, and testing product alternatives, constructing prototypes, and operating pilot plants. They do not include routine improvements to existing products and operations, however, nor do they include market research activities. (SFAS 2, par. 8) The following activities typically are considered research and development activities: (SFAS 2, par. 9)

   a. Laboratory research aimed at discovering new knowledge

   b. Searching for ways to apply new research findings or other knowledge

   c. Conceptualizing and designing product or process alternatives

   d. Evaluating product or process alternatives

   e. Modifying the concept or design of a product or process

f. Designing, constructing, and testing preproduction prototypes and models

g. Designing tools, jigs, molds, and dies involving new technology

h. Designing, constructing, and operating a pilot plant (so long as the plant is not of a scale that is economically feasible to the entity for commercial production)

i. Engineering activity to advance the product's design to the point of manufacture

47.201 Conversely, the following activities usually are *not* considered research and development activities: (SFAS 2, par. 10)

a. Engineering follow-through in an early phase of commercial production

b. Quality control during commercial production

c. Trouble-shooting in connection with breakdowns during commercial production

d. Routine efforts to improve the quality of an existing product

e. Adapting an existing capability to a specific requirement or customer need as part of a continuing commercial activity

f. Seasonal or periodic changes to existing products

g. Routine design of tools, jigs, molds, and dies

h. Constructing, relocating, rearranging, or starting facilities or equipment other than pilot plants or facilities or equipment whose sole use is for a particular research and development project

i. Legal work in connection with patent applications, patent defense, or patent sale or licensing

> **Practical Consideration.** The guidance in this chapter does not apply to activities unique to entities in extractive industries, such as prospecting, acquiring mineral rights, exploration, drilling, mining, and related mineral development. However, it does apply to research and development activities of those entities, such as developing a technique used in exploration, drilling, or extraction.

ACCOUNTING FOR RESEARCH AND DEVELOPMENT COSTS

47.202   Research and development costs include the following:

a. Intangibles purchased from others

b. Materials, equipment, and facilities acquired or constructed for a particular research and development project

c. Salaries and related costs of personnel engaged in research and development activities

d. Services performed by others in connection with research and development

e. Reasonable allocations of indirect costs (except general and administrative costs not clearly related to research and development activities)

Generally, research and development costs should be charged to expense when incurred rather than recorded as inventory, elements of overhead, or otherwise deferred to future periods. However, intangibles purchased from others and materials, equipment, and facilities should be capitalized and depreciated over their useful lives if they have alternative future uses (including use in other research and development projects). Depreciation expense related to capitalized research and development costs should be considered a research and development cost. (SFAS 2, paras. 11–12)

47.203   Research and development costs acquired in a purchase business combination should be assigned a portion of the purchase price based on their fair values. (See Chapter 3.) Subsequently, the costs should be accounted for as described in the preceding paragraph. That is, those costs that have alternative future uses should be capitalized and amortized and all other costs should be expensed when incurred. (FASBI 4, paras. 4–5)

Computer Software Costs

47.204   Generally, the guidelines in Paragraphs 47.200–.203 apply to the cost of software developed or purchased for internal use or for sale to others. The following paragraphs provide additional guidance on applying those guidelines.

47.205   **Software Purchased or Developed for Internal Use.** The guidance in Paragraphs 47.200–.203 should be followed when accounting for the cost of computer software purchased or developed for internal use. That is, if the software is used in research and development activities, its cost is a research and development cost and should be accounted for as follows:

a. Costs incurred to purchase software from others should be charged to expense when incurred unless it has an alternative future use. In that case, it should be capitalized and amortized over its useful life.

b. Costs incurred to internally develop software, including costs incurred during all phases of development, should be charged to expense when incurred. (The alternative future use test described in a. and in Paragraph 47.202 applies only to intangibles *purchased from others.* Consequently, none of the cost of software *developed internally* for research and development activities should be capitalized.) (FASBI 6, paras. 5–6 and 8)

Practical Consideration. Authoritative literature does not specifically address how software purchased or developed for internal use that is not considered a research and development cost should be treated. In practice, many companies expense such costs as they are incurred. The authors believe the costs should be treated the same as any other cost. That is, they should be charged to expense over the periods benefitted. For example, the cost incurred to develop software used in a company's general management information system should be capitalized and amortized to expense over the software's useful life. The authors' approach is consistent with a recently proposed SOP on accounting for software costs. (The AICPA expects to issue a final version of the SOP in late 1997 or early 1998.)

47.206   **Software Purchased or Developed to Be Sold, Leased, or Otherwise Marketed.** Costs incurred to establish the technological feasibility of software to be sold, leased, or otherwise marketed are research and development costs and should be charged to expense when incurred. (The cost of purchased software that has an alternative future use should be capitalized and accounted for according to its use, however.)

47.207   A software's technological feasibility is established when all activities necessary to produce the product in accordance with its design specifications have been performed. If the development process includes a detail program design, those activities include the following at a minimum:

a. Completing the product design and the detail program design and determining that the necessary skills, hardware, and software technology are available to the entity to produce the product

47.206

b. Confirming that the detail program design is complete and consistent with the product design by documenting and tracing the detail program design to product specifications

c. Reviewing the detail program design for high-risk development issues and resolving any uncertainties that are identified

If the development process does not include a detail program design with the preceding features, the activities necessary to produce a product include completing and testing a product design and working model. (SFAS 86, paras. 3–4)

> **Practical Consideration.** Software development costs incurred after technological feasibility has been established are not research and development costs. Accounting for those costs is discussed in Chapter 56.

RESEARCH AND DEVELOPMENT ARRANGEMENTS

47.208   Research and development may be partially or entirely funded by others through a research and development arrangement. For example, in a typical arrangement, an entity might form a limited partnership through which research and development will be conducted. The entity acts as general partner, managing the research and development activities, and limited partners provide all or a part of the funds needed to complete the research project. Normally, the entity performs the research under a contract with the limited partnership, and the limited partnership retains the rights to the results of the research and development. The entity may purchase the results from the partnership or pay a royalty to the partnership for the rights to use the results, however. Accounting for such arrangements depends on the nature of the obligation the entity incurs when it enters into the arrangement. (SFAS 68, par. 4)

> **Practical Consideration.** The limited partnership form is used for illustrative purposes only. In practice, research and development arrangements exist in a variety of forms.

Obligation Is a Liability to Repay the Other Parties

47.209   If the entity is obligated to repay all of the funds provided by the other parties, regardless of the outcome of the research and development, the financial risks associated with the research and development arrangement have not been transferred to others. In such cases, the entity should estimate and accrue the liability to repay others and charge research and development costs to expense as incurred.

47.210   In some instances, written agreements or contracts may not require the entity to repay the funds provided by the other parties, but circumstances indicate that it is probable the entity will repay the funds. In that event, the entity is presumed to have incurred a liability to repay. Examples of circumstances that may indicate that the entity will repay funds provided by others include the following:

a. The entity has indicated that it intends to repay the funds provided by others regardless of the success of the research and development.

b. The entity would suffer a severe economic penalty if it failed to repay the funds. For example, an entity that provided proprietary information to a limited partnership formed to conduct research and development may have to purchase the partnership's interest in the research to recover the proprietary information or prevent it from being transferred to others.

c. At the time the entity enters into the research and development arrangement, a significant related party relationship exists between the entity and a party providing the funding.

d. The entity has essentially completed the research and development before entering into the arrangement.

47.211   If the entity is obligated to repay some but not all of the funds provided by other parties, it should charge its portion of research and development costs to expense as the liability is incurred. (SFAS 68, paras. 5–9)

Obligation Is to Perform Contractual Services

47.212   If the entity is not obligated to repay any of the funds provided by the other parties or if repayment depends solely on the results of the research having some future economic benefit, the financial risks associated with the research and development arrangement have been transferred to others. In such cases, the entity should account for the arrangement as a contract to perform research and development for others. Consequently, any research and development costs incurred should be capitalized as inventory and charged to cost of sales when revenue is recognized. (SFAS 68, par. 10)

47.213   If the entity's obligation is to perform research and development for others and it subsequently decides to purchase the other parties' interests in the arrangement or to obtain the rights to use the research results, the purchase of the interest or rights should be accounted for in accordance with existing GAAP. (SFAS 68, par. 11) (Chapter 3 discusses accounting for assets acquired in a business combination and Chapter 26 discusses accounting for purchased intangible assets.)

Other Issues

47.214 **Loans or Advances to the Other Parties.** The entity may loan funds to the other parties, the repayment of which depends solely on the future economic benefits of the research and development. For example, the loan may be repaid by reducing the price the entity must pay to purchase the results of the project or by reducing the royalties the entity must pay to use the results of the project. Such loans should be charged to research and development expense unless they specifically relate to another activity, such as marketing or advertising. (SFAS 68, par. 12)

47.215 **Issuance of Warrants or Similar Instruments.** If the entity issues stock purchase warrants or similar instruments in connection with a research and development arrangement, a portion of the funds received from the other parties should be recorded as additional paid-in capital. The amount that should be recorded is the fair value of the instruments on the date of the arrangement. (SFAS 68, par. 13)

47.216 **Acquiring the Results of a Research and Development Arrangement by Issuing Stock.** The entity should record stock issued to acquire the results of a research and development arrangement at its fair value or the fair value of the consideration received, whichever is more clearly evident. Fair value should be determined at the date the entity exercises its option to purchase the results of the arrangement. (FTB 84-1, par. 7)

DISCLOSURE REQUIREMENTS

47.500 The total research and development costs charged to expense should be disclosed for each period for which an income statement is presented. (SFAS 2, par. 13) In addition, an entity that accounts for a research and development arrangement as a contract to provide research and development services for others should disclose the following:

a. Terms of significant agreements under the arrangement (including royalty agreements, purchase provisions, license agreements, and commitments to provide additional funding) as of the date of each balance sheet presented

b. Amount of compensation earned and costs incurred under such contracts for each period for which an income statement is presented (SFAS 68, par. 14)

AUTHORITATIVE LITERATURE AND RELATED TOPICS

AUTHORITATIVE LITERATURE

SFAS No. 2, *Accounting for Research and Development Costs*
SFAS No. 68, *Research and Development Arrangements*
SFAS No. 86, *Accounting for the Costs of Computer Software to Be Sold, Leased, or Otherwise Marketed*
FASB Technical Bulletin 84-1, *Accounting for Stock Issued to Acquire the Results of a Research and Development Arrangement*
FASB Interpretation No. 4, *Applicability of FASB Statement No. 2 to Business Combinations Accounted for by the Purchase Method*
FASB Interpretation No. 6, *Applicability of FASB Statement No. 2 to Computer Software*

RELATED PRONOUNCEMENTS

EITF Issue No. 85-35, *Transition and Implementation Issues for FASB Statement No. 86*
EITF Issue No. 86-14, *Purchased Research and Development Projects in a Business Combination*

RELATED TOPICS

Chapter 3—Business Combinations
Chapter 18—Development Stage Enterprises
Chapter 26—Intangible Assets
Chapter 56—Computer Software Developers

REVENUE RECOGNITION

Table of Contents

REVENUE RECOGNITION

OVERVIEW

48.100   Generally, revenue should be recognized (and an appropriate provision for uncollectible amounts should be made) when a transaction is completed. When the buyer has the right to return the merchandise sold, revenue should be recognized only if certain criteria are met. Revenue and cost of sales recognized when a right of return exists should be reduced for estimated returns, and expected costs or losses related to sales returns should be accrued.

48.101   Revenue related to separately priced extended warranty and product maintenance contracts should be deferred and generally recognized over the life of the contracts on a straight-line basis. Costs directly related to the acquisition of the contracts should be charged to expense in proportion to the revenue recognized. All other costs, including costs associated with performing services under the contracts, should be charged to expense as incurred.

ACCOUNTING REQUIREMENTS

48.200   Statement of Financial Accounting Concepts No. 5, *Recognition and Measurement in Financial Statements of Business Enterprises,* states that revenue is recorded in financial statements when the following conditions are met:

a. Amounts are realized or realizable (that is, they are converted or convertible into cash or claims to cash).

b. Amounts are earned (that is, activities prerequisite to obtaining benefits have been completed).

Thus, as a general rule, revenue from selling products should be recognized at the date of sale, and revenue from rendering services should be recognized when the services have been performed and are billable. In addition, an appropriate allowance for uncollectible amounts should be provided. (Chapter 10 discusses providing an estimate for uncollectible receivables.)

48.201   Ordinarily, the preceding conditions occur when the transaction is completed. As a result, recognizing revenue under the installment method (which recognizes a portion of the transaction's profit as revenues are collected) generally is not acceptable. In some exceptional cases, however, the terms of a transaction are such that receivables are collectible over an extended period of time and their collectibility cannot be reasonably estimated. Under those conditions, the installment method or cost-recovery method may be used to recognize revenue. (When the cost-recovery method is used, no profit is recognized until all costs have been recovered.) In addition, specific pronouncements, such as those dealing with sales of real estate (see Chapter 45) or construction contractors (see Chapter 57), may permit the use of the installment, cost-recovery, or percentage-of-completion method. (APB 10, par. 12)

Practical Consideration. To illustrate recognizing revenue under the installment and cost-recovery methods, assume that a company sold inventory costing $72,000 for $120,000. Under the terms of the sales contract, the sales proceeds will be received in 60 monthly installments of $2,000. Under both the installment and cost-recovery methods, the profit would be deferred at the time of the sale through the following entry:

Accounts receivable	120,000	
Inventory		72,000
Deferred gross profit		48,000

The deferred profit would be recognized differently under each method, however.

Installment method

Under the installment method, profit is recognized as proceeds are received. Thus, the profit would be recognized as follows:

Monthly installment	$2,000
Gross profit percentage ($48,000 ÷ $120,000)	× 40%
Profit recognized each month	$ 800

Each month, the profit would be recognized through the following entry:

Cash	2,000	
Cost of sales	1,200	
Deferred gross profit	800	
Accounts receivable		2,000
Sales		2,000

Practical Consideration (Continued).

Cost-recovery method

Under the cost-recovery method, no profit is recognized until all costs have been recovered, which, in this example, would not occur until the 36th payment is received. Thus, profit would be recognized through the following entries:

Installments 1–36:

Cash	2,000	
Cost of sales	2,000	
Accounts receivable		2,000
Sales		2,000

Installments 37–60:

Cash	2,000	
Deferred gross profit	2,000	
Accounts receivable		2,000
Sales		2,000

48.202 Various pronouncements discuss recognizing revenue related to specific transactions or industries. This chapter discusses general revenue recognition requirements, including those concerning recognizing revenue when the buyer has the right to return the merchandise, and recognizing revenue related to warranty and maintenance contracts.

RECOGNIZING REVENUE WHEN A RIGHT OF RETURN EXISTS

48.203 A customer may be allowed to return merchandise for refund, credit, or exchange during a specified period following the sale. In such cases, ownership essentially has not been transferred from the seller to the buyer. Consequently, the sale has not been completed and revenue generally should not be recognized. Revenue may be recognized at the time of sale when a right of return exists, however, if all of the following conditions are met:

    a. The seller's price to the buyer is substantially fixed or determinable at the date of sale.

    b. The buyer has paid the seller or is obligated to pay the seller and the obligation is not contingent on reselling the merchandise.

    c. The buyer's obligation to the seller would not change if the merchandise were stolen, damaged, or destroyed.

   d. The buyer has economic substance. (That is, the buyer is not a front established by the seller primarily to recognize sales revenue.)

   e. The seller has no significant obligation to help the buyer resell the merchandise.

   f. The amount of returns can be reasonably estimated. (SFAS 48, par. 6)

Practical Consideration. The guidance in Paragraphs 48.203–.205 on accounting for revenues when the right of return exists generally applies to all transactions except—

- revenue in service industries that may be returned under cancellation privileges,

- transactions involving real estate (see Chapter 45), and

- customer rights to return defective goods, such as under warranty provisions (see Paragraphs 48.206–.208).

48.204   If all of the preceding conditions are met and sales revenue is recognized, a contingency exists for the costs or losses that may occur from merchandise returns. The contingency should be accrued through a reduction to sales and cost of sales if—

   a. information available prior to issuing the financial statements indicates it is probable that an asset has been impaired or a liability incurred as of the balance sheet date and

   b. the amount of the loss can be reasonably estimated. (SFAS 5, par. 8 and SFAS 48, par. 7)

Practical Consideration. To illustrate accruing estimated sales returns, assume a company estimates that $100,000 of sales will be returned and the cost of sales related to those returns is $60,000. Assume further that the company estimates that it will incur $5,000 of additional costs to process the returns. The entry needed to accrue sales returns would be as follows:

Sales returns	100,000	
Inventory	60,000	
Cost of processing sales returns	5,000	
Allowance for estimated returns		100,000
Cost of sales		60,000
Accrued cost of processing		
sales returns		5,000

48.205 The ability to reasonably estimate the amount of future returns depends on a variety of factors that change from one case to the next. Factors that may impair a seller's ability to reasonably estimate returns include the following:

- Susceptibility of the merchandise to external factors such as changes in demand or technological obsolescence

- Right of return period that lasts for a relatively long time

- Lack of experience with similar types of sales or products

- Inability to apply prior experience due to changes in marketing policies or customer relationships (SFAS 48, par. 8)

> **Practical Consideration.** In practice, sellers generally estimate returns using a percentage of sales based on their past experience or the past experience of similar companies selling similar products.

SEPARATELY PRICED EXTENDED WARRANTY AND PRODUCT MAINTENANCE CONTRACTS

48.206 Many retailers offer a separately priced service contract when products are sold. The contract covers a stated period and may entitle the customer to warranty protection, routine periodic maintenance services, or both. Revenue from separately priced extended warranty and product maintenance contracts should be deferred at the point of sale and recognized on a straight-line basis over the life of the contract. Revenues may be recognized over the contract period in proportion to costs, however, if sufficient historical evidence indicates that the costs of performing services under the contracts are incurred on other than a straight-line basis. (FTB 90-1, par. 3)

> **Practical Consideration.** The portion of the deferred gross profit that is expected to be amortized within the next year should be classified as a current liability. The remaining amount should be classified as noncurrent.

48.207 Incremental direct acquisition costs (that is, those directly related to the acquisition of the contract that would not have been incurred if the contract had not been acquired) should also be deferred and charged to expense in proportion to the revenue recognized. Other costs related to the contracts, including the costs of services performed under the contract, general and administrative expenses, advertising expenses, and costs associated with the negotiation of a contract that is not consummated, should be charged to expense when incurred. (FTB 90-1, par. 4)

48.208   If the expected costs of providing services under separately priced extended warranty and product maintenance contracts plus unamortized acquisition costs exceed the related unearned revenue, a loss should be recognized. The loss should first be recognized by charging any unamortized acquisition costs to expense. A liability should be recognized for any loss that is greater than the unamortized acquisition costs. (FTB 90-1, par. 5)

> **Practical Consideration.** The guidance in Paragraphs 48.206–.208 applies only to warranty and maintenance agreements that are *separately priced*. An agreement is separately priced if its purchase is optional and its purchase price is stated separately from the price of the product.

DISCLOSURE REQUIREMENTS

48.500   Generally accepted accounting principles do not require specific disclosures about revenues in general, revenues recognized when a right of return exists, or revenues related to separately priced warranty and maintenance contracts. However, pronouncements covered in other chapters of this *Guide* may require disclosures about revenues related to specific types of transactions or industries (for example, revenues related to real estate transactions, computer software revenues, etc.). In addition, because a loss contingency generally arises when revenues are recognized and a right of return exists and when product warranty or product maintenance contracts are sold, the contingency and risks and uncertainties disclosures discussed in Chapter 10 may apply.

> **Practical Consideration.** APB Opinion No. 22, *Disclosure of Accounting Policies,* requires disclosure of the principles used that are (a) a selection from existing acceptable alternatives, (b) peculiar to the industry in which the entity operates, or (c) unusual or innovative applications of GAAP. (See Chapter 2.) Thus, the authors believe an entity should disclose its method of recognizing revenues if it involves recognizing revenues at other than the point of sale.

AUTHORITATIVE LITERATURE AND RELATED TOPICS

AUTHORITATIVE LITERATURE

APB Opinion No. 10, *Omnibus Opinion—1966*
SFAS No. 5, *Accounting for Contingencies*
SFAS No. 48, *Revenue Recognition When Right of Return Exists*
FASB Technical Bulletin 90-1, *Accounting for Separately Priced Extended Warranty and Product Maintenance Contracts*

RELATED PRONOUNCEMENTS

EITF Issue No. 91-6, *Revenue Recognition of Long-Term Power Sales Contracts*

EITF Issue No. 91-9, *Revenue and Expense Recognition for Freight Services in Process*

EITF Issue No. 95-1, *Revenue Recognition on Sales with Guaranteed Minimum Resale Value*

EITF Issue No. 95-4, *Revenue Recognition on Equipment Sold and Subsequently Repurchased Subject to an Operating Lease*

EITF Issue No. 96-17, *Revenue Recognition under Long-Term Power Sales Contracts That Contain both Fixed and Variable Pricing Terms*

SOP 81-1, *Accounting for Performance of Construction-Type and Certain Production-Type Contracts*

SOP 91-1, *Software Revenue Recognition*

SOP 92-1, *Accounting for Real Estate Syndication Income*

RELATED TOPICS

Chapter 2—Accounting Policies, Nature of Operations, and Use of Estimates Disclosures

Chapter 10—Contingencies

Chapter 23—Income Statement

Chapter 45—Real Estate Transactions

Chapter 56—Computer Software Developers

Chapter 57—Construction Contractors

Chapter 58—Franchisors

SEGMENT REPORTING

Table of Contents

SEGMENT REPORTING

OVERVIEW

49.100   A publicly traded company must disclose the following information about its reportable operating segments when it presents a complete set of financial statements:

- General information about factors used to identify reportable segments, the basis of organization, and sources of revenues

- Information about reported profit or loss (including certain revenues and expenses included in segment profit or loss) and segment assets

- Reconciliations of certain reported segment information to consolidated amounts

The entity also is required to disclose certain information on an entity-wide basis about products and services, geographic areas, and sales to major customers.

DISCLOSURE REQUIREMENTS

Practical Consideration. The guidance in this chapter is based on SFAS No. 131, *Disclosures about Segments of an Enterprise and Related Information,* which is effective for fiscal years beginning after December 15, 1997, with early application encouraged. Segment information for prior years, if presented, should be restated to conform with the guidance in this chapter unless it is impracticable to do so. Interim financial statements issued in the year SFAS No. 131 is initially applied do not have to comply with the required disclosures in this chapter. However, comparative information about the initial year's interim periods should be reported in interim financial statements in the year following SFAS No. 131's adoption.

Segment reporting requirements under previous authoritative literature are discussed in depth in the 1997 edition of *Guide to GAAP.*

49.500   Entities that issue debt or equity securities traded in a public market (and those required to file financial statements with the Securities and Exchange Commission) must disclose certain information about their operating segments in the complete sets of financial statements or condensed interim period financial statements they issue to shareholders. Segment information need not be disclosed in the following situations, however:

     a. Nonpublic companies and nonprofit organizations are not required to present segment information.

     b. Separate financial statements of a parent, subsidiary, joint venture, or equity method investee presented in another entity's financial report need not disclose segment information if (1) the separate financial statements are consolidated or combined in a complete set of financial statements and (2) both sets of financial statements are presented in the same financial report. (The consolidated or combined entity would be subject to the segment disclosure requirements, however. A publicly held parent, subsidiary, joint venture, or equity method investee would only be required to disclose segment information in its separately issued financial statements. (SFAS 131, par. 9)

SEGMENT DISCLOSURES

What Is an Operating Segment?

49.501   An operating segment is a component of an entity that has the following characteristics: (SFAS 131, paras. 9–10)

     a. It is involved in business activities from which it may earn revenues and incur expenses (including revenues and expenses from transactions with other components of the entity)

     b. Its operating results are regularly reviewed by the entity's management to evaluate the performance of the segment and make decisions about the allocation of resources to the segment.

     c. Separate financial information about it is available.

Practical Consideration. Regularly reviewing the segment's operating results and making decisions about how resources are allocated is a function of the *chief operating decision maker.* A chief operating decision maker may be the chief executive officer, chief operating officer, or a group of management (for example, the president, executive vice presidents, and others). Throughout this chapter, the term *chief executive* refers to the chief operating decision maker.

49.502   For some companies, the criteria in Paragraph 49.501 may be easily applied to determine what operations of the business are operating segments. However, other companies may produce financial and operating reports in a variety of different ways, and the chief executive may use more than one set of segment information. In such cases, the following factors may identify a single set of components that constitute the company's operating segments:

     a. The nature of each component's business activities

     b. The existence of managers responsible for each component

     c. Information presented to the board of directors (SFAS 131, par. 13)

Practical Consideration. Sometimes, not every part of an entity is included in an operating segment. For example, a corporate headquarters' or other department's activities may be intended to generate no revenue (or only incidental revenue) and would not be part of an operating segment. Furthermore, pension and postretirement benefit plans are not considered operating segments.

49.503   Operating segments generally have a segment manager who is accountable to and communicates operating activities, financial results, forecasts and other plans to the chief executive. The chief executive may also be the segment manager for one or more operating segments. If the criteria in Paragraph 49.501 can be applied to more than one set of components of the company, but there is only one set for which segment managers are held responsible, the operating segments would be comprised of the set of components for which component managers are held responsible. (SFAS 131, par. 14) If the company has overlapping sets of components for which segment managers are responsible (that is, a matrix form of organization), the components based on products and services would make up the operating segments. For example, a company may have managers responsible for specific product lines world-wide and managers responsible for specific geographic areas, with the chief executive regularly reviewing operating results for both sets of components. In that case, the operating segments would be the set of components based on product lines. (SFAS 131, par. 15)

49.504   A company may decide to combine two or more operating segments into a single segment if the segments have similar:

    a. economic characteristics,

    b. products and services,

    c. production processes,

    d. types or classes of customers,

    e. methods of distributing products or providing services, and

    f. regulatory environments, if applicable. (SFAS 131, par. 17)

Practical Consideration. SFAS No. 131 prescribes a *management approach* to identifying segments rather than the *industry approach* required by previous standards. That is, it requires a company to determine reportable segments based on the way management organizes segments for decision making and performance assessment purposes rather than along industry lines. (Previous requirements are discussed in depth in the 1997 edition of *Guide to GAAP*.) The management approach is expected to reduce the cost of providing segment information. It relies on information that generally is already available rather than industry or geographic information that may have to be generated specifically for the segment disclosures.

Selecting Reportable Segments

49.505   Generally, information should be reported separately for an operating segment (or aggregation of segments if two or more operating segments are combined as discussed in Paragraph 49.504) that meets any of the following quantitative tests: (SFAS 131, par. 18)

    a. *Its revenue, including intersegment sales or transfers, is 10% or more of the combined revenue of all of the entity's operating segments.*

    b. *Its reported profit or loss is 10% or more of the greater of the absolute amount of (in absolute terms)—*

       (1) the combined reported profit of all operating segments that did not report a loss or

       (2) the combined reported loss of all operating segments that reported a loss.

Practical Consideration. To illustrate applying the 10% of operating profit test, assume that an entity has identified the following industry segments:

Operating Segment	Reported Profit (Loss)
A	$ 5,000
B	6,000
C	600
D	1,000
	12,600
E	(7,500)
F	(4,400)
G	(800)
	(12,700)
Total	$ (100)

The test would be based on the combined loss of segments E, F, and G since the absolute value of their combined losses is greater than the absolute value of the combined profit of all segments that did not incur an operating loss. Thus, segments A, B, E, and F are considered reportable segments because they each had an operating profit or loss of at least $1,270 ($12,700 × 10%).

---

    c. *Its assets are 10% or more of the combined assets of all of the entity's operating segments.*

49.506   Reportable segments should represent a substantial portion of the entity's operations. Reportable segments are considered to represent a substantial portion of operations if their combined revenue is at least 75% of the entity's consolidated revenues. If the 75% test is not met, additional operating segments should be identified as reportable segments until the 75% test is met. (SFAS 131, par. 20) When adding reportable segments, the following should be considered:

    a. If management determines that an operating segment identified as a reportable segment in the prior period is of continuing significance, the entity should continue to report information about that segment separately even if it no longer meets the criteria in Paragraph 49.505. (SFAS 131, par. 21)

    b. An entity may combine information about operating segments that do not meet the thresholds discussed in Paragraph 49.505 with information about other operating segments that do not meet the thresholds only if they share a majority of the criteria for aggregation discussed in Paragraph 49.504. (SFAS 131, par. 19)

Practical Consideration. Material operating segments can only be combined if they meet *all* of the criteria in Paragraph 49.504. GAAP is more liberal in allowing immaterial segments to be combined if they meet only a *majority* of the criteria in Paragraph 49.504. However, aggregation of dissimilar operating segments is prohibited.

---

c. If an operating segment is determined to be a reportable segment in the current period, prior period information should be restated to reflect the newly identified segment as a separate segment (even if the segment did not meet the criteria in Paragraph 49.505 in the prior period). (SFAS 131, par. 23)

d. Information about operating segments that are not reportable segments should be aggregated and disclosed in an "all other" category separate from the reportable segment information. The sources of revenue for those segments should be disclosed. (SFAS 131, par. 21) A company may also elect to disclose information about nonreportable segments separately. (SFAS 131, par. 18)

As a practical matter, the total number of reportable segments should be kept to 10 or less since information about more segments than that may become overly detailed. (SFAS 131, par. 24)

Required Disclosures

49.507   A company should disclose the following information about its operating segments for each period for which a complete set of financial statements is presented:

General Information (SFAS 131, par. 26)

a. The factors used to identify the company's operating segments, including the basis of organization (for example, whether the company is organized by product or service lines, geographic regions, regulatory environment, or a combination of those factors and whether any segments have been aggregated)

b. The source of revenue (i.e., types of products or services) for each reportable segment

Profit or Loss Information (SFAS 131, par. 27)

c. Total profit or loss for each reportable segment (See Paragraph 49.508.)

d. Total assets for each reportable segment

e. The following *if such amounts are included in the measure of profit or loss reviewed by the chief executive—*

    (1) Revenues from external customers

    (2) Revenues from other operating segments

    (3) Interest revenue

    (4) Interest expense

Practical Consideration. Interest revenue and expense should be reported separately. However, if the majority of the segment's revenues are from interest and the chief executive relies on net interest revenue when evaluating performance and making decisions about resources allocated to the segment, then the company may report interest revenue net of interest expense for that segment. In such a case, the company should disclose the fact that interest revenue is reported net of interest expense.

---

    (5) Depreciation, depletion, and amortization expense

    (6) Unusual items or infrequent items (See Chapter 23.)

    (7) Equity in net income of equity method investees

    (8) Income tax expense or benefit

    (9) Extraordinary items

    (10) Significant noncash items (other than depreciation, depletion, and amortization)

Asset Information (SFAS 131, par. 28)

f. The following *if such amounts are included in the determination of segment assets reviewed by the chief executive—*

(1) Amount of the company's investment in equity method investees

(2) Total expenditures for investments in long-lived assets (other than financial instruments, long-term customer relationships of a financial institution, mortgage or other servicing rights, deferred tax assets, and deferred policy acquisition costs of an insurance enterprise)

Measurement Information (SFAS 131, par. 31)

g. The basis of accounting used for transactions between reportable segments

h. The nature of any differences between the methods used to measure segment profit or loss and the company's consolidated income before tax, extraordinary items, discontinued operations, and the cumulative effect of an accounting change (Differences consist of different accounting policies and any policies for allocating costs that would help users better understand the segment information.)

i. The nature of any differences between the methods used to measure segment assets and the company's consolidated assets (The disclosure should discuss differing accounting policies or any policies for allocating jointly used assets that would help users better understand the segment information.)

j. The nature of any change from prior periods in the method of measuring reportable segment profit or loss and its effect on the segment's profit or loss in the period of change

k. The nature and effect of any asymmetrical allocations to reportable segments (For example, a company may allocate accounts receivable to a segment but not losses on uncollectible accounts.)

49.508   The amounts reported for segment information should be the amounts used by the chief executive to measure segment performance and to make decisions about allocating resources to the operating segments. That is, adjustments and eliminations necessary to prepare the company's general purpose financial statements and allocations of revenues, expenses, and gains and losses should be included in determining segment profit and loss only if they are included in the amounts used by the chief executive. Likewise, only assets that are included in the measure of a segment's assets used by the chief executive should be reported for that segment. Any amounts allocated to reported segment profit or loss or assets should be allocated on a reasonable basis. (SFAS 131, par. 29) If the chief executive uses more than one measure of a segment's profit, loss, or assets, the amounts reported for that segment should be the amounts most consistent with the measurements used to prepare the company's consolidated financial statements. (SFAS 131, par. 30)

Practical Consideration. In other words, GAAP does not prescribe how segment information should be measured, but rather requires the entity to report the information in its financial statements in the same manner in which it is reported to the chief operating decision maker for purposes of making operating decisions.

49.509   **Reconciliations.** A company's disclosures should include reconciliations of segment information to consolidated company information. Specifically, the following reconciliations should be presented: (SFAS 131, par. 32)

    a. Total reportable segments' revenues to consolidated revenue

    b. Total reportable segment profit or loss to consolidated income before taxes, extraordinary items, discontinued operations, and cumulative effect of accounting changes (If the company allocates income taxes and extraordinary items to the reportable segments, the company may reconcile total reportable segment profit or loss to consolidated income after taxes and extraordinary items.)

    c. Total reportable segments' assets to consolidated assets

    d. Total reportable segments' amounts for other significant segment disclosures to consolidated amounts for those items (For example, if the company chooses to report long-term debt for reportable segments, then the company should disclose a reconciliation of total reportable segments' long-term debt to consolidated long-term debt.)

All reconciling items should be separately identified and adequately described.

49.510   **Interim Periods.** The following information should be presented for each reportable segment in the interim condensed financial statements issued to shareholders: (SFAS 131, par. 33)

a. Revenues from external customers

b. Revenues from other operating segments

c. Segment profit or loss

d. Total segment assets for which there has been a material change from the amount disclosed in the previous annual financial statements

e. If applicable, any differences from the previous annual financial statements in the basis for determining reportable segments or in the basis of measuring segment profit or loss

f. A reconciliation of the total reportable segment profit or loss to consolidated income before taxes, extraordinary items, discontinued operations, and cumulative effect of accounting changes (If the company allocates income taxes and extraordinary items to the reportable segments, the company may reconcile total reportable segment profit or loss to consolidated income after taxes and extraordinary items.)

49.511   Restating Previously Reported Segment Information. If an entity's internal restructuring causes its reportable segments to change, the segment information for earlier periods (including interim periods) should be restated. In such cases, the entity also should disclose whether it has restated the segment information for prior periods. (SFAS 131, par. 34) If prior period information is not restated (because it is impracticable to do so), the entity should present segment information for the current period under both the old basis and the new basis of segmentation if it is practicable to do so. (SFAS 131, par. 35)

Practical Consideration. Previously reported segment information must only be restated if it is practicable to do so. (Presumably, restatement would not be practicable if it would cause the company significant effort and expense.) If certain disclosures can be practicably restated but others cannot, the entity must restate those amounts that can be practicably restated.

49.512   Example Disclosure. EXHIBIT 49-1 illustrates disclosing information about operating segments.

EXHIBIT 49-1

ILLUSTRATION OF OPERATING SEGMENT DISCLOSURES

NOTE H—OPERATING SEGMENTS

Conglomerate, Inc. organizes its business units into six reportable segments: professional publications, domestic newspapers, foreign newspapers, paper products, software, and construction. The professional publications segment publishes professional literature for the accounting, legal, and medical professions. The domestic newspapers segment publishes primarily weekly community newspapers throughout the United States. The foreign newspapers segment publishes English-language newspapers throughout Europe. The paper products segment produces quality papers and newsprint for sale to the printing and publishing industries. The software segment produces packaged business application software for sale to small and large businesses. The construction segment builds bridges and highways for state and local governments. Conglomerate, Inc. also has operating segments in the real estate development and aircraft maintenance industries that do not meet the quantitative thresholds for reportable segments.

The segments' accounting policies are the same as those described in the summary of significant accounting policies except that interest expense is not allocated to the individual operating segments when determining segment profit or loss. Conglomerate, Inc. evaluates performance based on profit or loss from operations before interest and income taxes not including nonrecurring gains and losses. Retail prices are used to report intersegment sales.

Conglomerate, Inc.'s reportable business segments are strategic business units that offer different products and services. Each segment is managed separately because they require different technologies and market to distinct classes of customers.

EXHIBIT 49-1 (Continued)

	Professional Publications	Domestic Newspapers	Foreign Newspapers	Paper Products	Software	Construction	All Other	Total
Sales to external customers	$ 450,000	$ 385,000	$ 125,000	$ 400,000	$ 325,000	$ 250,000	$ 10,000	$1,945,000
Intersegment revenues	—	—	—	100,000	25,000	—	—	125,000
Interest revenue	30,000	10,000	5,000	25,000	20,000	10,000	—	100,000
Interest expense[a]	—	—	—	—	—	—	—	—
Depreciation and amortization	25,000	12,000	5,000	40,000	35,000	50,000	2,500	169,500
Segment profit	100,000	50,000	20,000	45,000	100,000	25,000	500	340,500
Other significant noncash items: Cost in excess of billings on long-term contracts	—	—	—	—	—	12,500	—	12,500
Segment assets	200,000	150,000	65,000	450,000	100,000	300,000	20,000	1,285,000
Expenditures for segment assets	25,000	10,000	5,000	75,000	20,000	40,000	2,000	177,000

Note:

a   Interest expense is not allocated to the operating segments.

EXHIBIT 49-1 (Continued)

Reconciliation of Segment Information

Revenues

Total revenues for reportable segments	$ 1,935,000
Other revenues	10,000
Elimination of intersegment revenues	(125,000)
Consolidated revenues	$ 1,820,000

Profit

Total reportable segment profit	$ 340,000
Other profit	500
Unallocated amounts:	
Interest expense	(125,000)
Gain on sale of corporate investments	25,000
Other corporate expenses	(30,000)
Income before income taxes and extraordinary items	$ 210,500

Assets

Total assets for reportable segments	$ 1,265,000
Other assets	20,000
Elimination of intercompany receivables	(125,000)
Goodwill not allocated to segments	75,000
Other unallocated amounts	100,000
Consolidated Assets	$ 1,335,000

Other Significant Adjustments	Segment Totals	Adjustments	Consolidated Total
Interest revenue	$ 100,000	$ 10,000	$ 110,000
Interest expense	—	125,000	125,000
Expenditures for assets	175,000	17,000	192,000
Depreciation and amortization	167,000	15,000	182,000
Cost in excess of billing on long-term contracts	12,500	—	12,500

The reconciling item to adjust interest expense is the amount of interest expense incurred by the Company, but not allocated to the operating segments. The other adjustments reflect amounts incurred at the parent not allocated to the operating segments and amounts incurred by nonreportable segments. None of the other adjustments are considered significant.

ENTITY-WIDE INFORMATION

49.513 An entity must make the following entity-wide disclosures if it does not provide the information in its segment disclosures: (The amounts should be determined using the same methods used to prepare the company's consolidated financial statements.)

Products and Services (SFAS 131, par. 37)

a. Revenues from external customers for each product or service or group of products and services if practicable to do so. (If not practicable, that fact should be disclosed.)

Geographic Information (SFAS 131, par. 38)

b. Revenues from external customers from (1) the company's home country, and (2) all foreign countries in total should be disclosed if practicable. (If not practicable, that fact should be disclosed.) Material revenues from a single foreign country should be separately disclosed. An entity must also disclose how it attributes revenues from external customers to individual countries.

Practical Consideration. GAAP does not prescribe a method of allocating revenues to particular geographic areas. Thus, for example, revenues may be assigned to countries based on the location of customers or the location from which the products were shipped.

---

c. Long-lived assets (other than financial instruments, long-term customer relationships of a financial institution, mortgage or other servicing rights, deferred tax assets, and deferred policy acquisition costs of an insurance enterprise) located in (1) the company's home country, and (2) all foreign countries in which the company holds assets should be disclosed if practicable. (If not practicable, that fact should be disclosed.) If assets held in a single foreign country are material, those amounts should be separately disclosed.

Major Customers

d. If 10% or more of the entity's revenue is derived from a single customer, that fact, the total revenue from each such customer, and the identity of the segment or segments reporting such revenue should be disclosed. (The identity of the customer need not be disclosed, however.) In applying that requirement, a group of entities under common control should be considered a single customer. Thus, for example, the federal government, a state government, a local government, or a foreign government should each be considered a single customer. (SFAS 131, par. 39)

49.514 Applicability of Foreign Operations Disclosure Requirements to a U.S. Company's Operations in Puerto Rico and Other U.S. Sovereignties. Due to the proximity, economic affinity, and similarities in business environments, a U.S. company should consider its operations in Puerto Rico and U.S. territories, such as the Virgin Islands and American Samoa, to be domestic operations. (FTB 79-4, par. 3)

49.515 Customers of Health Care Facilities. Generally, the patient, rather than the insurer, should be considered a customer of a health care facility. In most cases, the insurer is merely a paying agent of the patient and does not decide the doctor or types of services to be purchased. (FTB 79-5, par. 3)

Practical Consideration. Some health maintenance organizations (HMOs) require their participants to use a particular doctor or health care facility. In such cases, the authors believe the HMO should be considered the customer of the health care facility since the HMO, not the patient, decides which doctor or facility is used.

AUTHORITATIVE LITERATURE AND RELATED TOPICS

AUTHORITATIVE LITERATURE

SFAS No. 131, *Disclosures about Segments of an Enterprise and Related Information*
FASB Technical Bulletin 79-4, *Segment Reporting of Puerto Rican Operations*
FASB Technical Bulletin 79-5, *Meaning of the Term "Customer" as it Applies to Health Care Facilities*

RELATED PRONOUNCEMENTS

APB No. 28, *Interim Financial Reporting*

RELATED TOPICS

Chapter 9—Consolidated Financial Statements
Chapter 20—Equity Method Investments
Chapter 22—Foreign Operations and Currency Translation
Chapter 23—Income Statement
Chapter 29—Interim Financial Reporting

STOCK OPTION AND PURCHASE PLANS

Table of Contents

STOCK OPTION AND PURCHASE PLANS

OVERVIEW

EMPLOYEE STOCK OPTION AND PURCHASE PLANS

50.100 Accounting for an employee stock option or purchase plan differs depending on whether the plan is noncompensatory or compensatory. Under a noncompensatory plan, no compensation cost is recognized, and any difference between the option price and the stock's market price merely increases or decreases the proceeds received from issuing the stock. When stock is issued under a compensatory employee stock option or purchase plan, however, the company should recognize compensation costs equal to the difference between the quoted market price of the stock at the measurement date less the amount, if any, the employee must pay (referred to as the "intrinsic value method").

- The measurement date is the date on which the company knows both the number of shares the employee is to receive and the option price of the shares. For many plans, that date is the date the options are granted. For plans whose terms are variable, however, the measurement date may be later.

- Compensation costs should be accrued through a charge to stockholders' equity. The deferred compensation recorded in stockholders' equity should then be charged to expense over the periods the required employee services are performed.

50.101 Companies are encouraged to use the fair value method to account for transactions involving stock-based compensation that are entered into in fiscal years beginning after December 15, 1995. (The fair value method may be applied to earlier transactions, if desired.) Under the fair value method—

- compensation cost related to compensatory plans is the fair value of the options at the grant date less any amounts paid by the employee for the options. (That differs from compensation cost under the intrinsic value method, which is the quoted market price of the underlying stock at the measurement date less any cash or other assets the employee is required to pay.)

- compensation cost is accrued over the periods in which related employee services are rendered by debiting expense and crediting paid-in capital. (That differs from the intrinsic value method, which requires compensation cost to be recorded in stockholders' equity as a deferred charge and then amortized to expense over the employee service period.)

50.102   Regardless of the method used to account for stock-based compensation, certain disclosures generally are required.

EMPLOYEE STOCK OWNERSHIP PLANS

50.103   An employee stock ownership plan (ESOP) is a plan that primarily invests in the employer's stock. In a nonleveraged ESOP (i.e., one that does not borrow money to purchase the employer's stock), the employer should record compensation cost equal to the fair value of the shares it contributes. An employer's accounting for a leveraged ESOP differs, however. The employer should debit unearned ESOP shares (an equity account) for the shares issued to the ESOP, and, as the shares are committed to be released, (a) unearned ESOP shares should be credited for the cost of the shares, (b) compensation expense should be debited for the average fair value of the shares during the period, and (c) equity should be charged for any difference similar to accounting for gains and losses on sales of treasury stock. In addition, the employer should report loans to the ESOP from outsiders, including indirect loans, as liabilities on its balance sheet, accrue interest expense on the debt, and reduce the debt and accrued interest for payments made by the ESOP.

TRANSACTIONS WITH NONEMPLOYEES

50.104   The issuance of equity instruments to nonemployees in exchange for goods or services should be accounted for based on the fair value of the goods or services received or the fair value of the equity instruments issued, whichever is more reliably measured.

ACCOUNTING REQUIREMENTS

50.200   Companies often adopt plans in which officers and employees receive shares of the company's stock. Some of the more common plans include—

a. *plans with fixed terms.* The number of shares that may be acquired, required cash payments, and other terms are fixed and determinable at the date of the grant or award. Generally, the plans assume the employee will provide current or future services, and restrict the employee's right to transfer the stock received for a specified period. (APB 25, par. 24)

b. *stock option and purchase plans.* Under such plans, an employee receives the right to purchase a specified number of shares at a stated price during a stated period. (APB 25, par. 25)

c. *stock bonus or award plans.* An employer awards a fixed number or dollar amount of its shares to an employee, usually in return for no or a nominal cash payment from the employee. (APB 25, par. 26)

d. *plans with variable terms.* The number of shares, their price, and other terms vary depending on factors such as the market performance of the stock, dividends paid, or the employer's earnings.

e. *combination and elective plans.* The employee is allowed to select from alternatives under a plan or receives rights in more than one plan. For example, an employee may be given options to purchase a fixed number of shares at a fixed price during a specified period or elect to (a) receive the same number of shares at a different price during a different period or (b) receive a reduced number of shares without paying any cash. Such plans sometimes are referred to as "tandem stock" or "alternate stock" plans.

50.201   Accounting for stock option and purchase plans depends on whether they are noncompensatory or compensatory.

NONCOMPENSATORY PLANS

50.202   Some stock option and purchase plans are not intended to compensate employees for services. Instead, they are designed to raise capital or expand the company's ownership to include officers and employees. Generally, a plan is noncompensatory if the shares are offered at a price that is not lower than the price at which a similar number of shares would be offered to all stockholders. In addition, noncompensatory plans contain the following essential characteristics:

a. Substantially all full-time employees meeting limited employment qualifications may participate in the plan. (Employees who own a specified percent of the company's outstanding stock and executives may be excluded from such plans, however.)

b. Stock is offered to eligible employees equally or based on a uniform percentage of wages. (The plan may limit the number of shares that an employee may purchase, however.)

c. The time permitted to exercise an option or purchase right is limited to a reasonable period.

d. The stock is not offered at a discount from market price that is greater than the discount at which stock would be offered to all stockholders or others.

An employer should not recognize compensation expense when stock is issued through a noncompensatory plan. (ARB 43, Ch. 13B, paras. 4–7)

COMPENSATORY PLANS

50.203   Many plans include an element of compensation. They grant certain employees the right to purchase a specified number of shares of stock at a specified price that generally is below market. In some cases, the options may be exercised only under certain conditions. For example, the employee may be required to continue employment with the company for a specified period or to retain the stock for a specified length of time before selling it. (ARB 43, Ch. 13B, par. 3)

Measuring and Accruing Compensation Cost

50.204   **General Requirements.** An employer who issues stock through a compensatory plan should recognize compensation expense equal to the quoted market price of the stock at the measurement date less any cash or other assets the employee is required to pay. The measurement date is the first date on which the employer knows (a) the number of shares the employee is to receive and (b) the option or purchase price. Usually, the measurement date is the grant date. When determining compensation expense, the following should be considered:

a. The cost of purchasing treasury stock to distribute through the plan should not be used to measure compensation expense. (An exception to that rule exists for plans described in c., however. Such plans may measure compensation based on the cost of treasury stock acquired during the period the grant is made, provided the treasury stock is distributed shortly after the end of the year.)

b. The measurement date should not change from the grant date to a later date solely because an employee's termination reduces the number of shares that the employee is entitled to receive.

c. The measurement date may be the end of the fiscal period, rather than the date the grant is determined, if (1) the grant is provided for under the terms of an established formal plan, (2) the plan states the factors used to determine the total dollar amount of the grant for the period, and (3) the grant relates to services performed during the period.

d. If a stock option or purchase right is renewed or extended, a new measurement date is established.

e. If stock is transferred to an agent, trustee, or other third party for distribution to employees, the measurement date is the transfer date if the stock will not—

    (1) revert to the employer,

    (2) be granted later to the same employee on terms or for services different from those specified in the original grant, and

    (3) be granted later to another employee.

f. The measurement date for a grant of convertible stock is the date on which the conversion ratio is known. In addition, compensation expense should be based on the higher of the quoted market price of the convertible stock or the securities into which the stock may be converted.

g. If cash is paid to an employee to settle an earlier grant or award, compensation expense is the cash paid. Any difference between that amount and the amount previously measured should be accounted for prospectively as a change in accounting estimate.

h. Compensation expense for a plan that is a combination of two or more types of plans may need to be determined by measuring the compensation related to each part of the plan. If the plan allows an employee to select from various alternatives, compensation expense should be measured using the terms the employee is most likely to choose based on the current facts and circumstances. (APB 25, par. 11)

50.205   Compensation expense related to compensatory plans should be recognized over the period the services related to the grant are performed. If the measurement date is later than the date of the grant, compensation expense for each period between the grant date and measurement date should be measured based on the quoted market price of the stock at the end of each period.

50.206   In some cases, stock may be issued before the employee has rendered all the required services. In that event, compensation costs should be recognized as the services are performed as follows:

a. The portion related to services already performed should be charged to expense.

b. The portion related to future services should be recorded as deferred compensation and presented in the balance sheet as a reduction of stockholders' equity. The deferred compensation should be charged to expense during the periods the required future services are performed.

50.207   Amounts accrued as compensation expense are estimates and may differ from amounts that ultimately should be recorded. An adjustment of an amount recorded in a prior period should be treated as a change in accounting estimate. (See Chapter 1.) (APB 25, paras. 12–15)

50.208   **Stock Appreciation Rights and Other Variable Stock Option or Award Plans.** Employers sometimes offer variable stock option plans in which the number of shares awarded, the price, or both are not specified until after the date of grant. An example of such a plan is one that awards stock appreciation rights to employees. Stock appreciation rights entitle employees to receive cash, stock, or both as the market value of the company's stock increases over a specified price. (FASBI 28, par. 2)

50.209   Compensation expense related to stock appreciation rights and other variable plan awards should be recognized over the periods the employee performs the related services (i.e., the service period). If the awards are granted for past services, compensation expense should be recognized in the period the awards are granted. If the plan or agreement does not define the service period, the service period should be presumed to be the vesting period. (Generally, the vesting period is the period from the date of the grant to the date the employee's right to receive the award is not contingent on providing future services.) (FASBI 28, par. 3)

50.210 Determining compensation expense related to variable plan awards generally involves the use of estimates. Amounts accrued should be adjusted in subsequent periods as needed. For example, compensation expense related to stock appreciation rights increases or decreases as the market value of the company's stock increases or decreases. Accrued compensation and compensation expense should be adjusted accordingly in the period the increases or decreases occur. Similarly, accrued compensation related to a right that is forfeited or canceled should be adjusted by decreasing compensation expense in the period the right is forfeited or canceled. (FASBI 28, par. 4)

50.211 **Junior Stock Plans.** Junior stock is a separate class of stock, usually with fewer voting rights and lower dividend rates than common stock, that may be converted to common stock when the employee achieves certain performance goals. A junior stock plan is a variable plan since the number of shares of common stock an employee will receive upon conversion of the junior stock generally is not known until the performance goals are achieved. Thus, a junior stock plan should be accounted for as follows:

    a. Compensation expense should be determined on the measurement date, which, as discussed in Paragraph 50.204, is the date on which the company knows (1) the number of shares of common stock the employee will receive in exchange for the junior stock and (2) the option or purchase price. It is calculated as the excess of the market value of the common stock the employee is entitled to receive over the amount the employee pays for the junior stock and its conversion to common stock, if any.

    b. Compensation expense should not be accrued until it becomes probable that the performance goals will be achieved and the employee will be entitled to convert the junior stock to common stock. (Thus, expense may or may not be accrued when the junior stock is issued.)

> **Practical Consideration.** The term "probable" is used in the same context as in SFAS No. 5, *Accounting for Contingencies.* (See Chapter 10.) That is, achievement of the performance goals is probable if it is likely to occur.

    c. If cash is paid to an employee to reacquire junior stock, compensation expense is the amount by which the cash paid to the employee for the junior stock exceeds the amount the employee paid for the junior stock. (FASBI 38, paras. 2–6)

Accounting for Income Tax Benefits

50.212   Usually, an employer can claim a tax deduction related to its stock option or purchase plan for any amount the employees report as ordinary income. The deduction is allowed in the period the amount is included in the employees' gross income, which may or may not be the same period compensation expense is recognized for financial reporting. Consequently, a temporary difference may exist for which deferred taxes should be provided. (Recording deferred tax assets and liabilities is discussed in Chapter 24.)

50.213   Sometimes, the *amounts* deducted for tax purposes differ from the amounts expensed for financial reporting. If the tax deduction is higher than the amount expensed for financial reporting, the tax effect of the difference should be added to paid-in capital rather than income. Conversely, if the tax deduction is lower than the amount expensed for financial reporting, the tax effect of the difference should be subtracted from paid-in capital, but only to the extent tax benefits under the same or similar plans increased paid-in capital.

50.214   If an employer reimburses an employee for the tax effects of stock option plans, the reimbursement should be recognized as an additional expense. (APB 25, paras. 16–18)

RULES EFFECTIVE FOR YEARS BEGINNING AFTER DECEMBER 15, 1995

50.215   In practice, companies typically do not record compensation expense related to stock option and purchase plans since the fair value of the stock that ultimately will be issued is seldom higher than the option or purchase price at the measurement date. Consequently, the FASB issued SFAS No. 123, *Accounting for Stock-Based Compensation.* The Statement prescribes a fair value based method of accounting for stock options and other stock-based compensation. The following paragraphs discuss Statement 123's requirements and how they differ from the old rules.

> **Practical Consideration.** SFAS No. 123 encourages, rather than requires, employers to use the fair value method. Thus, an employer may continue to account for stock-based employee compensation following the old rules discussed in Paragraphs 50.204–.214. If the old rules are followed, however, pro forma disclosures of net income (and earnings per share if presented) must be made as if the fair value based method prescribed by SFAS No. 123 had been applied. (See Paragraph 50.502.) In addition—
>
> - once the fair value based method is adopted, an employer may not switch back to the old rules.
>
> - the employer must use the same method to account for all of its stock-based compensation plans.
>
> SFAS No. 123's accounting requirements are effective for transactions entered into in fiscal years beginning after December 15, 1995. Early adoption is permitted. The Statement's disclosure requirements are effective for financial statements for fiscal years beginning after December 15, 1995, or the date its accounting requirements are adopted, if earlier. For companies that continue to measure compensation cost under the old rules, pro forma disclosures are required for all awards granted in fiscal years beginning after December 15, 1994. The pro forma disclosures need not be presented in financial statements of the first fiscal year beginning after December 15, 1994, but they should be presented if those financial statements are subsequently presented for comparative purposes with financial statements of a later fiscal year.

Noncompensatory Plans

50.216   Under SFAS No. 123, a plan is noncompensatory if it meets the following criteria:

a. Substantially all full-time employees meeting limited employment qualifications may participate in the plan.

b. The plan has no option features other than the following:

   (1) Employees may enroll in the plan up to 31 days after the purchase price has been fixed.

   (2) The purchase price is based solely on the stock's market price at the date of the purchase, and employees are allowed to drop out of the plan before the purchase date and receive a refund of amounts previously paid.

c. The stock is not offered at a discount from market price that is higher than the greater of (1) the discount per share at which stock would be offered to all stockholders or others or (2) the stock issuance costs per share avoided by not having to raise a significant amount of capital through a public offering. (A discount of 5% or less would meet that criterion.)

If a plan is noncompensatory, compensation cost should not be recorded. The discount from market price merely reduces the proceeds received from issuing the stock. (SFAS 123, par. 23)

Compensatory Plans

50.217 Measuring Compensation Cost under the Fair Value Method. Under the fair value method prescribed by SFAS No. 123, compensation cost is the fair value of the *stock options or other equity instruments* at the grant date, less any amounts paid by the employee for the stock options or equity instruments. (SFAS 123, par. 16) (That differs from compensation cost under the old rules, which is equal to the quoted market price of the *underlying stock* at the measurement date less any cash or other assets the employee is required to pay.) When measuring compensation cost, the following should be considered:

a. The grant date is the date on which the employer and employee have a mutual understanding of the terms of the award and the employer becomes obligated to issue equity instruments or transfer assets to an employee who fulfills vesting requirements. The grant date of an award may be the end of the fiscal period, rather than a subsequent date when the award is actually made to the employee if (1) the grant is provided for under the terms of an established formal plan, (2) the plan states the factors used to determine the total dollar amount of grant for the period, and (3) the grant relates to services performed during the period. (SFAS 123, par. 395)

b. The fair value of nonvested stock awarded to an employee is the market price of the stock as if it were vested and issued on the grant date. (SFAS 123, par. 18)

c. The fair value of a stock option should be estimated using an option-pricing model that considers (1) the option's exercise price and expected life, (2) the underlying stock's current price and expected volatility (nonpublic companies need not consider volatility), (3) expected dividends, (4) and the risk-free interest rate for the expected term of the option. Examples of such an option-pricing model include the Black-Scholes model or a binomial model. (SFAS 123, par. 19)

d. If the fair value of a stock option or other equity instrument cannot be reasonably estimated at the grant date (for example, because the exercise price changes as the underlying stock's value changes), fair value should be measured at the first date it is reasonably possible to do so. Until then, compensation cost should be based on the award's value as if the option had been currently exercised. (SFAS 123, par. 22)

e. Each award should be measured separately based on terms, current stock prices, and related factors at the grant date. If an award is modified so that it is more valuable, the modification should be treated as the exchange of the original award for a new award. The additional compensation cost incurred is measured as the difference between the option's fair values before and after the modification. (SFAS 123, par. 35)

50.218 Recognizing Compensation Cost under the Fair Value Method. Under SFAS No. 123, compensation cost is recognized as follows:

a. Total compensation cost should be estimated based on the number of equity instruments that will eventually vest. (Previously recognized compensation cost should not be reversed if a vested stock option expires before it is exercised, however.) To estimate total compensation, the employer may either (a) estimate at the grant date the number of stock options or other equity instruments that will vest and revise that estimate as needed or (b) record compensation as if there will be no forfeitures and recognize forfeitures as they occur. (SFAS 123, paras. 26–28)

b. Compensation cost should be recorded during the periods in which related employee services are rendered by debiting expense and crediting paid-in capital. If the employee service period is not defined, it should be presumed to be the period from the grant date to the date the award becomes vested. If the award relates to past services, compensation cost should be recorded in the period the award is granted.

c. Dividends paid on awards of stock or other equity instruments that vest should be charged to retained earnings. Nonforfeitable dividends paid on stock that does not vest should be recorded as additional compensation cost. If dividends are paid only on stock that is vested, compensation cost should be reduced by the present value of dividends expected to be paid on the stock during the vesting period, discounted at an appropriate risk-free interest rate. Compensation cost should not be reduced for dividends paid or applied to reduce the exercise price pursuant to antidilution provisions, however. (SFAS 123, paras. 30–33)

d. When an option is exercised, the sum of the cash proceeds received and the amounts credited to paid-in capital for employee services should be credited to common stock.

Practical Consideration. To illustrate accounting for stock-based compensation under SFAS No. 123, assume that a company issued 5,000 stock options on December 31, 19X6. The fair value of each option on that date was $15, and each option entitles its holder to receive one share of $10 par common stock at an exercise price of $50 per share. Furthermore, the options vest in five years. Total compensation cost at the grant date is $75,000 (5,000 × $15) and would be recognized by making the following entry during each year of the vesting period: (For simplicity, the illustration ignores the effect of the accruals on deferred taxes.)

Compensation expense ($75,000 ÷ 5)	15,000	
Additional paid-in capital—stock		
options		15,000

Assuming the options are exercised at the end of the five-year vesting period, the following entry would be needed to record the issuance of common stock:

Cash (5,000 × $50)	250,000	
Additional paid-in capital—stock		
options	75,000	
Common stock (5,000 × $10)		50,000
Additional paid-in capital—		
common stock		275,000

50.219   Similar to accounting for stock-based compensation under the old rules, amounts accrued as compensation expense are estimates and may differ from amounts that ultimately should be recorded. An adjustment of an amount recorded in a prior period should be treated as a change in accounting estimate. (See Chapter 1.) (SFAS 123, par. 29)

50.220   **Cash Settlements.** If the company repurchases equity instruments issued to employees, the cash or other assets paid should be charged to equity to the extent the payment does not exceed the value of the instruments repurchased. Any excess payment represents additional compensation cost. (For example, if an option with a fair value of $15 is repurchased for $20, additional compensation cost of $5 has been incurred.) A nonvested award that is settled in cash has, in effect, become vested and any compensation cost measured at the grant date that has not been recognized should be recognized. (SFAS 123, par. 37)

50.221 **Accounting for Income Tax Benefits under the Fair Value Method.** Under SFAS No. 123, the income tax effect of stock-based compensation is accounted essentially in the same manner as under the old rules. That is, if amounts deducted for tax purposes in a period differ from the amounts expensed for financial reporting, deferred taxes should be provided. If the cumulative tax deduction is higher than the cumulative amount expensed for financial reporting, the tax effect of the difference should be added to paid-in capital rather than income. Conversely, if the cumulative tax deduction is lower than the cumulative amount expensed for financial reporting, the tax effect of the difference should be subtracted from paid-in capital, but only to the extent tax benefits under the same or similar plans increased paid-in capital. (SFAS 123, paras. 41–44)

TRANSACTIONS WITH NONEMPLOYEES

50.222 When an entity issues equity instruments to nonemployees in exchange for goods or services, the transaction should be accounted for based on the fair value of the goods or services received or the fair value of the equity instrument issued, whichever can be more reliably measured. Frequently, the fair value of goods or services received from suppliers can be reliably measured and therefore indicates the fair value of the equity instruments issued. However, in some situations the fair value of the equity instruments issued may be more reliably determined. For example, the fair value of tradeable equity instruments issued in a purchase business combination may be more reliably measured than the fair value of the business acquired. (SFAS 123, par. 8) (See Chapter 3 for guidance on business combinations.)

Measuring Fair Value

50.223 Fair value is the amount at which the asset could be bought or sold in a current transaction between willing parties, other than in a forced sale or liquidation. Fair value should be based on quoted market prices, if available. Otherwise, it should be estimated using the best available information and should consider prices for similar assets and the results of valuation techniques. Techniques that may be used to estimate fair value include the following: (SFAS 123, par. 9)

     a. Net present value of future cash flows (Cash flows should be discounted using a discount rate consistent with the risks involved.)

     b. Option pricing models

     c. Matrix pricing

     d. Option-adjusted spread models

Practical Consideration. SFAS 123 does not prescribe a measurement date (that is, the date of the stock price on which the fair value of the equity instrument is based) for a transaction with a nonemployee. As a practical matter, determining the appropriate measurement date is a minor issue because the issuer of equity instruments generally receives consideration (whether in the form of another financial instrument or goods or services) almost immediately after the parties agree to the transaction. Generally, if a long period elapses between the agreement and receipt of consideration, neither party has an obligation under the contract during that period. Thus, the distinction between grant date and vesting date generally is not present in many situations other than stock-based employee compensation.

EMPLOYEE STOCK OWNERSHIP PLANS

50.224   An employee stock ownership plan (ESOP) is described by the Employee Retirement Income Security Act of 1974 (ERISA) and the Internal Revenue Code as a stock bonus plan (or combination stock bonus and money purchase pension plan) that primarily invests in the employer's stock. How an employer accounts for an ESOP depends on whether the plan is leveraged or nonleveraged.

Leveraged ESOPs

50.225   An ESOP is leveraged if it borrows money to invest in the company's stock. Generally, the ESOP borrows the money (a) from the company (employer loan), (b) from the company with a related loan from an outsider to the company (indirect loan), or (c) from an outsider (direct loan). The debt, which usually is collateralized by the employer's stock, typically is repaid from the employer's contributions to the ESOP and dividends on the employer's stock. Generally, an employer should account for a leveraged ESOP as follows:

     a. When shares are issued to an ESOP (or the ESOP buys the company's shares on the open market), the employer should debit unearned ESOP shares (an equity account) and credit—

         (1) notes payable if the ESOP borrows money from an outside lender to purchase the company's shares or

         (2) cash if the company loans money to the ESOP to purchase the shares. (SOP 93-6, par. 13)

     b. When the ESOP's shares are committed to be released (that is, they are released for allocation to participants' accounts), (1) the cost of the shares should be credited to unearned ESOP shares, (2) the average fair value of the shares during the period should be debited to either compensation cost (or compensation payable) or dividends payable, depending on the purpose of the release, and (3) the difference should be charged or credited to equity similar to gains and losses on sales of treasury stock. (See Chapter 51.) (SOP 93-6, paras. 14 and 19)

c. The company should report loans to the ESOP from outsiders (including indirect loans) as liabilities, accrue interest expense on the debt, and reduce the debt and accrued interest payable for payments made by the ESOP to the outside lender. (SOP 93-6, par. 25)

d. The company should not report loans it makes to the ESOP as assets and, thus, should not recognize interest income on the receivable. (SOP 93-6, par. 26)

Nonleveraged ESOPs

50.226   In a nonleveraged ESOP, the employer makes periodic contributions of its shares or cash to the ESOP. In each period, the employer should record compensation cost equal to the fair value of the shares contributed or committed to be contributed. Dividends on shares held by nonleveraged ESOPs generally should be charged to retained earnings. (SOP 93-6, paras. 41–42)

> **Practical Consideration.** SOP 93-6, *Employers' Accounting for Employee Stock Ownership Plans,* provides additional guidance on accounting for the termination of a leveraged ESOP, reporting redemption of ESOP shares, and accounting for pension reversion ESOPs.

DISCLOSURE REQUIREMENTS

STOCK PURCHASE AND STOCK OPTION PLANS

50.500   A company that has not adopted SFAS No. 123 must disclose the status of the option or plan at the end of the period, including the number of shares under option, the option price, and the number of shares that would be issued if the options were exercised. The financial statements also should disclose information about options exercised during the period, including the number of shares involved and the option price of the shares. (ARB 43, Ch. 13B, par. 15)

Practical Consideration. SFAS No. 123's disclosure requirements are effective for financial statements for fiscal years beginning after December 15, 1995, or the date its accounting requirements are adopted, if earlier. Once effective, the Statement's disclosure requirements apply to all companies, including those that elect to account for stock-based compensation under the old rules rather than the fair value method.

50.501   A company that has adopted SFAS No. 123 must disclose the following about its stock-based compensation plans for each year for which an income statement is presented: (The information should be disclosed separately for each type of award granted by the company to the extent separate disclosure would be useful.)

   a. A description of the plan, including the general terms of awards (such as, vesting requirements, maximum term of options granted, and number of shares authorized for grants of options or other equity instruments)

   b. Number and weighted-average exercise prices of options that were—

      (1) outstanding at the beginning of the year

      (2) outstanding at the end of the year

      (3) exercisable at the end of the year

      (4) granted, exercised, forfeited, or expired during the year

   c. Weighted-average grant-date fair value of options granted during the year (If the exercise prices of some options differ from the market price of the stock on the grant date, those options' weighted-average exercise prices and weighted-average fair values should be disclosed separately.)

   d. Number and weighted-average grant-date fair value of equity instruments other than options granted during the year

   e. Description of the method and significant assumptions used during the year to estimate the fair values of options, including the risk-free interest rate, expected life, expected volatility, and expected dividends

   f. Total compensation cost recognized in income for stock-based employee compensation awards

g. Terms of significant modifications of outstanding awards

h. For options outstanding at the date of the latest balance sheet presented, the range of exercise prices, the weighted-average exercise price, and the weighted-average remaining contractual life (Exercise prices should be segregated into ranges that will help the financial statement user assess the number and timing of additional shares that may be issued and the cash that may be received from option exercises. Information disclosed about each range should include (1) the number, weighted-average exercise price, and weighted-average remaining contractual life of options outstanding and (2) the number and weighted-average exercise price of options currently exercisable.) (SFAS 123, paras. 46–48)

A company that issues equity instruments to acquire goods or services other than employee services should make similar disclosures if they would help financial statement readers better understand the effects of the transactions on the financial statements. (SFAS 123, par. 46)

50.502 Companies that continue to apply the old rules when accounting for stock-based compensation should also disclose pro forma net income (and pro forma earnings per share if earnings per share is presented) as if the fair value based method prescribed by SFAS No. 123 had been applied. The pro forma amounts should reflect only the effect the fair value method would have had on the compensation cost included in net income, net of tax. It should not reflect other adjustments to net income or earnings per share. (SFAS 123, par. 45)

> **Practical Consideration.** Companies that continue to measure compensation cost under the old rules must make the pro forma disclosures for all awards granted in fiscal years beginning after December 15, 1994. The pro forma disclosures need not be presented in financial statements of the first fiscal year beginning after December 15, 1994, but they should be presented if those financial statements are subsequently presented for comparative purposes with financial statements of a later fiscal year.

EMPLOYEE STOCK OWNERSHIP PLANS

50.503 A company should disclose the following information about its ESOP:

a. A description of the plan, including how contributions are determined, the employee groups covered, and the nature and effect of matters affecting the comparability of information for all periods presented (A company should include in its disclosures about leveraged ESOPs the basis for releasing shares and how dividends on allocated and unallocated shares are used.)

b. Accounting policies followed for ESOP transactions, including the method of measuring compensation, classification of dividends on ESOP shares, and treatment of ESOP shares for earnings per share computations (See Chapter 19.)

c. Compensation cost recognized during the period

d. Number of allocated shares, committed-to-be-released shares, and suspense shares held by the ESOP at the balance sheet date

e. Fair value of unearned ESOP shares at the balance sheet date

f. Existence and nature of any repurchase obligation, including the fair value of the shares allocated as of the balance sheet date that are subject to a repurchase obligation (SOP 93-6, par. 53)

Practical Consideration. The disclosures in a.–f. are required by SOP 93-6, *Employers' Accounting for Stock Ownership Plans.* Although the SOP's guidance need not be applied to shares acquired on or before December 31, 1992, the information in a.–f. should be disclosed, if applicable, about shares *not* accounted for under SOP 93-6. In addition, if SOP 93-6 has not been applied and the employer has, in substance, guaranteed the debt of an ESOP, the following should be disclosed:

  a. The compensation element and the interest element of annual contributions to the ESOP

  b. The interest rate and debt terms

AUTHORITATIVE LITERATURE AND RELATED TOPICS

AUTHORITATIVE LITERATURE

ARB No. 43, *Restatement and Revision of Accounting Research Bulletins* (Chapter 13B—Compensation Involved in Stock Option and Stock Purchase Plans)
APB Opinion No. 25, *Accounting for Stock Issued to Employees*
SFAS No. 123, *Accounting for Stock-Based Compensation*
FASB Interpretation No. 28, *Accounting for Stock Appreciation Rights and Other Variable Stock Option or Award Plans*

FASB Interpretation No. 38, *Determining the Measurement Date for Stock Option, Purchase, and Award Plans Involving Junior Stock*

SOP 93-6, *Employers' Accounting for Stock Ownership Plans*

RELATED PRONOUNCEMENTS

EITF Issue No. 84-13, *Purchase of Stock Options and Stock Appreciation Rights in a Leveraged Buyout*

EITF Issue No. 84-18, *Stock Option Pyramiding*

EITF Issue No. 84-34, *Permanent Discount Restricted Stock Purchase Plans*

EITF Issue No. 85-11, *Use of an Employee Stock Ownership Plan in a Leveraged Buyout*

EITF Issue No. 86-27, *Measurement of Excess Contributions to a Defined Contribution Plan or Employee Stock Ownership Plan*

EITF Issue No. 87-6, *Adjustments Relating to Stock Compensation Plans*

EITF Issue No. 87-23, *Book Value Stock Purchase Plans*

EITF Issue No. 87-33, *Stock Compensation Issues Related to Market Decline*

EITF Issue No. 88-6, *Book Value Stock Plans in an Initial Public Offering*

EITF Issue No. 88-27, *Effect of Unallocated Shares in an Employee Stock Ownership Plan on Accounting for Business Combinations*

EITF Issue No. 89-11, *Sponsor's Balance Sheet Classification of Capital Stock with a Put Option Held by an Employee Stock Ownership Plan*

EITF Issue No. 90-4, *Earnings-per-Share Treatment of Tax Benefits for Dividends on Stock Held by an Employee Stock Ownership Plan*

EITF Issue No. 90-7, *Accounting for Reload Stock Option*

EITF Issue No. 90-9, *Changes to Fixed Employee Stock Option Plans as a Result of Equity Restructuring*

EITF Issue No. 92-3, *Earnings-per-Share Treatment of Tax Benefits for Dividends on Unallocated Stock Held by an Employee Stock Ownership Plan (Consideration of the Implications of FASB Statement No. 109 on Issue 2 of EITF Issue No. 90-4)*

EITF Issue No. 94-6, *Accounting for the Buyout of Compensatory Stock Options*

EITF Issue No. 95-16, *Accounting for Stock Compensation Arrangements with Employer Loan Features under APB Opinion No. 25*

EITF Issue No. 96-3, *Accounting for Equity Instruments That Are Issued for Consideration Other Than Employee Services under FASB Statement No. 123*

EITF Issue No. 97-12, *Accounting for Increased Share Authorizations in an IRS Section 423 Employee Purchase Plan under APB Opinion No. 25, "Accounting for Stock Issued to Employees"*

Accounting Interpretations of APB Opinion No. 25, *Accounting for Stock Issued to Employees*

RELATED TOPICS

STOCKHOLDERS' EQUITY

Table of Contents

STOCKHOLDERS' EQUITY

OVERVIEW

51.100   The components of stockholders' equity include contributed capital (such as capital stock, additional paid-in capital, stock subscriptions receivable, and treasury stock) and retained earnings. Generally, capital transactions should not be included in the determination of income.

ACCOUNTING REQUIREMENTS

51.200   Stockholders' equity represents the owners' interests in a corporation's assets and liabilities. It is the residual amount of a corporation's assets less its liabilities and results from owner contributions, cumulative losses, and cumulative undistributed profits. The following paragraphs discuss the components of stockholders' equity and the methods used to account for them.

> **Practical Consideration.** Although this chapter primarily deals with corporate entities, many of its concepts may be applied to other forms of entities. For example, partners' equity and proprietor's equity, like stockholders' equity, represents an owner's interest in an entity's assets and liabilities. Unlike corporate entities, however, the equity sections of partnership and proprietorship financial statements typically include, for each owner or class of owner, a capital account, drawing account, and contribution account.

CONTRIBUTED CAPITAL

51.201   Contributed capital represents the investment made by the owners. It consists of amounts paid by owners when they purchased the company's stock and amounts arising from subsequent transactions with owners (for example, treasury stock transactions).

Capital Stock

51.202   Capital stock represents the legal capital provided by stockholders. It is the minimum investment in the business that must, under state law, be retained for the protection of creditors. Capital stock may consist of common or preferred shares. Common stock is the basic share issued and confers upon its owner the right to (a) vote on corporate matters, (b) share in profits,

(c) purchase a proportionate share of additional common stock issued, and (d) share in the corporation's assets upon liquidation. Preferred stock carries certain specified preferences or privileges (defined in the corporation's charter) over common stock. For example, preferred stock may be—

    a. voting or nonvoting;

    b. cumulative or noncumulative and fully participating, partially participating, or nonparticipating with respect to dividends;

    c. callable by the corporation for redemption at a specified price; and

    d. convertible to common stock.

Also, if the corporation is liquidated, preferred stockholders may have a higher priority to the corporation's assets than common stockholders.

51.203   When capital stock is issued, its par value (or stated value in the case of nopar stock) is recorded to common or preferred stock and any proceeds received in excess of par or stated value is recorded to additional paid-in capital. For example, the following entry would be required to record the sale of 1,000 shares of $10 par value common stock for $15 per share:

Cash ($15 × 1,000)	15,000	
Common stock ($10 × 1,000)		10,000
Additional paid-in capital		5,000

Costs of issuing stock should be deducted from the proceeds of the issue and should not be reported as an asset or expense.

51.204   **Stock Issued for Property and Subsequently Contributed Back to the Corporation.** A corporation may issue capital stock in exchange for property and, at about the same time and pursuant to a previous agreement or understanding, receive a portion of the issued stock back as a donation. In such cases, the property should be recorded at its fair value rather than at the par value of the stock. (ARB 43, Ch. 1A, par. 6)

Additional Paid-in Capital

51.205   Additional paid-in capital represents contributed capital in excess of legal capital. Consequently, it is affected by capital related-transactions such as the following:

a. Selling stock at an amount in excess of par or stated value

b. Purchasing or selling treasury stock

c. Capitalizing retained earnings, for example, as a result of stock dividends

d. Receiving donated assets

e. Undergoing a corporate readjustment or quasi-reorganization (See Chapter 44.)

f. Issuing detachable stock purchase warrants in connection with debt (APB 14, par. 16) (See Chapter 13.)

51.206   Current or future charges that would ordinarily be charged to expense should not be charged to additional paid-in capital except in a reorganization or quasi-reorganization. (ARB 43, Ch. 1A, par. 2) (Accounting for a quasi-reorganization is discussed in Chapter 44.)

Stock Subscriptions Receivable

51.207   A stockholder may agree to purchase a specified number of shares of stock and pay for the stock at one or more specified dates in the future. Such agreements, referred to as stock subscriptions, normally are recorded by debiting subscriptions receivable and crediting either stock subscribed or common (or preferred) stock issued and additional paid-in capital. Stock subscriptions may be formal or informal, and stock may be issued in advance of collection or as the receivable is collected.

> **Practical Consideration.** The authors believe that stock subscriptions receivable generally should be reported as a deduction from stockholders' equity. They should be shown as an asset only in rare circumstances when (a) there is substantial evidence of ability and intent to pay, such as when notes for stock are secured by irrevocable letters of credit or have been discounted at a bank, and (b) the receivables mature in a reasonably short period of time.

Treasury Stock

51.208   Treasury stock refers to a corporation's own stock that it holds. Generally, treasury stock should be reported as a deduction from stockholders' equity. (Treasury stock may be shown as an asset, however, when the corporation purchases it as part of a systematic method of fulfilling its requirements to issue shares in connection with an employee stock option plan. See

Chapter 50.) Dividends on treasury stock should not be reported as income. (ARB 43, Ch. 1A, par. 4)

51.209   When stock is retired or purchased for constructive retirement, the par value of the shares should be charged to the specific stock issue. Any difference between par value and the cost of the shares should be recorded as follows:

    a. An excess of the purchase price over par value may be charged either—

        (1) to additional paid-in capital related to the specific stock issue (limited to paid-in capital from previous retirements or sales of treasury stock plus a pro rata portion of other paid-in capital related to the issue) with any remaining excess charged to retained earnings (APB 6. par. 12) or

        (2) entirely to retained earnings. (ARB 43, Ch. 1B, par. 7)

    b. An excess of par value over purchase price should be credited to additional paid-in capital. (APB 6, par. 12)

51.210   When stock is acquired for purposes other than retirement, or when ultimate disposition has not been decided, the cost of the stock may be handled in either of the following ways:

    a. A deduction from the sum of capital stock, additional paid-in capital, and retained earnings

    b. Treated the same as retired stock (See Paragraph 51.209.)

If the treasury stock was not accounted for as retired and is subsequently sold, gains should be credited to additional paid-in capital and losses should be charged to additional paid-in capital to the extent there is additional paid-in capital related to that class of stock and then to retained earnings. (APB 6, par. 12)

51.211   **Acquiring Treasury Stock at a Price Significantly in Excess of Market Price.** If treasury stock is acquired at a price significantly in excess of its current market price, it is presumed that the purchase price includes amounts attributable to rights and privileges other than the shares purchased. (For example, the seller may agree to settle litigation or settle an employment contract.) In such cases, the purchase price should be allocated between the treasury stock and the other rights and privileges as follows:

a. The allocation should be based on the fair value of the treasury stock or the rights and privileges, whichever is more clearly evident. If the fair value of the treasury stock is more clearly evident, the treasury stock should be valued at fair value with any remaining cost assigned to the other rights and privileges. On the other hand, if the fair value of the rights and privileges is more clearly evident, (e.g. because the corporation's shares are not publicly traded) the rights and privileges should be valued at fair value with any remaining cost assigned to the treasury stock.

b. If no rights and privileges can be identified, the entire purchase price should be allocated to the treasury stock.

The cost assigned to the other rights and privileges should be accounted for according to their substance. (FTB 85-6, par. 3)

51.212   Costs incurred to defend against a takeover attempt or to pay a stockholder for a "standstill" agreement (i.e., an agreement in which the former stockholder agrees not to purchase additional shares of the corporation) should be charged to expense when incurred since they do not provide future economic benefits. (FTB 85-6, par. 7)

RETAINED EARNINGS

51.213   Retained earnings represent the undistributed earnings of an entity. Changes in retained earnings generally are limited to—

a. net income or loss,

b. distribution of earnings (dividends), and

c. adjustments to the opening balance as a result of prior period adjustments or certain changes in accounting principle.

Practical Consideration. Dividends are distributions of accumulated assets to stockholders typically in the form of cash, property, or stock. Generally, they are recorded on the date they are declared by debiting retained earnings and crediting dividends payable.

Stock Dividends

51.214   Transfers of shares of the corporation's capital stock as dividends are essentially no more than a realignment of stockholders' equity. However, the public views stock dividends as distributions of corporate earnings, usually in an amount equal to the fair value of the shares received. So long as the number of shares issued in a stock dividend is so small in comparison to the number of shares outstanding that they have no apparent effect on the market price of the shares, the stock dividend should be accounted for by transferring an amount equal to the fair value of the shares issued from retained earnings to capital stock and additional paid-in capital. Thus, stock dividends reduce retained earnings, but they do not reduce total stockholders' equity. (ARB 43, Ch. 7B, par. 10)

51.215   In a closely-held company, however, there is no need to capitalize retained earnings (other than to meet legal requirements). It is presumed the stockholders are intimately knowledgeable of the company's affairs and do not consider stock dividends as a distribution of earnings. Thus, stock dividends of closely-held companies may be treated as stock splits as discussed in Paragraph 51.216. (ARB 43, Ch. 7B, par. 12)

Stock Splits

51.216   Stock splits refer to stock dividends that generally are in excess of 20 to 25% of currently outstanding shares. In a stock split, no part of retained earnings should be transferred to capital stock or additional paid-in capital, other than as required by state law. Instead, the number of shares of stock outstanding is increased and the par value per share is decreased accordingly. (ARB 43, Ch. 7B, paras. 11 and 13–16)

Dividends-in-kind

51.217   Transfers of nonmonetary assets to owners (referred to as "dividends-in-kind") should be recorded at fair value (and a gain or loss on disposition of the assets recorded) if the fair values of the assets distributed are objectively measurable and could have been realized in an outright sale at or near the time of the distribution. However, distributions in a reorganization or liquidation (including spin-offs) or in a rescission of a prior business combination should be based on recorded amounts less any necessary reduction for impairment of value. (A pro rata distribution to owners of the shares of a company that has been or is being consolidated or accounted for under the equity method is considered to be the equivalent of a spinoff.) (APB 29, paras. 18 and 23)

DISCLOSURE REQUIREMENTS

CAPITAL STOCK

51.500 A corporation should disclose the following information about its capital stock:

General Information

Information about various rights and privileges of the various securities outstanding, such as: (SFAS No. 129, par. 4)

    a.   Dividend and liquidation preferences

    b.   Participation rights.

    c.   Call prices and dates

    d.   Conversion or exercise prices or rates and relevant dates

    e.   Sinking fund requirements

    f.   Unusual voting rights

    g.   Significant terms of obligations to issue additional shares

Preferred Stock

    a.   Liquidation preferences, disclosed in the aggregate (rather than on a per share basis) in the equity section of the balance sheet (SFAS No. 129, par. 6)

    b.   Aggregate or per share amounts at which preferred shares may be called or subject to redemption through sinking fund operations or otherwise (SFAS No. 129, par. 7)

    c.   Aggregate and per share amount of cumulative preferred dividends in arrears (SFAS No. 129, par. 7)

Practical Consideration. Most companies include the following disclosures on their balance sheets for each class of common and preferred stock:

- Title of issue

- Par or stated value per share

- Shares authorized

- Shares issued

Treasury Stock

a.   Restrictions of state laws, if any (APB 6, par. 13)

b.   In the rare situation when treasury stock is shown as an asset, the circumstances for such classification (ARB, Ch. 1A, par. 4)

c.   If the purchase of treasury stock involves the receipt or payment of consideration in exchange for stated or unstated rights and privileges, the amount allocated to the rights and privileges and their accounting treatment (FTB 85-6, par. 3)

Redeemable Stock

51.501   Corporations that issue redeemable stock should disclose total required redemption (separately or combined) for all classes of capital stock that are redeemable at determinable prices on determinable dates for each of the five years following the latest balance sheet presented. (SFAS No. 129, par. 8)

CHANGES IN CAPITAL ACCOUNTS

51.502   When both a balance sheet and an income statement are presented, changes in accounts comprising stockholders' equity (including retained earnings) and changes in the number of shares of equity securities should be disclosed. The disclosure may be presented in a separate statement, on the face of the financial statements, or in the notes to the financial statements. (APB 12, par. 10 and SFAS No. 129, par. 5)

DIVIDENDS-IN-KIND

51.503   When nonmonetary assets are distributed as dividends, the nature of the distribution, the basis of accounting for the assets transferred, and the gains and losses recognized should be disclosed. (APB 29, par. 28)

AUTHORITATIVE LITERATURE AND RELATED TOPICS

AUTHORITATIVE LITERATURE

ARB No. 43, *Restatement and Revision of Accounting Research Bulletins* (Chapter 1A—Rules Adopted by Membership, Chapter 1B—Opinion Issued by Predecessor Committee, and Chapter 7B—Stock Dividends and Stock Split-ups)

APB Opinion No. 6, *Status of Accounting Research Bulletins*

APB Opinion No. 12, *Omnibus Opinion—1967*

APB Opinion No. 14, *Accounting for Convertible Debt and Debt Issued with Stock Purchase Warrants*

APB Opinion No. 29, *Accounting for Nonmonetary Transactions*

SFAS No. 129, *Disclosure Information about Capital Structure*

FASB Technical Bulletin 85-6, *Accounting for a Purchase of Treasury Shares at a Price Significantly in Excess of the Current Market Price of the Shares and the Income Statement Classification of Costs Incurred in Defending against a Takeover Attempt*

RELATED PRONOUNCEMENTS

EITF Issue No. 84-40, *Long-Term Debt Repayable by a Capital Stock Transaction*

EITF Issue No. 85-1, *Classifying Notes Received for Capital Stock*

EITF Issue No. 85-25, *Sale of Preferred Stocks with a Put Option*

EITF Issue No. 86-32, *Early Extinguishment of a Subsidiary's Mandatorily Redeemable Preferred Stock*

EITF Issue No. 86-45, *Imputation of Dividends on Preferred Stock Redeemable at the Issuer's Option with Initial Below-Market Dividend Rate*

EITF Issue No. 87-17, *Spinoffs or Other Distributions of Loans Receivable to Shareholders*

EITF Issue No. 87-31, *Sale of Put Options on Issuer's Stock*

EITF Issue No. 88-6, *Book Value Stock Plans in an Initial Public Offering*

EITF Issue No. 89-11, *Sponsor's Balance Sheet Classification of Capital Stock with a Put Option Held by an Employee Stock Ownership Plan*

EITF Issue No. 94-7, *Accounting for Financial Instruments Indexed to, and Potentially Settled in, a Company's Own Stock*

EITF Issue No. 96-1, *Sale of Put Options on Issuer's Stock That Require or Permit Cash Settlement*

EITF Issue No. 96-13, *Accounting for Derivative Financial Instruments Indexed to, and Potentially Settled in, a Company's Own Stock*

RELATED TOPICS

TRANSFERS AND SERVICING OF FINANCIAL ASSETS

Table of Contents

TRANSFERS AND SERVICING OF FINANCIAL ASSETS

OVERVIEW

52.100   After a transfer of financial assets, an entity recognizes the financial and servicing assets it controls and liabilities it has incurred. When control of financial assets has been surrendered, the entity removes the financial assets from its balance sheet. A transfer of financial assets in which the transferor has surrendered control over those assets is accounted for as a sale to the extent consideration other than beneficial interests in the transferred assets is received in exchange. A transferor has surrendered control over transferred assets if (a) the transferred assets have been isolated from the transferor, (b) each transferee receives the right to pledge or exchange the transferred assets or the transferee is a qualifying special purpose entity and the holders of beneficial interest in that entity have the right to pledge or exchange the transferred assets, *and* (c) the transferor does not maintain effective control over transferred assets through a repurchase agreement. Liabilities and derivatives incurred or obtained by the entity as a result of a transfer of financial assets should be initially measured at their fair value. Servicing assets and other retained interests in the transferred assets should be measured by allocating the financial assets' previous carrying value between the assets sold and retained interests based on their relative fair values at the date of transfer.

52.101   In certain circumstances in which a secured party has taken control of financial assets, the debtor should reclassify financial assets pledged as collateral and the secured party (lender) should recognize those assets and the obligation to return them.

ACCOUNTING REQUIREMENTS

> **Practical Consideration.** The guidance in this chapter is based on SFAS No. 125, *Accounting for Transfers and Servicing of Financial Assets and Extinguishments of Liabilities.* SFAS No. 125 is effective for most transfers and servicing of financial assets occurring after December 31, 1996, and must be applied prospectively. Early or retroactive application of SFAS No. 125 is not permitted. (Extinguishment of liabilities is discussed in Chapter 14.)

Practical Consideration (Continued).

SFAS No. 127, *Deferral of the Effective Date of Certain Provisions of FASB Statement No. 125,* delays the effective date for certain provisions of SFAS No. 125. Specifically, the guidance in Paragraph 52.213 is effective for transactions occurring after December 31, 1997 and the guidance in Paragraphs 52.201–.208 and 52.212, as it is applied to repurchase agreements, dollar rolls, securities lending, and similar transactions, is effective for transactions occurring after December 31, 1997.

DEFINITION OF A FINANCIAL ASSET

52.200   A financial asset is cash, evidence of ownership in an entity, or a contract that conveys to another entity the right to: (SFAS 107, par. 3)

   a. receive cash or another financial instrument from the first entity
      or

   b. exchange other financial instruments on potentially favorable terms with the first entity.

Practical Consideration. Financial assets are types of financial instruments, which are discussed further in Chapter 21.

ACCOUNTING FOR TRANSFERS OF FINANCIAL ASSETS

52.201   A transfer of financial assets in which the transferor surrenders control over the financial assets should be accounted for as a sale to the extent that consideration (other than beneficial interests in the transferred assets) is received in exchange. Control over transferred assets has been surrendered if and only if *all* of the following conditions have been met: (SFAS 125, par. 9)

   a. The transferred assets have been isolated from the transferor (that is, put beyond the reach of the transferor and its creditors, even if the transferor is in bankruptcy or receivership).

   b. Either (1) the transferee obtains the right (free of conditions that prevent it from taking advantage of that right) to pledge or exchange the transferred assets or (2) the transferee is a qualifying special-purpose entity and the holders of beneficial interests in that entity have the right (free of conditions that prevent them from taking advantage of that right) to pledge or exchange those interests.

c. Effective control over the transferred assets is not maintained by the transferor through (1) an agreement that both entitles and obligates the transferor to repurchase or redeem the assets before their maturity or (2) an agreement that entitles the transferor to repurchase or redeem transferred assets that are not readily obtainable.

> **Practical Consideration.** In some industries, such as the mortgage banking industry, it is common for the transferor to securitize financial assets and retain all of the beneficial interests in the qualifying special purpose entity as securities. The retained securities provide the transferor with more financial flexibility because they can more easily be sold or pledged as collateral on borrowed funds than the transferred assets. However, the transfer does not meet the criteria to be accounted for as a sale (discussed in Paragraph 52.201) because the transferor has not received consideration other than the beneficial interests in the transferred assets. Consequently, the transfer should be accounted for as a secured borrowing and pledge of collateral. (See Paragraph 52.213.)

52.202   A qualifying special-purpose entity (discussed in Paragraph 52.201, item b.) must meet *both* of the following criteria:

a. It is a trust, corporation, or other legal entity whose activities are permanently limited by the legal documents establishing the special-purpose entity to: (SFAS 125, par. 26)

(1) Holding title to transferred financial assets.

(2) Issuing beneficial interests.

(3) Collecting cash proceeds from assets held, reinvesting proceeds pending distribution to owners of beneficial interests, and otherwise servicing assets held.

(4) Distributing proceeds to the holders of beneficial interests.

b. It has a legal standing separate from the transferor.

> **Practical Consideration.** Generally, under U.S. law, if the transferor holds all the beneficial interests in a special-purpose trust, the transferor can unilaterally dissolve the trust and resume control of the assets held by the trust. In that case, the entity does not have separate legal standing and therefore would not qualify as a special-purpose entity for purposes of complying with item b. of Paragraph 52.201.

52.203   After financial assets are transferred, the transferor should continue to carry on its balance sheet any retained interest in the transferred assets. The previous carrying amount should be allocated between the assets sold and any retained interests based on their relative fair values at the date of transfer. (SFAS 125, par. 10)

52.204   For transfers that meet the conditions to be accounted for as a sale (see Paragraph 52.201), the transferor (seller) should: (SFAS 125, par. 11)

  a. Derecognize (that is, remove from the balance sheet) all assets sold.

  b. Record all assets received and liabilities incurred as proceeds from the sale.

  c. Measure the assets received and liabilities incurred at fair value. (See Paragraphs 52.207–.208.)

  d. Recognize any gain or loss on the sale.

The transferee should record any assets obtained and liabilities incurred at fair value.

52.205   If financial assets are exchanged for cash or other consideration, but the transfer does not meet the criteria for sale discussed in Paragraph 52.201, the transferor and transferee should account for the transfer as a secured borrowing and pledge of collateral. (SFAS 125, par. 12) (See Paragraph 52.213.)

Agreements That Maintain Effective Control over Transferred Assets

52.206   When financial assets are transferred, the transferor may enter into an agreement with the transferee that in substance results in the transferor maintaining effective control over the assets. If so, the transaction should be accounted for as a secured borrowing. (See Paragraph 52.213.) An agreement maintains the transferor's effective control over transferred assets if it both entitles and requires the transferor to repurchase or redeem transferred assets from the transferee and meets *all* of the following conditions: (SFAS 125, par. 27)

  a. The transferor is able to repurchase or redeem the assets on substantially the agreed upon terms even in the event of default by the transferee.

  b. The agreement is for the repurchase or redemption of the assets prior to maturity at a fixed or determinable price.

  c. The agreement is entered into concurrently with the transfer.

d. The assets to be repurchased or redeemed are the same (or substantially the same) as the transferred assets.

Practical Consideration. The assets transferred and the assets to be repurchased or redeemed are substantially the same if they have all of the following characteristics:

    a. Generally, the same primary obligor (For debt guaranteed by a government, central bank, or governmental agency, the guarantor and the terms of the guarantee must be the same.)

    b. Identical form and type, resulting in the same risks and rights

    c. The same maturity (similar average weighted maturities that result in the same approximate market yield for mortgage backed pass-through and pay-through securities)

    d. Contractual interest rates that are identical

    e. Similar collateral

    f. The same aggregate unpaid principal amounts or principal amounts within accepted standards for the type of security involved

---

Fair Value

52.207   Fair value of financial assets should be based on quoted market prices when available. If quoted market prices are not available, fair value is based on the best information available. Fair value of similar assets and liabilities and the results of valuation techniques (such as the present value of estimated future cash flows using a discount rate commensurate with the risks involved, option pricing models, matrix pricing, option-adjusted spread models, and fundamental analysis) should be considered when estimating fair value. (SFAS 125, par. 43)

Not Practicable to Estimate Fair Values

52.208   Assets obtained should be recorded at zero if it is not practicable for the transferor to estimate their fair values. If it is not practicable for the transferor to estimate the fair values of liabilities incurred, no gain should be recognized on the transfer and the liabilities incurred should be recorded at the greater of: (SFAS 125, par. 45)

    a. The excess, if any, of (1) the fair values of assets obtained less the fair value of other liabilities incurred (that is, those liabilities for which it is practicable to estimate fair value) over (2) the total carrying value of the assets transferred.

b. The amount that would be recognized under SFAS No. 5, *Accounting for Contingencies* as interpreted by FASBI 14, *Reasonable Estimation of the Amount of a Loss.* SFAS No. 5 requires an entity to accrue a liability for loss contingencies that are both probable and reasonably estimable. If a loss is probable, but only a range of loss can be reasonably estimated, the minimum amount of the range should be accrued unless another amount is a better estimate. (See Chapter 10 for further guidance on accounting for contingencies.)

Servicing Assets and Liabilities

52.209   When an entity is obligated to service financial assets, it should recognize a servicing asset or a servicing liability for the servicing contract. The contract to service financial assets should be accounted for separately from the financial assets as follows: (SFAS 125, par. 37)

a. Servicing assets and servicing liabilities should be reported separately in the statement of financial position.

b. Servicing assets retained in the sale or securitization of the assets being serviced should be recorded at their allocated carrying amount based on relative fair values (if practicable) at the date of sale or securitization.

c. Servicing assets purchased or servicing liabilities assumed should be recorded at fair value.

d. Servicing liabilities undertaken in a sale or securitization should be recorded at fair value, if practicable.

e. Rights to future interest income from serviced assets in excess of contractually specified servicing fees should be accounted for separately from servicing assets.

f. Servicing assets should be amortized into income in proportion to and over the period of estimated net servicing income.

g. Servicing assets should be subsequently measured for impairment. Impairment should be recognized by recording a valuation allowance.

h. Servicing liabilities should be amortized into income in proportion to and over the period of estimated net servicing loss. However, if subsequent events (such as higher servicing expenses than originally estimated) result in an increase in the fair value of the servicing liability, the increased liability should be charged to earnings.

EXHIBIT 52-1 illustrates accounting for a transfer of financial assets with servicing retained.

Practical Consideration. SFAS 125 does not require a servicing asset or liability to be recorded when an entity securitizes the financial assets, retains all the resulting securities, and classifies them as debt securities held to maturity under SFAS No. 115. (Chapter 35 discusses classifying debt securities.)

52.210   **Servicing Contracts Prior to January 1, 1997.** For servicing contracts entered into prior to January 1, 1997, previously recognized servicing rights and excess servicing receivables (receivables for fees that do not exceed servicing fees specified in the contract) should be combined (net of any previously recorded servicing liabilities recorded under the contract) as an asset or liability. Previously recognized servicing receivables that exceed fees specified in the contract should be reclassified as interest-only strips receivable. Resulting servicing assets or liabilities should be subsequently measured as discussed in Paragraph 52.209. Resulting interest-only strips receivable should be subsequently measured as discussed in Paragraph 52.211. (SFAS 125, par. 20)

Financial Assets Subject to Prepayment

52.211   Financial assets (such as interest-only strips, other receivables, or retained interests in securitizations) that contractually can be prepaid or otherwise settled in a manner that the holder would not recover substantially all of its carrying value should be subsequently measured like investments in debt securities classified as available-for-sale or trading. (SFAS 125, par. 14) Consequently, changes in fair value (i.e., unrealized holding gains and losses) should be accounted for as follows: (SFAS 115, par. 13)

     a. *Trading securities.* Unrealized gains and losses should be included in earnings in the period they arise.

     b. *Available-for-sale securities.* Unrealized gains and losses should be reported as other comprehensive income. Realized gains and losses should be included in income in the period they are realized.

Chapter 35 discusses accounting for investments in marketable securities in more detail.

EXHIBIT 52-1

ILLUSTRATION OF THE ACCOUNTING FOR A TRANSFER OF FINANCIAL ASSETS WITH SERVICING RETAINED

To illustrate a transfer of financial assets with servicing retained, assume ABC, Inc. originates $10,000 of loans that yield 10% interest income for their estimated lives of 9 years. ABC, Inc. sells the $10,000 principal plus the right to receive interest income of 8% to XYZ, Inc. for $10,000. Servicing of the loans will continue to be handled by ABC, Inc. for compensation equal to half of the interest income not sold. The remaining half of the interest income not sold is considered to be an interest-only strip receivable. The fair value of the loans and servicing is $11,000 at the date of transfer. ABC, Inc. estimates the fair value of the servicing asset to be $400.

Fair Values

Cash proceeds	$	10,000
Servicing asset		400
Interest-only strip receivable		600

Allocation of Carrying Amount Based on Relative Fair Values

	Fair Value	Percentage of Total Fair Value	Allocated Carrying Amount
Loans sold	$ 10,000	91.0%	$ 9,100
Servicing Asset	400	3.6	360
Interest-only strip receivable	600	5.4	540
Total	$ 11,000	100.0%	$ 10,000

Gain on Sale

Net proceeds	$	10,000
Carrying amount of loans sold		9,100
Gain on sale	$	900

Journal Entries

Cash	10,000	
Loans		9,100
Gain on sale		900

To record transfer

EXHIBIT 52-1 (Continued)

Servicing asset	360	
Interest-only strip receivable	540	
Loans		900

To record servicing asset and interest-only strip receivable.

Transfers of Receivables with Recourse

52.212 When an entity transfers receivables to another entity (the transferee), it often does so with recourse. In such a case, the transferee has the right to receive payment from the transferor or the transferor must repurchase the receivables if the debtor defaults. Transfers of receivables with recourse must meet the conditions in Paragraph 52.201 to be accounted for as a sale. The effect of recourse provisions on the application of Paragraph 52.201 may vary by jurisdiction. In some jurisdictions, the transfer of receivables with full recourse may not place the transferred assets beyond the reach of the transferor and its creditors (however, transfers with limited recourse may). If the transfer of receivables with recourse does not meet the conditions in Paragraph 52.201, the transfer should be accounted for as a secured borrowing. (SFAS 125, par. 83) (Secured borrowings are discussed in Paragraph 52.213).

ACCOUNTING FOR SECURED BORROWINGS

52.213 A debtor may grant a security interest in assets to a lender to serve as collateral for its debt, and the lender may be allowed to sell or repledge the collateral. The accounting for collateral depends on the whether the lender has taken control of the collateral and on the terms of the collateral arrangement, as follows: (SFAS 125, par. 15)

    a. If the lender is allowed (by contract or custom) to sell or repledge the collateral and the debtor does not have the right to redeem the collateral on short notice (e.g., by substituting other collateral or terminating the collateral arrangement),

        (1) the debtor should report the collateral as a restricted asset in its balance sheet, and

        (2) the lender should recognize the collateral as its asset at fair value, and also recognize a liability for its obligation to return the collateral.

b. If the lender sells or repledges the collateral on terms that do not give it the right to repurchase or redeem the collateral on short notice (and thus may impair the debtor's right to redeem the collateral), the lender should recognize the proceeds from the sale or repledge of the collateral and its liability for returning the collateral if it is has not already done so.

c. A debtor that defaults under the terms of the secured borrowing and is no longer entitled to redeem the collateral should remove the collateral from its balance sheet. The lender should record the collateral as its asset to the extent it has not already done so.

d. Otherwise, the debtor should continue to carry the collateral as its asset, and the lender should not recognize the pledged collateral.

DISCLOSURE REQUIREMENTS

55.500   The following information should be disclosed about transfers and servicing of financial assets: (SFAS 125, par. 17)

a. The entity's policy for requiring collateral or other security interests for repurchase agreements or securities lending transactions.

b. The nature of restrictions placed on assets set aside solely for satisfying scheduled payments on a specific liability.

c. A description of financial assets obtained or liabilities incurred during the period for which it is not practicable to estimate the fair value and the reasons why it is not practicable to estimate fair value.

d. For all servicing assets and liabilities:

(1) The amounts of servicing assets and liabilities recorded and amortized during the period.

(2) The fair value of recorded servicing assets and liabilities (for which it is practicable to estimate fair value) and the significant assumptions used in estimating fair value.

(3) For any valuation allowances for impairment of recorded servicing assets, the beginning and ending balances,

aggregate additions charged to operations and the aggregate reductions credited to operations, and the aggregate direct write-downs charge to the allowance for all periods in results of operations are reported.

(4) The risk characteristics of the underlying financial assets used to group recognized servicing assets for purposes of measuring impairment (for example, whether servicing assets were grouped for impairment evaluation based on the underlying assets' type, size, interest rate, term, etc.)

AUTHORITATIVE LITERATURE AND RELATED TOPICS

AUTHORITATIVE LITERATURE

SFAS No. 107, *Disclosures about Fair Value of Financial Instruments*
SFAS No. 115, *Accounting for Certain Investments in Debt and Equity Securities*
SFAS No. 125, *Accounting for Transfers and Servicing of Financial Assets and Extinguishments of Liabilities*
SFAS No. 127, *Deferral of the Effective Date of Certain Provisions of FASB Statement No. 125*

RELATED PRONOUNCEMENTS

EITF Issue No. 84-5, *Sale of Marketable Securities with a Put Option*
EITF Issue No. 84-20, *GNMA Dollar Rolls*
EITF Issue No. 84-21, *Sale of a Loan with Partial Participation Retained*
EITF Issue No. 84-30, *Sales of Loans to Special-Purpose Entities*
EITF Issue No. 84-36, *Interest Rate Swap Transactions*
EITF Issue No. 84-39, *Transfers of Monetary and Nonmonetary Assets among Individuals and Entities Under Common Control*
EITF Issue No. 85-30, *Sale of Marketable Securities at a Gain with a Put Option*
EITF Issue No. 86-8, *Sale of Bad-Debt Recovery Rights*
EITF Issue No. 87-17, *Spin-Offs or Other Distributions of Loans Receivable to Shareholders*
EITF Issue No. 87-25, *Sale of Convertible, Adjustable-Rate Mortgages with Contingent Payment Agreement*
EITF Issue No. 87-30, *Sale of a Short-Term Loan Made under a Long-Term Credit Commitment*
EITF Issue No. 88-20, *Differences between Initial Investment and Principal Amount of Loans in a Purchased Credit Card Portfolio*
EITF Issue No. 88-22, *Securitization of Credit Card and Other Receivable Portfolios*

EITF Issue No. 90-18, *Effect of a "Removal of Accounts" Provision on the Accounting for a Credit Card Securitization*

EITF Issue No. 92-2, *Measuring Loss Accruals by Transferors for Transfers of Receivables with Recourse*

EITF Issue No. 96-10, *Impact of Certain Transactions on the Held-to-Maturity Classification under FASB Statement No. 115*

EITF Issue No. 96-20, *Impact of FASB Statement No. 125 on Consolidation of Special-Purpose Entities*

EITF Issue No. 97-3, *Accounting for Fees and Costs Associated with Loan Syndications and Loan Participations after the Issuance of FASB Statement No. 125*

EITF Issue No. 97-6, *Application of EITF Issue No. 96-20 to Qualifying SPEs Receiving Transferred Financial Assets Prior to the Effective Date of Statement 125*

RELATED TOPICS

INDUSTRY STANDARDS

Table of Contents

BANKING AND THRIFT INSTITUTIONS

Table of Contents

BANKING AND THRIFT INSTITUTIONS

OVERVIEW

53.100 Generally accepted accounting principles provide specific guidance on accounting for the intangible assets acquired and regulatory assistance received when banks and savings and loan associations are acquired in business combinations accounted for under the purchase method. In general, it requires an acquiring company to—

a. amortize goodwill to expense using the straight-line method over a period not exceeding the estimated remaining life of the long-term interest-bearing assets acquired. An accelerated method may be used, however, if the institution can demonstrate (1) the amount assigned to goodwill represents an amount paid for identifiable intangible assets whose fair value could not be individually determined and (2) the benefits expected to be received from the assets decline over their expected lives.

b. account for any regulatory assistance that is probable and reasonably estimable as part of the combination.

53.101 GAAP also provides specific guidance on accounting for the income tax effect of savings and loan associations' bad debt reserves. Generally, a savings and loan association should not record deferred taxes related to bad debt reserves for tax purposes that arose in tax years beginning before December 31, 1987.

ACCOUNTING REQUIREMENTS

ACCOUNTING FOR ACQUISITIONS OF BANKS AND SAVINGS AND LOAN ASSOCIATIONS

53.200 In a business combination accounted for by the purchase method, each asset acquired and liability assumed should be assigned a portion of the purchase price based on their fair values at the acquisition date. That method, referred to as the separate valuation method, should be applied to the tangible and intangible assets acquired. (See Chapter 3.)

> **Practical Consideration.** GAAP precludes the use of the net-spread method to account for acquisitions. Under the net-spread method, the acquisition is viewed as the purchase of an entire institution rather than the purchase of its separate assets and liabilities. Thus, if the spread between the rates received on the acquired institution's mortgage loan portfolio and the rates paid on its savings accounts is normal for the particular market, the acquired institution's loan portfolio and savings accounts are recorded at their carrying amounts rather than fair value.

Identifiable Intangible Assets

53.201   In an acquisition of a banking or thrift institution, a portion of the amount paid may relate to the purchase of core deposits. Core deposits are accounts that tend to remain in the financial institution regardless of changes in interest rates and are a dependable, long-term source of funds for the institution. They are considered to have a value that is separate from the institution's other assets. Consequently, in a business combination accounted for by the purchase method, a portion of the purchase price should be allocated to core deposits and other factors, such as the following: (FASBI 9, par. 8)

- Capacity of existing savings accounts and loan accounts to generate future income

- Capacity of existing savings accounts and loan accounts to generate additional business or new business

- Nature of territory served

Core deposits or any of the previous factors should be accounted for as identifiable intangible assets and should not be included in goodwill if their values can be separately identified. The portion of the purchase price allocated to identifiable intangible assets should be based on the fair value of the estimated benefits attributable to depositor or borrower relationships that exist at the acquisition date. Subsequent to the acquisition, the assets should be amortized over the estimated lives of the related existing depositor or borrower relationships. (SFAS 72, par. 4)

Unidentifiable Intangible Asset

53.202   Under the purchase method, the excess of the purchase price paid to acquire a financial institution over the fair value of the identifiable tangible and intangible assets and liabilities acquired should be recorded as goodwill. Goodwill is an unidentifiable intangible asset and should be amortized to expense over a period not exceeding the estimated remaining life of the long-term interest-bearing assets acquired or, if no significant long-term interest-bearing assets were acquired, the existing deposit base acquired. (SFAS 72, par. 6) Goodwill generally should be amortized using the straight-line method. However, an accelerated method may be more appropriate for an acquired savings and loan or similar institution that can demonstrate (a) the amount assigned to goodwill represents an amount paid for identifiable intangible assets whose fair value could not be individually determined and (b) the benefits expected to be received from the assets decline over their expected lives. (FASBI 9, par. 9)

> **Practical Consideration.** The goodwill amortization period should be determined at the acquisition date and normally should not exceed 40 years. The amortization period should be continually evaluated to determine whether later events and circumstances warrant a change in the estimated useful life of goodwill. The amortization period should not be adjusted upward, however. Amortization of goodwill and other intangibles is discussed further in Chapter 26.

53.203   If a large segment or branch of an acquired financial institution is sold or liquidated, the portion of the goodwill attributable to that segment or branch should be included in the cost of the assets sold. If the benefits of the remaining goodwill have been significantly reduced by the sale or liquidation, the reduction should be charged to income. (SFAS 72, par. 7)

Regulatory-assisted Combinations

53.204   A regulatory authority (such as the Federal Deposit Insurance Corporation or the Federal Savings and Loan Insurance Corporation) may provide assistance in the acquisition of a financial institution by agreeing to pay the difference between the interest cost of carrying the interest-bearing assets acquired and the future interest receivable on those assets. The acquiring company should consider the projected assistance as additional interest on the interest-bearing assets acquired when determining their fair values under the purchase method. Once determined, the carrying value of the interest-bearing assets should not be adjusted for subsequent changes in the estimated amount of assistance to be received. Also, interest-bearing assets should not be valued above their current market values if the acquiring company intends to sell them. Actual assistance should be reported in income in the period in which it accrues. (SFAS 72, par.8)

53.205   A regulatory authority may provide other forms of assistance in the acquisition of a financial institution. Under the purchase method, if receipt of other forms of financial assistance is probable and the amount is reasonably estimable, the acquiring company should assign part of the acquisition cost to the assistance received. If receipt of regulatory assistance is not probable or the amount is not reasonably estimable at the time of acquisition, any assistance subsequently recognized should be reported as a reduction of the goodwill that was recognized in the acquisition. Assistance recognized in excess of that goodwill should be reported in income. (SFAS 72, par. 9)

53.206   The acquiring company should not assign part of the acquisition cost to any assets or liabilities transferred to or assumed by a regulatory authority as part of the assistance. (SFAS 72, par. 9)

53.207   The acquiring company may agree to repay all or part of the regulatory assistance if certain criteria related to future operations are met. In that case, the repayment should be recognized as a liability and as a charge to income when the repayment is probable and the amount can be reasonably estimated. (SFAS 72, par. 10)

BAD DEBT RESERVES OF SAVINGS AND LOAN ASSOCIATIONS

53.208   Often, a savings and loan's bad debt reserve for tax purposes differs significantly from its GAAP basis reserve. The bad debt expense deduction under the Internal Revenue Code is based on specified limits while bad debt expense under GAAP is based on actual and expected losses. A savings and loan should not record deferred taxes for taxable temporary differences related to bad debt reserves for tax purposes that arose in tax years beginning before December 31, 1987. However, if circumstances indicate the savings and loan is likely to pay income taxes, either currently or in later years because of known or expected reductions in the bad debt reserve, deferred taxes attributable to that reduction should be accrued in the current period. (The related tax expense should not be reported as an extraordinary item.) Amounts of bad debt deductions for income tax purposes are includable in taxable income of later years if the bad debt reserves are subsequently used for purposes other than to absorb bad debt losses. (APB 23, paras. 19–23 and SFAS 109, par. 288)

DISCLOSURE REQUIREMENTS

53.500   An acquiring company should disclose the nature and amounts of any regulatory financial assistance granted or recognized during the period in connection with the acquisition of a banking or thrift institution. (SFAS 72, par. 11)

AUTHORITATIVE LITERATURE AND RELATED TOPICS

AUTHORITATIVE LITERATURE

APB Opinion No. 23, *Accounting for Income Taxes—Special Areas*
SFAS No. 72, *Accounting for Certain Acquisitions of Banking or Thrift Institutions*
SFAS No. 109, *Accounting for Income Taxes*
FASB Interpretation No. 9, *Applying APB Opinions No. 16 and 17 When a Savings and Loan Association or a Similar Institution is Acquired in a Business Combination Accounted for by the Purchase Method*

RELATED PRONOUNCEMENTS

SFAS No. 125, *Accounting for Transfers and Servicing of Financial Assets and Extinguishments of Liabilities*
AICPA Audit and Accounting Guide, *Banks and Savings Institutions*
AICPA Audit and Accounting Guide, *Audits of Credit Unions*
AICPA Audit and Accounting Guide, *Audits of Finance Companies*
SOP 92-3, *Accounting for Foreclosed Assets*
EITF Issue No. 84-4, *Acquisition, Development, and Construction Loans*
EITF Issue No. 84-9, *Deposit Float of Banks*
EITF Issue No. 84-21, *Sale of a Loan with a Partial Participation Retained*
EITF Issue No. 84-22, *Prior Years' Earnings per Share Following a Savings and Loan Association Conversion and Pooling*
EITF Issue No. 84-30, *Sales of Loans to Special-Purpose Entities*
FASB Technical Bulletin 85-1, *Accounting for the Receipt of Federal Home Loan Mortgage Corporation Participating Preferred Stock*

RELATED TOPICS

Chapter 3—Business Combinations
Chapter 24—Income Taxes
Chapter 26—Intangible Assets
Chapter 52—Transfers and Servicing of Financial Assets
Chapter 61—Lending and Mortgage Banking Activities

BROADCASTERS

Table of Contents

BROADCASTERS

OVERVIEW

54.100   A broadcaster should record acquired rights to broadcast program materials as an asset and the related obligation as a liability. The asset should be amortized to expense based on the estimated number of showings or over the period of the license agreement if the number of future showings cannot be determined. If the asset's estimated net realizable value is less than its unamortized cost, the asset should be written down to estimated net realizable value through a charge to current period income.

54.101   Barter transactions involving the exchange of unsold advertising time for products or services should be accounted for as nonmonetary transactions. Accordingly, they should be recorded at the estimated fair value of the products or services received.

54.102   A broadcaster should report a network affiliation agreement as an intangible asset. If the affiliation is terminated, the unamortized cost of the intangible asset should be charged to current period expense to the extent it exceeds the fair value of any new affiliation agreement.

ACCOUNTING REQUIREMENTS

LICENSE AGREEMENTS FOR PROGRAM MATERIAL

54.200   License agreements for program materials grant the broadcaster (licensee) the right to broadcast a specified program or package of programs for a certain number of showings or for a certain period of time. In return, the licensee pays a nonrefundable fee to the licensor, typically in installments over a period shorter than the license period. (SFAS 64, par. 14)

54.201   The licensee should record the broadcast rights acquired as an asset and the related obligation under the license agreement as a liability when the license period begins and all of the following conditions have been met:

a. The cost of each program is known or can be reasonably determined.

b. The licensee has accepted the program material in accordance with the conditions of the license agreement.

c. The program is available for its first showing or telecast. (This condition is considered to be met even though the license agreement or another license agreement with the same licensor imposes restrictions on the timing of subsequent showings. The condition is not met, however, if a conflicting license prevents the licensee from broadcasting the program.)

The asset should be classified on the balance sheet as current or noncurrent based on when it is expected to be used. Similarly, the liability should be classified as current or noncurrent based on when it is required to be paid. (SFAS 63, par. 3)

54.202   The asset and liability related to the license agreement should be reported at either the liability's gross amount or its present value. If the present value method is used, the difference between the net and gross liability should be accounted for as interest in accordance with APB Opinion No. 21, *Interest on Receivables and Payables.* (SFAS 63, par. 4) (Computing the present value of a liability and amortizing the discount to interest is discussed in Chapter 28.)

Practical Consideration. GAAP allows broadcasters to elect to record the liability at its gross amount or at a discounted amount following APB Opinion No. 21. However, APB Opinion No. 21 is relevant only when the liability is due in over one year and bears an unreasonable rate of interest or no interest at all. If the license agreement already requires payment of an appropriate rate of interest, the liability's present value would be equal to its gross amount.

Amortizing Program Rights

54.203   The cost of the license asset should be allocated to individual programs within a package based on the relative value of each program to the licensee. The asset then should be amortized based on (a) the estimated number of future showings of each program or (b) the period of the agreement if the estimated number of future showings cannot be determined. Generally, the licensee should amortize feature programs on a program-by-program basis and amortize program series and other syndicated products as a series. The straight-line amortization method should be used if each showing is expected to generate similar revenues. An accelerated method should be used if the first showing is more valuable than reruns. (SFAS 63, paras. 5–6)

54.204   The licensee should report the license agreement asset in the balance sheet at the lower of unamortized cost or estimated net realizable value. If the asset's estimated net realizable value on either a program-by-program, series, package, or daypart basis is less than its unamortized cost, the licensee should reduce the unamortized cost to estimated net realizable value through a charge to current period income. In that event, the written-down cost becomes the asset's new cost. (SFAS 63, par. 7)

BARTER TRANSACTIONS

54.205   A broadcaster may trade (or barter) unsold advertising time for products or services. Barter transactions should be recorded at the estimated fair value of the products or services received in accordance with APB Opinion No. 29, *Accounting for Nonmonetary Transactions*. (See Chapter 36.) Barter revenue should be reported when the advertising is broadcast. Consequently, a receivable should be recorded if the advertising is broadcast before the products or services are received, and a liability should be recorded if the products or services are received before the advertising is broadcast. (SFAS 63, par. 9)

NETWORK AFFILIATION AGREEMENTS

54.206   Under a network affiliation agreement, a network pays the broadcaster to carry network programing and advertising sold on a network basis. A broadcaster should report a network affiliation agreement in its balance sheet as an intangible asset (SFAS 63, par. 9). The asset should be amortized to expense over the lesser of its useful life or 40 years. (APB 17, paras. 29–30) (Amortizing intangible assets is discussed further in Chapter 26.)

54.207   If a network affiliation is terminated and immediately replaced (or is under agreement to be replaced), the broadcaster should recognize a loss to the extent that the unamortized cost of the terminated affiliation agreement exceeds the fair value of the new affiliation. (A gain should not be recognized, however.) If a network affiliation is terminated and not immediately replaced or is not under agreement to be replaced, the broadcaster should charge the unamortized cost of the terminated affiliation to expense. (SFAS 63, par. 9)

DISCLOSURE REQUIREMENTS

54.500   As discussed in Paragraph 54.201, a broadcaster should record an asset and liability for a license agreement when (a) the cost of each program can be reasonably determined, (b) it has accepted the program material under the terms of the license agreement, and (c) the program is available for its first showing. Any commitment for a license agreement that has been executed but not recorded because it does not meet all of those criteria should be disclosed. (SFAS 63, par. 10)

AUTHORITATIVE LITERATURE AND RELATED TOPICS

AUTHORITATIVE LITERATURE

SFAS No. 63, *Financial Reporting by Broadcasters*

RELATED PRONOUNCEMENTS

EITF Issue No. 87-10, *Revenue Recognition by Television "Barter" Syndicators*

RELATED TOPICS

Chapter 26—Intangible Assets
Chapter 28—Interest: Imputed
Chapter 36—Nonmonetary Transactions

CABLE TELEVISION COMPANIES

Table of Contents

CABLE TELEVISION COMPANIES

OVERVIEW

55.100   While a cable television system is partially in use and partially under construction (referred to as the "prematurity period"), cable television plant costs should be capitalized and subscriber-related costs should be charged to period expense. Programming and other system costs should be allocated between current and future operations, however. The portion that relates to current operations should be charged to current period expense and the remainder should be capitalized.

55.101   Initial hookup fees should be recognized as revenue to the extent of direct selling costs. Remaining hookup fees should be deferred and amortized to income in future periods. Initial hookup costs should be capitalized and depreciated. Subsequent costs to disconnect and reconnect subscribers should be charged to expense.

55.102   Successful franchise applications should be capitalized and amortized as an intangible asset. Unsuccessful applications should be charged to current period expense.

ACCOUNTING REQUIREMENTS

ACCOUNTING FOR INITIAL COSTS

Prematurity Period

55.200   The prematurity period is the time during which the cable television system is partially under construction and partially in service. It begins when subscriber revenue is first earned and ends when the first major stage of construction is completed or a predetermined subscriber level is reached. A cable television company should determine the beginning and end of its prematurity period prior to earning revenue from the first subscriber. Generally, the period should not exceed two years, although a longer period may be justified in major urban markets. Once established, the prematurity period should not be changed except under unusual circumstances. (SFAS 51, paras. 4 and 17)

Accounting for Costs during the Prematurity Period

55.201   The portion of the cable television system that is in the prematurity period and can be distinguished from the remainder of the system should be accounted for separately. A portion of the cable television system is clearly distinguished from the remainder of the system when it has most of the following characteristics:

   a. It is located in a separate geographic area or franchise area.

   b. It has separate facilities and equipment.

   c. Its construction or marketing begin at a significantly later date.

   d. Investing in the portion is a separate decision. (For example, it has its own break-even point and return on investment analysis or it requires separate approval to start construction.)

   e. It has separate accounting records, forecasts, budgets, etc. (SFAS 51, par. 5)

55.202   **Cable Television Plant.** The cable television plant consists of the equipment needed to provide service to subscribers. It includes satellite and microwave installations, studio facilities, cable and amplifiers, and converters and descramblers. A cable company should capitalize the costs of its cable television plant, including materials, direct labor, and construction overhead. (SFAS 51, paras. 6 and 17) In addition, interest on the portion of the system that is being readied for its intended use and not yet placed in service should be capitalized in accordance with SFAS No. 34, *Capitalization of Interest.* (SFAS 51, par. 9) (Capitalizing interest is discussed in Chapter 27.)

Practical Consideration. Because, as discussed in Paragraph 55.200, a portion of a cable system is being used in the company's earnings activities during the prematurity period, only part of the system qualifies for interest capitalization under SFAS No. 34. The portion that qualifies is the excess of (a) accumulated expenditures over (b) the total estimated cost of the system multiplied by the fraction described in Paragraph 55.203, item b.

55.203   During the prematurity period, the monthly depreciation of the cable television plant should be determined as follows:

   a. Compute a monthly depreciation amount by applying the company's normal depreciation policies to the *total estimated cost* of the cable television plant.

b. Multiply the amount computed in a. by a fraction whose denominator is the total number of subscribers expected at the end of the prematurity period and whose numerator is the greater of (1) the average number of subscribers expected that month as estimated at the beginning of the prematurity period, (2) the average number of subscribers that would be attained if equal amounts of subscribers were added each month toward the total expected subscribers during the prematurity period, or (3) the average number of actual subscribers. (SFAS 51, par. 8)

55.204 Subscriber-related Costs. Subscriber-related costs (i.e., costs necessary to obtain and retain subscribers to the system) and general and administrative expenses should be charged to expense in the period they are incurred. (SFAS 51, par. 6) The following are examples of subscriber-related costs:

- Billing and collecting costs

- Bad debts

- Mailings

- Repairs and maintenance of taps and connections

- Franchise fees related to revenues or number of subscribers

- Salary of the system manager

- Office rent

- Programing costs for additional channels used in the marketing effort

- Costs related to the revenues from or subscribers to per channel or per program services

- Direct selling costs

55.205 Programming and Other System Costs. Programming and other system costs include leases on poles, underground ducts, satellite installations, or microwave installations; property taxes; and local origination programming. Such costs that (a) are incurred in anticipation of servicing a fully operating system and (b) will not vary significantly based on the number of subscribers should be allocated between current and future operations. The portion related to current operations should be expensed currently and the remainder should be capitalized. The portion related to current operations is computed by applying the fraction described in Paragraph 55.203, item b. to total programming and other system costs for the month. In other words, the amount of programming and other system costs that should be charged to expense is the total of such costs incurred during the month divided by the total number of subscribers expected at the end of the prematurity period and multiplied by the greater of—

a. the average number of subscribers expected that month as estimated at the beginning of the prematurity period,

b. the average number of subscribers that would be attained if equal amounts of subscribers were added each month toward the total expected subscribers during the prematurity period, or

c. the average number of actual subscribers. (SFAS 51, paras. 6–7)

55.206   Programming and other system costs capitalized during the prematurity period should be amortized over the same period used to depreciate the main cable television plant. (SFAS 51, par. 10)

HOOKUP REVENUE AND COSTS

55.207   A cable company should recognize initial hookup fees as revenue to the extent of direct selling costs. (Direct selling costs are costs incurred to obtain and set up new subscribers. They include compensation paid to sales staff for obtaining new subscribers, advertising, and costs of processing documents related to new subscribers. They do not include supervisory and administrative or other indirect expenses, however.) Remaining hookup fees should be deferred and amortized to income over the estimated average period that subscribers are expected to remain connected to the system. (SFAS 51, par. 11)

55.208   Costs to initially connect a new subscriber to the system, including material, labor, and overhead costs, should be capitalized and depreciated over a period no longer than the depreciation period used for the cable television plant. Subsequent costs to disconnect and reconnect subscribers should be charged to expense. (SFAS 51, par. 12)

FRANCHISE COSTS

55.209   Usually, a cable television company applies to a local government for the rights to provide cable services in the geographic area. The costs of successful franchise applications should be capitalized and amortized as an intangible asset. (See Chapter 26 for a discussion on accounting for intangible assets.) The cost of unsuccessful franchise applications or abandoned franchises should be charged to current period expense. (SFAS 51, par. 13)

RECOVERABILITY

55.210   Changing conditions may raise doubts about whether a cable company will be able to recover the carrying amounts of its capitalized plant and intangible assets. Such capitalized costs should be evaluated for impairment in accordance with SFAS No. 121, *Accounting for the Impairment of Long-Lived Assets and for Long-Lived Assets to Be Disposed Of.* (Evaluating impairment is discussed in Chapter 33.) A cable company should continue to capitalize plant and intangible asset costs even if it determines that the assets have been impaired. In such cases, however, the provision required to reduce capitalized costs to recoverable value should be correspondingly increased. (SFAS 51, par. 14)

AUTHORITATIVE LITERATURE AND RELATED TOPICS

AUTHORITATIVE LITERATURE

SFAS No. 51, *Financial Reporting by Cable Television Companies*

RELATED TOPICS

Chapter 26—Intangible Assets
Chapter 33—Long-lived Assets, Depreciation, and Impairment

COMPUTER SOFTWARE DEVELOPERS

Table of Contents

COMPUTER SOFTWARE DEVELOPERS

OVERVIEW

56.100   The costs incurred to internally create computer software are considered research and development costs (and, thus, should be charged to expense) until the product's technological feasibility has been established. A software product's technological feasibility is established when a detail program design or working model has been completed. After that point, all production costs should be capitalized and (a) amortized over the product's economic life and (b) reported at the lower of unamortized cost or net realizable value.

56.101   The developer should stop capitalizing software production costs when the product is available for general release to the public. Costs incurred to duplicate the software and related materials from product masters and package them for distribution should be capitalized as inventory and charged to cost of sales as revenue is recognized.

56.102   The costs purchased software should be accounted for based on its future use.

ACCOUNTING REQUIREMENTS

ACCOUNTING FOR INTERNALLY-DEVELOPED COMPUTER SOFTWARE COSTS

Research and Development Costs

56.200   The expenses incurred by a computer software developer to establish the technological feasibility of a computer software product to be sold, leased, or otherwise marketed are research and development costs and should be charged to expense when incurred. (SFAS 86, par. 3) The technological feasibility of a computer software product is established when the developer completes all the planning, designing, coding, and testing activities necessary to determine that the product can be produced according to its design specifications. Consequently, a developer must have completed the activities in a. or b. below to prove that technological feasibility has been established:

a. *Developing the software includes a detail program design.* (A detail program design takes the product's features and technical requirements to their most detailed level and is ready for coding.)

  (1) The developer has completed the product design and the detail program design and has established that it has the necessary skills, hardware, and software technology available to produce the product.

  (2) The developer has confirmed the detail program design's completeness and consistency with the product design by documenting and tracing the detail program design to product specifications.

  (3) The developer has reviewed the detail program design for high-risk issues (such as, unproven features or technical innovations) and uncertainties related to the issues have been resolved through coding and testing.

b. *Developing the software does not include a detail program design.*

  (1) The developer has completed a product design and a working model of the software program.

  (2) The developer has confirmed that the working model is complete and consistent with the product design by testing it. (SFAS 86, par. 4)

56.201   Expenses incurred to internally develop computer software for use in research and development activities are also research and development costs that should be expensed when incurred. (FASBI 6, par. 8) (Chapter 47 discusses accounting for research and development costs in further detail.)

Practical Consideration. Currently, generally accepted accounting principles do not address accounting for the cost of internally developed computer software to be used in a company's selling or administrative activities. However, SFAS No. 86, *Accounting for the Costs of Computer Software to Be Sold, Leased, or Otherwise Marketed,* does state that most companies expense such costs in the period they are incurred even though they are not research and development costs. In addition, the AICPA has recently issued an exposure draft of an SOP that would require direct costs of software purchased or internally developed for internal use to be capitalized and amortized over its estimated useful life.

Production Costs

56.202   Production costs for computer software should not be capitalized until (a) technological feasibility has been established and (b) all research and development activities for any other components of the product or process in which the software will be used have been completed. After that point, costs to produce product masters, including coding and testing, should be capitalized. (SFAS 86, par 5)

56.203   A developer should stop capitalizing its computer software costs when the product is available for general release to customers. Maintenance and customer support costs should be charged to expense when they are incurred or when the related revenue is recognized, whichever occurs first. When the price of customer support is included in the product's sales price, customer support costs should be estimated and accrued in the same period the sales price is recognized. (SFAS 86, paras. 6 and 45)

Amortization and Evaluation of Software Costs

56.204   Capitalized software should be amortized on a product-by-product basis. The annual amortization amount is the greater of—

a. amortization computed using the straight-line method over the remaining estimated economic life of the product or

b. amortization computed using the ratio of the product's current gross revenues to its total current and anticipated future gross revenues. (SFAS 86, par. 8)

56.205   Capitalized software costs should be evaluated for recoverability at each balance sheet date. A product's unamortized capitalized cost should be written off to the extent it exceeds the product's net realizable value. The product's net realizable value is the estimated future gross revenues from the product less the estimated future costs of completing and disposing of the product. Asset write-downs should not be subsequently restored. (SFAS 86, par. 10)

Inventory Costs

56.206   The costs of duplicating the software and related materials from the product masters and packaging them for distribution should be capitalized as inventory on a unit-specific basis. The inventory costs should be charged to cost of sales when the revenue from the sale of the units is recognized. (SFAS 86, par. 9)

ACCOUNTING FOR PURCHASED COMPUTER SOFTWARE COSTS

56.207   Many companies purchase computer software rather than develop it internally. The cost of purchased software should be accounted for in the same manner as the cost of internally developed software. That is, it should be accounted based on its future use as follows:

a. Purchased software with no alternative future use except to be sold, leased, or otherwise marketed should be accounted for the same as costs incurred to internally develop software. (See Paragraphs 56.200–.206.)

b. Purchased or leased computer software that has no alternative future use except to be used in research and development activities are research and development costs and should be expensed when incurred.

c. Purchased software that has an alternative future use (for example, as a tool in developing another product or for resale) should be capitalized when acquired and accounted for based on the future use. (SFAS 86, paras. 7 and 37–39)

DISCLOSURE REQUIREMENTS

56.500   A company's financial statements should disclose the following information about computer software costs:

a. Unamortized computer software costs included in each balance sheet presented

b. Amount charged to expense in each income statement for amortization of software costs and for amounts written down to net realizable value (SFAS 86, par. 11)

Additional disclosures may be required about research and development costs incurred in connection with computer software to be sold, leased, or otherwise marketed. Disclosures about research and development costs are discussed in Chapter 47.

AUTHORITATIVE LITERATURE AND RELATED TOPICS

AUTHORITATIVE LITERATURE

SFAS No. 86, *Accounting for the Costs of Computer Software to Be Sold, Leased, or Otherwise Marketed*

FASB Interpretation No. 6, *Applicability of FASB Statement No. 2 to Computer Software*

RELATED PRONOUNCEMENTS

SOP 91-1, *Software Revenue Recognition*

EITF Issue No. 85-35, *Transition and Implementation Issues for FASB Statement No. 86*

EITF Issue No. 96-6, *Accounting for the Film and Software Costs Associated with Developing Entertainment and Educational Software Products*

EITF Issue No. 96-14, *Accounting for the Costs Associated with Modifying Computer Software for the Year 2000*

RELATED TOPICS

Chapter 47—Research and Development Costs

CONSTRUCTION CONTRACTORS

Table of Contents

CONSTRUCTION CONTRACTORS

OVERVIEW

57.100 Construction contractors should use the percentage-of-completion method to account for revenues from long-term construction contracts if they can make reasonably dependable estimates of costs to complete and the extent of progress toward completion. Under the percentage-of-completion method, income generally is recognized based on the ratio of costs incurred to date to estimated total costs.

57.101 If dependable estimates are not available or if inherent hazards cause forecasts to be doubtful, construction contractors should recognize revenue from long-term construction contracts using the completed-contract method. Under that method, income is not recognized until the contract is substantially completed.

ACCOUNTING REQUIREMENTS

57.200 Revenue recognition issues for construction contractors are different from those for most other commercial entities. Generally, commercial companies recognize revenue when a product is delivered to a customer at the conclusion of a sale. If construction contractors followed that general rule, however, revenue would not be recognized until the construction project is completed and delivered at the conclusion of the construction process. Under generally accepted accounting principles, construction contractors should recognize revenues from construction contracts under either the percentage-of-completion or the completed-contract method.

PERCENTAGE-OF-COMPLETION METHOD

57.201 The percentage-of-completion method recognizes income in each accounting period as the contract progresses to completion. The recognized income should be the estimated total income multiplied by either:

- the percentage of incurred costs to date to the most recently estimated total completion costs, or

- a percentage indicated by some other measure of progress toward completion that is appropriate with regard to the work performed.

Particularly in the early stages of a contract, costs may include items such as materials and subcontracts that distort the project's percentage of completion. (For example, materials may be purchased in the early stages of construction but not used until much later.) Such costs may be excluded from the percentage-of-completion calculation if that would result in a more meaningful allocation of periodic income. (ARB 45, par. 4)

> **Practical Consideration.** The principal advantage of the percentage-of-completion method is that income is recognized as work is performed rather than as contracts are completed. The principal disadvantage of the percentage-of-completion method is that it depends on estimates of ultimate costs and income, which are subject to inherent uncertainties in long-term contracts.

COMPLETED-CONTRACT METHOD

57.202   The completed-contract method recognizes income only when the project is complete (or substantially complete if no significant costs remain). Accordingly, costs of contracts in process and current billings are accumulated but there are no charges or credits to income (other than provisions for losses) prior to completion. (ARB 45, par. 9)

57.203   When the completed-contract method is used, it may be appropriate to allocate general and administrative expenses to contract costs rather than to periodic income if a better matching of costs and revenues would result, particularly in years when no contracts are completed. If the contractor is engaged in numerous projects, however, it may be preferable to charge general and administrative expenses to periodic income as incurred. (ARB 45, par. 10)

> **Practical Consideration.** The principal advantage of the completed-contract method is that it is based on actual results upon completion, rather than on estimates for unperformed work, which may involve unforeseen costs and possible losses. The principal disadvantage of the completed-contract method is that revenue related to work performed in the current period is not recognized until a later period when a contract extends into more than one accounting period. Thus, it may result in irregular income recognition.

SELECTION OF METHOD

57.204   The percentage-of-completion and completed-contract methods are not alternatives from which a contractor may select. Instead, GAAP specifies when each method should be used. In general, the percentage-of-completion method should be used when estimates of costs to complete and extent of progress toward completion of long-term contracts are reasonably dependable. The completed-contract method may be used, however, if lack of dependable estimates causes forecasts to be doubtful. (ARB 45, par. 15)

Practical Consideration. A contractor may be reasonably assured that it will not incur a loss on a contract but be unable to reasonably estimate the final profit that will be earned. In such cases, SOP 81-1, *Accounting for Performance of Construction-Type and Certain Production-Type Contracts,* recommends that the percentage-of-completion method be used assuming zero profit until more dependable estimates can be made.

PROVISION FOR ANTICIPATED LOSSES

57.205   Regardless of the revenue recognition method used by a contractor, GAAP requires a loss to be accrued whenever it becomes apparent that the total estimated contract costs (costs incurred to date plus estimated costs to complete) will materially exceed the total estimated contract revenue. If a loss on a particular contract is expected after comparing the total estimated contract revenue to the total estimated contract costs, the full loss should be charged to a special loss account and credited to a corresponding liability account. The contractor should accrue the full amount of the estimated loss in the period it is determined, and the accrued liability should be disclosed separately in the balance sheet, if material. If there is a close relationship between profitable and unprofitable contracts (for example, if the contracts are part of the same project), they may be considered as a group when determining whether a loss provision is necessary. (ARB 45, paras. 6 and 11)

BALANCE SHEET ACCOUNTS

57.206   Under the percentage-of-completion method, current assets may include an account for costs and recognized income not yet billed with respect to some contracts, and current liabilities may include an account for billings in excess of costs and recognized income with respect to other contracts. (ARB 45, par. 5) Under the completed-contract method, current assets may include an account for an excess of accumulated costs over related billings, and current liabilities may include an account for an excess of accumulated billings over related costs. (ARB 45, par. 12)

57.207   If costs exceed billings on some contracts and billings exceed costs on others, the contracts should usually be segregated so that assets include only those contracts on which costs exceed billings, and liabilities include only those on which billings exceed costs. (ARB 45, par. 12)

DISCLOSURE REQUIREMENTS

57.500 The method used to account for long-term construction contracts should be disclosed. (ARB 45, par. 15) In special cases, a contractor also should disclose extraordinary commitments. However, commitments to complete contracts in process generally are in the ordinary course of a contractor's business and need not be disclosed. (ARB 45, par. 16)

Practical Consideration. SOP 81-1, *Accounting for Performance of Construction-Type and Certain Production-Type Contracts,* also requires construction contractors to make certain disclosures. Those disclosures include the following:

- Methods used to report revenue from construction contracts

- Methods of measuring the extent of progress toward completion

- Criteria for determining substantial completion

- Information on revenues and costs arising from claims

- Effects of changes in estimates

AUTHORITATIVE LITERATURE AND RELATED TOPICS

AUTHORITATIVE LITERATURE

ARB No. 45, *Long-Term Construction-Type Contracts*

RELATED PRONOUNCEMENTS

AICPA Audit and Accounting Guide, *Construction Contractors*
SOP 81-1, *Accounting for Performance of Construction-Type and Certain Production-Type Contracts*
EITF Issue No. 86-7, *Recognition by Homebuilders of Profit from Sales of Land and Related Construction Contracts*

FRANCHISORS

Table of Contents

FRANCHISORS

OVERVIEW

58.100   A franchisor should recognize initial franchise fees from a franchise sale when it has substantially performed or satisfied all material services or conditions relating to the sale. If the initial franchise fee covers the sale of tangible assets, a portion of the fee should be allocated to the assets. The portion allocated to the assets should be recognized when title to the assets passes, even if the portion of the franchise fee related to initial services has not been recognized. Continuing franchise fees generally should be recognized as they are earned and become receivable from the franchisee.

58.101   Direct franchising costs should be recognized in the same period as related revenues.

58.102   Generally accepted accounting principles also address accounting for agency transactions, repossessed franchises, and the acquisition of an operating franchise by the franchisor.

ACCOUNTING REQUIREMENTS

58.200   Under a franchise agreement, one party (the franchisor) transfers the rights to operate a business for a specified period to another party (the franchisee) in exchange for a fee. Both parties to the agreement contribute to the arrangement. The franchisor typically provides trademarks, patents, a reputation for quality goods and services, advertising, consulting services, products, and/or equipment while the franchisee provides the capital, labor, and management necessary to operate the business.

58.201   Generally accepted accounting principles address several accounting issues unique to franchisors. Specifically, they address accounting for franchise fees and costs, "bargain price" product sales, relationships involving affiliates or agencies, purchase options, franchise repossessions, and business combinations.

FRANCHISE FEES

Individual Franchise Sales

58.202   The franchisor should recognize initial franchise fee revenue from an individual franchise sale when it has substantially performed or satisfied all material services or conditions relating to the sale. Substantial performance has occurred when the franchisor has—

     a. no remaining obligation or intent to refund any cash received or to forgive any unpaid notes or receivables;

     b. performed substantially all of the initial services required by the franchise agreement (such as providing assistance in site selection, obtaining facilities, advertising, training, preparing operating manuals, bookkeeping, or quality control); and

     c. met all other material conditions or obligations.

Substantial performance generally occurs when the franchisee begins operations. It may occur at an earlier date, however, if the franchisor can demonstrate that it satisfied all material services or conditions related to the sale prior to the commencement of operations. (SFAS 45, par. 5)

Practical Consideration. Although not required to by the franchise agreement, a franchisor may voluntarily perform certain initial services due to established business practices or regulatory requirements. In such cases, substantial performance does not occur until the voluntarily rendered services have been provided or a reasonable assurance exists that the services will not be provided.

58.203   A provision for estimated uncollectible initial franchise fees should be recorded when necessary. In rare cases in which the initial franchise fee is collectible over an extended period and there is no reasonable basis for estimating the receivable's collectibility, the installment or cost recovery methods may be used to account for franchise fee revenue. (SFAS 45, par. 6) (Chapter 48 discusses recognizing revenue under the installment and cost recovery methods and the circumstances under which those methods may be appropriate.)

58.204   A portion of the initial franchise fee should be deferred and amortized over the life of the franchise if it is probable that continuing franchise fees will not cover the franchisor's cost of providing continuing services plus a reasonable profit. The amount deferred should be sufficient to cover the estimated cost in excess of continuing fees and provide a reasonable profit on the continuing services. (SFAS 45, par. 7) (Accounting for continuing franchise fees is discussed in paragraphs 58.207–.208.)

Area Franchise Sales

58.205   An area franchise agreement transfers franchise rights within a geographical area and permits the opening of a number of franchised outlets in that area. A franchisor should account for initial area franchise fees as follows:

    a. If the franchisor's obligations and total cost relating to initial services are not affected significantly by the number of outlets opened in an area, initial area franchise fees should be accounted for like initial individual franchise fees and substantial performance should be determined using the same criteria. (See Paragraphs 58.202–.204.)

    b. If the franchisor's obligations and cost for initial services depend on the number of outlets opened in an area, initial area franchise fees should be recognized in proportion to the initial services provided. (For example, a franchisor that has substantially performed the required services related to 25% of the outlets to be opened would recognize 25% of the area franchise fee.) The franchisor may need to estimate the number of outlets involved (based on the terms of the franchise agreement) to recognize revenue in proportion to the outlets for which the required services have been substantially performed. Any change in estimate resulting from a change in circumstances should result in recognizing remaining fees as revenue in proportion to remaining services to be performed.

In any event, the franchisor should not recognize revenue that may have to be refunded because future services are not performed until the franchisee has no right to receive a refund. (SFAS 45, paras. 8–9)

Affiliate Relationships

58.206   The relationship between a franchisor and franchisee may be such that a franchisee not otherwise affiliated with the franchisor is considered an affiliate. For example, the franchisor may guarantee the franchisee's borrowings, have a credit interest in the franchisee, or control the franchisee's operations by sales or other agreements. The same revenue recognition criteria that apply to franchise sales to nonaffiliates apply to sales to affiliates. That is, franchise sale revenue from a franchisee who is an affiliate should not be recognized until the franchisor has satisfied or substantially performed all material services, conditions, or obligations relating to the sale. (SFAS 45, par. 10)

Continuing Franchise Fees

58.207   A franchisee may pay additional fees for continuing rights granted by the franchise agreement and for services during the life of the agreement. A franchisor should (a) report continuing franchise fees as revenue as the fees are earned and become receivable from the franchisee and (b) expense related costs as they are incurred. That is true even if a portion of the continuing fee is designated for a particular purpose, such as an advertising program. An exception to that rule exists if the franchise agreement establishes an agency relationship and a portion of the continuing fee is required to be segregated and used for a specified purpose. In that event, the franchisor should record the designated amount as a liability and charge costs incurred for the specified purpose against it. (SFAS 45, par. 14)

58.208   In some cases, continuing franchise fees are small in relation to the continuing services required by the franchise agreement. As discussed in Paragraph 58.204, if it is probable that continuing franchise fees will not cover the franchisor's cost of providing the continuing services plus a reasonable profit, a portion of the initial franchise fee should be deferred and amortized over the life of the franchise agreement. The amount deferred should be sufficient to cover the estimated cost in excess of continuing fees plus a reasonable profit on the continuing services. (SFAS 45, par. 7)

Commingled Revenue

58.209   **Tangible Assets Included in Franchise Fees.** In addition to the franchisor's initial services, the initial franchise fee may cover the sale of tangible assets, such as signs, equipment, inventory, land, or buildings. In such cases, a portion of the initial franchise fee should be allocated to the tangible assets. The amount allocated should be based on the fair value of the assets and may be recognized before or after recognizing the portion applicable to the initial services. For example, a franchisor should recognize the portion of the initial fee related to equipment when title to the equipment passes to the franchisee, even if the portion related to the initial services has not been recognized because substantial performance has not occurred. (SFAS 45, par. 12).

58.210   **Allocating Fees to Specific Services.** A franchise agreement may allocate portions of the total fee to the specific services the franchisor will provide. If the services are interrelated to such an extent that the amount that applies to each service cannot be objectively segregated, revenue for a specific service should not be recognized until all services under the franchise agreement have been substantially performed. On the other hand, if actual prices are available for individual services (for example, through recent sales of the separate services), a portion of the franchise fee may be recognized when a specific service is substantially performed. (SFAS 45, par. 13)

"Bargain Price" Product Sales

58.211   Payment of the initial franchise fee may give the franchisee the right to purchase equipment or supplies from the franchisor at a bargain price. A portion of the initial franchise fee should be deferred and accounted for as an adjustment of the selling price of the equipment or supplies if (a) the bargain price is lower than the selling price of the same product to other customers or (b) the price does not provide the franchisor a reasonable profit on the equipment or supply sales. The portion deferred should be either—

    a. the difference between the selling price to other customers and the bargain purchase price or

    b. an amount sufficient to cover any cost in excess of the bargain purchase price and provide a reasonable profit on the sale. (SFAS 45, par. 15)

Purchase Options

58.212   The franchise agreement may give the franchisor an option to purchase the franchisee's business. In such cases, the likelihood of the franchisor's acquiring the business should be considered when accounting for the initial franchise fee. If it is understood that the option will be exercised or probable that the business ultimately will be acquired, the franchisor should defer the initial franchise fee rather than recognize it as revenue. When the option is exercised, the deferred amount should reduce the franchisor's investment in the business. (SFAS 45, par. 11)

FRANCHISING COSTS

58.213   Direct franchising costs should be recognized in the same period as related revenues. Consequently, a franchisor should defer direct financing costs until related revenue is recognized (or accrue costs not yet incurred as of the date related revenue is recognized). Deferred costs should not exceed anticipated revenue less estimated additional related costs, however.

58.214   Regular and recurring indirect costs that are incurred regardless of the level of sales should be expensed when incurred. (SFAS 45, par. 17)

AGENCY RELATIONSHIPS

58.215 A franchisor may act as an agent for the franchisee by placing orders for inventory and equipment and selling to the franchisee at no profit. The franchisor should account for such transactions as receivables and payables in its balance sheet and not as revenue and expenses. (SFAS 45, par. 16)

REPOSSESSED FRANCHISES

58.216 A franchisor may repossess franchise rights if, for example, the franchisee does not open an outlet. Accounting for the repossession depends on whether consideration previously paid by the franchisee is refunded.

    a. *Consideration is refunded.* The franchisor should treat the repossession as a cancellation of the original sale if the consideration previously received is refunded. Any revenue previously recognized should be recorded as a reduction of revenue in the period the franchise is repossessed.

    b. *Consideration is not refunded.* The franchisor should not treat the repossession as a canceled sale if the consideration is not refunded. Consequently, no adjustment should be made for previously recognized revenue. Instead, the franchisor should (1) review any unpaid receivables from the franchisee for collectibility and record a provision for uncollectible amounts if necessary and (2) recognize in full any deferred revenue related to the original sale. (SFAS 45, par. 18)

BUSINESS COMBINATIONS

58.217 A franchisor that acquires the business of an operating franchisee should account for the transaction as a business combination in accordance with APB Opinion No. 16, *Business Combinations.* Consequently, accounting for the transaction depends on whether the combination is accounted for as a pooling of interests or a purchase.

    a. *Pooling of interests.* If the transaction is accounted for as a pooling of interests, the franchisor should (1) combine the financial statements of the two entities as of the beginning of the year and (2) eliminate the effects of the original sales transaction and any product sales between the two entities. Prior period financial statements, if presented, also should be restated to reflect the business combination.

b. *Purchase.* If the transaction is accounted for as a purchase, the franchisor should combine the financial statements of the two entities as of the date of the purchase. Transactions between the two entities occurring prior to the combination generally should not be eliminated. If the transaction is, in substance, a cancellation of the original franchise sale, however, the combination should be accounted for as a sales cancellation for a repossessed franchise as discussed in Paragraph 58.216. (SFAS 45, par. 19)

Accounting for business combinations under the pooling of interests method and purchase method is discussed further in Chapter 3.

DISCLOSURE REQUIREMENTS

58.501   Franchisors should disclose the following information in their financial statements or notes to the financial statements:

a. Nature of all significant commitments and obligations resulting from franchise agreements, including a description of the services that have not yet been substantially performed (SFAS 45, par. 20)

b. If the installment or cost recovery method is used to account for franchise fee revenue—

     (1) Method used to account for franchise fee revenue

     (2) Sales price

     (3) Revenue and related costs deferred (on both a current and cumulative basis)

     (4) Periods in which the fees become payable by the franchisee

     (5) Amounts originally deferred but later recognized because uncertainties about the collectibility of franchise fees are resolved (SFAS 45, par. 21)

c. Amount of initial franchise fees, if significant, disclosed separately from other franchise fee revenue (SFAS 45, par. 22)

d. When practicable, revenue and costs related to franchisor-owned outlets disclosed separately from revenue and costs related to franchised outlets (SFAS 45, par. 23)

e. If significant changes in the ownership of franchises occurs during the period—

(1) Number of franchises sold during the period

(2) Number of franchises purchased during the period

(3) Number of franchised outlets in operation during the period

(4) Number of franchisor-owned outlets in operation during the period (SFAS 45, par. 23)

58.502   In addition, the following disclosures are desirable, but not required:

a. If probable, the fact that initial franchise fee revenue will decline in the future because sales will reach a saturation point

b. Relative contribution to net income of initial franchise fee revenue if not otherwise apparent (SFAS 45, par. 22)

AUTHORITATIVE LITERATURE AND RELATED TOPICS

AUTHORITATIVE LITERATURE

SFAS No. 45, *Accounting for Franchise Fee Revenue*

RELATED TOPICS

Chapter 3—Business Combinations
Chapter 48—Revenue Recognition

GOVERNMENT CONTRACTORS

Table of Contents

GOVERNMENT CONTRACTORS

OVERVIEW

59.100   Generally, a government contractor should recognize revenues from government cost-plus-fixed-fee contracts when it incurs allowable costs and can bill fees to the government. If the cost-plus-fixed-fee contract is a supply contract, revenues should include the contractor's fees and reimbursable costs. If the contract is a service contract, revenues should include only the contractor's fees. In any event, revenue should be accrued based on the full billable fee rather than full fees less retainage.

59.101   Refunds due to the government as a result of renegotiated contracts should be accrued if they are probable and can be reasonably estimated. Generally, the provision should be presented as a reduction of contract revenues.

59.102   Any profit resulting from a fixed-price contract that is terminated by the government should be recognized if the amount of the termination claim can be reasonably determined. The profit should be recorded on the effective date of the termination, which is the date the contractor obtains the right to receive payment on the terminated contract.

ACCOUNTING REQUIREMENTS

59.200   Generally accepted accounting principles address unique accounting issues related to government contracts. Specifically, they address the contractor's recording of revenue and costs for cost-plus-fixed-fee contracts, contracts subject to renegotiation, and terminated fixed-price contracts.

COST-PLUS-FIXED-FEE CONTRACTS

What Are Cost-plus-fixed-fee Contracts?

59.201   Under cost-plus-fixed-fee (CPFF) contracts, the government periodically reimburses contractors for their expenditures plus a specified fixed fee. Generally, payment amounts are based on the percentage of expenditures incurred to the total estimated expenditures. CPFF contracts usually transfer title to materials to the government as soon as the contractor's expenditures are reimbursed, regardless of actual delivery of the materials. If the government cancels or terminates a CPFF contract, the contractor is entitled to reimbursement for all expenditures made and an equitable portion of the fixed fee. (ARB 43, Ch. 11A, paras. 6–8)

When Should Fees Be Accrued?

59.202   CPFF contracts are similar to long-term construction contracts, which allow recognition of profit as the work progresses so long as total profits and costs can be estimated with reasonable accuracy and ultimate collection is reasonably assured. Under government CPFF contracts, the contractor's risk of loss is minimal, the total profit is fairly definite, and pro-rata profit is reasonably assured even upon cancellation of the contract. Due to those circumstances, fees under CPFF contracts are usually considered to be earned when allowable costs are incurred by the contractor and the fees become billable to the government under the terms of the contract. Therefore, the contractor may actually accrue revenue for the fees as they become billable, which is usually prior to the time they are actually billed. (ARB 43, Ch. 11A, par. 16)

59.203   In some circumstances, factors may indicate that the contractor should not accrue revenue from CPFF contracts as the contract fees become billable to the government. For example, costs that substantially exceed estimates may indicate that the contractor should use a percentage-of-completion method to accrue fees or even wait until the product is delivered, depending on the circumstances. (ARB 43, Ch. 11A, par. 17)

What Should Be Included in Revenue?

59.204   If the CPFF contract is a supply contract, revenue reported in the contractor's income statement usually should include reimbursable costs as well as fees. If the CPFF contract is a service contract, however, revenue usually includes only the fee. Under either type of contract, the revenue for the fee should be accrued based on the full billable fee, rather than the full fee less the retainage amount withheld by the government to ensure complete performance. (ARB 43, Ch. 11A, paras. 18 and 20)

How Should Costs Be Reported in the Balance Sheet?

59.205   The contractor should report costs that have been incurred but not yet billed as receivables. The balance sheet should distinguish between receivables for unbilled costs and billed receivables. (ARB 43, Ch. 11A, par. 21)

59.206   Generally, a contractor should not offset government advances on CPFF contracts against contract receivables unless the advances are expected to be applied as partial payment of those particular receivables. (Typically, that does not occur until the contract is completed or nears completion.) The contractor should disclose any offset amounts in the financial statements. (ARB 43, Ch. 11A, par. 22)

CONTRACTS SUBJECT TO RENEGOTIATION

59.207 Some government contracts are subject to renegotiation and allow for refunds involving an adjustment of the original contract or selling price. The contractor's current liabilities should include a provision for probable renegotiation refunds that can be reasonably estimated. Since such a provision indicates that the collection or retention of the selling price is not reasonably assured, the contractor should correspondingly deduct the provision amount from sales revenue. If the actual renegotiation refund materially differs from the provision made in a prior year's financial statements, the difference between the actual renegotiation refund and the provision should be reported as a separate item in the current income statement. (ARB 43, Ch. 11B, paras. 6–7 and 9)

TERMINATED FIXED-PRICE CONTRACTS

When Is Profit Recognized?

59.208 The government can terminate war and defense supply contracts at its convenience to meet the changing requirements of the military. Upon termination of a contract, the contractor has the right to make a claim for fair compensation, and the government has the right to acquire any of the inventories included in the contractor's claim. The contractor does not have to perform any further service under a terminated contract to enforce its claim, except to negotiate settlements and protect and dispose of property. If the termination claim amount can be reasonably determined, the contractor should record any profit resulting from a terminated fixed-price contract at the effective date of the termination, which is the date the contractor acquires the right to receive payment on the terminated contract. (ARB 43, Ch. 11C, paras. 12–13)

How Is the Claim Amount Determined?

59.209 The total claim, particularly the profit allowance, is subject to negotiation in a terminated contract. The contract's termination articles often provide for a settlement formula that allows for definite profit percentages based on costs if the government and the contractor fail to reach agreement during the negotiations. A contractor who is unable to determine a more appropriate profit allowance may accrue the minimum amount determined by those formula percentages. The profit recorded upon termination is usually the difference between (a) the amount of the contractor's recorded claim and (b) the total currently recorded costs of the inventory, capital items, and other expenses applicable to the terminated contract. The recorded profit amount may exceed the amount specified as profit in the claim because the claim may include reimbursable costs that have been charged to expense in prior periods. (ARB 43, Ch. 11C, paras. 16–17)

59.210   If it is impossible to reasonably estimate a termination claim in time for inclusion in the financial statements of the period in which the termination occurs, the statements should reflect those parts of the termination claim that are reasonably determinable and disclose the status of the remainder. If the total undeterminable amount is material, the circumstances regarding the uncertainty of the claim should be disclosed in the financial statements. (ARB 43, Ch. 11C, paras. 18–19)

Financial Statement Presentation

59.211   The termination claim is a receivable that should be classified as a current asset, unless there is an indication of an extended delay in receiving payment. The claim may consist of several components, such as reimbursable costs for inventories and expenses as well as claims for profit. It is preferable to record the claim in one account, however. Material termination claims should be disclosed separately from other receivables. In addition, claims against the government should be segregated from claims against other contractors if amounts are significant. (ARB 43, Ch. 11C, paras. 20–21)

59.212   The contractor should record partial payments received between the effective date of the termination and final settlement as reductions of the termination claim receivable. Likewise, if advance payments had previously been received on a terminated contract, the contractor's financial statements issued before final collection of the termination claim should reflect any balance of those advances as a deduction from the claim receivable. Financial statements issued before the termination claim is recorded should disclose the relationship of the liability for such advances to a possible termination claim receivable. Loans negotiated on the security of the termination claim should be reflected as liabilities, with appropriate cross-reference to the related claim. (ARB 43, Ch. 11C, par. 22)

59.213   The amount of the termination claim representing the contractor's own reimbursable costs and profit components should be recorded as a sale. Costs related to the sale should be correspondingly recorded as expenses in the income statement. Because termination claims are viewed differently than normal revenues, however, they should be presented separately in the income statement. Items for which the contractor does not seek reimbursement should be left on the balance sheet as inventory or deferred charges. (ARB 43, Ch. 11C, par. 23)

Subcontractors' Claims

59.214   Subcontractors' claims are a contractor's obligations resulting from subcontractors incurring costs on billable materials or services that were not transferred to the contractor before contract termination. The termination articles of government contracts usually require the contractor to settle all subcontractors' claims affected by the termination and the government to pay the contractor the cost of settling and paying those claims. The subcontractors' claims are included in the contractor's termination claim but often are not paid to the subcontractors until after the contractor's claim has been settled. (ARB 43, Ch. 11C, paras. 24–25)

59.215   If the subcontractors' claims exceed the amount included in the contractor's termination claim, the contractor should record a liability and a provision for known or probable losses resulting from unrecoverable subcontractors' claims. (ARB 43, Ch. 11C, par. 27) Contractors may account for recoverable subcontractors' claims in either of two ways.

     a. Recoverable subcontractors' claims that are reasonably determinable may be reported as a current liability and the amounts recoverable by the contractor may be included in the termination claim receivable. (ARB 43, Ch. 11C, par. 29)

     b. Recoverable subcontractors' claims may be accounted for like contingent liabilities, which are not recorded as either an asset or a liability (except when a loss is expected) but which are disclosed in the financial statements. (ARB 43, Ch. 11C, par. 28)

Disposal Credits

59.216   Disposal credits are deducted from the termination claim receivable because the contractor retains or sells to outsiders some or all of the termination inventory for which the claim was made. The credit amount for retained inventory is determined by agreement between the contractor and a government representative. Since the contractor initially records a sale for the amount of inventory costs in the termination claim, the contractor's decision to retain and use that inventory is, in effect, a reacquisition of the inventory. Accordingly, it should be recorded as a purchase and as a reduction of the termination claim receivable at the agreed upon amount. Amounts the contractor receives for inventory items sold to others with the government's approval are collections on behalf of the government and should be applied as a reduction of the claim receivable. (ARB 43, Ch. 11C, par. 31)

No-cost Settlements

59.217   In no-cost settlements, the contractor retains the termination inventory and waives the right to make a claim against the government. Therefore, there is no sale of inventory to record and no reason to accrue any profit resulting from the termination. (ARB 43, Ch. 11C, par. 32)

DISCLOSURE REQUIREMENTS

59.500   The following disclosures are unique to government contractors:

a. For contracts subject to renegotiation, the uncertainties involved in estimating the renegotiation liability, the possibility that a greater liability may ultimately be negotiated, and the basis used to determine the amount of the liability (ARB 43, Ch. 11B, par. 5)

b. For termination claims, (1) a description of the portion of the claim that cannot be reasonably estimated and the circumstances surrounding the uncertainty (ARB 43, Ch. 11C, par. 19) and (2) the relationship between the possible termination claim receivable and any liability for advance payments received by the contractor (ARB 43, Ch. 11C, par. 22)

AUTHORITATIVE LITERATURE AND RELATED TOPICS

AUTHORITATIVE LITERATURE

ARB No. 43, *Restatement and Revision of Accounting Research Bulletins* (Chapter 12—Government Contracts)

RELATED PRONOUNCEMENTS

AICPA Audit and Accounting Guide, *Audits of Federal Government Contractors*

INSURANCE COMPANIES

Table of Contents

INSURANCE COMPANIES

Table of Contents (Continued)

INSURANCE COMPANIES

OVERVIEW

60.100   Insurance contracts are classified as either short-duration or long-duration. Long-duration contracts include whole-life, universal life, guaranteed renewable term life, endowment, annuity, title insurance, and participating life insurance contracts that are expected to remain in force for an extended period. All other insurance contracts, such as most property and liability contracts, are considered short-duration contracts.

REVENUE AND COST RECOGNITION

Short-duration Contracts

60.101   Generally, premiums from short-duration contracts are recognized as revenue over the contract period in proportion to the amount of insurance protection provided. Claim costs (including the estimated costs of claims related to insured events that have occurred but have not been reported to the insurer) should be recognized when insured events occur.

Long-duration Contracts

60.102   Premiums from long-duration contracts (other than universal life-type contracts) should be recognized when they are due from policyholders. Claim costs should be recognized when insured events occur. In addition, when revenues are recognized, an accrual should be made equal to the present value of estimated future policy benefits to be paid to policyholders less the present value of estimated future net premiums to be collected from policyholders.

60.103   Premiums collected on universal life-type contracts should not be reported as revenue. Rather, amounts assessed against policyholders for contract services should be reported as revenue. Generally, revenues should be reported in the period they are assessed.

INVESTMENT CONTRACTS

60.104   Some contracts issued by insurance companies do not subject the insurer to risks arising from policyholder mortality or morbidity. Such contracts are considered investment contracts rather than insurance contracts and should be accounted for like interest-bearing or other financial instruments.

ACQUISITION COSTS

60.105　Acquisition costs should be capitalized and reported as an asset. The costs should be amortized to expense in proportion to the related premium revenue recognized.

INVESTMENTS

60.106　An insurance company's investments in debt and equity securities with readily determinable fair values should be accounted for following the generally accepted accounting principles that apply to any other entity. Investments in equity securities whose fair values are not readily determinable should be reported at fair value with unrealized gains and losses, net of income taxes, reported as other comprehensive income. Investments in mortgage loans should be reported at outstanding principal or amortized cost, and investments in real estate should be reported at depreciated cost.

REINSURANCE

60.107　Reinsurance receivables and prepaid reinsurance premiums should be reported as assets. Amounts paid for prospective short-duration reinsurance should be amortized over the remaining contract period in proportion to the amount of insurance protection provided. Amounts paid for retroactive short-duration reinsurance should be reported as reinsurance receivables to the extent they do not exceed the recorded liabilities related to the underlying reinsured contracts. The estimated cost of long-duration reinsurance contracts should be amortized to expense over the remaining life of the underlying reinsured contracts.

ACCOUNTING REQUIREMENTS

60.200　Generally accepted accounting principles provide guidance for insurance companies on recognizing premium revenue and related liabilities and costs. In addition, GAAP addresses accounting for investment, limited-payment, and universal life-type contracts, contracts issued by mutual life insurance companies, reinsurance contracts, and recognition of catastrophe losses.

Practical Consideration. Generally, the guidance in this chapter applies to the following types of entities:

- Stock life insurance companies

- Property and liability insurance companies

- Title insurance companies

- Mutual life insurance companies

- Assessment enterprises

- Fraternal benefit societies

In addition, except for the guidance on premium revenue recognition, claim cost recognition, and acquisition costs, the chapter also applies to mortgage guaranty insurance companies.

CLASSIFICATION OF INSURANCE CONTRACTS

60.201　　Accounting for insurance contracts generally depends on how long the policies are expected to remain in force. Thus, insurance contracts should be classified as either short-duration or long-duration as follows: (SFAS 60, paras. 7–8)

- *Short-duration contracts.* Short-duration contracts provide insurance protection for a fixed period of short duration and enable the insurer to cancel the contract or revise its terms at the end of any contract period. Examples of short-duration contracts include most property and liability insurance contracts and certain term life insurance contracts, such as credit life insurance. Accident and health insurance contracts may be short-duration or long-duration depending on whether the contracts are expected to remain in force for an extended period.

- *Long-duration contracts.* Long-duration contracts generally are not subject to unilateral changes in their provisions and remain in force for an extended period. Examples of long-duration contracts include whole-life, guaranteed renewable term life, endowment, annuity, title insurance, and certain accident and health insurance contracts.

PREMIUM REVENUE RECOGNITION

Short-duration Contracts

60.202   Insurance companies usually should recognize premiums from short-duration contracts as revenue over the contract period in proportion to the amount of insurance protection provided. If the risk period differs significantly from the contract period, however, revenue should be recognized over the risk period in proportion to the amount of insurance protection provided. As a result, premiums from short-duration contracts usually are recognized evenly over the contract or risk period. (SFAS 60, par. 13)

60.203   Premiums may be subject to adjustment. For example, workers' compensation insurance premiums are based on past experience and determined at the end of the contract period. In such cases, premium revenue should be recognized as follows:

a. If the ultimate premium can be reasonably estimated, it should be recognized over the contract period.

b. If the ultimate premium cannot be reasonably estimated, the cost recovery or deposit method should be used to recognize premium revenue until the amount of the ultimate premium can be reasonably estimated. (SFAS 60, par. 14) Under the cost recovery method, premiums are recognized only to the extent of estimated claim costs. Under the deposit method, premiums received are recorded as deposits and not recognized as revenue until the ultimate premium is reasonably estimable. (SFAS 60, par. 66)

Long-duration Contracts

60.204   Premiums from long-duration contracts (other than universal life-type contracts and limited-payment contracts) should be recognized as revenue when due from policyholders. (SFAS 97, par. 30) (Accounting for universal life-type contracts and limited-payment contracts is discussed in Paragraphs 60.213–.217 and 60.212, respectively.) Title insurance premiums are considered due from policyholders on the date the company is legally or contractually entitled to the premium, which is either the binder date or effective date of the policy. (SFAS 60, par. 16)

COST RECOGNITION

Unpaid Claim Costs

60.205   The insurance company should accrue a liability for unpaid claim costs, including estimates of costs relating to incurred but not reported claims, and related claim adjustment expenses when insured events occur. (An exception to that rule exists for liabilities under title insurance contracts. Those liabilities should be accrued when title insurance premiums are recognized as revenue.) The liability for unpaid claims should be based on the estimated ultimate cost of settling the claims. Changes in claim cost estimates and differences between estimates and actual claim payments should be recognized in income during the period in which the estimates are changed or payments are made. Estimated recoveries on unsettled claims (such as from salvage, subrogation, or acquisition of real estate) should be evaluated in terms of their estimated realizable value and deducted from the liability for unpaid claims. Generally, estimated recoveries on settled claims also should be deducted from the liability for unpaid claims. (SFAS 60, paras. 17–18 and 20)

60.206   Mortgage guaranty companies and title insurance companies sometimes acquire real estate when settling claims. Real estate acquired should be recorded at fair value and reported separately in the balance sheet. (It should not be classified as an investment.) Subsequent decreases in the reported amount and realized gains and losses should be recognized as adjustments to claim costs.

Liability for Future Policy Benefits

60.207   When premium revenue related to long-duration contracts other than title insurance contracts and universal life-type contracts is recognized, a liability for future policy benefits should be accrued. The liability represents the present value of future benefits to be paid and related expenses less the present value of future net premiums (the portion of gross premiums required to provide for all benefits and expenses). The insurance company should estimate the liability using assumptions (such as estimates of expected investment yields, mortality, and morbidity) applicable at the time the insurance contracts are made. Original assumptions usually should continue to be used in subsequent accounting periods to determine changes in the liability for future policy benefits. Changes in the liability for future policy benefits should be recognized in income in the period in which the changes occur. (SFAS 60, paras. 21–24)

Acquisition Costs

60.208   Acquisition costs are commissions and other costs that vary with and primarily relate to insurance contracts issued or renewed during the period. Acquisition costs should be capitalized and charged to expense in proportion to the premium revenue recognized. Unamortized acquisition costs should be classified as an asset. (SFAS 60, paras. 28–29)

Premium Deficiency Costs

60.209   **Short-duration Contracts.** A premium deficiency exists on short-duration contracts if unearned premiums are less than the total of expected claim costs, claim adjustment expenses, policyholder dividends, unamortized acquisition costs, and maintenance costs. An insurance company should first recognize a premium deficiency by charging any unamortized acquisition costs to expense to the extent required to eliminate the deficiency. If the premium deficiency is greater than unamortized acquisition costs, a liability should be accrued for the excess deficiency. (SFAS 60, par. 34)

60.210   **Long-duration Contracts.** A premium deficiency should be recognized on long-duration contracts if the insurance company's actual experience with respect to previous estimated liability assumptions indicates that existing contract liabilities, together with the present value of future gross premiums, will not be sufficient (a) to cover the present value of future benefits to be paid, settlement costs, and maintenance costs and (b) to recover unamortized acquisition costs. The insurance company should recognize a premium deficiency by charging income and (a) reducing unamortized acquisition costs or (b) increasing the liability for future policy benefits. A loss should not be recorded, however, if its effect would be to create future income. (SFAS 60, paras. 36–37)

ACCOUNTING FOR SPECIAL TYPES OF LONG-DURATION CONTRACTS

Investment Contracts

60.211   Investment contracts are long-duration contracts that do not subject the insurance company to risks arising from policyholder mortality or morbidity. A mortality or morbidity risk exists if the contract requires the company to make payments or forego premiums contingent upon the death, disability, or continued survival of a specific individual. Since investment contracts do not subject the issuing company to significant insurance risk, they should not be accounted for as insurance contracts. Payments received for investment contracts should not be reported as revenues, but as liabilities, and should be accounted for like interest-bearing or other financial instruments. (SFAS 97, paras. 7 and 15)

> **Practical Consideration.** Under certain annuity contracts, an insurance company may be required to make payments regardless of whether the beneficiary is alive or dead, followed by additional payments if the beneficiary is alive. Such policies should be considered insurance contracts rather than investment contracts unless (a) there is only a remote chance that the beneficiary will be alive when the additional payments are due or (b) the present value of the additional payments is insignificant compared to the present value of all payments due under the contract.

Limited-payment Contracts

60.212　Limited-payment contracts are long-duration insurance contracts with terms that (a) are fixed and guaranteed and (b) subject the insurer to risks from providing benefits for policyholder mortality and morbidity over a period that extends beyond the period in which premiums are collected. Under limited-payment contracts, the collection of premiums does not represent the completion of the earnings process. Therefore, insurance companies should recognize revenue from those contracts over the period that benefits are provided rather than over the period that premiums are collected. Gross premiums received in excess of net premiums should be deferred and amortized to income (a) in relation to the amount of insurance in force, for life insurance contracts, or (b) in relation to the estimated benefits to be paid, for annuity contracts. (SFAS 97, par. 16)

Universal Life-type Contracts

60.213　Universal life-type contracts are long-duration contracts with premium or benefit terms that are not fixed or guaranteed and typically provide either death or annuity benefits. They are characterized by the following features: (SFAS 97, par. 10)

- The contract's terms do not assess fixed or guaranteed amounts against the policyholder for mortality coverage, contract administration, initiation, or surrender.

- Interest and other amounts that accrue to the policyholder are not fixed or guaranteed.

- The policyholder may vary premiums, within limits specified by the contract, without the insurer's consent.

60.214 Insurance companies should not report premiums collected on universal life-type contracts as revenue. Revenue should be reported for any amounts assessed against policyholders and should be reported in the period that the amounts are assessed unless the assessments represent compensation to the insurance company for services to be provided in future periods. Those amounts should be reported as unearned revenue and recognized in income over the period benefited. (SFAS 97, paras. 19–20)

60.215 Insurance companies should not report payments to policyholders that represent a return of policyholder balances as expenses. Expenses should include benefit claims in excess of the related policyholder balances, contract administration expenses, interest accrued to policyholders, and amortization of capitalized acquisition costs. Capitalized acquisition costs should be amortized over the life of universal life-type contracts based on a constant percentage of the present value of the estimated gross profit amounts expected to be realized over the life of the contracts. Acquisition costs that vary in a constant relationship to premiums or insurance in force, are recurring in nature, or tend to be incurred in a level amount from period to period should be expensed as incurred. (SFAS 97, par. 21)

60.216 The liability for policy benefits related to universal life-type contracts should be the total of:

     a. the account balance that accrues to the benefit of policyholders at the financial statement date. (If there is no stated account balance or contract value, the policy's cash surrender value should be used.)

     b. any amounts assessed to compensate the insurer for services to be performed in the future.

     c. any amounts previously assessed against policyholders that are refundable upon contract termination.

     d. any probable loss (premium deficiency).

Amounts that may be assessed against policyholders in future periods, including surrender charges, should not be anticipated in determining the liability for policy benefits. (SFAS 97, paras. 17–18)

60.217 **Internal Replacement Transactions.** Policyholders often purchase universal life-type contracts as replacements for other insurance contracts issued by the same company. If the policyholder uses the cash surrender value of the previous contract to pay the initial premium of the replacement contract, unamortized acquisition costs associated with the replaced contract and the difference between the replaced contract's cash surrender value and its previously recorded liability should not be deferred in connection with the replacement contract. The insurance company should recognize any gain or loss from replacement transactions in income during the period in which the replacement occurs. (SFAS 97, par. 26)

POLICYHOLDER DIVIDENDS

60.218 Participating life insurance contracts pay dividends to policyholders based on the insurance company's performance with the particular class of contracts. (SFAS 120, par. 18) Policyholder dividends should be estimated and accrued. That should be accomplished by charging current operations and crediting a liability for participating policyholder dividends similar to the way a minority interest's share of net income is recorded. Dividends declared or paid should then be charged to the liability or to current operations to the extent they exceed the recorded liability. (SFAS 60, par. 42)

60.219 When policyholder dividends are unrelated to net income and gross premiums are based on anticipated or intended dividends, the projected dividends at the time the policy was issued should be accrued ratably over the periods in which premiums are collected. (SFAS 60, par. 43)

CONTINGENT COMMISSIONS

60.220 An insurance company may pay additional commissions to agents based on the loss experience of the policies the agents generate. Contingent commissions receivable or payable should be accrued during the period related income is recognized. (SFAS 60, par. 44)

INVESTMENTS

60.221 GAAP provides the following guidance on accounting for the investments of insurance companies:

    a. *Investments in debt and equity securities.* An insurance company should account for its investments in debt and equity securities with readily determinable fair values the same as any other entity. (An equity security's fair value is readily determinable if sales prices or bid-and-ask quotes are currently available. Accounting for such investments is discussed in Chapter 35.) Investments in equity securities whose fair values are not readily determinable should be reported at fair value with unrealized gains and losses, net of income taxes, reported as a separate component of owners' equity. (SFAS 124, par. 107) Declines in fair value that are other than temporary should be reported as realized losses. (SFAS 60, par. 51 and SFAS 115, par. 127)

Practical Consideration. SFAS No. 124, par. 107 states that unrealized gains and losses on investments in equity securities whose fair values are *not readily determinable* should be reported as a separate component of stockholders' equity. However, the authors believe such gains and losses meet the definition of comprehensive income in SFAS No. 130, *Reporting Comprehensive Income* (discussed in Chapter 8), and therefore should be reported as other comprehensive income.

---

     b. *Investments in mortgage loans.* Mortgage loans should be reported at their outstanding principal balances unless they were purchased at a discount or premium. In that case, they should be reported at amortized cost. An allowance for estimated uncollectible amounts should be provided. (SFAS 60, par. 47)

     c. *Real estate investments.* Real estate investments should be reported at cost less accumulated depreciation. (SFAS 60, par. 48)

60.222   Generally, realized investment gains and losses should be reported as a component of other income on a pretax basis. Realized gains and losses should not be deferred to future periods. (SFAS 97, par. 28)

SEPARATE ACCOUNTS

60.223   An insurance company may maintain assets and liabilities in separate accounts to fund fixed-benefit plans. In such cases, the insurance company, acting as a fiduciary, receives a fee for managing investments, administrative expenses, etc. while the contract holder assumes the investment risk. Investments in separate accounts should be reported at market, except for accounts in which the insurance company has guaranteed a specific investment return. Those accounts should be valued the same as any other of the insurance company's investments. The assets and liabilities of separate accounts should be reported in the financial statements as summary totals. (SFAS 60, paras. 53–54)

DEFERRED INCOME TAXES

60.224   Deferred income taxes should not be provided for temporary differences related to the policyholders' surplus of stock life insurance companies that arose in fiscal years beginning on or before December 15, 1992. However, if circumstances indicate that taxes are likely to be paid in the foreseeable future because of a known or expected reduction in policyholders' surplus, income taxes attributable to the reduction should be accrued. (SFAS 60, par. 59 as amended by SFAS 109, par. 288)

REINSURANCE

60.225   An insurance company may obtain indemnification against claims associated with contracts it has written by entering into a reinsurance contract with another insurance company (the reinsurer). The insurer (ceding company) pays an amount to the reinsurer, and the reinsurer agrees to reimburse the insurer for a specified portion of claims paid under the reinsured contracts. (SFAS 113, par. 1)

Has the Insurer Obtained Indemnification?

60.226   To apply reinsurance accounting, the insurer must determine whether it has truly obtained indemnification against claims. The criteria for making that determination are discussed in the following paragraphs.

60.227   **Short-duration Contracts.** In reinsurance of short-duration contracts, indemnification of the insurer generally requires both of the following:

     a. *The reinsurer must assume significant insurance risk under the reinsured portions of the underlying insurance contracts.* The reinsurer has not assumed significant risk if there is only a remote probability that the timing or amount of its payments to the insurer will vary significantly. This condition is not met if contractual provisions delay timely reimbursement to the insurer. (SFAS 113, par. 9)

     b. *It must be reasonably possible that the reinsurer may realize a significant loss from the transaction.* (SFAS 113, par. 9) The evaluation of whether it is reasonably possible that the reinsurer will realize a significant loss should be based on the present value of all cash flows between the ceding company and assuming companies under reasonably possible outcomes. The significance of the loss should be determined by comparing the present value of the cash flows to the present value of the amounts paid or deemed to have been paid to the reinsurer. (SFAS 113, paras. 10 and 11)

60.228   **Long-duration Contracts.** In reinsurance of long-duration contracts, indemnification of the insurer requires the reasonable possibility that the reinsurer may realize significant loss from assuming insurance risk. Long-duration contracts that do not subject an insurer to mortality or morbidity risks are investment contracts rather than insurance contracts. (SFAS 113, par. 12)

Accounting for Reinsurance Transactions

60.229 If the criteria for indemnification discussed in Paragraphs 60.227–.228 are met, the reinsurance accounting described in the following paragraphs should be applied. For contracts that do not meet the requirements for reinsurance accounting—

a. the premium paid less the premium to be retained by the reinsurer should be accounted for as a deposit by the ceding company. A liability should be reported if the contract results in a net credit and an asset should be reported if the contract results in a net charge.

b. proceeds that represent recoveries of acquisition costs should reduce unamortized acquisition costs in such a way that net acquisition costs are charged to expense in proportion to net revenue recognized. If the ceding company has agreed to service all of the related contracts without reasonable compensation, estimated excess future servicing costs under the reinsurance contract should be accrued as a liability. The net cost to the assuming company should be accounted for as an acquisition cost. (SFAS 113, par. 18)

60.230 **Reporting Assets and Liabilities Related to Reinsurance Transactions.** Reinsurance contracts that are legal replacements of one insurer by another extinguish the insurer's liability to the policyholder and result in removal of related assets and liabilities from the insurer's financial statements. Reinsurance contracts that do not relieve an insurer of the legal liability to its policyholder do not result in removal of the related assets and liabilities from the insurer's financial statements. Consequently, insurers should report estimated reinsurance receivables arising from such contracts separately as assets. (Reinsurance receivables should be recognized in a manner consistent with the liabilities related to the underlying reinsured contracts.) Amounts paid to the reinsurer relating to the unexpired portion of reinsured contracts (prepaid reinsurance premiums) also should be reported separately as assets. Amounts receivable and payable between the insurer and an individual reinsurer should be offset only when a right of setoff exists. (SFAS 113, paras. 14–15 and 20)

60.231 Earned premiums ceded and recoveries recognized under reinsurance contracts should be either (a) reported in the income statement as a separate line item (or parenthetically) or (b) disclosed in the notes to the financial statements. (SFAS 113, par 16)

60.232 **Revenue and Cost Recognition.** Revenue and cost recognition requirements vary depending on whether the reinsurance contracts are short-duration or long-duration.

a. *Short-duration contracts.* The insurer should report amounts paid for prospective reinsurance as prepaid reinsurance premiums and amortize them over the remaining contract period in proportion to the amount of insurance protection provided. If the amounts paid are subject to adjustment and can be reasonably estimated, amortization should be based on the estimate of the amount that will ultimately be paid. (SFAS 113, par. 21)

Amounts paid for retroactive reinsurance should be reported as reinsurance receivables to the extent those amounts do not exceed the recorded liabilities relating to the underlying reinsured contracts. If the recorded liabilities exceed the amounts paid, the insurer should increase the reinsurance receivables to reflect the difference and defer the resulting gain. The deferred gain should be amortized over the estimated remaining settlement period using the interest method (if amounts and timing of recoveries can be reasonably estimated) or the recovery method (if amounts or timing of recoveries cannot be reasonably estimated). If the amounts paid for retroactive reinsurance exceed the recorded liabilities relating to the underlying reinsured contracts, the insurer should increase the related liabilities or reduce the reinsurance receivable or both at the time the reinsurance contract is entered into so that the excess is charged to earnings. (SFAS 113, paras. 22–23)

Changes in the estimated amount of the liabilities related to underlying reinsured contracts should be recognized in income in the period of the change. Reinsurance receivables should be adjusted for the related change in the amount recoverable from the reinsurer and a resulting gain adjusted or established. (SFAS 113, par. 24)

When a reinsurance contract contains prospective and retroactive provisions, each provision should be accounted for separately if practicable. If a separate accounting is not practicable, the contract should be treated as a retroactive contract. (SFAS 113, par. 25)

b. *Long-duration contracts.* The insurer should amortize the estimated cost of long-duration contracts over the remaining life of the underlying reinsured contracts. Any difference between amounts paid for a reinsurance contract and the amount of the liabilities for policy benefits relating to the underlying reinsured contracts should be amortized as part of the estimated reinsurance cost. (SFAS 113, par. 26)

ACCOUNTING AND REPORTING BY MUTUAL LIFE INSURANCE COMPANIES

60.233   Mutual life insurance companies should apply all of the above guidelines, as appropriate, to participating life insurance contracts unless the contracts meet both of the following conditions: (SFAS 120, paras. 5)

a. The contracts are long-duration participating contracts that are expected to pay dividends to policyholders based on the insurer's actual experience.

b. Annual policyholder dividends are paid in a manner that identifies divisible surplus and distributes that surplus in approximately the same proportion as the contracts are considered to have contributed to divisible surplus.

60.234   Mutual and stock life insurance companies with participating life insurance contracts meeting the above conditions are permitted to account for those contracts in accordance with Statement of Position 95-1, *Accounting for Certain Insurance Activities of Mutual Life Insurance Enterprises*. The same accounting policy should be applied consistently to all such participating life insurance contracts. Disclosure of the specific accounting policy applied to the contracts should be made. (SFAS 120, par. 6)

60.235   Mutual life insurance companies that issue GAAP basis financial statements must apply all applicable authoritative accounting pronouncements when preparing those statements. Financial statements based on regulatory accounting practices that differ from generally accepted accounting principles and are issued to regulators should not be described as prepared "in conformity with generally accepted accounting principles." (SFAS 120, par. 4 and FASBI 40, par. 18)

CATASTROPHE LOSSES OF PROPERTY AND CASUALTY INSURANCE COMPANIES

60.236   A contingency arises when a property and casualty insurance company issues an insurance policy covering risk of loss from catastrophes. The contingency is the risk of loss assumed by the insurance company for catastrophes that may occur during, but not beyond, the term of the policy. A loss accrual is not appropriate for such a contingency because the risk of loss is not both probable and reasonably estimable. Deferral of unearned premiums within the terms of policies in force represents the "unknown liability" for catastrophe losses on unexpired policies. Therefore, it is inappropriate to accrue an additional amount as an estimated loss for that same unknown liability. GAAP does require, however, accrual of a net loss (a loss in excess of deferred premiums) that probably will be incurred on insurance policies that are in force, provided that the loss can be reasonably estimated. In addition, a property and casualty insurance company is not prohibited from accruing probable catastrophe losses that have been incurred on or before the date of its financial statements but that have not been reported by its policyholders as of that date. If the amount of the loss can be reasonably estimated, incurred-but-not-reported losses must be accrued. (SFAS 5, paras. 40–41)

Practical Consideration. As discussed further in Chapter 10, a loss contingency should be disclosed, but not accrued, if (a) it is probable that a loss has occurred but its amount cannot reasonably be estimated, or (b) it is reasonably possible (but not probable) that a loss has occurred. Additional disclosures also may be necessary as required by SOP 94-6, *Disclosure of Certain Significant Risks and Uncertainties.*

60.237   Insurance companies should not accrue estimated losses for catastrophes that may occur beyond the terms of policies in force. Since existing policyholders are insured only during the period covered by their insurance contracts, an insurance company is not presently obligated to policyholders for catastrophes that may occur after their policies expire. The fact that catastrophes are certain to occur over the long term does not justify accrual before the catastrophes occur. Even though the costs of catastrophes to insurance companies are large and incurred irregularly and insurance companies recoup those costs in the long run through periodic adjustments in the premiums charged to policyholders, the accrual of a loss for catastrophes that may occur beyond the terms of policies in force is not appropriate. In addition, no portion of premium income should be deferred beyond the terms of policies in force. (SFAS 5, par. 42)

DISCLOSURE REQUIREMENTS

60.500   Insurance companies should disclose the following in their financial statements: (SFAS 60, par. 60 and SFAS 113, par. 27)

     a. Basis for estimating liabilities for unpaid claims and claim adjustments

     b. Methods and assumptions used to estimate the liability for future policy benefits (Although not required, insurance companies are encouraged to also disclosed the average rate of assumed investment yields in effect for the current year.)

c. Nature of capitalized acquisition costs, method of amortizing those costs, and amount amortized during the period

d. Carrying amount of liabilities for unpaid claims and claim adjustment expenses related to short-duration contracts presented at present value in the financial statements, including the range of interest rates used to discount the liabilities

e. Whether anticipated investment income is considered when determining if a premium deficiency exists related to short-duration contracts

f. Relative percentage of participating insurance, method of accounting for policyholder dividends, amount of dividends, and amount of any additional income allocated to participating policyholders

g. Amount of statutory capital and surplus

h. Amount of statutory capital and surplus necessary to satisfy regulatory requirements (based on current operations) if significant to the company's statutory capital and surplus

i. Nature of statutory restrictions on dividend payments and the amount of retained earnings that may not be used to pay dividends

j. Nature, purpose, and effect of ceded reinsurance transactions on operations, including the fact that the insurer is not relieved of its primary obligation to the policyholder in a reinsurance transaction

k. For short-duration contracts, premiums from direct business, reinsurance assumed, and reinsurance ceded, on both a written and an earned basis

l. For long-duration contracts, premiums and amounts assessed against policyholders from direct business, reinsurance assumed and ceded, and premiums and amounts earned

m. Methods used to recognize income on reinsurance contracts

In addition, ceding insurance companies must disclose concentrations of credit risk associated with reinsurance receivables and prepaid reinsurance premiums. (SFAS 113, par. 28) (Disclosing concentrations of credit risk is discussed further in Chapter 21.)

60.501 Mutual and stock life insurance companies also must disclose the policy for accounting for participating life insurance contracts. (SFAS 120, par. 6)

AUTHORITATIVE LITERATURE AND RELATED TOPICS

AUTHORITATIVE LITERATURE

SFAS No. 5, *Accounting for Contingencies*

SFAS No. 60, *Accounting and Reporting by Insurance Enterprises*

SFAS No. 97, *Accounting and Reporting by Insurance Enterprises for Certain Long-Duration Contracts and for Realized Gains and Losses from the Sale of Investments*

SFAS No. 113, *Accounting and Reporting for Reinsurance of Short-Duration and Long-Duration Contracts*

SFAS No. 120, *Accounting and Reporting by Mutual Life Insurance Enterprises and by Insurance Enterprises for Certain Long-Duration Participating Contracts*

SFAS No. 124, *Accounting for Certain Investments Held by Not-for-Profit Organizations*

FASB Interpretation No. 40, *Applicability of Generally Accepted Accounting Principles to Mutual Life Insurance and Other Enterprises*

SOP 94-6, *Disclosure of Certain Significant Risks and Uncertainties*

RELATED PRONOUNCEMENTS

AICPA Audit and Accounting Guide, *Audits of Property and Liability Insurance Companies*

SOP 92-5, *Accounting for Foreign Property and Liability Reinsurance*

SOP 94-5, *Disclosure of Certain Matters in the Financial Statements of Insurance Enterprises*

SOP 95-1, *Accounting for Certain Insurance Activities of Mutual Life Insurance Enterprises*

EITF Issue No. 92-9, *Accounting for the Present Value of Future Profits Resulting from the Acquisition of a Life Insurance Company*

EITF Issue No. 93-6, *Accounting for Multiple-Year Retrospectively Rated Contracts by Ceding and Assuming Enterprises*

EITF Issue No. 93-14, *Accounting for Multiple-Year Retrospectively Rated Insurance Contracts by Insurance Enterprises and Other Enterprises*

Practice Bulletin No. 8, *Application of FASB Statement No. 97, "Accounting and Reporting by Insurance Enterprises for Certain Long-Duration Contracts and for Realized Gains and Losses from the Sale of Investments," to Insurance Enterprises*

FASB Implementation Guide, *A Guide to Implementation of Statement 113, "Accounting and Reporting for Reinsurance of Short-Duration and Long-Duration Contracts"*

LENDING AND MORTGAGE BANKING ACTIVITIES

Table of Contents

LENDING AND MORTGAGE BANKING ACTIVITIES

OVERVIEW

61.100   Generally, loan origination fees, commitment fees and related direct loan costs for loans held for investment should be deferred and recognized as an adjustment to interest income over the life of the loan using the interest method. Fees and costs related to loans held for sale should be recognized when the loan is sold. If the loan commitment expires without the loan being made, the net commitment fee should be recognized in income upon expiration. Fees paid to permanent investors should be recognized when the loan is sold. Fees for services performed by third parties should be recognized when the service is performed.

61.101   The balance sheets of mortgage banking companies should distinguish between loans held for sale and mortgage loans held for long-term investment. Mortgage loans held for sale should be reported at the lower of cost or market value as of the balance sheet date. Mortgage-backed securities should be classified as trading securities under SFAS 115. Mortgage loans should be classified as long-term investments if the mortgage company has both the ability and intent to hold the loan for the foreseeable future or until maturity. A loss should be recognized if mortgage loans held as long-term investments are determined to be permanently impaired.

61.102   Mortgage banking companies buy or originate mortgage loans and may sell the loans but retain the right to service them in return for a fee. The rights to service mortgage loans are frequently purchased and sold because servicing fees often exceed the cost of performing servicing functions. The servicing fee, usually based on a percentage of the outstanding principal balance of the mortgage loan, is received for performing loan administration functions, such as collecting mortgage and escrow payments and maintaining loan payment records.

61.103   When a mortgage company is obligated to service mortgage loans, it should recognize a servicing asset or liability for that servicing contract. The servicing asset or liability should be accounted for separately from the mortgage loans. Servicing assets retained in a sale of mortgage loans should be recorded at their allocated carrying amount based on the relative fair value of the assets sold. Servicing assets purchased or servicing liabilities assumed should be recorded at fair value. Servicing assets and liabilities should be amortized into income in proportion to and over the period of estimated net servicing income or loss. Servicing assets should be subsequently measured for impairment. If subsequent events result in an increase in the estimated servicing liability, the increased liability should be charged to earnings.

ACCOUNTING REQUIREMENTS

61.200   Generally accepted accounting principles provide guidance on accounting for nonrefundable loan fees and costs. GAAP also provides guidance on accounting for mortgage loans, mortgage servicing fees and assets, and collateralized mortgage obligations. Generally, the guidance applies to all types of lenders.

ACCOUNTING FOR LOAN FEES AND COSTS

Loan Origination Fees and Costs

61.201   If a loan is held for resale, the lender should defer loan origination fees and related direct loan origination costs until the loan is sold. If a loan is held for investment, such fees and costs should be deferred and recognized over the life of the loan as an adjustment of interest income. (SFAS 91, par. 27) Loan origination fees and related direct loan origination costs for a specific loan should be offset and only the net amount should be deferred and amortized. (SFAS 91, par. 5)

61.202   Direct loan origination costs for a completed loan should include only (a) direct costs incurred in transactions with third parties and (b) employees' payroll and fringe benefit costs directly related to time spent performing the following activities for the loan: (SFAS 91, par. 6)

   a. Evaluating the prospective borrower's financial condition

   b. Evaluating and recording guarantees, collateral, and other security arrangements

   c. Negotiating loan terms

   d. Preparing and processing loan documents

   e. Closing the transaction

61.203   All other lending-related costs, including costs for unsuccessful loan origination efforts, advertising, soliciting potential borrowers, servicing existing loans, and establishing and monitoring credit policies, should be charged to expense as incurred. Indirect costs, such as administrative costs, rent, depreciation, and all other occupancy and equipment costs, should also be charged to expense as incurred. (SFAS 91, par. 7)

Commitment Fees and Costs

61.204   Fees received in return for guaranteeing the funding of mortgage loans to borrowers, builders, or developers are commitment fees. Lenders generally should offset commitment fees against any related direct loan origination costs incurred to make the commitment and defer the net amount. (SFAS 91, par. 9) If the commitment expires without the loan being made, the net commitment fee should be recognized in income upon expiration of the commitment. If the commitment is exercised, the net commitment fee should be recognized over the life of the loan as an adjustment of interest income. (SFAS 91, par. 8) Any unrecognized commitment fees should be recognized in income when the loan is repaid if repayment occurs before the expected repayment date. (SFAS 65, par. 27)

61.205   Available lines of credit under credit card arrangements also are loan commitments and fees collected in connection with such cards should be treated in part as loan commitment fees. Those fees should be deferred and recognized on a straight-line basis over the period the fee entitles the cardholder to use the card. (SFAS 91, par. 10)

61.206   Lenders should expense fees paid to permanent investors to ensure the ultimate sale of mortgage loans when the loans are sold or when it becomes evident the commitment will not be used. (SFAS 91, par. 27) Fees received for arranging a commitment directly between a permanent investor and a borrower (loan placement fees) should be recognized as revenue when all significant services have been performed. (SFAS 65, par. 24)

Fees for Services Rendered by Third Parties

61.207   Fees received from borrowers to reimburse the lender for the costs of specific loan origination services performed by third parties, such as appraisal fees, should be recognized as revenue when the services have been performed. (SFAS 65, par. 22)

Fees and Costs in Refinancings or Restructurings

61.208   If the terms of the new loan resulting from a loan refinancing or restructuring (other than a troubled debt restructuring) are at least as favorable to the lender as the terms for comparable loans to other customers with similar collection risks who are not refinancing or restructuring a loan with the lender, the lender should account for the refinanced loan as a new loan. Any unamortized net fees or costs and any prepayment penalties from the original loan should be recognized in interest income when the new loan is granted. (SFAS 91, par. 12)

61.209   If the terms of a refinanced or restructured loan are not as favorable to the lender as the terms for comparable loans to other customers, or if only minor modifications are made to the original loan contract, the lender should carry forward the unamortized net fees or costs from the original loan and any prepayment penalties as a part of the net investment in the new loan. In that case, the investment in the new loan should consist of the remaining net investment in the original loan, any additional amounts loaned, any fees received, and direct loan origination costs associated with the refinancing or restructuring. (SFAS 91, par. 13)

61.210   The lender should apply fees received in connection with a modification of terms of a troubled debt restructuring as a reduction of the recorded investment in the loan. All related costs, including direct loan origination costs, should be charged to expense as incurred. (SFAS 91, par. 14)

Purchased Loan Fees and Costs

61.211   The initial investment in a purchased loan should include the amount paid to the seller plus any fees paid or less any fees received. The purchaser may allocate the initial investment cost of loans purchased as a group to the individual loans or account for the initial investment in the aggregate. Any difference between the initial investment and the related loan's principal amount at the purchase date should be recognized as an adjustment of interest income over the life of the loan. All other costs incurred in connection with acquiring purchased loans or committing to purchase loans should be charged to expense as incurred. (SFAS 91, par. 15)

Syndication Fees

61.212   The company managing a loan syndication (the syndicator) should recognize loan syndication fees when the syndication is complete unless the syndicator retains a portion of the syndication loan. If the yield on the retained portion of the loan is less than the average yield (including fees) of the other syndication participants, the syndicator should defer part of the syndication fee to produce a yield on the retained portion of the loan that is at least equal to the average yield on the loans held by the other syndication participants. (SFAS 91, par. 11)

Amortization of Deferred Fees and Costs

61.213   Net fees or costs that are deferred and recognized as adjustments to interest income over the life of the related loan generally should be amortized by the interest method. The purpose of the interest method is to arrive at a constant effective rate of periodic interest income on the net investment in the loan. The difference between that periodic interest income and the stated interest on the outstanding principal amount of the loan should be the amount of periodic amortization recognized by the lender for deferred loan fees and costs. (SFAS 91, par. 18)

61.214   **Variable Loan Rates.** Special provisions for amortizing deferred fees and costs apply if the stated interest rate is not constant throughout the term of the loan. When that is the case, the interest method should be applied as follows: (SFAS 91, par. 18)

    a. *Loan's stated rate increases over the loan term.* Applying the interest method would result in interest accruing in the early periods in excess of the stated rate. However, interest should not be recognized to the extent that the net investment in the loan would increase to an amount greater than the amount for which the borrower could settle the debt. Prepayment penalties should be considered in determining the amount at which the borrower could settle the debt only to the extent such penalties are imposed throughout the loan term.

    b. *Loan's stated interest rate decreases over the loan term.* Interest received at the stated interest rate in the early periods of the loan term exceeds the interest income that is calculated using the interest method. As a result, the excess should be deferred and recognized in those future periods when the effective interest rate (i.e. the constant effective interest rate over the entire loan term) exceeds the stated interest rate.

    c. *Loan's stated rate varies based on independent factor.* If the loans stated rate varies based on an independent factor (rate or index, such as the prime rate), the calculation of the constant effective yield used to recognize deferred fees and costs should be based on either the rate or index in effect at the loan's inception or on the rate or index as it varies over the life of the loan.

61.215   In most cases, the calculation of the constant effective yield used in applying the interest method should be based on the payment terms stated in the loan contract and prepayment of principal should not be anticipated. However, if the lender holds a large number of similar loans for which principal prepayments are probable and the amount and timing of prepayments can be reasonably estimated, the lender may consider estimates of future prepayments in the calculation of the constant effective yield. If prepayments are considered in the calculation of constant effective yield and actual prepayments differ from anticipated prepayments, the constant effective yield should be recalculated to reflect actual prepayments to date and anticipated future prepayments. The net investment in the loans should be adjusted to reflect the amount that would have been recorded had the new effective yield been used from the inception of the loans with a corresponding charge or credit to interest income. (SFAS 91, par. 19)

61.216   Demand Loans. If a loan is payable at the lender's demand, the net fees or costs may be recognized as an adjustment to yield on the straight-line basis over either a period consistent with (a) the borrower's and lender's understanding for the term of the loan or (b) if no understanding exists, the lender's estimate of the period the loan will remain outstanding. Any unamortized amount should be recognized when the loan is paid in full. (SFAS 91, par. 20)

61.217   Revolving Lines of Credit. Net fees or costs related to revolving lines of credit should be recognized in income on the straight-line basis over the period the revolving line is active (assuming that debt is outstanding for the entire term of the contract). If the borrower pays off all debt and cannot reborrow under the line, any unamortized net fees or costs should be recognized in income when the debt is paid off. If the contract provides a schedule for payments and no additional borrowings are allowed under the credit agreement, the interest method should be used to recognize net unamortized fees or costs. (SFAS 91, par. 20)

Practical Consideration. For example, if the credit agreement provides for a two-year revolving line of credit with the option for the borrower to convert to a ten-year term loan, net loan fees or costs would be recognized in income as follows:

- During the term of the revolving line of credit, net fees or costs should be recognized on the straight-line basis over the combined term of the revolving line of credit and the term loan.

- If the borrower elects to convert to a term loan, unamortized net fees or costs should be recognized as an adjustment of yield using the interest method over the term of the loan.

- If the revolving line of credit expires and the debt is paid off, unamortized fees or costs should be recognized upon payment.

61.218 **Nonaccrual Loans.** Deferred net fees or costs should not be amortized during periods that interest income is not recognized on loans because of doubts about the realization of principal or interest. (SFAS 91, par. 17)

Financial Reporting

61.219 **Balance Sheet Classification.** The unamortized balance of loan origination, commitment, and other fees and costs being amortized by the interest method should be reported on the lender's balance sheet as part of the loan balance to which it relates. (SFAS 91, par. 21)

61.220 **Income Statement Classification.** The lender should report amortization of deferred loan origination, commitment, and other fees and costs being amortized by the interest method as part of interest income. Amortization of other fees should be reported as service fee income. (SFAS 91, par. 22)

ACCOUNTING FOR MORTGAGE LOANS AND MORTGAGE-BACKED SECURITIES

61.221 The balance sheets of mortgage banking companies should distinguish between mortgage loans held for sale and mortgage loans held for long-term investment.

Mortgages Held for Sale

61.222 Mortgage loans held for sale should be reported at the lower of cost or market value as of the balance sheet date. A valuation allowance should be used to account for any excess of cost over market value. Changes in the valuation allowance should be charged to income in the period the change occurs. (SFAS 65, par. 4) Mortgage-backed securities held for sale should be classified as trading securities and reported at fair value. (SFAS 115, par. 128) (Chapter 35 discusses accounting for investments in marketable securities.) Purchase discounts related to mortgage loans should not be amortized as interest revenue during the period the loans or securities are held for sale. (SFAS 65, par. 5)

61.223 The mortgage company should determine the market value of mortgage loans and mortgage-backed securities held for sale by type of loan. At a minimum, separate determinations of market value for residential and commercial mortgage loans should be made, as well as for loans subject to investor purchase commitments (committed loans) and loans held on a speculative basis (uncommitted loans). For each type of loan, the mortgage company may determine the lower of cost or market value for the aggregate of all loans within that category or for each individual loan. (SFAS 65, par. 9)

61.224   Market value should be determined separately for loans subject to investor purchase commitments (i.e. committed loans) and loans held on a speculative basis (i.e. uncommitted loans) as follows:

a. *Committed loans and mortgage backed securities.* Market value for loans subject to investor commitments should be based on the commitment price. (SFAS 65, par. 9) If the commitment price exceeds the fair value of mortgage backed securities subject to an investor purchase commitment, the implicit loss on the commitment should be recognized. (SFAS 115, par. 128)

b. *Uncommitted Loans.* Market value of uncommitted loans should be based on the market in which the mortgage banking entity normally operates. Consideration should be given to: (SFAS 65, par. 9)

   (1) Commitment prices (to the extent they reflect market conditions at the balance sheet date)

   (2) Market prices and yields obtained in the entities normal market outlets

   (3) Quoted GNMA security prices or other public market quotations for long-term mortgage rates

   (4) Current Federal Home Loan Mortgage Corporation and Federal National Mortgage Association delivery prices

c. *Uncommitted Mortgage-Backed Securities.* The fair value of uncommitted mortgage-backed securities collateralized by the entity's own loans generally should be based on the market value of the securities. If the trust holding the loans may be readily terminated and the loans sold directly, the fair value of the securities should be based on the market value of the loans or securities, depending on the mortgage entity's sales intent. Published mortgage-backed securities yields should be used to determine fair value of other mortgage-backed securities. (SFAS 65, par. 9)

61.225   Capitalized costs of servicing assets associated with the purchase or origination of mortgage loans should not be considered in the cost of mortgage loans when determining the lower of cost or market value of the loans. (SFAS 65, par. 10) Servicing assets or liabilities should be assessed for impairment or increased liability based on their fair value. (SFAS 125, par. 13) (See Paragraphs 61.230–.232.)

61.224

> **Practical Consideration.** To finance its mortgage loans or mortgage-backed securities held for sale, a mortgage banking company may temporarily transfer such loans or securities to banks or other financial institutions under repurchase agreements that indicate the mortgage company retains control over the loans' or securities' future economic benefits and risk of market loss. The mortgage company generally reacquires the same mortgage loans or securities from the financial institutions when the mortgage company sells the loans or securities to permanent investors. Transactions of that type fall under the requirements of SFAS 125, *Accounting for Transfers and Servicing of Financial Assets and Extinguishments of Liabilities,* which is discussed in Chapter 52.

Mortgages Held for Long-term Investment

61.226   A mortgage company should classify a mortgage loan as a long-term investment if the company has both the ability and the intent to hold the loan for the foreseeable future or until maturity. The mortgage company should use the lower of cost or market value on the transfer date to transfer a mortgage loan to a long-term investment classification. (SFAS 65, par. 6) Any difference between the loan's carrying amount and its outstanding principal balance should be recognized as an adjustment to interest income using the interest method. (SFAS 91, par. 27)

61.227   If ultimate recovery of the carrying amount of a mortgage loan held as a long-term investment is doubtful and the impairment is not considered to be temporary, the mortgage banker should reduce the carrying amount of the loan to its expected collectible amount, which becomes the new cost basis. The amount of the reduction should be reported as a loss. A recovery from the new cost basis should be reported as a gain only at the sale, maturity, or other disposition of the loan. (SFAS 65, par. 7)

Transactions with an Affiliated Company

61.228   The carrying amount of mortgage loans to be sold to an affiliated company should be adjusted to the lower of cost or market value as of the date management decides that a sale to an affiliated company will occur. Any adjustment amount should be charged to income. (SFAS 65, par. 12) If the loan originator is acting as an agent of an affiliated company by originating mortgage loans exclusively for that company, the loan transfers should be accounted for at the originator's acquisition cost. (SFAS 65, par. 13)

ACCOUNTING FOR MORTGAGE SERVICING FEES AND SERVICING ASSETS

> **Practical Consideration.** The following paragraphs are based on SFAS No. 125, *Accounting for Transfers and Servicing of Financial Assets and Extinguishments of Liabilities.* SFAS No. 125 is effective for transfers and servicing of financial assets occurring after December 31, 1996, and must be applied prospectively. Early or retroactive application of SFAS No. 125 is not permitted.

61.229   Mortgage banking companies buy or originate mortgage loans and may sell the loans but retain the right to service them in return for a fee. The rights to service mortgage loans are frequently purchased and sold because servicing fees often exceed the cost of performing servicing functions. The servicing fee, usually based on a percentage of the outstanding principal balance of the mortgage loan, is received for performing loan administration functions, such as collecting mortgage and escrow payments and maintaining loan payment records.

61.230   When a mortgage company is obligated to service mortgage loans, it should recognize a servicing asset or a servicing liability for the servicing contract. The contract to service the mortgage loans should be accounted for separately from the loans as follows: (SFAS 125, par. 37)

a. Servicing assets and servicing liabilities should be reported separately in the statement of financial position.

b. Servicing assets retained in the sale or securitization of the mortgage loans being serviced should be recorded at their allocated carrying amount based on relative fair values (if practicable) at the date of sale or securitization.

c. Servicing assets purchased or servicing liabilities assumed should be recorded at fair value.

d. Servicing liabilities undertaken in a sale or securitization should be recorded at fair value, if practicable.

e. Rights to future interest income from serviced loans in excess of contractually specified servicing fees should be accounted for separately from servicing assets (i.e. as interest-only strips).

f. Servicing assets should be amortized into income in proportion to and over the period of estimated net servicing income.

g. Servicing assets should be subsequently measured for impairment. (See Paragraph 61.231.)

h. Servicing liabilities should be amortized into income in proportion to and over the period of estimated net servicing loss. However, if subsequent events (such as higher servicing expenses than originally estimated) result in an increase in the fair value of the servicing liability, the increased liability should be charged to earnings.

Practical Consideration. SFAS 125 does not require a servicing asset or liability to be recorded when an entity securitizes the mortgage loans, retains all the resulting securities, and classifies them as debt securities held to maturity under SFAS No. 115. (Chapter 35 discusses accounting for debt securities held to maturity.)

Impairment

61.231   A mortgage company should evaluate and measure possible impairment of capitalized mortgage servicing assets by stratifying those assets based on the risk characteristics of the underlying loans. Risk characteristics may include loan type, size, note rate, origination date, term, and geographic location. The mortgage company should recognize impairment through a valuation allowance for an individual stratum. The impairment amount should be the excess of the capitalized mortgage servicing assets for a stratum over their fair value. The fair value of mortgage servicing rights that have not been capitalized should not be used in the evaluation of impairment. The mortgage company should subsequently adjust the valuation allowance to reflect changes in the measurement of impairment. Fair value in excess of the amount capitalized as mortgage servicing rights (net of amortization), however, should not be recognized. (SFAS 125, par. 37)

Fair Value

61.232   Fair value of servicing assets should be based on quoted market prices when available. If quoted market prices are not available, fair value is based on the best information available. Fair value of similar assets and liabilities and the results of valuation techniques (such as the present value of estimated future cash flows using a discount rate commensurate with the risks involved, option pricing models, matrix pricing, option-adjusted spread models, and fundamental analysis) should be considered when estimating fair value. (SFAS 125, par. 43)

Transition Guidance

61.233   For servicing contracts entered into prior to January 1, 1997, previously recognized servicing rights and excess servicing receivables (receivables for fees that do not exceed servicing fees specified in the contract) should be combined (net of any previously recorded servicing liabilities recorded under the contract) as an asset or liability. Previously recognized servicing receivables that exceed fees specified in the contract should be reclassified as interest-only strips receivable. Resulting servicing assets or liabilities should be subsequently measured as discussed in Paragraphs 61.230–.32. Resulting interest-only strips receivable should be subsequently measured like investments in debt securities classified as available-for-sale or trading. (SFAS 125, paras. 14 and 20). That is, they should be reported at fair value and unrealized holding gains and losses should be accounted for as follows: (SFAS 115, par. 13)

a. *Trading securities.* Unrealized gains and losses should be included in earnings in the period they arise.

b. *Available-for-sale securities.* Unrealized gains and losses should be reported as other comprehensive income (see Chapter 8). Realized gains and losses should be included in income in the period they are realized.

DISCLOSURE REQUIREMENTS

61.500   The following disclosures are unique for entities engaged in lending and mortgage banking activities:

a. The method used to determine the lower of cost or market value for mortgage loans (i.e. aggregate or individual loan basis). (SFAS 65, par. 29)

b. For entities that anticipate prepayments in their calculation of constant effective yield for purposes of applying the interest method when amortizing net loan fees or costs (see Paragraph 61.215), the policy and assumptions underlying the prepayment estimates. (SFAS 91, par. 19)

c. For all servicing assets and liabilities: (SFAS 125, par. 17)

    (1) The amounts of servicing assets and liabilities recorded and amortized during the period

(2) The fair value of recorded servicing assets and liabilities (for which it is practicable to estimate fair value) and the significant assumptions used in estimating fair value

(3) For any valuation allowances for impairment of recorded servicing assets, the beginning and ending balances, aggregate additions charged to operations and the aggregate reductions credited to operations, and the aggregate direct write-downs charge to the allowance for all periods in which results of operations are reported

(4) The risk characteristics of the underlying financial assets used to group recognized servicing assets for purposes of measuring impairment (for example, whether servicing assets were grouped for impairment evaluation based on the underlying assets' type, size, interest rate, term, etc.)

AUTHORITATIVE LITERATURE AND RELATED TOPICS

AUTHORITATIVE LITERATURE

SFAS No. 65, *Accounting for Certain Mortgage Banking Activities*
SFAS No. 91, *Accounting for Nonrefundable Fees and Costs Associated with Originating or Acquiring Loans and Initial Direct Costs of Leases*
SFAS No. 115, *Accounting for Certain Investments in Debt and Equity Securities*
SFAS No. 125, *Accounting for Transfers and Servicing of Financial Assets and Extinguishments of Liabilities*
FASB Technical Bulletin 87-3, *Accounting for Mortgage Servicing Fees and Rights*

RELATED PRONOUNCEMENTS

EITF Issue No. 84-19, *Mortgage Loan Payment Modifications*
EITF Issue No. 85-13, *Sale of Mortgage Service Rights on Mortgages Owned by Others*
EITF Issue No. 85-20, *Recognition of Fees for Guaranteeing a Loan*
EITF Issue No. 85-26, *Measurement of Servicing Fee under FASB Statement No. 65 When a Loan Is Sold with Servicing Retained*
EITF Issue No. 85-28, *Consolidation Issues Relating to Collateralized Mortgage Obligations*
EITF Issue No. 86-24, *Third-Party Establishment of Collateralized Mortgage Obligations*
EITF Issue No. 87-25, *Sale of Convertible, Adjustable-Rate Mortgages with Contingent Repayment Agreement*

EITF Issue No. 87-30, *Sale of a Short-Term Loan Made under a Long-term Credit Commitment*

EITF Issue No. 87-34, *Sale of Mortgage Servicing Rights with a Subservicing Agreement*

EITF Issue No. 89-4, *Accounting for a Purchased Investment in a Collateralized Mortgage Obligation Instrument or in a Mortgage-Backed Interest-Only Certificate*

EITF Issue No. 90-21, *Balance Sheet Treatment of a Sale of Mortgage Servicing Rights with a Subservicing Agreement*

EITF Issue No. 93-18, *Recognition of Impairment for an Investment in a Collateralized Mortgage Obligation Instrument or in a Mortgage-Backed Interest-Only Certificate*

EITF Issue No. 95-5, *Determination of What Risks and Rewards, If Any, Can Be Retained and Whether Any Unresolved Contingencies May Exist in a Sale of Mortgage Loan Servicing Rights*

EITF Issue No. 97-3, *Accounting for Fees and Costs Associated with Loan Syndications and Loan Participations after the Issuance of FASB Statement No. 125*

AcSEC Practice Bulletin No. 6, *Amortization of Discounts on Certain Acquired Loans*

FASB Implementation Guide, *A Guide to Implementation of Statement 91, "Accounting for Nonrefundable Fees and Costs Associated with Originating or Acquiring Loans and Initial Direct Costs of Leases"*

SOP 97-1, *Accounting by Participating Mortgage Loan Borrowers*

RELATED TOPICS

Chapter 8—Comprehensive Income
Chapter 28—Interest: Imputed
Chapter 45—Real Estate Transactions
Chapter 52—Transfers and Servicing of Financial Assets

MOTION PICTURE INDUSTRY

Table of Contents

MOTION PICTURE INDUSTRY

OVERVIEW

62.100   Revenues from the sale or license of motion picture exhibition rights to a movie theater generally should be recognized on the dates the film is shown. Revenues from film license agreements with television broadcasters should be recognized when the license period begins and certain conditions are met. Production costs should be capitalized as film cost inventory and amortized to expense based on related revenues.

62.101   Generally accepted accounting principles address other issues unique to motion picture producers and distributors, including accounting for loans to independent producers and classifying capitalized film costs in the balance sheet.

ACCOUNTING REQUIREMENTS

REVENUE

62.200   Generally, motion picture companies, independent producers, or distributors (licensors) recognize revenue following the same basic accounting concept as other industries. That is, they recognize revenue when amounts are realized and earned. The following paragraphs provide specific guidance on applying that basic concept to the sale or license of film exhibition rights to movie theaters or television networks (or stations).

Films Licensed to Movie Theaters

62.201   Motion picture exhibition rights typically are sold (licensed) to movie theaters based on either a percentage of the box office receipts or a flat fee. As a general rule, revenue from the sale of exhibition rights should be recognized on the date the film is shown. Thus, any nonrefundable guarantee received against a percentage of box office receipts normally should be deferred and not recognized as revenue until the dates the film is shown. However, in some markets (such as foreign markets), the licensor may not reasonably expect revenue from a percentage of box office receipts to exceed the nonrefundable guarantee. In that event, the nonrefundable guarantee is considered an outright sale of the exhibition rights and may be recognized as revenue when all of the following conditions are met: (SFAS 53, paras. 3–4)

a. The license fee for each film is known.

b. The cost of each film is known or reasonably determinable.

c. Collectibility of the full license fee is reasonably assured.

d. The film has been accepted by the licensee in accordance with the conditions of the license agreement.

e. The film is available for its first showing. (This criterion is met regardless of restrictions on the timing of subsequent showings. The condition is not met if a conflicting license agreement prevents the licensee from showing the film.)

Films Licensed to Television

62.202   A license agreement for television program material usually covers several films and grants a broadcaster the right to telecast either a specified number or an unlimited number of showings over a maximum time period for a specified fee. The agreement usually contains a separate license for each film in the package, and the broadcaster pays the required license fee whether or not the right to broadcast a film is exercised. Licensors should consider a license agreement for television program material as a sale of a right and should recognize revenue from the agreement when the license period begins and all of the following conditions have been met: (SFAS 53, par. 6)

- The license fee for each film is known.

- The cost of each film is known or reasonably determinable.

- Collectibility of the full license fee is reasonably assured.

- The film has been accepted by the licensee in accordance with the conditions of the license agreement.

- The film is available for its first showing or telecast. (This condition is met regardless of restrictions on the timing of subsequent showings. The condition is not met if a conflicting license agreement prevents the licensee from showing the film.)

If there are significant doubts about either party's obligation or ability to perform under the agreement, however, revenue recognition should be postponed until the doubts no longer exist. (SFAS 53, par. 7)

62.202

62.203   Revenue should be recognized in the same sequence as the market-by-market exploitation of the film and at the time the licensee can exercise its rights under the agreement. That occurs at the later of the beginning of the contract period or the expiration of a conflicting license. (SFAS 53, par. 8) The sales price for each film is the present value of the licensee fee specified in the agreement, computed in accordance with APB Opinion No. 21, *Interest on Receivables and Payables*. (SFAS 53, par. 9) (Imputing interest on receivables and payables is discussed in Chapter 28.)

COSTS AND EXPENSES

Production Costs

62.204   Production costs include the following costs of writing and producing a film:

     a. Salaries of cast, directors, producers, and extras

     b. Set construction, wardrobe, and prop costs

     c. Photography, sound synchronization, and editing costs

     d. Production overhead costs, including depreciation and amortization of studio equipment and leasehold improvements used in production.

     e. Rental of facilities on location

Production costs should be capitalized as film cost inventory and amortized using the individual-film-forecast-computation method or the periodic-table-computation method. Amortization should reasonably relate the film costs to the gross revenues reported and should begin when a film is released and revenues on that film are recognized. (SFAS 53, par. 10)

62.205   **Individual-film-forecast-computation Method.** The individual-film-forecast-computation method amortizes film costs based on the ratio of current gross revenues to anticipated total gross revenues. In determining that ratio, the motion picture company should divide the actual current period gross revenues from the film by the anticipated total gross revenues from the film during its useful life in all markets. The resulting ratio should be applied to production and other capitalized film costs to determine the amortization for each period. (SFAS 53, par. 11)

> **Practical Consideration.** As discussed in Paragraph 62.203, the amount recognized as revenue related to the sale of long-term, noninterest-bearing television exhibition rights is the present value of the license fee specified in the agreement. Thus, the present value of the revenues from television rights, rather than the gross proceeds, should be included in the numerator and denominator of the amortization ratio.

62.206 Estimates of anticipated total gross revenues should be reviewed periodically and revised as necessary to reflect more current information. When revenue estimates are revised, a new amortization ratio should be determined by dividing the actual gross revenues for the current period by the anticipated total gross revenues from the beginning of the current year. The revised ratio should be applied to the unrecovered capitalized film costs as of the beginning of the current year. (SFAS 53, par. 12)

62.207 **Periodic-table-computation Method.** The periodic-table-computation method should only be used if its result would approximate the result achieved using the individual-film-forecast-computation method. The periodic-table-computation method amortizes film costs using tables prepared from the historic revenue patterns of a large group of films. The method should only be used to amortize the portion of film costs relating to film rights licensed to movie theaters. It should not be used for a film whose distribution pattern differs significantly from the patterns of the films used in compiling the table, however. (SFAS 53, par. 13)

Participations

62.208 Persons involved in the production of a motion picture film frequently are compensated, in part or in full, with a participation in the income from the film. The compensation amount payable to the participant is usually based on percentages of revenues or profits from the film. If the motion picture company anticipates that compensation will be payable under a participation agreement, the total expected participation should be charged to expense in the same ratio that current gross revenues bear to anticipated total gross revenues. (SFAS 53, par. 14)

Exploitation Costs

62.209 Exploitation costs are incurred during the final production phase and during the release periods of films in both primary and secondary markets. They include such costs as film prints, prerelease and early release advertising expected to benefit the film in future markets, and other distribution expenses. Motion picture companies should capitalize exploitation costs that clearly benefit future periods as film cost inventory and amortize the costs in the same ratio that current gross revenues bear to anticipated total gross revenues. Local advertising and distribution expenses that are not clearly expected to benefit the film in future markets should be charged to expense in the period incurred. (SFAS 53, par. 15)

Inventory Valuation

62.210   A motion picture company should compare the cost of its inventory (unamortized production and exploitation costs) with the inventory's net realizable value each reporting period on a film-by-film basis. The company should write down the unamortized film costs to net realizable value if estimated future gross revenues from a film are not sufficient to recover the unamortized film costs, other direct distribution expenses, and participations. Film costs written down during a fiscal year may be written back up during the same fiscal year if warranted by subsequent increases in estimated future gross revenues. (Such write-ups should not exceed the current year write-down.) Film costs reduced to net realizable value at the end of a fiscal year should not be written back up in subsequent fiscal years, however. (SFAS 53, par. 16)

62.211   **Story Costs.** Film inventory costs ordinarily include expenditures for properties, such as film rights to books, stage plays, and original screenplays. The cost of adapting a story to the production techniques used in motion picture films should be included in the cost of the particular property. Properties should be reviewed periodically to determine whether they will be recovered. The cost of any property that will not be used in the production of a film should be charged to production overhead in the period that determination was made. Story costs generally should be charged to production overhead if the property has been held for three years and has not been set for production. Once charged off, story costs should not be reinstated. (SFAS 53, par. 17)

Advances and Loans to Independent Producers

62.212   Motion picture companies frequently advance funds or guarantee loans for the production of films by independent producers. In such cases, the independent producer and the motion picture company generally both have specified ownership rights in the film. In addition, the motion picture company frequently has a participation in the net revenues from the film. A motion picture company should include cash advances or loans made to independent producers in film cost inventory. Similarly, it should record loans that it guarantees on behalf of independent producers as film cost inventory and as liabilities when funds are disbursed. (SFAS 53, par. 18)

BALANCE SHEET CLASSIFICATION

62.213   A motion picture company may present either a classified or unclassified balance sheet. If a classified balance sheet is presented, film costs should be segregated between current and noncurrent assets. The following film costs should be classified as current assets:

a. Unamortized costs of film inventory released and allocated to the primary market

b   Completed films not released

c. Television films in production that are under a sales contract

All other capitalized film costs should be classified as noncurrent assets. (SFAS 53, par. 20)

62.214   A motion picture company should not report a license agreement for the sale of film rights for television exhibition as an asset until the time revenue from the agreement is recognized. Amounts received from such agreements prior to revenue recognition should be reported as advance payments and included in current liabilities if the advance payments relate to film cost inventory classified as current assets. (SFAS 53, par. 19)

HOME VIEWING MARKET

62.215   Often, films are licensed to the home viewing market, for example, on video cassette, pay-per-view, or laser disc. Such licensing agreements may have the characteristics of license agreements with movie theaters or television broadcasters. Consequently, they should be accounted for following the guidance in Paragraphs 62.201–.214 as appropriate. (SFAS 53, par. 22)

DISCLOSURE REQUIREMENTS

62.500   A motion picture company should disclose the components of its film inventories, including films released, completed but not released, and in process and story rights. (SFAS 53, par. 23)

AUTHORITATIVE LITERATURE AND RELATED TOPICS

AUTHORITATIVE LITERATURE

SFAS No. 53, *Financial Reporting by Producers and Distributors of Motion Picture Films*

RELATED PRONOUNCEMENTS

EITF Issue No. 87-10, *Revenue Recognition by Television (Barter) Syndicators*

NOT-FOR-PROFIT ORGANIZATIONS

Table of Contents

NOT-FOR-PROFIT ORGANIZATIONS

OVERVIEW

63.100   A complete set of financial statements for a not-for-profit organization includes a statement of financial position, statement of activities, statement of cash flows, and accompanying notes. Voluntary health and welfare organizations should also include a statement of functional expenses. An organization's net assets, revenues, expenses, gains, and losses should be classified based on donor restrictions—that is, as either unrestricted, temporarily restricted, or permanently restricted.

63.101   Generally accepted accounting principles provide guidance on accounting for certain events, transactions, and accounting issues that are unique to nonprofit organizations. That guidance includes the following:

   a. *Investments.* Not-for-profit organizations should report investments in equity securities with readily determinable fair values and all investments in debt securities at fair value. Realized and unrealized gains and losses should be included in the statement of activities.

   b. *Depreciation.* Not-for-profit organizations are required to depreciate long-lived tangible assets other than works of art or historical treasures that have indefinite or extraordinarily long useful lives.

GAAP also provides specific guidance on accounting for contributions. The guidance applies to all entities that make or receive contributions, including not-for-profit organizations, and is discussed in Chapter 11.

ACCOUNTING REQUIREMENTS

GAAP FOR NOT-FOR-PROFIT ORGANIZATIONS

63.200   Generally, not-for-profit organizations must follow the relevant generally accepted accounting principles that apply to for-profit businesses. Thus, nonprofit organizations must follow all ARBs, APB Opinions, and FASB Statements and Interpretations unless the pronouncement explicitly exempts them.

The Financial Accounting Standards Board has issued the following Statements that specifically deal with issues affecting nonprofit organizations:

- SFAS No. 93, *Recognition of Depreciation by Not-for-Profit Organizations*

- SFAS No. 116, *Accounting for Contributions Received and Contributions Made*

- SFAS No. 117, *Financial Statements of Not-for-Profit Organizations*

- SFAS No. 124, *Accounting for Certain Investments Held by Not-for-Profit Organizations*

Practical Consideration. This chapter focuses on the guidance contained in the preceding FASB Statements. Accountants also should consider the accounting guidance found in the AICPA Audit and Accounting Guide, *Not-for-Profit Organizations,* and SOP 94-3, *Reporting of Related Entities by Not-for-Profit Organizations,* to the extent it does not conflict with the principles discussed in this chapter. Alternatively, accountants may refer to PPC's *Guide to Nonprofit GAAP* for comprehensive coverage of the generally accepted accounting principles that apply to nonprofit organizations. In addition to its extensive coverage of the pronouncements written specifically for nonprofits, *Guide to Nonprofit GAAP* discusses, from a not-for-profit organization's perspective, the generally accepted accounting principles that all entities must follow.

DEPRECIATION

63.201   All not-for-profit organizations must depreciate their long-lived tangible assets. (SFAS 93, par 5) Depreciation need not be recognized on individual works of art or historical treasures that have indefinite or extraordinarily long useful lives, however. Works of art or historical treasures have indefinite or extraordinarily long useful lives if they (a) have cultural, aesthetic, or historical value that is worth preserving perpetually and (b) are being preserved by a holder that has the technological and financial ability to do so (for example, by placing art in a protective environment and limiting its use solely to display). (SFAS 93, par. 36) Works of art or historical treasures do not have indefinite or extraordinarily long useful lives (and thus should be depreciated) if their cultural aesthetic, or historical values can be preserved, if at all, only by periodically protecting, cleaning, and restoring them, usually at significant cost. (For example, the wear and tear of normal use, destructive effects of pollutants, vibrations, etc. may reduce the useful life of a monument or cathedral unless major preservation and restoration efforts are periodically made.) (SFAS 93, par. 35)

63.202   Capitalized costs of major preservation and restoration efforts should be depreciated, regardless of whether depreciation is recognized on the asset being protected or restored, if the efforts provide future economic benefits or service potential. (SFAS 93, par. 37)

INVESTMENTS

> **Practical Consideration.** The guidance on accounting for investments was derived from SFAS No. 124. The Statement was issued in November 1995 and is effective for fiscal years beginning after December 15, 1995 (and any interim periods within those years), with earlier application encouraged. A not-for-profit organization generally must apply its guidance to all investments in equity securities that have a readily determinable fair value and debt securities except the following:
>
> - Equity securities accounted for under the equity method (See Chapter 20.)
>
> - Investments in consolidated subsidiaries (See Chapter 9.)

63.203   Investments in equity securities with readily determinable fair values and all investments in debt securities should be reported in the statement of financial position at fair value with realized and unrealized gains and losses included in the statement of activities. Gains and losses should be reflected as increases or decreases in the unrestricted class of net assets unless the donor or relevant laws place temporary or permanent restrictions on the gains and losses. Investment income also should be reported as an increase in unrestricted net assets unless the donor placed restrictions on the income's use. If the income is restricted, it should be reported as an increase in temporarily or permanently restricted net assets, depending on the nature of the restrictions. (SFAS 124, paras. 7–9)

63.204   Donor-restricted investment income and gains whose restrictions are met in the same reporting period may be reported as unrestricted income and gains if the organization (a) reports consistently from period to period, (b) follows the same policy for reporting donor-restricted contributions, and (c) discloses its accounting policy. (SFAS 124, par. 10)

Reporting Losses on Endowment Fund Investments

63.205   Unless a donor or relevant law directs otherwise, any losses on investments that are donor-restricted for an endowment fund should first reduce any net appreciation reflected in temporarily restricted net assets rather than reduce permanently restricted net assets. Any remaining losses should reduce unrestricted net assets. Any future gains should be recorded as increases in unrestricted net assets until the total amount of the gains offsets the amount of the losses recorded (even if the losses reduced temporarily restricted net assets). Gains in excess of that amount should be recorded based on donor restrictions. (SFAS 124, paras. 11–12)

FINANCIAL STATEMENTS

63.206   A complete set of financial statements of a not-for-profit organization should include a statement of financial position as of the end of the reporting period, a statement of activities and a statement of cash flows for the reporting period, and accompanying notes. Voluntary health and welfare organizations also should present a statement of functional expenses. (SFAS 117, paras. 1 and 6)

Practical Consideration. Voluntary health and welfare organizations are nonprofit organizations that derive their revenue primarily from the general public and focus their efforts on health, welfare, or community services. Examples of voluntary health and welfare organizations include the Salvation Army, Red Cross, United Way, Boy Scouts, and organizations whose purpose is to find a cure for or help people deal with diseases such as cancer, diabetes, heart disease, or muscular dystrophy.

Statement of Financial Position

63.207   A statement of financial position should report total assets, liabilities, and net assets for the organization as a whole. Cash or other assets received with a donor-imposed restriction that limits their use to long-term purposes should not be classified with cash or other unrestricted assets that are available for current use. Information about liquidity should be provided by one or more of the following: (SFAS 117, paras. 10–12)

- Sequencing assets according to their nearness of conversion to cash and sequencing liabilities according to the nearness of their maturity and resulting use of cash

- Classifying assets and liabilities as current and noncurrent

- Disclosing relevant information about the liquidity or maturity of assets and liabilities, including restrictions on the use of particular assets, in notes to the financial statements

63.208   The statement of financial position should report the amounts for each of three classes of net assets: permanently restricted net assets, temporarily restricted net assets, and unrestricted net assets. Information about the nature and amounts of different types of permanent or temporary restrictions should be provided either by reporting their amounts on the face of the statement or by including relevant details in the notes to the financial statements. (SFAS 117, paras. 13–14)

> **Practical Consideration.** GAAP does not specifically require that the terms "unrestricted," "temporarily restricted," "permanently restricted," and "net assets" be used. Thus organizations may use "equity" for "net assets," and "other" or "not donor-restricted" for unrestricted net assets. However, the authors recommend using the terms "unrestricted," "temporarily restricted," and "permanently restricted," except in unusual situations, to avoid any confusion about their meaning or the nature of the restrictions.

63.209   **Permanently Restricted Net Assets.** An organization's use of permanently restricted net assets is limited by donor-imposed stipulations that do not expire with the passage of time and cannot be removed by the organization's actions. (SFAS 117, par. 168) Information about the amounts and types of restrictions on permanently restricted net assets may be disclosed by presenting secondary captions on the face of the statement of financial position or in the notes. Thus, an organization may present separate line items within permanently restricted net assets or the notes to distinguish between assets donated with stipulations that (a) they be used for a specified purpose, preserved, and not sold or (b) they be invested to provide a permanent source of income. (SFAS 117, par. 14)

63.210   **Temporarily Restricted Net Assets.** Temporarily restricted net assets are those whose use is restricted by donor-imposed stipulations that either expire with the passage of time or can be removed by the organization's actions. (SFAS 117, par. 168) Information about temporarily restricted net assets may be disclosed by presenting separate line items within temporarily restricted net assets or in the notes. Thus, separate line items may be used to distinguish between temporary restrictions for (a) support of particular operating activities, (b) investment for a specified term, (c) use in a specified future period, or (d) acquisition of long-lived assets. (SFAS 117, par. 15)

63.211   **Unrestricted Net Assets.** Changes in unrestricted net assets generally result from (a) revenues for providing services, producing and delivering goods, receiving unrestricted contributions, and receiving unrestricted dividends or interest from investments, (b) expenses incurred in providing services, producing and delivering goods, raising contributions, and performing administrative functions, and (c) reclassifications from other classes of net assets resulting from expiration of donor time or purpose restrictions. The only limits on using unrestricted net assets are the broad limits resulting from the organization's nature, purpose, and operating environment and limits resulting from contractual agreements. Information about significant contractual or self-imposed limits generally is provided in notes to the financial statements. (SFAS 117, par. 16)

63.212 **Format Considerations.** GAAP does not prescribe a specific format for the statement of financial position. Consequently, an organization may use a left-to-right or top-to-bottom balanced format or single-column, multi-column, single-page, or multi-page format. (SFAS 117, par. 86) EXHIBIT 63-1 presents an illustrative statement of financial position for a not-for-profit organization.

Statement of Activities

63.213 A statement of activities provided by a not-for-profit organization should report the amount of the change in net assets for the period for the organization as a whole. The net assets amount reported at the end of the period in the statement of activities should correspond to the net assets amount reported in the statement of financial position. The statement of activities should report the amount of change in each class of net assets (permanently restricted, temporarily restricted, and unrestricted) for the period. Events, such as expirations of donor-imposed restrictions, that simultaneously increase one class of net assets and decrease another should be reported as separate items. (SFAS 117, paras. 18–19)

63.214 **Revenues and Expenses.** Generally, a statement of activities should report revenues and expenses as increases and decreases, respectively, in unrestricted net assets. However, revenue generated by assets that have donor-imposed restrictions should be reported as an increase in either temporarily or permanently restricted net assets if the donor has imposed restrictions on the revenue. Otherwise, the revenue should be reported as an increase in unrestricted net assets. (SFAS 117, paras. 20 and 22)

63.215 Revenues and expenses generally should be reported at their gross amounts. Investment revenues may be reported net of related expenses if the amount of the expenses is disclosed either on the face of the statement or in the notes. Similarly, gains and losses resulting from peripheral or incidental transactions may be reported net. (For example, the sale of land and buildings no longer needed by ongoing activities normally is reported as a net gain or loss rather than as separate amounts for proceeds and costs of the assets sold. (SFAS 117, paras. 24–25)

EXHIBIT 63-1

EXAMPLE STATEMENT OF FINANCIAL POSITION

COMMUNITY PRESERVATION SOCIETY
STATEMENT OF FINANCIAL POSITION
June 30, 19X5

ASSETS		
Cash and cash equivalents	$	29,907
Short-term investments		1,337
Unconditional promises to give		
Unrestricted		37,906
Restricted for Hyden House renovation		117,032
Restricted to payment of long-term debt		36,300
Restricted to purchase of equipment		6,950
		198,188
Prepaid expenses		6,402
Long-term investments		64,875
Deposits on leased and other property		1,000
Property and equipment		648,410
TOTAL ASSETS	$	950,119
LIABILITIES		
Accounts payable	$	3,327
Compensation		3,089
Long-term debt		79,991
TOTAL LIABILITIES		86,407
NET ASSETS		
Unrestricted		601,518
Temporarily restricted		255,325
Permanently restricted		6,869
TOTAL NET ASSETS		863,712
TOTAL LIABILITIES AND NET ASSETS	$	950,119

63.216   To help donors, creditors, and others assess an organization's service efforts, the statement of activities or notes to the financial statements should report expenses by their functional classification (for example, by major classes of program services and supporting activities). Program services are the activities that fulfill the purposes for which the organization exists and that result in goods and services being distributed to beneficiaries, customers, or members. Those services are the major output of the organization and often relate to several major programs. Supporting activities are activities of a not-for-profit organization other than program services and generally include management and general, fundraising, and membership-development activities. (SFAS 117, paras. 26–27)

63.217   As discussed further in Paragraph 63.227, voluntary health and welfare organizations should report expenses by their functional classification, as well as by their natural classification in a matrix format in a separate financial statement. GAAP encourages, but does not require, other not-for-profit organizations to provide information about expenses by their natural classification. (SFAS 117, paras. 1–2)

63.218   **Contributions.** A not-for-profit organization should distinguish between contributions received (a) with permanent restrictions, (b) with temporary restrictions, and (c) without donor-imposed restrictions. A permanent or temporary restriction on the organization's use of the contributed assets results either from a donor's explicit stipulation or from circumstances surrounding the receipt of the contribution that make clear the donor's implicit restriction on use of the asset. Donor-restricted contributions should be reported as restricted revenues or gains, which increase either temporarily or permanently restricted net assets. Donor-restricted contributions whose restrictions are met in the same reporting period, however, may be reported as unrestricted revenues if the organization reports consistently from period to period and discloses its accounting policy. Contributions without donor-imposed restrictions should be reported as unrestricted revenues or gains, which increase unrestricted net assets. (SFAS 116, par. 14)

63.219   Receipts of unconditional promises to give payments in future periods should be reported as restricted revenues or gains unless (a) the donor explicitly stipulates that the receipt is to be used to support current period activities or (b) the circumstances surrounding the receipt of the promise make clear that the donor intended it to be used to support current period activities. (SFAS 116, par. 15)

63.220   A donor may give a long-lived asset to a not-for-profit organization without stipulating how long the donated asset must be used. Such a gift should be reported as restricted revenue or gain if the organization's accounting policy is to imply a time restriction that expires over the useful life of the donated asset.

An organization that adopts such a policy also should imply a time restriction on a long-lived asset acquired with gifts of cash or other assets restricted for the acquisition. In the absence of such a policy and other donor-imposed restrictions on the asset's use, an organization should report a gift of a long-lived asset as unrestricted revenue. An organization should disclose its accounting policy related to such gifts. (SFAS 116, par. 16)

63.221   A not-for-profit organization that receives transferred assets will be considered a donee and donor (instead of an agent, trustee, or intermediary) if the original donor has (a) directed the not-for-profit organization to distribute the transferred assets or income from the transferred assets to a third-party beneficiary *and* (b) explicitly granted the not-for-profit organization the power to distribute the transferred assets (or income) to any third-party beneficiary at the organization's own discretion. (FASBI 42, par. 2)

> **Practical Consideration.** Chapter 11 discusses accounting for contributions in further detail.

63.222   **Gains and Losses.** A statement of activities should report gains and losses recognized on investments and other assets or liabilities as increases or decreases in unrestricted net assets unless their use is temporarily or permanently restricted by explicit donor stipulations or by law. The statement may report gains and losses as net amounts if they result from peripheral or incidental transactions. (SFAS 117, par. 22)

63.223   **Additional Classifications.** In addition to classifying revenues, expenses, gains, and losses within the three classes of net assets, an organization may also classify items as operating and nonoperating, expendable and nonexpendable, earned and unearned, recurring and nonrecurring, or in other ways within a class of changes in net assets. (SFAS 117, par. 23)

63.224   **Format Considerations.** GAAP does not require a particular format for the statement of activities so long as revenues, expenses, gains, losses, and reclassifications are properly classified by net asset class and the change in net assets is presented by class of net assets and in total. EXHIBIT 63-2 presents an illustrative statement of activities for a nonprofit organization.

EXHIBIT 63-2

EXAMPLE STATEMENT OF ACTIVITIES

COMMUNITY PRESERVATION SOCIETY
STATEMENT OF CASH FLOWS
Year Ended June 30, 19X5

	Unrestricted	Temporarily Restricted	Permanently Restricted	Total
REVENUES AND OTHER SUPPORT				
Hyden House restoration campaign	$ —	$ 156,275	$ —	$ 156,275
Other contributions	133,209	50,964	2,704	186,877
Investment return	5,766	497	—	6,263
Special events and other	2,777	—	—	2,777
Net assets released from restrictions	158,343	(158,343)	—	—
TOTAL REVENUES AND OTHER SUPPORT	300,095	49,393	2,704	352,192
EXPENSES				
Program services	228,282	—	—	228,282
Supporting services	69,170	—	—	69,170
TOTAL EXPENSES	297,452	—	—	297,452
CHANGE IN NET ASSETS	2,643	49,393	2,704	54,740
NET ASSETS AT BEGINNING OF YEAR	598,875	205,932	4,165	808,972
NET ASSETS AT END OF YEAR	$ 601,518	$ 255,325	$ 6,869	$ 863,712

Statement of Cash Flows

63.225   A not-for-profit organization should prepare a statement of cash flows in accordance with SFAS No. 95, *Statement of Cash Flows,* giving special attention to the following cash flow activities that particularly relate to not-for-profit organizations:

- Cash flows from financing activities should include receipts from contributions and investment income that donors have restricted for long-term purposes, such as acquiring, constructing, or improving property, plant, equipment, or other long-lived assets or establishing or increasing an endowment. (SFAS 95, paras. 18–19 and SFAS 117, par. 20)

- Cash flow statements should reconcile the change in net assets to net cash flow from operating activities. (SFAS 95, par. 28 and SFAS 117, par. 20)

- Noncash investing and financing activities should include receiving a building or investment asset as a gift. (SFAS 95, par. 32 and SFAS 117, par. 20)

63.226   EXHIBIT 63-3 illustrates a statement of cash flows for a nonprofit organization.

EXHIBIT 63-3

EXAMPLE STATEMENT OF CASH FLOWS

COMMUNITY PRESERVATION SOCIETY
STATEMENT OF CASH FLOWS
Year Ended June 30, 19X5

CASH FLOWS FROM OPERATING ACTIVITIES	
Increase in net assets	$ 54,740
Adjustments to reconcile increase in net assets to net cash provided by operating activities:	
Depreciation	23,812
Unrealized gains on investments	(3,256)
(Increase) decrease in operating assets	
Unrestricted unconditional promises to give	(13,934)
Accounts receivable	1,355
Prepaid expenses	2,443
Increase (decrease) in operating liabilities	
Accounts payable	(3,445)
Compensation	(1,729)
Contributions restricted for long-term purposes	
Cash contributions	(42,947)
Restricted unconditional promises to give	(6,950)
Amortization of discount on unconditional promises to give	(3,771)
NET CASH PROVIDED BY OPERATING ACTIVITIES	6,318
CASH FLOWS FROM INVESTING ACTIVITIES	
Short-term investments, net	9,872
Purchases of long-term investments	(60,837)
Proceeds from maturity of long-term investments	12,500
Payments for property and equipment	(2,129)
NET CASH USED BY INVESTING ACTIVITIES	(40,594)
CASH FLOWS FROM FINANCING ACTIVITIES	
Capital campaign collections	17,771
Collection of support for Hyden House renovation	39,243
Collection of endowment fund support	2,704
Payments on Capital Bank notes	(11,190)
NET CASH PROVIDED BY FINANCING ACTIVITIES	48,528
NET INCREASE (DECREASE) IN CASH AND CASH EQUIVALENTS	14,252
BEGINNING CASH AND CASH EQUIVALENTS	15,655
ENDING CASH AND CASH EQUIVALENTS	$ 29,907

Expenses include interest paid of $253. Noncash investing and financing activities consist of financing the cost of acquiring a copier through a long-term note of $5,251, payable to Capital Bank.

Statement of Functional Expenses

63.227   Voluntary health and welfare organizations must present a statement of functional expenses that shows how the natural expense classifications (such as salaries, rent, electricity, interest expense, and depreciation) are allocated to significant program and supporting services. (Other nonprofit organizations may, but are not required to, present a statement of functional expenses.) A statement of functional expenses is, in short, a detailed analysis of the expense portion of the statement of activities presented in a matrix format. (SFAS 117, paras. 1–2) EXHIBIT 63-4 illustrates a statement of functional expenses for a nonprofit organization.

Practical Consideration. Expenses are required to be included in the statement of functional expenses while losses are not. Expenses result from a nonprofit organization's ongoing and major activities; losses result from peripheral or incidental transactions and from events and circumstances largely beyond the control of the organization. For example, unrealized losses on investments or a loss from a fire would not be included in the statement of functional expenses. However, expenses related to a senior citizen center cafeteria that is considered an ongoing activity would be included in the statement of functional expenses.

All expenses should be included in the statement of functional expenses regardless of where they are reported in the statement of activities. Thus, for example, investment expenses should be included in the statement of functional expenses even if they are reported as a reduction of investment income on the statement of activities.

EXHIBIT 63-4

EXAMPLE STATEMENT OF FUNCTIONAL EXPENSES

COMMUNITY PRESERVATION SOCIETY
STATEMENT OF FUNCTIONAL EXPENSES
Year Ended June 30, 19X5

| | Program Services | | Supporting Services | | |
	Hyden House	Advocacy	Management and General	Fundraising	Total
Compensation and related expenses					
Compensation	$ 70,061	$ 67,365	$ 38,720	$ 7,894	$184,040
Employee benefits	2,114	1,118	1,115	232	4,579
Payroll taxes	5,354	5,200	2,926	731	14,211
	77,529	73,683	42,761	8,857	202,830
Training	215	144	502	—	861
Depreciation	20,644	—	2,534	634	23,812
Insurance	8,119	591	1,548	387	10,645
Interest	—	—	248	—	248
Maintenance of equipment	324	—	733	—	1,057
Occupancy	16,996	14,978	1,586	314	33,874
Postage	68	39	997	996	2,100
Printing	434	138	968	1,450	2,990
Supplies	5,611	2,896	2,082	459	11,048
Telephone	2,293	874	581	387	4,135
Transportation	1,794	888	869	—	3,551
Other	24	—	220	57	301
	$134,051	$ 94,231	$ 55,629	$ 13,541	$297,452

DISCLOSURE REQUIREMENTS

63.500 Nonprofit organizations are subject to the same disclosure requirements as for-profit entities. In addition, GAAP specifically requires nonprofit
organizations to disclose the following in their general-purpose external financial statements:

Accounting policies

  a. Accounting policy for classifying gifts of long-lived assets (SFAS
     116, par. 16)

  b. If the use of the term operations is not apparent from the details
     provided on the face of the statement of activities, a description
     of the nature of the reported measure of operations or the items
     excluded from operations (SFAS 117, par. 23)

Long-lived assets

  a. Depreciation expense for the period

  b. Balances of major classes of depreciable assets, by nature or
     function, at the statement of financial position date

  c. Accumulated depreciation, by major classes of depreciable
     assets or in total, at the statement of financial position date

  d. A general description of the depreciation method used for major
     classes of depreciable assets (SFAS 93, par. 5)

Debt and equity securities

  a. For the most recent statement of financial position presented,
     information about investments with a significant concentration of
     market risk, including the nature and carrying amount of the
     investments (SFAS 124, par. 16)

  b. For each statement of financial position presented—

    (1) Aggregate carrying value of each major type of investment

    (2) Basis used to determine the carrying value for other invest-
        ments not required to be carried at fair value

    (3) For investments other than financial instruments carried at fair
        value, the methods and significant assumptions used to esti-
        mate fair value

(4) If the fair value of assets for all donor-restricted endowment funds at the reporting date is less than the amounts required by donors or law, the aggregate amount of the deficiencies (SFAS 124, par. 15)

c. For each period for which a statement of activities is presented—

(1) Information about the components of investment return included in the change in net assets

(2) If an intermediate measure of operations that includes only a portion of the investment return is presented on the statement of activities, the policy used in determining the portion included and a reconciliation of the investment return to amounts reported in the statement of activities (SFAS 124, par. 14)

AUTHORITATIVE LITERATURE AND RELATED TOPICS

AUTHORITATIVE LITERATURE

SFAS No. 93, *Recognition of Depreciation by Not-for-Profit Organizations*
SFAS No. 99, *Deferral of the Effective Date of Recognition of Depreciation by Not-for-Profit Organizations*
SFAS No. 116, *Accounting for Contributions Received and Contributions Made*
SFAS No. 117, *Financial Statements of Not-for-Profit Organizations*
SFAS No. 124, *Accounting for Certain Investments Held by Not-for-Profit Organizations*
FASB Interpretation No. 42, *Accounting for Transfers of Assets in Which a Not-for-Profit Organization is Granted Variance Power*

RELATED PRONOUNCEMENTS

AICPA Audit and Accounting Guide, *Not-for-Profit Organizations*
SOP 94-3, *Reporting of Related Entities by Not-for-Profit Organizations*

RELATED TOPICS

Chapter 4—Cash Flows Statement
Chapter 9—Consolidated Financial Statements
Chapter 11—Contributions
Chapter 20—Equity Method Investments
Chapter 33—Long-lived Assets, Depreciation, and Impairment

OIL AND GAS PRODUCING ACTIVITIES

Table of Contents

OIL AND GAS PRODUCING ACTIVITIES

OVERVIEW

64.100   GAAP describes the successful efforts method of accounting for oil and gas producing activities. Under that method, which is preferred but not required, the costs of oil and gas producing activities are accounted for as follows:

   a. Geological and geophysical costs and the costs of carrying and retaining undeveloped properties should be charged to expense when incurred since they do not result in the acquisition of assets.

   b. Costs incurred to drill exploratory wells and exploratory-type stratigraphic test wells that do not find proved reserves should be charged to expense when it is determined that the wells have not found proved reserves.

   c. Costs incurred to acquire properties and drill development wells, development-type stratigraphic test wells, successful exploratory wells, and successful exploratory-type stratigraphic wells should be capitalized.

   d. Capitalized costs of wells and related equipment should be amortized, depleted, or depreciated using the units-of-production method.

   e. Costs of unproved properties should be assessed periodically to determine if an impairment loss should be recognized.

64.101   Companies with oil and gas producing activities should disclose the method of accounting for costs incurred in those activities and the method of disposing of related capitalized costs. In addition, *publicly traded* companies must include the following as supplementary information when a complete set of annual financial statements are presented:

   a. Proved oil and gas reserve quantities

   b. Capitalized costs related to oil and gas producing activities

c. Costs incurred for property acquisition, exploration, and development activities

d. Results of operations for oil and gas producing activities

e. Standardized measure of discounted future net cash flows related to proved oil and gas reserve quantities

ACCOUNTING REQUIREMENTS

64.200   Oil and gas producing activities involve acquiring mineral interests in properties, exploration, development, and production. They do not include transporting, refining, or marketing oil and gas, however. (SFAS 19, par.1) Generally, oil and gas producing activities are accounted for under either of two methods—the full cost method or the successful efforts method. Under the full cost method, properties are divided into cost centers (such as U.S. operations, U.K. operations, etc.) and all acquisition, exploration, and development costs for properties within each cost center are capitalized when incurred. Under the successful efforts method, however, only exploration and development costs related to proved reserves are capitalized. Thus, the principal difference between the two methods is the treatment of acquisition and exploration costs that do not directly relate to the discovery of oil and gas reserves. The full cost method considers those costs as necessary for the discovery of general oil and gas reserves and capitalizes and amortizes them. The successful efforts method expenses those costs since they do not result in the actual discovery of reserves.

Practical Consideration. In 1977, the FASB issued SFAS No. 19, *Financial Accounting and Reporting by Oil and Gas Producing Companies,* which required companies to use the successful efforts method to account for costs incurred in oil and gas producing activities. Soon after, the Securities and Exchange Commission released rules allowing public companies to use either the successful efforts method prescribed by SFAS No. 19 or the full cost method. Consequently, the FASB suspended the effective date of most of SFAS No. 19's provisions thereby allowing all oil and gas producing companies (both public and nonpublic) to use either the successful efforts or full cost method of accounting. (SFAS No. 19's requirements for reporting accounting changes and allocating income taxes related to oil and gas producing activities were not suspended, however.)

The following paragraphs summarize the successful efforts method of accounting prescribed by authoritative literature. Rules for the full cost method of accounting can be found in Regulation S-X of the Securities and Exchange Commission.

ACQUISITION COSTS

64.201   Costs incurred to purchase or lease an unproved or proved property should be capitalized when incurred. Such costs include lease bonuses, purchase options, mineral rights, brokers' fees, recording fees, legal costs, and other costs incurred in acquiring properties.

Unproved Properties

64.202   Unproved properties are properties with no proved reserves. That is, they are properties on which oil and gas reserves either have not been found or have been found but cannot, with reasonable certainty, be recovered under existing economic and operating conditions. (SFAS 25, par. 34)

64.203   **Impairment Assessment.** Oil and gas producing companies should periodically assess unproved properties to determine whether they have been impaired. A property generally would be impaired if a dry hole has been drilled on it and the company has no firm plans to continue drilling. Also, the likelihood of impairment increases as the expiration of the lease term approaches if drilling activity has not begun on the property or on nearby properties. If the assessment indicates that a property has been impaired, the company should recognize a loss by providing a valuation allowance. Impairment of individual unproved properties with relatively significant acquisition costs should be assessed on a property-by-property basis. The valuation allowance for a company that has a relatively large number of unproved properties whose acquisition costs are not individually significant should be determined either in the aggregate or by groups. (SFAS 19, par. 28)

64.204   Information that becomes available after the balance sheet date but before the financial statements are issued should be considered when assessing impairment. For example, an unproved property may be considered impaired at the balance sheet date if, before the financial statements are issued, an exploratory well in progress at the balance sheet date is completed without finding proved reserves. (SFAS 19, par. 39) Previously issued financial statements should not be restated for such information, however. (FASBI 36, par. 2)

64.205   **Reclassification to Proved Properties.** A company should reclassify a property from unproved to proved when proved reserves are discovered on the property. For example, based on the results of an exploratory well, oil and gas reserves that can be produced under current economic conditions may be found on unproved properties. Similarly, if economic or operating conditions change (for example, oil prices increase or technological advances are made making reserve production economically feasible), oil and gas reserves that were previously believed to be unrecoverable may become recoverable. In either case, the unproved property should be reclassified to proved properties. For a property whose impairment has been individually assessed, the net carrying amount (acquisition cost less any valuation allowance) should be reclassified to proved properties; for properties whose impairment has been assessed on a group basis, the gross acquisition cost should be reclassified. (SFAS 19, par. 29)

Practical Consideration. When a single unproved property covers a vast area, proved reserves may only be found on a portion of the property. In such cases, only the portion of the property that relates to the proved reserves should be reclassified from unproved properties to proved properties.

64.206   Information that becomes available after the balance sheet date but before the financial statements are issued may be used to assess the conditions that existed at the balance sheet date. Thus, for example, if an exploratory well in progress at the balance sheet date discovers proved reserves before the financial statements are issued, the related unproved property should be reclassified to proved properties. (SFAS 19, par. 39) Previously issued financial statements should not be restated, however. (FASBI 36, par.2)

Proved Properties

64.207   Proved properties are those that contain known oil or gas reserves that can be recovered with reasonable certainty based on current economic and operating conditions. Generally, the determination that reserves can be recovered economically is based on (a) actual production or conclusive formation tests and (b) costs and oil or gas prices at the date the estimate is made (Changes in oil or gas prices should not be considered unless they are provided by existing contractual arrangements.) (SFAS 25, par. 34)

64.208   **Depletion of Acquisition Costs.** Capitalized acquisition costs of proved properties should be amortized (depleted) by the units-of-production method as the related oil and gas reserves are produced so that each unit of oil and gas produced is assigned a pro rata portion of the unamortized acquisition costs. The company may compute depletion on a property-by-property basis or on the basis of some reasonable aggregation of properties, such as a reservoir or field. The unit cost should be computed on the basis of the total estimated units of all proved oil and gas reserves. Units-of-production depletion rates should be revised at least once a year, and those revisions should be accounted for prospectively as changes in accounting estimates. (SFAS 19, par. 30)

64.206

64.209 The unit-of-production amortization method requires that the total number of units of oil or gas reserves in a property or group of properties be estimated and that the number of units produced in the current period be determined. If properties contain both oil and gas reserves, the reserves and the oil and gas produced should be converted to a common unit of measure on the basis of their approximate relative energy content. Alternatively, if it expects the relative proportion of oil and gas extracted in the current period to continue throughout the remaining productive life of the property, the company may compute amortization on the basis of either the oil or gas produced. Similarly, if either oil or gas clearly dominates both the reserves and current production, amortization may be computed based on production of the dominant mineral only. (SFAS 19, par. 35)

64.210 **Impairment Assessment.** The costs of proved properties, including related wells, equipment, and facilities should be reviewed for impairment if events or changes in circumstances indicate that they may not be fully recoverable. The method of determining whether proved properties have been impaired is the same as for other long-lived assets. That method is discussed in detail in Chapter 33.

Surrender or Abandonment of Properties

64.211 **Unproved Properties.** When a company surrenders or abandons an unproved property, its capitalized acquisition costs, less any related impairment allowance, should be written off and a loss recognized. (SFAS 19, par. 40)

64.212 **Proved Properties.** If only an individual well, piece of equipment, or single lease is abandoned or retired, no gain or loss should be recognized so long as the remainder of the property continues to produce oil or gas. Instead, the company should treat the abandoned or retired asset as if it were fully amortized and charge its cost to accumulated depreciation, depletion, or amortization. Generally, a gain or loss should be recognized when the last well on an individual property or group of properties ceases to produce and the entire property or group is abandoned. If a proved property or group of properties is partially abandoned or retired as a result of a catastrophic event or other major abnormality, however, a loss should be recognized at the time of abandonment or retirement. (SFAS 19, par. 41)

EXPLORATION COSTS

64.213 Exploration involves identifying and examining specific areas that have prospects of containing oil and gas reserves, as well as drilling exploratory wells and exploratory-type stratigraphic test wells. Exploration costs may be incurred both before and after acquiring the related property. The principal types of exploration costs relate to:

- topographical, geological, and geophysical studies,

- carrying and retaining undeveloped properties,

- dry hole and bottom hole contributions,

- drilling and equipping exploratory wells, and

- drilling exploratory-type stratigraphic test wells (wells drilled to obtain information about a specific geologic condition). (SFAS 19, paras. 16–17)

Geological and Geophysical Studies

64.214 Exploration costs for geological and geophysical studies, carrying and retaining undeveloped properties, and dry hole and bottom hole contributions do not result in the acquisition of an asset and therefore should be charged to expense when incurred. (SFAS 19, par. 18)

Practical Consideration. An oil and gas company may conduct geological and geophysical studies and other exploration activities on property it does not own. In exchange, the company will either (a) receive an interest in the property if proved reserves are found or (b) be reimbursed by the owner if proved reserves are not found. In such cases, the geological and geophysical studies and other costs do result in the acquisition of an asset. Thus, they should be recorded as a receivable when they are incurred and reclassified to proved properties if proved reserves are found.

Uncompleted Wells

64.215 An oil and gas producing company should capitalize the costs of drilling exploratory wells and exploratory-type stratigraphic test wells as part of its uncompleted wells, equipment, and facilities until it determines whether the well has found proved reserves. At that time, the capitalized costs of drilling the well should be charged to expense if proved reserves are not found or reclassified as part of the costs of the company's wells and related equipment and facilities if proved reserves are found (even though the well may not yet be completed as a producing well). (SFAS 19, par. 19)

64.216 Classification of reserves as proved may depend on whether a major capital expenditure can be justified which, in turn, may depend on whether additional wells find a sufficient quantity of additional reserves. In that case, the cost of drilling the well should continue to be carried as an asset pending determination of whether proved reserves have been found only so long as both of the following conditions are met:

    a. The well has found a sufficient quantity of reserves to justify its completion as a producing well if the required capital expenditure is made.

    b. Drilling of the additional wells is under way or firmly planned for the near future.

If both of the above conditions are not met, the company should treat the well as impaired and charge its costs to expense. If the company cannot determine that proved reserves have been found within one year after the completion of drilling, the well should be treated as impaired and its costs charged to expense. (SFAS 19, par. 31)

64.217   Events occurring after the balance sheet date may be used to determine whether a well has found proved reserves. (SFAS 19, par. 39) Consequently, if an exploratory well or exploratory-type stratigraphic test well is in progress at the end of a period and, subsequent to the balance sheet date but before the financial statements are issued, the well is determined not to have found proved reserves, the costs incurred as of the balance sheet date, net of any salvage value, should be charged to expense for that period. (If information becomes available after the financial statements have been issued, however, the previously issued financial statements should not be restated.) (FASBI 36, par. 2)

DEVELOPMENT COSTS

64.218   Oil and gas producing companies incur development costs to obtain access to proved reserves and to provide facilities for extracting, treating, gathering, and storing the oil and gas. Development costs include—

    • gaining access to and preparing well locations for drilling.

    • drilling and equipping development wells, development-type stratigraphic test wells, and service wells.

    • acquiring, constructing, and installing production facilities.

    • providing improved recovery systems. (SFAS 19, par. 21)

64.219   All costs incurred to drill and equip development wells, development-type stratigraphic test wells, and service wells should be capitalized, whether the wells are successful or unsuccessful. Costs of drilling those wells and constructing production equipment and facilities should be included in the company's uncompleted wells, equipment, and facilities until drilling or construction is completed. After that time, development costs should be capitalized as part of the cost of a company's wells and related equipment and facilities. (SFAS 19, par. 22)

Depreciation of Development Costs

64.220   Capitalized costs of exploratory wells and exploratory-type stratigraphic test wells that have found proved reserves and capitalized development costs should be depreciated using the units-of-production method described in Paragraphs 64.208–.209. Unit cost should be computed on the basis of the total estimated units of proved developed reserves, rather than on the basis of all proved reserves, however. (That differs from the depletion of acquisition costs of proved properties discussed in Paragraph 64.208, which is based on estimated units of all proved reserves.) Future development costs should not be considered when determining the amortization rate. Thus, if significant development costs related to a group of development wells (such as the cost of an offshore production platform) are incurred before all of the development wells in the group have been drilled, a portion of the development costs should be excluded from the amortization rate until the additional development wells are drilled. Similarly, proved developed reserves that will be produced only after significant additional development costs have been incurred should not be included in the amortization rate. (SFAS 19, par. 35)

64.221   Estimated salvage values and estimated dismantlement, restoration, and abandonment costs should be considered when determining depreciation and amortization rates. (SFAS 19, par. 37)

PRODUCTION COSTS

64.222   Production costs are incurred to operate and maintain a company's wells and related equipment and facilities. They include lifting the oil and gas to the surface as well as gathering, treating, field processing, and field storing the oil and gas. The following are specific examples of production costs: (SFAS 19, par. 24)

   a. Labor to operate the wells and related equipment and facilities

   b. Repairs and maintenance

   c. Materials, supplies, and fuel consumed and services utilized in operating the wells and related equipment and facilities

d. Property taxes and insurance applicable to proved properties and wells and related equipment and facilities

e. Severance taxes

64.223   Production costs (and related depreciation, depletion, and amortization of capitalized acquisition, exploration, and development costs) should be treated as part of the cost of oil and gas produced. (SFAS 19, par. 25)

SUPPORT EQUIPMENT AND FACILITIES

64.224   Support equipment and facilities include seismic, drilling, construction, and grading equipment, as well as vehicles, repair shops, warehouses, supply points, camps, and division, district, or field offices. A company should capitalize the cost of acquiring or constructing support equipment and facilities used in oil and gas producing activities. The depreciation and operating costs of such support equipment and facilities should be accounted for as exploration, development, or production costs, as appropriate. (SFAS 19, par. 26)

MINERAL PROPERTY CONVEYANCES

64.225   Mineral interests in properties are frequently conveyed to others and those conveyances may involve the transfer of all or part of the rights and responsibilities of operating a property. The transferor should not recognize a gain or loss at the time of the conveyance when—

a. assets used in oil and gas producing activities are transferred in exchange for other assets also used in oil and gas producing activities, or

b. assets are pooled in a joint undertaking intended to find, develop, or produce oil or gas from a particular property or group of properties.

The transferor also should not recognize a gain at the time of conveyance if a part of an interest is sold and—

a. substantial uncertainty exists about whether the costs of the retained interest will be recovered, or

b. the seller has a substantial obligation for future performance.

If a conveyance is not one of the types described above, gain or loss generally should be recognized unless there are other aspects of the transaction that would prohibit such recognition under GAAP. (SFAS 19, paras. 42–46)

INCOME TAXES

64.226   Oil and gas producing companies should recognize deferred income taxes for temporary differences related to intangible drilling and development costs and other incurred costs that enter into the determination of taxable income and pretax accounting income in different periods. When assessing whether deferred tax assets are likely to be realized, the company should consider the possibility that statutory depletion in future periods will reduce or eliminate taxable income in future years. However, the tax benefit of the excess of statutory depletion over cost depletion for tax purposes should not be recognized until the period in which the excess is deducted for income tax purposes. (SFAS 19, paras. 60–62 and SFAS 109, par. 288)

INTEREST CAPITALIZATION UNDER THE FULL COST METHOD

64.227   The full cost method generally capitalizes acquisition, exploration, and development costs associated with a particular cost center when the costs are incurred. If the cost center is producing, all of the related capitalized costs are subject to amortization. For oil and gas producing operations accounted for by the full cost method, capitalized costs that are currently being amortized do not qualify for interest capitalization since they are assets in use in the company's earning activities (i.e., they are considered to be placed in production). However, exploration or development costs qualify for interest capitalization if they are related to projects in progress that are not being currently amortized because the related cost center is not producing. In some cases, significant costs related to unusually major development projects (such as those associated with offshore operations) are deferred separately and not amortized until the related property is determined to be either productive or nonproductive. Those deferred exploration or development costs also are assets qualifying for interest capitalization since they are not being currently amortized for such projects in progress. (FASBI 33, par. 2)

DISCLOSURE REQUIREMENTS

64.500   All companies engaged in oil and gas producing activities must disclose the method of accounting for the costs of those activities and the manner of disposing of capitalized costs related to those activities. (SFAS 69, par. 6) In addition, *publicly traded companies* that have significant oil and gas producing activities must disclose the following as supplementary information for each period for which they present a balance sheet, income statement, statement of cash flows, and related notes: (SFAS 69, par. 7)

a. Proved oil and gas reserve quantities

b. Capitalized costs related to oil and gas producing activities

c. Costs incurred for property acquisition, exploration, and development activities

d. Results of operations for oil and gas producing activities

e. Standardized measure of discounted future net cash flows related to proved oil and gas reserve quantities

The disclosures are not required in interim financial statements. However, interim financial statements should disclose any major discovery or other event that causes a significant change from the oil and gas reserve quantities information presented in the most recent annual financial statements. (SFAS 69, par. 9)

64.501   A company's oil and gas producing activities are considered significant during the year if—

a. revenues from oil and gas producing activities are 10 percent or more of the company's total revenues;

b. results of operations for oil and gas activities before income taxes are 10 percent or more of (1) the combined operating profit of all industry segments that did not incur an operation loss or (2) the combined operating loss of all industry segments that incurred an operating loss; or

c. the identifiable assets related to oil and gas producing activities are 10 percent or more of the combined identifiable assets of all industry segments. (SFAS 69, par. 8)

PROVED OIL AND GAS RESERVE QUANTITIES

64.502   Public companies required to disclose information about their proved oil and gas quantities should present the following as supplementary information:

a. *Net quantities of proved and proved developed reserves of oil (including natural gas condensate and natural gas liquids) and natural gas as of the beginning and end of the year.* Generally, oil reserve amounts include reserves of condensate and natural gas liquids. If significant, however, natural gas liquids reserves should be disclosed separately. In addition, net quantities include operating and nonoperating interests, although reserves related to royalty interests need not be disclosed if the information is unavailable. (If royalty interest reserve information is unavailable, that fact and the company's share of oil and gas produced for royalty interests during the year should be disclosed.) Information about net quantities should not include outside interests in reserves owned by the company. (SFAS 69, par. 10)

b. *Changes in the net quantities of proved oil and gas reserves.* Changes that should be disclosed and explained include those resulting from (1) revisions of previous estimates, (2) use of improved recovery techniques, (3) purchases of minerals in place, (4) extensions of old reservoirs through additional drilling and discoveries of new proved reserves, (5) production, and (6) sales of minerals in place. (SFAS 69, par. 11)

64.503   The preceding information should be disclosed for the company's home country and each foreign geographic area in which significant reserves are located. (SFAS 69, par. 12) In addition, the following should be considered:

- Oil reserves and natural gas liquids reserve information should be stated in barrels and natural gas reserves should be stated in cubic feet. (SFAS 69, par. 15)

- The net quantities disclosed should not include oil or gas subject to purchase under long-term supply, purchase, or similar agreements. (Quantities subject to such agreements with governments or authorities at the end of the year and received during the year should be separately disclosed, however, if the company participates in the operation of the properties or otherwise serves as the producer of those reserves.) (SFAS 69, par. 13)

- If the company issues consolidated financial statements, all of the reserves attributable to the parent and all of the reserves attributable to consolidated subsidiaries (whether or not wholly owned) should be included. (However, if a significant portion of the reserves at the end of the year relates to a subsidiary in which there is a significant minority interest, that fact and the approximate portion should be disclosed.) (SFAS 69, par. 14)

- If the company's financial statements include investments that are proportionately consolidated, the company's proportionate share of such investee's oil and gas reserves should be included. (SFAS 69, par. 14)

- Oil and gas reserves of equity method investees should not be included. Instead, the company should separately disclose its share of the investees' oil and gas reserve quantities at the end of the year. (SFAS 69, par. 14)

- Economic factors or significant uncertainties affecting proved reserves should be explained. For example, unusually high development costs or lifting costs may be expected, a major pipeline or other facility may need to be constructed before production can begin, or the company may be contractually obligated to sell production at below market prices. (SFAS 69, par. 16)

- If a government restricts the disclosure of reserve amounts or requires disclosure of reserves other than proved, the company should disclose the fact that reserve quantity information does not include amounts from that country or that the reserve estimates include amounts other than proved reserves. (SFAS 69, par. 17)

CAPITALIZED COSTS RELATED TO OIL AND GAS PRODUCING ACTIVITIES

64.504   Publicly held companies must disclose the capitalized costs and related accumulated depreciation, amortization, and depletion of their oil and gas producing activities. Generally, capitalized amounts are separately disclosed for mineral interests; wells and related equipment and facilities; support equipment and facilities; and uncompleted wells, equipment, and facilities. However, those categories may be combined if appropriate. In any event, significant capitalized costs of unproved properties should be separately disclosed. (SFAS 69, par. 19)

64.505   A company's share of an equity method investee's capitalized costs related to oil and gas producing activities should be separately disclosed. (SFAS 69, par. 20)

COSTS INCURRED FOR PROPERTY ACQUISITION, EXPLORATION, AND DEVELOPMENT ACTIVITIES

64.506   Publicly traded companies must disclose the costs incurred during the year (whether capitalized or expensed) for property acquisition, exploration, and development. (SFAS 69, par. 21) When disclosing that information, the following should be considered:

- The amounts should be disclosed for each geographic area for which reserve quantities are disclosed. (SFAS 69, par. 22)

- Costs incurred to acquire proved reserves (if significant) should be disclosed separately from those incurred to acquire unproved reserves. (SFAS 69, par. 22)

- The company's share of costs incurred by equity method investees should be separately disclosed, in the aggregate and for each geographic area for which reserve quantities are disclosed. (SFAS 69, par. 23)

RESULTS OF OPERATIONS FOR OIL AND GAS PRODUCING ACTIVITIES

64.507   Publicly traded companies should disclose, as supplemental information, the results of operations of oil and gas producing activities, in the aggregate and for each geographic area for which reserves quantities are disclosed. The disclosure should include information about the following: (SFAS 69, paras. 24–28)

a. *Revenues.* Revenues should include sales to third parties and sales or transfers to the company's other operations. (Sales or transfers to other operations should be reported separately, however.) Revenues should not include production or severance taxes, royalty payments, and net profits disbursements.

b. *Production (lifting) costs.* Production costs include, labor, fuel, supplies, repairs, property taxes, and insurance incurred to operate producing wells. They also include production and severance taxes.

c. *Exploration expenses.*

d. *Depreciation, depletion, and amortization.*

e. *Income tax expense.* Income taxes should be based on statutory tax rates applied to revenue less production costs, exploration expenses, depreciation, depletion, and amortization. It should include all the deductions, credits, and allowances related to oil and gas producing activities that are reflected in the company's consolidated income tax expense for the period.

f. *Results of operations of oil and gas producing activities (excluding corporate overhead and interest costs).* Some expenses incurred by a company's corporate office may be oil and gas operating expenses rather than general corporate overhead. Thus, the nature of the expense, not the location of its incurrence, should dictate whether it is included in results of operations of oil and gas producing activities.

64.508   The company should not include its share of equity method investees' oil and gas activities in its results of operations information. Instead, the company should separately disclose its share of equity method investees' results of operations of oil and gas producing activities, in the aggregate and for each geographic area for which reserve quantities are disclosed. (SFAS 69, par. 29)

> **Practical Consideration.** The preceding information need not be presented as supplementary information if it can be found elsewhere in the financial statements. For example, the information would already be disclosed in the income statement and would not need to be presented separately if substantially all of the company's business activities consist of oil and gas producing activities and those activities are located in substantially one geographic area. Similarly, if oil and gas producing activities comprise a segment and are located in substantially one geographic area, the required information may already be disclosed in the information about business segments.

STANDARDIZED MEASURE OF DISCOUNTED FUTURE NET CASH FLOWS RELATED TO PROVED OIL AND GAS RESERVE QUANTITIES

64.509   Publicly traded companies must disclose the following information, in the aggregate and for each geographic area for which reserve quantities are disclosed:

a. *Future cash inflows.* Future cash inflows are computed by applying year-end prices to year-end quantities of proved reserves. Future price changes should be considered only if they are provided by contracts existing at year end. (SFAS 69, par. 30)

b. *Future development and production costs.* The costs are determined by estimating, based on year-end costs and existing

economic conditions, the expenses that will be incurred to produce the company's proved oil and gas reserves at the end of the
year. Estimated development costs should be presented separately if they are significant. (SFAS 69, par. 30)

c. *Future income tax expense.* Future income tax expense is computed by applying appropriate year-end statutory tax rates to
future pretax net cash flows related to oil and gas reserves, less
the tax basis of the properties involved. Changes in future tax
rates should be considered based on enacted tax laws at the end
of the year. (SFAS 69, par. 30)

d. *Future net cash flows.* Future net cash flows are determined by
subtracting future development and production costs and future
income tax expense from future cash inflows. (SFAS 69, par. 30)

e. *Discount.* A discount rate of 10 percent per year should be
applied to future net cash flows. (SFAS 69, par. 30)

f. *Standardized measure of discounted future net cash flows.* This
amount is computed by subtracting the computed discount from
future net cash flows. (SFAS 69, par. 30)

g. *Aggregate change during the year in the standardized measure
of discounted future net cash flows.* Sources of the change that
should be separately presented (if significant) include (1) net
change in sales prices and production costs related to future production, (2) changes in estimated future development costs,
(3) sales and transfers of oil and gas produced during the period,
(4) net change due to extensions, discoveries, and improved
recovery techniques, (5) net change due to purchases and sales
of minerals in place, (6) net change due to revisions of estimated
reserve quantities, (7) previously estimated production costs that
were incurred during the period, (8) accretion of discount, and
(9) net change in income taxes. When computing those amounts,
the effects of price and cost changes should be considered
before the effects of changes in quantities. (In other words, the
changes in quantities should be stated at year-end prices and
costs.) (SFAS 69, par. 33)

64.510   When disclosing the preceding information, the following should be
considered:

- If a significant portion of the consolidated standardized measure of future net cash flows relates to a subsidiary in which there is a significant minority interest, that fact and the approximate portion should be disclosed. (SFAS 69, par. 31)

- The standardized measure of future net cash flows should not include the company's share of the standardized measure of future net cash flows of equity method investees. The company's share of equity method investees' standardized measure of net future cash flows should be separately disclosed, however, in the aggregate and for each geographic areas for which reserve quantities are disclosed. (SFAS 69, par. 32)

AUTHORITATIVE LITERATURE AND RELATED TOPICS

AUTHORITATIVE LITERATURE

SFAS No. 19, *Financial Accounting and Reporting by Oil and Gas Producing Companies*

SFAS No. 25, *Suspension of Certain Accounting Requirements for Oil and Gas Producing Companies*

SFAS No. 69, *Disclosures about Oil and Gas Producing Activities*

FASB Interpretation No. 33, *Applying FASB Statement No. 34 to Oil and Gas Producing Operations Accounted for by the Full Cost Method*

FASB Interpretation No. 36, *Accounting for Exploratory Wells in Progress at the End of a Period*

RELATED PRONOUNCEMENTS

AICPA Audit and Accounting Guide, *Audits of Entities with Oil and Gas Producing Activities*

EITF Issue No. 90-22, *Accounting for Gas-Balancing Arrangements*

RELATED TOPICS

Chapter 24—Income Taxes
Chapter 27—Interest: Capitalized
Chapter 33—Long-lived Assets, Depreciation, and Impairment

RECORD AND MUSIC INDUSTRY

Table of Contents

RECORD AND MUSIC INDUSTRY

OVERVIEW

65.100   The owner of a record master or music copyright may license the right to distribute records or music. If the terms of the license agreement are such that (a) the agreement is, in effect, an outright sale of rights and (b) collection of the license fee is reasonably assured, the licensor should recognize the fee as revenue. Also, a licensor should record any minimum guarantee received in advance as a liability and recognize it as revenue as it is earned. Similarly, the licensee should report the minimum guarantee paid as an asset and amortize it to expense according to the terms of the license agreement.

65.101   As a general rule, royalties earned by artists should be adjusted for anticipated returns and charged to expense in the period in which related record sales occur. In addition, the cost of record masters generally should be charged to expense over the estimated life of the recorded performance.

ACCOUNTING REQUIREMENTS

65.200   Generally accepted accounting principles establish accounting and reporting standards for licensors and licensees in the record and music industry. GAAP specifically addresses accounting and reporting for license revenues and expenses, artist compensation costs, and the costs of record masters.

LICENSOR ACCOUNTING

Revenues

65.201   **License Agreements.** The owner (licensor) of a record master or music copyright may realize substantial revenues by entering into license agreements. A license agreement grants the licensee the right to sell or distribute records or music for a fixed fee or for a fee based on record or music sales. In some cases, a license agreement is, in effect, an outright sale of rights. Generally, a sale has occurred and revenue from a license agreement may be recognized in full (assuming the fee's collectibility is reasonably assured) when the licensor has:

- signed a noncancelable contract,

- agreed to a fixed fee,

- delivered the rights to the licensee and the licensee may exercise them without restriction, and

- met all significant obligations to furnish music or records. (SFAS 50, par. 7)

65.202   Fees under the license agreement that are not fixed in amount should not be recognized as revenue until they can be reasonably estimated or the licence agreement expires. (SFAS 50, par. 9)

65.203   **Minimum Guarantees.** Often, a licensee will pay the licensor a minimum guarantee in advance for the right to sell or distribute the records or music. The licensor should initially report a minimum guarantee as a liability and recognize it as revenue as it is earned under the agreement. If the amount earned cannot be determined, however, the licensor should recognize the minimum guarantee as revenue equally over the remaining term of the license agreement. (SFAS 50, par. 8)

Artist Compensation Cost

65.204   Royalties earned by artists should be adjusted for anticipated returns and charged to expense in the period in which related record sales occur. Often, contracts with artists require record companies to pay nonrefundable royalties before related record sales occur. In such cases, a record company should record the advance royalties as follows:

a. The record company should record the advance royalty payment as an asset if the artist's past performance and current popularity indicate that the advance royalties will be recovered from future royalties to be earned by the artist. The asset should be appropriately classified as current and noncurrent and charged to expense as the artist earns royalties. Any portion of the advance that subsequently does not appear to be fully recoverable from the artist's future royalties should be charged to expense in the period the loss becomes evident.

b. The record company should charge the advance royalty payment to current period expense if the artist's past performance and current popularity do not indicate that future earned royalties will be sufficient to cover the advance royalty (for example, advance royalties paid to new artists, previously unsuccessful artists, or previously successful artists that are not currently popular). (SFAS 50, par. 10)

Cost of Record Masters

65.205   Under many recording contracts, the record company bears a portion of the costs of record masters and recovers a portion of the costs from the artist out of royalties the artist earns. In such cases, the cost of record masters should be accounted for as follows:

    a. The record company's portion of the cost of a record master should be reported as an asset if the past performance and current popularity of the artist provide a sound basis for recovering the cost from future sales. Otherwise, the cost should be charged to expense. Any amount recognized as an asset should be amortized to expense over the estimated life of the recorded performance.

    b. The record company should account for the portion of the record master cost recoverable from the artist's royalties as an advance royalty following the guidance in Paragraph 65.204. (SFAS 50, paras. 11–12)

LICENSEE ACCOUNTING

65.206   As discussed in Paragraph 65.203, a licensee will sometimes pay the licensor a minimum guarantee in advance for the right to sell or distribute the records or music. A licensee should report such minimum guarantees as assets and subsequently charge them to expense in accordance with the terms of the license agreement. Any portion of the guarantees that subsequently does not appear to be recoverable should be charged to expense in the period that determination is made. (SFAS 50, par. 15)

65.207   Other fees may be required by the license agreement. Such fees that are not fixed in amount before the agreement expires should be estimated and accrued on a license-by-license basis. (SFAS 50, par. 15)

DISCLOSURE REQUIREMENTS

65.500 A record company should disclose the following information in its financial statements (or notes to the financial statements):

    • Commitments for artist advances that are payable in future years and future royalty guarantees (SFAS 50, par. 13)

- The record company's portion of the cost of record masters that is recorded as an asset (SFAS 50, par. 14)

AUTHORITATIVE LITERATURE AND RELATED TOPICS

AUTHORITATIVE LITERATURE

SFAS No. 50, *Financial Reporting in the Record and Music Industry*

RELATED TOPICS

Chapter 48—Revenue Recognition

REGULATED OPERATIONS

Table of Contents

REGULATED OPERATIONS

OVERVIEW

66.100   Public utility companies and other entities are sometimes regulated by independent third parties or governing boards. The regulators set the rates that those entities may charge customers so that sufficient revenue is generated to cover certain allowable costs.

66.101   Because allowable costs may include costs incurred in the current period, prior periods or costs expected to be incurred in future periods, revenues frequently recover costs before or after the costs have been incurred. Consequently, a regulated entity should—

   a. capitalize costs incurred if it is probable that future revenue will be provided to recover the costs.

   b. record a liability for revenue that provides recovery of expected future costs.

Capitalized costs should be charged to expense when it is no longer probable that they will be recovered by future revenue. Revenue recorded as a liability should be recognized in income as related costs are incurred.

66.102   GAAP for regulated entities also includes the following requirements:

   a. A regulator may require an entity to determine the cost of financing construction as if it were financed by borrowings and equity. Thus, for rate-making purposes, an entity must capitalize imputed interest and a designated cost of equity and include those amounts in the asset's depreciable cost. In such cases, the entity generally should also capitalize those amounts in its GAAP basis financial statements rather than capitalize interest in accordance with SFAS No. 34, *Capitalization of Interest Cost.*

   b. When it is probable that an operating asset or asset under construction will be abandoned, a regulated entity should reduce the cost of the asset to the present value of the future revenues that are expected to be allowed as a result of the abandonment. Costs in excess of the present value of the future revenues should

66.102

be recognized as a loss. Similarly, costs of a recently completed plant that will be disallowed for rate-making purposes should be recognized as a loss.

c. Allowable costs deferred for future recovery under a phase-in plan related to plants completed before January 1, 1988 (and plants on which substantial physical construction had occurred before that date) should be capitalized if certain criteria are met.

66.103   If an entity determines that it no longer has regulated operations, it should discontinue applying GAAP for regulated entities. The effects of any regulator's actions that had been previously recognized as assets and liabilities for regulated entities, but that would not have been recognized for entities in general, should be removed from the balance sheet. Plant, equipment, and inventory should not be adjusted, however, unless those assets are impaired. The net effect of the adjustments that result from the discontinuation should be reported in the current period income statement as an extraordinary Item.

ACCOUNTING REQUIREMENTS

66.200   The guidelines in this chapter apply to most public utilities and other enterprises that have regulated operations and meet all of the following criteria: (SFAS 71, par. 5)

- An independent, third-party regulator, or the enterprise's own appropriately empowered governing board, establishes or approves the enterprise's rates for regulated services or products provided to its customers.

- The regulated rates are designed to recover the specific enterprise's costs of providing the regulated services or products.

- In view of the demand for the regulated services or products and the level of competition, rates set at levels sufficient to recover the enterprise's costs can be charged to and collected from customers.

Practical Consideration. This chapter discusses the GAAP requirements that apply to a regulated entity's external, general purpose financial statements. Its guidance should be applied only to the portion of an entity's operations that are regulated. Regulated entities should also follow GAAP for entities in general to the extent it does not conflict with the guidance discussed in this chapter.

Practical Consideration (Continued).

Regulators may impose other accounting or financial statement presentation requirements that are not discussed in this chapter. For example, a regulator may require an entity to capitalize certain costs that would normally be charged to expense under GAAP. An entity may prepare financial statements following such regulatory requirements, but the financial statements should not be described as being in conformity with generally accepted accounting principles.

66.201   In addition to providing general guidance on financial reporting for regulated enterprises, GAAP also provides guidance for regulated enterprises on accounting for plant abandonments, cost disallowances for recently completed plants, phase-in plans, and discontinuance of regulated operations.

ACCOUNTING FOR REGULATED OPERATIONS IN GENERAL

66.202   Regulators sometimes determine allowable costs (i.e., the costs that should be recovered by revenue) and allow the enterprise to charge rates that will produce revenue approximately equal to those costs. In some cases, regulators include costs incurred in prior periods or costs expected to be incurred in future periods in allowable costs. Thus, revenues may recover costs before or after the costs are actually incurred. As discussed in the following paragraphs, costs that would otherwise be charged to expense generally should be capitalized if it is probable that future revenue will be provided to recover the costs. The portion of current revenue that provides for recovery of expected future costs should be recorded as a liability and recognized in income as the costs are incurred. (SFAS 71, paras. 1–3)

Capitalizing Costs

66.203   A regulated enterprise should capitalize all or part of an incurred cost that would otherwise be charged to expense if both of the following criteria are met:

a. It is probable that future revenue at least equal to the capitalized cost will result from including that cost in allowable costs for rate-making purposes.

b. Based on available evidence, future revenue will provide for recovery of previously incurred costs rather than expected levels of similar future costs. (If the future revenue will be provided by an automatic rate-adjustment clause, the regulator must clearly have intended the future revenue to provide for the recovery of previously incurred costs.) (SFAS 71, par. 9)

The incurred cost should be charged to earnings when it no longer meets the above criteria. (SFAS 121, par. 32)

66.204   A regulator's rate actions can reduce or eliminate the value of an incurred cost that has been capitalized as an asset. If the regulator excludes all or part of the cost from allowable costs, the carrying amount of any related asset should be reduced to the extent of the excluded cost. A new asset should be recognized if the regulator subsequently allows costs previously excluded from allowable costs to be recovered through rates. (SFAS 121, par. 32)

Recording Liabilities

66.205   A regulator's rate actions can impose a liability on a regulated enterprise by requiring customer refunds or reducing future rates. The regulated enterprise should account for such liabilities as follows:

- A regulator may require refunds to customers. A regulated enterprise should record refunds that are both probable and reasonably estimable as liabilities and as expenses or reductions of revenue.

- A regulator may allow current rates to recover expected future costs and require future rates to be reduced by the amounts of the expected future costs if those costs are not incurred. Until the regulated enterprise incurs the specified costs, revenues collected for such costs should not be recognized. Instead, the revenues should be recorded as liabilities and recognized as the associated costs are incurred.

66.206   A regulator may require an enterprise to pass a gain or reduction of net allowable costs through to customers over future periods. For rate-making purposes, that might be accomplished by amortizing the gain or cost reduction over those future periods and reducing rates so that revenue will be reduced by approximately the amortization amount. If a gain or cost reduction is amortized over future periods for rate-making purposes, the regulated enterprise should not recognize the gain or cost reduction in current period income. Instead, it should record the gain or cost reduction as a liability for expected future customer rate reductions. (SFAS 71, par. 11)

ALLOWANCE FOR FUNDS USED DURING CONSTRUCTION

66.207   A regulator sometimes requires an enterprise to capitalize an "allowance for funds used during construction" as part of the acquisition cost of plant and equipment. The regulator may require the enterprise to determine the cost of financing construction as if it were financed partially by borrowings and partially by equity. Consequently, the enterprise must capitalize a computed interest cost and a designated cost of equity funds and correspondingly increase current period net income. After construction is complete, the enterprise must use the resulting capitalized cost as the basis for depreciation and unrecovered investment costs for rate-making purposes. In such cases, the cost of financing construction for rate-making purposes should be used for financial reporting purposes rather than interest capitalized in accordance with SFAS No. 34, *Capitalization of Interest Cost.* (SFAS 71, par. 15) (The cost should be capitalized for financial reporting purposes only if its subsequent inclusion in allowable costs for rate-making purposes is probable, however.) (SFAS 90, par. 9) The amount capitalized should be reflected in the enterprise's income statement as an item of other income, a reduction of interest expense, or both. (SFAS 71, par. 15)

SALES TO AFFILIATES

66.208   An enterprise should not eliminate profit on sales to regulated affiliates in its general-purpose financial statements if both of the following criteria are met:

- The sales price is reasonable.

- It is probable that, through the rate-making process, future revenue approximating the sales price will result from the regulated affiliate's use of the products.

The enterprise usually should consider the sales price to be reasonable if the price is accepted or not challenged by the regulator that governs the regulated affiliate. (SFAS 71, paras. 16–17)

INCOME TAXES

66.209   Regulated enterprises are not exempt from the requirements of SFAS No. 109, *Accounting for Income Taxes.* SFAS No. 109 specifically requires regulated enterprises to recognize a deferred tax liability for (a) tax benefits that flow through to customers when temporary differences originate and (b) the equity component of the allowance for funds used during construction. If, as a result of a regulator's action, it is probable that the related future increase in taxes payable will be recovered from customers through future rates, an asset should be recognized for that probable future revenue. That asset also is a temporary difference for which deferred taxes should be recognized. (SFAS 109, par. 29)

ABANDONMENTS AND DISALLOWANCES OF PLANT COSTS

Abandonments

66.210   When it becomes probable that an operating asset or an asset under construction will be abandoned, the enterprise should remove the cost of that asset from construction work-in-process or plant-in-service. The enterprise should determine whether the regulator is likely to provide recovery of any allowed cost with full, partial, or no return on investment between the time abandonment becomes probable and recovery is completed.

66.211   **Full Return Is Likely.** If full return on investment is likely to be provided between the time abandonment becomes probable and recovery is completed, the enterprise should recognize any probable and reasonably estimable disallowed costs on the abandoned plant as a loss and correspondingly reduce the carrying amount of the recorded asset. The remaining cost of the abandoned plant should be reported as a separate new asset (SFAS 90, par. 3) and, during the period between the date when the new asset is recognized and recovery begins—

   a. the new asset's carrying amount should be increased by accruing a carrying charge. (A rate equal to the allowed overall cost of capital in the jurisdiction in which recovery is expected should be used to accrue the carrying charge.) (SFAS 90, par. 5)

   b. the new asset should be amortized in the same manner as that used for rate-making purposes. (SFAS 90, par. 6)

   c. the recorded amount of the new asset should be adjusted as necessary if new information indicates that the estimates used to record the asset have changed. (Any adjustment should be recognized in current period income as a loss or gain.) (SFAS 90, par. 4)

66.212   **Partial or No Return Is Likely.** If partial or no return on investment is likely to be provided between the time when abandonment becomes probable and recovery is completed—

   a. the enterprise should recognize any probable and reasonably estimable disallowed costs of the abandoned plant as a loss.

   b. the present value of the future revenues expected to recover the allowable cost of the abandoned plant and any return on investment should be reported as a separate new asset.

> **Practical Consideration.** When determining the present value of expected future revenues, the discount rate used should be the rate the entity would have to pay to borrow an equivalent amount for the expected recovery period. In addition, present value calculations should consider the period before recovery is expected and the period over which recovery is expected. If the estimate of either period is a range, the most likely period within the range should be used. If no estimate within the range is better than another, the minimum period within the range should be used.

    c. any excess of the remaining cost of the abandoned plant over that present value should be recognized as a loss. (SFAS 90, par. 3)

    d. during the period between the dates when the new asset is recognized and when recovery begins, the new asset's carrying amount should be increased by accruing a carrying charge. (The rate that was used to compute the present value should be used to accrue the carrying charge.) (SFAS 90, par. 5)

    e. the new asset should be amortized to produce a constant return on the unamortized investment in the new asset that is equal to the rate at which the expected revenues were discounted. (SFAS 90, par. 6)

    f. the recorded amount of the new asset should be adjusted as necessary if new information indicates that the estimates used to record the asset have changed. (Any adjustment should be recognized in current period income as a loss or gain.) (SFAS 90, par. 4)

66.213 Income Taxes. When an enterprise recognizes a loss on abandonment, the deferred income tax liabilities related to the remaining asset should be (a) the amount of income taxes that will be payable in future years as a result of recovering the recorded amount of the remaining asset and (b) any additional income taxes that will result from recovery of a separate asset recognized for the expected future revenue to be provided in rates by the regulator when the related income taxes become payable. (FTB 87-2, par. 14)

66.214   When a regulator allows recovery of cost without return on investment, the enterprise usually should compute the net loss on abandonment by discounting the after-tax future revenues expected to be allowed by the regulator at an after-tax incremental borrowing rate and compare the result to the recorded net investment in the abandoned plant (the recorded investment reduced by allocable deferred income tax amounts). If that discounted present value is less than the recorded net investment, a net loss should be recognized.

However, losses are not allowed to be reported on a net-of-tax basis. As a result, the enterprise should "gross up" the loss for financial reporting purposes. (FTB 87-2, par. 17)

Disallowances of Costs of Recently Completed Plants

66.215　A disallowance is a rate-making action that prevents the regulated enterprise from recovering either some amount of its investment or some amount of return on its investment. When it becomes probable that part of the cost of a recently completed plant will be disallowed for rate-making purposes and a reasonable estimate of the disallowed cost can be made, the enterprise should deduct the estimated disallowed cost from the reported cost of the plant and recognize the amount as a loss. (SFAS 90, par. 7)

ACCOUNTING FOR PHASE-IN PLANS

66.216　A phase-in plan is a rate-making method intended to moderate a sudden increase in rates while providing the regulated enterprise with recovery of its investment and a return on that investment during the recovery period. Phase-in plans typically are used by public utility regulators to reduce the impact of "rate spikes" by spreading the allowable costs of newly completed utility plants over future periods. A phase-in plan meets all of the following criteria:

a. The regulator adopts the plan in connection with a major, newly completed plant of the regulated enterprise or of one of its suppliers, or a major plant scheduled for completion in the near future.

b. The plan defers the rates intended to recover allowable costs beyond the period in which the allowable costs would be charged to expense under GAAP applicable to enterprises in general.

c. The plan defers the rates intended to recover allowable costs beyond the period in which the rates would have been ordered under the rate-making methods routinely used by the regulator prior to 1982 for similar allowable costs of the enterprise. (SFAS 92, par. 3)

66.217　If a regulator orders a phase-in plan in connection with a plant on which substantial physical construction was not performed before January 1, 1988, the regulated enterprise cannot capitalize, for financial reporting purposes, any of the allowable costs that the regulator deferred for future recovery for rate-making purposes. (SFAS 92, par. 4) Similarly, if the plant was completed or if substantial physical construction was performed prior to January 1, 1988, allowable costs deferred for future recovery under a phase-in plan should not be capitalized for financial reporting unless each of the following four criteria is met: (SFAS 92, par. 5)

    a. The regulator has agreed to the phase-in plan.

    b. The plan specifies when recovery will occur.

    c. All allowable costs deferred under the plan are scheduled for recovery within 10 years of the date when deferrals begin.

    d. The percentage increase in rates scheduled for each future year under the plan is not greater than the percentage increase in rates scheduled for each immediately preceding year.

66.218   If an existing phase-in plan is modified (or replaced or supplemented by a new plan), the preceding criteria should be applied to the combined plans. The date deferrals begin (item c.) is the date of the earliest deferral under either plan and the final recovery date is the date all deferred amounts under the plans are recovered. (SFAS 92, par. 6)

Interrelationship of Phase-in Plans and Disallowances

66.219   If a rate-making method that meets the criteria for a phase-in plan includes an indirect disallowance of plant costs (such as failing to provide the enterprise a return on the deferred costs), the disallowance should be accounted for as described in Paragraph 66.215. (SFAS 92, par. 7)

Financial Statement Classification

66.220   Regulated enterprises should report cumulative amounts capitalized under phase-in plans as a separate asset in the balance sheet. Amounts capitalized during the period should not be shown as a reduction of a particular expense. Rather, the net amount capitalized during the period (or the net amount of previously capitalized allowable costs recovered during the period) should be reported as a separate item of other income or expense in the income statement. (SFAS 92, par. 10)

ALLOWANCE FOR EARNINGS ON SHAREHOLDERS' INVESTMENT

66.221   As described in Paragraph 66.207, regulators sometimes require the capitalization of an "allowance for funds used during construction." One component of that allowance is the designated cost of equity funds, also referred to as an "allowance for earnings on shareholders' investment." If an allowance for earnings on shareholders' investment is capitalized for rate-making purposes other than during construction or as part of a phase-in plan, the amount capitalized for rate-making purposes should not be capitalized for financial reporting. (SFAS 92, par. 9)

DISCONTINUATION OF REGULATED OPERATIONS

66.222   When an enterprise determines that all or a portion of its regulated operations no longer meet the criteria in Paragraph 66.200, the enterprise should discontinue applying GAAP for regulated enterprises to that portion of its operations. For financial reporting purposes, an enterprise that discontinues accounting for all or part of its operations as a regulated enterprise should elimi-nate from its balance sheet the effects of any regulator's actions that had been previously recognized as assets and liabilities for regulated enterprises, but that would not have been recognized as assets and liabilities by enterprises in general. The carrying amounts of plant, equipment, and inventory measured and reported according to GAAP for regulated enterprises should not be adjusted unless those assets are impaired, however. In that event, the carrying amounts of the assets should be reduced to reflect the impairment. Whether those assets have been impaired should be judged in the same manner as for enterprises in general. (See Chapter 33.) The enterprise should include the net effect of the adjustments required for discontinuation (including any adjustment related to impaired assets) in income of the period in which the discontinuation occurs and classify the net effect as an extraordinary item. (SFAS 101, paras. 5–6)

SALE-LEASEBACK TRANSACTIONS

66.223   Accounting for a regulated entity's sale-leaseback transactions in accordance with GAAP (see Chapter 31) may result in income and expenses being recognized in different periods for financial reporting and rate-making purposes. Timing differences that relate to phase-in plans should be accounted for following the guidance on phase-in plans in Paragraphs 66.216–.220. (SFAS 98, par. 14) Timing differences not related to phase-in plans should be accounted for as follows:

    a. If the sale-leaseback transaction is accounted for under the deposit method, but the sale is recognized for rate making pur-poses, the asset's amortization should be adjusted so that it equals the total of the rental expense and the gain or loss allow-able for rate-making purposes. (SFAS 98, par 15)

    b. If the sale-leaseback transaction is accounted for as a financing and the sale is recognized for rate-making purposes, interest imputed for the financing and the asset's amortization should be adjusted so that their total equals total rent expense and gain or loss allowable for rate-making purposes. (SFAS 98, par. 15)

c. An asset or liability should be recorded for the difference between the income and expense amounts recognized under the deposit method or financing method and amounts recognized for rate-making purposes if the criteria discussed in Paragraphs 66.203–.206 are met. (SFAS 98, par. 16)

DISCLOSURE REQUIREMENTS

66.500   Like other entities, a regulated entity should disclose the significant accounting policies used to prepare its financial statements. In addition, a regulated entity must disclose the following:

a. *Refunds.* If refunds and related revenues are recognized in different periods and the effect of the refunds on net income is material, a regulated entity must disclose (1) the effect of the refunds on net income and (2) the year in which the related revenue was recognized. The effect may be presented, net of taxes, as a separate line item in the income statement, but it should not be presented as an extraordinary item. (SFAS 71, par. 19)

b. *Recovery that does not provide a return on investment.* A regulator may provide for recovery of a cost, but not for a related return on investment during the recovery period. For example, amortization of a capitalized cost may be included in allowable costs for rate-making purposes but the unamortized (and unrecovered) cost is not. If recovery of a major cost does not provide for a return on investment during the recovery period, a regulated entity must disclose the asset's unamortized cost and remaining recovery period. (SFAS 71, par. 20)

c. *Phase-in plans.* A regulated entity should disclose the terms of any phase-in plan in effect during the year or ordered for future years. In addition, the net amount allowable costs deferred for future recovery for rate-making purposes at the balance sheet (and the net change in the deferral during the year) should be disclosed. (SFAS 92, par. 11)

d. *Allowance for earnings on shareholders' investment.* A regulated entity must disclose the nature and amount of any allowance for earnings on shareholders' investment that is capitalized for rate-making purposes but not for financial reporting.

e. *Discontinuance of regulated operations.* If the entity is no longer required to apply the specialized accounting requirements for regulated operations, it should disclose, in the period the discontinuance occurs, (1) the reasons the specialized requirements no longer apply and (2) the identity of the portion of its operations to which the specialized requirements are no longer being applied.

AUTHORITATIVE LITERATURE AND RELATED TOPICS

AUTHORITATIVE LITERATURE

SFAS No. 71, *Accounting for the Effects of Certain Types of Regulation*
SFAS No. 90, *Regulated Enterprises—Accounting for Abandonments and Disallowances of Plant Costs*
SFAS No. 92, *Regulated Enterprises—Accounting for Phase-in Plans*
SFAS No. 98, *Accounting for Leases:*
- *Sale-Leaseback Transactions Involving Real Estate*
- *Sales-Type Leases of Real Estate*
- *Definition of the Lease Term*
- *Initial Direct Costs of Direct Financing Leases*

SFAS No. 101, *Regulated Enterprises—Accounting for the Discontinuation of Application of FASB Statement No. 71*
SFAS No. 109, *Accounting for Income Taxes*
SFAS No. 121, *Accounting for the Impairment of Long-Lived Assets and for Long-Lived Assets to Be Disposed of*
FASB Technical Bulletin 87-2, *Computation of a Loss on an Abandonment*

RELATED PRONOUNCEMENTS

EITF Issue No. 92-7, *Accounting by Rate-Regulated Utilities for the Effects of Certain Alternative Revenue Programs*
EITF Issue No. 92-12, *Accounting for OPEB Costs by Rate-Regulated Enterprises*
EITF Issue No. 93-4, *Accounting for Regulatory Assets*
EITF Issue No. 96-17, *Revenue Recognition under Long-Term Power Sales Contracts That Contain both Fixed and Variable Pricing Terms*
EITF Issue No. 97-4, *Deregulation of Electricity—Issues Related to the Application of FASB Statement No. 71 and No. 101*

RELATED TOPICS

Chapter 24—Income Taxes
Chapter 33—Long-lived Assets, Depreciation, and Impairment

66.500

TITLE PLANT

Table of Contents

TITLE PLANT

OVERVIEW

67.100   Direct costs to construct or acquire a title plant should be capitalized until the plant can be used to perform title searches. Capitalized costs should not be depreciated. Costs to maintain the title plant or to perform title searches should be expensed when incurred.

ACCOUNTING REQUIREMENTS

67.200   A title plant is a historical record of all ownership, encumbrances, and other matters affecting title to land in a particular geographic area. Title plants are updated frequently by adding information related to the current title status of particular parcels of real estate. Title insurance companies (underwriters), title abstract companies, title agents, and other companies use a title plant in their operations. The following paragraphs discuss the accounting issues related to maintaining a title plant.

CAPITALIZATION OF TITLE PLANT

67.201   A title plant may be constructed by summarizing and indexing information from the public records of a specific geographic area for a specific period of time. (For example, a title plant might cover ownership information about a particular city or county for the period January 1, 1945 to the present.) Alternatively, a company could purchase a copy of, an undivided interest in, or exclusive ownership of an existing title plant. Regardless, the direct costs incurred to construct or otherwise acquire a title plant should be capitalized until the plant can be used to perform title searches. (SFAS 61, paras. 3–5)

> **Practical Consideration.** A company may construct or acquire a title plant covering the same geographic area as its existing title plant but for an earlier period of time (referred to as an "antecedent plant" or "backplant"). For example, a company whose title plant covers the period January 1, 1945 to the present might acquire a title plant covering the period January 1, 1900 to December 31, 1944. In such cases, the same capitalization rules apply. That is, the direct, identifiable costs of a backplant should be capitalized until the plant can be used to perform title searches.

67.202   A title plant typically has an indefinite estimated useful life. Thus, a plant's capitalized costs should not be depreciated or charged to income unless circumstances indicate that its carrying amount has been impaired. The following circumstances may indicate impairment: (SFAS 61, par. 6 and SFAS 121, par. 9)

- Changes in legal requirements or statutory practices

- Effects of obsolescence, demand, and other economic factors

- Actions of competitors and others that may affect competitive advantages

- Failure to maintain the title plant properly on a current basis

- Abandonment of the title plant or other circumstances that indicate obsolescence

The above circumstances indicate that the carrying amount of the capitalized costs may not be recoverable, and the impairment provisions discussed in Chapter 33 should be followed.

TITLE PLANT MAINTENANCE AND TITLE SEARCHES

67.203   Costs incurred to maintain a title plant and perform title searches should be expensed as incurred. Maintaining a title plant involves the frequent updating of records either to add information about sales or transfers of real estate, or to document the addition or release of liens and other encumbrances. A title search involves reviewing title plant records to determine whether any defects in or liens against an owner's title to a property exist. (SFAS 61, par. 7)

STORAGE AND RETRIEVAL

67.204   After a title plant is operational, its information may be converted from one storage and retrieval system to another. For example, a company may convert from a manual, index card-based system to a computerized system. Costs to convert title plant information from one storage and retrieval system to another or to modify or modernize the storage and retrieval system should not be capitalized as part of the title plant. The costs may be capitalized separately, however, and charged to expense in a systematic and rational manner. (SFAS 61, par. 8)

SALE OF TITLE PLANT

67.205   The sale of a title plant should be reported separately in the financial statements as follows:

a. A company that sells its title plant and relinquishes all rights to its future use should report a gain or loss equal to the amount received less the adjusted cost of the title plant.

b. A company that sells an undivided ownership interest in its title plant should report a gain or loss equal to the amount received less a pro rata portion of the adjusted cost of the title plant.

c. A company that sells a copy of its title plant or the right to use it should report a gain equal to the amount received. Ordinarily, no costs should be allocated to the sale unless the value of the title plant decreases below its adjusted cost as a result of the sale.

DISCLOSURE REQUIREMENTS

67.500   There are no disclosure requirements unique to title plants. However, the authors believe many of the disclosures related to other assets are relevant to title plants. For example, if costs incurred to convert title plant information from one storage and retrieval system to another are separately capitalized and amortized (see Paragraph 67.204), the amortization period and method generally should be disclosed. In addition, if circumstances indicate that the plant's carrying amount has been impaired, the disclosures discussed in Chapter 33 should be made.

AUTHORITATIVE LITERATURE AND RELATED TOPICS

AUTHORITATIVE LITERATURE

SFAS No. 61, *Accounting for Title Plant*

RELATED TOPICS

Chapter 33—Long-lived Assets, Depreciation, and Impairment

DISCLOSURE REQUIREMENTS FOR FINANCIAL STATEMENTS OF NONPUBLIC BUSINESSES
(Long-form Disclosure Checklist)

Company: _____   Balance Sheet Date: _____

Prepared by: _____   Date: _____

Explanatory Comments

The following is a list of the primary disclosure requirements for financial statements of a *nonpublic business (organized for profit)* as required by generally accepted accounting principles. Note, this is a disclosure checklist, not a GAAP application checklist; accordingly, GAAP application and measurement questions are not included. Consideration has been given to Statements of Financial Accounting Standards (SFAS), Financial Accounting Standards Board Interpretations (FASBI), Opinions of the Accounting Principles Board (APB), Accounting Research Bulletins (ARB), FASB Technical Bulletins (FTB), AICPA Statements of Position of the Accounting Standards Division (SOP), AICPA Industry Audit and Accounting Guides, consensus positions of the FASB Emerging Issues Task Force (EITF), Practice Bulletins of the AICPA Accounting Standards Executive Committee (AcSEC PB), AICPA Accounting Interpretations (AI), and FASB "Qs and As" (QA).

An occasional reference is made to Statements on Auditing Standards (AU sections) published by the AICPA. Disclosure guidelines for certain financial statement items, e.g., subsequent events, are in auditing pronouncements. Inclusion of those disclosures without regard to whether the financial statements are audited or unaudited is generally accepted practice.

Some checklist questions do not cite a specific authoritative reference but indicate that the disclosure is "generally accepted." Most firms disclose that information even though a specific requirement in authoritative literature cannot be identified.

This checklist is divided into two parts: Part I—Most Frequent Disclosures, and Part II—Other Disclosures. See separate instructions for Part I and Part II.

Additional disclosures may be required for entities in certain industries as discussed in the Specialized Accounting and Reporting Principles section in Part 1 of this checklist. PPC publishes the following supplemental industry disclosure checklists: (The supplemental checklists are not substitutes for this checklist. They present only the disclosures unique to the particular industry. They should only be used in conjunction with this checklist.)

- **Construction contractors and homebuilders—See PPC's *Guide to Construction Contractors* or *Guide to Preparing Financial Statements.***

- **Real estate companies—See PPC's *Guide to Real Estate* or *Guide to Preparing Financial Statements.***

This checklist is current through the following pronouncements:

- SFAS No. 131 (June 1997)
- FASB TB 94-1 (April 1994)
- Consensuses reached by the EITF through its July 1997 meeting.
- FASBI No. 42 (September 1996)

- AICPA SOP 97-1 (May 1997)
- AcSEC PB No. 15 (January 1997)
- FASB Qs and As on SFAS No. 115 (November 1995)

For a list of disclosures required by subsequent pronouncements, visit PPC's home page on the World Wide Web at *http://www.ppcinfo.com.*

PART I—MOST FREQUENT DISCLOSURES

Instructions

Part I should be completed in its entirety. A block ☐ has been provided for each major disclosure caption. If the major caption is not applicable to your client, simply place a (✓) in the block. It will then not be necessary to check N/A for each question under the major caption. Otherwise, respond to each question with a (✓) in the appropriate column: (a) Yes— disclosure made; (b) No—item present but no disclosure made (any item checked "No" should be explained in the checklist or in a separate memorandum); or (c) N/A—either the item is not present or it is immaterial to the financial statements.

PART I—TABLE OF CONTENTS

BALANCE SHEET

CURRENT ASSETS

☐

1. If a classified balance sheet is used, is a total of current assets presented? (Generally accepted)

—   —   —

CASH

☐

1. Are restrictions on cash properly disclosed (SFAS No. 5, paras. 18 and 19) and are restricted amounts appropriately segregated from other cash items, showing restricted cash as a noncurrent asset if appropriate? (ARB No. 43, ch. 3A, para. 6)

—   —   —

2. Are material bank overdrafts presented as a separate caption among current liabilities? Similarly, are material dollar amounts of held checks (checks on the bank reconciliation but not released until after the balance sheet date) reclassified as accounts payable? (Generally accepted)

—   —   —

3. Are significant concentrations of credit risk arising from cash deposits in excess of federally insured limits disclosed in accordance with SFAS No. 105? (See FINANCIAL INSTRUMENTS, Question No. 3, page 22.)

—   —   —

NOTES AND ACCOUNTS RECEIVABLE

☐

1. Are all significant categories of receivables segregated from normal trade receivables, e.g., tax refunds, contract termination claims, advance payments on purchases, amounts due from officers, employees, directors, stockholders, affiliates? (ARB No. 43, ch. 1A, para. 5)

—   —   —

2. Are amounts due from affiliates or subsidiaries classified as current only if it is the entity's practice to liquidate them periodically and the current financial position of the affiliate or subsidiary warrants that treatment? (ARB No. 43, ch. 3A, para. 4)

—   —   —

3. Is the allowance for doubtful accounts disclosed? (APB No. 12, para. 3)

—   —   —

	Disclosure Made?		
	Yes	**No**	**N/A**

4. Are unearned discounts, finance charges, and imputed interest that are included in the face amount of receivables deducted from the related receivable and appropriately disclosed? (APB No. 6, para. 14, and APB No. 21, para. 16)
    — — —

5. For transfers of receivables with recourse reported as sales, do the transferor's financial statements disclose the following:

   a. The proceeds to the transferor during each period for which an income statement is presented? (Generally accepted)
    — — —
   b. The information required by SFAS No. 105? (See FINANCIAL INSTRUMENTS, Question Nos. 1–3, page 21.)
    — — —
   c. If the recourse obligation related to a transfer occurring prior to January 1, 1997 is discounted, the undiscounted amount and the interest rate used? (EITF 92-2)
    — — —

6. Are contingent liabilities associated with sold or discounted receivables disclosed (guarantees to repurchase receivables or related property)? (SFAS No. 5, para. 12)
    — — —

7. Are significant concentrations of credit risk arising from receivables disclosed in accordance with SFAS No. 105? (See FINANCIAL INSTRUMENTS, Question No. 3, page 22.)
    — — —

8. If impairment of loans has been recognized, have the disclosures required by SFAS No. 114, as amended by SFAS No. 118, been made? (See TROUBLED DEBT RESTRUCTURINGS—CREDITORS, Question No. 2, page 61.)
    — — —

9. Have the necessary fair value disclosures been made? (See FINANCIAL INSTRUMENTS, Question Nos. 4–7, page 22.)
    — — —

MARKETABLE DEBT AND EQUITY SECURITIES

1. Are separate disclosures of the following made for all major security types classified as available for sale or classified as held to maturity as of each date for which a balance sheet is presented: (SFAS No. 115, para. 19)

   a. Aggregate fair value?
    — — —
   b. Gross unrealized holding gains and losses?
    — — —
   c. Amortized cost basis?
    — — —

[Financial institutions should disclose the preceding information for the following types of securities: (a) equity securities, (b) debt securities issued by the U.S. Treasury and other U.S. government corporations and agencies, (c) debt securities issued by U.S. states and political subdivisions of the states, (d) debt securities issued by foreign governments, (e) corporate debt securities, (f) mortgage-backed securities, and (g) other debt securities.]

2. For each category of securities, are the amounts reported as cash equivalents in the balance sheet and statement of cash flows disclosed? (SFAS No. 115, para. 117)   — — —

3. Are separate disclosures of the following made for all investments in debt securities classified as available for sale or as held to maturity: (SFAS No. 115, para. 20)

   a. Information about the contractual maturities as of the most recent balance sheet presented (disclosure can be by appropriate groups)?   — — —
   b. Method used to allocate securities into maturity groups, if necessary?   — — —

   (Financial institutions should disclose the fair value and amortized cost of the investments based on at least four maturity groupings— within one year, after one year through five years, after five years through 10 years, and after 10 years.)

4. For each period for which an income statement is presented, have the following been disclosed: (SFAS No. 115, para. 21)

   a. Proceeds from sales of securities available for sale?   — — —
   b. Gross realized gains and losses from sales of securities available for sale?   — — —
   c. Method used to determine cost when calculating realized gains or losses (average cost or other method)?   — — —
   d. Gross gains and gross losses included in earnings from transfers of securities from the available for sale category into the trading category?   — — —
   e. Change in net unrealized holding gain or loss on securities available for sale that has been included in other comprehensive income during the period?   — — —
   f. Change in net unrealized holding gain or loss on trading securities that has been included in earnings during the period?   — — —

	Disclosure Made?		
	Yes	**No**	**N/A**

5. For each period for which an income statement is presented have the following for sales of or transfers from securities classified as held to maturity been disclosed: (SFAS No. 115, para. 22)

    a. Amortized cost of the sold or transferred security?

    b. Related realized or unrealized gain or loss?

    c. Circumstances leading to the decision to sell or transfer the security?

6. Have the following been disclosed about futures contracts accounted for as hedges: (SFAS No. 80, para. 12)

    a. Nature of the assets, liabilities, firm commitments, or anticipated transactions that are hedged with futures contracts?

    b. Method of accounting for futures contracts including a description of the events or transactions that cause changes in the contracts' values to be recognized in income?

7. Has the policy for accounting for the premium paid to acquire an option classified as held to maturity or available for sale been disclosed? (EITF 96-11)

8. If the entity enters into repurchase agreements or securities lending transactions, has its policy for requiring collateral or other security been disclosed? (SFAS No. 125, para. 17)

9. Have the necessary fair value disclosures been made? (See FINANCIAL INSTRUMENTS, Question Nos. 4–7, page 22.)

INVENTORIES

1. Is the basis for stating inventories disclosed, including the method of determining cost? (ARB No. 43, ch. 3A, para. 9, and ch. 4, paras. 4–16; and APB No. 22, para. 13)

2. Are unusual losses from write-down to market disclosed separately from cost of goods sold in the income statement? (ARB No. 43, ch. 4, paras. 14 and 17)

3. If practicable, are the major classes of inventories such as finished goods, work-in-process, materials, and supplies disclosed? (Generally accepted)

4. For conformity with IRS Regulations for entities using LIFO, are disclosures of annual income, profit, or loss on any inventory basis other than LIFO *excluded* from presentation on the face of the financial statements? (Such disclosures may be made only in the notes to the financial statements or in a supplementary schedule.) [CAUTION: Read IRS Reg. 1.472-2(e) to become familiar with LIFO conformity disclosure and reporting subtleties.]   — — —

PROPERTY AND EQUIPMENT

1. Are the following disclosed relating to depreciable assets:

   a. Balances of major classes of depreciable assets, by nature or function, at the balance sheet date? (APB No. 12, para. 5b)   — — —

   b. Accumulated depreciation, by class or in total, at the balance sheet date? (APB No. 12, para. 5c)   — — —

   c. A general description of the method or methods used in computing depreciation with respect to major classes of depreciable assets? (APB No. 12, para. 5d, and APB No. 22, para. 13)   — — —

   d. Depreciation expense for the period? (APB No. 12, para. 5a)   — — —

2. Is the carrying amount of property not a part of long-term operating assets, e.g., idle or held for investment, segregated? (Generally accepted)   — — —

3. If property and equipment is impaired or is being held for disposal, have the disclosures required by SFAS No. 121 been made? (See IMPAIRED LONG-LIVED ASSETS AND LONG-LIVED ASSETS TO BE DISPOSED OF, page 46.)   — — —

CURRENT LIABILITIES (EXCEPT INCOME TAXES)

1. If a classified balance sheet is used, is a total of current liabilities presented? (SFAS No. 6, para. 15)   — — —

2. Are significant categories segregated, e.g., accounts payable, accrued expenses, customer deposits, dividends payable, interest payable, amounts due to officers or employees? (Generally accepted)   — — —

	Disclosure Made?	
	Yes	**No**	**N/A**

3. If the entity has not accrued compensated absences because the amount cannot be reasonably estimated, has that fact been disclosed? (SFAS No. 43, paras. 6 and 7)   __   __   __

4. If real and personal property tax accruals are subject to a substantial measure of uncertainty, has the liability been disclosed as an estimate? (ARB No. 43, ch. 10A, para. 16)   __   __   __

NOTES PAYABLE, LONG-TERM DEBT, AND OTHER OBLIGATIONS   ☐

1. Are significant categories of debt identified in the balance sheet or related notes, e.g., notes to banks, mortgage notes, or related party notes? (Generally accepted)   __   __   __

2. Are interest rates, maturity dates, subordinate features (Generally accepted), pledged assets, and restrictive covenants (SFAS No. 5, paras. 18–19) disclosed?   __   __   __

3. Have the necessary fair value disclosures been made? (See FINANCIAL INSTRUMENTS, Question Nos. 4–7, page 22.)   __   __   __

4. If a note is noninterest bearing or has an unreasonable stated interest rate: (APB No. 21, para. 16)

    a. Is the discount or premium presented as a deduction from or addition to the face amount of the note?   __   __   __
    b. Does the disclosure include the effective interest rate and face amount of the note?   __   __   __
    c. Is amortization of the discount or premium reported as interest in the income statement?   __   __   __

5. Are current portions of debt obligations presented as current liabilities? (ARB No. 43, ch. 3A, paras. 7–8; SFAS No. 78, para. 5; and EITF 86-30)

    a. Does the current liability classification include obligations that, by their terms, are due on demand or will be due on demand within one year (or operating cycle, if longer) from the balance sheet date, even though liquidation may not be expected within that period?   __   __   __

	Disclosure Made?		
	Yes	**No**	**N/A**

b. Does the current liability classification include long-term obligations that are or will be callable by the creditor either because the debtor's violation of a provision of a debt agreement at the balance sheet date makes the obligation callable or because the violation, if not cured within a specified grace period, will make the obligation callable unless one of the following conditions is met:

    (1) The creditor has waived or subsequently lost the right to demand payment for more than one year from the balance sheet date?

    (2) It is probable the debtor will cure the violation within the grace period?

c. If obligations under b.(2) are classified as long-term liabilities, are the circumstances disclosed?

6. Are the combined aggregate amounts of maturities and sinking fund requirements for all long-term borrowings disclosed for each of the five years following the date of the latest balance sheet presented? (SFAS No. 47, para. 10)

7. If a short-term obligation expected to be refinanced is to be excluded from current liabilities, do disclosures include: (SFAS No. 6, para. 15; FASBI No. 8, para. 3; and FTB 79-3)

    a. General description of the financing agreement?

    b. Terms of any new obligation incurred or expected to be incurred, or equity securities issued or expected to be issued as a result of the refinancing?

8. If assets are set aside after December 30, 1996, solely for satisfying scheduled payments of a specific debt, has the nature of restrictions placed on those assets been disclosed? (SFAS No. 125, para.17)

9. Are conversion features for convertible debt appropriately accounted for and disclosed? (Generally accepted)

INCOME TAXES

1. If the entity is an S corporation, partnership, or proprietorship, do disclosures explain why income tax expense is not recorded? (Generally accepted)

Disclosure Made?

	Yes	No	N/A

2. Are the following amounts appropriately classified in the balance sheet:

    a. Taxes currently payable or refundable? (ARB No. 43, ch. 3A; and APB No. 2, para. 14)

    b. Current and noncurrent deferred tax assets and liabilities, including a valuation allowance, if any, related to deferred tax assets? (SFAS No. 109, para. 41)

3. Within each tax jurisdiction (e.g., federal, state, and local), have current deferred tax assets and liabilities been offset and presented as a single amount and noncurrent deferred tax assets and liabilities been offset and presented as a single amount? (SFAS No 109, para. 42)

4. If the entity includes more than one taxpaying component, have the net current deferred tax asset or liability and the net noncurrent deferred tax asset or liability within each tax jurisdiction been shown separately for each taxpaying component? (SFAS No. 109, para. 42)

5. Have the following components of the net deferred tax asset or liability recognized in the balance sheet been disclosed: (SFAS No. 109, para. 43)

    a. Total deferred tax liability for all taxable temporary differences?

    b. Total deferred tax asset for all deductible temporary differences, operating loss carryforwards, and tax credit carryforwards?

    c. Total valuation allowance recognized for deferred tax assets?

6. Has the amount of income tax expense or benefit allocated to the following items been disclosed for each year for which they are presented: (SFAS No. 109, para. 46; APB No. 9, para. 26; and APB No. 20, para. 20)

    a. Continuing operations?
    b. Discontinued operations?
    c. Extraordinary items?
    d. Items charged or credited directly to stockholders' equity?
    e. Prior-period adjustments?

7. Have the following significant components of income tax expense attributable to continuing operations been disclosed for each year presented either in the financial statements or notes: (SFAS No. 109, para. 45)

    a. Current tax expense or benefit?   ___   ___   ___
    b. Deferred tax expense or benefit, exclusive of the effects of other components listed in (c) through (h)?   ___   ___   ___
    c. Investment tax credits?   ___   ___   ___
    d. Government grants to the extent recognized as a reduction of income tax expense?   ___   ___   ___
    e. Benefits of operating loss carryforwards?   ___   ___   ___
    f. Tax expense that results from allocating certain tax benefits either directly to contributed capital or to reduce goodwill or other noncurrent intangible assets of an acquired entity?   ___   ___   ___
    g. Adjustments of a deferred tax asset or liability for enacted changes in tax laws or rates or a change in the entity's tax status?   ___   ___   ___
    h. Adjustments of the beginning-of-the-year balance of a valuation allowance because of a change in circumstances that causes a change in judgment about the realizability of the related deferred tax asset in future years?   ___   ___   ___

8. Has the net change during the year in the total valuation allowance been disclosed? (SFAS No. 109, para. 43)   ___   ___   ___

9. Have the types of temporary differences and carryforwards that result in significant portions of deferred tax assets (before allocation of a valuation allowance) or liabilities been disclosed? (SFAS No. 109, para. 43)   ___   ___   ___

10. Do disclosures regarding income taxes include: (SFAS No. 109, paras. 47 and 48)

    a. Amounts and expiration dates of operating loss and tax credit carryforwards for tax purposes?   ___   ___   ___
    b. Any portion of the valuation allowance for deferred tax assets for which subsequently recognized tax benefits will be allocated (1) to reduce goodwill or other noncurrent intangible assets of an acquired entity or (2) directly to contributed capital?   ___   ___   ___

	Disclosure Made?		
	Yes	**No**	**N/A**

    c.   Significant reconciling items between income tax expense attributable to continuing operations for the year and the amount of income tax expense that would result from applying domestic federal statutory rates to pretax income from continuing operations?   —   —   —

11.   Do disclosures regarding investment tax credits include: (SFAS No. 109, para. 48; APB No. 4, para. 11; and AI-APB 4, No. 2)

    a.   The accounting method used and the amounts involved?   —   —   —
    b.   Amounts of any unused investment credits and expiration dates?   —   —   —

12.   If the entity is part of a group that files a consolidated tax return, have the following amounts been disclosed in its separately issued financial statements: (SFAS No. 109, para. 49)

    a.   The aggregate amount of current and deferred tax expense for each income statement presented?   —   —   —
    b.   The amount of any tax-related balances due to or from affiliates as of the date of each balance sheet presented?   —   —   —
    c.   The principal provisions of the method by which the consolidated amount of current and deferred tax expense is allocated to members of the group?   —   —   —
    d.   The nature and effect of any changes in the method of allocating current and deferred tax expense to members of the group and in determining the related balances due to or from affiliates during each year for which the disclosures in (a) and (b) above are presented?   —   —   —

13.   Have the nature and effect of any other significant matters affecting comparability of information for all periods presented been disclosed if not otherwise apparent from the disclosures in items 3–10? (SFAS No. 109, para. 47)   —   —   —

STOCKHOLDERS' (MEMBERS') EQUITY   ☐

1.   Are classes of capital stock presented in order of priority in liquidation? (Generally accepted)   —   —   —

2.   Are the legal title of securities; par or stated values; and number of shares authorized, issued, and outstanding disclosed? (Generally accepted)   —   —   —

3. Are changes in separate accounts comprising stockholders' equity and changes in the number of shares of equity securities disclosed? (APB No. 12, para. 10; and AcSEC PB No. 14, paras. 8 and 12)

      —   —   —

4. Are changes in the equity accounts of S corporations, partnerships, and proprietorships, including limited liability companies and limited liability partnerships, disclosed? (NOTE: GAAP does not require S corporations or limited liability companies and partnerships to disclose changes in the components of retained earnings or equity.) (Generally accepted)

      —   —   —

5. Are all compensation arrangements involving stock, regardless of the name given, accounted for according to their substance? (APB No. 25, para. 8, fn. 2)

      —   —   —

NOTE: Nonpublic companies must make the disclosures in Question Nos. 6–7 in financial statements for periods ending after December 15, 1997. (The disclosures, which previously applied only to publicly held companies, may be included in financial statements for earlier periods, however. In practice, many nonpublic companies already make the disclosures.)

6. Have the pertinent rights and privileges of the various securities outstanding been disclosed (for example, a description of dividend and liquidation preferences, participation rights, call prices and dates, conversion or exercise prices or rates and pertinent dates, sinking fund requirements, unusual voting rights, and significant terms of contracts to issue additional shares)? (SFAS No. 129, para. 4)

      —   —   —

7. Have the number of shares issued on conversion, exercise, or otherwise during at least the most recent annual fiscal period and any subsequent interim period presented been disclosed? (SFAS No. 129, para. 5)

      —   —   —

8. Has the amount of redemption requirements been disclosed, separately by issue or combined, for all issues of capital stock that are redeemable at fixed or determinable prices on fixed or determinable dates in each of the five years following the latest balance sheet presented? (SFAS No. 47, para. 10 and SFAS No. 129, para. 8)

      —   —   —

9. Are the following disclosures made for preferred stock:

   a. The liquidation preference of preferred stock (or other senior stock) that has a preference in involuntary liquidation considerably in excess of its par or stated value? (The disclosure should be made in the equity section of the balance sheet rather than the notes.) (APB No. 10, para. 10 and SFAS No. 129, para. 6)   —   —   —

   b. Aggregate or per-share amounts at which preferred stock may be called or redeemed? (APB No. 10, para. 11 and SFAS No. 129, para. 7)   —   —   —

   c. Aggregate and per-share amounts of arrearages in cumulative preferred dividends? (APB No. 10, para. 11 and SFAS No. 129, para. 7)   —   —   —

10. Are the following disclosures made for treasury stock:

   a. The number of shares and the basis of carrying the stock? (Generally accepted)   —   —   —

   b. Restrictions of state laws, if any? (APB No. 6, para. 13)   —   —   —

   c. If treasury stock is purchased for purposes other than retirement or if the ultimate disposition has not been decided:

      (1) Has the cost been shown separately as a deduction from stockholders' equity, or

      (2) Has the par value of the shares been charged to the specific stock issue and the difference charged or credited to additional paid-in capital? An excess of purchase price over the par value and any amount charged to additional paid-in capital should be charged to retained earnings. (Alternatively, the excess may be charged entirely to retained earnings.) (APB No. 6, para. 12b)   —   —   —

   d. In the rare situation when treasury stock is shown as an asset, have the circumstances for such classification been disclosed? (ARB No. 43, ch. 1A, para. 4)   —   —   —

   e. If the purchase of treasury stock also involves the receipt or payment of consideration in exchange for stated or unstated rights or privileges, have the allocation of amounts paid and the accounting treatment for such amounts been disclosed? (FTB 85-6, para. 3)   —   —   —

Disclosure
Made?

	Yes	No	N/A

11. For financial statements of periods beginning after December 15, 1997, is each classification of accumulated other comprehensive income presented either (a) on the face of the balance sheet as a separate component of equity, (b) on the statement of changes in equity, or (c) in the notes to the financial statements? (SFAS No. 130, para. 26)

STATEMENT OF INCOME (Some income statement disclosures have already been addressed in the section on balance sheet related disclosures.)

1. Are the major categories of revenue and expense items, such as sales, cost of goods sold, and selling and administrative expenses, shown separately on the face of the income statement? (Generally accepted)

2. Are sales or operating revenues shown net of discounts, allowances, etc.? (Generally accepted)

3. Are sales revenues and cost of goods sold shown net of estimated returns? (SFAS No. 48, para. 7)

4. Are cost of goods sold and expenses shown net of purchase discounts? (Generally accepted)

5. For each accounting period presented, have the following been disclosed: (SFAS No. 34, para. 21, and SFAS No. 49, para. 9)

   a. The total amount of interest costs incurred, with separate identification of interest costs associated with product financing arrangements?
   b. The total amount of interest charged to expense?
   c. The total amount of interest capitalized?

6. Are all accrued net losses on firm purchase commitments for inventory separately disclosed in the income statement? (ARB No. 43, ch. 4, para. 17)

7. Are material events or transactions that are either unusual in nature or of infrequent occurrence, but not both (and thus not meeting the criteria for extraordinary items): (APB No. 30, para. 26; and FTB 82-1, para. 6)

   a. Reported as a separate component of income from continuing operations?

b.   Accompanied by disclosure of the nature and financial effects of each event?

    —   —   —

8.   Have the nature of the event or transaction and the principal items entering into the determination of an extraordinary gain or loss been disclosed? (APB No. 30, para.11)

    —   —   —

9.   Are all extraordinary items segregated from results of ordinary operations? (APB No. 30, paras. 10–12)

    —   —   —

10. Are descriptive captions and amounts (including applicable income taxes) presented for individual extraordinary events or transactions, preferably on the face of the income statement if practicable? (APB No. 30, para. 11)

    —   —   —

11. Is the adjustment in the current period of a previously presented extraordinary item presented properly? (APB No. 30, para. 25)

    —   —   —

12. Is the following information about comprehensive income disclosed for financial statements of periods beginning after December 15, 1997:

a.   Components of comprehensive income and total comprehensive income for the period, presented either in a separate statement of comprehensive income that begins with net income, on the income statement below the total for net income, or in the statement of changes in equity? (SFAS No. 130, paras. 14 and 22)

    —   —   —

b.   Reclassification adjustments, displayed on the face of the statement that presents comprehensive income or disclosed in the notes to the financial statements? (SFAS No. 130, para. 20)

    —   —   —

c.   Income tax expense or benefit allocated to each component of comprehensive income, including reclassification adjustments? (SFAS No. 130, para. 25)

    —   —   —

STATEMENT OF CASH FLOWS

1.   Are noncash investing and financing transactions disclosed either in narrative form or summarized in a schedule? (SFAS No. 95, para. 32)

    —   —   —

2.   Is the accounting policy for determining which items are treated as cash and cash equivalents disclosed? (SFAS No. 95, para. 10)

    —   —   —

3. If the indirect method of reporting cash flows from operating activities is used, are amounts of interest paid (net of amounts capitalized) and income taxes paid during the period disclosed? (SFAS No. 95, para. 29)

—   —   —

4. If cash flows from futures contracts, forward contracts, option contracts, or swap contracts that are accounted for as hedges are classified in the same category as cash flows from the item being hedged, is that accounting policy disclosed? (SFAS No. 104, para. 7)

—   —   —

GENERAL FINANCIAL STATEMENT DISCLOSURES (These are additional note disclosures that have not been addressed in previous checklist questions.)

NATURE OF OPERATIONS   ☐

1. Have the following disclosures about the entity's products or services been made: (SOP 94-6, para. 10)

   a. A description of the major products or services the entity sells or provides and its principal markets, including the location of those markets?

   —   —   —

   b. If the entity operates in more than one business, the relative importance of its operations in each business and the basis for that determination (e.g., based on assets, revenues, or earnings)?

   —   —   —

USE OF ESTIMATES   ☐

1. Has the fact that preparation of financial statements in conformity with GAAP requires the use of management's estimates been disclosed? (SOP 94-6, para. 11)

   —   —   —

ACCOUNTING POLICIES   ☐

1. Are all significant accounting policies presented in the first note or in a separate schedule? (Such policies should include those for which there is a selection from existing acceptable alternatives, principles and methods peculiar to the industry in which the entity operates, and unusual or innovative applications of GAAP or methods of application.) (APB No. 22, paras. 8–15)

   —   —   —

	Disclosure Made?		
	Yes	No	N/A

2. Is there disclosure of any material changes in classifications made to previously issued financial statements? (AU Section 420.16)   ___ ___ ___

RELATED PARTY TRANSACTIONS AND COMMON CONTROL

☐

1. Do disclosures of material related party transactions include: (SFAS No. 57, para. 2)

 a. The nature of the relationship(s)? (If necessary to an understanding of the effects of the transactions, the related party should be identified by name.)   ___ ___ ___

 b. A description of the transactions, including transactions to which no amounts or nominal amounts were ascribed, for each of the periods for which an income statement is presented and such other information deemed necessary to an understanding of the effects of the transactions on the financial statements?   ___ ___ ___

 c. The dollar amounts of transactions for each of the periods for which income statements are presented and the effects of any change in the method of establishing the terms from that used in the preceding period?   ___ ___ ___

 d. Amounts due from or to related parties as of the date of each balance sheet presented and, if not otherwise apparent, the terms and manner of settlement?   ___ ___ ___

 e. The disclosures required by SFAS No. 109? (See INCOME TAXES, Question No. 12.)   ___ ___ ___

2. If representations are made that the related party transactions were consummated on terms equivalent to those that prevail in arm's length transactions, can such representations be substantiated? (SFAS No. 57, para. 3)   ___ ___ ___

3. If the entity and one or more other entities are under common control and the existence of that control could result in operating results or financial position of the entity significantly different from those that would have been obtained if the entities were autonomous, has disclosure been made of the nature of the control relationship, even though there have been no transactions between the entities? (SFAS No. 57, para. 4)   ___ ___ ___

PENSION PLANS—DEFINED CONTRIBUTION (Profit-sharing Plans) (See Part II for defined benefit pension plan disclosures.)   ☐

1. Is the following information about the entity's defined contribution plan disclosed separately from defined benefit plan disclosures: (SFAS No. 87, para. 65)

     a. A description of the plan(s) including employee groups covered, the basis for determining contributions, and the nature and effect of significant matters affecting comparability of information for all periods presented?

     b. The amount of cost recognized during the period?

LEASES IN STATEMENTS OF LESSEES   ☐

1. General disclosures:

     a. Have the nature and extent of leasing transactions with related parties been disclosed? (SFAS No. 13, para. 29)

     b. Has a general description of the entity's leasing arrangements been disclosed, including the following: (SFAS No. 13, para. 16d)

         (1) The basis on which contingent rental payments are determined?

         (2) The existence and terms of renewal or purchase options and escalation clauses?

         (3) Restrictions imposed by lease agreements such as those concerning dividends, additional debt, and further leasing?

2. Operating leases:

     a. Has disclosure of the following been made for operating leases having initial or remaining noncancelable lease terms in excess of one year: (SFAS No. 13, para. 16b)

         (1) Future minimum rental payments required as of the date of the latest balance sheet presented, in the aggregate and for each of the five succeeding fiscal years?

     (2)   The total amount of minimum rentals to be received in the future under noncancelable subleases as of the date of the latest balance sheet presented? — — —

  b. Has disclosure been made of rental expense for each period for which an income statement is presented, with separate amounts for minimum rentals, contingent rentals, and sublease rental income? (NOTE: Rental payments under leases with terms of one month or less that were not renewed need not be included.) (SFAS No. 13, para. 16c) — — —

3. Capital leases:

  a. Have the following been separately identified in each balance sheet presented or disclosed in the notes: (SFAS No. 13, paras. 13 and 16)

     (1)   The gross amount of assets in the balance sheet recorded under capital leases and the accumulated amortization by major classes according to nature or function? — — —

     (2)   The lease obligations classified as current and long-term? — — —

  b. Has disclosure been made of future minimum lease payments as of the latest balance sheet presented, in the aggregate and for each of the five succeeding fiscal years, with appropriate separate deductions therefrom for executory costs and imputed interest to reduce net minimum lease payments to present value? (SFAS No. 13, paras. 10 and 16a) — — —

  c. Has disclosure been made of minimum sublease rentals to be received in the future under noncancelable subleases? (SFAS No. 13, para. 16a) — — —

  d. Have the following been disclosed for each income statement presented: (SFAS No. 13, paras. 13 and 16a, and SFAS No. 29, para. 12)

     (1)   Amortization expense, unless it is included in depreciation expense and that fact has been disclosed? — — —

     (2)   Total contingent rentals actually incurred? — — —

4. Sales-leaseback transactions:

    a. Has the seller-lessee disclosed the terms of the transaction, including any future commitments, obligations, provisions, or circumstances that require or result in the seller-lessee's continuing involvement? (SFAS No. 98, para. 17)   ___ ___ ___

    b. For transactions accounted for under the deposit method or as a financing, has the seller-lessee disclosed the following, in the aggregate and for each of the five years succeeding the latest balance sheet date: (SFAS No. 98, para. 18)

        (1) Obligation for future minimum lease payments as of the date of the latest balance sheet presented?   ___ ___ ___
        (2) Total minimum sublease rentals to be received in the future under noncancelable subleases?   ___ ___ ___

FINANCIAL INSTRUMENTS   ☐

1. For financial instruments with off-balance-sheet risk, have the following disclosures been made by class of financial instrument: (SFAS No. 105, para. 17)

    a. The face or contract amount?   ___ ___ ___
    b. The nature and terms of the financial instruments, including the credit and market risk, the cash requirements, and the related accounting policy?   ___ ___ ___

    c. Have the disclosures in Question Nos. 1a and 1b: (SFAS No. 119, paras. 8 and 14)

        (1) Included a description of the leverage features and their general effect on the credit and market risk, cash requirements, and related accounting policy?   ___ ___ ___
        (2) Also been made for options and other derivatives that do not have off-balance-sheet risk?   ___ ___ ___
        (3) Been made by category of financial instrument (e.g., class of financial instrument, business activity, or risk), distinguishing between those held for trading purposes and those held for purposes other than trading?   ___ ___ ___
        (4) If categorization of financial instruments referred to in Question No. 1c(2) is other than by class, does the disclosure describe the classes of financial instruments included in each category?   ___ ___ ___

2. For financial instruments with off-balance-sheet credit risk, have
    the following disclosures been made: (SFAS No. 105, para. 18)

    a. The amount of accounting loss the entity would incur if any
        party to the financial instrument failed to perform according
        to the terms of the contract and the collateral, if any, proved
        to be of no value?   —   —   —
    b. The entity's policy of requiring collateral to support financial
        instruments subject to credit risk?   —   —   —
    c. Information about the entity's access to collateral?   —   —   —
    d. A description of the collateral?   —   —   —

3. Have significant concentrations of credit risk from all financial
    instruments been disclosed, including the following about each
    significant concentration: (SFAS No. 105, para. 20)

    a. Information about the activity, region, or economic charac-
        teristic that identifies the concentration?   —   —   —
    b. The amount of accounting loss due to credit risk the entity
        would incur if parties to the financial instruments that make
        up the concentration failed to perform according to the
        terms of the contracts and the collateral, if any, proved to be
        of no value?   —   —   —
    c. The entity's policy of requiring collateral to support financial
        instruments subject to credit risk?   —   —   —
    d. Information about the entity's access to collateral?   —   —   —
    e. A description of the collateral?   —   —   —

    NOTE: The disclosure requirements in Question Nos. 4. and 5.
    are optional for nonpublic companies that (a) have total assets on
    the financial statement date of less than $100 million and (b) have
    not held or issued any derivative financial instruments during the
    reporting period. (SFAS No.126, para. 2)

4. Have the following disclosures about the fair value of financial
    instruments been made: (SFAS No. 107, paras. 10 and 14)

    a. Fair value of financial instruments for which it is practicable
        to estimate fair value? (NOTE: For trade receivables and
        payables, no disclosure is required when the carrying
        amount approximates fair value.)   —   —   —
    b. The methods and significant assumptions used to estimate
        the fair value of financial instruments?   —   —   —

c. If it is not practicable to estimate the fair value of a financial instrument or a class of financial instruments, the reasons it is not practicable and information pertinent to estimating the fair value of the financial instrument or class of financial instruments, such as the carrying amount, effective interest rate, and maturity?   —   —   —

5. Do the disclosures in Question No. 4a: (SFAS No. 119, para. 15)

a. Include the related carrying amounts in a format that makes it clear (1) whether the fair value and carrying amount represent assets or liabilities and (2) how the carrying amounts relate to what is reported in the balance sheet?   —   —   —

b. Appear in a single note or, if disclosed in more than a single note, does one note include a summary table containing the fair value and related carrying amounts and refer to the other disclosures required by SFAS No. 107?   —   —   —

c. Distinguish between derivative and nonderivative financial instruments?   —   —   —

d. Distinguish between financial instruments held or issued for trading purposes and those held or issued for purposes other than trading?   —   —   —

6. For entities that hold or issue financial instruments for trading or other purposes, have the disclosures required by SFAS No. 119 been made? (See DERIVATIVE FINANCIAL INSTRUMENTS, page 38.)   —   —   —

7. If the entity transfers financial instruments during the period and it is not practicable to estimate the fair values of the assets obtained or liabilities incurred in the transfer, have the assets and liabilities been described and the reasons why it is not practicable to estimate their fair value been disclosed? (SFAS No. 125, para. 17)   —   —   —

OTHER COMMITMENTS   ☐

1. Are the following types of commitments disclosed:

a. Obligations to reduce debts, maintain working capital, or restrict dividends? (SFAS No. 5, paras. 18–19)   —   —   —

b. Unused letters of credit? (SFAS No. 5, paras. 18–19; also see FINANCIAL INSTRUMENTS, page 21)   —   —   —

c. Net losses on inventory purchase commitments? (ARB No. 43, ch. 4, para. 17)   —   —   —

Disclosure Made?

	Yes	No	N/A

d. Existence, nature, and amount of any guarantees, even if the possibility of loss is remote? (SFAS No. 5, para. 12; and FASBI No. 34; also see FINANCIAL INSTRUMENTS, page 21)   — — —

CONTINGENCIES, RISKS, AND UNCERTAINTIES   ☐

SFAS No. 5 Contingencies   ☐

1. Are the nature and amount of an accrued loss contingency disclosed in the financial statements if the following is true: (SFAS No. 5, paras. 9–10)

   a. Exposure to loss in excess of the amount accrued exists, or   — — —
   b. Disclosure is necessary to keep the financial statements from being misleading?   — — —

2. For loss contingencies not accrued, but when at least a reasonable possibility exists that a loss (or additional loss in excess of amounts accrued) may have occurred, do disclosures indicate: (SFAS No. 5, para. 10)

   a. Nature of contingency?   — — —
   b. Estimate of possible loss or range of loss, or a statement that such estimate cannot be made?   — — —

3. Have contingencies that might result in gains been adequately disclosed but not reflected in the accounts so as not to recognize revenue prior to its realization? (SFAS No. 5, para. 17)   — — —

4. If it is at least reasonably possible that the effect on the financial statements of significant estimates involving SFAS No. 5 contingencies (as referred to in Question Nos. 1–3) will change within one year of the date of the financial statements due to one or more future confirming events and the effect of that change would be material to the financial statements, do the disclosures include an indication that it is at least reasonably possible that a change in estimate will occur in the near term? (SOP 94-6, paras. 13–15) (NOTE: If the entity uses risk reduction techniques to mitigate losses or the uncertainty that may result from future events and, as a result, the preceding criteria are not met, the disclosures are encouraged but not required.)   — — —

5. Has disclosure been made of loss contingencies relating to guar-
    antees made for outside parties including the nature and amounts
    thereof? [Also, consider disclosing, if estimable, the value of any
    recovery that could be expected to result. Examples include (a)
    guarantees of indebtedness of others, and (b) indirect guarantees
    of the indebtedness of others. (SFAS No. 5, para. 12; also see
    FINANCIAL INSTRUMENTS, page 21)]   __ __ __

Significant Estimates Other Than SFAS No. 5 Contingencies   ☐

6. Have the following disclosures been made for significant estimates
    if it is at least reasonably possible that the estimates will change
    within one year of the date of the financial statements due to one or
    more confirming events and the effect of that change would be
    material: (SOP 94-6, paras. 13–15) (NOTE: If the entity uses risk
    reduction techniques to mitigate losses or the uncertainty that may
    result from future events and, as a result, the preceding criteria are
    not met, the disclosures are encouraged but not required.)

    a. The nature of the estimate?   __ __ __
    b. An indication that it is at least reasonably possible that a
        change in the estimate will occur in the near term?   __ __ __

Concentrations   ☐

7. Have the following concentrations and the general nature of the risk
    associated with each been disclosed if (a) the concentration exists
    at the financial statement date, (b) the concentration makes the
    entity vulnerable to the risk of a near-term severe impact, and (c) it
    is at least reasonably possible that the events that could cause the
    severe impact will occur in the near term: (SOP 94-6, paras. 21, 22,
    and 24)

    a. Concentrations in the volume of business transacted with a
        particular customer, supplier, lender, grantor, or contributor?
        (NOTE: It is always considered at least reasonably possible
        that any customer, grantor, or contributor will be lost in the
        near term.)   __ __ __
    b. Concentrations in revenue from particular products, ser-
        vices, or fund-raising events?   __ __ __
    c. Concentrations in the available sources of supply of materi-
        als, labor, or services, or of licenses or other rights used in
        the entity's operations?   __ __ __
    d. Concentrations in the market or geographic area?   __ __ __

	Disclosure Made?		
	Yes	**No**	**N/A**

e. Concentrations of labor subject to collective bargaining agreements, including the percentage of the labor force covered by those agreements and the percentage covered by agreements that will expire within one year? — — —

f. Concentrations of operations outside the entity's home country, including the carrying amounts of net assets and the geographic areas in which they are located? (NOTE: It is always considered at least reasonably possible that operations located outside an entity's home country will be disrupted in the near term.) — — —

Going Concern

8. If substantial doubt exists about the entity's ability to continue as a going concern for a period not to exceed one year beyond the balance sheet date, do the financial statements adequately disclose the following matters: (AU Section 341.10)

a. Pertinent conditions and events giving rise to the assessment of substantial doubt about the entity's ability to continue as a going concern for a period not to exceed one year from the balance sheet date? — — —

b. The possible effects of such conditions and events? — — —

c. Management's evaluation of the significance of those conditions and events and any mitigating factors? — — —

d. Possible discontinuance of operations? — — —

e. Management's plans (including relevant prospective financial information)? — — —

f. Information about the recoverability or classification of recorded asset amounts or the amounts or classification of liabilities? — — —

9. If substantial doubt about the entity's ability to continue as a going concern for a period not to exceed one year from the balance sheet date is alleviated, do the financial statements adequately disclose the following matters: (AU Section 341.11)

a. The conditions and events that initially caused the substantial doubt? — — —

b. The possible effects of such conditions and events? — — —

c. Any mitigating factors, including management's plans? — — —

☐

ILLEGAL ACTS

1. If material revenue or earnings are derived from transactions involving illegal acts, or if illegal acts create significant unusual risks associated with material revenue or earnings, such as loss of a significant business relationship, has that information been disclosed? (AU Section 317.15)   ___ ___ ___

☐

CHANGES IN PRESENTATION OF COMPARATIVE STATEMENTS

1. If, because of reclassifications or other reasons, changes have occurred in the manner of or the basis for presenting corresponding items in comparative statements, are the changes explained? (ARB No. 43, ch. 2A, para. 3)   ___ ___ ___

☐

SUBSEQUENT EVENTS

1. Are subsequent events that provide evidence about conditions that *did not exist* at the date of the balance sheet, but arose subsequent to the date, adequately disclosed to keep the financial statements from being misleading? (SFAS No. 5, para.11; and AU Sections 560.05–.07 and .09)   ___ ___ ___

2. If a change in the entity's tax status becomes effective after year end but before the financial statements are issued, are proper disclosures made? (QA-SFAS No. 109, No. 11)   ___ ___ ___

☐

OTHER POSSIBLE DISCLOSURES

SPECIALIZED ACCOUNTING AND REPORTING PRINCIPLES— Have appropriate disclosures been made for: (These specialized disclosures are not included in Part II. If present, consult the appropriate pronouncement. Preparers should also refer to pronouncements of the Governmental Accounting Standards Board for disclosure requirements of governmental entities.)

1. Agricultural producers and cooperatives (SOP 85-3 and AICPA Industry Audit and Accounting Guide, *Audits of Agricultural Producers and Agricultural Cooperatives*)?   ___ ___ ___
2. Airlines (AICPA Industry Audit and Accounting Guide, *Audits of Airlines*)?   ___ ___ ___

	Disclosure Made?		
	Yes	**No**	**N/A**

3. Banking and thrift institutions (SFAS Nos. 72 and 91; SOPs 83-1 and 90-11; EITF 92-5; and AICPA Industry Audit and Accounting Guides, *Banks and Savings Institutions* and *Audits of Credit Unions*)?—See the disclosure checklist in PPC's *Guide to Audits of Financial Institutions*. ⎯ ⎯ ⎯

4. Broadcasting industry (SFAS No. 63)? ⎯ ⎯ ⎯

5. Brokers and dealers in securities (AICPA Industry Audit and Accounting Guide, *Brokers and Dealers in Securities*)? ⎯ ⎯ ⎯

6. Cable television companies (SFAS No. 51)? ⎯ ⎯ ⎯

7. Casinos (AICPA Industry Audit and Accounting Guide, *Audits of Casinos*)? ⎯ ⎯ ⎯

8. Coal industry (EITF 92-13)? ⎯ ⎯ ⎯

9. Common interest realty associations (AICPA Audit and Accounting Guide, *Audits of Common Interest Realty Associations*)?—See the disclosure checklist in PPC's *Guide to Homeowners' Associations*. ⎯ ⎯ ⎯

10. Construction contractors (ARB No. 45; SOP 81-1; and AICPA Industry Audit and Accounting Guide, *Construction Contractors*)?—See the supplemental disclosure checklist in PPC's *Guide to Construction Contractors* or *Guide to Preparing Financial Statements*. ⎯ ⎯ ⎯

11. Contributions received from nonowners (SFAS No. 116)? ⎯ ⎯ ⎯

12. Defined benefit pensions plans (SFAS No. 35; and AICPA Industry Audit and Accounting Guide, *Audits of Employee Benefit Plans*)?—See the disclosure checklist in PPC's *Guide to Audits of Employee Benefit Plans*. ⎯ ⎯ ⎯

13. Defined contribution retirement plans (SOP 94-4; AICPA Audit and Accounting Guide, *Audits of Employee Benefit Plans*, and AcSEC PB 12)?—See the disclosure checklist in PPC's *Guide to Audits of Employee Benefit Plans*. ⎯ ⎯ ⎯

14. Entities in reorganization under the bankruptcy code (SOP 90-7; and AcSEC PB No. 11)? ⎯ ⎯ ⎯

15. Finance companies (SOP 90-11; and AICPA Industry Audit and Accounting Guide, *Audits of Finance Companies*)? ⎯ ⎯ ⎯

16. Franchise fee revenue (SFAS No. 45)? ⎯ ⎯ ⎯

17. Government contractors (SOP 81-1; and AICPA Industry Audit and Accounting Guide, *Audits of Federal Government Contractors*)? ⎯ ⎯ ⎯

18. Governmental colleges and universities (SOPs 74-8 and 92-9; and AICPA Industry Audit and Accounting Guide, *Audits of Colleges and Universities*)? ⎯ ⎯ ⎯

19. Health and welfare benefit plans (SOPs 92-6 and 94-4; and AICPA Audit and Accounting Guide, *Audits of Employee Benefit Plans*)?—See the disclosure checklist in PPC's *Guide to Audits of Employee Benefit Plans*. ⎯ ⎯ ⎯

20. Health care providers (AICPA Audit and Accounting Guide, *Health Care Organizations*)? ⎯ ⎯ ⎯

	Disclosure Made?		
	Yes	No	N/A
21. Insurance industry (SFAS Nos. 60, 91, 97, 113, and 120; FASBI No. 40; SOPs 90-11, 92-5, 94-5, and 95-1; AICPA Industry Audit and Accounting Guides, *Audits of Property and Liability Insurance Companies* and *Audits of Stock Life Insurance Companies*; and AcSEC PB Nos. 8, 9, and 15)?	—	—	—
22. Investment companies and partnerships (SOPs 93-2, 95-2, and 95-3; and AICPA Industry Audit and Accounting Guide, *Audits of Investment Companies*)?	—	—	—
23. Investments in real estate joint ventures (SOP 78-9)?—See the supplemental disclosure checklist in PPC's *Guide to Real Estate.*	—	—	—
24. Mortgage banking activities (SFAS Nos. 65, 91, and 125 and SOP 97-1)?—See the disclosure checklist in PPC's *Guide to Audits of Financial Institutions.*	—	—	—
25. Motion picture film industry (SFAS Nos. 53 and 89)?	—	—	—
26. Motor carriers (SFAS No. 44)?	—	—	—
27. Oil and gas operations (SFAS Nos. 19, 25, and 69; FASBI Nos. 33 and 36; and AICPA Industry Audit and Accounting Guide, *Audits of Entities with Oil and Gas Producing Activities*)?	—	—	—
28. Public utility industry (SFAS Nos. 71, 90, 92, and 101; and EITF 92-12 and 97-4)?	—	—	—
29. Record and music industry (SFAS No. 50)?	—	—	—
30. Railroad industry (SFAS No. 73)?	—	—	—
31. Real estate investment trusts (SOPs 75-2 and 78-2)?	—	—	—
32. Real estate projects (costs and initial rental operations)(SFAS No. 67)?—See the supplemental disclosure checklist in PPC's *Guide to Real Estate.*	—	—	—
33. Real estate sales (SFAS No. 66)?—See the supplemental disclosure checklist in PPC's *Guide to Real Estate.*	—	—	—
34. Servicing assets and liabilities (SFAS No. 125)?	—	—	—
35. State and local governmental units (AICPA Industry Audit and Accounting Guide, *Audits of State and Local Governmental Units*)?—See the disclosure checklist in PPC's *Guide to Audits of Local Governments* or *Guide to Preparing Governmental Financial Statements.*	—	—	—
36. Title plant costs (SFAS No. 61)?	—	—	—

	Part II Page	Item Present	Item Not Present

PART II DISCLOSURES—Review the following list of disclosures for applicability to your client. Indicate either "item present" or "item not present." If the item is present, attach and complete the appropriate checklist entries from Part II.

		Part II Page	Item Present	Item Not Present
1.	Accounting changes and correction of an error?	33	___	___
2.	Advertising costs?	35	___	___
3.	Business combinations—pooling of interests?	35	___	___
4.	Business combinations—purchase?	36	___	___
5.	Computer software revenues and costs?	38	___	___
6.	Consolidations?	38	___	___
7.	Derivative financial instruments?	38	___	___
8.	Development stage companies?	40	___	___
9.	Discontinued operations?	41	___	___
10.	Employee stock ownership plans (ESOPs)?	42	___	___
11.	Employee termination benefits and other costs to exit an activity (including certain restructuring costs)?	43	___	___
12.	Environmental remediation obligations and contingencies?	44	___	___
13.	Extinguishment of debt?	45	___	___
14.	Foreign operations?	45	___	___
15.	Impaired long-lived assets and long-lived assets to be disposed of?	46	___	___
16.	Income taxes—special areas?	47	___	___
17.	Intangibles?	47	___	___
18.	Interim financial statements?	48	___	___
19.	Investments accounted for by the equity method?	49	___	___
20.	Leases in financial statements of lessors?	50	___	___
21.	Lending activities and loan purchases?	51	___	___
22.	Limited liability companies or partnerships (LLCs or LLPs)?	51	___	___
23.	Long-term contracts?	52	___	___
24.	Nonmonetary transactions?	52	___	___
25.	Pension plans—defined benefit?	52	___	___
26.	Postemployment benefits?	54	___	___
27.	Postretirement benefits other than pensions—defined benefit plans?	54	___	___
28.	Postretirement benefits other than pensions—defined contribution plans?	57	___	___
29.	Quasi-reorganization?	57	___	___

SUBSEQUENT PRONOUNCEMENTS ISSUED. This checklist is current through the pronouncements listed on page 1. Use the space provided below to list additional requirements as they are issued by authoritative bodies until this checklist is revised. (A list of disclosure requirements issued subsequent to the date of this checklist can be found at PPC's World Wide Web site at *http://www.ppcinfo.com*.)

Technical Pronouncement	Description of Topic	Have the Disclosure Requirements Been Considered?		
		Yes	No	N/A

PART II—OTHER DISCLOSURES

Instructions

Part I contains a checklist of Part II disclosures common to nonpublic entities. If any of those Part II disclosures are present, print them and attach to Part I the appropriate disclosure page(s) in Part II, then complete the added pages. Occasionally the appropriate pages selected from Part II will include disclosure topics not applicable to the entity. If that occurs, either check the N/A sections for the nonapplicable topics or "cut and paste" from the printed pages of Part II only those checklist topics applicable to your client.

**Disclosure
Made?**

<u>Yes</u>   <u>No</u>   <u>N/A</u>

□

ACCOUNTING CHANGES AND CORRECTION OF AN ERROR

1. Change in accounting principle:

    a. Have the nature of and justification for a change in accounting principle (clearly explaining why the change is preferable) and its effect on income before extraordinary items and net income of the period of the change been disclosed? (APB No. 20, para. 17)   —   —   —

    b. Have changes that have no material effect on current financial statements but are reasonably certain to have a substantial effect in later years been disclosed? (APB No. 20, para. 38)   —   —   —

    c. If an entity changes its method of amortization for newly acquired, identifiable, long-lived assets and uses that method for all additional new assets of the same class, but continues to use the previous method for existing assets of that class, have the nature of the change, effect on income before extraordinary items, and effect on net income been disclosed? (APB No. 20, para. 24)   —   —   —

2. For a change in accounting principle accounted for by restating prior statements, has the effect on income before extraordinary items and net income for all prior periods presented been disclosed? (APB No. 20, para. 28)   —   —   —

3. Change in accounting principle accounted for as a cumulative effect adjustment:

    a. Has the cumulative effect of a change in accounting principle been shown as a separate item in the income statement between the captions "extraordinary items" and "net income," and has the related tax effect also been shown? (APB No. 20, para. 20)   —   —   —

b. Have pro forma amounts of income before extraordinary items and net income been shown on the face of the income statement for all periods presented as if the newly adopted accounting principle had been applied during all periods affected? (If an income statement is presented for the current period only, the actual and pro forma amounts for the immediately preceding period should be disclosed.) (APB No. 20, paras. 19 and 21)

    —   —   —

c. If the pro forma amounts cannot be computed or reasonably estimated for individual prior periods although the cumulative effect on retained earnings at the beginning of the period of change can be determined, has the reason for not showing the pro forma amounts been disclosed? (APB No. 20, para. 25)

    —   —   —

d. If it is considered impossible to compute the effect on retained earnings at the beginning of the period of change (principally changes from FIFO to LIFO), do the financial statements disclose: (APB No. 20, para. 26)

   (1) The effects of the change on the results of operations of the period of change?

    —   —   —

   (2) The reason for omitting accounting for the cumulative effect and disclosure of pro forma amounts for prior years?

    —   —   —

4. Change in accounting estimate:

a. For a change in an estimate that affects several future periods, has the effect on income before extraordinary items and net income of the current period been disclosed? (APB No. 20, para. 33)

    —   —   —

b. Has disclosure been made of the effect, if material, on income before extraordinary items and net income for changes in estimates made each period in the ordinary course of accounting for items such as uncollectible accounts or inventory obsolescence? (APB No. 20, para. 33)

    —   —   —

5. For a change in reporting entity, do financial statements for the period in which a change has occurred describe the nature of the change, the reason for it, and the effect of the change on income before extraordinary items and net income? (APB No. 20, para. 35)

    —   —   —

6. For a correction of an error, have the following been disclosed:

a. The nature of the error? (APB No. 20, para. 37)

    —   —   —

b. Effect of the correction on income before extraordinary items and net income in the period of correction? (APB No. 20, para. 37)

    —   —   —

	Disclosure Made?		
	Yes	**No**	**N/A**

    c. For comparative financial statements, adjusted net income and its components, retained earnings balances, and other affected balances for all periods presented to reflect retroactive application of the prior-period adjustment? (APB No. 9, para. 18) —   —   —

    d. For single period financial statements, the effect of restatement (gross and net of tax) on beginning retained earnings and on net income of the preceding year? (APB No. 9, para. 26) —   —   —

    e. The amount of income tax applicable to each prior-period adjustment? (APB No. 9, para. 26) —   —   —

    f. If a restated historical financial summary (commonly 5 or 10 years) is presented, disclosure of the restatements in the first summary after the restatements? (APB No. 9, para. 27) —   —   —

ADVERTISING COSTS

1. Have the following disclosures about direct-response advertising been made: (SOP 93-7, para. 49)

    a. A description of the direct-response advertising that is capitalized? —   —   —

    b. The accounting policy for it? —   —   —

    c. The amortization period? —   —   —

2. For nondirect-response advertising costs, has the policy about whether those costs are expensed as incurred or expensed the first time the advertising takes place been disclosed? (SOP 93-7, para. 49) —   —   —

3. Have the total advertising costs charged to expense for each income statement presented been disclosed? (SOP 93-7, para. 49) —   —   —

4. Have any write-downs of capitalized advertising to net realizable value been disclosed? (SOP 93-7, para. 49) —   —   —

5. Has the total amount of capitalized advertising included in each balance sheet presented been disclosed? (SOP 93-7, para. 49) —   —   —

BUSINESS COMBINATIONS—POOLING OF INTERESTS

1. Have the following required disclosures been made: (APB No. 16, para. 64)

    a. Name and description of entities? —   —   —

    b. Method of accounting used (pooling of interests)? —   —   —

    c. Description and number of shares of stock issued? —   —   —

d. Revenue, extraordinary items, net income, and other changes in stockholders' equity for each of the entities from beginning of period to date of combination, including the amount and manner of accounting for any interentity items?

e. Description of adjustments of net assets and effects on net income reported previously by the separate entities when combined entities conform accounting practices?

f. Details of an increase or decrease in retained earnings from changing the fiscal year of a combining entity? (Show at least revenue, expenses, extraordinary items, net income, and other changes in stockholders' equity for the period excluded from reported operations.)

g. Reconciliation of amounts of revenue and earnings previously reported by the acquiring entity with the combined amounts currently presented?

2. Have details of the effects of a business combination consummated before financial statements are issued but that is either incomplete as of the balance sheet date or is initiated after that date been disclosed? (APB No. 16, para. 65)

3. If a transaction expected to be treated as a pooling has been initiated, and a portion of the stock has been acquired, but the pooling is not consummated at the date of the financial statements, have combined results of operations of all prior periods and the entire current period been disclosed in the manner that would be presented if the combination is later accounted for as a pooling? (APB No. 16, para. 62)

BUSINESS COMBINATIONS—PURCHASE

1. Have the following required disclosures been made: (APB No. 16, para. 95)

a. Name and description of acquired entity?

b. Method of accounting used (purchase)?

c. Period for which results of operations of the acquired entity are included in income statement?

d. Cost of the acquired entity?

e. If applicable, number of shares of stock issued or issuable and amounts assigned thereto?

f. If goodwill resulted from the acquisition, description of amortization method and period?

g. Contingent payments, options, or commitments and their proposed accounting treatment?

h. Consideration that is issued or issuable at the end of a contingency period or that is held in escrow? (APB No. 16, para. 78)

2. If the combined entity plans to incur costs from exiting an activity of an acquired entity, involuntarily terminating employees of an acquired entity, or relocating employees of an acquired entity and the activities of the acquired entity that will not be continued are significant to the combined entity's revenues or operating results or the cost recognized from those activities as of the consummation date are material to the combined entity:

    a. Have the following disclosures been made for the period in which a purchase business combination occurs: (EITF No. 95-3)

        (1) When the plans to exit an activity or involuntarily terminate (relocate) employees of the acquired entity are not final as of the balance sheet date, a description of any unresolved issues, the types of additional liabilities that may result in an adjustment to the purchase price allocation, and how any adjustment will be reported?

        (2) A description of the type and amount of liabilities assumed in the purchase price allocation for costs to exit an activity or involuntarily terminate (relocate) employees?

        (3) A description of the major actions comprising the plan to exit an activity or involuntarily terminate (relocate) employees of an acquired entity?

        (4) A description of activities of the acquired entity that will not be continued, including the method of disposition, and the anticipated date of completion and description of employee group(s) to be terminated (relocated)?

    b. Have the following disclosures been made for all periods presented subsequent to the acquisition date in which a purchase business combination occurred, until a plan to exit an activity or involuntarily terminate or relocate employees of an acquired entity is fully executed: (EITF No. 95-3)

        (1) A description of the type and amount of exit costs, involuntary employee termination costs, and relocation costs paid and charged against the liability?

        (2) The amount of any adjustment(s) to the liability account and whether the corresponding entry was an adjustment of the costs of the acquired entity or included in the determination of net income for the period?

	Disclosure Made?		
	Yes	No	N/A

COMPUTER SOFTWARE REVENUES AND COSTS ☐

1. Have the policies for recognizing revenue from selling, leasing, or otherwise marketing computer software been disclosed? (SOP 91-1, para. 42) — — —

2. Have the following been disclosed for computer software costs to be sold, leased, or otherwise marketed, whether internally developed, produced, or purchased (except costs incurred for computer software created for others under a contractual arrangement): (SFAS No. 86, para. 11)

   a. Unamortized computer software costs included in each balance sheet presented? — — —
   b. The total amount charged to expense in each income statement presented for amortization of capitalized computer software costs and for amounts written down to net realizable value? — — —

3. Are research and development costs incurred for a computer software product to be sold, leased, or otherwise marketed disclosed (either separately or as part of total research and development costs) for each period presented? (SFAS No. 86, para.12) — — —

CONSOLIDATIONS ☐

1. If consolidated statements are presented:

   a. Is the consolidation policy disclosed? (ARB No. 51, para. 5; and APB No. 22, para. 13) — — —
   b. Are interentity balances and transactions eliminated? (ARB No. 51, para. 6) — — —
   c. If the financial reporting periods of subsidiaries differ from that of the parent, is recognition given by disclosure or otherwise to the effect of intervening events that materially affect financial position or the results of operations? (ARB No. 51, para. 4; SFAS No. 12, paras. 18–20; and FASBI No. 13) — — —

DERIVATIVE FINANCIAL INSTRUMENTS ☐

1. Have the following disclosures about derivatives held or issued for purposes other than trading been made: (SFAS No. 119, para. 11) — — —

   a. A description of the entity's objectives for holding or issuing the derivatives, the context needed to understand those objectives, and the entity's strategies for achieving those objectives? — — —
   b. The classes of derivatives used? — — —

    c. A description of how each class of derivatives is reported in the financial statements, including the entity's accounting policies about:

        (1) How derivatives are recognized and measured or reasons for not recognizing them?   — — —

        (2) Where derivatives are reported in the balance sheet?   — — —

        (3) Where gains and losses related to derivatives are reported in the income statement?   — — —

    d. For derivatives held or issued for hedging purposes (both firm commitments and forecasted transactions for which there is no firm commitment):

        (1) A description of anticipated transactions whose risks are hedged, including the period until the anticipated transactions are expected to occur?   — — —

        (2) A description of the classes of derivatives used to hedge the anticipated transactions?   — — —

        (3) The amount of hedging gains and losses explicitly deferred?   — — —

        (4) A description of the transactions or other events that result in the recognition in earnings of gains or losses deferred by hedge accounting?   — — —

2. Have the following disclosures about derivatives held or issued for trading purposes been made: (SFAS No. 119, para. 10)

    a. The average fair value of the derivatives during the period, distinguishing between those that are assets and those that are liabilities?   — — —

    b. The fair value of derivatives at the balance sheet date, distinguishing between those that are assets and those that are liabilities?   — — —

    c. The net gains or losses (i.e., net trading revenues) resulting from trading activities during the period categorized by class, business activity, risk, or other categories used in managing those activities?   — — —

    d. Where the gains and losses are reported in the income statement?   — — —

    e. If disaggregation of net gains or losses is other than by class, a description for each category of the classes of derivatives, other financial instruments, and nonfinancial assets and liabilities from which the net trading gains or losses arose?   — — —

	Disclosure Made?		
	Yes	**No**	**N/A**

3. Unless FASB Interpretation No. 39, *Offsetting of Amounts Related to Certain Contracts,* permits the carrying amounts to be offset in the statement of financial position, does the entity disclose the fair value of derivative financial instruments without: (SFAS No. 119, para. 15)

    a. Combining, aggregating, or netting the fair value with the fair value of nonderivative financial instruments?   — — —

    b. Netting the fair value with the fair value of other derivative financial instruments?   — — —

DEVELOPMENT STAGE COMPANIES   ☐

1. Do the financial statements of development stage companies disclose: (SFAS No. 7, paras. 11–13)

    a. Balance Sheet—any cumulative net losses reported with a descriptive caption such as "deficit accumulated during the development stage" in the stockholders' equity section?   — — —

    b. Income Statement—amounts of revenues and expenses for each individual period presented as well as cumulative amounts from the entity's inception?   — — —

    c. Statement of Cash Flows—cash inflows and outflows for each period for which an income statement is presented and, in addition, cumulative amounts from the entity's inception?   — — —

    d. Statement of Stockholders' Equity—showing from the entity's inception:

        (1) For each issuance, the date and number of shares of stock, warrants, rights, or other equity securities issued for cash and for other consideration?   — — —

        (2) For each issuance, the dollar amounts (per share or other equity unit and in total) assigned to the consideration received for shares of stock, warrants, rights, and other equity securities? (Dollar amounts should be assigned to any noncash consideration received.)   — — —

        (3) For each issuance involving noncash consideration, the nature of the noncash consideration and the basis for assigning amounts?   — — —

    e. That the financial statements are those of a development stage company and a description of the nature of the development stage activities in which the entity is engaged?   — — —

    f. In the financial statements for the first fiscal year in which the entity is no longer considered to be in the development stage that in prior years it had been in the development stage? [If financial statements for prior years are presented for comparative purposes, the cumulative amounts and other additional disclosures required by (a) through (e) need not be shown.]   — — —

☐

DISCONTINUED OPERATIONS

1. For discontinued operations of a segment of a business, has disclosure been made for: [For periods subsequent to the measurement date and including the period of disposal, notes should disclose the information in items (e) through (i).] (APB No. 30, paras. 8 and 18)

    a. Income or loss of the discontinued segment (net of applicable income taxes) reported separately from income from continuing operations (before extraordinary items and cumulative effects of accounting changes)?   —   —   —

    b. Gain or loss from disposal of the discontinued segment (net of applicable income taxes) reported separately from income from continuing operations (before extraordinary items and cumulative effects of accounting changes)? (If the gain or loss cannot be reasonably estimated, that fact should be disclosed.)   —   —   —

    c. Amounts of income taxes applicable to income from discontinued operations and the gain or loss on disposal?   —   —   —

    d. Revenues applicable to the discontinued operations?   —   —   —

    e. The identity of the segment of business that has been or will be discontinued?   —   —   —

    f. The expected disposal date, if known?   —   —   —

    g. The expected manner of disposal?   —   —   —

    h. A description of the remaining assets and liabilities of the segment at the balance sheet date (may instead be disclosed by segregating the net assets and liabilities in the balance sheet)?   —   —   —

    i. Income or loss from discontinued operations and any proceeds from disposal of the segment during the period from the measurement date to the balance sheet date, and for periods subsequent to the measurement date including the period of disposal, those amounts compared to previously disclosed estimates?   —   —   —

2. For each adjustment in the current period of a loss on disposal of a business segment that was reported in a prior period, has the following been disclosed separately in the current period as a gain or loss on disposal of a segment: (APB No. 30, para. 25, and SFAS 16, para. 16)

    a. Year of origin and nature?   —   —   —

    b. Amount of adjustment?   —   —   —

	Disclosure Made?		
	Yes	**No**	**N/A**

EMPLOYEE STOCK OWNERSHIP PLANS (ESOPs)

☐

The disclosures listed in items (1) through (6) are required by SOP 93-6, and apply to shares acquired by an ESOP after December 31, 1992 (new shares). Shares acquired on or before December 31, 1992 (old shares), may be accounted for following SOP 96-3, or SOP 76-3. If SOP 76-3 is followed, the applicable disclosures in items (1) through (4) and (6) through (7) should be made.

SOP 93-6

☐

1. Do the financial statements disclose the following general information regarding the plan: (SOP 93-6, para. 53a)

   a. A description of the plan?
   b. The basis for determining contributions to the plan?
   c. The employee groups covered by the plan?
   d. The nature and effect of significant matters affecting comparability of information for the periods presented?
   e. The basis for releasing shares and how dividends on allocated and unallocated shares are used (applies to leveraged ESOPs and pension reversion ESOPs)?

2. Have the following accounting policy disclosures been made: (The disclosures are required for both *old shares* and *new shares* if the employer does not adopt SOP 93-6 guidance for old shares) (SOP 93-6, para. 53b)

   a. The method of measuring compensation?
   b. The classification of dividends on ESOP shares?
   c. How ESOP shares are treated in the employer's earnings per share calculations?

3. Do the financial statements disclose the amount of plan compensation cost recognized during the period? (SOP 93-6, para. 53c)

4. Do the financial statements disclose the number of allocated shares, committed-to-be-released shares, and suspense shares held by the plan at the balance sheet date? (Separate disclosure is required for both old shares and new shares if the employer does not adopt SOP 93-6 guidance for the old shares.) (SOP 93-6, para. 53d)

5. Is the fair value of unearned ESOP shares at the balance sheet date disclosed? (This disclosure need not be made for old ESOP shares if the employer does not adopt SOP 93-6 guidance for the old shares.) (SOP 93-6, para. 53e)

	Disclosure Made?		
	Yes	**No**	**N/A**

6. Do the financial statements disclose the existence and nature of any repurchase obligations, including the fair value of any shares subject to a repurchase obligation and allocated as of the balance sheet date? (SOP 93-6, para. 53f) | — | — | — |

SOP 76-3

7. If an employer has, in substance, guaranteed the debt of an ESOP, do the employer's financial statements disclose: (SOP 76-3, para. 10)

    a. The compensation element and the interest element of annual contributions to the ESOP? | — | — | — |

    b. The interest rate and debt terms? | — | — | — |

EMPLOYEE TERMINATION BENEFITS AND OTHER COSTS TO EXIT AN ACTIVITY (INCLUDING CERTAIN RESTRUCTURING COSTS)

1. Have the following disclosures about accrued employee termination benefits been made: (EITF 94-3)

    a. The amount of the termination benefits accrued and charged to expense and the classification of those costs in the income statement? | — | — | — |

    b. The number of employees to be terminated? | — | — | — |

    c. A description of the employee group(s) to be terminated? | — | — | — |

    d. The amount of actual termination benefits paid and charged against the liability accrued for employee termination benefits? | — | — | — |

    e. The number of employees actually terminated as a result of the termination plan? | — | — | — |

    f. The amount of any adjustment(s) to the liability accrued for employee termination benefits? | — | — | — |

2. Have the following disclosures about the entity's plan to exit an activity been made in the financial statements of all periods until the exit plan is fully executed if the activities that will not be continued are significant to the entity's revenue or operating results or the exit costs recognized at the commitment date are material: (EITF 94-3)

    a. A description of the major actions included in the exit plan and the particular activities that will not be continued, including method of disposition? | — | — | — |

    b. When the major actions of the exit plan are expected to be completed? | — | — | — |

    c. A description of the type and amount of exit costs recognized as liabilities? | — | — | — |

    d. The classification of the exit costs in the income statement? | — | — | — |

	Disclosure Made?		
	Yes	No	N/A

e. A description of the type and amount of exit costs paid and charged against the liability? — — —

f. The amount of any adjustments to the liability? — — —

g. For all periods presented, the revenues and net operating income or losses from activities that will not be continued if those activities have separately identifiable operations? — — —

ENVIRONMENTAL REMEDIATION OBLIGATIONS AND CONTINGENCIES ☐

1. Has the following information been disclosed about recorded accruals for environmental remediation loss contingencies and related assets for third-party recoveries: (SOP 96-1, paras. 7.11 and 7.20)

   a. Whether the accrual for environmental remediation liabilities is measured on a discounted basis? — — —

   b. The nature and amount of the accrual (if necessary for the financial statements not to be misleading)? — — —

   c. If any portion of the accrued obligation is discounted, the undiscounted amount of the obligation and the discount rate used? — — —

   d. If it is at least reasonably possible that the accrued obligation or any recognized asset for third-party recoveries will change within one year of the date of the financial statements and the effect is material, an indication that it is at least reasonably possible that a change in the estimate will occur in the near term? — — —

2. Have the following disclosures been made about unaccrued environmental remediation contingencies (including exposures in excess of amounts accrued): (SOP 96-1, para. 7.21)

   a. A description of the reasonably possible loss contingency and an estimate of the possible loss (or the fact that such an estimate cannot be made)? — — —

   b. If it is at least reasonably possible that the estimated loss (or gain) contingency will change within one year of the date of the financial statements and the effect is material, an indication that it is at least reasonably possible that a change in the estimate will occur in the near term? — — —

3. If an environmental liability for a specific clean-up site is discounted because it meets the criteria for discounting in EITF 93-5 and the effect of discounting is material, do the financial statements disclose the undiscounted amounts of the liability and any related recovery and the discount rate used? (EITF 93-5) — — —

☐

EXTINGUISHMENT OF DEBT

1. If debt is considered to be extinguished prior to December 31, 1996, under the provisions of SFAS No. 76, para. 3(c) relating to cash or other assets placed in trust, is a general description of the transaction and the amount of debt that is considered extinguished at the end of the period disclosed so long as the debt remains outstanding? (SFAS No. 125, para. 17)   — — —

2. If assets are set aside after December 30, 1996, solely for satisfying scheduled payments of a specific debt, has the nature of restrictions placed on those assets been disclosed? (SFAS No. 125, para. 17)   — — —

3. When a gain or loss from the extinguishment of debt is classified as an extraordinary item, has the transaction been described either on the statement or in a separate note (including the source of any funds used to extinguish the debt, if identifiable), and has the income tax effect in the period of extinguishment been disclosed? (SFAS No. 4, para. 9)   — — —

4. Has the aggregate gain or loss from the extinguishment of debt not classified as an extraordinary item, e.g., sinking fund transactions, been identified in the income statement as a separate item, if material? (SFAS No. 4, para. 8)   — — —

FOREIGN OPERATIONS

☐

1. Are significant foreign operations disclosed, including foreign earnings reported in excess of amounts received in the U.S. (or available for unrestricted transmittal to the U.S.)? (ARB 43, Ch. 12, paras. 5–6)   — — —

2. Has the following information about foreign currency translations been disclosed: (SFAS No. 52, paras. 30–32)

    a. Aggregate foreign currency transaction gain or loss included in net income?   — — —

    b. Analysis of the changes during the period in other comprehensive income for cumulative translation adjustments, including at a minimum—

        (1) Beginning and ending amount of cumulative translation adjustments?   — — —

        (2) Aggregate adjustment for the period resulting from translation adjustments and gains and losses from hedges of a net investment in a foreign entity and long-term intercompany foreign currency transactions?   — — —

        (3) Amount of taxes for the period allocated to translation adjustments?   — — —

	Disclosure Made?		
	Yes	**No**	**N/A**

      (4) Amounts transferred from cumulative translation adjustments and included in net income as a result of the sale or liquidation of an investment in a foreign entity? — — —

  c. Exchange rate changes occurring after the balance sheet date (if their effects are material), including their effects on unsettled foreign currency transactions? (If it is not practicable to determine the effect of the rate changes, that fact should be stated.) — — —

IMPAIRED LONG-LIVED ASSETS AND LONG-LIVED ASSETS TO BE DISPOSED OF

1. Have the following disclosures been made about impaired assets that will continue to be used (SFAS No. 121, para. 14):

  a. A description of the impaired assets and the facts and circumstances leading to the impairment? — — —

  b. The amount of the impairment loss and how fair value was determined? — — —

  c. The caption in the income statement in which the impairment loss is aggregated if that loss has not been presented as a separate caption or reported parenthetically on the face of the statement? — — —

  d. The business segment(s) affected, if applicable? — — —

2. Have the following disclosures been made for all assets to be disposed of in each period that those assets are held (SFAS No. 121, para. 19):

  a. A description of assets to be disposed of, the facts and circumstances leading to the expected disposal, the expected disposal date, and the carrying amount of those assets? — — —

  b. The business segment(s) in which assets to be disposed of are held, if applicable? — — —

  c. The loss, if any, resulting from writing down the assets to fair value less cost to sell? — — —

  d. The gain or loss, if any, resulting from subsequent changes in the carrying amounts of assets to be disposed of? — — —

  e. The caption in the income statement in which the gains or losses (from c. and d.) are aggregated if those gains or losses have not been presented as a separate caption or reported parenthetically on the face of the statement? — — —

  f. The results of operations for assets to be disposed of to the extent that those results are included in the entity's results of operations for the period and can be identified? — — —

☐

INCOME TAXES—SPECIAL AREAS

1. Have the following disclosures been made whenever a deferred tax liability is not recognized for any of the areas addressed by APB No. 23 (undistributed earnings of subsidiaries or corporate joint ventures, bad debt reserves of savings and loan associations, or policy holders' surplus of life insurance companies), for deposits in statutory reserve funds by U.S. steamship companies, or for inside basis differences of foreign subsidiaries in the consolidated financial statements of the parent and its foreign subsidiaries: (SFAS No. 109, para. 44; and EITF 93-16)

   a. A description of the types of temporary differences for which a deferred tax liability has not been recognized and the types of events that would cause those temporary differences to become taxable?

   b. The cumulative amount of each type of temporary difference?   ___   ___   ___

   c. The amount of the unrecognized deferred tax liability for temporary differences related to investments in foreign subsidiaries and foreign corporate joint ventures that are essentially permanent in duration if determination of that liability is practicable or a statement that determination is not practicable?   ___   ___   ___

   d. The amount of the unrecognized deferred tax liability for temporary differences related to undistributed domestic earnings, the bad debt reserve for tax purposes of a U.S. savings and loan association or other qualified thrift lender, the policy holders' surplus of a life insurance company, and the statutory reserve funds of a U.S. steamship company?   ___   ___   ___

2. If the tax benefits of deductible temporary differences and carryforwards arising prior to a quasi-reorganization are recognized in net income rather than contributed capital, have the following been disclosed: (SFAS No. 109, para. 39)

   a. The date of the quasi-reorganization?   ___   ___   ___

   b. The manner of reporting the tax benefits and that it differs from present accounting requirements for other entities?   ___   ___   ___

   c. The effect of the tax benefits on income from continuing operations, income before extraordinary items, and on net income?   ___   ___   ___

INTANGIBLES

☐

1. Are the method and period of amortization of intangible assets disclosed? (APB No. 16, para. 95, and APB No. 17, para. 30)   ___   ___   ___

2. Are the reasons for significant reductions relating to intangible assets disclosed? (APB No. 17, para. 31)   ___   ___   ___

	Disclosure Made?		
	Yes	No	N/A

INTERIM FINANCIAL STATEMENTS   ☐

1. Do the notes disclose the method used to determine inventory and cost of sales amounts if physical inventories as of the interim date have not been used to determine those amounts? (APB No. 28, para. 14)

2. If seasonal variations affect revenues, has that fact been disclosed and consideration been given to supplemental reporting of interim information for the 12-month period ended as of the interim date for the current and preceding years? (APB No. 28, para. 18)

3. If there are significant variations in the customary relationship between income tax expenses and pretax accounting income, and the reasons the variations exist are not apparent, has appropriate disclosure been made? (APB No. 28, para. 19, fn. 2)

4. Do the notes disclose contingencies and other uncertainties that are necessary to make the interim financial statements not misleading? (APB No. 28, para. 22)

5. If there is a retroactive application of a change in accounting principle, is the effect on all periods presented disclosed? (APB No. 28, para. 25)

6. Have appropriate disclosures been made for changes in accounting principles when neither the cumulative effect of the change nor pro forma amounts can be computed (principally changes to the LIFO method of inventory pricing)? (SFAS No. 3, para. 12)

7. Are extraordinary items and unusual or infrequently occurring transactions and events that are material to the operating results of the interim period reported separately in the period they occurred? (APB No. 28, para. 21)

8. Has disclosure been made of any change in accounting principles or practices from those applied in the prior annual report, the preceding interim period of the current year, or the comparable interim period of the prior year? (APB No. 28, para. 23)

9. Has the effect of a change in accounting estimate been disclosed if it is material to any interim period presented? (APB No. 28, para. 26)

10. Have the nature and amount of costs and expenses incurred in an interim period that cannot be readily identified with the activities or benefits of other interim periods been disclosed? (APB No. 28, para. 15)

11. If the cumulative effect of an accounting change or correction of an error was not reported because the amounts were not material to the annual financial statements, have such amounts been disclosed if they are material to the interim financial statements? (APB No. 28, para. 29)

    —   —   —

12. Have the following disclosures been made for the interim period in which an adjustment related to prior interim periods of the current fiscal year occurs: (SFAS No. 16, para. 15)

    a. The effect on income from continuing operations and net income for each prior interim period of the current fiscal year?

    —   —   —

    b. The income from continuing operations and net income for each prior interim period restated in accordance with SFAS No. 16, para. 14?

    —   —   —

13. Have appropriate disclosures been made for the cumulative effect-type accounting changes other than changes to LIFO in the interim financial statements? (SFAS No. 3, para. 11)

    —   —   —

14. Has disclosure of prior-period adjustments been made in interim financial statements during the year subsequent to the date of recording the adjustments? (APB No. 9, para. 26, fn. 3)

    —   —   —

INVESTMENTS ACCOUNTED FOR BY THE EQUITY METHOD

1. Have the following been disclosed if the investor owns 20% or more of the common stock and uses the equity method: (APB No. 18, para. 20)

    a. The name of each investee and percentage of ownership of common stock, if significant?

    —   —   —

    b. Accounting policies of the investor relative to investments in common stock?

    —   —   —

    c. Difference, if any, between the amount at which the investment is carried and the amount of underlying equity in net assets for the latest balance sheet presented and the accounting treatment of the difference?

    —   —   —

    d. The aggregate market value of each identified investment for which a market value is available? (Not required for investments in common stock of subsidiaries.)

    —   —   —

    e. When investments in common stock, corporate joint ventures, or other investments accounted for under the equity method are, in the aggregate, material, has summarized information as to assets, liabilities, and results of operations been presented either individually or in groups as appropriate?

    —   —   —

    f. Material effects of possible conversions, exercises, or contingent issuances of the investee?

    —   —   —

	Disclosure Made?		
	Yes	No	N/A

2. If the investor does not use the equity method, is disclosure made of the names of any significant investee corporations in which the investor owns 20% or more of the voting stock, together with the reasons the equity method is not considered appropriate? (APB No. 18, para. 20, fn. 13) — — —

3. Is disclosure made of the names of any significant investee corporations in which the investor owns less than 20% of the voting stock and the common stock is accounted for on the equity method, together with the reasons the equity method is considered appropriate? (APB No. 18, para. 20, fn. 13) — — —

4. Are investments in common stock shown in the balance sheet of an investor as a single amount, and the investor's share of earnings or losses of investees shown in the income statement as a single amount, except for extraordinary items, prior-period adjustments, etc.? (APB No. 18, para. 19) — — —

LEASES IN FINANCIAL STATEMENTS OF LESSORS

1. Have the following disclosures been made when leasing, other than leveraged leasing, is a significant part of the lessor's business activities in terms of revenue, net income, or assets: (SFAS No. 13, para. 23, and SFAS No. 91, para. 25)

    a. General description of the lessor's leasing arrangements? — — —

    b. Sales-type and direct financing leases:

        (1) For each balance sheet presented, have the components of the net investments in sales-type and direct financing leases been disclosed:

            (a) Aggregate minimum future lease payments to be received? — — —

            (b) Amount of aggregate minimum future lease payments representing:

                • Executory costs, including any profit thereon? — — —

                • Accumulated allowance for uncollectible minimum lease payments receivable? — — —

            (c) Unguaranteed residual values accruing to the lessor's benefit? — — —

            (d) Unearned income? — — —

            (e) For direct financing leases only, initial direct costs? — — —

| | Disclosure Made? | | |
| | Yes | No | N/A |

(2) Have future minimum lease payments to be received for each of the five succeeding fiscal years as of the date of the latest balance sheet presented been disclosed?   — — —

(3) For each income statement presented, have contingent rentals included in income been disclosed?   — — —

  c. Operating leases:

    (1) For the latest balance sheet presented, have the following been disclosed:

      (a) Cost and carrying amount, if different, of property of the lessor held for leasing by major classes of property according to nature or function, and the total amount of accumulated depreciation thereon?   — — —

      (b) Future minimum rentals on noncancelable leases in the aggregate and for each of the next five fiscal years?   — — —

    (2) Have contingent rentals included in income for each income statement presented been disclosed?   — — —

  d. Have appropriate disclosures been made for leveraged leases? (SFAS No. 13, para. 47)   — — —

  e. Have the nature and extent of leasing transactions with related parties been disclosed? (SFAS No. 13, para. 29)   — — —

LENDING ACTIVITIES AND LOAN PURCHASES   ☐

1. If the entity anticipates prepayments of loan principal, has that policy and the significant assumptions underlying prepayment estimates been disclosed? (SFAS No. 91, para. 19)   — — —

LIMITED LIABILITY COMPANIES OR PARTNERSHIPS (LLCs or LLPs)   ☐

1. If members' liability is limited, has that fact been disclosed? (AcSEC PB 14, para. 15)   — — —

2. Have the different classes of members' interests and the respective rights, preferences, and privileges of each class been disclosed? (AcSEC PB 14, para. 15)   — — —

3. Has the amount of each class of members' equity been disclosed, either on the face of the balance sheet or in the notes? (AcSEC PB 14, para. 15)   — — —

	Disclosure Made?		
	Yes	**No**	**N/A**

4. If the LLC or LLP has a finite life, has the date it will cease to exist been disclosed? (AcSEC PB 14, para. 15) — — —

5. If the LLC or LLP was formed by combining entities under common control or by conversion from another type of entity, has the fact that the assets and liabilities were previously held by a predecessor entity or entities been disclosed in the year of formation? (AcSEC PB 14, para. 16) — — —

LONG-TERM CONTRACTS (This section need not be completed when preparing the financial statements of a construction contractor or homebuilder. Instead, refer to the Supplemental Disclosure Checklist for Construction Contractors and Homebuilders in PPC's *Guide to Construction Contractors* or *Guide to Preparing Financial Statements*.) ☐

1. Have the unbilled costs and fees under cost-type contracts been shown separately from billed accounts receivable? (ARB No. 43, ch. 11A, para. 21) — — —

2. Have the advances offset against cost-type contract receivables been disclosed? (ARB No. 43, ch. 11A, para. 22) — — —

3. Has the method used to account for long-term construction contracts been disclosed? (ARB No. 45, para. 15) — — —

NONMONETARY TRANSACTIONS ☐

1. Are nonmonetary transactions disclosed adequately, including the nature of the transactions, the basis of accounting, and any related gains or losses? (APB No. 29, para. 28) — — —

PENSION PLANS—DEFINED BENEFIT (See Part I for defined contribution plans.) ☐

1. Has the following information about defined benefit plans been disclosed: (For single-employer defined benefit plans, the following disclosures may be combined for all of the entity's plans, or information about plans may be presented in groups, whichever is more useful. However, disclosures for plans outside the U.S. should not be combined with those for U.S. plans unless all plans use similar economic assumptions.) (SFAS No. 87, paras. 54 and 56)

    a. A description of the plan including employee groups covered, type of benefit formula, funding policy, types of assets held, and significant nonbenefit liabilities (such as unsettled security purchases, unsecured borrowings, or borrowings secured by investments in real estate), if any, and the nature and effect of significant matters affecting comparability of information for all periods presented? — — —

b. The amount of net periodic pension cost for the period showing separately the service cost component, the interest cost
component, the actual return on assets for the period, and the
net total of other components?

    — — —

c. A schedule reconciling the funded status of the plan with
amounts reported in the employer's balance sheet, showing
the following amounts separately: (Plans with assets in
excess of the accumulated benefit obligation should not be
combined with plans that have accumulated benefit obligations that exceed plan assets.)

  (1) The fair value of plan assets?

    — — —

  (2) The projected benefit obligation identifying the accumulated benefit obligation and the vested benefit
obligation?

  (3) The amount of unrecognized prior service cost?

    — — —

  (4) The amount of unrecognized net gain or loss (including asset gains and losses not yet reflected in market-
related value)?

    — — —

  (5) The amount of any remaining unrecognized net
obligation or net asset existing at the date of initial
application of SFAS No. 87?

    — — —

  (6) The amount of any additional liability recognized pursuant to SFAS No. 87, para. 36?

    — — —

  (7) The amount of net pension asset or liability recognized
in the balance sheet pursuant to SFAS No. 87, paras.
35 and 36 (which is the net result of combining the preceding six items)?

    — — —

d. The weighted-average assumed discount rate and rate of
compensation increase (if applicable) used to measure the
projected benefit obligation and the weighted-average
expected long-term rate of return on plan assets?

    — — —

e. If applicable, the amounts and types of securities of the
employer and related parties included in plan assets, and the
approximate amount of annual benefits of employees and
retirees covered by annuity contracts issued by the employer
and related parties?

    — — —

f. If applicable, the alternative amortization methods used pursuant to SFAS No. 87, paras. 26 and 33, and the existence
and nature of the commitment discussed in SFAS No. 87,
para. 41?

    — — —

	Disclosure Made?		
	Yes	No	N/A

2. For multi-employer plans, has the following information been disclosed separately from disclosures for a single-employer plan: (SFAS No. 87, para. 69)

    a. A description of the multi-employer plan(s) including the employee groups covered, the type of benefits provided (defined benefit or defined contribution), and the nature and effect of significant matters affecting comparability of information for all periods presented?

    b. The amount of cost recognized during the period?

3. If a gain or loss has been recognized as a result of the settlement or curtailment of a defined benefit plan or of termination benefits, have the following been disclosed: (SFAS No. 88, para. 17)

    a. A description of the nature of the event(s)?

    b. The amount of gain or loss recognized?

4. If a gain or loss from settlement or curtailment has not been recognized in the current fiscal year and the employer's financial position or results of operations would have been materially different had it been recognized, have appropriate disclosures been made? (QA-SFAS No. 88, No. 28)

POSTEMPLOYMENT BENEFITS

1. If the entity has not accrued postemployment benefits solely because the amount cannot be reasonably estimated (such as salary continuation, supplemental unemployment benefits, severance benefits, disability-related benefits, job training and counseling, and continuation of health insurance coverage), has that been disclosed? (SFAS No. 112, para. 7)

POSTRETIREMENT BENEFITS OTHER THAN PENSIONS—DEFINED BENEFIT PLANS

1. Has the following information about defined benefit plans been disclosed: (For single-employer defined benefit plans, the following disclosures may be combined for all of the entity's plans, or information about plans may be presented in groups, whichever is more useful. However, disclosures for plans that provide primarily postretirement health care benefits should not be combined with those for plans that provide other postretirement benefits. In addition, disclosures for plans outside the U.S. should not be combined with those for U.S. plans.) (SFAS No. 106, paras. 74, 77, and 78)

    a. A description of the substantive plan that is the basis for the accounting, including the following:

        (1) The nature of the plan?

	Disclosure Made?		
	Yes	**No**	**N/A**

(2) Any modifications of the existing cost-sharing provisions encompassed by the plan? — — —

(3) The existence and nature of any commitment to increase monetary benefits provided by the plan? — — —

(4) Employee groups covered? — — —

(5) Types of benefits provided? — — —

(6) Funding policy? — — —

(7) Types of assets held and significant nonbenefit liabilities? — — —

(8) The nature and effect of significant matters affecting the comparability of information for all periods presented, such as the effect of a business combination or divestiture? — — —

b. The amount of net periodic postretirement benefit cost showing separately the service cost component, the interest cost component, the actual return on plan assets for the period, amortization of the unrecognized transition obligation or transition asset, and the net total of other components? — — —

c. A schedule reconciling the funded status of the plan with amounts reported in the employer's balance sheet, showing the following amounts separately: (The disclosures of aggregate plan assets and the aggregate accumulated postretirement benefit obligation for underfunded plans should not be combined with those for fully funded plans.)

(1) The fair value of plan assets? — — —

(2) The accumulated postretirement benefit obligation, identifying separately the portion attributable to retirees, other fully eligible plan participants, and other active plan participants? — — —

(3) The amount of unrecognized prior service cost? — — —

(4) The amount of unrecognized net gain or loss (including plan asset gains and losses not yet reflected in market-related value)? — — —

(5) The amount of any remaining unrecognized transition obligation or transition asset? — — —

(6) The amount of net postretirement benefit asset or liability recognized in the balance sheet (which is the net result of combining the preceding five items)? — — —

d. The assumed health care cost trend rate used to measure the expected cost of benefits covered by the plan (gross eligible charges) for the next year and a general description of the direction and pattern of change in the assumed trend rates thereafter, together with the ultimate trend rate and when that rate is expected to be achieved? — — —

	Disclosure Made?		
	Yes	**No**	**N/A**

e. The weighted-average of the assumed discount rate and rate of compensation increase (for pay-related plans) used to measure the accumulated postretirement benefit obligation? — — —

f. The weighted-average of the expected long-term rate of return on plan assets and, for plans whose income is segregated from the employer's investment income for tax purposes, the estimated income tax rate included in that rate of return? — — —

g. The effect of a one-percentage-point increase in the assumed health care cost trend rates for each future year on (1) the aggregate of the service and interest cost components of net periodic postretirement health care benefit cost and (2) the accumulated postretirement benefit obligation for health care benefits? — — —

h. The amounts and types of securities of the employer and related parties included in plan assets, and the approximate amount of future annual benefits of plan participants covered by insurance contracts issued by the employer and related parties? — — —

i. Any alternative amortization method used pursuant to SFAS No. 106, para. 53 or 60? — — —

j. The amount of gain or loss recognized during the period for a settlement or curtailment and a description of the nature of the event? — — —

k. The cost of providing special or contractual termination benefits recognized during the period and a description of the nature of the event? — — —

2. For multi-employer plans, has the following information been disclosed separately from disclosures for a single-employer plan: (SFAS No. 106, para. 82)

a. A description of the multi-employer plan including the employee groups covered, the type of benefits provided (defined benefits or defined contribution), and the nature and effect of significant matters affecting comparability of information for all periods presented? — — —

b. The amount of postretirement benefit cost recognized during the period, if available. Otherwise, the amount of the aggregate required contribution for the period to the general health and welfare benefit plan that provides health and welfare benefits to both active employees and retirees? — — —

**POSTRETIREMENT BENEFITS OTHER THAN PENSIONS—DEFINED
CONTRIBUTION PLANS**   ☐

1. Is the following information about the entity's defined contribution
    plan disclosed separately from defined benefit plan disclosures:
    (SFAS No. 106, para. 106)

    a. A description of the plan, including employee groups cov-
        ered, the basis for determining contributions, and the nature
        and effect of significant matters affecting comparability of
        information for all periods presented?

    b. The amount of cost recognized during the period?   — — —

QUASI-REORGANIZATION   ☐

1. Following a corporate readjustment (quasi-reorganization), has a
    retained earnings account been established and dated to show that
    it runs from the time of the readjustment? (This dating generally
    should not continue for more than 10 years following the readjust-
    ment.) (ARB No. 43, ch. 7A, para. 10, and ARB No. 46, para. 2) — — —

2. If conservative estimates are used for assets, has that fact been dis-
    closed and the assets properly accounted for on realization? (ARB
    No. 43, ch. 7A, para. 4)   — — —

RESEARCH AND DEVELOPMENT   ☐

1. If the entity accounts for its obligations under a research and devel-
    opment arrangement as a contract to perform research and devel-
    opment for others, have the following been disclosed: (SFAS No. 68,
    para. 14)

    a. Terms of significant agreements under the research and
        development arrangements as of each balance sheet date
        presented?   — — —

    b. Amount of compensation earned and cost incurred for each
        period for which an income statement is presented?   — — —

2. Is disclosure made of total research and development costs
    charged to expense in each period presented including research
    and development costs incurred for computer software costs to be
    sold, leased, or otherwise marketed? (SFAS No. 2, para. 13; SFAS
    No. 86, para. 12; and FASBI Nos. 4 and 6)   — — —

	Disclosure Made?		
	Yes	No	N/A

RETAINED EARNINGS RESTRICTIONS

☐

1. Are the following restrictions on retained earnings disclosed:

   a. Restrictions as to dividend payments? (SFAS No. 5, paras. 18–19)

   b. If state laws relating to acquisition of stock restrict the availability of retained earnings for payment of dividends or have other effects of a significant nature, have those facts been disclosed? (APB No. 6, para. 13)

   c. If a portion of retained earnings is "appropriated" for loss contingencies, is the appropriation clearly shown as an appropriation of retained earnings within the stockholders' equity section of the balance sheet? (SFAS No. 5, para. 15)

STOCK-BASED COMPENSATION (INCLUDING COMPENSATION FOR NONEMPLOYEE SERVICES)

☐

SFAS No. 123's disclosure requirements apply to all entities, but its accounting requirements for measuring compensation cost need not be followed unless the entity elects to do so. Entities that continue to measure compensation cost under the old rules must make the pro forma disclosures listed in item (2) for all awards granted in fiscal years beginning after December 15, 1994. The pro forma disclosures need not be presented in financial statements of the first fiscal year beginning after December 15, 1994, but they should be presented if those financial statements are subsequently presented for comparative purposes with financial statements of a later fiscal year.

SFAS No. 123 Disclosures

☐

1. Have the following been disclosed about the entity's stock-based compensation plans (separately for each type of award granted to the extent separate disclosure would be useful): (SFAS No. 123, paras. 46–48)

   a. A description of the plan, including the general terms of awards (such as, vesting requirements, maximum term of options granted, and number of shares authorized for grants of options or other equity instruments)?

   b. Number and weighted-average exercise prices of options that were—

      (1) Outstanding at the beginning of the year?
      (2) Outstanding at the end of the year?
      (3) Exercisable at the end of the year?
      (4) Granted, exercised, forfeited, or expired during the year?

	Disclosure Made?		
	Yes	**No**	**N/A**

c. Weighted-average grant-date fair value of options granted during the year? (Amounts related to options whose exercise price differ from the market price of the stock on the grant date should be disclosed separately.)

d. Number and weighted-average grant-date fair value of equity instruments other than options granted during the year?

e. Description of the method and significant assumptions used during the year to estimate the fair values of options, including the risk-free interest rate, expected life, expected volatility, and expected dividends?

f. Total compensation cost recognized in income for stock-based employee compensation awards?

g. Terms of significant modifications of outstanding awards?

h. For options outstanding at the date of the latest balance sheet presented, the range of exercise prices, the weighted-average exercise price, and the weighted-average remaining contractual life, and for each range (1) the number, weighted-average exercise price, and weighted-average remaining contractual life of options outstanding; and (2) the number and weighted-average exercise price of options currently exercisable?

2. If the entity continues to apply the old rules when accounting for stock-based compensation rather than SFAS No. 123, has pro forma net income (and pro forma earnings per share if earnings per share is presented) as if the fair-value-based method prescribed by SFAS No. 123 had been applied been disclosed? (SFAS No. 123, para. 45)

ARB No. 43 Disclosures

3. Are the following disclosed concerning stock option plans involving stock appreciation rights and other variable plan awards and stock purchase plans: (ARB No. 43, ch. 13B, para. 15; APB No. 25, para. 15; and FASBI No. 28, paras. 2–5)

a. A statement that a plan exists?

b. The number of shares under option?

c. The option price?

d. The number of shares to which options were exercisable?

e. Exercised options (numbers of shares and exercise price)?

	Disclosure Made?		
	Yes	**No**	**N/A**

TAX LEASES ☐

1. Have the entities involved in the sale or purchase of tax benefits through tax leases disclosed the method(s) of: (FTB No. 82-1, para. 4)

   a. Recognizing revenue? — — —
   b. Allocating the income tax benefits and asset costs to current and future periods? — — —

2. If unusual or infrequent, have the nature and financial effects of sales or purchases of tax benefits through tax leases been disclosed on the face of the income statement or in a note to the financial statements? (FTB No. 82-1, para. 6) — — —

3. Have significant contingencies existing with respect to sales or purchases of tax benefits through tax leases been disclosed? (FTB No. 82-1, para. 7) — — —

4. If comparative financial statements are presented, has any change in the method of accounting for sales or purchases of tax benefits through tax leases that significantly affects comparability been disclosed? (FTB No. 82-1, para. 7) — — —

TERMINATION CLAIMS RECEIVABLE ☐

1. If the total of the undeterminable parts of a termination claim is believed to be material, have the essential facts been disclosed? (ARB No. 43, ch. 11C, para. 19) — — —

2. Have material termination claims been separately disclosed in the balance sheet? (ARB No. 43, ch. 11C, para. 21) — — —

3. Has disclosure been made of the relationship between advances or other loans received on terminated contracts and the potential termination claim receivable? (ARB No. 43, ch. 11C, para. 22) — — —

4. If the amount of termination sales is material, has it been separately disclosed in the income statement? (ARB No. 43, ch. 11C, para. 23) — — —

TROUBLED DEBT RESTRUCTURINGS—CREDITORS ☐

1. Has the amount of any commitments to lend additional funds to debtors owing receivables whose terms have been modified in troubled debt restructurings been disclosed? (SFAS No. 15, para. 40b) — — —

	Disclosure Made?		
	Yes	No	N/A

2. Has the following information about impaired loans been disclosed: (Restructured loans are not required to be included in disclosures 2a. and 2b. in years after the restructuring, if the restructured loan's interest rate was comparable to a rate that the creditor would have accepted on other loans with similar risks and the restructured loan is not considered impaired based on the new terms.) (SFAS No. 118, para. 6i)

    a. As of the date of each balance sheet presented:

        (1) The total recorded investment in impaired loans as defined by SFAS No. 114?   ___ ___ ___

        (2) The recorded investment in impaired loans that have a related allowance for credit losses determined in accordance with SFAS No. 114 and the recorded investment in impaired loans that do not have an allowance for credit losses determined in accordance with SFAS No. 114?   ___ ___ ___

        (3) The total allowance for credit losses on impaired loans?   ___ ___ ___

    b. For each period for which an income statement is presented:

        (1) The average recorded investment in the impaired loans?   ___ ___ ___

        (2) The related amount of interest income recognized for the time that the loans were impaired during the period?   ___ ___ ___

        (3) The amount of interest income recognized using a cash-basis method for the time that the loans were impaired during the period, unless that is not practical to determine?   ___ ___ ___

    c. The creditor's policy for recognizing interest income on impaired loans, including how cash receipts are recorded?   ___ ___ ___

3. For each period for which an income statement is presented, has the following activity in the total allowance for credit loss account (i.e., determined in accordance with SFAS Nos. 5 and 114) been disclosed: (SFAS No. 118, para. 6i)

    a. Balance at the beginning and end of the year?   ___ ___ ___
    b. Additions charged to income?   ___ ___ ___
    c. Write-downs charged against the allowance?   ___ ___ ___
    d. Recoveries of amounts previously charged off?   ___ ___ ___

Disclosure Made?

	Yes	No	N/A

TROUBLED DEBT RESTRUCTURINGS—DEBTORS

☐

1. When troubled debt restructurings have occurred during a period for which financial statements are presented, have the following disclosures been made: (SFAS No. 15, para. 25)

   a. A description of the principal changes in terms, the major features of settlement, or both, for each restructuring? (Separate restructurings within a fiscal period for the same categories of payable may be grouped.) — — —

   b. The aggregate gain on restructuring of payables and the related income tax effect? — — —

   c. The aggregate gain or loss on transfers of assets recognized during the period? — — —

2. Have the following been disclosed for periods after a troubled debt restructuring has occurred: (SFAS No. 15, para. 26)

   a. The extent to which amounts contingently payable are included in the carrying amount of restructured payables? — — —

   b. Total amounts that are contingently payable on restructured payables and the conditions under which those amounts would become payable or would be forgiven when there is at least a reasonable possibility that a liability for contingent payments will be incurred? — — —

UNCONDITIONAL PURCHASE OBLIGATIONS

☐

1. For unconditional purchase obligations that are not recorded on the purchaser's balance sheet, is the following information disclosed: (SFAS No. 47, para. 7)

   a. Nature and term of the obligation(s)? — — —

   b. Amount of the fixed and determinable portion of the obligation(s) as of the latest balance sheet presented and, if determinable, for each of the five succeeding fiscal years? — — —

   c. Nature of any variable components of the obligation(s)? — — —

   d. Amounts purchased under the obligation(s) for each period for which an income statement is presented? — — —

2. For unconditional purchase obligations that are recorded on the purchaser's balance sheet, have the following disclosures been made for each of the five years following the date of the latest balance sheet presented: (SFAS No. 47, para. 10)

    a. The aggregate amount of payments for unconditional purchase obligations?   —   —   —

    b. The combined aggregate amount of maturities and sinking fund requirements for all long-term borrowings?   —   —   —

    c. The amount of redemption requirements for all issues of capital stock that are redeemable at fixed or determinable prices on fixed or determinable dates, separately by issue or combined?   —   —   —

SUPPLEMENTAL DISCLOSURE CHECKLIST FOR PUBLIC ENTITIES

Company: _____   Balance Sheet Date: _____

Prepared by: _____   Date: _____

Explanatory Comments

The following is a checklist of supplemental disclosure requirements that are unique to public entities. The checklist, which should be considered in addition to the nonpublic entities disclosure checklist at CX-1, includes disclosures required by the following sources of GAAP:

- Statements of Financial Accounting Standards (SFAS)
- Financial Accounting Standards Board Interpretations (FASBI)
- Opinions of the Accounting Principles Board (APB)
- Accounting Research Bulletins (ARB)
- FASB Technical Bulletins (FTB)
- AICPA Statements of Position of the Accounting Standards Division (SOP)
- AICPA Industry Audit and Accounting Guides
- consensus positions of the FASB Emerging Issues Task Force (EITF)
- Practice Bulletins of the AICPA Accounting Standards Executive Committee (AcSEC PB)
- AICPA Accounting Interpretations (AI)
- FASB "Q & As" (QA)

This checklist is intended to be a summary of the public entity disclosures required by generally accepted accounting principles. *Consequently, it does not include additional disclosures required by the Securities and Exchange Commission or other regulatory agencies.*

This checklist is current through the following pronouncements:

- SFAS No. 131 (June 1997)
- FASB TB 94-1 (April 1994)
- Consensuses reached by the EITF through its July 1997 meeting
- FASBI No. 42 (September 1996)

- AICPA SOP 97-1 (May 1997)
- AcSEC PB No. 15 (January 1997)
- FASB Qs and As on SFAS No. 115 (November 1995)

For a list of disclosures required by subsequent pronouncements, visit PPC's home page on the World Wide Web at *http://www.ppcinfo.com*.

INSTRUCTIONS

A block ☐ has been provided for each major disclosure caption. If the major caption does not apply, place a (✓) in the block. It will then not be necessary to check N/A for each question under the major caption. Otherwise, respond to each question with a (✓) in the appropriate column: (a) Yes—disclosure made, (b) No—item present but no disclosure made (any item checked "No" should be explained in the checklist or in a separate memorandum), or (c) N/A— either the item is not present or it is immaterial to the financial statements.

TABLE OF CONTENTS

Disclosure
Made?

Yes   No   N/A

EARNINGS PER SHARE ☐

The disclosures in items (1) through (10) are required by APB No. 15 and apply to public company financial statements for fiscal years ending on or before December 15, 1997. The disclosures in items (11) through (19) are required by SFAS No. 128, which supersedes APB No. 15. SFAS No. 128 is effective for periods ending after December 15, 1997. Early application is not permitted. All prior period earnings per share information should be restated when SFAS No. 128 is adopted.

APB No. 15 ☐

1. Are per share amounts included on the face of the income statement for—

   a. income from continuing operations? (APB No. 30, para. 9)   — — —

   b. income before extraordinary items? (APB No. 15, para. 13)   — — —

   c. cumulative effect of a change in accounting principle? (APB No. 20, para. 20)   — — —

   d. net income? (APB No. 15, para. 13)   — — —

   e. extraordinary items? (APB No. 15, para. 13)   — — —

   f. results of discontinued operations? (APB No. 30, para. 9)   — — —

   g. gain or loss from disposal of a business segment? (APB No. 30, para. 9)   — — —

2. Have the pertinent rights and privileges of the various securities outstanding been disclosed (for example, a description of dividend and liquidation preferences, participation rights, call prices and dates, conversion or exercise prices or rates and pertinent dates, sinking fund requirements, unusual voting rights, etc.)? (APB No. 15, para. 19)   — — —

3. Do the notes to the financial statements disclose the bases on which both primary and fully diluted earnings per share are calculated, including (1) the common stock equivalents included in primary earnings per share and the securities included in fully diluted earnings per share, (2) the assumption used, and (3) the number of shares issued on conversion, exercise, or otherwise during at least the most recent annual fiscal period and any subsequent interim periods presented? (APB No. 15, para. 20)   — — —

**Disclosure
Made?**

<u>Yes</u>   <u>No</u>   <u>N/A</u>

4. If prior year income is presented and has been restated due to a prior period adjustment, have restated prior year earnings per share and the effects of the restatement, expressed in per share amounts, been disclosed? (APB No. 15, para. 18)   —   —   —

5. If a conversion occurs during the year (or after the year but before financial statements are issued) and the conversion would have affected primary earnings per share if it had taken place at the beginning of the year, has supplementary information showing what primary earnings per share would have been if the conversion had occurred at the beginning of the year (or date the convertible security was issued, if later) been presented? (APB No. 15, para. 22)   —   —   —

6. If common stock or common stock equivalents are sold during the year (or after the year but before financial statements are issued) and proceeds have been or will be used to retire debt or preferred stock, has the following been presented: (APB No. 15, para. 23)

    a. Supplementary information showing what earnings per share amounts would have been for the latest fiscal year and any interim period presented as if the retirement had taken place at the beginning of the period (or date the retired security was issued, if later)?   —   —   —

    b. Bases for the calculations?   —   —   —

7. Has the fact that per share calculations reflect the effects of stock dividends or splits occurring after the balance sheet date but before the financial statements are issued been disclosed, if applicable? (APB No. 15, para. 48)   —   —   —

8. Have any adjustments made to net income used in per share calculations for the rights of senior securities been disclosed? (APB No. 15, para. 50)   —   —   —

9. Have per share and aggregate amounts of cumulative preferred dividends in arrears been disclosed? (APB No. 15, para. 50)   —   —   —

10. For troubled debt restructurings that have occurred during a period for which financial statements are presented, has the per share amount of the aggregate gain on restructuring payables, net of related income tax effect, been disclosed? (SFAS No. 15, para. 25)   —   —   —

**Disclosure
Made?**

Yes   No   N/A

☐

SFAS No. 128

11. Are per share amounts included on the face of the income statement for—

    a. income from continuing operations? (SFAS No. 128, para. 36)   —   —   —

    b. net income? (SFAS No. 128, para. 36)   —   —   —

12. Are per share amounts included on the face of the income statement or in the notes to the financial statements for—

    a. results of discontinued operations? (SFAS No. 128, para. 37)   —   —   —

    b. extraordinary items? (SFAS No. 128, para. 37)   —   —   —

    c. cumulative effect of a change in accounting principle? (SFAS No. 128, para. 37)   —   —   —

13. Do the notes to the financial statements include a reconciliation of the numerators and denominators (including income and share amounts for all securities that affect earnings per share) of the basic and diluted earnings per share computations for income from continuing operations? (SFAS No. 128, para. 40)   —   —   —

14. Do the financial statements disclose the effect of preferred dividends on the income available to common shareholders amount used in the basic earnings per share calculation? (SFAS No. 128, para. 40)   —   —   —

15. Do the notes to the financial statements disclose any securities (including those that could be issued under contingent stock agreements) that could potentially dilute earnings per share but were not included in the diluted earnings per share computation because their effect was antidilutive for the periods presented? (SFAS No. 128, para. 40)   —   —   —

16. If any transactions occurred after the end of the period but before issuance of the financial statements that would have a material effect on the number of common shares or potential common shares outstanding at the end of the period, have they been disclosed? (SFAS No. 128, para. 41)   —   —   —

17. If prior year income is presented and has been restated due to a prior period adjustment, have restated prior year earnings per share and the effects of the restatement, expressed in per share amounts, been disclosed? (SFAS No. 128, para. 57)   —   —   —

	Disclosure Made?		
	Yes	**No**	**N/A**

18. Has the fact that per share calculations reflect the effects of stock dividends, stock splits, or reverse stock splits been disclosed, if applicable? (SFAS No. 128, para. 54)   —   —   —

19. If per share amounts other than those required to be presented are disclosed, do the notes to the financial statements disclose whether they are net of tax? (SFAS No. 128, para. 37)   —   —   —

APB No. 15 and SFAS No. 128

20. Have the effects of the following on per share amounts of income before extraordinary items and net income been disclosed:

   a. Change in accounting principle? (The effects on per share amounts in the period of the change and in all restated prior periods presented should be disclosed.) (APB No. 20, paras. 17 and 28)   —   —   —

   b. Change in the method of amortizing newly acquired, identifiable, long-lived assets when the previous method continues to be used for existing assets of that class? (APB No. 20, para. 24)   —   —   —

   c. Change in accounting estimate that affects several future periods? (The effect on per share amounts of the current period should be disclosed.) (APB No. 20, para. 33)   —   —   —

   d. Change in reporting entity? (APB No. 20, para. 35)   —   —   —

   e. Correction of an error? (The effect on per share amounts in the period of correction should be disclosed.) (APB No. 20, para. 37)   —   —   —

21. For a change in accounting principle accounted for as a cumulative effect adjustment, have pro forma per share amounts of income before extraordinary items and net income been shown on the face of the income statement for all periods presented as if the newly adopted accounting principle had been applied during all periods affected? (If an income statement is presented for the current period only, the actual and pro forma per share amounts for the immediately preceding period should be disclosed.) (APB No. 20, paras. 19 and 21)   —   —   —

22. If the tax benefits of deductible temporary differences and carryforwards arising prior to a quasi-reorganization are recognized in net income rather than contributed capital, has the effect of the tax benefits on the per share amounts of income from continuing operations, income before extraordinary items, and net income been disclosed? (SFAS No. 109, para. 39)   —   —   —

**Disclosure
Made?**

<u>Yes</u>   <u>No</u>   <u>N/A</u>

SEGMENT INFORMATION, MAJOR CUSTOMERS, FOREIGN OPERATIONS, AND EXPORT SALES

The disclosures in items (1) through (9) are required by SFAS Nos. 14 and 30 and apply to public company financial statements for fiscal years beginning on or before December 15, 1997 that have not adopted SFAS No. 131. The disclosures in items (10) through (23) are required by SFAS No. 131, which supersedes SFAS Nos. 14 and 30. SFAS No. 131 is effective for fiscal years beginning after December 15, 1997, with early application encouraged. Segment information for prior years should be restated to conform with the disclosures in items (10) through (23) unless it is impracticable to do so.

SFAS Nos. 14 and 30

1. Have the following been presented for each reportable segment and in the aggregate for remaining segments not deemed reportable segments: (SFAS No. 14, paras. 14 and 22–27)

    a. Sales to unaffiliated customers?
    b. Sales or transfers to other industry segments, including the basis of accounting for the sales or transfers, the nature of any change in that basis, and the effect of any change in that basis on the reportable segment's operating profit or loss in the period of the change?
    c. Operating profit or loss?
    d. Nature and amount of any unusual or infrequently occurring items included in the segment's operating profit or loss?
    e. Nature of any change in the method of allocating operating expenses among industry segments and its effect on the segment's operating profit or loss in the period of the change?
    f. If another measure of profitability also is presented (for example, net income), the method used to determine those amounts, including the nature of and effect of any change in that method?
    g. Aggregate carrying amount of identifiable assets?
    h. Aggregate amount of depreciation, depletion, and amortization expense?
    i. Amount of capital expenditures (i.e., additions to property, plant, and equipment)?
    j. Equity in net income from and net assets of equity method investees whose operations are vertically integrated with the segment's operations, including the geographic areas in which the investees operate?

	Disclosure Made?		
	Yes	**No**	**N/A**

k. In the period in which a change in accounting principle occurs, the effect of the change on the segment's operating profit?   — — —

l. Types of products and services from which revenue is derived?   — — —

m. Accounting policies relevant to the reportable segment to the extent they are not adequately explained by the disclosures of the entity's accounting policies?   — — —

n. If foreign operations are identified as a segment and the segment is a reportable segment, the types of industry operations included in the foreign operations?   — — —

2. Has the entity disclosed the reasons why (a) a segment that fails to meet one of the tests for reportable segments has been identified as a reportable segment and (b) a segment that meets one of the tests for reportable segments has not been identified as a reportable segment? (SFAS No. 14, para. 16)   — — —

3. If the entity operates predominately or exclusively in a single industry, is that industry identified? (SFAS No. 14, para. 20)   — — —

4. Have the nature and effect of any restatement of prior period segment information been disclosed? (SFAS No. 14, para. 40)   — — —

5. If 10% or more of the entity's revenue is derived from a single customer, has that fact and the amount of revenue from each customer been disclosed? (SFAS No. 30, para. 6)   — — —

6. Have the nature and effect of any restatement of prior period information about major customers been disclosed? (SFAS No. 14, para. 40)   — — —

7. If (a) revenue generated by foreign operations from sales to unaffiliated customers is 10% or more of the entity's reported consolidated revenue or (b) identifiable assets of foreign operations are 10% or more of the entity's reported consolidated total assets, has the following information about its foreign operations (either in the aggregate or by significant geographic area) and its domestic operations been disclosed: (SFAS No. 14, par. 32–37)

a. Revenue from sales to unaffiliated customers and revenue from sales or transfers between geographic areas, including the basis of accounting for intraentity sales or transfers and the nature of any change in that basis and its effect in the period of the change?   — — —

b. Operating profit or loss, net income, or some other measure of profitability?   — — —

	Disclosure Made?		
	Yes	No	N/A

    c.   Identifiable assets? — — —

    d.   Geographic areas into which the entity's foreign operations have been disaggregated? — — —

8.   If export sales from the entity's home country to unaffiliated customers in foreign countries is 10% or more of total revenue from sales to unaffiliated customers, has the amount of those export sales been reported, in the aggregate and by appropriate geographic areas? (SFAS No. 14, para. 36) — — —

9.   Have the nature and effect of any restatement of prior period foreign operation or export sales information been disclosed? (SFAS No. 14, para. 40) — — —

☐

SFAS No. 131

10.   Do the financial statements disclose the factors used to identify the company's operating segments, including the basis of organization? (SFAS No. 131, para. 26) — — —

11.   Is the source of revenue (i.e., types of products or services) for each reportable operating segment disclosed? (SFAS No. 131, para. 26) — — —

12.   Have the following been disclosed for each reportable operating segment: (SFAS No. 131, para. 27)

    a.   A measure of total profit or loss? — — —

    b.   Total assets? — — —

13.   Have the following been disclosed if included in the measure of profit or loss reviewed by the entity's chief operating decision maker: (SFAS No. 131, para. 27)

    a.   Revenues from external customers? — — —

    b.   Revenues from other operating segments? — — —

    c.   Interest revenue? — — —

    d.   Interest expense? — — —

    e.   Nature and amount of any unusual or infrequently occurring item? — — —

    f.   Depreciation, depletion, and amortization expense? — — —

    g.   Amount of capital expenditures (i.e., additions to property, plant, and equipment)? — — —

    h.   Equity in net income from equity method investees? — — —

    i.   Income tax expense or benefit? — — —

    j.   Extraordinary items?

    k.   Significant non-cash items (other than depreciation, depletion, and amortization)?

14.   If the company meets the criteria in SFAS No. 131 for reporting interest revenue net of interest expense, do the financial statements disclose that interest is reported net? (SFAS No. 131, par. 27)

15.   Have the following been disclosed if included in the determination of segment assets reviewed by the chief operating decision maker— (SFAS No. 131, para. 28)

    a.   Amount of the company's investment in equity method investees?

    b.   Total expenditures for investments in long-lived assets (other than financial instruments, long-term customer relationships of a financial institution, mortgage or other servicing rights, deferred tax assets, and deferred policy acquisition costs of an insurance enterprise)?

16.   Do the financial statements disclose the following related to the measurement of operating segment profit or loss and segment assets— (SFAS No. 131, para. 31)

    a.   The basis of accounting used for transactions between reportable segments?

    b.   The nature of any differences between the methods used to measure segment profit or loss and the company's consolidated income before tax, extraordinary items, discontinued operations, and the cumulative effect of an accounting change?

    c.   The nature of any differences between the methods used to measure segment assets and the company's consolidated assets?

    d.   The nature of any change from prior periods in the method of measuring reportable segment profit or loss and its effect on the segment's profit or loss in the period of change?

    e.   The nature and effect of any asymmetrical allocations to reportable segments (for example, if the company allocates accounts receivable to a segment but not losses on uncollectible accounts)?

17.   Do the company's financial statements disclose the following reconciliations of segment information to consolidated company information— (SFAS No. 131, para. 32)

    a.   Total reportable segment revenue to consolidated revenue?

**Disclosure
Made?**

<u>Yes</u>   <u>No</u>   <u>N/A</u>

b. Total reportable segment profit or loss to consolidated income before taxes, extraordinary items, discontinued operations, and cumulative effect of accounting changes? (If the company allocates income taxes and extraordinary items to the reportable segments, the company may reconcile total reportable segment profit or loss to consolidated income after taxes and extraordinary items.)   __ __ __

c. Total reportable segments' assets to consolidated assets?   __ __ __

d. Total reportable segments' amounts for other significant segment disclosures to consolidated amounts for those items?   __ __ __

18. If the company's internal restructuring has caused its reportable segments to change and prior period segment information has been restated as a result, has that fact been disclosed in the financial statements? (SFAS No. 131, para. 34)   __ __ __

19. If the company's internal restructuring has caused its reportable segments to change and prior period segment information has been restated as a result, is segment information for the current period presented under both the old basis and the new basis of segmentation, unless it is impracticable to do so? (SFAS No. 131, para. 35)   __ __ __

The separate disclosures listed in items 20–23 are required if the company does not provide the information in the segment disclosures listed in items 10–19.

20. Do the financial statements disclose revenues from external customers for each product or service or group of products or services, if practicable to do so? (SFAS No. 131, par. 37)   __ __ __

21. If applicable, do the financial statements disclose— (SFAS No. 131, para. 38)

a. Revenues from external customers for the company's home country?   __ __ __

b. Revenues from external customers for all foreign countries in total?   __ __ __

c. How the company attributes revenue from external customers to individual countries?   __ __ __

22. If applicable, do the financial statements disclose long-lived assets (other than financial instruments, long-term customer relationships of a financial institution, mortgage or other servicing rights, deferred tax assets, and deferred policy acquisition costs of an insurance enterprise) located in— (SFAS No. 131, para. 38)

a. The company's home country?   __ __ __

	Disclosure Made?		
	Yes	No	N/A

b. All foreign countries in which the company holds assets, if practicable? (If not practicable, that fact should be disclosed.)

c. In a single foreign country, if material?

23. If 10% or more of the entity's revenue is derived from a single customer, has that fact, the amount of revenue from each customer, and the identity of the segment or segments reporting such revenue (if applicable) been disclosed? (SFAS No. 131, para. 39)

INCOME TAXES

1. If the entity is a public entity not subject to income taxes because its income is taxed directly to its owners, has that fact and the net difference between the tax and financial bases of its assets and liabilities been disclosed? (SFAS No. 109, para. 43)

2. Have the approximate tax effects each type of temporary difference and carryforward that results in significant portions of deferred tax assets (before allocation of a valuation allowance) or liabilities been disclosed? (SFAS No. 109, para. 43)

BUSINESS COMBINATIONS

1. In a business combination accounted for under the purchase method, has the acquiring entity disclosed the following supplemental pro forma information: (APB No. 16, para. 96 and SFAS No. 79, para. 6)

a. Results of operations (including, at a minimum, revenue, income before extraordinary items, net income, and earnings per share amounts) for the current period as though the companies had combined at the beginning of the period (unless the acquisition was at or near the beginning of the period)?

b. If comparative statements are presented, the results of operations (including, at a minimum, revenue, income before extraordinary items, net income, and earnings per share amounts) for the immediately preceding period as though the companies had combined at the beginning of the period?

2. In a business combination accounted for as a pooling of interests, have the nature and effects on earnings per share of nonrecurring intercompany transactions involving long-term assets and liabilities that were not eliminated from current period income been disclosed? (APB No. 16, para. 56)

	Disclosure Made?		
	Yes	**No**	**N/A**

3. If dividends per share are reported following a business combination accounted for as a pooling of interests, are the following disclosed: (APB 15, par. 70)

    a. The circumstances involved? — — —

    b. Dividends declared per share by the principle constituent? — — —

    c. Total dividends declared per share (or amount per current equivalent) for the other constituent? — — —

    d. Basis of presentation if other than on a historical basis? — — —

INTERIM FINANCIAL STATEMENTS

1. Have the following disclosures been made for the interim period in which an adjustment related to prior interim periods of the current fiscal year occurs: (SFAS No. 16, para. 15)

    a. The effect on income from continuing operations, net income, and related per share amounts for each prior interim period of the current fiscal year? — — —

    b. The income from continuing operations, net income, and related per share amounts for each prior interim period restated in accordance with SFAS No. 16, para. 14? — — —

2. If the entity reports summarized financial information at interim dates, have the following been disclosed: (APB No. 28, para. 30)

    a. Gross revenues, provision for income taxes, extraordinary items, cumulative effect of changes in accounting principles, net income, and comprehensive income? — — —

    b. Primary and fully diluted earnings per share data for each period presented? — — —

    c. Seasonal revenue, costs, or expenses? — — —

    d. Significant changes in estimates or provisions for income taxes? — — —

    e. Disposal of a segment of a business and extraordinary, unusual or infrequently occurring items? — — —

    f. Contingent items? — — —

    g. Changes in accounting principles or estimates? — — —

    h. Significant changes in financial position? — — —

3. Does the interim financial information disclose the following information for each reportable operating segment— (SFAS No. 131, para. 33)

    a. Revenues from external customers? — — —

    b. Revenues from other operating segments? — — —

 c. Segment profit or loss?

 d. Total segment assets for which there has been a material change from the amount disclosed in the previous annual financial statements?

 e. If applicable, any differences from the previous annual financial statements in the basis for determining reportable segments or in the basis for measuring segment profit or loss?

 f. A reconciliation of the total reportable segment profit or loss to consolidated income before taxes, extraordinary items, discontinued operations, and cumulative effect of accounting changes? (If the company allocates income taxes and extraordinary items to the reportable segments, the company may reconcile total reportable segment profit or loss to consolidated income after taxes and extraordinary items.)

4. If the entity presents summarized financial information at interim dates but does not present summarized financial data separately for the fourth quarter, have the following been disclosed in the annual financial statements: (APB No. 28, para. 31)

 a. Accounting changes, disposals of segments of a business, and extraordinary, unusual, or infrequently occurring items that were recognized in the fourth quarter?

 b. The aggregate effects of year-end adjustments that are material to the fourth quarter?

CROSS-REFERENCE TO AUTHORITATIVE PRONOUNCEMENTS

Authoritative Pronouncement	Guide to GAAP Reference
ACCOUNTING RESEARCH BULLETINS (ARB):	
ARB Nos. 1–42	Superseded by ARB No. 43
ARB No. 43, *Restatement and Revision of Accounting Research Bulletins*	
Chapter 1A: Rules Adopted by Membership	Ch. 46—Related Party Disclosures Ch. 51—Stockholders' Equity
Chapter 1B: Opinion Issued by Predecessor Committee	Ch. 51—Stockholders' Equity
Chapter 2A Comparative Financial Statements	Ch. 6—Comparative Financial Statements
Chapter 2B: Combined Statement of Income and Earned Surplus	Superseded by APB Opinion No. 9
Chapter 3A: Current Assets and Current Liabilities	Ch. 12—Current Assets and Current Liabilities
Chapter 3B: Application of United States Government Securities against Liabilities for Federal Taxes on Income	Superseded by APB Opinion No. 10
Chapter 4: Inventory Pricing	Ch. 30—Inventory
Chapter 5: Intangible Assets	Superseded by APB Opinion Nos. 16 and 17
Chapter 6: Contingency Reserves	Superseded by SFAS No. 5
Chapter 7A: Quasi-Reorganization or Corporate Readjustment	Ch. 44—Quasi-reorganizations
Chapter 7B: Stock Dividends and Stock Split-ups	Ch. 51—Stockholders' Equity
Chapter 7C: Business Combinations	Superseded by ARB No. 48
Chapter 8: Income and Earned Surplus	Superseded by APB Opinion No. 9
Chapter 9A: Depreciation and High Costs	Ch. 33—Long-lived Assets, Depreciation, and Impairment
Chapter 9B: Depreciation on Appreciation	Superseded by APB Opinion No. 6
Chapter 9C: Emergency Facilities—Depreciation, Amortization, and Income Taxes	Ch. 33—Long-lived Assets, Depreciation, and Impairment
Chapter 10A: Real and Personal Property Taxes	Ch. 43—Property Taxes

Authoritative Pronouncement	*Guide to GAAP* **Reference**
ACCOUNTING RESEARCH BULLETINS (ARB): (Continued)	
ARB No. 43 (Continued)	
Chapter 10B: Income Taxes	Superseded by APB Opinion No. 11 and SFAS Nos. 96 and 109
Chapter 11A: Cost-Plus-Fixed-Fee Contracts	Ch. 59—Government Contractors
Chapter 11B: Renegotiation	Ch. 59—Government Contractors
Chapter 11C: Terminated War and Defense Contracts	Ch. 59—Government Contractors
Chapter 12: Foreign Operations and Foreign Exchange	Ch. 22—Foreign Operations and Currency Translation
Chapter 13A: Pension Plans—Annuity Costs Based on Past Service	Superseded by APB Opinion No. 8
Chapter 13B: Compensation Involved in Stock Option and Stock Purchase Plans	Ch. 50—Stock Option and Purchase Plans
Chapter 14: Disclosure of Long-Term Leases in Financial Statements of Lessees	Superseded by APB Opinion No. 5
Chapter 15: Unamortized Discount, Issue Cost, and Redemption Premium on Bonds Refunded	Superseded by APB Opinion No. 26
ARB No. 44, *Declining-balance Depreciation*	Superseded by ARB No. 44(R)
ARB No. 44R, *Declining-balance Depreciation*	Superseded by SFAS Nos. 96 and 109
ARB No. 45, *Long-Term Construction-Type Contracts*	Ch. 57—Construction Contractors
ARB No. 46, *Discontinuance of Dating Earned Surplus*	Ch. 44—Quasi-reorganizations
ARB No. 47, *Accounting for Costs of Pension Plans*	Superseded by APB Opinion No. 8
ARB No. 48, *Business Combinations*	Superseded by APB Opinion No. 16
ARB No. 49, *Earnings per Share*	Superseded by APB Opinion No. 9
ARB No. 50, *Contingencies*	Superseded by SFAS No. 5
ARB No. 51, *Consolidated Financial Statements*	Ch. 9—Consolidated Financial Statements
ACCOUNTING PRINCIPLES BOARD OPINIONS (APB):	
APB Opinion No. 1, *New Depreciation Guidelines and Rules*	Superseded by SFAS Nos. 96 and 109
APB Opinion No. 2, *Accounting for the "Investment Credit"*	Ch. 24—Income Taxes

Authoritative Pronouncement	*Guide to GAAP* **Reference**

ACCOUNTING PRINCIPLES BOARD OPINIONS (APB): (Continued)

APB Opinion No. 3, *The Statement of Source and Application of Funds*	Superseded by APB Opinion No. 19
APB Opinion No. 4, *Accounting for the "Investment Credit"*	Ch. 24—Income Taxes
APB Opinion No. 5, *Reporting of Leases in Financial Statements of Lessee*	Superseded by SFAS No. 13
APB Opinion No. 6, *Status of Accounting Research Bulletins*	Ch. 33—Long-lived Assets, Depreciation, and Impairment Ch. 51—Stockholders' Equity
APB Opinion No. 7, *Accounting for Leases in Financial Statements of Lessors*	Superseded by SFAS No. 13
APB Opinion No. 8, *Accounting for the Cost of Pension Plans*	Superseded by SFAS No. 87
APB Opinion No. 9, *Reporting the Results of Operations*	Ch. 23—Income Statement Ch. 42—Prior Period Adjustments
APB Opinion No. 10, *Omnibus Opinion—1966*	Ch. 24—Income Taxes Ch. 37—Offsetting Assets and Liabilities Ch. 48—Revenue Recognition
APB Opinion No. 11, *Accounting for Income Taxes*	Superseded by SFAS Nos. 96 and 109
APB Opinion No. 12, *Omnibus Opinion—1967*	Ch. 12—Current Assets and Current Liabilities Ch. 17—Deferred Compensation Arrangements Ch. 33—Long-lived Assets, Depreciation, and Impairment Ch. 51—Stockholders' Equity
APB Opinion No. 13, *Amending Paragraph 6 of APB Opinion No. 9, Application to Commercial Banks*	Ch. 23—Income Statement
APB Opinion No. 14, *Accounting for Convertible Debt and Debt Issued with Stock Purchase Warrants*	Ch. 13—Debt: Convertible Debt Ch. 51—Stockholders' Equity
APB Opinion No. 15, *Earnings per Share*	Superseded by SFAS No. 128

Authoritative Pronouncement	*Guide to GAAP* **Reference**
ACCOUNTING PRINCIPLES BOARD OPINIONS (APB): (Continued)	
APB Opinion No. 16, *Business Combinations*	Ch. 1—Accounting Changes Ch. 3—Business Combinations Ch. 9—Consolidated Financial Statements Ch. 26—Intangible Assets Ch. 30—Inventory Ch. 39—Pension Plans: Accounting by Employers
APB Opinion No. 17, *Intangible Assets*	Ch. 26—Intangible Assets
APB Opinion No. 18, *The Equity Method of Accounting for Investments in Common Stock*	Ch. 20—Equity Method Investments
APB Opinion No. 19, *Reporting Changes in Financial Position*	Superseded by SFAS No. 95
APB Opinion No. 20, *Accounting Changes*	Ch. 1—Accounting Changes Ch. 42—Prior Period Adjustments
APB Opinion No. 21, *Interest on Receivables and Payables*	Ch. 28—Interest: Imputed
APB Opinion No. 22, *Disclosure of Accounting Policies*	Ch. 2—Accounting Policies, Nature of Operations, and Use of Estimates Disclosures Ch. 29—Interim Financial Reporting
APB Opinion No. 23, *Accounting for Income Taxes—Special Areas*	Ch. 24—Income Taxes Ch. 53—Banking and Thrift Institutions
APB Opinion No. 24, *Accounting for Income Taxes—Investments in Common Stock Accounted for by the Equity Method (Other Than Subsidiaries and Corporate Joint Ventures)*	Superseded by SFAS Nos. 96 and 109
APB Opinion No. 25, *Accounting for Stock Issued to Employees*	Ch. 50—Stock Option and Purchase Plans
APB Opinion No. 26, *Early Extinguishment of Debt*	Ch. 14—Debt Extinguishments
APB Opinion No. 27, *Accounting for Lease Transactions by Manufacturer or Dealer Lessors*	Superseded by SFAS No. 13
APB Opinion No. 28, *Interim Financial Reporting*	Ch. 29—Interim Financial Reporting Ch. 30—Inventory
APB Opinion No. 29, *Accounting for Nonmonetary Transactions*	Ch. 36—Nonmonetary Transactions Ch. 51—Stockholders' Equity

Authoritative Pronouncement	*Guide to GAAP* **Reference**

ACCOUNTING PRINCIPLES BOARD OPINIONS (APB): (Continued)

APB Opinion No. 30, *Reporting the Results of Operations—Reporting the Effects of Disposal of a Segment of a Business, and Extraordinary, Unusual and Infrequently Occurring Events and Transactions*	Ch. 19—Earnings per Share Ch. 23—Income Statement
APB Opinion No. 31, *Disclosure of Lease Commitments by Lessees*	Superseded by SFAS No. 13

STATEMENTS OF THE FINANCIAL ACCOUNTING STANDARDS BOARD (SFAS):

SFAS No. 1, *Disclosure of Foreign Currency Translation Information*	Superseded by SFAS Nos. 8 and 52
SFAS No. 2, *Accounting for Research and Development Costs*	Ch. 47—Research and Development Costs
SFAS No. 3, *Reporting Accounting Changes in Interim Financial Statements*	Ch. 1—Accounting Changes Ch. 29—Interim Financial Reporting
SFAS No. 4, *Reporting Gains and Losses from Extinguishment of Debt*	Ch. 14—Debt Extinguishments
SFAS No. 5, *Accounting for Contingencies*	Ch. 10—Contingencies Ch. 25—Insurance Costs Ch. 48—Revenue Recognition Ch. 60—Insurance Companies
SFAS No. 6, *Classification of Short-Term Obligations Expected to Be Refinanced*	Ch. 12—Current Assets and Current Liabilities
SFAS No. 7, *Accounting and Reporting by Development Stage Enterprises*	Ch. 18—Development Stage Enterprises
SFAS No. 8, *Accounting for the Translation of Foreign Currency Transactions and Foreign Currency Financial Statements*	Superseded by SFAS No. 52
SFAS No. 9, *Accounting for Income Taxes—Oil and Gas Producing Companies*	Superseded by SFAS No. 19
SFAS No. 10, *Extension of "Grandfather" Provisions for Business Combinations*	Ch. 3—Business Combinations
SFAS No. 11, *Accounting for Contingencies—Transition Method*	Not discussed
SFAS No. 12, *Accounting for Certain Marketable Securities*	Superseded by SFAS No. 115
SFAS No. 13, *Accounting for Leases*	Ch. 31—Leases
SFAS No. 14, *Financial Reporting for Segments of a Business Enterprise*	Superseded by SFAS No. 131

Authoritative Pronouncement	*Guide to GAAP* Reference
STATEMENTS OF THE FINANCIAL ACCOUNTING STANDARDS BOARD (SFAS): (Continued)	
SFAS No. 15, *Accounting by Debtors and Creditors for Troubled Debt Restructurings*	Ch. 16—Debt Restructurings
SFAS No. 16, *Prior Period Adjustments*	Ch. 10—Contingencies Ch. 29—Interim Financial Reporting Ch. 42—Prior Period Adjustments
SFAS No. 17, *Accounting for Leases—Initial Direct Costs*	Superseded by SFAS No. 91
SFAS No. 18, *Financial Reporting for Segments of a Business Enterprise—Interim Financial Statements*	Superseded by SFAS No. 131
SFAS No. 19, *Financial Accounting and Reporting by Oil and Gas Producing Companies*	Ch. 64—Oil and Gas Producing Activities
SFAS No. 20, *Accounting for Forward Exchange Contracts*	Superseded by SFAS No. 52
SFAS No. 21, *Suspension of the Reporting of Earnings per Share and Segment Information by Nonpublic Enterprises*	Superseded by SFAS No. 131
SFAS No. 22, *Changes in the Provisions of Lease Agreements Resulting from Refundings of Tax-Exempt Debt*	Ch. 14—Debt Extinguishments Ch. 31—Leases
SFAS No. 23, *Inception of the Lease*	Ch. 31—Leases
SFAS No. 24, *Reporting Segment Information in Financial Statements That Are Presented in Another Enterprise's Financial Report*	Superseded by SFAS No. 131
SFAS No. 25, *Suspension of Certain Accounting Requirements for Oil and Gas Producing Companies*	Ch. 64—Oil and Gas Producing Activities
SFAS No. 26, *Profit Recognition on Sales-Type Leases of Real Estate*	Superseded by SFAS No. 98
SFAS No. 27, *Classification of Renewals or Extensions of Existing Sales-Type or Direct Financing Leases*	Ch. 31—Leases
SFAS No. 28, *Accounting for Sales with Leasebacks*	Ch. 31—Leases
SFAS No. 29, *Determining Contingent Rentals*	Ch. 31—Leases
SFAS No. 30, *Disclosure of Information about Major Customers*	Superseded by SFAS No. 131

Authoritative Pronouncement	*Guide to GAAP* Reference

STATEMENTS OF THE FINANCIAL ACCOUNTING STANDARDS BOARD (SFAS): (Continued)

Authoritative Pronouncement	*Guide to GAAP* Reference
SFAS No. 31, *Accounting for Tax Benefits Related to U.K. Tax Legislation concerning Stock Relief*	Superseded by SFAS Nos. 96 and 109
SFAS No. 32, *Specialized Accounting and Reporting Principles and Practices in AICPA Statements of Position and Guides on Accounting and Auditing Matters*	Superseded by SFAS No. 111
SFAS No. 33, *Financial Reporting and Changing Prices*	Superseded by SFAS No. 89
SFAS No. 34, *Capitalization of Interest Cost*	Ch. 27—Interest: Capitalized
SFAS No. 35, *Accounting and Reporting by Defined Benefit Pension Plans*	Ch. 38—Pension Plan Financial Statements
SFAS No. 36, *Disclosure of Pension Information*	Superseded by SFAS No. 87
SFAS No. 37, *Balance Sheet Classification of Deferred Income Taxes*	Ch. 24—Income Taxes
SFAS No. 38, *Accounting for Preacquisition Contingencies of Purchased Enterprises*	Ch. 3—Business Combinations Ch. 10—Contingencies
SFAS No. 39, *Financial Reporting and Changing Prices: Specialized Assets—Mining Oil and Gas*	Superseded by SFAS No. 89
SFAS No. 40, *Financial Reporting and Changing Prices: Specialized Assets—Timberlands and Growing Timber*	Superseded by SFAS No. 89
SFAS No. 41, *Financial Reporting and Changing Prices: Specialized Assets—Income-Producing Real Estate*	Superseded by SFAS No. 89
SFAS No. 42, *Determining Materiality for Capitalization of Interest Cost*	Ch. 27—Interest: Capitalized
SFAS No. 43, *Accounting for Compensated Absences*	Ch. 7—Compensated Absences
SFAS No. 44, *Accounting for Intangible Assets of Motor Carriers*	Ch. 26—Intangible Assets
SFAS No. 45, *Accounting for Franchise Fee Revenue*	Ch. 58—Franchisors
SFAS No. 46, *Financial Reporting and Changing Prices: Motion Picture Films*	Superseded by SFAS No. 89
SFAS No. 47, *Disclosure of Long-Term Obligations*	Ch. 34—Long-term Obligation Disclosures

Authoritative Pronouncement	*Guide to GAAP* Reference

STATEMENTS OF THE FINANCIAL ACCOUNTING STANDARDS BOARD (SFAS): (Continued)

SFAS No. 48, *Revenue Recognition When Right of Return Exists*	Ch. 48—Revenue Recognition
SFAS No. 49, *Accounting for Product Financing Arrangements*	Ch. 15—Debt: Product Financing Arrangements
SFAS No. 50, *Financial Reporting in the Record and Music Industry*	Ch. 65—Record and Music Industry
SFAS No. 51, *Financial Reporting by Cable Television Companies*	Ch. 55—Cable Television Companies
SFAS No. 52, *Foreign Currency Translation*	Ch. 22—Foreign Operations and Currency Translation
SFAS No. 53, *Financial Reporting by Producers and Distributors of Motion Picture Films*	Ch. 62—Motion Picture Industry
SFAS No. 54, *Financial Reporting and Changing Prices: Investment Companies*	Superseded by SFAS No. 89
SFAS No. 55, *Determining whether a Convertible Security Is a Common Stock Equivalent*	Superseded by SFAS No. 111
SFAS No. 56, *Designation of AICPA Guide and Statement of Position (SOP) 81-1 on Contractor Accounting and SOP 81-2 concerning Hospital-Related Organizations as Preferable for Purposes of Applying APB Opinion No. 20*	Superseded by SFAS No. 111
SFAS No. 57, *Related Party Disclosures*	Ch. 46—Related Party Disclosures
SFAS No. 58, *Capitalization of Interest Cost in Financial Statements That Include Investments Accounted for by the Equity Method*	Ch. 27—Interest: Capitalized
SFAS No. 59, *Deferral of the Effective Date of Certain Accounting Requirements for Pension Plans of State and Local Governmental Units*	Superseded by SFAS No. 75
SFAS No. 60, *Accounting and Reporting by Insurance Enterprises*	Ch. 60—Insurance Companies
SFAS No. 61, *Accounting for Title Plant*	Ch. 67—Title Plant
SFAS No. 62, *Capitalization of Interest Cost in Situations Involving Certain Tax-Exempt Borrowings and Certain Gifts and Grants*	Ch. 27—Interest: Capitalized
SFAS No. 63, *Financial Reporting by Broadcasters*	Ch. 54—Broadcasters
SFAS No. 64, *Extinguishments of Debt Made to Satisfy Sinking-Fund Requirements*	Ch. 14—Debt Extinguishments

Authoritative Pronouncement	**Guide to GAAP Reference**
STATEMENTS OF THE FINANCIAL ACCOUNTING STANDARDS BOARD (SFAS): (Continued)	
SFAS No. 65, *Accounting for Certain Mortgage Banking Activities*	Ch. 61—Lending and Mortgage Banking Activities
SFAS No. 66, *Accounting for Sales of Real Estate*	Ch. 45—Real Estate Transactions
SFAS No. 67, *Accounting for Costs and Initial Rental Operations of Real Estate Projects*	Ch. 45—Real Estate Transactions
SFAS No. 68, *Research and Development Arrangements*	Ch. 47—Research and Development Costs
SFAS No. 69, *Disclosures about Oil and Gas Producing Activities*	Ch. 64—Oil and Gas Producing Activities
SFAS No. 70, *Financial Reporting and Changing Prices: Foreign Currency Translation*	Superseded by SFAS No. 89
SFAS No. 71, *Accounting for the Effects of Certain Types of Regulation*	Ch. 66—Regulated Operations
SFAS No. 72, *Accounting for Certain Acquisitions of Banking or Thrift Institutions*	Ch. 3—Business Combinations Ch. 53—Banking and Thrift Institutions
SFAS No. 73, *Reporting a Change in Accounting for Railroad Track Structures*	Ch. 1—Accounting Changes
SFAS No. 74, *Accounting for Special Termination Benefits Paid to Employees*	Superseded by SFAS No. 88
SFAS No. 75, *Deferral of the Effective Date of Certain Accounting Requirements for Pension Plans of State and Local Governmental Units*	Ch. 38—Pension Plan Financial Statements
SFAS No. 76, *Extinguishment of Debt*	Superseded by SFAS No. 125
SFAS No. 77, *Reporting by Transferors for Transfers of Receivables with Recourse*	Superseded by SFAS No. 125
SFAS No. 78, *Classification of Obligations That Are Callable by the Creditor*	Ch. 12—Current Assets and Current Liabilities
SFAS No. 79, *Elimination of Certain Disclosures for Business Combinations by Nonpublic Enterprises*	Ch. 3—Business Combinations
SFAS No. 80, *Accounting for Futures Contracts*	Ch. 35—Marketable Securities
SFAS No. 81, *Disclosure of Postretirement Health Care and Life Insurance Benefits*	Superseded by SFAS No. 106
SFAS No. 82, *Financial Reporting and Changing Prices: Elimination of Certain Disclosures*	Superseded by SFAS No. 89

Authoritative Pronouncement	*Guide to GAAP* Reference
STATEMENTS OF THE FINANCIAL ACCOUNTING STANDARDS BOARD (SFAS): (Continued)	
SFAS No. 83, *Designation of AICPA Guides and Statement of Position on Accounting by Brokers and Dealers in Securities, by Employee Benefit Plans, and by Banks as Preferable for Purposes of Applying APB Opinion No. 20*	Superseded by SFAS No. 111
SFAS No. 84, *Induced Conversions of Convertible Debt*	Ch. 13—Debt: Convertible Debt
SFAS No. 85, *Yield Test for Determining whether a Convertible Security Is a Common Stock Equivalent*	Superseded by SFAS No. 128
SFAS No. 86, *Accounting for the Costs of Computer Software to Be Sold, Leased, or Otherwise Marketed*	Ch. 47—Research and Development Costs Ch. 56—Computer Software Developers
SFAS No. 87, *Employers' Accounting for Pensions*	Ch. 3—Business Combinations Ch. 39—Pension Plans: Accounting by Employers
SFAS No. 88, *Employers' Accounting for Settlements and Curtailments of Defined Benefit Pension Plans and for Termination Benefits*	Ch. 39—Pension Plans: Accounting by Employers
SFAS No. 89, *Financial Reporting and Changing Prices*	Ch. 5—Changing Prices: Reporting Their Effects
SFAS No. 90, *Regulated Enterprises—Accounting for Abandonments and Disallowances of Plant Costs*	Ch. 66—Regulated Operations
SFAS No. 91, *Accounting for Nonrefundable Fees and Costs Associated with Originating or Acquiring Loans and Initial Direct Costs of Leases*	Ch. 31—Leases Ch. 61—Lending and Mortgage Banking Activities
SFAS No. 92, *Regulated Enterprises—Accounting for Phase-in Plans*	Ch. 33—Long-lived Assets, Depreciation, and Impairment Ch. 66—Regulated Operations
SFAS No. 93, *Recognition of Depreciation by Not-for-Profit Organizations*	Ch. 33—Long-lived Assets, Depreciation, and Impairment Ch. 63—Not-for-profit Organizations
SFAS No. 94, *Consolidation of All Majority-Owned Subsidiaries*	Ch. 9—Consolidated Financial Statements Ch. 20—Equity Method Investments
SFAS No. 95, *Statement of Cash Flows*	Ch. 4—Cash Flows Statement Ch. 19—Earnings per Share Ch. 27—Interest: Capitalized
SFAS No. 96, *Accounting for Income Taxes*	Superseded by SFAS No. 109

Authoritative Pronouncement	*Guide to GAAP* Reference

STATEMENTS OF THE FINANCIAL ACCOUNTING STANDARDS BOARD (SFAS): (Continued)

SFAS No. 97, *Accounting and Reporting by Insurance Enterprises for Certain Long-Duration Contracts and for Realized Gains and Losses from the Sale of Investments*

Ch. 60—Insurance Companies

SFAS No. 98, *Accounting for Leases:*
* *Sale-Leaseback Transactions Involving Real Estate*
* *Sales-Type Leases of Real Estate*
* *Definition of the Lease Term*
* *Initial Direct Costs of Direct Financing Leases*

Ch. 31—Leases
Ch. 45—Real Estate Transactions
Ch. 66—Regulated Operations

SFAS No. 99, *Deferral of the Effective Date of Recognition of Depreciation by Not-for-Profit Organizations*

Ch. 63—Not-for-profit Organizations

SFAS No. 100, *Accounting for Income Taxes—Deferral of the Effective Date of FASB Statement No. 96*

Superseded by SFAS Nos. 103, 108, and 109

SFAS No. 101, *Regulated Enterprises—Accounting for the Discontinuation of Application of FASB Statement No. 71*

Ch. 66—Regulated Operations

SFAS No. 102, *Statement of Cash Flows—Exemption of Certain Enterprises and Classification of Cash Flows from Certain Securities Acquired for Resale*

Ch. 4—Cash Flows Statement
Ch. 38—Pension Plan Financial Statements

SFAS No. 103, *Accounting for Income Taxes—Deferral of the Effective Date of FASB Statement No. 96*

Superseded by SFAS Nos. 108 and 109

SFAS No. 104, *Statement of Cash Flows—Net Reporting of Certain Cash Receipts and Cash Payments and Classification of Cash Flows from Hedging Transactions*

Ch. 4—Cash Flows Statement
Ch. 35—Marketable Securities

SFAS No. 105, *Disclosure of Information about Financial Instruments with Off-Balance-Sheet Risk and Financial Instruments with Concentrations of Credit Risk*

Ch. 21—Financial Instrument Disclosures

SFAS No. 106, *Employers' Accounting for Postretirement Benefits Other Than Pensions*

Ch. 3—Business Combinations
Ch. 17—Deferred Compensation Arrangements
Ch. 39—Pension Plans: Accounting by Employers
Ch. 41—Postretirement Benefits Other Than Pensions

Authoritative Pronouncement	*Guide to GAAP* **Reference**
STATEMENTS OF THE FINANCIAL ACCOUNTING STANDARDS BOARD (SFAS): (Continued)	
SFAS No. 107, *Disclosures about Fair Value of Financial Instruments*	Ch. 21—Financial Instrument Disclosures Ch. 52—Transfers and Servicing of Financial Assets
SFAS No. 108, *Accounting for Income Taxes— Deferral of the Effective Date of FASB Statement No. 96*	Superseded by SFAS No. 109
SFAS No. 109, *Accounting for Income Taxes*	Ch. 3—Business Combinations Ch. 9—Consolidated Financial Statements Ch. 24—Income Taxes Ch. 33—Long-lived Assets, Depreciation, and Impairment Ch. 42—Prior Period Adjustments Ch. 44—Quasi-reorganizations Ch. 46—Related Party Disclosures Ch. 53—Banking and Thrift Institutions Ch. 66—Regulated Operations
SFAS No. 110, *Reporting by Defined Benefit Pension Plans of Investment Contracts*	Ch. 38—Pension Plan Financial Statements
SFAS No. 111, *Rescission of FASB Statement No. 32 and Technical Corrections*	Ch. 1—Accounting Changes Ch. 42—Prior Period Adjustments
SFAS No. 112, *Employers' Accounting for Post-employment Benefits*	Ch. 7—Compensated Absences Ch. 40—Postemployment Benefits
SFAS No. 113, *Accounting and Reporting for Reinsurance of Short-Duration and Long-Duration Contracts*	Ch. 60—Insurance Companies
SFAS No. 114, *Accounting by Creditors for Impairment of a Loan*	Ch. 16—Debt Restructurings Ch. 32—Loan Impairment
SFAS No. 115, *Accounting for Certain Investments in Debt and Equity Securities*	Ch. 12—Current Assets and Current Liabilities Ch. 35—Marketable Securities Ch. 52—Transfers and Servicing of Financial Assets Ch. 61—Lending and Mortgage Banking Activities
SFAS No. 116, *Accounting for Contributions Received and Contributions Made*	Ch. 11—Contributions Ch. 63—Not-for-profit Organizations
SFAS No. 117, *Financial Statements of Not-for-Profit Organizations*	Ch. 63—Not-for-profit Organizations
SFAS No. 118, *Accounting by Creditors for Impairment of a Loan—Income Recognition and Disclosures*	Ch. 32—Loan Impairment

Authoritative Pronouncement	***Guide to GAAP* Reference**
STATEMENTS OF THE FINANCIAL ACCOUNTING STANDARDS BOARD (SFAS): (Continued)	
SFAS No. 119, *Disclosure about Derivative Financial Instruments and Fair Value of Financial Instruments*	Ch. 21—Financial Instrument Disclosures
SFAS No. 120, *Accounting and Reporting by Mutual Life Insurance Enterprises and by Insurance Enterprises for Certain Long-Duration Participating Contracts*	Ch. 60—Insurance Companies
SFAS No. 121, *Accounting for the Impairment of Long-Lived Assets and for Long-Lived Assets to Be Disposed Of*	Ch. 3—Business Combinations Ch. 26—Intangible Assets Ch. 33—Long-lived Assets, Depreciation, and Impairment Ch. 45—Real Estate Transactions Ch. 66—Regulated Operations
SFAS No. 122, *Accounting for Mortgage Servicing Rights*	Superseded by SFAS No. 125
SFAS No. 123, *Accounting for Stock-Based Compensation*	Ch. 50—Stock Option and Purchase Plans
SFAS No. 124, *Accounting for Certain Investments Held by Not-for-Profit Organizations*	Ch. 63—Not-for-profit Organizations
SFAS No. 125, *Accounting for Transfers and Servicing of Financial Assets and Extinguishments of Liabilities*	Ch. 14—Debt Extinguishments Ch. 31—Leases Ch. 35—Marketable Securities Ch. 52—Transfers and Servicing of Financial Assets Ch. 61—Lending and Mortgage Banking Activities
SFAS No. 126, *Exemption from Certain Required Disclosures about Financial Instruments for Certain Nonpublic Entities*	Ch. 21—Financial Instrument Disclosures
SFAS No. 127, *Deferral of the Effective Date of Certain Provisions of FASB Statement No. 125*	Ch. 52—Transfers and Servicing of Financial Assets
SFAS No. 128, *Earnings per Share*	Ch. 19—Earnings per Share
SFAS No. 129, *Disclosure of Information about Capital Structure*	Ch. 34—Long-term Obligation Disclosures Ch. 51—Stockholders' Equity
SFAS No. 130, *Reporting Comprehensive Income*	Ch. 8—Comprehensive Income Ch. 20—Equity Method Investments Ch. 22—Foreign Operations and Currency Translation Ch. 35—Marketable Securities
SFAS No. 131, *Disclosures about Segments of an Enterprise and Related Information*	Ch. 49—Segment Reporting

Authoritative Pronouncement	*Guide to GAAP* Reference

FINANCIAL ACCOUNTING STANDARDS BOARD INTERPRETATIONS (FASBI):

FASB Interpretation No. 1, *Accounting Changes Related to the Cost of Inventory*	Ch. 1—Accounting Changes
FASB Interpretation No. 2, *Imputing Interest on Debt Arrangements Made under the Federal Bankruptcy Act*	Superseded by SFAS No. 15
FASB Interpretation No. 3, *Accounting for the Cost of Pension Plans Subject to the Employee Retirement Income Security Act of 1974*	Superseded by SFAS No. 87
FASB Interpretation No. 4, *Applicability of FASB Statement No. 2 to Business Combinations Accounted for by the Purchase Method*	Ch. 3—Business Combinations Ch. 47—Research and Development Costs
FASB Interpretation No. 5, *Applicability of FASB Statement No. 2 to Development Stage Enterprises*	Superseded by SFAS No. 7
FASB Interpretation No. 6, *Applicability of FASB Statement No. 2 to Computer Software*	Ch. 47—Research and Development Costs Ch. 56—Computer Software Developers
FASB Interpretation No. 7, *Applying FASB Statement No. 7 in Financial Statements of Established Operating Enterprises*	Ch. 18—Development Stage Enterprises
FASB Interpretation No. 8, *Classification of a Short-Term Obligation Repaid Prior to Being Replaced by a Long-Term Security*	Ch. 12—Current Assets and Current Liabilities
FASB Interpretation No. 9, *Applying APB Opinions No. 16 and 17 When a Savings and Loan Association or Similar Institution Is Acquired in a Business Combination Accounted for by the Purchase Method*	Ch. 3—Business Combinations Ch. 53—Banking and Thrift Institutions
FASB Interpretation No. 10, *Application of FASB Statement No. 12 to Personal Financial Statements*	Superseded by SFAS No. 83
FASB Interpretation No. 11, *Changes in Market Value after the Balance Sheet Date*	Superseded by SFAS No. 115
FASB Interpretation No. 12, *Accounting for Previously Established Allowance Accounts*	Superseded by SFAS No. 115
FASB Interpretation No. 13, *Consolidation of a Parent and Its Subsidiaries Having Different Balance Sheet Dates*	Superseded by SFAS No. 115
FASB Interpretation No. 14, *Reasonable Estimation of the Amount of a Loss*	Ch. 10—Contingencies

Authoritative Pronouncement	***Guide to GAAP* Reference**
FINANCIAL ACCOUNTING STANDARDS BOARD INTERPRETATIONS (FASBI): (Continued)	
FASB Interpretation No. 15, *Translation of Unamortized Policy Acquisition Costs by a Stock Life Insurance Company*	Superseded by SFAS No. 52
FASB Interpretation No. 16, *Clarification of Definitions and Accounting for Marketable Equity Securities That Become Nonmarketable*	Superseded by SFAS No. 115
FASB Interpretation No. 17, *Applying the Lower of Cost or Market Rule in Translated Financial Statements*	Superseded by SFAS No. 52
FASB Interpretation No. 18, *Accounting for Income Taxes in Interim Periods*	Ch. 24—Income Taxes
FASB Interpretation No. 19, *Lessee Guarantee of the Residual Value of Leased Property*	Ch. 31—Leases
FASB Interpretation No. 20, *Reporting Accounting Changes under AICPA Statements of Position*	Ch. 1—Accounting Changes
FASB Interpretation No. 21, *Accounting for Leases in a Business Combination*	Ch. 31—Leases
FASB Interpretation No. 22, *Applicability of Indefinite Reversal Criteria to Timing Differences*	Superseded by SFAS Nos. 96 and 109
FASB Interpretation No. 23, *Leases of Certain Property Owned by a Governmental Unit or Authority*	Ch. 31—Leases
FASB Interpretation No. 24, *Leases Involving Only Part of a Building*	Ch. 31—Leases
FASB Interpretation No. 25, *Accounting for an Unused Investment Tax Credit*	Superseded by SFAS Nos. 96 and 109
FASB Interpretation No. 26, *Accounting for Purchase of a Leased Asset by the Lessee during the Term of the Lease*	Ch. 31—Leases
FASB Interpretation No. 27, *Accounting for a Loss on a Sublease*	Ch. 31—Leases
FASB Interpretation No. 28, *Accounting for Stock Appreciation Rights and Other Variable Stock Option or Award Plans*	Ch. 19—Earnings per Share Ch. 50—Stock Option and Purchase Plans
FASB Interpretation No. 29, *Reporting Tax Benefits Realized on Disposition of Investments in Certain Subsidiaries and Other Investees*	Superseded by SFAS Nos. 96 and 109

Authoritative Pronouncement	*Guide to GAAP* **Reference**
FINANCIAL ACCOUNTING STANDARDS BOARD INTERPRETATIONS (FASBI): (Continued)	
FASB Interpretation No. 30, *Accounting for Involuntary Conversions of Nonmonetary Assets to Monetary Assets*	Ch. 36—Nonmonetary Transactions
FASB Interpretation No. 31, *Treatment of Stock Compensation Plans in EPS Computations*	Superseded by SFAS No. 128
FASB Interpretation No. 32, *Application of Percentage Limitations in Recognizing Investment Tax Credit*	Superseded by SFAS Nos. 96 and 109
FASB Interpretation No. 33, *Applying FASB Statement No. 34 to Oil and Gas Producing Operations Accounted for by the Full Cost Method*	Ch. 27—Interest: Capitalized Ch. 64—Oil and Gas Producing Activities
FASB Interpretation No. 34, *Disclosure of Indirect Guarantees of Indebtedness of Others*	Ch. 10—Contingencies
FASB Interpretation No. 35, *Criteria for Applying the Equity Method of Accounting for Investments in Common Stock*	Ch. 20—Equity Method Investments
FASB Interpretation No. 36, *Accounting for Exploratory Wells in Progress at the End of a Period*	Ch. 64—Oil and Gas Producing Activities
FASB Interpretation No. 37, *Accounting for Translation Adjustments upon Sale of Part of an Investment in a Foreign Entity*	Ch. 22—Foreign Operations and Currency Translation
FASB Interpretation No. 38, *Determining the Measurement Date for Stock Option, Purchase, and Award Plans Involving Junior Stock*	Ch. 19—Earnings per Share Ch. 50—Stock Option and Purchase Plans
FASB Interpretation No. 39, *Offsetting of Amounts Related to Certain Contracts*	Ch. 37—Offsetting Assets and Liabilities
FASB Interpretation No. 40, *Applicability of Generally Accepted Accounting Principles to Mutual Life Insurance and Other Enterprises*	Ch. 60—Insurance Companies
FASB Interpretation No. 41, *Offsetting of Amounts Related to Certain Repurchase and Reverse Repurchase Agreements*	Ch. 37—Offsetting Assets and Liabilities
FASB Interpretation No. 42, *Accounting for Transfers of Assets in Which a Not-for-Profit Organization Is Granted Variance Power*	Ch. 11—Contributions Ch. 63—Not-for-profit Organizations

Authoritative Pronouncement	*Guide to GAAP* **Reference**
FINANCIAL ACCOUNTING STANDARDS BOARD TECHNICAL BULLETINS (FTB):	
FASB Technical Bulletin 79-1, *Purpose and Scope of FASB Technical Bulletins and Procedures for Issuance*	Superseded by FTB 79-1(R)
FASB Technical Bulletin 79-1R, *Purpose and Scope of FASB Technical Bulletins and Procedures for Issuance*	Not discussed
FASB Technical Bulletin 79-2, *Computer Software Costs*	Superseded by SFAS No. 86
FASB Technical Bulletin 79-3, *Subjective Acceleration Clauses in Long-Term Debt Agreements*	Ch. 12—Current Assets and Current Liabilities
FASB Technical Bulletin 79-4, *Segment Reporting of Puerto Rican Operations*	Ch. 49—Segment Reporting
FASB Technical Bulletin 79-5, *Meaning of the Term "Customer" as It Applies to Health Care Facilities under FASB Statement No. 14*	Ch. 49—Segment Reporting
FASB Technical Bulletin 79-6, *Valuation Allowances Following Debt Restructuring*	Superseded by SFAS No. 114
FASB Technical Bulletin 79-7, *Recoveries of a Previous Writedown under a Troubled Debt Restructuring Involving Modification of Terms*	Superseded by SFAS No. 114
FASB Technical Bulletin 79-8, *Applicability of FASB Statements 21 and 33 to Certain Brokers and Dealers in Securities*	Superseded by SFAS No. 131
FASB Technical Bulletin 79-9, *Accounting in Interim Periods for Changes in Income Tax Rates*	Ch. 24—Income Taxes
FASB Technical Bulletin 79-10, *Fiscal Funding Clauses in Lease Agreements*	Ch. 31—Leases
FASB Technical Bulletin 79-11, *Effect of a Penalty on the Term of a Lease*	Superseded by SFAS No. 98
FASB Technical Bulletin 79-12, *Interest Rate Used in Calculating the Present Value of Minimum Lease Payments*	Ch. 31—Leases
FASB Technical Bulletin 79-13, *Applicability of FASB Statement No. 13 to Current Value Financial Statements*	Ch. 31—Leases
FASB Technical Bulletin 79-14, *Upward Adjustment of Guaranteed Residual Values*	Ch. 31—Leases

Authoritative Pronouncement	*Guide to GAAP* **Reference**
FINANCIAL ACCOUNTING STANDARDS BOARD TECHNICAL BULLETINS (FTB): (Continued)	
FASB Technical Bulletin 79-15, *Accounting for Loss on a Sublease Not Involving the Disposal of a Segment*	Ch. 31—Leases
FASB Technical Bulletin 79-16, *Effect of a Change in Income Tax Rate on the Accounting for Leveraged Leases*	Superseded by FTB 79-16(R)
FASB Technical Bulletin 79-16(R), *Effect of a Change in Income Tax Rate on the Accounting for Leveraged Leases*	Ch. 31—Leases
FASB Technical Bulletin 79-17, *Reporting Cumulative Effect Adjustment from Retroactive Application of FASB Statement No. 13*	Ch. 31—Leases
FASB Technical Bulletin 79-18, *Transition Requirement of Certain FASB Amendments and Interpretations of FASB Statement No. 13*	Ch. 31—Leases
FASB Technical Bulletin 79-19, *Investor's Accounting for Unrealized Losses on Marketable Securities Owned by an Equity Method Investee*	Ch. 20—Equity Method Investments Ch. 35—Marketable Securities
FASB Technical Bulletin 80-1, *Early Extinguishment of Debt through Exchange for Common or Preferred Stock*	Ch. 14—Debt Extinguishments
FASB Technical Bulletin 80-2, *Classification of Debt Restructurings by Debtors and Creditors*	Ch. 16—Debt Restructurings
FASB Technical Bulletin 81-1, *Disclosure of Interest Rate Futures Contracts and Forward and Standby Contracts*	Superseded by SFAS No. 80
FASB Technical Bulletin 81-2, *Accounting for Unused Investment Tax Credits Acquired in a Business Combination Accounted for by the Purchase Method*	Superseded by SFAS Nos. 96 and 109
FASB Technical Bulletin 81-3, *Multiemployer Pension Plan Amendments Act of 1980*	Superseded by SFAS No. 87
FASB Technical Bulletin 81-4, *Classification as Monetary or Nonmonetary Items*	Superseded by SFAS No. 89
FASB Technical Bulletin 81-5, *Offsetting Interest Cost to Be Capitalized with Interest Income*	Superseded by SFAS No. 62
FASB Technical Bulletin 81-6, *Applicability of Statement 15 to Debtors in Bankruptcy Situations*	Ch. 16—Debt Restructurings

Authoritative Pronouncement	*Guide to GAAP* **Reference**
FINANCIAL ACCOUNTING STANDARDS BOARD TECHNICAL BULLETINS (FTB): (Continued)	
FASB Technical Bulletin 82-1, *Disclosure of the Sale or Purchase of Tax Benefits through Tax Leases*	Ch. 24—Income Taxes
FASB Technical Bulletin 82-2, *Accounting for the Conversion of Stock Options into Incentive Stock Options as a Result of the Economic Recovery Tax Act of 1981*	Superseded by SFAS No. 123
FASB Technical Bulletin 83-1, *Accounting for the Reduction in the Tax Basis of an Asset Caused by the Investment Tax Credit*	Superseded by SFAS Nos. 96 and 109
FASB Technical Bulletin 84-1, *Accounting for Stock Issued to Acquire the Results of a Research and Development Arrangement*	Ch. 47—Research and Development Costs
FASB Technical Bulletin 84-2, *Accounting for the Effects of the Tax Reform Act of 1984 on Deferred Income Taxes Relating to Domestic International Sales Corporations*	Superseded by SFAS Nos. 96 and 109
FASB Technical Bulletin 84-3, *Accounting for the Effects of the Tax Reform Act of 1984 on Deferred Income Taxes of Stock Life Insurance Enterprises*	Superseded by SFAS Nos. 96 and 109
FASB Technical Bulletin 84-4, *In-Substance Defeasance of Debt*	Superseded by SFAS No. 125
FASB Technical Bulletin 85-1, *Accounting for the Receipt of Federal Home Loan Mortgage Corporation Participating Preferred Stock*	Ch. 36—Nonmonetary Transactions
FASB Technical Bulletin 85-2, *Accounting for Collateralized Mortgage Obligations*	Superseded by SFAS No. 125
FASB Technical Bulletin 85-3, *Accounting for Operating Leases with Scheduled Rent Increases*	Ch. 31—Leases
FASB Technical Bulletin 85-4, *Accounting for Purchases of Life Insurance*	Ch. 25—Insurance Costs
FASB Technical Bulletin 85-5, *Issues Relating to Accounting for Business Combinations, Including* • *Costs of Closing Duplicate Facilities of an Acquirer* • *Stock Transactions between Companies under Common Control* • *Downstream Mergers* • *Identical Common Shares for a Pooling of Interests* • *Pooling of Interests by Mutual and Cooperative Enterprises*	Ch. 3—Business Combinations

Authoritative Pronouncement	**_Guide to GAAP_ Reference**

FINANCIAL ACCOUNTING STANDARDS BOARD TECHNICAL BULLETINS (FTB): (Continued)

FASB Technical Bulletin 85-6, _Accounting for a Purchase of Treasury Shares at a Price Significantly in Excess of the Current Market Price of the Shares and the Income Statement Classification of Costs Incurred in Defending against a Takeover Attempt_

Ch. 51—Stockholders' Equity

FASB Technical Bulletin 86-1, _Accounting for Certain Effects of the Tax Reform Act of 1986_

Superseded by SFAS Nos. 96 and 109

FASB Technical Bulletin 86-2, _Accounting for an Interest in the Residual Value of a Leased Asset:_
- _Acquired by a Third Party or_
- _Retained by a Lessor That Sells the Related Minimum Rental Payments_

Ch. 31—Leases
Ch. 37—Offsetting Assets and Liabilities

FASB Technical Bulletin 87-1, _Accounting for a Change in Method of Accounting for Certain Postretirement Benefits_

Superseded by SFAS No. 106

FASB Technical Bulletin 87-2, _Computation of a Loss on an Abandonment_

Ch. 66—Regulated Operations

FASB Technical Bulletin 87-3, _Accounting for Mortgage Servicing Fees and Rights_

Ch. 61—Lending and Mortgage Banking Activities

FASB Technical Bulletin 88-1, _Issues Relating to Accounting for Leases:_
- _Time Pattern of the Physical Use of the Property in an Operating Lease_
- _Lease Incentives in an Operating Lease_
- _Applicability of Leveraged Lease Accounting to Existing Assets of the Lessor_
- _Money-Over-Money Lease Transactions_
- _Wrap Lease Transactions_

Ch. 31—Leases

FASB Technical Bulletin 88-2, _Definition of a Right of Setoff_

Superseded by FASBI 39

FASB Technical Bulletin 90-1, _Accounting for Separately Priced Extended Warranty and Product Maintenance Contracts_

Ch. 48—Revenue Recognition

FASB Technical Bulletin 94-1, _Application of Statement 115 to Debt Securities Restructured in a Troubled Debt Restructuring_

Ch. 35—Marketable Securities

SELF-STUDY CPE

Guide to GAAP

Table of Contents

Registered with the National Association of State Boards of Accountancy as a sponsor of continuing professional education on the National Registry of CPE Sponsors. State boards of accountancy have final authority on the acceptance of individual courses. Complaints regarding sponsors may be addressed to NASBA, 150 Fourth Avenue North, Suite 700, Nashville, TN 37219-2417, (615) 880-4200.

State Board Registration Numbers

Indiana	CE92000369
Illinois	158-000837
New York	E96-740
NASBA	91-00221-97

SELF-STUDY CONTINUING
PROFESSIONAL EDUCATION

INTRODUCTION

Four 10-hour Courses Included

This section of your *Guide* contains four 10-hour self-study CPE courses. The first and second are new courses, while the third and fourth are updated from last year. You may complete any or all of the courses. Completing the courses is optional: however, there is a separate charge for grading and processing your examination questions for each course. To obtain credit, the courses must be postmarked by December 31, 1998.

Taking the Courses

For each course, you will be asked to complete a reading assignment, review the key points, and take a short self-study quiz. After completing the quiz, you can evaluate your progress by comparing your answers with the correct answers provided. References are cited so you can refer to the *Guide* if you have answered any questions incorrectly.

Obtaining CPE Credit

The AICPA's *Statement on Standards for Formal Continuing Professional Education (CPE) Programs* allows CPE credit equal to half of the average completion time for noninteractive self-study courses. Because of that ruling, each course provides 10 hours of CPE credit even though it is designed to take approximately 20 hours to complete (measured in 50-minute contact hours).

After completing a course, you can receive CPE credit by completing an **Examination for CPE Credit Answer Sheet** (located behind the Self-study CPE 4) and sending your completed answer sheet to PPC for grading. Payment for $42 (by check or credit card) must accompany each examination submitted. We cannot process examinations that do not include payment. If you submit the examinations for more than one course, a single check covering payment of all examinations submitted is acceptable. A certificate documenting 10 hours of CPE credit will be issued for each examination score of 75% or higher. The Examination contains instructions for obtaining CPE credit. Also, please take a few minutes to complete the **Course Evaluation** (located behind each **Examination for CPE Credit Answer Sheet**) and return it to us so that we can provide you with the best possible CPE.

If more than one person wants to complete this self-study course, each person should complete a separate Examination for CPE Credit Answer Sheet. We would also appreciate their completing a separate Course Evaluation. Payment of $42 must accompany each examination submitted.

Retaining CPE Records

For all scores of 75% or higher, PPC will send a *Certificate of Completion*. You should retain it and a copy of these materials for at least five years.

In-firm Training

PPC also offers a number of in-firm training classes that provide up to eight hours of CPE credit. Please call our Sales Department at (800) 323-8724 for more information.

Section I

Chapters 27–39

OVERVIEW

RECOMMENDED FOR: Users of PPC's *Guide to GAAP*

PREREQUISITE: None

CPE CREDIT: 10 Hours

SUBJECT CATEGORY: Accounting and Auditing

EXPIRATION DATE: Postmarked by December 31, 1998

KNOWLEDGE LEVEL: Basic

MAJOR SUBJECTS:

Chapter 27—Interest: Capitalized

Chapter 28—Interest: Imputed

Chapter 29—Interim Financial Reporting

Chapter 30—Inventory

Chapter 31—Leases

Chapter 32—Loan Impairment

Chapter 33—Long-lived Assets, Depreciation, and Impairment

Chapter 34—Long-term Obligation Disclosures

Chapter 35—Marketable Securities

Chapter 36—Nonmonetary Transactions

Chapter 37—Offsetting Assets and Liabilities

Chapter 38—Pension Plan Financial Statements

Chapter 39—Pension Plans: Accounting by Employers

Self-study
CPE
1

SELF-STUDY CPE 1

CHAPTERS 27–39

LEARNING OBJECTIVES

After completing the reading assignment below, you should be able to:

- identify assets that qualify for interest capitalization and determine the amount of interest cost to capitalize.

- determine the appropriate interest rate for imputed interest and account for the related discount or premium.

- account for revenues, expenses, inventories, changes in accounting principles, adjustments, and income taxes in interim periods.

- value inventory.

- classify and account for leases.

- determine when a loan is impaired, measure impairment, and recognize income on impaired loans.

- account for the cost, depreciation, and impairment of long-lived assets.

- disclose required information for long-term obligations.

- account for debt and equity securities, as well as futures contracts.

- account for nonmonetary transactions and involuntary conversions of nonmonetary assets to monetary assets.

- understand the criteria for offsetting assets and liabilities.

- understand the required pension plan financial statements, including the statement of net assets available for benefits and the statement of changes in net assets available for benefits.

- account for defined benefit and defined contribution pension plans.

READING ASSIGNMENT

Read Chapters 27–39 of the *Guide*.

KEY POINTS

After reading the assigned material, you should understand the following key points. If any of them are unclear, review the **READING ASSIGNMENT** again.

Interest: Capitalized

✓ The capitalization period for interest generally begins when all of the following conditions are met:

   a. Expenditures have been made.

   b. Activities necessary to prepare the asset for its intended use are in progress.

    c.   Interest cost is being incurred.

✓   The interest capitalization period ends when the asset is substantially complete and ready for its intended use.

✓   The interest capitalization rate used should be based on rates that apply to outstanding borrowings during the period, as follows:

    a.   If debt can be directly associated with a qualifying asset, the rate on that debt should be applied to the average accumulated expenditures up to the debt amount.

    b.   If average accumulated expenditures exceed directly associated debt, a weighted average of the rates applicable to other debt should be applied to the average accumulated expenditures that exceed the directly associated debt.

✓   If no specific borrowing was incurred to acquire the asset, interest should be capitalized in accordance with the prior procedure.

✓   Interest capitalized during a period should not exceed the interest costs actually incurred during the period.

✓   The following disclosures about interest costs should be included in the financial statements or related notes:

    a.   The amount of interest costs incurred and charged to expense during the period

    b.   The amount of interest costs capitalized during the period, if any

✓   SFAS No. 95, *Statement of Cash Flows,* requires the amount of interest paid, net of amounts capitalized, to be disclosed. The disclosure may be made on the face of the cash flow statement or in the notes.

Interest: Imputed

✓   When imputing interest on a note whose interest rate is not reasonable in comparison to prevailing market conditions, the interest rate used to determine the present value of future payments should approximate the rate that an independent borrower and an independent lender would have negotiated in a similar transaction.

✓   If the present value of a note's future cash flows exceeds the face amount of the note, a premium exists. A discount exists if the present value of the note's future cash flows is less than the face amount of the note. Amortization of a discount or premium should be reported as interest expense or income over the life of the note.

✓   A discount or premium on a note should not be reported on the balance sheet as a separate asset or liability. Instead, it should be added to or subtracted from the related note balance.

✓   The financial statements or notes to the financial statements should include a description of any notes, including their effective interest rates and the face amounts of the notes.

Interim Financial Reporting

✓   The results of each interim period should be based on the accounting principles and practices used by a company in preparing its latest annual financial statements, unless a change in accounting practice or policy has been adopted during the current year.

✓   Some difficulties in applying GAAP in interim periods may arise and certain accounting principles may require modification at interim dates so that the interim period's results better relate to annual results. Therefore, modifications to GAAP are permitted or required for interim periods in certain circumstances. For example—

a. inventories may be estimated at interim dates using the gross profit method when interim physical inventory counts are not taken.

b. income taxes may be estimated at interim dates by applying an estimated annual effective tax rate.

c. other modifications of accounting principles, such as estimating depreciation expense and assigning a portion to interim periods, may be necessary to properly recognize revenues and expenses.

✓ For interim financial statements, a change in an accounting principle occurs if an accounting principle or the method of applying a principle differs from that used in the preceding interim period, the prior annual period, or the comparable interim period of the prior year.

✓ With certain exceptions, disclosures required in interim financial statements generally are the same as those required in annual financial statements.

Inventory

✓ Generally, inventory should be recorded at cost, which includes all direct and indirect costs incurred to prepare it for sale or use. Allocating indirect costs between inventory and period expense is a key factor in determining inventory cost.

✓ The following methods of determining the sequence of inventory costs to be charged to cost of sales are permitted under GAAP:

a. Specific identification

b. First-in, first-out

c. Last-in, first-out

d. Average cost

✓ GAAP recognizes that in some cases, it may be preferable to use variations of the above methods, such as the retail inventory method or the standard cost method.

✓ Obsolescence, deterioration, damage, changing prices, or other factors may cause an inventory's recorded cost to exceed its market value. In such cases, GAAP requires inventory to be written down to market value and an unrealized loss to be recognized in current period income.

✓ Generally, the lower of cost or market rule should be applied to each item in inventory. However, it may be applied to each inventory item, total inventory, or the total of the components of each major category of inventory depending on the method that most fairly presents current period income.

✓ A company should include the following disclosures about inventories in its financial statements:

a. Basis for stating inventories

b. Method of determining costs

c. Unusual losses resulting from lower of cost or market adjustments

Leases

✓ A lessee should classify a lease as a capital lease if the lease meets at least one of the following criteria:

a. The lease passes title to the lessee by the end of the lease term.

Self-study
CPE 1

    b. The lease contains a bargain purchase option.

    c. The lease term is at least 75% of the property's estimated remaining economic life.

    d. The present value of the minimum lease payments is at least 90% of the property's fair value.

✓   The 75% and 90% tests do not apply if the lease term begins within the last 25% of the leased property's total estimated economic life.

✓   Direct financing and sales-type leases are the lessor's equivalent of a capital lease.

✓   In a sales-type lease—

    a. the leased property's book value is different from its fair value.

    b. the transaction provides a profit or loss to the lessor.

    c. both a profit element and a financing element are recognized.

✓   In a direct financing lease—

    a. the fair value and book value of the leased asset are the same.

    b. there is no profit or loss involved for the lessor.

    c. the lease is accounted for as a financing.

    d. the difference between the total lease payments to be received and the book value of the property is assumed to be the equivalent of interest that would have been paid had the lessee borrowed the money from the lessor to purchase the property.

✓   A lessor should classify a lease as a sales-type or direct financing lease if the lease meets at least one of the lessee's criteria for a capital lease and both of the following criteria:

    a. Collectibility of the minimum lease payments is reasonably predictable.

    b. There are no important uncertainties about additional unreimbursed costs the lessor will incur.

✓   A leveraged lease is structured primarily to provide certain tax benefits (and the temporary use of funds due to taxes saved in the early years of the lease) to the lessor without the lessor being entirely at risk for nonperformance by the lessee.

✓   A leveraged lease must meet the criteria for classification as a direct financing lease and possess all of the following additional characteristics:

    a. It involves a lessee, a lessor, and a long-term creditor.

    b. The financing provided by the long-term creditor is nonrecourse to the general credit of the lessor.

    c. The amount of financing provided by the long-term creditor is substantial to the transaction.

    d. The lessor's net investment in the lease declines in the early years of the lease and rises during the later years before it is finally eliminated.

    e. Any investment tax credit retained by the lessor is deferred and allocated to income over the lease term.

✓   A lessee should account for a capital lease as if the leased asset was purchased and the entire purchase price was financed, as follows:

Self-study CPE 1

    a. The lessee should record a leased asset and a lease obligation of the same amount.

    b. The amount recorded should be the lesser of the fair value of the leased asset at the inception of the lease or the present value of the minimum lease payments as of the beginning of the lease term.

    c. The lessee should depreciate the leased asset over its estimated useful life down to its expected value to the lessee at the end of the lease term. The period over which the asset should be depreciated and the value to which it should be depreciated depend on why the lease was capitalized.

    d. The lessee's capital lease obligation should be accounted for using the interest method of accounting. Consequently, a portion of each minimum lease payment should be allocated to interest expense, and the remainder applied to reduce the obligation, so that a constant rate of interest is produced on the outstanding liability.

✓ A lessee should account for an operating lease by charging the lease payments to expense, generally on a straight-line basis over the lease term.

✓ A lessor should account for a sales-type lease as follows:

    a. The gross investment in the lease and the present value of the gross investment in the lease should be determined.

    b. The present value of the gross investment should be recorded as a receivable and classified as current or noncurrent.

    c. The difference between the gross investment and its present value should be recorded as unearned income and amortized over the lease term using the interest method.

    d. The present value of the minimum lease payments to be received should be recognized as income.

    e. The carrying amount of the leased property, plus any initial direct costs and less the present value of the unguaranteed residual value, should be charged against income.

✓ A lessor should account for a direct financing lease as follows:

    a. The gross investment in the lease should be determined.

    b. The difference between the gross investment and the book value of the property represents unearned interest income. The unearned interest income and any initial direct costs should be amortized to income over the lease term using the interest method.

    c. The net investment in the lease (the gross investment plus any unamortized initial direct costs minus the unearned interest income) should be shown as a single line item on the balance sheet and classified as current and noncurrent.

✓ A lessor should account for a leveraged lease as follows:

    a. The net investment (rents receivable, investment tax credit receivable, the estimated residual value of the leased asset, and unearned and deferred income) should be recorded net of the principal and interest on the nonrecourse debt.

    b. The total net income over the lease term is determined by subtracting the original investment from total cash receipts.

    c. The total net income over the lease term should only be recognized in periods in which the net investment net of deferred taxes is positive.

    d. If, at any time, projected cash receipts over the remaining term of the lease are less than the lessor's investment in the lease, a loss should be recognized immediately.

Self-study CPE 1

✓   A lessor should account for an operating lease as follows:

a. The leased asset should continue to be carried in the lessor's balance sheet and depreciated according to the lessor's normal depreciation policy.

b. Rent income should be reported as it becomes receivable, generally on a straight-line basis.

✓   If the provisions of a capital lease are changed (other than by renewing or extending the term), the lessee should account for the lease as follows:

a. If the revised lease would have been an operating lease, the asset and obligation are written off and a gain or loss is recognized for the difference.

b. If the revised lease is still a capital lease, but the revision changes the remaining minimum lease payments, the lease obligation should be adjusted to the present value of the remaining minimum lease payments. The asset should be adjusted by the same amount, and no gain or loss should be recorded.

✓   If a sales-type or direct financing lease is revised, and the revised lease would have been an operating lease had the revised terms existed at inception, the lessor should account for the lease as follows:

a. The net investment in the lease should be written off.

b. The leased asset should be recorded on the lessor's books at the lower of its original cost, present fair value, or present carrying amount.

c. Any difference in the net investment and the amount at which the asset is recorded on the lessor's books should be recognized as a loss in the period of the change.

✓   If a sales-type or direct financing lease is revised, the revision changes the remaining minimum lease payments, and the revised lease would still have been a sales-type or direct financing lease had the revised terms existed at inception, the lessor should account for the lease as follows:

a. The gross investment in the lease should be adjusted to reflect the new minimum lease payments receivable and the new estimated residual value, if affected.

b. The net adjustment should be charged or credited to unearned income.

✓   When a capital lease is terminated because the lessee purchases the leased asset from the lessor, the lessee should remove the lease obligation and record the difference between the purchase price and the obligation as an adjustment to the carrying amount of the asset.

✓   When a capital lease is terminated other than due to the purchase of the leased asset by the lessee, the lessee should write off the leased asset and obligation and record any difference as a gain or loss. The lessor should account for the termination in the same way as for a change in the provisions of a sales-type or direct financing lease.

✓   Changes in circumstances or estimates, such as changes in the estimated economic life or residual value of leased assets, do not require the classification of the lease to be reconsidered.

✓   Classifying real estate leases depends on whether they involve land only; land and buildings; land, buildings, and equipment; or only part of a building.

✓   If a new lessee is substituted for the original lessee under a new agreement, and the original lease agreement is terminated, the transaction is accounted for by both the original lessee and the original lessor as a termination.

Self-study CPE **1**

✓   If a new lessee is substituted under the original lease agreement for the original lessee, and the new lessee is primarily obligated for the lease, the lessor's accounting for the original lease is unchanged. The original lessee, however, should account for the transaction as a termination.

✓   If the lessee subleases the property, the original lessor's and lessee's accounting for the original lease should not change. The original lessee (new sublessor) should classify and account for the sublease as a new agreement.

✓   A sale-leaseback transaction occurs when an owner sells property and then leases all or part of it back from the new owner.

    a.   The buyer-lessor should treat the sale-leaseback as two separate transactions—the purchase of an asset and the lease (either operating or direct financing) of an asset.

    b.   The seller-lessee should account for the lease portion of the sale-leaseback as a capital lease (if it meets the applicable criteria), or as an operating lease. Except in certain situations, any profit or loss on the sale of the asset should be deferred and amortized in proportion to the amortization of the leased asset (if the lease is classified as a capital lease) or in proportion to the gross rental charged to expense over the lease term (if the lease is classified as an operating lease).

Loan Impairment

✓   A loan is considered impaired if it is probable that the creditor will be unable to collect at least some of the scheduled principal or interest payments under the contractual terms of the loan agreement.

✓   The value of an impaired loan should be measured based on the present value of expected future cash flows discounted at the loan's effective interest rate, the loan's market price, or the fair value of the loan's collateral (less discounted estimated costs to sell).

✓   If the value of the loan is less than the recorded investment in the loan, a loss should be recognized by recording or adjusting a valuation allowance and charging bad debt expense.

Long-lived Assets, Depreciation, and Impairment

✓   A tangible long-lived capital asset should be recorded at acquisition cost, including all costs necessary to bring the asset to its location in working condition.

    a.   The asset should not be written up to reflect appraisal, market, or current values that are above cost.

    b.   The cost of the asset, less salvage value, should be depreciated over the asset's estimated useful life.

✓   Prior period financial statements should not be adjusted for changes in the estimated useful life or salvage value of a capital asset. Instead, the dollar amount of the change should be recorded entirely in current year earnings or current and future earnings if the change affects both.

✓   A change in accounting principle due to a change in the method used to depreciate previously recorded assets is recorded by including the cumulative effect of the change as of the beginning of the year of the change in current period earnings.

✓   When it is determined that the carrying value of a capital asset will not be fully recovered, the asset is considered impaired. Accounting for impaired assets depends on whether the company intends to dispose of the asset or continue to use the asset.

    a.   An asset that will be sold or abandoned should be stated at the lower of carrying value or fair value less costs to sell.

Self-study
CPE   **1**

      (1)   The carrying amount of the asset should be adjusted (either up or down) for subsequent changes in fair value, but should never be adjusted above the asset's original carrying amount.

      (2)   Assets to be disposed of should not be depreciated while held for disposal.

  b. If the carrying amount of an asset that will be held and used in the company's operations exceeds the expected undiscounted cash flows from continuing to use the asset:

      (1)   An impairment loss should be recorded for the amount by which the asset's carrying amount exceeds its fair value.

      (2)   The asset's reduced carrying amount becomes its new cost. Subsequent recoveries of the impairment loss due to increases in the asset's fair value should not be recognized.

✓   Impairment losses related to long-lived assets should be reported as a component of income from continuing operations before income taxes.

Long-term Obligation Disclosures

✓   An unconditional purchase obligation requires one party to transfer funds to another party in the future in return for specified quantities of goods and services at specified prices.

✓   The following information should be disclosed about unconditional purchase obligations that have not been recognized in the balance sheet:

  a. Nature and term of the obligations

  b. Total amount of the fixed and determinable portion of the obligations as of the date of the latest balance sheet presented and, if determinable, for each of the five succeeding fiscal years

  c. Nature of any variable components of the obligations

  d. Amounts actually purchased under the obligations for each period for which an income statement is presented

✓   If an unconditional purchase obligation has been recorded, the total payments required for each of the five years following the latest balance sheet date presented should be disclosed.

Marketable Securities

✓   A debt security for which the entity has both the positive intent and ability to hold to maturity should be classified as held-to-maturity and reported in the balance sheet at its amortized cost.

✓   Debt and equity securities with readily determinable fair values should be classified as trading securities if they are purchased and held principally for the purpose of selling them in the near term.

  a. Trading securities should be reported in the balance sheet at fair value.

  b. Realized and unrealized gains and losses on trading securities should be included in earnings in the period they arise.

✓   Investments not classified as held-to-maturity or trading should be classified as available-for-sale.

  a. Available-for-sale investments should be reported in the balance sheet at fair value.

  b. Unrealized gains and losses on available-for-sale securities should be reported as other comprehensive income.

Self-study
CPE 1

    c.   Realized gains and losses should be included in income in the period they are realized.

✓   If the fair value of an available-for-sale or held-to-maturity security is less than its carrying amount and the decline is other than temporary, the carrying amount of the investment should be reduced to fair value. The amount of the writedown should be included in earnings as if it were a realized loss.

✓   In a futures contract, an investor agrees to purchase or sell specified amounts of a commodity on a specified future date at a specified price. Generally, the deposit paid to the commodities broker for the futures contract should be recorded as an asset and the recorded amount increased or decreased as the market value of the contract changes.

Nonmonetary Transactions

✓   As a general rule, the amount recorded for an asset received in a nonmonetary exchange should be the fair value of the asset given up (or the fair value of the asset received if it is more clearly evident) and a gain or loss should be recognized on the transaction.

    a.   Exceptions to the general rule relate to exchanges in which fair value is not determinable, like-kind exchanges, and nonreciprocal transfers to owners.

    b.   If neither the fair value of the asset given up nor the fair value of the asset received can be determined within reasonable limits, the recorded amount of the asset transferred should be used to measure the transaction.

✓   A like-kind exchange involving only nonmonetary assets should be based on recorded amounts and no gain or loss recognized. If the exchange involves monetary consideration—

    a.   The entity receiving the monetary consideration should recognize a portion of any gain on the transaction in the ratio of cash received to total consideration received.

    b.   The entity paying the monetary consideration should record the new asset at the surrendered asset's book value plus the cash payment and not recognize any gain.

    c.   Any losses on the exchange should be recognized by the entity receiving the monetary consideration.

✓   Generally, nonreciprocal transfers of nonmonetary assets to owners should be recorded at fair value if the fair value of the assets distributed are objectively measurable and could have been realized in an outright sale at or near the time of the distribution.

Offsetting Assets and Liabilities

✓   Assets and liabilities should not be offset (reported at a net amount) in a statement of financial position unless a right of setoff exists.

✓   A right of setoff exists when all of the following conditions are met:

    a.   Each of two parties owes the other determinable amounts.

    b.   The reporting party has the right to set off the amount owed with the amount owed by the other party.

    c.   The reporting party intends to set off.

    d.   The right of setoff is enforceable at law.

Pension Plan Financial Statements

✓   GAAP does not require defined benefit pension plans to prepare or distribute financial statements. If annual financial statements are prepared, however, GAAP requires that they include the following:

   a. Statement of net assets available for benefits as of the plan's year end

   b. Statement of changes during the year in net assets available for benefits

   c. Information about the actuarial present value of accumulated plan benefits as of either the beginning or end of the plan's year

   d. Information about significant factors affecting the change during the year in the actuarial present value of accumulated plan benefits

✓ The primary purpose of the statement of net assets available for benefits is to identify the resources that are available to pay benefits to plan participants. The statement, which should be prepared on the accrual basis of accounting, includes information about the plan's liabilities as well as its assets.

✓ SFAS No. 35 requires the statement of changes in net assets available for benefits to identify the significant changes in net assets and to disclose the following:

   a. The net change in fair value for each significant class of investments

   b. Investment income, excluding the separately reported net change in fair value

   c. Contributions from the employer, segregated between cash and noncash contributions

   d. Contributions from participants

   e. Contributions from other identified sources

   f. Benefits paid to participants

   g. Payments to insurance companies to purchase contracts that are excluded from plan assets

   h. Administrative expenses

✓ The benefit obligation information may be presented either as a separate statement, on the face of another statement, or in the notes to the financial statements, as long as it is presented all in one place.

✓ Significant changes affecting the actuarial present value of accumulated plan benefits should be identified. Information about the changes may be presented as a separate statement, on the face of another statement, or in notes to the financial statements, as long as it is presented all in one place. At a minimum, the significant effects of the following should be disclosed:

   a. Plan amendments

   b. Changes in the nature of the plan

   c. Changes in actuarial assumptions

   d. Actuarial present value of accumulated plan benefits as of the preceding benefit information date, if the three preceding items are presented in other than a statement format

Pension Plans: Accounting by Employers

✓ The following are the two basic types of pension plans:

   a. A defined benefit plan provides specified benefits to plan participants. The benefits are based on a variety of factors including a participant's age, years of service, and compensation.

b. A defined contribution plan provides an individual account for each participant and specifies how contributions to the individual's account are to be determined. Defined contribution plans do not define specific benefit amounts that participants are to receive. Instead, they provide benefits based solely on (1) the amount contributed to a participant's account, (2) the returns earned on the investment of those contributions, and (3) forfeitures of other participants' benefits that may be allocated to the participant's account.

✓ The annual pension cost of a defined benefit pension plan consists of the following six components:

     a. Service cost

     b. Interest cost on the projected benefit obligation

     c. Actual return on plan assets

     d. Amortization of unrecognized prior service cost

     e. Amortization of unrecognized gains and losses

     f. Amortization of the unrecognized net asset or net obligation for the plan at the time SFAS No. 87 was first adopted

✓ Service cost relates only to employee service rendered during the year and is computed as the actuarial present value of benefits attributed by the pension benefit formula to employee service during the period. It requires assumptions about the attrition of present participants and future changes in their compensation and ignores participants that may be added to the plan in the future.

✓ Interest cost reflects interest for the year on the plan's obligation to provide benefits. The information needed to compute interest cost is (a) the projected benefit obligation and (b) an assumed discount rate.

✓ Actual return on plan assets generally represents realized and unrealized investment gains and losses as well as any interest and dividends received.

✓ Amortization of unrecognized prior service cost is determined by amortizing the cost of providing benefits related to services rendered before a plan was adopted or amended over the remaining service lives of participants who are active at the date of the plan adoption or amendment.

✓ Gains and losses arise when the following occur:

     a. Assumptions used to compute the projected benefit obligation change.

     b. Actual results differ from the expected return on plan assets.

✓ Generally, gains and losses are not required to be included in pension expense in the period they arise. Instead, they may be deferred until amortization is required in a future year, as follows:

     a. Amortization is required in any year in which the beginning of the year unrecognized net gain or loss exceeds the greater of 10% of the projected benefit obligation or the market-related value of plan assets.

     b. In such years, the amount of net gain or loss that must be included in net pension cost is the excess net gain or loss divided by the average remaining service lives of active employees.

✓ GAAP allows an employer to amortize the difference between the fair value of plan assets and the projected benefit obligation to earnings over future years, as follows:

Self-study
CPE

   a. As it is amortized, the difference is charged or credited to pension cost and credited or charged to accrued pension cost (or to prepaid pension cost if there is no accrual).

   b. The difference should be amortized using the straight-line method.

   c. The amortization period should be the average remaining service period of participants that were employed when SFAS No. 87 was adopted, except in certain circumstances.

✓   Plan assets and pension obligations generally should be measured as of the employer's financial statement date or, if used consistently from year to year, as of a date not more than three months prior to the date of the financial statements.

✓   An employer that sponsors a defined contribution plan should disclose the following items separately from disclosures about its defined benefit pension plan:

   a. A description of the plan

   b. The amount of pension cost recognized during the period

Self-study CPE 1

SELF-STUDY QUIZ

Select the best answer for each question below and circle the corresponding letter. Then check your answers with the correct answers in the following section.

1. **Which of the following conditions must be met before the capitalization period for interest begins?**

   a. Interest cost is being incurred.

   b. Expenditures have been made.

   c. Activities necessary to prepare the asset for its intended use are in progress.

   d. All of the above.

2. **Which of the following rates should NOT be used to determine the interest capitalization rate?**

   a. The interest rate on borrowings for previous debt not associated with the qualifying asset when that interest rate is twice as high as the current interest rate that could have been obtained.

   b. A weighted average of the rates applicable to other debt applied to the average accumulated expenditures that exceed the directly associated debt.

   c. The rate on debt directly associated with a qualifying asset.

   d. A weighted average of the rates applicable to other debt applied to the average accumulated expenditures if no specific borrowing was incurred to acquire the asset.

3. **Which of the following is NOT a required financial statement disclosure about interest costs?**

   a. The amount of interest paid during the period, net of amounts capitalized

   b. The present value of future interest costs on debt incurred during the period

   c. The amount of interest costs capitalized during the period

   d. The amount of interest costs incurred and charged to expense during the period

4. **Which of the following is correct regarding a discount or premium on a note?**

   a. A discount or premium should be reported on the balance sheet as a separate asset or liability.

   b. A discount exists if the face amount of the note is less than the note's future cash flows.

   c. A premium exists if the face amount of the note exceeds the present value of the note's future cash flows.

   d. A discount or premium should be amortized to interest expense or income over the life of the note.

5. **Which of the following should be disclosed about a note in the financial statements?**

   a. Effective interest rate

   b. Face amount

   c. Description of the note

   d. All of the above

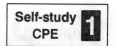

Self-study
CPE   1

6. **Which of the following does NOT apply to interim financial reporting?**

   a. A change in accounting principle occurs if an accounting principle differs from that used in the comparable interim period of the prior year.

   b. Disclosures required in interim financial statements generally are the same as those required in annual financial statements.

   c. Modifications to GAAP are not permitted for interim periods.

   d. In general, the results of each interim period should be based on the accounting principles used in preparing the latest annual financial statements.

7. **Which of the following modifications to GAAP are NOT permitted for interim periods?**

   a. Income taxes may be estimated at interim dates.

   b. Adjustments may be made to annualize seasonal revenue.

   c. Inventories may be estimated at interim dates using the gross profit method.

   d. Depreciation expense may be estimated and a portion assigned to interim periods.

8. **Which of the following statements correctly describes the lower of cost or market rule?**

   a. The lower of cost or market rule must be applied to each item in inventory.

   b. Inventory should be recorded at market value if that amount exceeds recorded cost.

   c. When inventory is written down to market value, an unrealized loss should be recognized in current period income.

   d. All of the above.

9. **Which of the following is NOT a required financial statement disclosure for inventories?**

   a. The market value of the inventories

   b. Unusual losses resulting from lower of cost or market adjustments

   c. The basis for stating inventories

   d. The method of determining costs

10. **Which of the following is NOT a criteria for a lessee to classify a lease as a capital lease?**

    a. The lease contains a bargain purchase option.

    b. The lease reverts title to the lessor at the end of the lease term.

    c. The present value of the minimum lease payments is at least 90% of the property's fair value.

    d. The lease term is at least 75% of the property's estimated remaining economic life.

11. **Which of the following is a characteristic of a direct financing lease?**

    a. The transaction provides a profit or loss to the lessor.

    b. The leased property's book value is different from its fair value.

    c. The fair value and book value of the leased asset are the same.

    d. The lease is accounted for as a sale.

Self-study CPE 1

12. **Which of the following is NOT a characteristic of a leveraged lease?**

    a. The amount of financing provided by the long-term creditor gives the lessor substantial leverage.

    b. The lease involves at least three parties.

    c. Collectibility of the minimum lease payments is reasonably predictable.

    d. Both a profit element and a financing element are recognized.

13. **Which of the following is NOT correct regarding a lessee's accounting for a capital lease?**

    a. The entire amount of each lease payment should be charged to expense.

    b. The leased asset should be depreciated over its estimated useful life.

    c. A portion of each lease payment should be allocated to interest expense.

    d. The leased asset and liability initially should be recorded at the same amount.

14. **Which of the following is correct regarding a lessor's accounting for a sales-type lease?**

    a. The present value of the minimum lease payments should be recorded as a receivable.

    b. The difference between the gross investment and the book value of the property should be recorded as unearned income.

    c. The total net income over the lease term is determined by subtracting the original investment from total cash receipts.

    d. None of the above.

15. **Which of the following is correct with regard to the termination of a capital lease?**

    a. The reason for the termination determines the lessee's accounting treatment.

    b. The lessor should account for a termination that is not due to the lessee's purchase of the leased asset in the same way as for a change in the provisions of a sales-type or direct financing lease.

    c. If the lessee purchases the leased asset from the lessor, the lessee should remove the lease obligation and adjust the carrying amount of the asset.

    d. All of the above.

16. **If the lessor sells the property subject to a direct financing lease after the lease is entered into, which of the following is correct?**

    a. The original accounting for the lease should not be reversed.

    b. The net investment in the lease should be written off.

    c. The sales price should be amortized to income over the remaining term of the lease.

    d. None of the above.

Self-study
CPE
1

17. **Which of the following is correct when accounting for a sale-leaseback transaction?**

    a. The buyer-lessor should treat the transaction as the purchase of an asset and the sales-type lease of an asset.

    b. The seller-lessee should immediately recognize any profit or loss on the sale of the asset.

    c. The seller-lessee must account for the lease portion of the transaction as a capital lease.

    d. None of the above.

18. **Which of the following correctly describes an impaired loan?**

    a. The value must be measured based on the present value of expected future cash flows discounted at the loan's effective interest rate.

    b. Bad debt expense should be charged if the recorded investment in the loan is more than the value of the loan.

    c. A loan is considered impaired if there is a delay in payment, but the creditor expects to collect all amounts due.

    d. All of the above.

19. **Which of the following correctly describes the accounting for a tangible long-lived asset?**

    a. The cost of the asset, less salvage value, should be depreciated over the asset's estimated useful life.

    b. The asset should be recorded at acquisition cost.

    c. The asset should not be written up to reflect market values that are above cost.

    d. All of the above.

20. **Which of the following correctly describes the accounting for an impaired asset?**

    a. If the impaired asset will be held and used in the company's operations, the carrying amount of the asset should be adjusted for subsequent increases in fair value.

    b. An impaired asset to be disposed of should be depreciated while held for disposal.

    c. An impaired asset that will be abandoned should be stated at the lower of carrying value or fair value less costs to sell.

    d. A subsequent increase in the fair value of an impaired asset to be disposed of can result in adjusting the carrying amount above the asset's original carrying amount.

21. **Which of the following information must be disclosed about an unrecorded unconditional purchase obligation?**

    a. The total amount of the fixed portion of the obligation as of the date of the latest balance sheet presented

    b. The nature and term of the obligation

    c. The nature of any variable components of the obligation

    d. All of the above

22. **Which of the following does NOT correctly describe accounting for trading securities?**

    a. Unrealized gains on trading securities should be included in earnings in the period they arise.

    b. Trading securities should be reported in the balance sheet at fair value.

    c. Realized gains on trading securities should be reported as other comprehensive income.

    d. Both debt and equity securities can be classified as trading securities.

23. **Which of the following correctly describes available-for-sale investments?**

    a. Unrealized losses on available-for-sale investments should be included in income in the period they arise.

    b. Realized losses on available-for-sale investments should be included in income in the period they are realized.

    c. Available-for-sale investments should be reported in the balance sheet at cost.

    d. Realized gains on available-for-sale investments should be reported as other comprehensive income.

24. **Which of the following statements about like-kind exchanges involving monetary consideration is correct?**

    a. The entity receiving monetary consideration should recognize any loss on the exchange that it incurs.

    b. The entity paying monetary consideration should not recognize a gain on the exchange.

    c. The entity paying the monetary consideration should record the new asset at the surrendered asset's book value plus the cash payment.

    d. All of the above.

25. **Which of the following conditions is required before assets and liabilities may be offset and reported as a net amount?**

    a. The right of setoff is enforceable at law.

    b. The reporting party has the right and intent to set off the amount owed with the amount owed by the other party.

    c. Each of two parties owes the other determinable amounts.

    d. All of the above.

26. **GAAP does NOT require annual financial statements for defined benefit pension plans to include which of the following?**

    a. Statement of cash flows

    b. Statement of changes during the year in net assets available for benefits

    c. Information about the actuarial present value of accumulated plan benefits

    d. Statement of net assets available for benefits as of the plan's year end

Self-study
CPE **1**

27. **Which of the following must be disclosed in the statement of changes in net assets available for benefits?**

    a. Administrative expenses

    b. Investment income

    c. Contributions from participants and the employer

    d. All of the above

28. **Which of the following correctly describes defined contribution pension plans?**

    a. They define specific benefit amounts that participants are to receive.

    b. They provide benefits based on the contributions to a participant's account, the returns on those contributions, and other participants' forfeitures allocated to the participant's account.

    c. They provide benefits based on the participant's age, years of service, and compensation.

    d. They do not provide an individual account for each participant.

29. **Which of the following statements correctly describes the components of the annual pension cost of a defined benefit pension plan?**

    a. Actual return on plan assets represents only realized investment gains and losses.

    b. The calculation of service cost should not consider assumptions about participants that may be added to the plan in the future.

    c. Amortization of unrecognized prior service cost is determined by amortizing the actuarial present value of benefits attributed by the pension benefit formula to employee service during prior periods.

    d. None of the above.

30. **Which of the following should be disclosed for a defined contribution pension plan?**

    a. The amortization method used for unrecognized prior service cost

    b. The amount of pension cost recognized during the period

    c. The assumptions used to compute the projected benefit obligation

    d. All of the above

ANSWERS

This section lists the correct answers to the self-study quiz for Self-study CPE 1. If you answered a question incorrectly, reread the appropriate section in Chapters 27–39 of the *Guide*. (Paragraph numbers are in parentheses.)

1. Which of the following conditions must be met before the capitalization period for interest begins?

   d. All of the above. (27.207)

2. Which of the following rates should NOT be used to determine the interest capitalization rate?

   a. The interest rate on borrowings for previous debt not associated with the qualifying asset when that interest rate is twice as high as the current interest rate that could have been obtained. (27.205 and 27.210)

   If average accumulated expenditures exceed directly associated debt or if no specific borrowing was incurred to acquire the asset, a weighted average of the rates applicable to other debt should be applied to the average accumulated expenditures that exceed the directly associated debt. When determining the debt to include in the weighted average rate, judgment should be used to ensure that the rate used reasonably reflects the interest cost that could have been avoided.

3. Which of the following is NOT a required financial statement disclosure about interest costs?

   b. The present value of future interest costs on debt incurred during the period (27.500–.502)

4. Which of the following is correct regarding a discount or premium on a note?

   d. A discount or premium should be amortized to interest expense or income over the life of the note. (28.204–.205)

5. Which of the following should be disclosed about a note in the financial statements?

   d. All of the above (28.500)

6. Which of the following does NOT apply to interim financial reporting?

   c. Modifications to GAAP are not permitted for interim periods. (29.100–.101 and 29.200–.201)

   Certain accounting principles may require modification at interim dates so that the interim period's results better relate to annual results.

7. Which of the following modifications to GAAP are NOT permitted for interim periods?

   b. Adjustments may be made to annualize seasonal revenue. (29.100 and 29.200)

   Revenue should be recognized during interim periods on the same basis as followed for the full year.

8. Which of the following statements correctly describes the lower of cost or market rule?

   c. When inventory is written down to market value, an unrealized loss should be recognized in current period income. (30.207 and 30.209)

9. Which of the following is NOT a required financial statement disclosure for inventories?

   a. The market value of the inventories (30.500)

10. Which of the following is NOT a criteria for a lessee to classify a lease as a capital lease?

    b. The lease reverts title to the lessor at the end of the lease term. (31.101 and 31.202)

11. Which of the following is a characteristic of a direct financing lease?

    c. The fair value and book value of the leased asset are the same. (31.102 and 31.201)

12. Which of the following is NOT a characteristic of a leveraged lease?

    d. Both a profit element and a financing element are recognized. (31.102–.103, 31.201, 31.208, and 31.222)

    A leveraged lease must meet the criteria for classification as a direct financing lease. In a direct financing lease, there is no profit involved for the lessor, and the lease is accounted for as a financing.

13. Which of the following is NOT correct regarding a lessee's accounting for a capital lease?

    a. The entire amount of each lease payment should be charged to expense. (31.105 and 31.210–.213)

    A lessee should only charge lease payments related to operating leases to expense. In a capital lease, a portion of each minimum lease payment should be allocated to interest expense, and the remainder applied to reduce the lease obligation.

14. Which of the following is correct regarding a lessor's accounting for a sales-type lease?

    d. None of the above. (31.107 and 31.220)

    The present value of the minimum lease payments to be received should be recognized as income. The difference between the gross investment and its present value should be recorded as unearned income and amortized over the lease term.

15. Which of the following is correct with regard to the termination of a capital lease?

    d. All of the above. (31.241–.242)

16. If the lessor sells the property subject to a direct financing lease after the lease is entered into, which of the following is correct?

    a. The original accounting for the lease should not be reversed. (31.244)

17. Which of the following is correct when accounting for a sale-leaseback transaction?

    d. None of the above. (31.275–.277)

    The buyer-lessor should treat the sale-leaseback as the purchase of an asset and the lease of an asset and must classify the lease as either an operating or direct financing lease. The seller-lessee should defer and amortize any profit or loss on the sale of the asset. The seller-lessee should account for the lease portion of a sale-leaseback as a capital lease if it meets the appropriate capital lease criteria. Otherwise, it should account for the lease as an operating lease.

18. Which of the following correctly describes an impaired loan?

    b. Bad debt expense should be charged if the recorded investment in the loan is more than the value of the loan. (32.201–.203)

19. Which of the following correctly describes the accounting for a tangible long-lived asset?

    d. All of the above. (33.200–.201)

20. Which of the following correctly describes the accounting for an impaired asset?

    c. An impaired asset that will be abandoned should be stated at the lower of carrying value or fair value less costs to sell. (33.212–.216)

Self-study CPE 1

21. Which of the following information must be disclosed about an unrecorded unconditional purchase obligation?

    d. All of the above (34.503)

22. Which of the following does NOT correctly describe accounting for trading securities?

    c. Realized gains on trading securities should be reported as a separate component of stockholders' equity. (35.100, 35.204, and 35.207)

    Realized gains on trading securities should be included in current period income.

23. Which of the following correctly describes available-for-sale investments?

    b. Realized losses on available-for-sale investments should be included in income in the period they are realized. (35.205 and 35.207)

24. Which of the following statements about like-kind exchanges involving monetary consideration is correct?

    d. All of the above. (36.204)

25. Which of the following conditions is required before assets and liabilities may be offset and reported as a net amount?

    d. All of the above. (37.200)

26. GAAP does NOT require annual financial statements for defined benefit pension plans to include which of the following?

    a. Statement of cash flows (38.202 and 38.204)

    Defined benefit pension plans are exempt from the requirement to present a statement of cash flows. (4.201)

27. Which of the following must be disclosed in the statement of changes in net assets available for benefits?

    d. All of the above (38.214)

28. Which of the following correctly describes defined contribution pension plans?

    b. They provide benefits based on the contributions to a participant's account, the returns on those contributions, and other participants' forfeitures allocated to the participant's account. (39.200)

29. Which of the following statements correctly describes the components of the annual pension cost of a defined benefit pension plan?

    b. The calculation of service cost should not consider assumptions about participants that may be added to the plan in the future. (39.203, 39.206, and 39.208)

30. Which of the following should be disclosed for a defined contribution pension plan?

    b. The amount of pension cost recognized during the period (39.504)

Self-study
CPE 1

EXAMINATION FOR CPE CREDIT

Chapters 27–39

Test Instructions

1. The questions on the next pages are TRUE/FALSE. Choose the best answer for each question and mark the appropriate box on the answer sheet. Answer sheets are located behind Self-study CPE 4.

2. If you change your answer, erase completely. Do not make any stray marks, as they may be misinterpreted.

3. Photocopies of this form are acceptable. However, each examination submitted must be accompanied by a payment of $42.

4. To receive CPE credit, completed answer sheets must be submitted by December 31, 1998. Send the completed **Examination for CPE Credit Answer Sheet** along with your payment to the address listed below. CPE credit will be given for examination scores of 75% or higher.

5. Only the **Examination for CPE Credit Answer Sheet** should be submitted for grading. **DO NOT SEND YOUR SELF-STUDY MATERIALS.** Be sure to keep a completed copy for your records.

6. Please allow a minimum of three weeks for grading.

7. Please direct any questions or comments to our Customer Service department at (800) 323-8724.

Send your completed **Examination for CPE Credit Answer Sheet** and your payment to:

Practitioners Publishing Company
GAP Self-study CPE
P.O. Box 966
Fort Worth, TX 76101

If you are paying by credit card, you may fax your completed **Examination for CPE Credit Answer Sheet** to PPC at (817) 877-3694.

EXAMINATION QUESTIONS

1. The capitalization period for interest ends when the debt associated with the qualifying asset is retired.

2. Interest capitalized during a period should equal the interest costs actually incurred during the period.

3. The amount of interest paid during the period disclosed on the statement of cash flows should be reported net of amounts capitalized.

4. Interest must be imputed on a note whose interest rate is NOT reasonable in comparison to prevailing market conditions.

5. A premium exists if the face amount of a note is less than the present value of the note's future cash flows.

6. A premium on a note receivable should be reported on the balance sheet as an addition to the related note balance.

7. Revenues should be recognized in interim periods on the same basis as followed for the full year.

8. A change in accounting principle occurs if an accounting principle in an interim period differs from that used in the preceding interim period.

9. Interim financial statements generally require the same disclosures as annual financial statements.

10. The cost of inventory should include all indirect costs incurred to prepare it for sale or use.

11. The average cost method is NOT allowed under GAAP in determining the amount of inventory costs to be charged to cost of sales.

12. Losses resulting from the writedown of inventory to market value should NOT be recognized until they are realized.

13. The lower of cost or market rule should be applied to each inventory item, total inventory, or the total components of each major category of inventory depending on the method that most fairly presents current period income.

14. A leased asset's fair value is the same as its book value in a sales-type lease.

15. A lessor should classify a lease as an operating lease if collectibility of the minimum lease payments is NOT reasonably predictable.

16. A characteristic of a leveraged lease is that it meets the criteria for classification as a direct financing lease.

17. A lessee should record an asset acquired under a capital lease at the lesser of the present value of the minimum lease payments at the beginning of the lease term or the fair value of the asset at the start of the lease.

18. A lessee should charge the entire amount of the lease payments for a capital lease to expense over the lease term.

19. The lessee should capitalize and depreciate the leased asset in an operating lease.

20. The lessee should write off the leased asset under a capital lease if the lease is revised and the revised lease would have been an operating lease.

Self-study
CPE **1**

21. A change in the estimated economic life of a leased asset does NOT require the classification of the lease to be reconsidered.

22. The seller-lessee should account for a sale-leaseback transaction as the sale of an asset and immediately recognize any profit or loss on the sale.

23. In certain circumstances, the value of an impaired loan can be measured based on the loan's market price.

24. If the fair value of an impaired loan's collateral is less than the recorded investment in the loan (and the collateral is the sole source of repayment), a loss should be recognized.

25. Prior period financial statements should be adjusted for changes in the estimated useful life of a capital asset.

26. A change in the method used to depreciate previously recorded assets is a change in accounting principle that does NOT result in adjusting prior period financial statements.

27. Impairment losses related to long-lived assets should be reported as extraordinary items in the income statement.

28. If an unconditional purchase obligation has been recorded, the total amounts paid under the obligation for each of the five years preceding the latest balance sheet date presented should be disclosed.

29. A held-to-maturity debt security should be reported in the balance sheet at its fair value.

30. The writedown of an available-for-sale security due to a nontemporary decline in its fair value should be accounted for as if it were a realized loss.

31. An investor in a futures contract generally should record the deposit amount paid to a commodities broker as a liability.

32. A company that exchanges machinery for land should recognize any gain or loss on the nonmonetary exchange if the fair values of the assets are determinable.

33. Nonreciprocal transfers of nonmonetary assets to owners generally should be recorded at fair value.

34. Assets and liabilities can be offset and reported at a net amount in a balance sheet if a right of setoff exists.

35. GAAP requires defined benefit pension plans to prepare financial statements that include information about significant factors affecting the change in the actuarial present value of accumulated plan benefits during the year.

36. If annual GAAP basis financial statements for defined benefit pension plans are prepared, they must include a statement of changes in net assets available for benefits during the year.

37. A statement of net assets available for benefits should be prepared on the accrual basis of accounting.

38. The statement of changes in net assets available for benefits should disclose employer contributions, but NOT participant contributions.

39. A defined benefit pension plan provides benefits based on the amount contributed to a participant's account.

40. Pension plan obligations must be measured as of the employer's financial statement date.

Self-study CPE 1

Section II

Chapters 40–52

OVERVIEW

RECOMMENDED FOR: Users of PPC's *Guide to GAAP*

PREREQUISITE: None

CPE CREDIT: 10 Hours

SUBJECT CATEGORY: Accounting and Auditing

EXPIRATION DATE: Postmarked by December 31, 1998

KNOWLEDGE LEVEL: Basic

MAJOR SUBJECTS:

Chapter 40—Postemployment Benefits

Chapter 41—Postretirement Benefits Other Than Pensions

Chapter 42—Prior Period Adjustments

Chapter 43—Property Taxes

Chapter 44—Quasi-reorganizations

Chapter 45—Real Estate Transactions

Chapter 46—Related Party Disclosures

Chapter 47—Research and Development Costs

Chapter 48—Revenue Recognition

Chapter 49—Segment Reporting

Chapter 50—Stock Option and Purchase Plans

Chapter 51—Stockholders' Equity

Chapter 52—Transfers and Servicing of Financial Assets

Self-study
CPE **2**

SELF-STUDY CPE 2

CHAPTERS 40–52

LEARNING OBJECTIVES

After completing the reading assignment below, you should be able to:

- account for and disclose postemployment benefits.

- account for and disclose defined benefit and defined contribution postretirement plans.

- define and account for prior-period adjustments.

- account for and disclose property taxes.

- account for quasi-reorganizations.

- account for real estate transactions.

- define a related party and disclose related party transactions.

- define research and development activities and account for research and development costs (including computer software costs).

- recognize revenue when a right of return exists and recognize revenue on separately priced extended warranty and product maintenance contracts.

- disclose operating segments, geographic information, and major customers.

- account for stock option and purchase plans.

- account for contributed capital and retained earnings.

- account for transfers and serving of financial assets.

READING ASSIGNMENT

Read Chapters 40–52 of the *Guide*.

KEY POINTS

After reading the assigned material, you should understand the following key points. If any of them are unclear, review the **READING ASSIGNMENT** again.

Postemployment Benefits

✓ An employer should accrue a liability for postemployment benefits if all of the following conditions are met:

    a. The employee's right to the benefits is attributable to services already performed.

    b. The employee's right to be paid postemployment benefits vests or accumulates.

    c. It is probable that the benefits will be paid.

    d. The amount that will be paid is reasonably estimable.

Self-study
CPE **2**

Postretirement Benefits Other Than Pensions

✓ The two basic types of postretirement benefit plans are defined benefit plans and defined contribution plans:

     a. Defined benefit plans provide specified benefits stated in terms of monetary amounts or benefit coverage and based on a benefit formula.

     b. Defined contribution plans provide an individual account for each participant and specify how contributions to the individual's account are to be determined, but do not define specific benefit amounts that participants are to receive.

✓ The cost of providing postretirement benefits under defined benefit plans should be charged to operations during the period the related employee services are rendered. That is accomplished through a combination of current accruals for employee service rendered during the period and amortization of prior period results.

✓ The annual cost of a defined benefit postretirement plan consists of the following components:

     a. Service cost

     b. Interest cost

     c. Actual return on plan assets

     d. Amortization of unrecognized prior service cost

     e. Amortization of unrecognized gains and losses

     f. Amortization of the unrecognized net asset or net obligations for the plan at the time SFAS No. 106 was first adopted

✓ Postretirement plan assets and benefit obligations generally should be measured as of the employer's financial statement date or, if used consistently from year to year, as of a date not more than three months prior to the date of the financial statements.

✓ When a defined benefit postretirement plan is acquired as part of a business combination accounted for under the purchase method, a liability should be recorded for any accumulated benefit obligation in excess of plan assets and an asset should be recorded for an excess of plan assets over the accumulated benefit obligation.

✓ A plan settlement eliminates the employer's responsibility for its postretirement benefit obligation. Therefore, a gain or loss should be recognized at the time of settlement. To be considered a settlement, the transaction must—

     a. be an irrevocable action;

     b. relieve the company or the plan of primary responsibility for a benefit obligation; and

     c. eliminate significant risks related to the obligation and the assets used to effect the settlement.

✓ A plan curtailment occurs when a portion of future postretirement benefits are reduced for current participants. A curtailment generally prevents the accumulated benefit obligation from growing for all or a portion of the plan's participants. It may eliminate coverage for certain participants, eliminate future defined benefit accruals, or both. The following two components comprise the effects of a plan curtailment:

     a. Decrease in unrecognized prior service cost (Such costs should be written off in proportion to the reduction in the remaining future years of service at the date of the curtailment.)

Self-study CPE 2

    b. Curtailment gain or loss (If a curtailment causes a plan's accumulated benefit obligation to decrease, a gain would result. Conversely, a loss results if a curtailment causes the accumulated benefit obligation to increase.)

✓   If employers provide benefits to employees when employment is terminated, the date on which termination benefits should be accrued depends on the type of termination benefits, as follows:

    a. Special termination benefits are offered for only a short period of time and should be accrued when an employee accepts the employer's offer and the amount of benefits can be reasonably estimated.

    b. Contractual termination benefits are those required by the terms of a separate agreement or the terms of an existing employee benefit plan and are provided only as the result of a specified event. Recognition of contractual termination benefits occurs in the employer's financial statements when (a) it is probable that employees will be entitled to benefits and (b) the amount of benefits to be provided can be reasonably estimated.

✓   Defined contribution postretirement plan benefits are equal to the value of each individual participant's account balance. The postretirement benefit cost to be recorded as expense normally should be the contribution that applies to that period accounted for on the accrual basis. Required contributions for periods after the employee retires or terminates should be estimated and accrued during the employee's service period.

✓   An employer that sponsors a defined contribution postretirement benefit plan should disclose the following items separately from disclosures about its defined benefit postretirement plan:

    a. A description of the plan including employee groups covered, the basis for determining contributions, and the nature and effect of significant matters affecting comparability of information for all periods presented

    b. The amount of cost recognized during the period

Prior Period Adjustments

✓   Profits and losses related to the correction of an error in previously issued prior period financial statements should not be included in current period net income. Instead, the prior period's financial statements (and beginning retained earnings of the current period) should be adjusted to correct the error.

✓   An error may result from any of the following:

    a. Making a mathematical mistake

    b. Using an accounting principle that is not in conformity with GAAP

    c. Applying a GAAP principle incorrectly

    d. Disregarding or misusing facts that existed at the date the financial statements were prepared

✓   A prior period adjustment is made by:

    a. Adjusting the current period's beginning retained earnings balance for the error's effect on prior years' earnings.

    b. Restating balance sheets and income statements of the affected prior periods, if presented, to show the correct amounts.

✓   The following disclosures are required when previously issued prior period financial statements are adjusted due to the correction of an error:

Self-study
CPE **2**

a. Nature of the error

b. For all periods presented, the effect of the error on income before extraordinary items, net income, and, for public companies, related per share amounts

c. For single period financial statements, the effect of restatement (gross and net of tax) on beginning retained earnings and on net income of the preceding year

d. The amount of income tax applicable to each prior period adjustment

e. If a restated historical financial summary is presented, disclosure of the restatements in the first summary published after the restatements

Property Taxes

✓ The most appropriate basis for recording real and personal property taxes is to accrue them monthly over the fiscal period of the related taxing authority, regardless of whether the exact amount owed can be determined.

Quasi-reorganizations

✓ A corporation with a significant accumulated deficit and unrealistic carrying values for its assets may undergo a quasi-reorganization when it appears that operations are turning around and profits are likely. A corporation electing to restate its accounts through a quasi-reorganization should record the following adjustments:

a. Assets should be written down to their fair values.

b. Unknown losses incurred prior to the readjustment should be estimated and accrued.

c. The above adjustments should be charged first to retained earnings to the extent there is retained earnings, and then to additional paid-in capital. Any deficit in retained earnings also should be charged to additional paid-in capital.

✓ Retained earnings should be "dated" in the financial statements to show that the account was readjusted in a quasi-reorganization. The corporation should continue to date retained earnings until the effective date of the quasi-reorganization no longer has significance, generally a period of 10 years.

Real Estate Transactions

✓ Sales of real estate (other than retail land sales) should be accounted for under one of the following six methods, each of which recognizes profit differently:

a. Full accrual method

b. Deposit method

c. Cost recovery method

d. Installment method

e. Reduced profit method

f. Percentage-of-completion method

✓ The full accrual method assumes that all conditions necessary for a sale have been met (i.e. the earnings process is complete) and thus, all profit is recognized.

✓ Under the deposit method, the seller should not recognize any profit or notes receivable at the sale date. Instead, the seller should continue to report the property, any related existing debt (even debt assumed by the buyer), and depreciation in its financial statements.

Self-study CPE 2

✓   Under the cost recovery method, the seller defers all profit until the buyer's total payments (including principal and interest on debt due to the seller and on existing debt assumed by the buyer) exceed the seller's cost of the property sold.

✓   The seller recognizes profit proportionately as the sales value is collected under the installment method. A profit percentage (total profit on the sale divided by the sales value) is normally calculated as of the sale date and that percentage is applied to the principal payments received to calculate the profit to be recognized each period.

✓   Under the reduced profit method, the seller determines a reduced profit by discounting the receivable from the buyer to the present value of the minimum annual payments due under the sales contract over 20 years for land debt or over the normal loan term for other real estate. The profit recognized at the sale date is the total profit on the sale less the discount. The seller defers the portion of the profit equal to the discount and none of the deferred profit is recognized until the end of the period used in the present value calculation. At that time, the deferred profit is recognized as payments are collected.

✓   Profit is recognized based on the percentage of cost incurred to the total costs expected to be incurred under the percentage-of-completion method.

✓   For retail land sales, the full accrual method should be applied if all of the following conditions have been met:

    a.   Expiration of the refund period

    b.   Sufficient cumulative payments

    c.   Collectibility of receivables

    d.   Nonsubordination of receivables

    e.   Completion of development

✓   Payments to obtain an option to acquire real property should be capitalize as incurred. Developers should capitalize other preacquisition costs if all of the following conditions are met:

    a.   The costs are directly identifiable with the specific property.

    b.   The costs would be capitalized if the property were already acquired.

    c.   Acquisition of the property or of an option to acquire the property is probable.

✓   The capitalized costs associated with abandoned real estate should be written off. The costs of an abandoned property that is only part of a project should not be allocated to the rest of the project or to other projects.

✓   Selling costs related to a real estate project should be capitalized if they are reasonably expected to be recovered from the project's sale or from incidental operations and are incurred for (a) tangible assets that are used directly during the selling period to aid in the sale of the project or (b) services that have been performed to obtain regulatory approval of sales.

✓   Costs incurred to rent real estate projects (other than initial direct costs) under operating leases should be capitalized if the costs relate to future rental operations and recovery of the costs is reasonably expected from those operations.

✓   If a loan agreement allows a lender to participate in the appreciation of the mortgaged real estate's market value, the borrower should determine the fair value of the participation feature and record a participation liability for that amount at the loan's origination. The

Self-study
CPE   **2**

offsetting debit to a debt discount account should be amortized under the interest method using the effective interest rate.

Related Party Disclosures

✓   A related party is an entity that can control or significantly influence the management or operating policies of another entity to the extent one of the entities may be prevented from pursuing its own interests. Transactions between related parties should be recorded in the same manner as transactions between unrelated parties.

✓   The following information about material related party transactions should be disclosed:

   a.   Nature of the relationship involved

   b.   Description of the transactions, including those for which no or nominal amounts were recorded, for each period for which an income statement is presented

   c.   Dollar amounts of the transactions for each period for which an income statement is presented

   d.   Amounts due from or to related parties as of the date of each balance sheet presented

Research and Development Costs

✓   Generally, research and development costs should be charged to expense when incurred. However, intangibles purchased from others should be capitalized and depreciated over their useful lives if they have alternative future uses (including use in other research and development projects).

✓   Computer software costs should be accounted for as follows:

   a.   Costs incurred to purchase software from others for a company's internal research and development use should be charged to expense when incurred unless the software has an alternative future use. In that case, it should be capitalized and amortized over its useful life.

   b.   Costs incurred to internally develop software for a company's internal use (in research and development activities) should be charged to expense when incurred.

   c.   Costs incurred to establish the technological feasibility of purchased or internally developed software to be sold, leased, or otherwise marketed are research and development costs and should be charged to expense when incurred.

✓   The total research and development costs charged to expense should be disclosed for each period for which an income statement is presented.

Revenue Recognition

✓   A right of return exists when the customer is allowed to return merchandise for refund, credit, or exchange during a specified period following the sale. Revenue may be recognized at the time of sale when a right of return exists, if all of the following conditions are met:

   a.   The seller's price to the buyer is substantially fixed or determinable at the date of sale.

   b.   The buyer has paid the seller or is obligated to pay the seller and the obligation is not contingent on reselling the merchandise.

   c.   The buyer's obligation to the seller would not change if the merchandise were stolen, damaged, or destroyed.

   d.   The buyer has economic substance.

    e.   The seller has no significant obligation to help the buyer resell the merchandise.

    f.   The amount of returns can be reasonably estimated.

✓   Revenue from separately priced extended warranty and product maintenance contracts should be deferred at the point of sale and generally recognized on a straight-line basis over the life of the contract.

Segment Reporting

✓   Entities that issue publicly traded debt or equity securities (and those required to file financial statements with the Securities and Exchange Commission) must disclose certain information about their operating segments in the complete sets of financial statements or condensed interim financial information issued to shareholders.

✓   An operating segment is a component of an entity that has the following characteristics:

    a.   It is involved in business activities from which it may earn revenues and incur expenses (including revenues and expenses from transactions with other components of the entity).

    b.   Its operating results are regularly reviewed by the entity's management to evaluate the performance of the segment and make decisions about the allocation of resources to the segment.

    c.   Separate financial information about it is available.

✓   Generally, information should be reported separately for an operating segment (or aggregation of segments if two or more operating segments are combined) that meets any of the following quantitative tests:

    a.   Its revenue, including intersegment sales or transfers, is 10% or more of the combined revenue of all of the entity's operating segments.

    b.   Its reported profit or loss is 10% or more of the greater of the absolute amount of (1) the combined reported profit of all operating segments that did not report a loss or (2) the combined reported loss of all operating segments that reported a loss.

    c.   Its assets are 10% or more of the combined assets of all of the entity's operating segments.

✓   A company's disclosures should include reconciliations of the segment information to consolidated company information. Specifically, the following reconciliations should be presented:

    a.   Total reportable segments' revenues to consolidated revenue

    b.   Total reportable segment profit or loss to consolidated income before taxes, extraordinary items, discontinued operations, and cumulative effect of accounting changes. (If the company allocates income taxes and extraordinary items to the reportable segments, the company may reconcile total reportable segment profit or loss to consolidated income after taxes and extraordinary items)

    c.   Total reportable segments' assets to consolidated assets

    d.   Total reportable segments' amounts for other significant segment disclosures to consolidated amounts for those items

✓   If an entity's internal restructuring causes its reportable segments to change, the segment information for earlier periods (including interim periods) should be restated. If prior period information is not restated because it is impracticable to do so, the entity should present

Self-study CPE 2

segment information for the current period under both the old basis and the new basis of segmentation if it is practicable to do so.

✓ An entity must make entity-wide disclosures related to the following if it does not provide the information in its segment disclosures:

 a. Products and services

 b. Geographic information

 c. Major customers

Stock Option and Purchase Plans

✓ Noncompensatory stock option and purchase plans are not intended to compensate employees for services. Instead, they are designed to raise capital or expand the company's ownership to include officers and employees. Generally, a plan is noncompensatory if the shares are offered at a price that is not lower than the price at which a similar number of shares would be offered to all stockholders.

✓ An employer should not recognize compensation expense when stock is issued through a noncompensatory plan.

✓ Compensatory stock option and purchase plans grant certain employees the right to purchase a specified number of shares of stock at a specified price that generally is below market. In some cases, the options may be exercised only under certain conditions, such as continuing employment with the company for a specified period.

✓ An employer who issues stock through a compensatory plan should recognize compensation expense equal to the quoted market price of the stock at the measurement date less any cash or other assets the employee is required to pay.

✓ Compensation expense related to compensatory plans should be accrued through a charge to stockholders' equity. The deferred compensation recorded in stockholders' equity should then be charged to expense over the periods the required employee services are performed.

✓ Companies are encouraged to use the fair value method to account for transactions involving stock-based compensation that are entered into in fiscal years beginning after December 15, 1995. Under the fair value method for compensatory plans, compensation cost—

 a. is the fair value of the stock options or other equity instruments at the grant date, less any amounts paid by the employee for the stock options or equity instruments.

 b. is accrued over the periods in which related employee services are rendered by debiting expense and crediting paid-in capital.

✓ When an entity issues equity instruments to nonemployees in exchange for goods or services, the transaction should be accounted for based on the fair value of the goods or services received or the fair value of the equity instrument issued, whichever can be more reliably measured.

✓ An employee stock ownership plan (ESOP) primarily invests in the employer's stock. An ESOP is leveraged if it borrows money to invest in the company's stock. The debt, which usually is collateralized by the employer's stock, typically is repaid from the employer's contributions to the ESOP and dividends on the employer's stock. In a nonleveraged ESOP, the employer makes periodic contributions of its shares or cash to the ESOP.

Self-study CPE 2

✓ For a leveraged ESOP, the employer should debit unearned ESOP shares (an equity account) for the shares issued to the ESOP, and, as the shares are committed to be released for allocation to participant's accounts—

   a. credit unearned ESOP shares for the cost of the shares,

   b. debit compensation expense for the average fair value of the shares during the period, and

   c. charge equity for any difference.

✓ For a nonleveraged ESOP, the employer should record compensation cost equal to the fair value of the shares contributed or committed to be contributed in each period.

Stockholders' Equity

✓ The components of stockholders' equity include contributed capital (such as capital stock, additional paid-in capital, stock subscriptions receivable, and treasury stock) and retained earnings. The components of contributed capital are defined as follows:

   a. Capital stock represents the legal capital provided by stockholders. It is the minimum investment in the business that must, under state law, be retained for the protection of creditors. Capital stock may consist of common or preferred shares.

   b. Additional paid-in capital represents contributed capital in excess of legal capital.

   c. Stock subscriptions receivable represent a stockholder's agreement to purchase a specified number of shares of stock and pay for the stock at one or more specified dates in the future.

   d. Treasury stock refers to a corporation's own stock that it holds.

✓ Retained earnings represent the undistributed earnings of an entity. Changes in retained earnings generally are limited to—

   a. net income or loss,

   b. distribution of earnings (dividends), and

   c. adjustments to the opening balance as a result of prior-period adjustments or certain changes in accounting principles.

✓ So long as the number of shares issued in a stock dividend is so small in comparison to the number of shares outstanding that they have no apparent effect on the market price of the shares, the stock dividend should be accounted for by transferring an amount equal to the fair value of the shares issued from retained earnings to capital stock and additional paid-in capital. Thus, stock dividends reduce retained earnings, but they do not reduce total stockholders' equity.

Transfers and Servicing of Financial Assets

✓ A transfer of financial assets in which the transferor surrenders control over the financial assets should be accounted for as a sale to the extent that consideration (other than beneficial interests in the transferred assets) is received in exchange.

✓ For transfers that meet the conditions to be accounted for as a sale, the transferor (seller) should:

   a. Derecognize (that is, remove from the balance sheet) all assets sold

   b. Record all assets received and liabilities incurred as proceeds from the sale

Self-study CPE 2

    c.   Measure assets received and liabilities incurred at fair value

    d.   Recognize any gain or loss

✓   When financial assets are transferred, the transferor may enter into an agreement with the transferee that in substance results in the transferor maintaining effective control over the assets. If so, the transaction should be accounted for as a secured borrowing.

✓   When an entity is obligated to service financial assets, it should recognize a servicing asset or servicing liability for the servicing contract. The contract to service the financial assets should be accounted for separately from the financial assets.

✓   Financial assets (such as interest-only strips, other receivables, or retained interests in securitizations) that contractually can be prepaid or otherwise settled in a manner that the holder would not recover substantially all of its carrying value should be subsequently measured like investments in debt securities classified as available-for-sale or trading.

✓   In certain circumstances in which a secured party has taken control of financial assets, the debtor should reclassify financial assets pledged as collateral and the secured party (lender) should recognize those assets and the obligation to return them.

SELF-STUDY QUIZ

Select the best answer for each question below and circle the corresponding letter. Then check your answers with the correct answers in the following section.

1. **Which of the following is NOT required before an employer may accrue a liability for postemployment benefits?**

   a. The amount that will be paid must be known.

   b. It is probable that the benefits will be paid.

   c. The employee's right to the benefits relates to services already performed.

   d. The employee's right to be paid the benefits vests or accumulates.

2. **Which of the following is a component of the annual cost of a defined benefit postretirement plan?**

   a. Amortization of unrecognized prior service cost

   b. Interest cost

   c. Amortization of unrecognized gains and losses

   d. All of the above

3. **Which of the following is required for a transaction to be considered a settlement of a postretirement plan benefit obligation?**

   a. Significant risks related to the obligation must be eliminated.

   b. The transaction must be irrevocable.

   c. The company or the plan must be relieved of primary responsibility for the benefit obligation.

   d. All of the above.

4. **Which of the following is NOT true regarding a postretirement benefit plan curtailment?**

   a. The curtailment may eliminate coverage for certain participants.

   b. The curtailment cannot affect current participants.

   c. A curtailment generally prevents the accumulated benefit obligation from growing for certain plan participants.

   d. The curtailment may eliminate future defined benefit accruals.

5. **Which of the following is true for the accrual of termination benefits?**

   a. A condition for accruing termination benefits is that the amount of benefits to be provided be reasonably estimable.

   b. Contractual termination benefits may not be accrued until it is probable that employees will be entitled to the benefits.

   c. Special termination benefits should be accrued when an employee accepts the employer's offer and the amount of benefits can be reasonably estimated.

   d. All of the above.

6. **Which of the following is NOT a required disclosure for an employer that sponsors a defined contribution postretirement benefit plan?**

   a. The difference between the contribution allowable for the period and actual contributions made to the plan during that period

   b. The basis for determining contributions

   c. The amount of cost recognized during the period ·

   d. Employee groups covered by the plan

7. **Which of the following statements about prior period adjustments is FALSE?**

   a. Using an accounting principle that is not in conformity with GAAP in previously issued prior period financial statements can result in a prior period adjustment.

   b. The current period's beginning retained earnings balance should be adjusted for an error's effect on the prior years' earnings.

   c. Current period net income should be adjusted to reflect the correction of an error in previously issued prior period financial statements.

   d. Any prior period financial statements that are presented should be restated to show the correct amount.

8. **Which of the following disclosures is required when previously issued prior period financial statements are adjusted due to the correction of an error?**

   a. The amount of income tax applicable to each prior period adjustment

   b. The effect of the error on net income

   c. The nature of the error

   d. All of the above

9. **Which of the following is correct about accruing real and personal property taxes?**

   a. The exact amount owed must be determined prior to accrual.

   b. The taxes should be accrued on an annual basis, after being levied by the taxing authority.

   c. The taxes should be accrued monthly over the fiscal period of the related taxing authority.

   d. None of the above.

10. **Which of the following adjustments should NOT be recorded by a corporation restating its accounts through a quasi-reorganization?**

    a. Additional paid-in capital should be adjusted for any deficit in retained earnings.

    b. Additional paid-in capital should be adjusted for any excess of fair value over cost for assets.

    c. Assets should be written down to their fair values.

    d. Retained earnings, if any, should be adjusted for estimated unknown losses incurred prior to the quasi-reorganization.

Self-study CPE 2

11. **Which of the following methods may be used (depending on the nature of the transaction) to account for sales of real estate (other than retail land sales)?**

     a.   Cost recovery method

     b.   Completed contract method

     c.   Last-in, first-out method

     d.   Average cost method

12. **Which of the following statements is FALSE when describing a method of accounting for sales of real estate?**

     a.   Under the cost recovery method, the seller defers all profit until the buyer's total payments (including principal and interest on debt due to the seller and on existing debt assumed by the buyer) exceed the seller's cost of the property sold.

     b.   The full accrual method assumes that all conditions necessary for a sale have been met and thus, all profit is recognized.

     c.   Under the deposit method, a proportion of the profit is recognized as payments are received.

     d.   Under the percentage-of-completion method, profit is recognized based on the percentage of cost incurred to the total costs expected to be incurred.

13. **Which of the following statements is TRUE when describing a method of accounting for sales of real estate?**

     a.   The seller recognizes profit proportionately as the sales value is collected under the installment method.

     b.   Under the deposit method, the seller continues to report the property, any related existing debt, and depreciation in its financial statements.

     c.   All profit is recognized at the sale date under the full accrual method.

     d.   All of the above.

14. **Which of the following are conditions that must be met in order to use the full accrual method for retail land sales?**

     a.   Completion of development

     b.   Collectibility of receivables

     c.   Expiration of refund period

     d.   Nonsubordination of receivables

     e.   All of the above

15. **Which of the following statements is TRUE?**

     a.   The capitalized costs associated with abandoned real estate that is only part of a project should be allocated to the rest of the project or other projects.

     b.   Selling costs related to a real estate project should never be capitalized.

     c.   Cost incurred to rent real estate projects (other than initial direct costs) under operating leases should be capitalized if the costs relate to future rental operations and recovery of the costs is reasonably expected from those operations.

     d.   All of the above.

Self-study
CPE
2

16. **Which of the following disclosures is NOT required for material related party transactions?**

    a. A representation that the transactions were made on an arm's length basis

    b. Amounts due to related parties as of the balance sheet date

    c. A description of the nonmonetary transactions for each period for which an income statement is presented

    d. Dollar amounts of the transactions for each period for which an income statement is presented

17. **Which of the following computer software costs should be capitalized?**

    a. Costs incurred to establish the technological feasibility of purchased software to be sold

    b. Cost of software purchased for a company's internal use in research and development that also has an alternative future use

    c. Costs incurred to establish the technological feasibility of internally developed software to be sold

    d. Cost of software developed internally for a company's internal use

18. **Which of the following is required to recognize revenue at the time of sale when a right of return exists?**

    a. The buyer has paid the seller or is obligated to pay the seller.

    b. The seller has no significant obligation to help the buyer resell the merchandise.

    c. The seller's price to the buyer must be substantially fixed or determinable at the date of the sale.

    d. All of the above.

19. **An operating segment is a component of an entity that has which of the following characteristics?**

    a. Separate financial information is available.

    b. Its operating results are regularly reviewed by the entity's management to evaluate the performance of the segment and make decisions about the allocation of resources to the segment.

    c. It is involved in business activities from which it may earn revenues and incur expenses.

    d. All of the above.

20. **Generally, which of the following operating segments should NOT be identified as a reportable segment?**

    a. An operating segment whose total assets are 20% of the combined assets of all the entity's operating segments.

    b. An operating segment whose revenues is 10% of the combined revenue of all the entity's operating segments.

    c. An operating segment whose total revenues are 5% of total revenue from all of the entity's operating segments.

    d. An operating segment whose reported profit is $20,000 when the combined reported profit of all operating segments is $100,000 and no operating segments reported a loss.

Self-study
CPE 2

21. **A company's segment disclosure should include which of the following?**

    a. Total assets for each reportable segment.

    b. The source of revenue for each reportable segment.

    c. Factors used to identify the company's operating segments.

    d. All of the above.

    e. None of the above.

22. **Which of the following reconciliations of segment information should be disclosed in an entity's financial statements?**

    a. Total reportable segments' assets to consolidated assets

    b. Total reportable segments' current liabilities to consolidated current liabilities (if segment current liabilities are disclosed)

    c. Total reportable segments' revenues to consolidated revenue

    d. All of the above

23. **An entity must disclose information about which of the following if not included in the segment disclosures?**

    a. Geographic information

    b. Major customers

    c. Products and services

    d. All of the above

    e. None of the above

24. **Which of the following is correct for companies using the fair value method to account for compensatory stock option and purchase plans?**

    a. When stock options are granted, compensation expense should be debited for the options' average fair value of the stock, even if the options relate to the employee's future service.

    b. Compensation cost should be recorded in stockholders' equity as a deferred charge and then amortized to expense over the employee service period.

    c. Paid-in capital should be credited as compensation cost is accrued over the period in which related employee services are rendered.

    d. Compensation cost is the quoted market price of the underlying stock at the measurement date less any cash or other assets the employee is required to pay.

25. **Which of the following is correct for a leveraged ESOP?**

    a. Compensation expense should be debited for the average fair value of the shares committed to be released during the period.

    b. Compensation expense should be debited for the fair value of the shares contributed in each period.

    c. Unearned ESOP shares should be *credited* for the cost of the shares when the shares are issued to the ESOP.

    d. None of the above.

Self-study CPE 2

26. **Which of the following is NOT a component of contributed capital?**

    a. Retained earnings

    b. Additional paid-in capital

    c. Treasury stock

    d. Capital stock

27. **Which of the following does NOT contribute to a change in retained earnings?**

    a. Dividends

    b. Prior period adjustments

    c. Net loss

    d. Issuance of capital stock

28. **Which of the following statements is TRUE related to transfers of financial assets?**

    a. If the transferor enters into an agreement with the transferee that in substance results in the transferor maintaining effective control over the assets, the transaction should be accounted for as a sale.

    b. If the transferor enters into an agreement with the transferee that in substance results in the transferor maintaining effective control over the assets, the transaction should be accounted for as a secured borrowing.

    c. If a company transfers financial assets to a special-purpose entity and the company retains all of the beneficial interests in the special-purpose entity as securities, the transfer should be accounted for as a sale.

    d. All of the above.

29. **Which of the following describes the accounting for a contract to service financial assets?**

    a. Servicing assets and liabilities should be reported separately in the statement of financial position.

    b. Servicing liabilities undertaken in a sale or securitization should be recorded at fair value, if practicable.

    c. Servicing assets should be amortized into income in proportion to and over the period of estimated net servicing income.

    d. All of the above.

30. **In a secured borrowing, if the lender has taken control of the collateral and is allowed to sell or repledge the collateral and the debtor does not have the right to redeem the collateral on short notice, which of the following statements is TRUE?**

    a. The debtor should derecognize the collateral.

    b. The lender should not record the collateral.

    c. The debtor should report the collateral as a restricted asset in its balance sheet.

    d. All of the above.

Self-study
CPE **2**

ANSWERS

This section lists the correct answers to the self-study quiz for Self-study CPE 2. If you answered a question incorrectly, reread the appropriate section in Chapters 40–52 of the *Guide*. (Paragraph numbers are in parentheses.)

1. Which of the following is NOT required before an employer may accrue a liability for postemployment benefits?

   a. The amount that will be paid must be known. (40.201)

   The amount that will be paid need not be known, but must be reasonably estimable.

2. Which of the following is a component of the annual cost of a defined benefit postretirement plan?

   d. All of the above (41.202)

3. Which of the following is required for a transaction to be considered a settlement of a postretirement plan benefit obligation?

   d. All of the above. (41.226)

4. Which of the following is NOT true regarding a postretirement benefit plan curtailment?

   b. The curtailment cannot affect current participants. (41.230)

   A plan curtailment occurs when a portion of future postretirement benefits are reduced for current participants.

5. Which of the following is true for the accrual of termination benefits?

   d. All of the above. (41.232)

6. Which of the following is NOT a required disclosure for an employer that sponsors a defined contribution postretirement benefit plan?

   a. The difference between the contribution allowable for the period and actual contributions made to the plan during that period (41.501)

7. Which of the following statements about prior period adjustments is FALSE?

   c. Current period net income should be adjusted to reflect the correction of an error in previously issued prior period financial statements. (42.200–.201)

   Profits and losses related to the correction of an error in previously issued prior period financial statements should not be included in current period net income. Instead, the prior period's financial statements (and beginning retained earnings of the current period) should be adjusted to correct the error.

8. Which of the following disclosures is required when previously issued prior period financial statements are adjusted due to the correction of an error?

   d. All of the above (42.500)

9. Which of the following is correct about accruing real and personal property taxes?

   c. The taxes should be accrued monthly over the fiscal period of the related taxing authority. (43.201–.202)

Self-study
CPE 2

10. Which of the following adjustments should NOT be recorded by a corporation restating its accounts through a quasi-reorganization?

    b. Additional paid-in capital should be adjusted for any excess of fair value over cost for assets. (44.201)

    No adjustment should be made for the excess of assets' fair value over cost. Assets should be written down for any excess of cost over fair value. That adjustment should be charged first to retained earning to the extent there is retained earnings, and then to additional paid-in capital.

11. Which of the following methods may be used (depending on the nature of the transaction) to account for sales of real estate (other than retail land sales)?

    a. Cost recovery method (45.200)

12. Which of the following statements is FALSE when describing a method of accounting for sales of real estate?

    c. Under the deposit method, a proportion of the profit is recognized as payments are received. (45.202)

    Under the deposit method, the seller should not recognize any profit or notes receivable at the sale date. Instead, the seller should continue to report the property, any related existing debt (even debt assumed by the buyer), and depreciation in its financial statements.

13. Which of the following statements is TRUE when describing a method of accounting for sales of real estate?

    d. All of the above. (45.207, 45.202, 45.201)

14. Which of the following are conditions that must be met in order to use the full accrual method for retail land sales?

    e. All of the above (45.224)

15. Which of the following statements is TRUE?

    c. Cost incurred to rent real estate projects (other than initial direct costs) under operating leases should be capitalized if the costs relate to future rental operations and recovery of the costs is reasonably expected from those operations. (45.244, 45.246, 45.248)

16. Which of the following disclosures is NOT required for material related party transactions?

    a. A representation that the transactions were made on an arm's length basis (46.502)

    Because related party transactions cannot be presumed to be conducted under competitive, free-market conditions, the disclosures should not imply that the transactions were made on an arm's-length basis unless that representation can be substantiated. (46.503)

17. Which of the following computer software costs should be capitalized?

    b. Cost of software purchased for a company's internal use in research and development that also has an alternative future use (47.205–.206)

18. Which of the following is required to recognize revenue at the time of sale when a right of return exists?

    d. All of the above. (48.203)

Self-study
CPE 2

19. An operating segment is a component of an entity that has which of the following characteristics?

    d. All of the above. (49.501)

20. Generally, which of the following operating segments should NOT be identified as a reportable segment?

    c. An operating segment whose total revenues are 5% of total revenue from all of the entity's operating segments. (49.505)

21. A company's segment disclosure should include which of the following?

    d. All of the above. (49.507)

22. Which of the following reconciliations of segment information should be disclosed in an entity's financial statements?

    d. All of the above (49.509)

23. An entity must disclose information about which of the following if not included in the segment disclosures?

    d. All of the above (49.513)

24. Which of the following is correct for companies using the fair value method to account for compensatory stock option and purchase plans?

    c. Paid-in capital should be credited as compensation cost is accrued over the period in which related employee services are rendered. (50.101 and 50.217–.218)

25. Which of the following is correct for a leveraged ESOP?

    a. Compensation expense should be debited for the average fair value of the shares committed to be released during the period. (50.103 and 50.225)

26. Which of the following is NOT a component of contributed capital?

    a. Retained earnings (51.100)

27. Which of the following does NOT contribute to a change in retained earnings?

    d. Issuance of capital stock (51.213)

28. Which of the following statements is TRUE related to transfers of financial assets?

    b. If the transferor enters into an agreement with the transferee that in substance results in the transferor maintaining effective control over the assets, the transaction should be accounted for as a secured borrowing. (52.206)

29. Which of the following describes the accounting for a contract to service financial assets?

    d. All of the above. (52.209)

30. In a secured borrowing, if the lender has taken control of the collateral and is allowed to sell or repledge the collateral and the debtor does not have the right to redeem the collateral on short notice, which of the following statements is TRUE?

    c. The debtor should report the collateral as a restricted asset in its balance sheet. (52.213)

Self-study
CPE **2**

EXAMINATION FOR CPE CREDIT

Chapters 40–52

Test Instructions

1. The questions on the next pages are TRUE/FALSE. Choose the best answer for each question and mark the appropriate box on the answer sheet. Answer sheets are located behind Self-study CPE 4.

2. If you change your answer, erase completely. Do not make any stray marks, as they may be misinterpreted.

3. Photocopies of this form are acceptable. However, each examination submitted must be accompanied by a payment of $42.

4. To receive CPE credit, completed answer sheets must be submitted by December 31, 1998. Send the completed **Examination for CPE Credit Answer Sheet** along with your payment to the address listed below. CPE credit will be given for examination scores of 75% or higher.

5. Only the **Examination for CPE Credit Answer Sheet** should be submitted for grading. **DO NOT SEND YOUR SELF-STUDY MATERIALS.** Be sure to keep a completed copy for your records.

6. Please allow a minimum of three weeks for grading.

7. Please direct any questions or comments to our Customer Service department at (800) 323-8724.

Send your completed **Examination for CPE Credit Answer Sheet** and your payment to:

Practitioners Publishing Company
GAP Self-study CPE
P.O. Box 966
Fort Worth, TX 76101

If you are paying by credit card, you may fax your completed **Examination for CPE Credit Answer Sheet** to PPC at (817) 877-3694.

EXAMINATION QUESTIONS

1. An employer should NOT accrue a liability for postemployment benefits if the amount that will be paid cannot be reasonably estimated.

2. The annual cost of providing postretirement benefits under defined contribution plans consists of current accruals for employee service rendered during the period as well as amortization of prior period results.

3. Postretirement plan benefit obligations must be measured as of the employer's financial statement date.

4. An asset should be recorded for an excess of plan assets over the accumulated benefit obligation when a defined benefit postretirement plan is acquired as part of a purchase business combination.

5. A gain results if a postretirement benefit plan curtailment causes a plan's accumulated benefit obligation to increase.

6. Special termination benefits are required by the terms of an existing employee benefit plan and are provided only as the result of a specified event.

7. Contributions to a defined contribution postretirement benefit plan for periods after an employee retires should be estimated and accrued during the employee's service period.

8. An employer that sponsors both a defined contribution and a defined benefit postretirement plan should separately disclose information about the two plans.

9. An error due to a mathematical mistake in previously issued financial statements should NOT result in a prior period adjustment.

10. No disclosures regarding adjustment of errors in previously issued prior period financial statements are required for single period financial statements issued during the current period.

11. Real and personal property taxes should NOT be accrued until the exact amount owed can be determined.

12. Retained earnings should be "dated" in the financial statements to show that the account was readjusted in a quasi-reorganization.

13. The reduced profit method should be used in certain cases to account for the sale of real estate.

14. A gain should be recorded at the sale date when using the deposit method to account for the sale of real estate.

15. Under the cost recovery method of accounting for real estate sales, the seller defers all profits until the buyer's total payments (including principal and interest on debt due to the seller and on existing debt assumed by the buyer) exceed the seller's cost of the property sold.

16. Under the reduced profit method of accounting for real estate sales, the seller recognizes profit proportionately as the sales value is collected.

17. The full accrual method can be used to account for retail land sales prior to the development's completion.

18. Payments to obtain an option to acquire real property should be expensed as incurred.

19. The cost of an abandoned property that is only part of a project should be allocated to the rest of the project.

Self-study
CPE   **2**

20. Tangible assets that are used directly in the selling period to aid in the sale of a real estate project should be capitalized if they are reasonably expected to be recovered from the project's sale.

21. Costs incurred to rent real estate projects should always be expensed.

22. If a lender participates in the appreciation of the mortgaged real estate's market value, at the loan's origination the borrower should record a participation liability for the fair value of the participation feature.

23. Transactions between related parties should be recorded in the same manner as transactions between unrelated parties.

24. A company's internal research and development costs generally should be capitalized and amortized.

25. A company's financial statements should disclose the total research and development costs charged to expense for each period for which an income statement is presented.

26. Revenue from a separately priced extended warranty contract should be recognized in its entirety at the point of sale.

27. ALL entities must disclose segment information.

28. An operating segment's revenues are derived exclusively from outside customers.

29. A company must make separate disclosures about a component of an entity regardless of whether its operating results are reviewed for internal decision making.

30. An operating segment whose assets are 10% of the combined assets of all of the entity's operating segments should NOT be identified as a reportable segment.

31. A company's segment disclosures should include a reconciliation of total reportable segment revenues to consolidated revenue.

32. If not included in the its segment disclosures, a company must include entity-wide disclosures about major customers.

33. Treasury stock represents a stockholder's agreement to purchase a specified number of shares of stock and pay for the stock at one or more specified future dates.

34. Stock dividends reduce retained earnings but do NOT reduce total stockholders' equity.

35. A transfer of financial assets in which the transferor surrenders control over the financial assets should be accounted for as a sale to the extent that consideration (other than beneficial interests in the transferred assets) is received in exchange.

36. If a transfer meets the conditions to be accounted for as a sale, the transferor (seller) should only record any assets received at the cost of the assets given up.

37. If the transferor enters into an agreement with the transferee that in substance results in the transferor maintaining effective control over the assets, the transaction should be accounted for as a secured borrowing.

38. Servicing assets and servicing liabilities should be offset and reported net in the balance sheet.

39. Financial assets that contractually can be prepaid or otherwise settled in a manner that the holder would not recover substantially all of its carrying value should be subsequently measured like investments in debt securities classified as held-to-maturity.

40. In a secured borrowing, if the lender is allowed to sell or repledge the collateral, the debtor should record a loss on the transfer of the collateral.

Self-study CPE **2**

Section III

Chapters 53–60

OVERVIEW

RECOMMENDED FOR: Users of PPC's *Guide to GAAP*

PREREQUISITE: None

CPE CREDIT: 10 Hours

SUBJECT CATEGORY: Accounting and Auditing

EXPIRATION DATE: Postmarked by December 31, 1998

KNOWLEDGE LEVEL: Basic

MAJOR SUBJECTS:

Chapter 53—Banking and Thrift Institutions

Chapter 54—Broadcasters

Chapter 55—Cable Television Companies

Chapter 56—Computer Software Developers

Chapter 57—Construction Contractors

Chapter 58—Franchisors

Chapter 59—Government Contractors

Chapter 60—Insurance Companies

SELF-STUDY CPE 3

CHAPTERS 53–60

LEARNING OBJECTIVES

After completing the reading assignment, you should be able to identify the unique accounting and disclosure requirements for various specialized industries.

READING ASSIGNMENT

Read Chapters 53–60 of the *Guide*.

KEY POINTS

After reading the assigned material, you should understand the following key points. If any of them are unclear, review the **READING ASSIGNMENT** again.

Banking and Thrift Institutions

✓   Core deposits are accounts that tend to remain in the financial institution regardless of changes in interest rates and are a dependable, long-term source of funds for the institution.

✓   Core deposits should be accounted for as identifiable assets and should not be included in goodwill if their values can be separately identified.

✓   Goodwill is an unidentifiable intangible asset and should be amortized to expense over a period not exceeding the estimated remaining life of the long-term interest-bearing assets acquired or, if no significant long-term interest-bearing assets were acquired, the existing deposit base acquired.

✓   Goodwill generally should be amortized using the straight-line method. However, an accelerated method may be more appropriate for an acquired savings and loan or similar institution that can demonstrate (a) the amount assigned to goodwill represents an amount paid for identifiable intangible assets whose fair value could not be individually determined and (b) the benefits expected to be received from the assets decline over their expected lives.

✓   A regulatory authority may provide assistance in the acquisition of a financial institution by agreeing to pay the difference between the interest cost of carrying the interest-bearing assets acquired and the future interest receivable on those assets.

✓   The acquiring company should consider the projected regulatory assistance as additional interest on the interest-bearing assets acquired when determining their fair values under the purchase method.

✓   Actual regulatory assistance should be reported in income in the period in which it accrues.

✓   If receipt of regulatory assistance is not probable or if the amount is not reasonably estimable at the time of acquisition, any assistance subsequently recognized should be reported as a reduction of the goodwill that was recognized in the acquisition. Assistance recognized in excess of that goodwill should be reported in income.

✓   Generally, a savings and loan should not record deferred taxes for taxable temporary differences related to bad debt reserves for tax purposes that arose in tax years beginning before December 31, 1987.

Self-study
CPE **3**

Broadcasters

✓   The licensee should record the broadcast rights acquired as an asset and the related obligation under the license agreement as a liability when the license period begins and if all the following conditions have been met:

   a.   The cost of each program is known or can be reasonably determined.

   b.   The licensee has accepted the program material in accordance with the conditions of the license agreement.

   c.   The program is available for its first showing or telecast.

✓   The asset and liability related to the license agreement should be reported at either the liability's gross amount or its present value.

✓   Generally, the licensee should amortize feature programs on a program-by-program basis and amortize program series and other syndicated products as a series.

✓   If the license agreement asset's estimated net realizable value on either a program-by-program, series, package, or day-part basis is less than its unamortized cost, the licensee should reduce the unamortized cost to estimated net realizable value through a charge to current period income.

✓   Barter transactions should be recorded at the estimated fair value of the products or services received in accordance with APB Opinion No. 29, *Accounting for Nonmonetary Transactions*.

✓   A broadcaster should report a network affiliation agreement in its balance sheet as an intangible asset, which should be amortized to expense over the lesser of its useful life or 40 years.

✓   If a network affiliation is terminated and not immediately replaced or is not under agreement to be replaced, the broadcaster should charge the unamortized cost of the terminated affiliation to expense.

Cable Television Companies

✓   The prematurity period is the time during which the cable television system is partially under construction and partially in service. It begins when subscriber revenue is first earned and ends when the first major stage of construction is completed or a predetermined subscriber level is reached.

✓   The portion of the cable television system that is in the prematurity period and can be distinguished from the reminder of the system should be accounted for separately.

✓   A cable company should capitalize the costs of its cable television plant, including materials, direct labor, and construction overhead.

✓   Subscriber-related costs (i.e., costs necessary to obtain and retain subscribers to the system) and general and administrative expenses should be charged to expense in the period they are incurred.

✓   A cable company should recognize initial hookup fees as revenue to the extent of direct selling costs. Direct selling costs include compensation paid to sales staff for obtaining new subscribers, advertising, and costs of processing documents related to new subscribers.

✓   Costs to initially connect a new subscriber to the system, including material, labor, and overhead costs, should be capitalized and depreciated over a period no longer than the depreciation period used for the cable television plant.

Self-study CPE **3**

✓ A cable company should continue to capitalize plant and intangible asset costs even if it determines that the assets have been impaired. In such cases, however, the provision required to reduce capitalized costs to recoverable value should be correspondingly increased.

Computer Software Developers

✓ The expenses incurred by a computer software developer to establish the technological feasibility of a computer software product to be sold, leased, or otherwise marketed are research and development costs and should be charged to expense when occurred.

✓ A developer must have completed the activities in a. or b. to prove that technological feasibility has been established:

   a. *Developing the software includes a detail program design.* The developer must have completed the detail program design, which takes the product's features and technical requirements to their most detailed level and is ready for coding.

   b. *Developing the software does not include a detail program design.* The developer must have completed a product design and a working model of the software program. The developer also must have confirmed that the working model is complete and consistent with product design by testing it.

✓ Production costs for computer software should not be capitalized until (a) technological feasibility has been established and (b) all research and development activities for any other components of the product or process in which the software will be used have been completed.

✓ A developer should stop capitalizing its computer software costs when the product is available for general release to customers.

✓ Maintenance and customer support costs should be charged to expense when they are incurred or when the related revenue is recognized, whichever occurs first.

✓ Capitalized software should be amortized on a product-by-product basis. The annual amortization is the greater of:

   a. amortization computed using the straight-line method over the remaining estimated economic life of the product, or

   b. amortization computed using the ratio of the product's current gross revenues to its total current and anticipated future gross revenues.

✓ A product's unamortized capitalized cost should be written off to the extent it exceeds the product's net realizable value. The product's net realizable value is the estimated future gross revenues from the product less the estimated future costs of completing and disposing of the product.

✓ The costs of duplicating the software and related materials from the product masters and packaging them for distribution should be capitalized as inventory on a unit-specific basis. Inventory costs should be charged to cost of sales when the revenue from the sale of the units is recognized.

✓ The cost of purchased software should be accounted for in the same manner as the cost of internally developed software.

Construction Contractors

✓ Under generally accepted accounting principles, construction contractors should recognize revenues from construction contracts under either the percentage-of-completion or the completed-contract method.

✓ The percentage-of-completion method recognizes income in each accounting period as the contract progresses to completion.

✓ The completed-contract method recognizes income only when the project is complete.

✓ The percentage-of-completion and completed-contract methods are not alternatives from which a contractor may select. In general, the percentage-of-completion method should be used when estimates of costs to complete and extent of progress toward completion of long-term contracts are reasonably dependable. The completed-contract method may be used, however, if lack of dependable estimates causes forecasts to be doubtful.

✓ Regardless of the revenue recognition method used by a contractor, GAAP requires a loss to be accrued whenever it becomes apparent that the total estimated contract costs will materially exceed the total contract revenue.

Franchisors

✓ The franchisor should recognize initial franchise fee revenue from an individual franchise sale when it has substantially performed or satisfied all material services or conditions relating to the sale.

✓ Substantial performance has occurred when the franchisor has:

    a. no remaining obligation or intent to refund any cash received or to forgive any unpaid notes or receivables;

    b. performed substantially all of the initial services required by the franchise agreement; and

    c. met all other material conditions or obligations.

✓ A portion of the initial franchise fee should be deferred and amortized over the life of the franchise if it is probable that continuing franchise fees will not cover the franchisor's cost of providing continuing services plus a reasonable profit.

✓ An area franchise agreement transfers franchise rights within a geographical area and permits the opening of a number of franchised outlets in that area.

✓ If the franchisor's obligations and total cost relating to initial services are not affected significantly by the number of outlets opened in a geographical area, initial area franchise fees should be accounted for like initial individual franchise fees. Substantial performance should be determined using the same criteria.

✓ If the franchisor's obligations and cost for initial services depend on the number of outlets opened in a geographical area, initial area franchise fees should be recognized in proportion to the initial services provided.

✓ A franchisor should (a) report continuing franchise fees as revenue as the fees are earned and become receivable from the franchisee and (b) expense related costs as they are incurred.

✓ A franchisor should recognize the portion of the initial fee related to equipment when title to the equipment passes to the franchisee, even if the portion related to the initial services has not been recognized because substantial performance has not occurred.

✓ If the services are interrelated to such an extent that the amount that applies to each service cannot be objectively segregated, revenue for a specific service should not be recognized until all services under the franchise agreement have been substantially performed.

✓ A portion of the initial franchise fee should be deferred and accounted for as an adjustment of the selling price of the equipment or supplies if (a) the bargain price is lower than the

selling price of the same product to other customers or (b) the price does not provide the franchisor a reasonable profit on the equipment or supply sales.

✓ Direct franchising costs should be recognized in the same period as related revenues.

Government Contractors

✓ Under cost-plus-fixed-fee (CPFF) contracts, the government periodically reimburses contractors for their expenditures plus a specified fee.

✓ CPFF contracts are similar to long-term construction contracts, which allow recognition of profit as the work progresses so long as total profits and costs can be estimated with reasonable accuracy and ultimate collection is reasonably assured.

✓ Fees under CPFF contracts are usually considered to be earned when allowable costs are incurred by the contractor and the fees become billable to the government under the contract terms. Therefore, the contractor may actually accrue revenue for the fees as they become billable, which is usually before they are actually billed.

✓ In some circumstances, factors may indicate that the contractor should not accrue revenue from CPFF contracts as the contract fees become billable to the government. For example, costs that substantially exceed estimates may indicate that the contractor should use a percentage-of-completion method to accrue fees or even wait until the product is delivered, depending on the circumstances.

✓ The contractor should report costs that have been incurred but not yet billed as receivables. The balance sheet should distinguish between receivables for unbilled costs and billed receivables.

✓ Some government contracts are subject to renegotiation and allow for refunds involving an adjustment of the original contract or selling price. The contractor's current liabilities should include a provision for probable renegotiation refunds that can be reasonable estimated.

✓ The government can terminate war and defense supply contracts at its convenience to meet changing military requirements. If the termination claim amount can be reasonably determined, the contractor should record any profit resulting from a terminated fixed-price contract at the effective date of the termination, which is the date the contractor acquires the right to receive payment on the terminated contract.

✓ The profit recorded upon termination is usually the difference between (a) the amount of the contractor's recorded claim and (b) the total currently recorded costs of the inventory, capital items, and other expenses applicable to the terminated contract.

✓ The amount of the terminated claim representing the contractor's own reimbursable costs and profit components should be recorded as a sale. Costs related to the sale should be correspondingly recorded as expenses in the income statement.

✓ Subcontractor's claims are a contractor's obligations resulting from subcontractors incurring costs on billable materials or services that were not transferred to the contractor before contract termination. The subcontractor's claims are included in the contractor's termination claim but often are not paid to the subcontractors until after the contractor's claim has been settled.

✓ If the subcontractor's claims exceed the amount included in the contractor's termination claim, the contractor should record a liability and a provision for known or probable losses resulting from unrecoverable subcontractor's claims.

✓ Disposal credits are deducted from the termination claim receivable because the contractor retains or sells to outsiders some or all of the termination inventory for which the claim was made.

✓   The following disclosures are unique to government contractors:

    a. For contracts subject to renegotiation, the uncertainties involved in estimating the renegotiation liability, the possibility that a greater liability may ultimately be negotiated, and the basis used to determine the amount of the liability.

    b. For termination claims, (1) a description of the portion of the claim that cannot be reasonably estimated and the circumstances surrounding the uncertainty and (2) the relationship between the possible termination claim receivable and any liability for advance payments received by the contractor.

Insurance Companies

✓   Short-duration contracts provide insurance protection for a fixed period of short duration and enable the insurer to cancel the contract or revise its terms at the end of any contract period. Examples of short-duration contracts include most property and liability insurance contracts and certain term life contracts, such as credit life insurance.

✓   Long-duration contracts generally are not subject to unilateral changes in their provisions and remain in force for an extended period. Examples of long-duration contracts include whole-life, guaranteed renewable term life, endowment, annuity, title insurance, and certain accident and health insurance contracts.

✓   Insurance companies usually should recognize premiums from short-duration contracts as revenue over the contract period in proportion to the amount of insurance protection provided. If the risk period differs significantly from the contract period, however, revenue should be recognized over the risk period in proportion to the amount of insurance protection provided.

✓   Premiums from long-duration contracts (other than universal life-type contracts and limited-payment contracts) should be recognized as revenue when due from policyholders.

✓   The insurance company should accrue a liability for unpaid claim costs, including estimates of costs relating to incurred but not reported claims, and related claim adjustment expenses when insured events occur.

✓   The liability for unpaid claims should be based on the estimated ultimate cost of settling the claims. Changes in claim cost estimates and differences between estimates and actual claim payments should be recognized in income during the period in which the estimates are changed or payments are made.

✓   When premium revenue related to long-duration contracts (other than title insurance contracts and universal life-type contracts) is recognized, a liability for future policy benefits should be accrued. The liability represents the present value of future benefits to be paid and related expenses less the present value of future net premiums.

✓   Acquisition costs are commissions and other costs that vary with and primarily relate to insurance contracts issued or renewed during the period. Acquisition costs should be capitalized and charged to expense in proportion to the premium revenue recognized.

✓   Payments received for investment contracts should not be reported as revenues, but as liabilities, and should be accounted for like interest-bearing or other financial instruments.

✓   Under limited-payment contracts, the collection of premiums does not represent the completion of the earnings process, therefore, revenue from those contracts should be recognized over the period benefits are provided rather than over the period that premiums are collected.

✓ Policyholder dividends should be estimated and accrued by charging operations and crediting a liability. Dividends declared or paid should then be charged to the liability or to current operations to the extent they exceed the recorded liability.

✓ In reinsurance of short-duration contracts, indemnification of the insurer generally requires both of the following:

   a. The reinsurer must assume significant insurance risk under the reinsured portions of the underlying insurance contracts.

   b. It must be reasonably possible that the reinsurer may realize a significant loss from the transaction.

✓ Financial statements based on regulatory accounting practices that differ from generally accepted accounting principles and are issued to regulators should not be described as prepared "in conformity with generally accepted accounting principles."

✓ A contingency arises when a property and casualty insurance company issues an insurance policy covering risk of loss from catastrophes. Deferral of unearned premiums within the terms of policies in force represents the "unknown liability" for catastrophe losses on unexpired policies. Therefore, it is inappropriate to accrue an additional amount as an estimated loss for that same unknown liability.

SELF STUDY QUIZ

Select the best answer for each question below and circle the corresponding letter. Then check your answers against the correct answers in the following section.

1. **Which of the following statements regarding core deposits at banking and thrift institutions is correct?**

   a. Core deposits fluctuate with changes in interest rates.

   b. Core deposits represent liabilities for customer demand accounts.

   c. Core deposits are a long-term source of funds.

   d. Core deposits are always a component of goodwill.

2. **Which of the following statements is NOT correct regarding goodwill amortization at banking and thrift institutions?**

   a. The amortization period should never exceed 25 years.

   b. The amortization period should not exceed the estimated remaining life of the long-term interest-bearing assets acquired or, if no significant long-term interest-bearing assets were acquired, the existing deposit base acquired.

   c. Goodwill may be amortized using a straight-line method.

   d. Goodwill may be amortized using an accelerated method.

3. **Under the purchase method, how should the acquiring bank or thrift record projected regulatory assistance?**

   a. Regulatory assistance should only be recorded when the actual amount is known.

   b. As a reduction to interest-bearing liabilities assumed.

   c. Projected assistance is an off-balance-sheet item which is reported in the notes to the financial statements.

   d. As additional interest on the interest-bearing assets acquired when determining their fair values.

4. **Which of the following statements is correct regarding assistance in regulatory-assisted banking and thrift institution combinations?**

   a. Actual assistance is an off-balance-sheet item that is reported in the notes to the financial statements.

   b. Actual assistance should be reported in income in the period in which it accrues.

   c. Actual assistance is always reported in income as of the combination date.

   d. None of the above.

5. **Which of the following is a condition to recording broadcast rights acquired and the related obligation under the license agreement?**

   a. The program is available for its first showing or telecast.

   b. The cost of each program is known or can be reasonably determined.

   c. The licensee has accepted the program material in accordance with the conditions of the license agreement.

   d. All of the above.

Self-study CPE 3

6. **The licensee should reduce the unamortized cost of broadcast rights when which of the following conditions is met?**

   a. Impairment has been determined in accordance with SFAS No. 121, *Accounting for the Impairment of Long-Lived Assets and for Long-Lived Assets to Be Disposed Of.*

   b. The related obligation under the license agreement has been met.

   c. The asset's estimated net realizable value is less than its amortized cost.

   d. None of the above.

7. **Barter transactions should be recorded in accordance with which of the following authoritative pronouncements?**

   a. APB Opinion No. 29, *Accounting for Nonmonetary Transactions.*

   b. ARB No. 50, *Contingencies.*

   c. APB No. 17, *Intangible Assets.*

   d. All of the above.

8. **A broadcaster's network affiliation agreement should be classified in its financial statements under which category?**

   a. Only disclosed in the notes to the financial statements.

   b. Component of goodwill.

   c. Tangible asset.

   d. Intangible asset.

9. **Which of the following is a definition of the prematurity period for cable television companies?**

   a. The cable television system is completely constructed but service has not begun.

   b. The cable television system is partially under construction and partially in service.

   c. Construction has not begun on the cable television system.

   d. The one-year period after construction of the cable television system has begun regardless of whether service is offered.

10. **Which of the following are cable television plant costs that a cable company should capitalize?**

    a. Materials.

    b. Direct labor.

    c. Construction overhead.

    d. All of the above.

11. **Which of the following subscriber-related costs are capitalized?**

    a. Costs necessary to obtain and retain subscribers.

    b. General expenses.

    c. Administrative expenses.

    d. None of the above.

Self-study **3**
CPE

12. **Which of the following statements is correct regarding the accounting for costs to initially connect a new subscriber to the system?**

    a. Related material, labor, and overhead costs should not be capitalized.

    b. The costs should be capitalized and depreciated over a period no longer than the depreciation period used for the cable television plant.

    c. The costs should be capitalized and depreciated over a period no longer than 60 months.

    d. Costs can only be capitalized during the prematurity period.

13. **Which of the following statements best defines a detail program design for a computer software developer?**

    a. It takes the product's features and technical requirements to their most detailed level and is ready for coding.

    b. It takes the product's features and technical requirements to their most detailed level but it is not ready for coding.

    c. It is a working model of the software program.

    d. It is a completed product design.

14. **A computer software developer should stop *capitalizing* software costs when which of the following occurs?**

    a. Technological feasibility has been established.

    b. All research and development activities have been completed.

    c. The product is available for general release to customers.

    d. All of the above.

15. **Which of the following statements regarding write-offs of unamortized capitalized software costs is correct?**

    a. A product's unamortized capitalized cost should be written off to the extent it exceeds the product's net realizable value.

    b. A product's unamortized capitalized cost should be written off to the extent it exceeds the product's fair value less estimated selling costs.

    c. A product's unamortized capitalized cost should be written off to the extent it exceeds the product's fair value.

    d. A product's unamortized capitalized cost should be written off to the extent it exceeds the estimated undiscounted future cash flows.

16. **How is purchased software accounted for?**

    a. Purchased software is always capitalized.

    b. Purchased software is always expensed.

    c. In the same manner as the cost of internally developed software.

    d. None of the above.

17. **Which of the following statements regarding the completed-contract method is correct?**

    a. The completed-contract method recognizes income in each accounting period as the contract progresses to completion.

    b. The completed-contract method always recognizes losses at the completion of the contract.

    c. The completed-contact method is used if a lack of dependable estimates causes forecasts to be doubtful.

    d. The completed-contact method or the percentage-of-completion method may be selected by the contractor regardless of the availability of estimates of costs to complete and extent of progress toward completion.

18. **Which of the following is a condition for substantial performance regarding a franchisor recognizing initial franchise fee revenue?**

    a. Franchisor has no remaining obligation or intent to refund any cash received or to forgive any unpaid notes or receivables.

    b. Franchisor has performed substantially all of the initial services required by the franchise agreement.

    c. Franchiser has met all material conditions or obligations.

    d. All of the above.

19. **Which of the following statements is correct if it is probable that continuing franchise fees will not cover the franchisor's cost of providing continuing services plus a reasonable profit?**

    a. A provision for estimated uncollected initial franchise fees should be recorded.

    b. No profit should be recognized for the franchise.

    c. A portion of the initial franchise fee should be deferred and amortized over the life of the franchise.

    d. The entire initial franchise fee should always be deferred and amortized over the life of the franchise.

20. **Which of the following statements is NOT correct regarding area franchise sales?**

    a. Area franchises transfer franchise rights within a geographical area.

    b. Area franchises permit the opening of a number of franchised outlets in a geographical area.

    c. Substantial performance criteria are never considered in recognizing initial area franchise fees.

    d. Initial area fees may be recognized in proportion to the initial services provided.

21. **Which of the following statements is correct regarding when a franchisor should recognize the portion of the initial fee related to equipment?**

    a. Substantial performance has occurred.

    b. Title to the equipment passes.

    c. Not before the franchisee commences operations.

    d. After the equipment is placed in service.

Self-study CPE 3

22. **Which of the following statements regarding when fees under government cost-plus-fixed-fee contracts are usually considered to be earned is correct?**

    a. Allowable costs are actually billed to the government.

    b. Allowable costs are incurred by the contractors regardless of the terms for billing under the contract.

    c. Fees become billable to the government under the terms of the contract regardless of whether the allowable costs have been incurred.

    d. Allowable costs are incurred by the contractors and the fees become billable to the government under the terms of the contract.

23. **Which of the following should be included in a government contractor's current liabilities?**

    a. Probable renegotiation refunds that can be reasonably estimated.

    b. Contractor costs that have been incurred but not yet billed.

    c. Profit on termination claims.

    d. None of the above.

24. **The profit recorded by a government contractor upon termination of a contract by the government is usually which of the following?**

    a. The difference between the amount of the contractor's recorded claim and the total currently recorded costs of the inventory, capital items, and other expenses applicable to the terminated contract.

    b. The sum of the amount of the contractor's recorded claim and the total currently recorded costs of the inventory, capital items, and other expenses applicable to the terminated contract.

    c. The difference between the amount of the contractor's recorded claim and the total currently recorded costs of the inventory, capital items, and other expenses applicable to the terminated contract plus a 10% penalty.

    d. The exact profit amount listed in the contract.

25. **Which of the following statements regarding disposal credits for government contractors is correct?**

    a. The disposal credit is only determined by the government.

    b. The disposal credit is only determined by the government contractor.

    c. Disposal credits represent the net realizable value of contractual inventory.

    d. Disposal credits are deducted from the termination claim receivable because the contractor retains or sells some or all of the terminated inventory for which the claim was made.

26. **Which of the following is NOT a long-duration insurance contract?**

    a. Guaranteed renewable term life.

    b. Annuity.

    c. Credit life insurance.

    d. Title insurance.

Self-study CPE 3

27. **The liability for unpaid claims should be based on which of the following?**

    a. A percentage of premium revenue.

    b. The estimated ultimate cost of settling the claims.

    c. The actual cost of settling claims in the previous year.

    d. None of the above.

28. **Which of the following statements regarding investment contracts at insurance companies is NOT correct?**

    a. Payments received should not be reported as revenues.

    b. Payments received should be reported as liabilities.

    c. Investment contracts should be accounted for like interest-bearing financial instruments.

    d. None of the above.

29. **In reinsurance of short-duration contracts, indemnification of the insurer generally requires which of the following?**

    a. It must be reasonably possible that the reinsurer may realize a significant loss from the transaction.

    b. It must be reasonably possible that the reinsurer may realize a significant gain from the transaction.

    c. The contractual provisions should delay timely reimbursement to the insured.

    d. The reinsurer only has a remote probability that the timing or amount of its payments to the insured will vary significantly

30. **Which of the following statements regarding insurance companies financial statements is correct?**

    a. All insurance companies financial statements must be prepared in accordance with generally accepted accounting principles.

    b. All insurance company financial statements provided to regulators must be described as being prepared "in conformity with generally accepted accounting principles."

    c. Regulatory financial statements requirements are always considered generally accepted accounting principles.

    d. None of the above.

ANSWERS

This section lists the correct answers to the self-study quiz for Self-study CPE 3. If you answered a question incorrectly, reread the appropriate paragraph in Chapters 53–60 of the *Guide*. (Paragraph references are in parentheses.)

1. Which of the following statements regarding core deposits at banking and thrift institutions is correct?

    c. Core deposits are a long-term source of funds. (53.201)

2. Which of the following statements is NOT correct regarding goodwill amortization at banking and thrift institutions?

    a. The amortization period should never exceed 25 years. (53.202)

3. Under the purchase method, how should the acquiring bank or thrift record projected regulatory assistance?

    d. As additional interest on the interest-bearing assets acquired when determining their fair values. (53.204)

4. Which of the following statements is correct regarding assistance in regulatory-assisted banking and thrift institution combinations?

    b. Actual assistance should be reported in income in the period in which it accrues. (53.204)

5. Which of the following is a condition to recording broadcast rights acquired and the related obligation under the license agreement?

    d. All of the above. (54.201)

6. The licensee should reduce the unamortized cost of broadcast rights when which of the following conditions is met?

    c. The asset's estimated net realizable value is less than its amortized cost. (54.204)

7. Barter transactions should be recorded in accordance with which of the following authoritative pronouncements?

    a. APB Opinion No. 29, *Accounting for Nonmonetary Transactions.* (54.205)

8. A broadcaster's network affiliation agreement should be classified in its financial statements under which category?

    d. Intangible asset. (54.206)

9. Which of the following is a definition of the prematurity period for cable television companies?

    b. The cable television system is partially under construction and partially in service. (55.200)

10. Which of the following are cable television plant costs that a cable company should capitalize?

    d. All of the above. (55.202)

11. Which of the following subscriber-related costs are capitalized?

    d. None of the above. (55.204)

12. Which of the following statements is correct regarding the accounting for costs to initially connect a new subscriber to the system?

    b. The costs should be capitalized and depreciated over a period no longer than the depreciation period used for the cable television plant. (55.208)

13. Which of the following statements best defines a detail program design for a computer software developer?

    a. It takes the product's features and technical requirements to their most detailed level and is ready for coding. (56.200)

14. A computer software developer should stop *capitalizing* software costs when which of the following statements occurs?

    c. The product is available for general release to customers. (56.203)

15. Which of the following statements regarding write-offs of unamortized capitalized software costs is correct?

    a. A product's unamortized capitalized cost should be written off to the extent it exceeds the product's net realizable value. (56.205)

16. How is purchased software accounted for?

    c. In the same manner as the cost of internally developed software. (56.207)

17. Which of the following statements regarding the completed-contract method is correct?

    c. The completed-contact method is used if a lack of dependable estimates causes forecasts to be doubtful. (57.204)

18. Which of the following is a condition for substantial performance regarding a franchisor recognizing initial franchise fee revenue?

    d. All of the above. (58.202)

19. Which of the following statements is correct if it is probable that continuing franchise fees will not cover the franchisor's cost of providing continuing services plus a reasonable profit?

    c. A portion of the initial franchise fee should be deferred and amortized over the life of the franchise. (58.204)

20. Which of the following statements is NOT correct regarding area franchise sales?

    c. Substantial performance criteria is never considered in recognizing initial area franchise fees. (58.205)

21. Which of the following statements is correct regarding when a franchisor should recognize the portion of the initial fee related to equipment?

    b. Title to the equipment passes. (58.209)

22. Which of the following statements regarding when fees under government cost-plus-fixed-fee contracts are usually considered to be earned is correct?

    d. Allowable costs are incurred by the contractors and the fees become billable to the government under the terms of the contract. (59.202)

23. Which of the following should be included in a government contractor's current liabilities?

    a. Probable renegotiation refunds that can be reasonably estimated. (59.207)

Self-study CPE 3

24. The profit recorded by a government contractor upon termination of a contract by the government is usually which of the following?

   a. The difference between the amount of the contractor's recorded claim and the total currently recorded costs of the inventory, capital items, and other expenses applicable to the terminated contract. (59.209)

25. Which of the following statements regarding disposal credits for government contractors is correct?

   d. Disposal credits are deducted from the termination claim receivable because the contractor retains or sells some or all of the terminated inventory for which the claim was made. (59.216)

26. Which of the following is NOT a long-duration insurance contract?

   c. Credit life insurance. (60.201)

27. The liability for unpaid claims should be based on which of the following?

   b. The estimated ultimate cost of settling the claims. (60.205)

28. Which of the following statements regarding investment contracts at insurance companies is NOT correct?

   d. None of the above. (60.211)

29. In reinsurance of short-duration contracts, indemnification of the insurer generally requires which of the following?

   a. It must be reasonably possible that the reinsurer may realize a significant loss from the transaction. (60.227)

30. Which of the following statements regarding insurance companies financial statements is correct?

   d. None of the above. (60.235)

EXAMINATION FOR CPE CREDIT

Chapters 53–60

Test Instructions

1. The questions on the next pages are TRUE/FALSE. Choose the best answer for each question and mark the appropriate box on the answer sheet. Answer sheets are located behind Self-study CPE 4.

2. If you change your answer, erase completely. Do not make any stray marks because they may be misinterpreted.

3. Photocopies of this form are acceptable. However, each examination must be accompanied by a payment of $42.

4. To receive CPE credit, completed answer sheets must be postmarked by December 31, 1998. Send the completed **Examination for CPE Credit Answer Sheet** along with your payment to the address listed below. CPE credit will be given for examination scores of 75% or higher.

5. Only the **Examination for CPE Credit Answer Sheet** should be submitted for grading. **DO NOT SEND YOUR SELF-STUDY MATERIALS.** Be sure to keep a completed copy for your records.

6. Please allow a minimum of three weeks for grading.

7. Please direct any questions or comments to our Customer Service department at (800) 323-8724.

Send your completed **Examination for CPE Credit Answer Sheet** and your payment to:

Practitioners Publishing Company
GAP Self-study CPE
P.O. Box 966
Fort Worth, TX 76101

If you are paying by credit card, you may fax your completed **Examination for CPE Credit Answer Sheet** to PPC at (817) 877-3694.

EXAMINATION QUESTIONS

1. Core deposits are identifiable tangible liabilities.

2. Goodwill at a banking or thrift institution must always be amortized using an accelerated method.

3. The Federal Savings and Loan Insurance Corporation may provide assistance in the acquisition of a financial institution by agreeing to pay the difference between the interest cost of carrying the interest-bearing assets acquired and the future interest receivable on those assets.

4. An acquiring company should consider the projected regulatory assistance as additional interest on the interest-bearing assets acquired when determining their fair value under the purchase method.

5. Regulatory assistance to an acquiror of a financial institution may reduce goodwill.

6. A savings and loan should not record deferred taxes for taxable temporary differences related to bad debt reserves for tax purposes that arose in any tax years.

7. One condition for a broadcast licensee to record broadcast rights acquired as an asset and the related obligation under the license agreement as a liability is that the cost of each program must be known or be reasonably determined.

8. A broadcaster's asset and liability related to a license agreement may be reported at either the liability's gross amount or its present value.

9. The licensee should ALWAYS amortize feature programs and program series on a program-by-program basis.

10. When a licensee reduces the unamortized cost of a license agreement asset to estimated net realizable value, a charge should be made to prior-period income.

11. If a network affiliation is terminated and not immediately replaced or is not under agreement to be replaced, the broadcaster should charge the unamortized cost of the terminated affiliation to expense.

12. For cable television companies, the prematurity period begins when subscriber revenue is first earned and ends when the first major stage of construction is completed or a predetermined subscriber level is reached.

13. The portion of the cable television system that is in the prematurity period and can be distinguished from the remainder of the system should be accounted for separately.

14. Direct selling costs for cable companies include compensation paid to sales staff for obtaining new subscribers.

15. Direct selling costs for cable companies do NOT include costs of processing documents related to new subscribers.

16. A cable company should continue to capitalize plant and intangible asset costs even if it determines that the assets have been impaired.

17. The expenses incurred by a computer software developer to establish the technological feasibility of a computer software product should be capitalized and amortized over the estimated life of the computer software product.

18. Production costs for computer software should not be capitalized until all research and development activities for any other components of the product or process in which the software will be used have been completed.

19. Maintenance and customer support costs for computer software developers should NOT be charged to expense when they are incurred or when the related revenue is recognized.

20. A software product's net realizable value is the estimated future gross revenues from the product less the estimated future costs of completing and disposing of the product.

21. Purchased software should always be expensed when incurred.

22. The percentage-of-completion method recognizes income in each accounting period as the contract progresses to completion.

23. The percentage-of-completion and completed-contract methods are NOT alternatives from which a contractor may select.

24. GAAP requires a loss to be accrued when it becomes apparent that the total estimated contract costs will materially exceed the total contract revenues ONLY under the percentage-of-completion method.

25. The franchisor should recognize all the initial franchise fee revenue from an individual franchise sale over the life of the franchise agreement.

26. A franchisor should report continuing franchise fees as revenues as the fees are earned and become receivable from the franchisee.

27. A franchisor should recognize the portion of the initial fee related to equipment only when substantial performance has occurred.

28. If the franchisor's services are interrelated to such an extent that the amount applies to each service cannot be objectively segregated, revenue for a specific service should be recognized in proportion to the initial services provided.

29. A portion of the initial franchise fee should be deferred and accounted for as an adjustment of the selling price of the equipment or supplies if the price does NOT provide the franchisor a reasonable profit on the equipment or supply sales.

30. Direct franchising costs should be recognized in the same period as related revenues.

31. A government contractor may actually accrue revenue for fees as they become billable, which may be before they are actually billed.

32. When costs substantially exceed estimates for a government contractor, the contractor should always use the net realizable value method to accrue fees.

33. A government contractor's balance sheet should NOT distinguish between receivables for unbilled costs and billed receivables.

34. The amount of the termination claim representing the contractor's own reimbursable costs and profit components should be recorded as a sale.

35. Disposal credits are deducted from the termination claim receivable because the contractor retains or sells to outsiders some or all of the termination inventory for which the claim was made.

36. Insurance companies should ALWAYS recognize premiums from short-duration contracts as revenue over the contract period in proportion to the amount of insurance protection provided.

37. Premiums from long-duration contracts should be recognized as revenue over the contract period in proportion to the amount of insurance protection provided.

Self-study
CPE   **3**

38. Payments received for investment contracts at insurance companies should NOT be reported as revenues, but as liabilities.

39. In reinsurance of short-duration contracts, indemnification of the insurer generally requires the reinsurer to assume significant insurance risk under the reinsured portions of the underlying insurance contracts.

40. Property and casualty insurance companies should accrue additional amounts for unidentifiable risk of loss from catastrophes.

Section IV

Chapters 61–67

OVERVIEW

RECOMMENDED FOR: Users of PPC's *Guide to GAAP*

PREREQUISITE: None

CPE CREDIT: 10 Hours

SUBJECT CATEGORY: Accounting and Auditing

EXPIRATION DATE: Postmarked by December 31, 1998

KNOWLEDGE LEVEL: Basic

MAJOR SUBJECTS:

Chapter 61—Lending and Mortgage Banking Activities

Chapter 62—Motion Picture Industry

Chapter 63—Not-for-profit Organizations

Chapter 64—Oil and Gas Producing Activities

Chapter 65—Record and Music Industry

Chapter 66—Regulated Operations

Chapter 67—Title Plant

Self-study
CPE
4

SELF-STUDY CPE 4

CHAPTERS 61–67

LEARNING OBJECTIVES

After completing the reading assignment, you should be able to identify the unique accounting and disclosure requirements for various specialized industries.

READING ASSIGNMENT

Read Chapters 61–67 of the *Guide.*

KEY POINTS

After reading the assigned material, you should understand the following key points. If any of them are unclear, review the **READING ASSIGNMENT** again.

Lending and Mortgage Banking Activities

✓ If a loan is held for resale, the lender should defer loan origination fees and related loan origination costs until the loan is sold. If a loan is held for investment, such fees and costs should be deferred and recognized over the life of the loan as an adjustment of interest income.

✓ Direct loan origination costs for a completed loan should include only (a) direct costs incurred in transactions with third parties and (b) employees' payroll and fringe benefit costs directly related to time spent performing the following activities for the loan:

   a. Evaluating the prospective borrower's financial condition

   b. Evaluating and recording guarantees, collateral, and other security arrangements

   c. Negotiating loan terms

   d. Preparing and processing loan documents

   e. Closing the transaction

✓ Fees received in return for guaranteeing the funding of mortgage loans to borrowers, builders, or developers are commitment fees. Lenders generally should offset commitment fees against any related direct loan origination costs incurred to make the commitment and defer the net amount.

✓ If the commitment expires without the loan being made, the net commitment fee should be recognized in income upon expiration of the commitment. If the commitment is exercised, the net commitment fee should be recognized over the life of the loan as an adjustment of interest income.

✓ The initial investment in a purchased loan should include the amount paid to the seller plus any fees paid or less any fees received. The purchaser may allocate the initial investment cost of loans purchased as a group to the individual loans or account for the initial investment in the aggregate.

✓ The company managing a loan syndication (the syndicator) should recognize loan syndication fees when the syndication is complete unless the syndicator retains a portion of

Self-study CPE 4

the syndication loan. If the yield on the retained portion of the loan is less than the average yield (including fees) of the other syndication participants, the syndicator should defer part of the syndication fee to produce a yield on the retained portion of the loan that is at least equal to the average yield on the loans held by the other syndication participants.

✓ Special provisions for amortizing deferred fees and costs apply if the stated interest rate is not constant throughout the term of the loan. When that is the case, the interest method should be applied.

✓ In most cases, the calculation of the constant effective yield used in applying the interest method should be based on the payment terms stated in the loan contract and prepayment of principal should not be anticipated. However, if the lender holds a large number of similar loans for which principal prepayments are probable and the amount and timing of prepayments can be reasonably estimated, the lender may consider estimates of future prepayments in the calculation of the constant yield effect.

✓ Net fees or costs related to revolving lines of credit should be recognized in income on the straight-line basis over the period the revolving line is active (assuming that debt is outstanding for the entire term of the contract). If the borrower pays off the debt and cannot reborrow under the line, any unamortized net fees or costs should be recognized in income when the debt is paid off.

✓ Deferred net fees or costs should not be amortized during periods that interest income is not recognized on loans because of doubts about the realization of principal or interest.

✓ The unamortized balance of loan origination, commitment, and other fees and costs being amortized by the interest method should be reported on the lender's balance sheet as part of the loan balance to which it relates.

✓ The lender should report amortization of deferred loan origination, commitment, and other fees and costs being amortized by the interest method as part of interest income. Amortization of other fees should be reported as service fee income.

✓ Mortgage loans held for sale should be reported at the lower of cost or market value. A valuation allowance should be used to account for any excess of cost over market value. Changes in the valuation allowance should be charged to income in the period the change occurs.

✓ Capitalized costs of servicing assets associated with the purchase or origination of mortgage loans should not be considered in the cost of mortgage loans for the purpose of determining the lower of cost or market value of the loans. Servicing assets or liabilities should be assessed for impairment or increased liability based on their fair value.

✓ A contract to service mortgage loans should be accounted for separately from the loans as follows:

   a.   Servicing assets and servicing liabilities should be reported separately in the statement of financial position.

   b.   Servicing assets retained in the sale or securitization of the mortgage loans being serviced should be recorded at their allocated carrying amount based on relative fair values (if practicable) at the date of sale or securitization.

   c.   Servicing assets purchased or servicing liabilities assumed should be recorded at fair value.

   d.   Servicing liabilities undertaken in a sale or securitization should be recorded at fair value, if practicable.

e. Rights to future interest income from serviced loans in excess of contractually specified servicing fees should be accounted for separately from servicing assets (i.e., as interest-only strips).

f. Servicing assets should be amortized into income in proportion to and over the period of estimated net servicing income.

g. Servicing assets should be subsequently measured for impairment.

h. Servicing liabilities should be amortized into income in proportion to and over the period of estimated net servicing loss.

Motion Picture Industry

✓ Motion picture exhibition rights typically are sold (licensed) to movie theaters based on either a percentage of the box office receipts or a flat fee. As a general rule, revenue from the sale of exhibition rights should be recognized on the date the film is shown.

✓ A license agreement for television program material usually covers several films and grants a broadcaster the right to telecast either a specified number or an unlimited number of showings over a maximum time period for a specified fee.

✓ Production costs include the following costs of writing and producing a film:

a. Salaries of cast, directors, producers, and extras.

b. Set construction, wardrobe, and prop costs.

c. Photography, sound synchronization, and editing costs.

d. Production overhead costs, including depreciation and amortization of studio equipment and leasehold improvements used in production.

e. Rental of facilities on location.

✓ Production costs should be capitalized as film cost inventory and amortized using the individual-film-forecast-computation method or the periodic-table-computation method.

✓ The individual-film-forecast-computation method amortizes film costs based on the ratio of current gross revenues to anticipated total gross revenues.

✓ The periodic-table-computation method should only be used if its result would approximate the result achieved using the individual-film-forecast-computation method. The periodic-table-computation method amortizes film costs using tables prepared from the historic revenue patterns of a large group of films.

✓ Exploitation costs are incurred during the final production phase and during the release periods of films in both primary and secondary markets. They include such costs as film prints, prerelease and early release advertising expected to benefit the film in future markets, and other distribution expenses.

✓ Motion picture companies should capitalize exploitation costs that clearly benefit future periods as film cost inventory and amortize the costs in the same ratio that current gross revenues bear to anticipated total gross revenues.

✓ The company should write down the unamortized film costs to net realizable value if estimated future gross revenues from a film are not sufficient to recover the unamortized film costs, other direct distribution expenses, and participations.

✓ A motion picture company should not report a license agreement for the sale of film rights for television exhibition as an asset until the time revenue from the agreement is recognized.

Self-study
CPE **4**

Not-for-profit Organizations

✓ All not-for-profit organizations must depreciate their long-lived tangible assets. Depreciation need not be recognized on individual works of art or historical treasures that have indefinite or extraordinary long useful lives, however.

✓ Capitalized costs of major preservation and restoration efforts should be depreciated, regardless of whether depreciation is recognized on the asset being protected or restored, if the efforts provide future economic benefits or service potential.

✓ Investments in equity securities with readily determinable fair values and all investments in debt securities should be reported in the statement of financial position at fair value with realized and unrealized gains and losses included in the statement of activities.

✓ Donor-restricted investment income and gains whose restrictions are met in the same reporting period may be reported as unrestricted income and gains if the organization (a) reports consistently from period to period, (b) follows the same policy for reporting donor-restricted contributions, and (c) discloses its accounting policy.

✓ The statement of financial position should report the amounts for each of three classes of net assets: permanently restricted net assets, temporarily restricted net assets, and unrestricted net assets. Information about the nature and amounts of different types of permanent or temporary restrictions should be provided either by reporting their amounts on the face of the statement of financial position or by including relevant details in the notes to the financial statements.

✓ An organization's use of permanently restricted net assets is limited by donor-imposed stipulations that do not expire with the passage of time and cannot be removed by the organization's actions.

✓ Temporarily restricted net assets are those whose use is restricted by donor-imposed stipulations that either expire with the passage of time or can be removed by the organization's actions.

✓ Changes in unrestricted net assets generally result from (a) revenues for providing services, producing and delivering goods, receiving unrestricted contributions, and receiving unrestricted dividends or interest from investments, (b) expensed incurred in providing services, producing and delivering goods, raising contributions, and performing administrative functions, and (c) reclassifications from other classes of net assets resulting from expiration of donor time or purpose restrictions.

✓ A statement of activities provided by a not-for-profit organization should report the amount of the change in net assets for the period for the organization as a whole.

✓ The statement of activities should report the amount of change in each class of net assets (permanently restricted, temporarily restricted, and unrestricted) for the period.

✓ To help donors, creditors, and others assess an organization's service efforts, the statement of activities or notes to the financial statements should report expenses by their functional classification.

✓ A not-for-profit organization should distinguish between contributions received (a) with permanent restrictions, (b) with temporary restrictions, and (c) without donor-imposed restrictions.

✓ Receipts of unconditional promises to give payments in future periods should be reported as restricted revenues or gains unless (a) the donor explicitly stipulates that the receipt is to be used to support current period activities or (b) the circumstances surrounding the receipt of

Self-study CPE 4

the promise make clear that the donor intended it to be used to support current period activities.

✓ A not-for-profit organization should prepare a statement of cash flows in accordance with SFAS 95, *Statement of Cash Flows.*

✓ Voluntary health and welfare organizations must present a statement of functional expenses that shows how the natural expense classifications (such as salaries, rent, electricity, interest expense, and depreciation) are allocated to significant program and supporting services.

Oil and Gas Producing Activities

✓ Generally, oil and gas producing activities are accounted for under either of two methods—the full cost method or the successful efforts method. Under the full cost method, properties are divided into cost centers and all acquisition, exploration, and development costs for properties within each cost center are capitalized when incurred. Under the successful efforts method, however, only exploration and development costs related to proved reserves are capitalized.

✓ Oil and gas producing companies should periodically assess unproved properties to determine whether they have been impaired. If the assessment indicates that an unproved property has been impaired, the company should recognize a loss by providing a valuation allowance.

✓ Capitalized acquisition costs of proved properties should be amortized (depleted) by the units-of-production method as the related oil and gas reserves are produced so that each unit of oil and gas produced is assigned a pro rata portion of the unamortized acquisition costs. Units-of-production depletion rates should be revised at least once a year, and those revisions should be accounted for prospectively as changes in accounting estimates.

✓ The costs of proved properties, including related wells, equipment, and facilities should be reviewed for impairment if events or changes in circumstances indicate that they may not be fully recoverable. The method of determining whether proved properties have been impaired is the same as for other long-lived assets.

✓ Exploration costs for geological and geophysical studies, carrying and retaining undeveloped properties, and dry hole and bottom hole contributions do not result in the acquisition of an asset and therefore should be charged to expense when incurred.

✓ An oil and gas producing company should capitalize the costs of drilling exploratory wells and exploratory-type stratigraphic test wells as part of its uncompleted wells, equipment, and facilities until it determines whether the well has found proved reserves. At that time, the capitalized costs of drilling the well should be charged to expense if proved reserves are not found or reclassified as part of the costs of the company's wells and related equipment and facilities if proved reserves are found.

✓ All costs incurred to drill and equip development wells, development-type stratigraphic test wells, and service wells should be capitalized, whether the wells are successful or unsuccessful. Costs of drilling those wells and constructing production equipment and facilities should be included in the company's uncompleted wells, equipment, and facilities until drilling or construction is completed. After that time, development costs should be capitalized as part of the cost of a company's wells and related equipment and facilities.

✓ Capitalized costs of exploratory wells and exploratory-type stratigraphic test wells that have found proved reserves and capitalized development costs should be depreciated using the units-of-production method.

✓ Production costs (and related depreciation, depletion, and amortization of capitalized acquisition, exploration, and development costs) should be treated as part of the cost of oil and gas produced.

Record and Music Industry

✓ Generally, a sale has occurred and revenue from a license agreement may be recognized in full (assuming the fee's collectibility is reasonably assured) when the licensor has:

    a. signed a noncancelable contract,

    b. agreed to a fixed fee,

    c. delivered the rights to the licensee and the licensee may exercise them without restriction, and

    d. met all significant obligations to furnish music or records.

✓ Often, a licensee will pay the licensor a minimum guarantee in advance for the right to sell or distribute the records or music. The licensor should initially report a minimum guarantee as a liability and recognize it as revenue as it is earned under the agreement.

✓ Royalties earned by artists should be adjusted for anticipated returns and charged to expense in the period in which related record sales occur.

✓ The record company should record the advance royalty payment as an asset if the artist's past performance and current popularity indicate that the advance royalties will be recovered from future royalties to be earned by the artist.

✓ The record company should charge the advance royalty payment to current period expense if the artist's past performance and current popularity do not indicate that future earned royalties will be sufficient to cover the advance royalty.

✓ The record company's portion of the cost of a record master should be reported as an asset if the past performance and current popularity of the artist provide a sound basis for recovering the cost from future sales.

✓ A record company should disclose the following information in its financial statements:

    a. Commitments for artist advances that are payable in future years and future royalty guarantees.

    b. The record company's portion of the cost of record masters that is recorded as an asset.

Regulated Operations

✓ Regulators sometimes determine allowable costs (i.e., the costs that should be recovered by revenue) and allow the enterprise to charge rates that will produce revenue approximately equal to those costs. In some cases, regulators include costs incurred in prior periods or costs expected to be incurred in future periods in allowable costs.

✓ Costs that would otherwise be charged to expense generally would be capitalized if it is probable that future revenue will be provided to recover the costs.

✓ The portion of current revenue that provides for recovery of expected future costs should be recorded as a liability and recognized in income as the costs are incurred.

✓ A regulated enterprise should capitalize all or part of an incurred cost that would otherwise be charged to expense if both of the following criteria are met:

    a. It is probable that future revenue at least equal to the capitalized cost will result from including that cost in allowable costs for rate-making purposes.

Self-study CPE 4

b. Based on available evidence, future revenue will provide for recovery of previously incurred costs rather than expected levels of similar future costs.

The incurred cost should be charged to earnings when it no longer meets the above criteria.

✓ A regulator's rate actions can reduce or eliminate the value of an incurred cost that has been capitalized as an asset.

✓ A regulator may allow current rates to recover expected future costs and require future rates to be reduced by the amounts of the expected future costs if those costs are not incurred. Until the regulated enterprise incurs the specified costs, revenues collected for such costs should not be recognized. Instead, the revenues should be recorded as liabilities and recognized as the associated costs are incurred.

✓ An enterprise should not eliminate profit on sales to regulated affiliates in its general-purpose financial statements if both of the following criteria are met:

a. The sales price is reasonable.

b. It is probable that, through the rate-making process, future revenues approximating the sales price will result from the regulated affiliate's use of the products.

✓ When it becomes probable that an operating asset or asset under construction will be abandoned, the enterprise should remove the cost of that asset from construction work-in-process or plant-in-service. The enterprise should determine whether the regulator is likely to provide recovery of any allowed cost with full, partial, or no return on investment between the times that abandonment becomes probable and recovery is completed.

✓ When it becomes probable that part of the cost of a recently completed plant will be disallowed for rate-making purposes and a reasonable estimate of the disallowed cost can be made, the enterprise should deduct the estimated disallowed cost from the reported cost of the plant and recognize the amount as a loss.

✓ A phase-in plan is a rate-making method intended to moderate a sudden increase in rates while providing the regulated enterprise with recovery of its investment and a return on that investment during the recovery period. A phase-in plan meets all of the following criteria:

a. The regulator adopts the plan in connection with a major, newly completed plant of the regulated enterprise or of one of its suppliers or a major plant scheduled for completion in the near future.

b. The plan defers the rates intended to recover allowable costs beyond the period in which the allowable costs would be charged to expense under GAAP applicable to enterprises in general.

c. The plan defers the rates intended to recover allowable costs beyond the period in which the rates would have been ordered under the rate-making methods routinely used by the regulator prior to 1982 for similar allowable costs of the enterprise.

✓ For financial reporting purposes, an enterprise that discontinues accounting for all or part of its operations as a regulated enterprise should eliminate from its balance sheet the effects of any regulator's actions that had been previously recognized as assets and liabilities for regulated enterprises, but that would not have been recognized as assets and liabilities by enterprises in general.

✓ Accounting for a regulated entity's sale-leaseback transactions in accordance with GAAP may result in income and expenses being recognized in different periods for financial reporting and rate-making purposes.

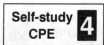

Title Plant

✓ A title plant is a historical record of all ownership, encumbrances, and other matters affecting title to land in a particular geographic area.

✓ The direct costs incurred to construct or otherwise acquire a title plant should be capitalized until the plant can be used to perform title searches.

✓ A title plant typically has an indefinite useful life. Thus, a plant's capitalized costs should not be depreciated or charged to income unless circumstances indicate that its carrying amount has been impaired. The following circumstances may indicate impairment:

    a. Changes in legal requirements or statutory practices.

    b. Effects of obsolescence, demand, and other economic factors.

    c. Actions of competitors and others that may affect competitive advantages.

    d. Failure to maintain the title plant on a current basis.

    e. Abandonment of the title plant or other circumstances that indicate obsolescence.

✓ Costs incurred to maintain a title plant and perform title searches, should be expensed as incurred.

✓ The sale of a title plant should be reported separately in the financial statements as follows:

    a. A company that sells its title plant and relinquishes all rights to its future use should report a gain or loss equal to the amount received less the adjusted cost of the title plant.

    b. A company that sells an undivided ownership interest in its title plant should report a gain or loss equal to the amount received less a pro rata portion of the adjusted cost of the title plant.

    c. A company that sells a copy of its title plant or the right to use it should report a gain equal to the amount received. Ordinarily, no costs should be allocated to the sale unless the value of the title plant decreases below its adjusted cost as a result of the sale.

SELF STUDY QUIZ

Select the best answer for each question below and circle the corresponding letter. Then check your answers against the correct answers in the following section.

1. **Direct loan origination costs include employees' payroll and fringe benefit costs directly related to time spent performing which of the following activities?**

   a. Evaluating and recording guarantees, collateral, and other security arrangements.

   b. Negotiating loan terms.

   c. Preparing and processing loan documents.

   d. All of the above.

2. **Which of the following statements regarding commitment fees for lending and mortgage banking activities is NOT correct?**

   a. If the commitment expires without the loan being made, the net commitment fee should be recognized in income upon expiration of the commitment.

   b. Lenders generally should offset commitment fees against any related direct loan origination costs incurred to make the commitment and defer the net amount.

   c. If the commitment is exercised, the net commitment fee should be recognized in income.

   d. If the commitment is exercised, the net commitment fee should be recognized over the life of the loan as an adjustment of interest income.

3. **Which of the following statements is correct regarding the initial investment in a purchased loan?**

   a. The initial investment in a purchased loan should include the amount paid to the seller plus any fees paid or less any fees received.

   b. The initial investment in a purchased loan should only include the amount paid to the seller.

   c. The purchaser must allocate the initial investment cost of loans purchased as a group to the individual loans.

   d. The purchaser must account for the initial investment cost in the aggregate.

4. **Which of the following statements is correct regarding accounting for deferred net fees or costs for nonaccrual loans?**

   a. Deferred net fees or costs should continue to be recognized as an adjustment of yield using the interest method over the term of the loan.

   b. Deferred net fees or costs should be recognized upon payment.

   c. Deferred net fees or costs should not be amortized during periods that interest income is not recognized.

   d. Deferred net fees or costs should continue to be amortized on a straight-line basis.

Self-study
CPE
4

5.   Which of the following statements is correct regarding the accounting for mortgage loans held for sale as of the balance sheet date?

   a.   Report separately at fair value.

   b.   Report separately at the lower of cost or market value.

   c.   Report as a long-term investment at amortized cost.

   d.   Report as a long-term investment at the lower of cost or market value.

6.   Which of the following statements regarding the accounting for contracts to service mortgage loans is correct?

   a.   Servicing assets purchased or servicing liabilities assumed should be recorded at fair value.

   b.   Servicing assets should be subsequently measured for impairment.

   c.   Servicing assets and servicing liabilities should be reported separately in the statement of financial position.

   d.   All of the above.

7.   Motion picture industry production costs include which of the following costs?

   a.   Photography, sound synchronization, and editing costs.

   b.   Prerelease advertising.

   c.   Distribution expenses.

   d.   All of the above.

8.   Which of the following statements is NOT correct regarding the accounting for motion picture industry production costs?

   a.   Production costs should be capitalized as film cost inventory.

   b.   Production costs may be amortized using the individual-film-forecast-computation method.

   c.   Production costs include the costs of writing and marketing a film.

   d.   Production costs include depreciation and amortization of studio equipment and leasehold improvements used in production.

9.   Which of the following statements regarding motion picture industry exploitation costs is NOT correct?

   a.   Exploitation costs are incurred *after* completion of the final production phase.

   b.   Exploitation costs should be amortized in the same ratio that current gross revenues bear to anticipated total gross revenue.

   c.   Exploitation costs include early release advertising expected to benefit the film in future markets.

   d.   All of the above.

Self-study
CPE   4

10. **If the estimated future gross revenues from a film are not sufficient to recover the unamortized film costs, which of the following statements is correct?**

     a.   The company should write down the unamortized film costs in accordance with SFAS No. 121, *Accounting for the Impairment of Long-Lived Assets and for Long-Lived Assets to Be Disposed Of.*

     b.   No write down is necessary; only disclosure of the estimated impairment in the financial statements is required.

     c.   The company should write down the unamortized film costs to net realizable value.

     d.   None of the above.

11. **Which of the following statements is correct regarding costs of major preservation and restoration efforts of a not-for-profit organization?**

     a.   Capitalized costs should be depreciated only if depreciation is recognized on the asset being protected or restored.

     b.   Capitalized costs should be depreciated if the efforts provide future economic benefits or service potential.

     c.   The costs of major preservation and restoration efforts should be expensed as incurred.

     d.   The costs of only the first major preservation or restoration effort should be capitalized and subsequent preservation and restoration efforts should be expensed as incurred.

12. **Which of the following conditions must be present for the organization to report donor-restricted investment income and gains as unrestricted income and gains if restrictions are met in the same reporting period?**

     a.   The organization reports consistently from period to period.

     b.   The organization follows the same policy for reporting donor-restricted contributions.

     c.   The organization discloses its accounting policy.

     d.   All of the above.

13. **Which statement is correct regarding the reporting of information about the nature and amounts of different types of permanent or temporary restrictions?**

     a.   Information is only reported in a statement of functional expenses.

     b.   Information may be reported by providing the amount on the face of the statement of financial position or by including relevant details in the notes to the financial statements.

     c.   Information may be reported only by providing the amount on the face of the statement of financial position.

     d.   Information may be reported only by including relevant details in the notes to the financial statements.

14. **Which of the following statements is correct regarding a statement of activities for a not-for-profit organization?**

     a.   GAAP proscribes a specific format for the statement.

     b.   Permanently restricted and temporarily restricted assets may be combined.

     c.   The statement should report the amount of the change in net assets for the period for the organization as a whole.

     d.   All of the above.

Self-study CPE 4

15. **Which of the following accounting methods is permissible for oil and gas producing activities?**

    a. Full cost method and successful efforts method.

    b. Full cost method and installment method.

    c. Successful efforts method and unit-of-production method.

    d. Full cost method and unit-of-production method.

16. **Which of the following statements is correct?**

    a. Units-of-production depletion rates should be revised at least once a year.

    b. Revisions in units-of-production rates are accounted for as changes in estimates.

    c. Capitalized acquisition costs of proved properties should be amortized using the units of production method.

    d. All of the above.

17. **Which of the following statements is correct regarding impairment of proved oil and gas properties?**

    a. The costs of proved properties should be reviewed for impairment if events or changes in circumstances indicate that they may not be fully recoverable.

    b. Oil and gas producing companies should annually calculate the net realizable value.

    c. The method of determining whether proved properties have been impaired is NOT the same as for other long-lived assets.

    d. Oil and gas producing companies should quarterly assess proved properties to determine whether they have been impaired.

18. **Which of the following is NOT an oil and gas development cost that should be capitalized?**

    a. Drill and equip development wells.

    b. Development-type stratigraphic test wells.

    c. Geological and geophysical studies.

    d. All of the above.

19. **Which of the following statements is a condition for revenue from a license agreement to be recognized in full in the record and music industry?**

    a. The fee's collectibility is reasonably assured.

    b. The signed contract is noncancelable.

    c. The licensee may exercise the rights to the license without restriction.

    d. All of the above.

20. **Which of the following statements is correct regarding a record and music industry licensor recording a minimum guarantee?**

    a. The minimum guarantee should be reported as a liability and recognized as revenue as it is earned under the agreement.

    b. The minimum guarantee should be reported as an asset and recognized as expense over the life of the agreement.

    c. Recorded as revenue when the noncancelable contract is signed.

    d. Recorded as revenue when the license agreement expires.

21. **The record company should charge the advance royalty payment to current-period expense in which of the following situations?**

    a. Advance royalty payments should always be charged to current period expense.

    b. The artist's current popularity indicates that the advance royalties will be recovered from future royalties to be earned by the artist.

    c. The artist's current popularity indicates that the advance royalties will NOT be recovered from future royalties to be earned by the artist.

    d. Advance royalty payments should be charged to expense over the estimated life of record sales.

22. **Which of the following statements is correct regarding a record company's reporting of the cost of a record master?**

    a. A record master should be reported as an asset regardless of the past performance and current popularity of the artist.

    b. A record master should be reported as an asset if the past performance and current popularity of the artist provide a sound basis for recovering the costs from future sales.

    c. A record company should record the entire record master cost as an asset regardless of its portion of the cost.

    d. None of the above.

23. **Which of the following statements is NOT correct regarding allowable costs for regulated operations?**

    a. Allowable costs are costs that should be recovered by revenue.

    b. Allowable costs may include costs expected to be incurred in future periods.

    c. Allowable costs may include costs incurred in prior periods.

    d. None of the above.

24. **Which of the following statements is correct if regulators allow current rates to recover expected future costs at a regulated operations?**

    a. The revenues should be recognized as collected.

    b. The revenues should be recorded as liabilities and recognized as the associated costs are incurred.

    c. An asset is recognized for the expected future costs.

    d. Regulators never allow current rates to recover expected future costs.

25. **Which of the following statements is correct regarding an abandoned asset at a regulated operation?**

    a. Regulators may provide for full, partial, or no return on the investment for the asset.

    b. Abandoned assets under construction remain in the construction work-in-process account until recovery is complete.

    c. Regulators never provide for full recovery of abandoned assets.

    d. Abandoned assets are accounted for the same at regulated and non-regulated enterprises.

26. **Which of the following is a criteria for a regulated operations phase-in plan?**

    a. The regulator adopts the plan in connection with a major, newly completed plant of the regulated enterprise or of one of its suppliers or a major plant scheduled for completion in the near future.

    b. The plan defers the rates intended to recover allowable costs beyond the period in which the allowable costs would be charged to expense under GAAP applicable to enterprises in general.

    c. The plan defers the rates intended to recover allowable costs beyond the period in which the rates would have been ordered under the rate-making methods routinely used by the regulator prior to 1982 for similar allowable costs of the enterprise.

    d. All of the above.

27. **Which of the following statements is correct regarding financial reporting of an enterprise that discontinues accounting for all or part of its operations as a regulated enterprise?**

    a. The enterprise should eliminate from its balance sheet the effects of any regulator's actions that had been previously recognized as assets and liabilities for regulated enterprises over a five-year phase-in period.

    b. The enterprise should eliminate from its balance sheet the effects of any regulator's actions that had been previously recognized as assets and liabilities for regulated enterprises over a 10-year phase-in period.

    c. The enterprise should eliminate from its balance sheet the effects of any regulator's actions that had been previously recognized as assets and liabilities for regulated enterprises, but that would not have been recognized as assets and liabilities by enterprises in general.

    d. The enterprise should eliminate from its balance sheet the effects of any regulator's actions that had been previously recognized as assets and liabilities for regulated enterprises, even if they would have been recognized as assets and liabilities by enterprises in general.

28. **Which of the following statements regarding the direct costs of a title plant is correct?**

    a. Only costs to construct a title plant may be capitalized.

    b. Costs to acquire a title plant are expensed as incurred.

    c. Title plant costs should be capitalized after the plant can be used to perform title searches.

    d. None of the above.

Self-study CPE 4

29. **Which of the following circumstances does NOT indicate impairment of a title asset?**

    a. Actions of competitors and others that may affect competitive advantages.

    b. Converting a title plant from one storage and retrieval system to another.

    c. Changes in legal requirements or statutory practices.

    d. Failure to maintain the title plant properly on a current basis.

30. **Which of the following statements is correct regarding the sale of a title plant being reported separately in the financial statements?**

    a. A company that sells its title plant and relinquishes all rights to its future use should report a gain or loss equal to the amount received less the adjusted cost of the title plant.

    b. A company that sells an undivided ownership interest in its title plant should report a gain or loss equal to the amount received less a pro rata portion of the adjusted cost of the title plant.

    c. A company that sells a copy of its title plant or the right to use it should report a gain equal to the amount received. Ordinarily, no costs should be allocated to the sale unless the value of the title plant decreases below its adjusted cost as a result of the sale.

    d. All of the above.

Self-study CPE 4

ANSWERS

This section lists the correct answers to the self-study quiz for Self-study CPE 4. If you answered a question incorrectly, reread the appropriate paragraph in Chapters 61–67 of the *Guide*. (Paragraph references are in parentheses.)

1. Direct loan origination costs include employees' payroll and fringe benefit costs directly related to time spent performing which of the following activities?

   d. All of the above. (61.202)

2. Which of the following statements regarding commitment fees for lending and mortgage banking activities is NOT correct?

   c. If the commitment is exercised, the net commitment fee should be recognized in income. (61.204)

3. Which of the following statements is correct regarding the initial investment in a purchased loan?

   a. The initial investment in a purchased loan should include the amount paid to the seller plus any fees paid or less any fees received. (61.211)

4. Which of the following statements is correct regarding accounting for deferred net fees or costs for nonaccrual loans?

   c. Deferred net fees or costs should not be amortized during periods that interest income is not recognized. (61.218)

5. Which of the following statements is correct regarding the accounting for mortgage loans held for sale as of the balance sheet date?

   b. Report separately at the lower of cost or market value. (61.222)

6. Which of the following statements regarding the accounting for contracts to service mortgage loans is correct?

   d. All of the above. (61.230)

7. Motion picture industry production costs include which of the following costs?

   a. Photography, sound synchronization, and editing costs. (62.204)

8. Which of the following statements is NOT correct regarding the accounting for motion picture industry production costs?

   c. Production costs include the costs of writing and marketing a film. (62.204)

9. Which of the following statements regarding motion picture industry exploitation costs is NOT correct?

   a. Exploitation costs are incurred *after* completion of the final production phase. (62.209)

10. If the estimated future gross revenues from a film are not sufficient to recover the unamortized film costs, which of the following statements is correct?

    c. The company should write down the unamortized film costs to net realizable value. (62.210)

11. Which of the following statements is correct regarding costs of major preservation and restoration efforts of a not-for-profit organization?

    b. Capitalized costs should be depreciated if the efforts provide future economic benefits or service potential. (63.202)

Self-study CPE **4**

12. Which of the following conditions must be present for the organization to report donor-restricted investment income and gains as unrestricted income and gains if restrictions are met in the same reporting period?

    d. All of the above. (63.204)

13. Which statement is correct regarding the reporting of information about the nature and amounts of different types of permanent or temporary restrictions?

    b. Information may be reported by providing the amount on the face of the statement of financial position or by including relevant details in the notes to the financial statements. (63.208)

14. Which of the following statements is correct regarding a statement of activities for a not-for-profit organization?

    c. The statement should report the amount of the change in net assets for the period for the organization as a whole. (63.213)

15. Which of the following accounting methods is permissible for oil and gas producing activities?

    a. Full cost method and successful efforts method. (64.200)

16. Which of the following statements is correct?

    d. All of the above. (64.208)

17. Which of the following statements is correct regarding impairment of proved oil and gas properties?

    a. The costs of proved properties should be reviewed for impairment if events or changes in circumstances indicate that they may not be fully recoverable. (64.210)

18. Which of the following is NOT an oil and gas development cost that should be capitalized?

    c. Geological and geophysical studies. (64.214 and 64.218)

19. Which of the following statements is a condition for revenue from a license agreement to be recognized in full in the record and music industry?

    d. All of the above. (65.201)

20. Which of the following statements is correct regarding a record and music industry licensor recording a minimum guarantee?

    a. The minimum guarantee should be reported as a liability and recognized as revenue as it is earned under the agreement. (65.203)

21. The record company should charge the advance royalty payment to current-period expense in which of the following situations?

    c. The artist's current popularity indicates that the advance royalties will NOT be recovered from future royalties to be earned by the artist. (65.204)

22. Which of the following statements is correct regarding a record company's reporting of the cost of a record master?

    b. A record master should be reported as an asset if the past performance and current popularity of the artist provide a sound basis for recovering the costs from future sales. (65.205)

Self-study CPE 4

23. Which of the following statements is NOT correct regarding allowable costs for regulated operations?

    d. None of the above. (66.202)

24. Which of the following statements is correct if regulators allow current rates to recover expected future costs at a regulated operations?

    b. The revenues should be recorded as liabilities and recognized as the associated costs are incurred. (66.205)

25. Which of the following statements is correct regarding an abandoned asset at a regulated operation?

    a. Regulators may provide for full, partial, or no return on the investment for the asset. (66.210)

26. Which of the following is a criteria for a regulated operations phase-in plan?

    d. All of the above. (66.216)

27. Which of the following statements is correct regarding financial reporting of an enterprise that discontinues accounting for all or part of its operations as a regulated enterprise?

    c. The enterprise should eliminate from its balance sheet the effects of any regulator's actions that had been previously recognized as assets and liabilities for regulated enterprises, but that would not have been recognized as assets and liabilities by enterprises in general. (66.222)

28. Which of the following statements regarding the direct costs of a title plant is correct?

    d. None of the above. (67.201)

29. Which of the following circumstances does NOT indicate impairment of a title asset?

    b. Converting a title plant from one storage and retrieval system to another. (67.202)

30. Which of the following statements is correct regarding the sale of a title plant being reported separately in the financial statements?

    d. All of the above. (67.205)

Self-study CPE 4

EXAMINATION FOR CPE CREDIT

Chapters 61–67

Test Instructions

1. The questions on the next pages are TRUE/FALSE. Choose the best answer for each question and mark the appropriate box on the answer sheet. Answer sheets are located behind Self-study CPE 4.

2. If you change your answer, erase completely. Do not make any stray marks because they may be misinterpreted.

3. Photocopies of this form are acceptable. However, each examination must be accompanied by a payment of $42.

4. To receive CPE credit, completed answer sheets must be postmarked by December 31, 1998. Send the completed Examination for CPE Credit Answer Sheet along with your payment to the address listed below. CPE credit will be given for examination scores of 75% or higher.

5. Only the **Examination for CPE Credit Answer Sheet** should be submitted for grading. **DO NOT SEND YOUR SELF-STUDY MATERIALS.** Be sure to keep a completed copy for your records.

6. Please allow a minimum of three weeks for grading.

7. Please direct any questions or comments to our Customer Service department at (800) 323-8724.

Send your completed **Examination for CPE Credit Answer Sheet** and your payment to:

Practitioners Publishing Company
GAP Self-study CPE
P.O. Box 966
Fort Worth, TX 76101

If you are paying by credit card, you may fax your completed **Examination for CPE Credit Answer Sheet** to PPC at (817) 877-3694.

EXAMINATION QUESTIONS

1. If a loan is held for investment, the lender should recognize deferred loan origination fees and related direct loan origination costs over the life of the loan as an adjustment of interest income.

2. The company managing a loan syndication (the syndicator) should recognize loan syndication fees when the syndication is complete regardless of whether the syndicator retains a portion of the syndication loan.

3. Special provisions for amortizing deferred fees and costs apply if the stated interest rate is not constant throughout the term of the loan.

4. If the lender holds a large number of similar loans for which principal prepayments are probable and the amount and timing of prepayments can be reasonably estimated, the lender may consider estimates of future prepayments in the calculation of the constant effective yield.

5. Net fees or costs related to revolving lines of credit by lenders should be recognized in income on the straight-line basis over the period the revolving line is active.

6. The unamortized balance of loan origination, commitment, and other fees and costs being amortized by the interest method should be reported on the lender's balance sheet as a separate line item.

7. Capitalized costs of servicing assets associated with the purchase or origination of mortgage loans should be considered in the cost of mortgage loans for the purpose of determining the lower of cost or market value of the loans.

8. As a general rule, revenue from the sale of exhibition rights in the motion picture industry should be recognized on the date the film is shown.

9. Motion picture industry production costs do NOT include rental of facilities on location.

10. The periodic-table-computation method amortizes film costs based on the ratio of current gross revenues to anticipated total gross revenues.

11. The individual-film-forecast-computation method of amortizing capitalized motion picture industry production costs should only be used if its result would approximate the periodic-table-computation method.

12. Exploitation costs are incurred during the release periods of films in both primary and secondary markets.

13. A motion picture company should not report a license agreement for the sale of film rights for television exhibition as an asset until the time revenue from the agreement is recognized.

14. Not-for-profit organizations do NOT need to recognize depreciation on individual works of art or historical treasures that have indefinite or extraordinarily long useful lives.

15. For not-for-profit organizations, investments in equity securities with readily determinable fair values and all investments in debt securities should be reported in the statement of financial position at cost.

16. The statement of activities for not-for-profit organizations should report the amount of change in each class of net assets (permanently restricted, temporarily restricted, and unrestricted) for the period.

17. To help donors, creditors, and others assess an organization's service efforts, the statement of activities or notes to the financial statements should report expenses by their functional classification.

Self-study
CPE 4

18. Receipts of unconditional promises to give payments in future periods should ALWAYS be reported as restricted revenues or gains.

19. Voluntary health and welfare organizations are NOT required to present a statement of functional expenses.

20. Under the full cost method, only exploration and development costs related to proved reserves are capitalized.

21. Oil and gas producing companies should periodically assess unproved properties to determine whether they have been impaired.

22. Under the units-of-production method, each unit of oil and gas produced is NOT assigned a pro rata portion of the unamortized acquisition costs.

23. Exploration costs for geological and geophysical studies, carrying and retaining underdeveloped properties, and dry hole and bottom hole contributions should be capitalized.

24. Once construction is completed, development costs should be capitalized as part of the cost of a company's wells and related equipment and facilities.

25. Production costs should be treated as part of the cost of oil and gas produced.

26. The only condition for a record company to record a sale and revenue from a license agreement is when the licensor has met all significant obligations to furnish music or records.

27. Royalties earned by artists should be adjusted for anticipated returns and charged to expense in the period in which related record sales occur.

28. Record companies should always record advance royalty payments as expenses.

29. A record company should disclose the commitments for artist advances that are payable in future years and future royalty guarantees in its financial statements or notes to the financial statements.

30. The record company's portion of the cost of record masters that is recorded as an asset must be reported as a separate line item on the balance sheet.

31. For a regulated operation, costs that would otherwise be charged to expense generally should be capitalized if it is probable that future revenue will be provided to recover the costs.

32. A regulator's rate actions can reduce or eliminate the value of an incurred cost that has been capitalized as an asset.

33. A regulator may allow current rates to recover expected future costs and require future rates to be reduced by the amounts of the expected future costs if those costs are not incurred.

34. A regulated enterprise should always eliminate profit on sales to regulated affiliates in its general-purpose financial statements.

35. When it becomes probable that part of the cost of a recently completed plant will be disallowed for rate-making purposes and a reasonable estimate of the disallowed cost can be made, the enterprise should deduct the estimated disallowed cost from the reported cost of the plant and recognize the amount as a loss.

36. Accounting for a regulated entity's sale-leaseback transactions in accordance with GAAP will *always* result in income and expenses being recognized in the same periods for financial reporting and rate-making purposes.

37. A title plant typically has a definite estimated useful life.

38. A title plant's capitalized costs should always be depreciated.

39. Costs incurred to maintain a title plant and perform title searches should be expensed as incurred.

40. A company that sells a copy of its title plant or the right to use it should report a gain equal to the amount received.

ANSWER SHEET INSTRUCTIONS
GAP 98/42

1. The answer sheet is on the reverse side of this page. Please carefully remove the page at the perforations.

2. Fill in all the information using a black pen or pencil and plain block letters. Avoid touching the sides of the boxes.

3. Under section "SSN," please write your social security number and bubble in the appropriate circles below.

4. Under the "Exam" Section, please write in the number of the self-study CPE section (1, 2, 3, or 4) that applies.

5. Please answer true or false to each question, bubbling in the appropriate circle under the "Answers" Section.

6. Fill in your CPE Reporting Deadline and return your answer sheet along with your payment of $42 for each exam.

7. Finally, please take a moment to fill out and return the Course Evaluation for the exam.

Send your completed Examination for CPE Credit Answer Sheet and your payment to:

Practitioners Publishing Company
GAP Self-study CPE
P.O. Box 966
Fort Worth, Texas 76101

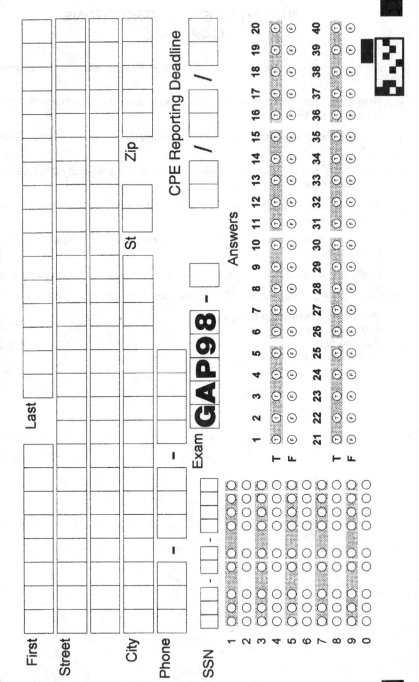

Examination for CPE Credit Answer Sheet

First

Street

Last

City

St   Zip

Phone   –   –

SSN   –   –

Exam **GAP98** –

CPE Reporting Deadline

/   /

Answers

| 1 | 2 | 3 | 4 | 5 | 6 | 7 | 8 | 9 | 10 | 11 | 12 | 13 | 14 | 15 | 16 | 17 | 18 | 19 | 20 |

T ⓣ
F ⓕ

| 21 | 22 | 23 | 24 | 25 | 26 | 27 | 28 | 29 | 30 | 31 | 32 | 33 | 34 | 35 | 36 | 37 | 38 | 39 | 40 |

T ⓣ
F ⓕ

Guide to GAAP

Course Evaluation

Place an "X" in the appropriate box to indicate the course taken.

☐ CPE 1—Chapters 27–39 (GAP 98-1/42)   ☐ CPE 3—Chapters 53–60 (GAP 98-3/42)

☐ CPE 2—Chapters 40–52 (GAP 98-2/42)   ☐ CPE 4—Chapters 61–67 (GAP 98-4/42)

1. Appropriateness of the material for your experience level.

   ☐ New material—over my head.   ☐ New material—challenging but not overwhelming.

   ☐ A good refresher, and I learned some new things.   ☐ Material was not challenging.

2. The stated learning objectives of this self-study course were met.

   ☐ Agree ☐ Neutral ☐ Disagree

3. The program materials contributed to the achievement of the stated learning objectives.

   ☐ Agree ☐ Neutral ☐ Disagree

4. The program content was timely and relevant.

   ☐ Agree ☐ Neutral ☐ Disagree

5. The examination questions related to the course material.

   ☐ Agree ☐ Neutral ☐ Disagree

6. The examination questions were clear and unambiguous.

   ☐ Agree ☐ Neutral ☐ Disagree

7. Please provide any constructive criticism you may have about the course materials, such as particularly difficult parts, hard to understand areas, unclear instructions, appropriateness of subjects, educational value, and ways to make it more fun. Please be as specific as you can.

   _____

   _____

   _____

   _____

   _____

   _____

Please send your completed Course Evaluation to:

Practitioners Publishing Company
GAP Self-study CPE
P.O. Box 966
Fort Worth, TX 76101

ANSWER SHEET INSTRUCTIONS
GAP 98/42

1. The answer sheet is on the reverse side of this page. Please carefully remove the page at the perforations.

2. Fill in all the information using a black pen or pencil and plain block letters. Avoid touching the sides of the boxes.

3. Under section "SSN," please write your social security number and bubble in the appropriate circles below.

4. Under the "Exam" Section, please write in the number of the self-study CPE section (1, 2, 3, or 4) that applies.

5. Please answer true or false to each question, bubbling in the appropriate circle under the "Answers" Section.

6. Fill in your CPE Reporting Deadline and return your answer sheet along with your payment of $42 for each exam.

7. Finally, please take a moment to fill out and return the Course Evaluation for the exam.

Send your completed Examination for CPE Credit Answer Sheet and your payment to:

Practitioners Publishing Company
GAP Self-study CPE
P.O. Box 966
Fort Worth, Texas 76101

Examination for CPE Credit Answer Sheet

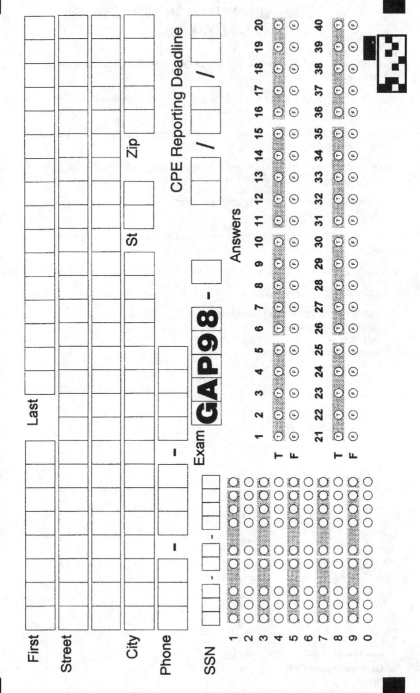

Guide to GAAP

Course Evaluation

Place an "X" in the appropriate box to indicate the course taken.

☐ CPE 1—Chapters 27–39 (GAP 98-1/42) ☐ CPE 3—Chapters 53–60 (GAP 98-3/42)

☐ CPE 2—Chapters 40–52 (GAP 98-2/42) ☐ CPE 4—Chapters 61–67 (GAP 98-4/42)

1. Appropriateness of the material for your experience level.

   ☐ New material—over my head. ☐ New material—challenging but not overwhelming.

   ☐ A good refresher, and I learned some new things. ☐ Material was not challenging.

2. The stated learning objectives of this self-study course were met.

   ☐ Agree ☐ Neutral ☐ Disagree

3. The program materials contributed to the achievement of the stated learning objectives.

   ☐ Agree ☐ Neutral ☐ Disagree

4. The program content was timely and relevant.

   ☐ Agree ☐ Neutral ☐ Disagree

5. The examination questions related to the course material.

   ☐ Agree ☐ Neutral ☐ Disagree

6. The examination questions were clear and unambiguous.

   ☐ Agree ☐ Neutral ☐ Disagree

7. Please provide any constructive criticism you may have about the course materials, such as particularly difficult parts, hard to understand areas, unclear instructions, appropriateness of subjects, educational value, and ways to make it more fun. Please be as specific as you can.

_____

_____

_____

_____

_____

_____

Please send your completed Course Evaluation to:

Practitioners Publishing Company
GAP Self-study CPE
P.O. Box 966
Fort Worth, TX 76101

ANSWER SHEET INSTRUCTIONS
GAP 98/42

1. The answer sheet is on the reverse side of this page. Please carefully remove the page at the perforations.

2. Fill in all the information using a black pen or pencil and plain block letters. Avoid touching the sides of the boxes.

3. Under section "SSN," please write your social security number and bubble in the appropriate circles below.

4. Under the "Exam" Section, please write in the number of the self-study CPE section (1, 2, 3, or 4) that applies.

5. Please answer true or false to each question, bubbling in the appropriate circle under the "Answers" Section.

6. Fill in your CPE Reporting Deadline and return your answer sheet along with your payment of $42 for each exam.

7. Finally, please take a moment to fill out and return the Course Evaluation for the exam.

Send your completed Examination for CPE Credit Answer Sheet and your payment to:

Practitioners Publishing Company
GAP Self-study CPE
P.O. Box 966
Fort Worth, Texas 76101

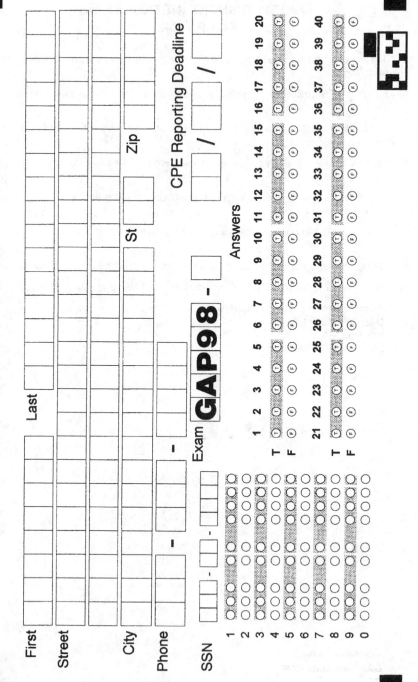

Examination for CPE Credit Answer Sheet

Guide to GAAP

Course Evaluation

Place an "X" in the appropriate box to indicate the course taken.

☐ CPE 1—Chapters 27–39 (GAP 98-1/42) ☐ CPE 3—Chapters 53–60 (GAP 98-3/42)

☐ CPE 2—Chapters 40–52 (GAP 98-2/42) ☐ CPE 4—Chapters 61–67 (GAP 98-4/42)

1. Appropriateness of the material for your experience level.

    ☐ New material—over my head. ☐ New material—challenging but not overwhelming.

    ☐ A good refresher, and I learned some new things. ☐ Material was not challenging.

2. The stated learning objectives of this self-study course were met.

    ☐ Agree ☐ Neutral ☐ Disagree

3. The program materials contributed to the achievement of the stated learning objectives.

    ☐ Agree ☐ Neutral ☐ Disagree

4. The program content was timely and relevant.

    ☐ Agree ☐ Neutral ☐ Disagree

5. The examination questions related to the course material.

    ☐ Agree ☐ Neutral ☐ Disagree

6. The examination questions were clear and unambiguous.

    ☐ Agree ☐ Neutral ☐ Disagree

7. Please provide any constructive criticism you may have about the course materials, such as particularly difficult parts, hard to understand areas, unclear instructions, appropriateness of subjects, educational value, and ways to make it more fun. Please be as specific as you can.

    _____

    _____

    _____

    _____

    _____

    _____

    _____

Please send your completed Course Evaluation to:

Practitioners Publishing Company
GAP Self-study CPE
P.O. Box 966
Fort Worth, TX 76101

ANSWER SHEET INSTRUCTIONS
GAP 98/42

1. The answer sheet is on the reverse side of this page. Please carefully remove the page at the perforations.

2. Fill in all the information using a black pen or pencil and plain block letters. Avoid touching the sides of the boxes.

3. Under section "SSN," please write your social security number and bubble in the appropriate circles below.

4. Under the "Exam" Section, please write in the number of the self-study CPE section (1, 2, 3, or 4) that applies.

5. Please answer true or false to each question, bubbling in the appropriate circle under the "Answers" Section.

6. Fill in your CPE Reporting Deadline and return your answer sheet along with your payment of $42 for each exam.

7. Finally, please take a moment to fill out and return the Course Evaluation for the exam.

Send your completed Examination for CPE Credit Answer Sheet and your payment to:

Practitioners Publishing Company
GAP Self-study CPE
P.O. Box 966
Fort Worth, Texas 76101

Examination for CPE Credit Answer Sheet

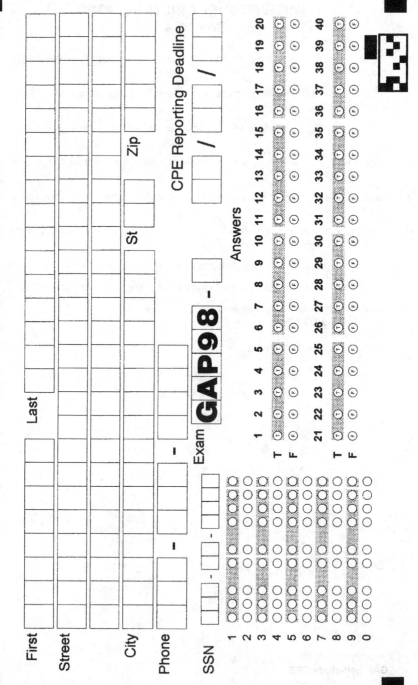

Guide to GAAP

Course Evaluation

Place an "X" in the appropriate box to indicate the course taken.

☐ CPE 1—Chapters 27–39 (GAP 98-1/42) ☐ CPE 3—Chapters 53–60 (GAP 98-3/42)

☐ CPE 2—Chapters 40–52 (GAP 98-2/42) ☐ CPE 4—Chapters 61–67 (GAP 98-4/42)

1. Appropriateness of the material for your experience level.

    ☐ New material—over my head. ☐ New material—challenging but not overwhelming.

    ☐ A good refresher, and I learned some new things. ☐ Material was not challenging.

2. The stated learning objectives of this self-study course were met.

    ☐ Agree ☐ Neutral ☐ Disagree

3. The program materials contributed to the achievement of the stated learning objectives.

    ☐ Agree ☐ Neutral ☐ Disagree

4. The program content was timely and relevant.

    ☐ Agree ☐ Neutral ☐ Disagree

5. The examination questions related to the course material.

    ☐ Agree ☐ Neutral ☐ Disagree

6. The examination questions were clear and unambiguous.

    ☐ Agree ☐ Neutral ☐ Disagree

7. Please provide any constructive criticism you may have about the course materials, such as particularly difficult parts, hard to understand areas, unclear instructions, appropriateness of subjects, educational value, and ways to make it more fun. Please be as specific as you can.

    _____

    _____

    _____

    _____

    _____

    _____

    _____

Please send your completed Course Evaluation to:

Practitioners Publishing Company
GAP Self-study CPE
P.O. Box 966
Fort Worth, TX 76101

TOPICAL INDEX

References are to paragraph numbers.

References are to paragraph numbers.